For UPSC/STATE PCS/ UGC-NET & University Exams

ANTHROPOLOGY
EXEMPLIFIED

PAPER-I&II

AF883465

RAJAT SAMBYAL, JKPS

Chief Editor
Shyam Salona

Read best Be best
KBC-NANO

Published by :
KBC Nano Publication Pvt. Ltd.
Publisher, Distributor & Order Supplier

Price : ₹ 580/-

KBC Nano Publication Pvt. Ltd.

Registered Office :

90-SFS, Mukherjee Nagar
Delhi-110009

Publication : 011-47557273

Correspondence Address :

13-B (Basement), Below HDFC Bank,
Old Rajinder Nagar
New Delhi-110060

Phone : 011-47000218, 8826403255
9968637044, 9968814135

Email : kbcnanopublication@gmail.com

Website: www.kumarbookcentre.com

Design & Layout by :

D. KBC-DTP Section (Delhi)

Printer :

Shanti Printer, Delhi

NOTE : *Due care and diligence has been taken while editing and printing the book, neither the author nor the Editor/Publisher of the book hold any responsibility for any mistakes that may have inadvertently crept in.*

In case of binding mistake, misprints, or for missing pages etc., Publisher's entre liability, and your exclusive remedy, is replacement of the book within one month of purchase by similar edition of the book. All disputes are subject to exclusive jurisdiction of Delhi Courts only.

PREFACE

Honestly speaking, I have never thought of writing a book on my optional subject, Anthropology. However, in my 6th and last attempt at UPSC CSE 2021, I was able to increase my overall score in optional by 53 marks vis-à-vis UPSC CSE 2020. I have one of the highest marks in anthropology in UPSC CSE 2021, i.e., an overall score of 307. In optional paper 1, I got 169 marks, and in optional paper 2, I got 138 marks. This urged me to put across my ideas and strategy, which helped me garner more marks. Recently, I cleared the JKPSC, CSE 2022 examination with a rank of 64. I have joined as Deputy Superintendent of Police (DySP) in the Jammu and Kashmir Police Service (JKPS).

Using relevant, current-based case studies is one of the keys to making any optional material relevant, and this can act as a topping over the cake. Though it is beyond the capacity of one individual to justify the diverse topics included in the subject, I have used many resources, which have been cited in the bibliography section. I honestly own all such mistakes that might have crept in due to swiftness and ignorance.

I will love to thank my mother, Jyoti Jamwal, my father, Mohinder Singh, my sister, Mehak Sambyal, and my friend Shivam, without whose support I would have never been in a position to bring this book to you. I also sincerely thank my anthropology teachers, especially Sudhir Kumar, Sanjeev Choudhary, and N.K. Vaid, for their material and moral support. There are many more teachers, friends, and role models who have acted as sources of inspiration in my journey, and they have indirectly pushed me. Last but not least, it is aspirants to the civil service who have acted as a source of strength to complete this book and give it my best shot.

"If everything around you seems dark, look again; you may be the light" - Rumi.

Dedicated to my parents,
who remain associated with my upbringing and
issues unless planned better and
solved like action anthropologists

CONTENTS

PAPER-I

PAPER-II

❑❑❑

INTRODUCTION

Anthropology as a subject covers the study of humans in totality, ranging from socio-cultural to biological to linguistic to archaeological aspects.

This book tries to cover the full syllabus of UPSC CSE Anthropology optional in question-answer format. It comes in handy when you have to remember such a vast syllabus and write a good answer within the specified time limit and space. A key aspect of this book is the inter linkages with scholars, diagrams, committees, current events, and much more.

Information given in boxes can be used to make the answer relevant and updated. It will act as a topping over the pizza base and increase the quality multi fold. At the end, a chapter named "Chapter 10: Ethnographic Profile of Tribes in Jammu and Kashmir UT and Ladakh UT" will help aspirants have in-depth knowledge about certain tribes.

No book can provide spoon-feeding covering the whole optional syllabus. It can be complemented with some standard books, as given in the bibliography section. Considering the changes in the pattern of questions asked by UPSC, an aspirant has to develop the ability to use this information in an efficient and effective manner.

An aspirant has to be both rigid and flexible, like the Indian constitution. Rigidity needs to prevail in remembering all questions. Flexibility is needed to use information from Anthropology Paper 1 in Paper 2, vice versa, and even from one topic to another within the same paper.

Last but not least, aspirants should practice UPSC anthropology's previous year's questions (at least the last 5–6 years) by using the information provided in this book. A chapter named "Unconventional UPSC Previous Year Questions" will help aspirants cover and get prepared for certain unconventional questions.

India has propagated the concept of "Vasudhaiva kutumbakam," meaning the world is one family. Anthropologists are strong believers and actionists in this concept, which tries to cover every aspect of human life both in time and space.

UPSC (Mains) ANTHROPOLOGY OPTIONAL PAPER-I (2024)

SECTION-A

1. Write notes on the following in about 150 words each: *10 × 5 = 50 Marks*
   (a) Attributes of culture
   (b) Harappan maritime trade
   (c) Critical perspective on avoidance and joking relationship
   (d) Lethal and sublethal genes
   (e) Hemoglobin in health and disease

2. (a) Discuss historical particularism as a critical development to the classical evolutionism. *20 Marks*
   (b) Describe the evidences of food production and domestication of animals with special reference to Mehrgarh. Throw light on its significance. *15 Marks*
   (c) Critically comment on the lifestyle diseases and their impact on human health. *15 Marks*

3. (a) What is meant by karyotype? How does its analysis help in diagnosis of the chromosomal aberrations in man? *20 Marks*
   (b) Define urbanization and discuss its impact on family in India with examples. *15 Marks*
   (c) Discuss the contemporary challenges in fieldwork method in anthropological research. *15 Marks*

4. (a) Critically discuss the characteristics of the psychological types in the cultures of the American South-West as observed by Ruth Benedict. *20 Marks*
   (b) Discuss the Acheulian and Oldowan traditions of Indian Paleolithic cultures with suitable illustrations. *15 Marks*
   (c) What is genetic counselling? Briefly discuss various steps involved in it. *15 Marks*

SECTION-B

5. Write notes on the following in about 150 words each: *10 × 5 = 50 Marks*
   (a) Chronometric dating
   (b) Cultural relevance of the Kula
   (c) Heritability and its estimation
   (d) Authority and forms of political organization
   (e) Single-gene mutation disorders in man

6. (a) Discuss the geographical distribution of Homo erectus. Taking into account its physical features, where does it fit in human evolutionary line? *20 Marks*
   (b) Discuss the applications of forensic anthropology with suitable examples. *15 Marks*
   (c) How does Lévi-Strauss look at the Tsimshian myth of Asdiwal? Critically discuss Lévi-Strauss' theory of structuralism in the light of his study of mythologies. *15 Marks*

7. (a) Critically explain the notion of 'deconstruction' in the light of the postmodern works of Jacques Derrida. *20 Marks*
   (b) What is a multifactorial trait? Illustrate your answer with suitable human examples. *15 Marks*
   (c) Discuss the applicability of various sampling techniques in selecting the study group. *15 Marks*

8. (a) Examine critically the concept of social stratification as a basis for sustaining social inequality. *20 Marks*
   (b) Describe the genetics and inheritance patterns of the ABO and Rh blood groups in man. *15 Marks*
   (c) Critically discuss the synergistic effect of biological and cultural factors in human evolution. 15 Marks

ANALYSIS OF UPSC Mains 2024 Anthropology Optional Paper-1

1. Equal emphasis on biological component and social component
2. Expected questions like postmodernism, Levi Strauss's myth, Malinowski's Kula exchange, Ruth Benedict, etc.
3. Current emphasis is laid by questions like contemporary challenges in fieldwork and lifestyle diseases.
4. Almost all the questions were from within the syllabus prescribed and can be found in 1st Edition of the Book "ANTHROPOLOGY EXEMPLIFIED".

Question No. of **UPSC Anthropology Mains 2024 Paper-I**	Covered in Page no. of Book **"ANTHROPOLOGY EXEMPLIFIED"**
Q.1.(a)	Page 63 and 66 of Paper-I
Q.1. (b)	Page 10 of Paper-II
Q.1.(c)	Page 73 of Paper-I
Q.1.(d)	Page 183 & 184 of Paper-I
Q.1.(e)	Page 217 of Paper-I
Q.2.(a)	Page 127 &128 of Paper-I
Q.2. (b)	Page 5 & 6 of Paper-II
Q.2. (c)	Page 224 & 225 of Paper-I
Q.3. (a)	Page 175 & 176 of Paper-I
Q.3. (b)	Page 82 & 83 of Paper-I
Q.3. (c)	Page 160 of Paper-I + 185 of Paper-II

Q.4. (a)	Page 140 & 141 of Paper-I
Q.4. (b)	Page 2 of Paper-II
Q.4. (c)	Page 202 of Paper-I
Q.5. (a)	Page 52 & 53 of Paper-I
Q.5. (b)	Page 96 of Paper-I
Q.5. (c)	Page 173 of Paper-I
Q.5. (d)	Page 104 of Paper-I
Q.5. (e)	Page 181 & 187 of Paper-I
Q.6. (a)	Page 33 & 34 of Paper-I
Q.6. (b)	Page 251, 252 & 253 of Paper-I
Q.6. (c)	Page 138 & 139 of Paper-I
Q.7. (a)	Page 154 of Paper-I
Q.7. (b)	Page 183 of Paper-I
Q.7. (c)	Not covered
Q.8. (a)	Page 68 & 69 of Paper-I
Q.8. (b)	Page 213, 214 & 215 of Paper-I
Q.8. (c)	Page 12, 13 & 14 of Paper-I

Q. 3 (c) Discuss the contemporary challenges in fieldwork method in anthropological research.

Ans. Contemporary anthropological fieldwork faces several challenges, as highlighted by anthropologists, governmental reports, and international organizations, with specific insights from Indian anthropologists.

1. **Ethical Challenges:** Ethical dilemmas have become more complex, particularly regarding informed consent and privacy. *George E. Marcus* (1998) stresses the need for transparency, while Indian anthropologist *N.K. Bose* highlights the importance of understanding local norms and cultural sensitivities when conducting research in indigenous communities. Reports from the *American Anthropological Association (AAA)* and *United Nations* also emphasize the need to protect vulnerable populations, a concern echoed by Indian scholars like *L.P. Vidyarthi*, who advocates for ethical standards that ensure indigenous communities' autonomy and avoid exploitation.
2. **Technological Challenges:** The use of social media and big data in fieldwork has raised ethical concerns regarding privacy and surveillance. *Alison G. O'Malley* (2021) points out the complexities of integrating technology into fieldwork, which is also discussed in Indian government reports, such as the Ministry of Tribal Affairs' reports, which highlight how technological interventions can affect marginalized communities' autonomy. During the COVID-19 pandemic, remote ethnography and virtual fieldwork have been increasingly used, though Indian anthropologists like *Suresh Sharma* caution about losing the immersion and direct engagement that traditional fieldwork offers.
3. **Access and Representation:** Accessing marginalized or politically sensitive communities has become difficult due to globalization. Indian anthropologists like *B.K. Roy Burman* have noted the challenges in accessing tribal communities, particularly due to growing governmental restrictions or fears of

cultural erosion. Reports from organizations like the United Nations and Indian Ministry of Tribal Affairs also stress that mistrust of outsiders can lead to misrepresentation or exclusion from research.

4. **Reflexivity:** Reflexivity is crucial in fieldwork, as the researcher's own identity influences the research process. *Clifford Geertz* (1973) and Indian anthropologists like *T.N. Madan* emphasize the need for self-awareness in understanding how cultural biases, gender, and social position shape the research. The *Indian Anthropological Society* has advocated for greater reflexivity to ensure that researchers are aware of their positionality and influence on the communities they study.

In conclusion, contemporary anthropological fieldwork in India and globally faces ethical, technological, and access-related challenges, which require adaptive, culturally sensitive methods. Insights from Indian anthropologists provide a localized understanding of these issues, highlighting the need for careful, ethical, and reflexive approaches in modern research.

Q. 7. (a) Critically explain the notion of 'deconstruction' in the light of the postmodern works of Jacques Derrida.

Ans. In anthropology, 'deconstruction' is a critical approach introduced by French philosopher *Jacques Derrida*, which challenges conventional ways of understanding culture, language, and meaning. Deconstruction critiques the assumptions inherent in structuralism, which views language and culture as systems of fixed and stable meanings. Derrida's theory, however, posits that meaning is always unstable, fragmented, and subject to constant change.

Central to Derrida's deconstruction is the concept of *differance* (a term combining the French words for "difference" and "deferral"), which suggests that meaning is never fully present but is always deferred, constantly shifting and contingent on its relation to other signs. This idea disrupts the structuralist belief that words or symbols have stable, inherent meanings. Derrida argues that meanings are never final; they are continually in flux and can never be fully grasped.

Deconstruction also critiques the binary oppositions that are foundational to Western thought and culture, such as mind/body, nature/culture, and raw/cooked. These binaries often create hierarchical relationships, where one side of the binary is privileged over the other. For example, in many Western cultures, speech is valued more than writing, as seen in philosophical traditions from Plato to Saussure. Derrida challenges this hierarchy by showing that the "privileged" term always depends on the "subordinate" one for meaning. For instance, writing is not merely a secondary representation of speech, but in fact, can be seen as undermining speech due to its capacity to preserve meaning beyond immediate presence.

For anthropologists, deconstruction is a tool to critically examine cultural texts, narratives, and practices, revealing their internal contradictions and power structures. It encourages a deeper understanding of how dominant cultural meanings are constructed, often by marginalizing alternative voices and experiences. Derrida's approach calls for a rejection of fixed, essentialist interpretations of culture and identity, offering instead a more fluid, contingent understanding of cultural practices.

While deconstruction has provided valuable insights in anthropology, it has also been criticized. Some argue that it leads to relativism and undermines the possibility of stable cultural meanings, making it difficult to address issues like social justice or equality. However, it remains influential, prompting anthropologists to question traditional methodologies and the ways in which knowledge is produced and represented in anthropological research.

Q.7 (c) Discuss the applicability of various sampling techniques in selecting the study group.

Ans. In anthropological research, selecting the right study group is crucial for ensuring reliable and meaningful data. Various sampling techniquesare employed based on the research objectives, population characteristics, and available resources.

1. **Random Sampling:** In this method, each individual has an equal chance of being selected. It is ideal for large populations where the goal is to ensure an unbiased and representative sample. However, it may be less applicable in smaller, more specific groups, such as tribes, where cultural context is vital.
2. **Stratified Sampling:** This involves dividing the population into subgroups based on specific characteristics (e.g., age, gender) and then randomly sampling from each group. It ensures that all relevant subgroups are represented. For instance, in studying an indigenous community, stratified sampling can ensure the inclusion of different age groups or genders.
3. **Systematic Sampling:** This method selects every "nth" individual from a list. It is easy to implement but can be biased if there is an underlying pattern in the population list.
4. **Convenience Sampling:** In this non-probability method, participants are selected based on ease of access. While practical for exploratory research, it may introduce bias and is less representative of the larger population.
5. **Purposive (Judgmental) Sampling:** Here, participants are selected based on specific criteria relevant to the research. It is often used in qualitative research where deep insights from knowledgeable informants are needed, such as when studying unique cultural practices in small communities.
6. **Snowball Sampling:** Useful for hidden or marginalized populations, snowball sampling relies on initial participants referring others. Though it helps access hard-to-reach groups, it can limit diversity in the sample.

The choice of sampling technique depends on the research goals, whether seeking broad generalization or in-depth, context-specific knowledge. Often, researchers combine methods to balance representation and depth.

UPSC (Mains) ANTHROPOLOGY OPTIONAL PAPER-II (2024)

SECTION-A

1. Write notes on the following in about 150 words each: *10 × 5 = 50 Marks*
   (a) Digitisation of rural economy
   (b) Origin of State Societies
   (c) Syro-Malabar Christians
   (d) Artisan tribes of Jharkhand
   (e) Causes of stunting and wasting among tribal children

2. (a) Critically discuss the recent welfare measures initiated by the Government for the Particularly Vulnerable Tribal Groups (PVTGs). Comment why PVTGs were erroneously called Primitive Tribal Groups (PTGs). *20 Marks*
   (b) How is PESA Act empowering local self-governance and impacting women's political participation? *15 Marks*
   (c) Deconstruct the colonial history of Indian Anthropology highlighting the critical role played by the Indian Anthropologists in sustaining its autonomy. *15 Marks*

3. (a) Critically describe evidences from Rakhi Garhi and its linkages to Harappan civilization. *20 Marks*
   (b) Compare and contrast the approaches of M.N. Srinivas and L.P. Vidyarthi to social change in village India. *15 Marks*
   (c) Examine the impact of Forest Policies from 1878 to 2006 on land alienation and deprivation of rights of tribal communities in India. *15 Marks*

4. (a) What are the ethical concerns in biological and socio-cultural anthropology because of recent advances in AI and genetic research? *20 Marks*
   (b) Write an essay on the life history of tribal activist and freedom fighter Birsa Munda. What was the impact of his sacrifice on tribal society? *15 Marks*
   (c) What are the demographic challenges of India's changing population dynamics in the next 50 years? *15 Marks*

SECTION-B

5. Write notes on the following in about 150 words each: *10 × 5 = 50 Marks*
   (a) B.K. Roy Burman's concept of 'Buffer Zone'

(b) Describe ILO's Convention No. 169 (1989) on Indigenous and Tribal people. Is India a signatory to it?

(c) Agricultural practices of the Apatani

(d) Status of Sixth Schedule Areas

(e) Constitutional Safeguards for Backward Classes

6. (a) Custodians of natural resources are the tribals, but they are the most deprived. Critically examine how climate change will impact their survival in future. *20 Marks*

(b) Elucidate the difference between secularism, religiosity, religious fundamentalism and spiritualism from an anthropological perspective. *15 Marks*

(c) Discuss the contribution of P.K. Bhowmick in decriminalising the status of the Lodha tribe. *15 Marks*

7. (a) Critically examine existing paradigms of holistic health for the marginalised sections of society drawing inferences from COVID-19 pandemic. *20 Marks*

(b) Discuss the theories on origin of caste system and its criticism in India. Differentiate between caste, class and race. *15 Marks*

(c) Elucidate the resurgence of ethno-nationalism from an anthropological lens. *15 Marks*

8. (a) Describe the important Paleolithic sites from South India with suitable examples. What is the significance of South Indian Paleolithic cultures? *20 Marks*

(b) Distinguish a "Theocratic State' from a secular, liberal, democratic state. Illustrate your answer with examples from tribal and contemporary societies. *15 Marks*

(c) Discuss the economic, social and developmental impacts on tribal communities with special reference to mining. *15 Marks*

ANALYSIS OF UPSC Mains 2024 Anthropology Optional Paper-II

1. Paper-II was more analytical, which requires a clear understanding of topics like autonomy of subjects by Indian anthropologists, theoretical and democratic states, etc.
2. Greater emphasis on contemporary topics like COVID-19, AI, the next 50 years demographic challenges, digitalisation, climate change, etc.
3. Around 170 marks come under the "easy" category, 50 marks under "average," and 30 marks paper under the "difficult" category.
4. Except 30 marks compulsory question, 230 marks paper can be attempted from the 1st Edition of the book **"ANTHROPOLOGY EXEMPLIFIED"**.

Question No. of **UPSC Anthropology Mains 2024 Paper-II**	Covered in Page no. of Book **"ANTHROPOLOGY EXEMPLIFIED"**
Q.1.(a)	Page 125, 126
Q.1. (b)	Page 104, 105 of Paper-I
Q.1.(c)	Not covered
Q.1.(d)	Page 100 of Paper-II
Q.1.(e)	Page 109, 110, 111 of Paper-II

Q.2.(a)	Page 178, 179 & 180 of Paper-II
Q.2. (b)	Page 137 of Paper-II
Q.2. (c)	Page 61, 62 & 71 of Paper-II
Q.3. (a)	Page 9 & 17 of Paper-II
Q.3. (b)	Page 67 & 68 of Paper-II
Q.3. (c)	Page 121,122 & 123 of Paper-II
Q.4. (a)	Not Covered
Q.4. (b)	Page 147 & 148 of Paper-II
Q.4. (c)	Page 30 & 31 of Paper-II
Q.5. (a)	Not covered
Q.5. (b)	Not covered
Q.5. (c)	Page 159 of Paper-II
Q.5. (d)	Page 166 & 167 of Paper-II
Q.5. (e)	Page 134 & 135 of Paper-II
Q.6. (a)	Page 126 & 127 of Paper-II
Q.6. (b)	Not covered
Q.6. (c)	Not covered
Q.7. (a)	Page 79, 109 & 110 of Paper-II
Q.7. (b)	Page 42 of Paper-II + Page 68 & 209 of Paper-I
Q.7. (c)	Page 144, 145 & 186 of Paper-II
Q.8. (a)	Page 2 & 3 of Paper-II
Q.8. (b)	Page 136 & 187 of Paper-II + Page 103 &104 of Paper-I
Q.8. (c)	Page 118, 119 & 120 of Paper-II

Q. 1 (c) Syro-Malabar Christians

Ans. Syro-Malabar Christians are an ethnoreligious group primarily found in Kerala, India, with roots tracing back to the evangelistic work of St. Thomas the Apostle in the 1st century AD. They belong to the Syro-Malabar Church, an Eastern Catholic Church in communion with the Roman Catholic Church. The Church follows the Syro-Malabar Rite, a distinctive liturgical tradition that blends Eastern Christian practices with Catholic doctrine.

Their social organization is heavily influenced by ancient Christian customs, yet deeply intertwined with the cultural traditions of Kerala. The community's language is primarily Malayalam, and their rituals, including the Holy Qurbana (Mass), reflect a rich blend of local customs and Christian theology.

Anthropologist *K. K. Aziz* has written on the social and cultural aspects of Syro-Malabar Christians, focusing on their historical roots, social organization, and the interplay between Christianity and local Kerala traditions.

L. M. Joshi, an anthropologist, has also written on the Syro-Malabar Christians, focusing on their religious practices and social structures. Additionally, *S. N. Eisenstadt* has studied the community in the context of Indian religious pluralism.

C. G. G. J. D'Cruz, a notable anthropologist, has written on the Syro-Malabar Christians, focusing on their social structure, religious practices, and the influence of Catholicism on Kerala's indigenous traditions.

Syro-Malabar Christians have a significant presence in Kerala's socio-economic and political spheres, particularly in education and healthcare. While they maintain strong religious and cultural ties, their adaptation to modern India showcases the dynamic interaction between tradition and contemporary life.

Q. 4. (a) What are the ethical concerns in biological and socio-cultural anthropology because of recent advances in AI and genetic research?

Ans. Ethical Concerns in Biological Anthropology:

Recent advances in AI and genetic research have raised significant ethical concerns in biological anthropology, particularly regarding issues of consent, privacy, and the potential for genetic determinism. With the advent of genomic sequencing and AI-powered data analysis, the ability to map human genetic diversity has vastly improved. While these developments offer new insights into human evolution and diversity, they also pose risks related to the misuse of genetic data. In India, the *National Ethical Guidelines for Biomedical Research Involving Human Participants* (2017), issued by the Indian Council of Medical Research (ICMR), emphasize the importance of informed consent, particularly in genetic research. However, the complexity of AI algorithms and genetic databases can lead to difficulties in ensuring participants fully understand how their data will be used, stored, and shared.

Additionally, concerns about privacy are heightened as genetic data, once shared, can be linked to individuals across generations, potentially revealing sensitive family history and predispositions. Anthropologists like *Nandini Sundar* have critiqued the use of genetic research to categorize people based on race, warning against the dangers of reinforcing biological determinism. Such practices could inadvertently contribute to harmful stereotypes or discriminatory practices, especially in societies like India, where caste and ethnicity-based identities are complex and historically entrenched. Moreover, AI systems trained on biased genetic datasets could perpetuate existing inequalities, raising questions about how these technologies are designed and whose interests they serve.

Ethical Concerns in Socio-Cultural Anthropology:

In socio-cultural anthropology, the intersection of AI and anthropological research introduces new ethical concerns, particularly in areas like cultural representation, data ownership, and the potential for exploitation of indigenous knowledge. With AI's growing role in analyzing cultural practices and behaviors through vast datasets, there is a risk of oversimplification and misrepresentation of complex cultures. For instance, AI algorithms, designed to process social media data or online cultural content, might misinterpret local customs or historical contexts, leading to a distorted understanding of cultural practices.

Reports like the *National Tribal Policy of India* (2006) highlight the need to protect indigenous cultural knowledge from exploitation, especially as AI technologies can easily be used to appropriate traditional knowledge for commercial or academic purposes without adequate compensation or consent. The use of AI in cultural research also raises the question of whose voice is being amplified. As *Clifford Geertz* noted in "The Interpretation of Cultures" (1973), cultural interpretation must be sensitive to the local context and lived experiences, something that AI may not adequately capture. This becomes especially problematic when AI is used to create representations of marginalized groups, potentially perpetuating stereotypes.

Furthermore, socio-cultural anthropologists like *Akhil Gupta* have critiqued the increasing role of AI in fieldwork, where digital tools and machine learning could replace traditional ethnographic methods.

This shift could marginalize human-centered research, where anthropologists build relationships with communities and understand cultures from an insider's perspective. AI's reliance on big data risks overlooking smaller, nuanced cultural narratives that might not be easily captured in datasets, raising concerns about the ethical integrity of the research process.

In conclusion, both biological and socio-cultural anthropology must confront the ethical implications of AI and genetic research, ensuring that these technologies are used responsibly, with respect for human dignity, cultural diversity, and historical context.

Q.5 (a) B.K. Roy Burman's concept of 'Buffer Zone'

Ans. B.K. Roy Burman's concept of the 'Buffer Zone' refers to the regions or communities that exist between traditional, isolated tribal groups and the larger, more dominant societies. These zones serve as intermediaries, where tribal and non-tribal populations interact, leading to the diffusion of cultures, practices, and values. Burman emphasized that these zones can help facilitate the integration of tribal communities into mainstream society while preserving their distinctiveness. The buffer zone plays a role in mediating conflicts and ensuring that tribal populations are not overwhelmed by external influences.

The concept of the 'Buffer Zone' offers several advantages for tribal communities. It provides a space where tribes can interact with external societies while maintaining a degree of cultural autonomy. By being positioned between isolated tribal groups and the dominant social systems, these buffer zones offer tribes the opportunity to engage with modern institutions, such as education, healthcare, and economic development, without completely losing their traditional ways of life. This intermediary position can reduce the direct pressure from mainstream society, offering tribes a controlled environment for gradual integration. It also allows for the preservation of tribal identity and customs while facilitating economic and social mobility, promoting a balance between tradition and modernization.

However, the concept has been criticized by some Indian anthropologists for oversimplifying the complexities of tribal integration. Critics argue that it overlooks the coercive aspects of state policies and the negative impact of such "buffer zones" on tribal autonomy. *N.K. Bose* and other scholars have pointed out that these intermediary spaces often lead to cultural erosion rather than preservation.

Q.5 (b) Describe ILO's Convention No. 169 (1989) on Indigenous and Tribal people. Is India a signatory to it?

Ans. *ILO Convention No. 169* (1989) is a comprehensive international treaty that aims to protect the rights of indigenous and tribal peoples. It focuses on their right to self-determination, land ownership, and participation in political, economic, and social decisions. The convention also emphasizes the protection of indigenous cultures, languages, and traditional practices, urging governments to respect their distinct identities and ways of life. It mandates consultation with indigenous communities before implementing projects that affect them, ensuring that their rights to land and resources are safeguarded, while promoting social, economic, and educational equality for these marginalized groups.

India is not a signatory to ILO Convention No. 169. *The Report of the Committee on the Welfare of Scheduled Tribes* (2004) and the *Report of the National Commission for Scheduled Tribes* (2018) suggest that while India has made efforts to protect tribal rights through domestic legislation like the *Forest Rights Act* (2006), concerns over sovereignty and practical challenges have prevented adoption of the convention.

Q.6 (a) Elucidate the difference between secularism, religiosity, religious fundamentalism and spiritualism from an anthropological perspective.

Ans. Here's a tabular comparison of secularism, religiosity, religious fundamentalism, and spiritualism from an anthropological perspective:

Concept	Secularism	Religiosity	Religious Fundamentalism	Spiritualism
Definition	Separation of religion from state and public life.	The extent of individual or communal religious practice and belief.	Literal and strict interpretation of religious texts and doctrines.	Focus on personal, mystical experiences of the divine or transcendent. transcendent.
Focus	Political and social governance.	Religious practices and observances.	Return to traditional beliefs and practices.	Individual, direct spiritual experiences.
Anthropological Insight	T.N. Madan in "Secularism in its Indian Context" (2009) discusses India's model of secularism, emphasizing religious tolerance rather than strict separation.	Clifford Geertz in "Religion as a Cultural System" (1973) explores how religiosity forms a cultural framework shaping community and identity.	Saba Mahmood in "Politics of Piety" (2005) examines Islamic fundamentalism and its reaction to modernity and its role in political and social life.	Victor Turner in "The Ritual Process" (1969) highlights how spiritualism fosters transformative communal bonds (communitas) beyond institutionalized religion.
Examples	Indian Constitution, Western secular models	Daily rituals, festivals, prayer practices	Radical religious groups, conservative movements	Mysticism, New Age practices, meditation

In summary:

- Secularism is the state's stance on religion.
- Religiosity reflects how religious beliefs are practiced.
- Religious fundamentalism seeks a return to strict, traditional practices.
- Spiritualism focuses on personal, mystical experiences beyond institutional religion.

These concepts shape individual and collective identities, social systems, and political structures in distinct ways, as explored by anthropologists through cultural and social lenses.

Q.6 (c) Discuss the contribution of P.K. Bhowmick in decriminalising the status of the Lodha tribe.

Ans. *P.K. Bhowmick*, an influential anthropologist, played a pivotal role in challenging the colonial-era categorization of the Lodha tribe as a "criminal tribe." Under the British colonial regime, the Lodhas were listed under the Criminal Tribes Act of 1871, which stigmatized them as inherently criminal and subjected them to punitive measures. This labeling deeply marginalized the tribe, limiting their access to education, healthcare, and economic opportunities.

Bhowmick's anthropological work, particularly in the 1950s and 1960s, focused on the social and cultural characteristics of the Lodha tribe, seeking to challenge the prejudiced assumptions surrounding their identity. He argued that the label "criminal" was a product of colonial policies and misinterpretations of their traditional way of life. Through his studies, Bhowmick highlighted that the Lodhas' practices, such as hunting and shifting cultivation, were misunderstood by colonial authorities, who framed them as criminal activities.

Bhowmick's efforts were instrumental in reshaping the perception of the Lodha tribe. His work, combined with advocacy from social reformers, led to the eventual removal of the Lodhas from the Criminal Tribes Act list in 1952. This decriminalization allowed the Lodhas to regain their dignity, access rights, and participate in national development. However, scholars like *Nandini Sundar* criticize Bhowmick for not sufficiently addressing the socio-economic exploitation and the deeper historical roots of the tribe's marginalization, focusing instead on legal reclassification.

Bhowmick's contribution remains a significant milestone in the anthropology of marginalized tribal communities in India.

Q. 8 (b) Distinguish a "Theocratic State" from a secular, liberal, democratic state. Illustrate your answer with examples from tribal and contemporary societies.

Ans. A "Theocratic State" is one where religious leaders control political power, and laws are based on religious doctrines. In ancient tribal societies, such as the Sentinalese and Andamanese, spiritual leaders held significant political authority. Governance was deeply intertwined with religious beliefs and rituals. Similarly, in North American tribes like the Navajo or Hopi, religious leaders guided political decisions based on spiritual traditions, creating a theocratic system where religion shaped laws and leadership.

In contrast, a "Secular, Liberal, Democratic State" operates on the principle of separating religion from governance. Modern states like Australia and North America exemplify this model, where laws are based on secular principles such as justice and equality, rather than religious doctrines. Indigenous groups like the Yolngu or Arrernte in Australia, and the Cree or Haida in Canada, practice their spiritual beliefs while living under secular governance that guarantees religious freedom and equal rights.

The *Xaxa Committee Report (2014)* on tribal development in India highlights the challenges tribal groups face in navigating modern governance systems. It emphasizes the need to integrate tribal communities into the democratic framework while respecting their cultural and religious identities. Similarly, anthropologists like *Clifford Geertz* have examined how religious systems govern tribal societies, such as in the Bali Aga community, showing how religion and politics are often inseparable in traditional societies. *Anthony Giddens* discusses the shift from tribal theocracies to secular, democratic states, noting the complex process of adapting tribal governance to modern legal systems.

Thus, while ancient tribes like the Sentinalese and Navajo operated under theocratic systems, contemporary Indigenous groups navigate secular, democratic states that protect their cultural rights and religious freedoms.

1

Meaning of Anthropology, Evolution of Man, Primates, Fossils and Archaeology

1.1

Meaning, Scope and Development of Anthropology

Q 1. Meaning, Scope and Development of Anthropology

Ans. Aristotle coined, defined, and explained anthropology for the first time and said that anthropology is gossip, which revolves around man, and an anthropologist is a gossiper who talks about himself.

- Herskovits, in his book "Man and His Works", says that anthropology is the study of man and his works.
- Kluckhone, in his book "Mirror for Man", says that anthropology is a mirror for man, which gives him the opportunity to look at himself in an infinite variety of ways.
- M. Harris, in his book "Theory of Culture in Postmodern Times", says that anthropology is the study of all aspects of humankind in all places at all times.
- Anthropology is the systematic, holistic, integrated, comparative, historical, and universal study of all aspects of mankind at all times and in all parts of the world.

Scope:

- M. Harris said that anthropology is the study of all aspects of mankind in all places at all times.
- According to Ember and Ember, anthropology has not always been as global and comprehensive as it is today.
- Traditionally, they concentrated on non-western culture and left the study of western civilization and complex societies to other disciplines. In recent years, this has disappeared, and anthropologists now work in their own complex societies.

It can be studied under five headings:

1. **Physical:**

1. Human evolution	2. Palaeoanthropology and Primatology
3. Anthropometric development	4. Demographic study
5. Human growth and development	6. Races study
7. Genetics: Eugenics and Euthenics	

2. **Socio-Cultural:**
   1. Formation of ethnography
   2. Origin and variation in cultural material
   3. Institutions study things like economy and kinship
   4. Emergent areas like human rights, migration crisis, and gender relations

3. Linguistic:

1. Origin and changes in language
2. Components of language like phonemes and morphs
3. Language and culture relations: Conklin study
4. Non-verbal communication
5. Change in language with change in social context

4. Archaeological:

1. Reconstruct past
2. Ethno archaeology
3. Public archaeology

5. Applied:

1. Kinanthropometry
2. Epidemological
3. Public archaeology
4. Protection of language
5. Welfare of vulnerable tribal

To handle new problems, sub-branches have emerged like slum anthropology, marine anthropology, and salvage anthropology. In anthropology, micro aspects are studied to improve macro aspects (policy-making).

Development:

Anthropology is as old as humanity itself. From the very beginning, humans have been interested in studying themselves.

- According to T.K. Penniman's classification,
  - Before 1859, Charles Darwin's work, there were two phases:
    - Formulatory: before 1835
    - Convergent: 1835–1859
  - After it, there are two phases:
    - Constructive (1859–1901): classical evolutionist
    - Critical: 1900–1935 based on Radcliffe, Malinowski, Redfield
- Firstly, there are unsystematic studies. Herodotus (5th century BC) was the first one who studied couvade, climatic, and diet effects on growth and the father's or mother's natural head. Later on, Aristotle coined the term anthropology which means gossip that revolves around men.
- During the enlightenment period, works by Immanuel Kant, Charles Darwin's Origin of Species, Herbert Spencer's Social Darwinism, and Wallace became the premise for the development of classical evolutionism and further schools of systematic study.
- In biological anthropology, the initial focus was on fossil studies of human races. Later on, works of Washburn and new technological development led to a shift towards biological (new physical) anthropology, which included the study of primates, genetics, etc.
- Initially, the works of Franz Boas related to the description of linguistics. Sapir made a study of comparative cultures based on language. However, later works of Dell Hymes and Gumberz led to ethnography of communication, the study of the social life of speech, etc.
- Archaeological anthropology has seen development from earlier surveying, excavation, identification, and classification. Later, the development of processual archaeology led by Binford and interpretative archaeology led by Ian Hodder took place.
- In India, anthropological development was related to British rule. The development of the Asiatic Society of Bengal (1874), the Anthropological Introduction at Calcutta University (1920), and the Anthropological Survey of India (1945) paved the way for growth. Scholars like SC Roy, Guha, Majumdar, and L.P. Vidyarthi contributed a lot.

Relevance:

Anthropologists study topics that are essential to understanding human well-being and what it means to be human. Moreover, most anthropologists apply their knowledge and skills to real-world problems.

For example, many anthropologists work at the intersection of law, policy, and ethics, considering such vital issues as migration. They help governments develop policies and advise businesses on analysing human behaviour using anthropological intelligence. Additionally, they can help illuminate the inner workings of politics and the nature of power. Further, they can spotlight how these power dynamics play out—for example, in the social construction of race.

Anthropologists also address human-caused issues related to the environment, such as plastic waste, climate change, deforestation, and destructive wildfires. They can uncover tensions between carbon credit programmes and indigenous communities. When archaeological sites lie in the path of development projects, they record and preserve objects found there.

When it comes to health issues, anthropologists can help design culturally specific strategies for combating epidemics, tuberculosis, and diabetes. They can offer insight into the evolution of exercise and the impacts of changes in human diets. They can provide guidance on controversies in genetics and medicine, such as the DNAediting tool CRISPR or pig organ transplants.

Anthropologists can answer persistent questions about violence, the nature of war, and the enduring hold death has over our lives. They can even give people a more hopeful view of humanity's ingenuity and imagination. In conclusion, because humans are so endlessly and wonderfully diverse, the work of anthropology is equally varied. As an anthropologist, if nothing else, you will rarely be bored.

1.2 Relationships with other disciplines : Social Sciences, behavioural Sciences, Life Sciences, Medical Sciences, Earth Sciences and Humanities.

Q 1. Anthropology and Sociology

Ans. The relationship between anthropology and sociology is very close. Both deal with various social aspects like marriage, family, kinship, religion, etc. Thus, *A.L. Kroeber* termed both anthropology and sociology "twin sisters".

Theme	Anthropology	Sociology
Aim and scope	Universal and Atomistic.	Limited to contemporary rural and urban societies.
Subject matter	Initially, it focuses on tribal and preindustrial societies. Now it studies historical, biological, and cultural aspects of preliterate, peasant and urban societies.	Initially, it studied only the industrial west. Now it conducts studies in both rural and urban societies throughout the world.
Approach	Interdisciplinary – linkage with biology, history, etc.	Sociological approaches are differentiated by the level of analysis. Macrosociology involves the study of widespread social processes. Microsociology involves the study of people at a more interpersonal level, as in face-to-face interactions.

Techniques for data collection	More focus on primary data collection by means of participant observation and prolonged stays. This is supplemented with the scientific techniques of forensics and radiocarbon dating to get concise and qualitative data for cross-cultural analysis.	More use of secondary data collection techniques like questionnaires, schedules, sampling methods, appraisals, statistics, etc. to get quantitative data. They rarely attempted to test their generalisations cross-culturally.

But now these differences are fading away because the subject matter and techniques of both sociologists and anthropologists are merging. Many sociologists also begin to study human groups as studied by anthropologists, and many anthropologists also adopt sociological methods as part of their studies. Many sociologists, for example, also work as anthropologists:

- G.S. Ghurye was a sociologist, but he spent his whole life studying tribes as done by anthropologists.
- M.N. Srinivas also occupied the position of professor of sociology, but he extensively studied tribal societies and conducted comparative studies of historical societies, simpler societies, and civilised societies. His works "Religion and Society among Coorgs" and "Indian Village" have an anthropological outlook.
- Similarly, sociologists like Andre Beteille, T.C. Das, Madan, D.N Majumdar, and S.C. Dube contributed not in the field of anthropology. Thus, now both anthropology and sociology exhibit approximate similarity in methods, theory, and approach.

Hence it is imperative to quote A.L. Kroeber who once said, "All in all, the differences between anthropology and sociology are only in emphasis because, in principle, both anthropology and sociology are difficult to keep apart from one another".

Q 2. Anthropology and History

Ans. History is a sequence of past events. Thus, in order to understand the past, it is necessary to seek the help of history. As anthropology studies all societies, even historical ones, a relationship is established between anthropology and history.

Theme	Anthropology	History
Scope	Universal and holistic. It is concerned with prehistoric, proto-historic, historic, and contemporary societies.	Limited to historic and literate societies which forms the major portion of study. There is less focus on prehistoric cultures.
Subject matter	There is less focus on specific individuals. It can be said to be relatively subaltern in nature. Local elements like folktales, myths, etc. form an important part of the study. It studies both material and immaterial aspects of culture.	It is more concerned with certain royal individuals, dynasties, and making a record of a chronology of events. It studies only the tangible parts of culture, like artifacts, manuscripts, etc. It is upside-down anthropology.
Approach It	It is nomothetic (ethnology) and generalising and aims to find out the general laws of culture and society, as well as ideographic (ethnography).	It is ideographic and particularizing. It aims to narrate historical events in chronological order.
Techniques for data collection	More focus on primary data collection by means of participant observation and prolonged stays. This is supplemented by the scientific techniques of forensics and radiocarbon dating to get concise and qualitative data for cross-cultural analysis.	The use of secondary source is a compulsion here, as the societies to be studied are already extinct. The societies are studied indirectly by the leftover material.

The historical approach of socio-cultural anthropology deals with social and cultural changes and social and cultural set-ups during historical periods. This approach to socio-cultural anthropology is related to history. In socio-cultural anthropology, there are theories of evolutionism and diffusionism. The evolutionists try to trace the origin of different institutions in societies, and the diffusionists deal with the diffusion of various cultural treats during different historical periods. Thus, evolutionist and diffusionist methodologies are related to history.

According to Evans Pritchard, it is difficult to understand the past without the help of history; thus, history helps anthropologists a lot to enhance their knowledge about past societies.

S.C. Dube remarked that it is difficult to understand the present social and cultural setups without knowledge of their pasts. Thus, anthropology cannot sustain itself without knowledge of history; particularly in India, both history and anthropology are closely related.

Q 3. Anthropology and Political science

Ans. Every society has devised certain mechanisms to manage public affairs, maintain public order, and promote welfare among the people. All three of these functions are performed by the political organisation of society. Political science studies political processes, political activities, administrative machinery, ways to elect or appoint an authority, etc., which is the subject matter of political science. But anthropologists, particularly political anthropologists, also study how people in simpler societies manage public affairs, maintain public order, elect or appoint their chiefs or heads, remain integrated and disciplined in the absence of codified laws, etc. This approach to anthropology brings it close to political science.

Theme	Anthropology	Political Science
Scope	Universal and holistic. It is concerned with political systems of primitive, peasant, pre-industrial and modern societies.	Limited to political systems of complex, advanced or modern societies. It pays little attention to the political systems of pre-industrial societies.
Subject matter	It studies why and how a political being evolved.	It assumes man to be a political being.
Approach	It studies political systems embedded in socio-cultural systems.	As a part science, it studies political systems independent of other systems of the society. It considers politics to be a distinct and independent activity.
Techniques for data collection	More focus on primary data collection by means of Participant Observation and prolonged stays. This is supplemented scientific techniques of forensics, radio-carbon dating to get concise and qualitative data for cross-cultural analysis.	Scholars study the constitutions and survey the political atmosphere. Then commentaries are written and comparative analysis is conducted for contemporary societies. There is less focus the political systems.

Now, many anthropologists seek the advice of many scholars of political science to understand the political set-up of many tribal groups. Similarly, political science seeks the help of anthropology to understand how political awareness can be created among tribes and how their political participation can be assumed. Thus, now both anthropology and political science are moving in the direction of strengthening their relationship.

Q 4. Anthropology and Psychology / Behavioural Sciences

Ans. Both subjects study human behaviour, human personality, human intelligence, socialisation processes, aggression, sexuality, sex roles, etc.

Two books by Margret Mead, "Coming of Age in Samoa" and "Growing Up in New Guinea," proved to be very helpful for psychologists.

Theme	Anthropology	Psychology
Scope	Universal and holistic. It is concerned with behavioural systems of primitive, peasant, preindustrial and modern societies.	Limited to present day societies.
Subject matter	It studies individuals, societies as a whole and even nation.	It is limited to individuals and groups.
Approach	It attempts to study conscious & unconscious phenomena along with external material aspects of culture such as social structure, economic systems etc.	As a part science, it studies only the mental facts. It dives into the internal constitution of an individual.
Techniques for data collection	More focus on primary data collection by means of participant observation and prolonged stays This is supplemented by the scientific techniques of psychological studies qualitative data for cross-cultural analysis.	Advanced techniques are used like: Cognitive remediation Cognitive restructuring Dream analysis Resistance analysis Transference analysis to get concise and The field for a psychologist is the clinic, where interviews take place.

In spite of these differences, both anthropology and psychology help each other in understanding human behaviour and personality.

Q 5. Anthropology and Economics

Ans. Anthropology, particularly economic anthropology, deals with modes of production, means of distribution, and ways of consumption. Production, distribution, and consumption are the main domains of economies. But because these areas are also covered by anthropology, anthropology comes closer to economics. Although anthropology dealt with certain economic aspects, it exhibited differences from the modern economy.

Theme	Anthropology	Economy
Scope	Universal and holistic. It is concerned with the economic patterns and systems of primitive, peasant, pre-industrial, and modern societies. In small-scale societies, where anthropologists mainly study, there may not be distinct economic transactions as found in advanced societies.	Limited to the economic systems of contemporary societies and studies only the transactional aspects of human relations.

Subject matter	It studies why and how economic systems evolve.	It assumes man to be Homo economics with natural qualities of rationalization.
Approach	It studies economic systems as embedded in socio-cultural systems. The norms of exchange and distribution are considered rooted in social values.	As a part science, it studies economic systems independent of other systems of the society. It considers economic causes to be the driving force of all human actions.
Techniques for data collection	More focus on primary data collection by means of participant observation, fieldwork and prolonged stays. This is supplemented by the scientific techniques to get concise and qualitative data for cross-cultural analysis.	The economists use statistical methods and advanced mathematics to derive trends and inferences.

But now many changes have been taking place in the tribal economy, particularly due to globalisation and contact with the mainstream. Therefore, anthropologists also begin to apply methods of modern economics to study tribal economies. Anthropologists also begin to study the economies of industrial and post-industrial societies.

Economists also seek the advice of anthropologists in order to frame many economic policies for simpler people. Due to this approach of anthropology and economics, close relations are developing between them.

Q 6. Anthropology and Medical Sciences

Ans. Like medical sciences, anthropology also deals with medicine, diseases, and their prevention, particularly with respect to similar societies, thus developing a relationship between anthropology and medical science. Due to the interest of anthropologists in the field of medical science, a particular branch of anthropology has emerged: medical anthropology. Medical anthropology deals with many diseases and syndromes like Down syndrome, Edward syndrome, Klinfelter syndrome, and Turner syndrome. They understand the genetic reasons behind the occurrence of such disorders and how they can be prevented. Many medical anthologists act as genetic counsellors and work in this direction.

Theme	Anthropology	Medical Sciences
Scope	Universal and holistic. It is concerned with epidemiological and medical systems of primitive, peasant, preindustrial and modern societies.	Limited to present day societies.
Subject matter	It studies individuals, societies as a whole and even nation.	Limited to individual and groups.
Approach	It studies medical systems as embedded in socio-cultural systems, along with genetic studies.	As a part science, it only deals with medicines, diseases and their prevention
Techniques for data collection	More focus on primary data collection by means of participant observation, fieldwork and prolonged stays. This is supplemented by the scientific techniques to get concise and qualitative data for cross-cultural analysis.	Advanced techniques are used like: Genetical analysis, DNA analysis, etc. The field for a doctor is the hospital, where research and operations take place.

Medical anthropology also analyses the role of witchcraft, sorcery, and magic in the health of simpler societies.

The medical doctors seek the help of anthropologists with the question of how diseases in simpler societies can be caused and how the simpler people can be motivated to adopt modern medicines.

Anthropologist suggestions include alternate methods of treatment and alternate medicines, including local herbs, to deal with the health issues of simpler people.

Medical doctors help the anthropologists maintain the hygiene, sanitation, and well-being of simpler people. Many doctors, after giving up their profession, work with tribes for their well-being. Dr. Nadine Peacock worked among the Ituri Pygmies of Zaire and helped this group get rid of many diseases.

Although there are certain differences between anthropology and medical science, both of them work together for the well-being of people.

Q 7. Anthropology and Earth Sciences

Ans. Both anthropology and geography study human relationships with the environment. After studying geography, anthropologists come to know that a number of supernatural events are actually natural, so they propagate this idea among people, particularly the simpler ones, so that they can no longer remain supernatural regarding certain happenings. For *example,* earlier it was believed, but now, with the help of geography, anthropologists are able to convey that earthquakes are natural events.

Geology is the study of rocks. The study of rocks is an important component of understanding human evolution because fossils are discovered between rocks. When geologists fix the age of rocks, the age of the concerned fossil is also estimated. An anthropologist also seeks the help of geologists to establish the age of different tools and to understand the type of stone to be used for making such tools. By studying rock stratigraphy, various evolutionary phases can be established.

Theme	Anthropology	Earth sciences
Scope	Universal and holistic. It is concerned with natural and supernatural patterns and systems of primitive, peasant, pre-industrial and modern societies.	Limited to the study of physical aspects of rocks, climate, environment, etc.
Subject matter	Cultural and natural events.	Rocks, atmosphere, hydrosphere, climate etc.
Approach	It uses a synchronic and diachronic approach to understand and disseminate natural laws via generalisations.	It involve the analysis of already existing natural phenomenon.
Techniques data collection	More focus on primary data collection by means of participant observation, fieldwork and prolonged stays. This is supplemented scientific stays. This is supplemented by the scientific techniques of forensics and radiocarbon dating to get concise and qualitative data for cross -cultural analysis.	Super-computers are used for advanced for modelling, remote sensing etc.

Today, following an interdisciplinary approach, we don't compare subjects but bring them together on a common platform. Humans are complex beings, and understanding them requires a multidisciplinary approach.

1.3

Main Branches of Anthropology, their Scope and Relevance:

(a) Social-cultural Anthropology. **(b) Biological Anthropology.**
(c) Archaeological Anthropology. **(d) Linguistic Anthropology.**

Q 1. Social-cultural Anthropology

Ans. Following Franz Boas classification, socio-cultural anthropology is one of the four subfields of anthropology. This branch of anthropology deals with socio–cultural evolution and variation. Earlier, the term socio-cultural anthropology was not used collectively, and social anthropology was used separately from cultural anthropology. Social anthropology originated and developed in England. It studied the origin, development, and factors behind the emergence of marriage, family, kinship, religious, political, and economic systems. In other words, it dealt with the characteristics of all social systems. On the other hand, cultural anthropology originated and developed in America. It studies human culture i.e. acquired custom, tradition, ethics, etc. and how they are acquired, learned, and transmitted in different societies. But we know there can be no culture without society, and no society without culture; hence, they should be studied collectively rather than individually. It was through the efforts of A.L. Kroeber that the terms were merged. It has scope in two sub branches: ethnography and ethnology. Ethnography means the extensive and intensive study of a single culture at a particular time. While ethnology is comparative as it utilises ethnographies and compares them, ethnology has two broad specialisations: topical specialisation and area specialisation. Topical anthropology covers areas like ethno zoology, ethno botany, and political anthropology. While area studies help to study different areas to know their specifications.

Approaches:

1. Holism
2. Emic and Etic approaches
3. Case study approach
4. Comparative approach
5. System and process approach

Starting from classical evolutionism, it has evolved through diffusionism, functionalism, structure functionalism, etc.

Applications:

1. Helpful in the field of public administration, rural development programmes, solving socio-cultural problems, etc.
2. Helps individuals become cultural relativists and bust the myth of social superiority.
3. To preserve cultures prone to extinction.
4. Contemporary areas: gender study, human rights, globalisation, multiculturalism, public health, corporate culture, etc.

Q 2. Biological Anthropology

Ans. Following Franz Boas classification, biological anthropology is one of the four subfields of anthropology. It is that branch of anthropology that deals not only with physical (morphological) man but also with genetics. It began in the late 18th century when scientists became curious to know about physical differences among humans, which laid the foundation for the study of race. In 1850, fossils of the ancestors of man were discovered, which prompted interest in human biological evolution. In 1871, Charles Darwin opined that human have evolved from apes, and thereafter, the study of man, monkeys, and apes, i.e., primates started. At this time, it was called physical anthropology as it studied only the morphology of primates; races too were studied morphologically. Fossils were anatomical structures, but they too were studied at face value. Changes began in the 20th century. The ABO blood group was discovered by Landsteiner in 1900. Cytology, cytogenetics, and biochemistry came in the second decade of the century. The synthetic theory of evolution was propounded in the 1930s. It brought about a change in scope and subject matter. Genetic studies started replacing morphological (physical) studies.

Studies started involving interactions between heredity and the environment. There have also been studies involving the interaction between genetic behaviour and culture. It was thereafter given the name "New Physical Anthropology" by Washburn.

Sub-Branches:

1. Human Genetics
2. Forensics
3. Demographics
4. Ecology and adaptation
5. Palaeo anthropology
6. Primatology

Applications

Designing sport equipment, medical equipment, nutritional plan, DNA technology, medical pluralism, genetic counselling, etc.

Today, biological anthropologists work with socio-cultural anthropologists to align their solutions with diverse cultures and societies.

Q 3. Archaeological Anthropology

Ans. Following Franz Boas classification, archaeological anthropology is one of four subfields of anthropology. It is concerned with the exploration, collection, identification, classification, and interpretation of antiquarian and environmental remains in order to reconstruct the chronological sequence of the human past. It originated and developed mainly in America. It studied pre history, history and proto history. It even studied tools and traditions like Acheulian, Mousterian, Levallosian, etc. The scope got widened with the works of Binfond, David Clarke, Willey, etc. They included a system approach to the study. Later, Ian Hodder emphasised internal innovative elements in culture rather than external environmental factors as agents of change.

Archaeological records include individual objects like jewellery, structures, monuments, tools, and art like pottery, painting, soil, and sediments.

Scope:

1. Environment archaeology
2. Tools and technology
3. Ethnology
4. Marine archaeology
5. Ethno archaeology
6. Settlement archaeology
7. Urban archaeology

Methods used:

1. Aerial, maps, and satellite images
2. Settlement archaeology: Institutions control via material study
3. Environment archaeology: Reconstructing past climate
4. Ethnoarchaeology: Reconstructing the past via present society
5. Bioarchaeology: Mortality and Epidemiology Study
6. Experimental archaeology: Test hypotheses

Case Study: Arizona's garbage project in Tucson helped evaluate how many beers were consumed in town (*Willian* Rathje).

Applications:

1. Reconstruct past
2. Help to know adaptations in the past
3. Public archaeology and cultural revenue management
4. Migration pattern of the past: East Africa dispersed
5. The prehistoric part of cultural anthropology is akin to archaeology.

The use of GIS, DNA, and genetic studies enhanced the interdisciplinary and holistic outlook of this discipline.

Q 4. Linguistic Anthropology

Ans. Following Franz Boas classification, linguistic anthropology is one of four subfields of anthropology. Due to their possession of language, humans have a unique position in the animal kingdom and remain cultural generation after generation. A branch of anthropology that studies languages, particularly the unwritten languages of non-western people, is known as linguistic anthropology. Until the early decade of the 20th century, it was called 'anthropological linguistics' as it dealt with the origin and classification of language. Following the Sapir-Whorf hypothesis and Levi Strauss, focus is on the link between language and the human thought process, along with its implications for behaviour. Post-1950, the focus is on language as a vehicle for culture. Dell Hymes was the first to rename the field to linguistic anthropology. He initiated 'ethnography of communications'.

Sub-Branches:

1. Historical linguistics: It studies the emergence and diversification of different languages. It also studies how particular languages have undergone changes since their inception.
2. Structural linguistics: It studies the structure of different languages, how words are arranged in a particular language, etc.
3. Comparative linguistics: Different languages are studied comparatively.
4. Socio linguistic: It studies how language is put into actual speech, how people speak differently in different contexts, and how language ascertains the social status of a human group.

It also studies the relationship between language and culture, like how language moulds personalities and how culture is transmitted from generation to generation. Another subject matter is to study language socialisation: "socialisation through language" and "socialisation to language". It studies not only major but also minor languages. Summing up, it studies the role of language in one's society, in one's personality, and actually in one's life. Linguistics even helps preserve culture by scripting languages through extensive field work.

Case Study

Vervet Monkey (Ember & Ember): They are not closely related to humans, as are African apes. However, they consider three different reactions to alarm calls for different predators: eagle, python, and leopard. They look up when they hear 'eagle' call.

Q 5. Action and Applied Anthropology

Ans. Pride of anthropology lies in the way it has applied its subject matter for betterment of humanity. The concept of action anthropology was given by Sol Tax in one of his papers, 'Values in Action', published in 1958. According to Sol Tax, an anthropologist who remains associated with a particular issue or problem for a prolonged period until the issue is solved is termed an action anthropologist. It replaced the traditional passive approach. Like an applied anthropologist, his knowledge and concepts are used. Not only does he act as an advisor or counsellor, but he remains associated at ground level at all three stages: before, during, and after. Action anthropologists include L.P. Vidyarthi, who studies among Malers of Jharkhand, and P.K. Bhowmick, who studies among Lodhas of Bengal. They consider the problem their own and work with sincerity to solve it. If the programme fails, they don't blame anyone but mend their own ways of working and introduce a solution in modified form. They act to solve problems like birth control, infant mortality, malnutrition, education promotion, etc. While applied anthropology is defined as an organised interaction between professional anthropologists and welfaremaking agencies in order to get the desired results of particular efforts. It developed mainly in America after WWII, when a number of anthropologists contributed to ameliorating the miseries of war victims. The term was coined by Daniel G. Briton in his paper 'The Aims of Anthropology' in 1875. The basic objective is to apply knowledge to solve various problems and bring welfare to neglected people. Another is to instruct agencies to bring about planned change. S.C. Roy applied his knowledge to solve problems among the Oraons of two villages who fought over the issue of the flag. Sachindra Narayan redesigned the hockey stick for Malers of Jharkhand and the archery game for Paharia of Jharkhand.

They work with a plan to solve issues like infant mortality, birth control, etc. with the help of agencies like UNICEF, UNESCO, WHO, etc.

By judging the importance of applied anthropology, Raymond Firth calls them "social engineers" because, like engineers, they mend social evils, whereas Kluckholn calls them "social doctors" because, like doctors, they cure social evils.

1.4

Human Evolution and emergence of Man:

(a) Biological and Cultural factors in human evolution.

(b) Theories of Organic Evolution (Pre-Darwinian, Darwinian and Post-Darwinian).

(c) Synthetic theory of evolution; Brief outline of terms and concepts of evolutionary biology (Doll's rule, Cope's rule, Gause's rule, parallelism, convergence, adaptive radiation, and mosaic evolution).

Q 1. Biological and cultural factors in Human evolution

Ans. Human evolution is the interplay of biological evolution and cultural evolution. Thus, *Washburn* termed this evolution "gene-cultural co-evolution". According to him, both biological evolution and cultural evolution are interrelated.

Biological Factors:

1. **Size and complexity of brain:** In hominids, the size of brain has almost tripled in the last three million years. There were strong selective pressures behind this, with this factor providing the basis for all other evolutionary transformations.
2. **Erect posture and bipedalism:** Bipedalism refers to walking and running on hindlegs that move alternately. It provided an upgrade in efficiency over knuckle-walking.

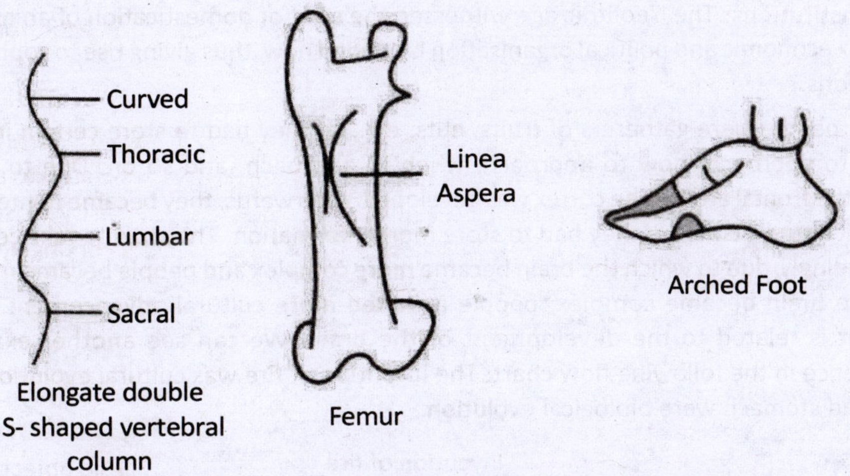

Anatomical features that make humans habitually bipedal

3. **Hyoid bone complex:** The shape of the hyoid bone in the neck is unique to hominids and reflects their ability to speak.

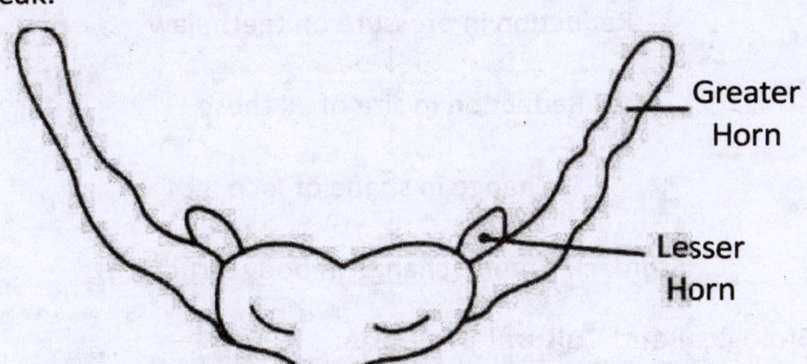

Hyoid Bone

Cultural Factors:

1. **Tool Making:** Bipedalism freed the hands for carrying objects and for making and using tools. This in turn improved coordination between eye and hand, along with the movement of the opposable thumb.

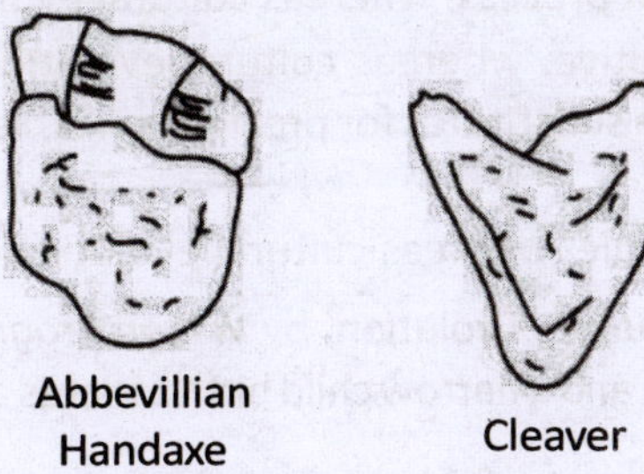

Early Human Tools

2. **Hunting and Gathering:** Humans require animal protein for their increasing brain sizes. Thus, through their tools and cooperative strategies, they began to hunt animals. To increase their survival chances, humans started to live in social groups.
3. **Speech development:** The development of the hyoid bone complex, along with increasing cognition and intellect, led to the onset of speech and language. This enhanced communication and social bonding.

4. **Social Institutions:** The Neolithic age witnessed the start of domestication of animals and plants. Complex economic and political organisation is needed now, thus giving rise to sophisticated social institutions.

Initially, people were gatherers of fruits, nuts, etc., so they had to store certain information like which plant to approach, how to approach, when to approach, and so on. Due to the storage of information, the frontal area of the cortex was developed. Afterwards, they became hunters, pastoralists, and then agriculturalists. Thus, they had to store more information. They had to take certain decisions and act accordingly, due to which the brain became more complex and people became more intelligent, but when the brain became complex, people acquired more cultural advancement. Thus, cultural advancement is related to the development of the brain. We can see another example of their interdependence in the following flow chart: The invention of fire was cultural evolution, but changes in the face and stomach were biological evolution.

Invention of fire
↓
Food became cooked
↓
Reduction in pressure on teeth, jaw
↓
Reduction in size of all these
↓
Change in shape of face
↓
Stomach simple (change in body structure)

Difference between Biological and Cultural Evolution:

1. Biological evolution is prior to cultural evolution because the biological evolution of humans was part of organic evolution, which was initiated billions of years ago, whereas cultural evolution began with the appearance of humans on earth.
2. Biological evolution signifies the transmission of genes, i.e., gene-generated transmission, whereas cultural evolution is a learning process.
3. Biological evolution is a natural process, whereas cultural evolution is a deliberate process.
4. Biological evolution is substitutive, whereas cultural evolution is additive because in biological evolution, successive stages are substitutes for previous ones, retain already existing cultural treats, and even add some more.
5. Biological evolution is irreversible, whereas cultural evolution may be reversible.

In an article named 'Scars of Human Evolution' by *Wilton Krogman*, it has described problems like back pain, a windpipe choked by food, and a narrow child birth canal as adaptations that were not successful.

Q 2. Lamarckism

Ans. A French-born biologist, Jean Baptiste De Lamarck, in his book entitled "Philosophie Zoologique" put forth his theory of organic evolution, which centred on the inheritance of acquired characters. The theory can be explained through the following postulates:

1. **Theory of Growth for Internal Urge:** Internal forces of life tend to increase the size of an organism through growth in organs and systems.

Criticism: It is true that large species are descendants of small ones, but it is not a rule. But it is not always true that small species give way to large ones; otherwise, how could we explain extinction?

2. **Theory of Need:** The growth of a new organ in a living being or the modification of an older one is need-based.

   Criticism: Need cannot direct the course of evolution; otherwise, man has always been thinking of flying but has never developed wings.

3. **Theory of Use:** The development of an organ is directly proportional to its use. Use leads to growth, while disuse leads to degeneration.

   Criticism: It is partially true that athletes can develop leg muscles by jogging, but if used beyond their limits, the results can be negative.

4. **Theory of Inheritance of Acquired Characters:** All changes that take place in an individual's life by chance, accident, or heredity are passed on to the next generation.

   Criticism: If person due to accident has to get legs computed, he/she still bears normal children and not lame ones. Theory of continuity of Germplasm by August Weismann - Characters influencing germplasm are only inherited.

Lamarck cited example like Giraffe had earlier short neck, lived upon grass. But when it became scarce, they have to stretch neck to reach leaves of tall plant. Continuous stretching modified it and it passed to next generation and today Giraffe had long necks.

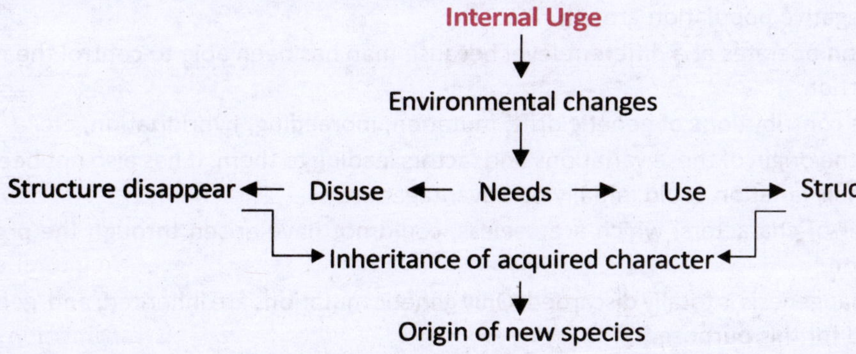

One basic drawback of this theory was that it lacks convincing data and evidence to support it.

Despite all criticism, Lamarck's work is commendable. He gave his theory when utterance of word 'evolution' was rebellious. He created interest in subject which led to development of modern scientific theories.

Q 3. Darwanisim

Ans. The term Darwinism is coined to elaborate on the theory of organic evolution as given by Charles Darwin, in his book 'Origin of Species by Natural Selection'. Inspired from: Flora and Fauna of the Galapagos, Malthus - Overpopulation, Lyell and Uniformitarian, Wallace Variation, and so on.

The Darwinian explanation rests on certain observed facts and certain inductions from these facts:

1. **Observed fact:** Malthusian principle says that there is an increase in the number of individuals in every species in the geometric ratio, but resources increase in arithmetic ratio while the total number remains constant generation after generation. Inferred fact: Struggle for existence says that lack of food and room creates competition among individuals having ecological relations to one another.

2. **Observed fact:** Variation: Always apparent slight variation exists among individuals of a species, even though they are of the same generation. Inferred fact: Natural selection: success in competition of those individuals whose slight differences are of such nature as to give them an advantage over their competitors in a particular environment.
3. **Observed fact:** Hereditary: Transmission by patients to offspring of form and physiology essentially like parents Inferred fact: Origin of Species: After 'n' number of generations, some individual would appear that would be different from the 1 st parental generation.

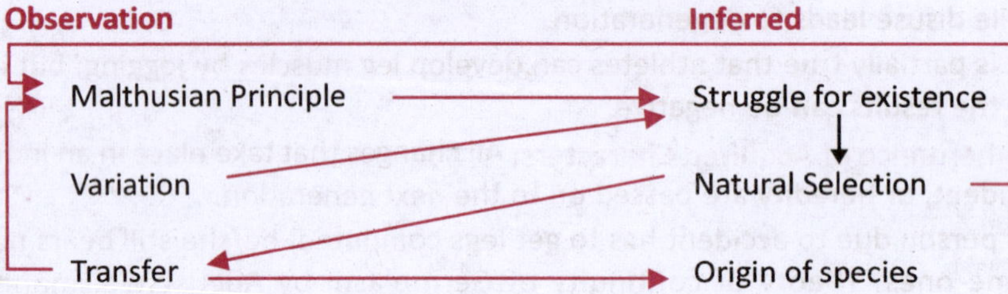

Example: Industrial melanism: increase in dark moths and decrease in grey moths, post-industrial revolution in England.

Criticism:

1. Increase in population in geometric progression is not applicable to man. Many countries now even have a negative population growth rate.
2. Natural selection operates at a different level because man has been able to control the negative effects of selection.
3. He ignored the contributions of genetic drift, mutation, inbreeding, hybridization, etc.
4. He is silent on the origin of these variations and factors leading to them. It has also not been made clear how a small variation could initially be advantageous.
5. A large number of characters, which are useless, could not have arisen through the process of natural selection.
6. The theory of pangenesis is totally discarded. Only genetic mutations are inherited, and 'gemmules' are not formed for this purpose.

In spite of criticism, it deserves credit as modern theories are based on Darwin and have contributed a lot to organic evolution via natural selection.

Case Study

- **Colour helps "Darwinian fitness" in nature; humans are impacting this too**

The change in the peppered moth's wing colour is a famous illustration; as the Industrial Revolution gained steam and more soot was created starting in the middle of the 19th century, trees in England turned darker. This was reflected in the prevalence of dark-coloured peppered moths, a renowned illustration of extremely quick colour evolution brought on by human influences. All the species occupying this place are being impacted by how people are changing the ecosystem right now. Both the evolution of colour and the visual environment that creatures may see are being impacted by us. Winters are becoming shorter, and there is less snow, which affects animals with seasonal colour changes, such as snowshoe hares, which are white in winter and brown in summer. Because of how this has changed their local environment, certain populations no longer change colour. Stickleback fish frequently have vivid colours, which is vital for their mate selection and reproduction. This is also occurring in waterbodies. However, the visual environment inside lakes and streams is altering as water bodies become more and more contaminated. These fish are also altering since their original hues and patterns can no longer be seen.

Q 4. Neo-lamarckism

Ans. Some evolutionist biologists, like McDougall, Packard, Cope, Herbert Spencer, Griffith, Detleofson, etc., further modified the Lamarckian theory, and this modified version of Lamarckism is termed neo-Lamarckism.

Neo-Lamarckists hold that adaptation is universal. Changing environmental conditions bring about changes in the habits of individuals, and to cope with changing environmental conditions and changing habits, individuals acquire new characters, and in certain cases, such characters also become time-span characters that become fully apparent in coming generations.

The Neo-Lamarckists conducted many experiments to prove that acquired characters can also be inherited.

McDougall conducted an experiment on rats by putting them in a water tank. The water tank was provided with two exits, one lighted and the other dark; the lighted exit was also provided with an electric shock. Now, it is natural that rats attempted to escape from lighted holes, but due to electric shock, they were not able to escape, and after repeated trials, they learned to escape from dark holes. Then, their offspring were put through the same trials, and this trial went on generation after generation. It was observed by McDougall that learning capability kept on increasing with every successive generation until rats directly escaped from the dark hole. Thus, he claimed that this learning process is an acquired quality that is inherited by offspring.

Griffith and Detleofson also conducted an experiment on rats by putting them on rotating tables for several months. Rats became adaptive to rotating conditions to such an extent that even when rotation was stopped, they showed signs of dizziness. Then these rats were interbred by themselves, and their offspring were put under the same conditions, and after certain generations, the offspring showed irregularities in gait even at the time of birth. Thus, both of them claimed that such irregularities were acquired characteristics that became part of heredity.

Many more experiments were conducted by other Neo-Lamarckists, which proved that acquired character can also be inherited. They even claim that acquired characters can also be inherited among humans, but generations are not able to observe them because such characters become apparent after a longer time and a particular generation is not able to observe such characters.

Therefore, neo-Lamarckism cannot be discarded completely because certain acquired characters can also become part of heredity.

Q 5. Synthetic theory of Evolution

Ans. Synthetic theory of human evolution is the most recent and most scientific of all existing theories and combines all genuine elements of hitherto existing theories. Exponents of the theory made use of modern scientific knowledge, such as cytology, cytogenetics, etc., and employed modern techniques of research. The theory propagated by several neo-Darwinians, including Stebbins, Simpson, Fisher, etc., basically aimed to clear Darwinism of drawbacks and criticism. As a result, Darwinism forms its core, but other evolutionary processes are also given credit.

Synthetic Theory proponents:

1. **Mutation:** Hugo De Vries, Dobzhansky
2. **Population Genetics:** Sewall Wright, Hardy
3. **Population Dynamics:** Julian Huxley

The basic features of synthetic theory are:

Mutation, genic recombination, change in chromosome number, natural selection, and isolation are the five essential evolutionary processes. The first three provide genetic variability, and the last two guide populations of organisms into adaptive channels.

1. New traits appear through mutation—radiation is the main source among humans—but they owe their existence and spread to natural selection.
2. Change in chromosome number leads to variations among lower forms of living organisms, but in humans, it leads to sex anomalies and autosomal anomalies like Turner Syndrome (44 + X) and Down syndrome (trisomy of the 21st chromosome).
3. Genic recombination results in a change in the sequence of genes on the chromosome. The new arrangement does result in new genic expression resulting in a new phenotype, but such deletion, inversion, duplication, etc., results in severe disability and even death among humans.
4. Isolation (reproductive) as well as geographic isolation form a strong base for the formation of new species.
   Reproductive isolation to work effectively requires the immense contributions of mutation, selection, and geographic isolation.
5. In addition to the above five, three ancillary processes affect evolution:
   a. **Migration:** movement from one place to another
   b. **Hybridization:** mating of two individuals of different genotypes
   c. **Chance factor**: due to sheer chance, a change in genetic material

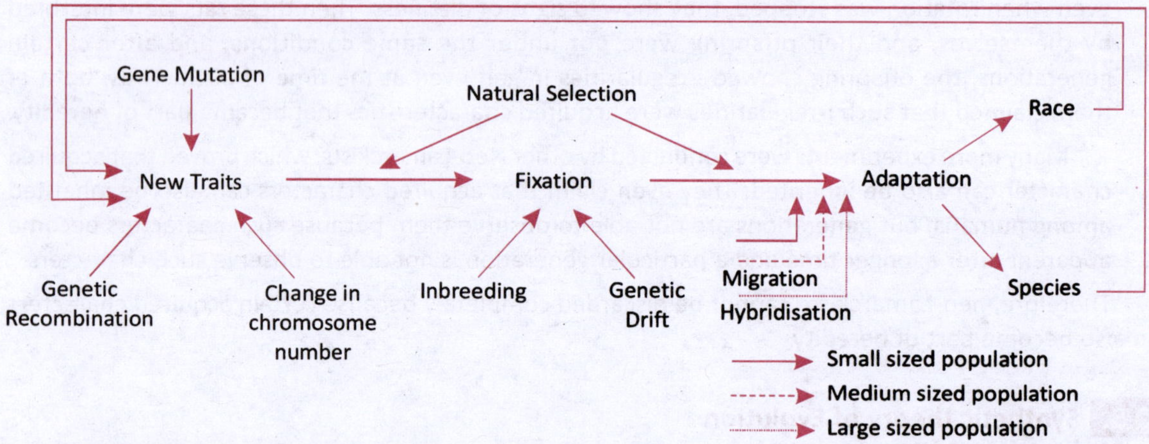

New species are formed by continuous action of micro evolutionary processes over long time span cutting through geographical span.

Limitation:

1. Scientific theory only explains the fixation stage, it ignored Lamarckism.
2. The theory explains evolution in the past but fails to explain it in terms of its future direction.
3. The factors of genic recombination and change in chromosome number do not warrant the importance given to them in this theory and downplay genetic drift and hybridization.
4. The punctuated equilibrium theory of Eldredge and Gould explained that evolution is sudden and not gradual.

5. The Kimura hypothesis explains that most mutant genes are selectively neutral.
6. Eugene Koonin stated that while the edifice of modern synthesis crumbled beyond repair. A new 21st-century synthesis can be glimpsed that ages advances in molecular biology, microbiology, and genomics.

   Biologists have continued to debate the need for replacement synthesis.

Case Study

- **Why do we love sugar so much? Here is a genetic connection to your sweet addiction:**

Getting enough food to eat was one of our ancient ancestors' main problems. Basic daily tasks like caring for children, finding housing, and obtaining enough food all require energy in the form of calories. All of these tasks appeared to be more successful for people who are better at gaining calories. They had superior fitness in terms of evolution because they lived longer and produced more children who survived. They could quickly taste food to determine its caloric content without spending a lot of time acquiring, preparing, and eating it. Early humans were able to find sweetness and eat a lot of calories with little effort. They could focus their efforts instead of haphazardly browsing, which would increase their chances of succeeding in evolution.

Sweet taste genes: A sugar-detection receptor protein named TAS1R2/3 is produced by sweet-detecting cells. When it does, the brain receives a neural signal for processing. This message describes how you experience sweetness in food. Every protein in the body is made according to instructions that are encoded in genes. A pair of conveniently named genes on chromosome 1 of the human genome, TAS1R2 and TAS1R3, encode the sugar-detecting receptor protein TAS1R2/3. Natural selection preserves genes with crucial jobs, while genes without them deteriorate and occasionally vanish entirely as organisms change. The use-it-or-lose-it hypothesis also explains the fascinating finding that animal species that do not typically consume sugar have lost their capacity to perceive it. For instance, many carnivores, which do not profit greatly from the perception of sugars, only contain degraded remnants of TAS1R2.

Q 6. Dollo's Rule

Ans. Louis Dollo was a Belgian paleontologist, who in 1893, proposed that "Evolution is irreversible and irrevocable." A structure that changes its form in the course of evolution does not revert to its earlier form. Dollo's law of irreversibility (also known as Dollo's law) states that "an organism never returns exactly to a former state, even if it finds itself placed in conditions of existence identical to those in which it has previously lived... it always keeps some trace of the intermediate stages through which it has passed".

The hypothesis was first advanced by a historian, Edgar Quinet. Stephen Jay Gould supported Dollo's law that irreversibility forecloses certain evolutionary pathways once broad forms have emerged. For example, once you adopt the ordinary body plan of a reptile, hundreds of options are forever closed, and future possibilities must unfold within the limits of inherited design.

Reasons of Irreversibility:

1. The same environment cannot be replicated. Doll's rule seeks to explain the course of evolution. This rule predicts that evolutionary changes cannot be reverted because every species is the product of its environment, and similar kinds of environments cannot be replicated.
2. More Functional Specialisation: When structural changes are responsible for functional specialisation, it confines a species to a narrow and restricted environment; there is no possibility of reversion to the primitive organisation from which it originally derived.

3. Because such evolving groups have a tendency to be more specialised and acquire more progressive useful variations, which lead to the irreversibility of evolution.

Examples:

1. Races, species, and genera are formed over a period of time through changes in genetic composition. All these alterations cannot be reversed back to their original stock.
2. Throughout the Pleistocene, humans adapted to changing environmental conditions with changes like the lower jaw, dentition, erect posture, brain size, etc., which cannot be reversed.
3. Land vertebrates, in the course of secondary adaptation to life in water, do not become fish again, nor do they acquire the characteristics peculiar to fish.
4. If a premolar is lost in the course of evolution, then it will never recur again as a premolar in subsequent evolution.
5. Ichthyosaurs, which became adapted to an aqueous environment, remained typical in all their structural features. Similarly, whales remained mammals with their own special structural features.

Exceptions:

1. In Stephen Jay Gould's interpretation of Dollo's law, it would not be possible to regain a coil after the coiling has been lost. Nevertheless, a few genera in the slipper snail family may have changed their developmental timing and regained a coiled shell from a limpet-like shell.
2. Dollo's law has since been refuted by evidence that evolutionary specialization can be undone. For instance, reversible evolution has been observed on a relatively short evolutionary time scale in the peppered moth (Biston betularia). In the 19th century, a dark morph of the moth emerged in response to air pollution during the Industrial Revolution and became the dominant colour morph, almost completely replacing the light-coloured form. By the late 20th century, however, the light morph was on the rise again, with its increase coincident with the decline of air pollution in England.

Q 7. Cope's Rule

Ans. *Edward de Cope*, an American paleontologist, gave this rule on the basis of his extensive study of the fossils of mammals. The rule states that organisms have a tendency to increase in size during evolution.

Reasons for the increase in size:

1. Decrease the body surface area: It is now presumed that increases in size in different mammalian lineages may be on account of different seasons. In the Pleistocene, it could have been a device to decrease body surface to conserve body heat in a cold environment.
2. To capture large prey: Among carnivores, increasing in size facilitates the capture of large herbivores on which they feed.
3. Mechanism to increase Fecundity: For egg-laying mammals, this would be a device to increase their fecundity, which means the number of offspring produced will be higher due to more eggs in a large body.

Examples: There are numerous examples throughout evolutionary history: mammals increasing in size after the demise of the dinosaurs; amphibians increasing in size after making it onto the land; all animals increasing in size after the Cambrian Explosion 540 million years ago; and so on. The evolution of the horse, camel, and all other herbivores exhibited an increase in size, so they attained gigantism. Dinosaurs provide the most interesting example of an increase in size.

Exceptions:

1. Insectivorous mammals: It is physically impossible for Mole to be very large because that will be a difficulty in borrowing.
2. Flying bat: The habit of flying imposes limitations on the body size of bats.
3. Many mammalian lineages exhibit a decline in size; for example, carnivores attained gigantic size in the Pliocene and Pleistocene but showed a decrease in size thereafter.
4. J. Arnold, who studied planktonic foraminifera, found that the newer species are of small size.
5. Hooijer has pointed out that progressive size decrease has been characteristic of many vertebrates during the quaternary period, which is now in progress.

This theory tried to explain organic evolution in a meaningful way, but it is not universally applicable.

Q 8. Gause's Rule

Ans. The competitive exclusion principle, sometimes referred to as Gause's law, is a proposition named for Georgy Gause that two species competing for the same limited resource cannot coexist at constant population values. When one species has even the slightest advantage over another, the one with the advantage will dominate in the long term. This leads either to the extinction of the weaker competitor or to an evolutionary or behavioural shift towards a different ecological niche.

The principle has been paraphrased in the maxim "complete competitors cannot coexist". His rule says that competition may occur between populations within an ecosystem for any available resources such as food, space, light or shelter.

Consequently, one species survives and the other gets eliminated because species are also ecological units.

Reasons:

1. If two species occur at the same trophic level, then they are likely to compete for food, space, etc. Adaptive radiation by one or more species may occur over a period of time. Consequently, they come to occupy separate niches within the trophic level, thus minimising the extent of competition.
2. Alternatively, if the competitors occupy the same trophic levels (food levels) in a strongly overlapping niche and an equilibrium situation has been reached where neither succeeds, then one of the competitors will decline in number to the point of extinction.

Examples:

1. Paramoecium aurelia and P. caudatum exist at the same trophic level and compete against each other. When cultured separately, both prosper. When cultured together, Caudatum is eliminated and Aurelia survives.
2. Two hunter-gatherer groups in the same eco niche will fight for resources but hunter-gatherers and agriculturists can coexist peacefully.

This principle is accepted because it explains organic evolution through the principles of struggle for existence and survival of the fittest.

Q 9. Parallelism and Convergence

Ans. If there is close similarity in the morphology of two organisms and there is a close phylogenetic relationship between them, it can be because of parallelism or convergence.

The term parallelism is usually applied when two organisms that are related through common ancestry develop similar adaptive characters in the course of evolution. In other words, the evolution of two related species in the same direction occurs and they resemble each other more than their common ancestor. Initial similarity is due to ancestral traits, but continuous similarity is due to adaptation to similar conditions. For example, loss of tail among humans and apes.

Parallelism leads to homologous evolution. Homology means similarity in the structure of an organ among organisms due to a common ancestor. E.g., the wings of a bat, the forelimbs of a horse, a monkey, and a man are homologous because they descended from the same ancestoral structure. Therefore, homologous organs have a common origin and are built in some fundamental pattern but perform varied functions and have different appearances.

Convergence: The term convergence is usually applied when two organisms that are not related through common ancestry develop similar adaptive characters in the course of evolution. In other words, the evolution of superficially similar traits by unrelated species occurs as a result of adaptation to a similar way of life. Two unrelated groups living in similar but separate environments develop superficially similar appearances and lifestyles.

For example, the Tasmanian wolf, a marsupial mammal, and the North American wolf, a placental mammal, are morphologically similar due to similar adaptations. They diverged more than 100 million years ago.

Convergence leads to an analogous evolution. Analogy means similarity in form and purpose, even though one is not a descendant of some ancestor. E.g., the wings of a bee, a bird, or a bat are analogous as they are from different ancestors but adopted in a similar way in a similar environment.

However, the presence of rods (photoreceptors) in nocturnal vertebrates like owls and bats may be due to convergence or parallelism. Hence, not all cases are easy to classify.

Q 10. Adaptive Radiation

Ans. The concept of adaptive radiation is given by *H.F. Osborn* for explaining evolution of number of new forms from ancestor form with great modification and adaptability in different environment conditions.

Charles Darwin defined adaptive radiation as the emergence of many species from one or a few ancient species. He compared it to how the spokes of a wheel emerge from the hub. *Janusch* defined adaptive radiation as the rapid increase in numbers and kinds of any evolving organism and their spread to different eco-niches according to their adaptability.

Major factors:

1. Increase in population size
2. Competition for food and shelter
3. Heterogenous environment
4. Splitting of the population
5. Migration and exposure to different environmental conditions
6. Formation of new organs
7. Origin of new species

Examples: Reptiles are cold-blooded, but mammals are warm-blooded. During the Holocene period, the climate became warmer, reptiles became extinct, but new forms involved adapting to different conditions. Similarly, among mammals, the primitive radiation of monkeys to trees, bats to air, whales to water, and ungulates to water led to the development of new organs for grazing and so on.

Mammals – Monkey	Bat	Whale	Human
↓	↓	↓	↓
Tree	Sky	Water	Earth

Methodology:

1. Morphological feature of a fossil
2. Comparative anatomy of living forms

Mechanism:

1. It operates above the species level and results in the formation of new genera, families, or orders.
2. The changes in organisation occur due to sudden mutations of large size, which are called macro mutations.
3. Micro mutations occur in a group of individuals who have entered a new adaptive zone free from competition.

Features:

1. Adaptive radiation results in evolutionary changes.
2. Adaptive radiation produces groups of specially adapted animals among divergent stocks.
3. Adaptive radiation leads to specialisation in a particular direction, which results in overspecialization and ultimately extinction. Because overly specialised forms are unable to modify when they enter a new adaptive zone.

Thus, adaptive radiation is one of the basic patterns of evolution. It reduces competition, helps in better exploitation of resources, and produces new diversity among organisms.

Q 11. Mosaic Evolution

Ans. Mosaic evolution refers to the differential evolution of component parts of an organism, *i.e.,* all organs do not change at the same rate in the course of evolution and also do not change at the same time.

As far as humans are concerned, there was an earlier occurrence of structure for bipedal locomotion, followed by a change in skull and brain size. These evolutionary pressures for upright posture took precedence over braindevelopment. Secondly, it took humans millions of years to acquire bipedal from quadrupedal locomotion but it took a few years to acquire a complex brain afterwards. Therefore, changes among humans occurred at different rates and at different times.

Significance:

1. Play a key note in macroevolution.
2. Shows an even adaptive pattern of evolution in organisms.
3. Stage-by-stage changes in parts of organs

The principle of mosaic evolution seems to indicate that natural selection acts differently on various organs of an organism. This variability makes it difficult to draw a conclusion about the relationship between two fossil forms or the basis of a single system.

It therefore helps resolve many practical and theoretical problems, among them questions about missing links.

1.5

Characteristics of Primates; Evolutionary Trend and Primate Taxonomy; Primate Adaptations; (Arboreal and Terrestrial) Primate Taxonomy; Primate Behaviour; Tertiary and Quaternary fossil primates; Living Major Primates; Comparative Anatomy of Man and Apes; Skeletal changes due to erect posture and its implications.

Q 1. Characteristics of Primates and their Taxonomy

Ans. The order primate is one of 16 orders of Mammalia, which include animals like squirrels, gorillas, men, etc. The classic definition of primates given by Mivart is that primates are unguiculate, claviculate, placental mammals with orbits encircled by bone, three kinds of teeth at least at one stage of life, brains always with posterior lobe and calcarine fissure, innermost digit of at least one pair of extremities opposable, hallux with a flat nail or more, well-developed caecum, penis pendulous, testis scrotal, and always two pectoral mammae.

Ashley Montagu has recognised two sub-orders of primates: Prosimii and Anthropoidea.

Taxonomy:

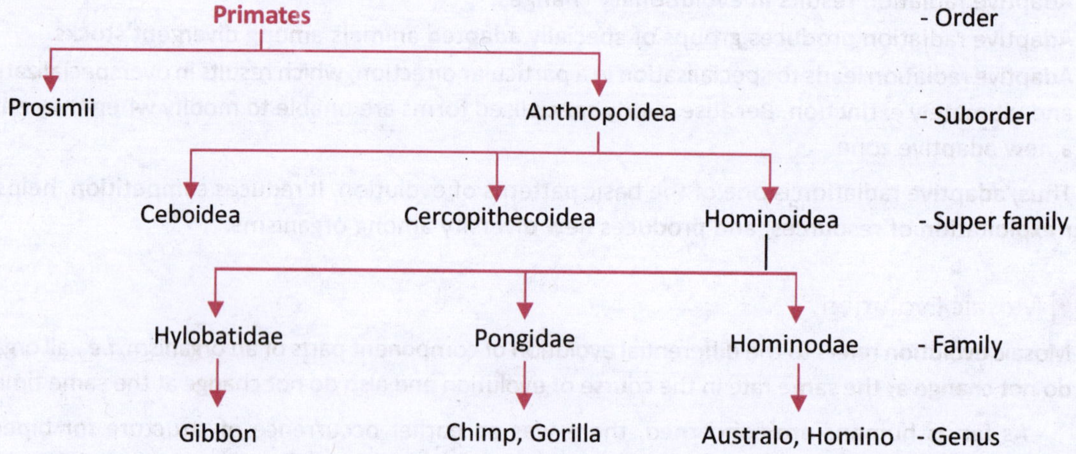

According to Clarke, the characteristics of primates can be subdivided into two categories. Among these, the presence of characters like dentition, five-digit fingers, orbits encircled by bones, etc. are general. Whereas there are certain specialized features of primates:

1. Comparatively large and complex brain
2. Stereoscopic vision
3. Prehensile limbs
4. Lumbar curve in V-column, forward position of V-column
5. Can sit straight on hips
6. Social interaction and prolonged gestation period.

They are not present in all primates. Specialized characters are more evolved in humans.

Relevance of primate study:

1. Understand similarities between primates and humans and the course of human evolution. E.g., genetic distance studies by *Sarish and Wilson.*

2. Human Evolution: Comparative studies of primates indicate that the large brains of the genus Homo evolved after bipedalism and human dental characteristics.
3. Cultural Evolution: *Jane Goodall's* Study of Chimpanzees in Tanzania. She cited the complex social life of chimpanzees, citing emotional depth and social hierarchies.
4. Origin of language: Different calls for different animals by the Vervet monkey show the language origin process.
5. Adaptations: the pre-stages of evolution and its process
6. Zoonosis: how disease spreads from primates to humans and prevention mechanisms

Q 2 Prosimii and Anthropoidea

Ans. The order Primate consists of two sub-orders: Prosimii and Anthropoidea. Prosimii includes lemurs, tarsiers, lorries, and tree shrews. Anthropoidea includes all monkeys, apes, and humans. Prosimii are called lower primates or primitive monkeys, while anthropoids are called higher primates.

Similarities: Based upon the following general mammalian features, both show:

1. Presence of a calcarine fissure and a posterior lobe in the brain.
2. At least at one stage of life, there are three kinds of teeth: incisors, canines, and molars.
3. Well-development clavicles.
4. Prehensile limbs adapted for arboreal life.
5. Pendulous penis and testes in the sac.

Differences: Due to the specialised primate characters being less developed in Prosimii than in Anthropoidea. Prosimii, when compared to Anthropoidea, have:

1. A smaller brain with a smaller cranium.
2. A foramen magnum that is relatively backward.
3. V-shaped dental arcade, as opposed to the U- or parabolic-shaped dental arcade found in Anthropoidea.
4. Less bipedalism capacity.
5. Nocturnal life, which is typically confined to remote areas.

Present-day Prosimii are the descendants of a 45 million-year-old large and mixed group, from which the evolutionary line of Anthropoidea separated about 35 million years ago.

Q 3. Monkeys and Hominoidea

Ans. As per Ashley Montague, the order Primate contains two sub-orders: Prosimii and Anthropoidea. Anthropoidea is divisible into two main series: Platyrrhini (new world monkeys), which comprises the superfamily Ceboidea, and Catarrhini (old world monkeys), which comprises the superfamilies Ceropithecoides and Hominoidea. Hominoidea includes apes and humans.

Similarities:

1. Large and comparatively rounded cranium.
2. For frontal vision, eyes are placed closer to each other.
3. Lack of wet rhinarium in the nasal cavity
4. Reduction in prognathism and size of the nasal cavity
5. Mobile upper lips detached from gums, resulting in facial expressions.
6. Prehensile hands, along with fingers of the hand and foot with nails
7. Great capacity for bipedalism.

Differences:

1. The cranial capacity of hominoids is much larger than that of monkeys.
2. The dental formula of hominoids is 2123/2123, whereas monkey families have either 2123/2123 or 2133/2133 or 2132/2132.
3. In contrast to hominoids, monkeys are generally small arboreal animals that make their way on all fours along tree branches and feed while sitting upright on a narrow limb.
4. Monkeys have a longer and prehensile tail, unlike hominoids.
5. Geographically, monkeys are less widely distributed than hominoids.

Thus, because of evolutionary forces, several differences exist between monkeys and hominoids.

Q 4. Comparative Anatomy of Man and Apes

Ans. As per Ashley Montague, the order Primate contains two sub-orders: Prosimii and Anthropoidea. Anthropoidea is divisible into two main series: Platyrrhini (new world monkeys) which comprises the superfamily Ceboidea, and Catarrhini (old world monkeys) which comprises the superfamilies Ceropithecoides and Hominoidea. Hominoidea includes apes and humans.

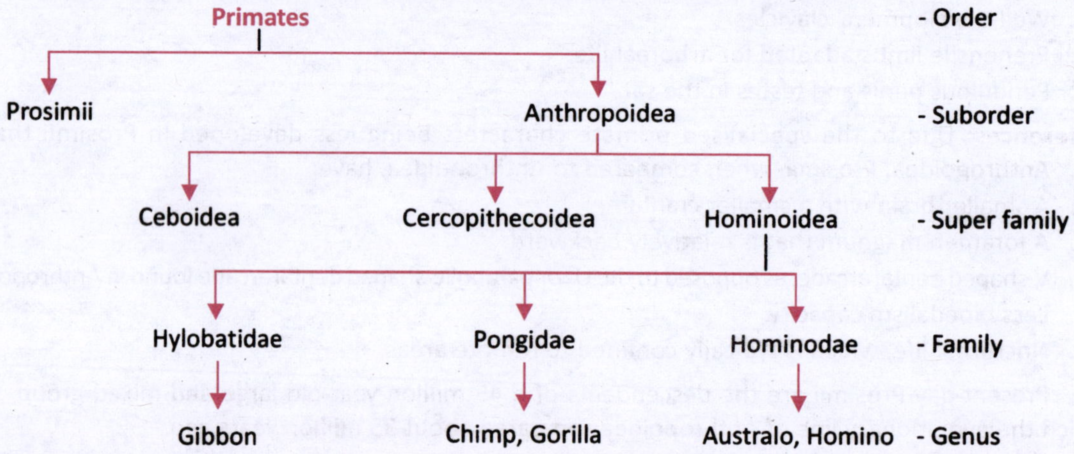

Feature	Apes	Human
Skull and teeth	Facial Region more than cranial region Prognathous Thick brow ridge Nuchal bone well marked Poor chin	Facial Region less than cranial region Orthognathous Brow ridge absent Nuchal bone absent Chin well marked
Spine and pelvis	Two curves only Less basin-shaped pelvis and narrower iliac blades	Double S-shaped spine, with four curve More basin-shaped pelvis and broader iliac blades
Limbs and foot	Femur is Short, thick and curved Linea aspera absent Legs are shorter than arms Flat footed Hallux opposable	Femur is Long, slender and elongated Linea aspera, a rough ridge on the back side of the femur, present Legs are longer than arms Arched feet Hallux non opposable

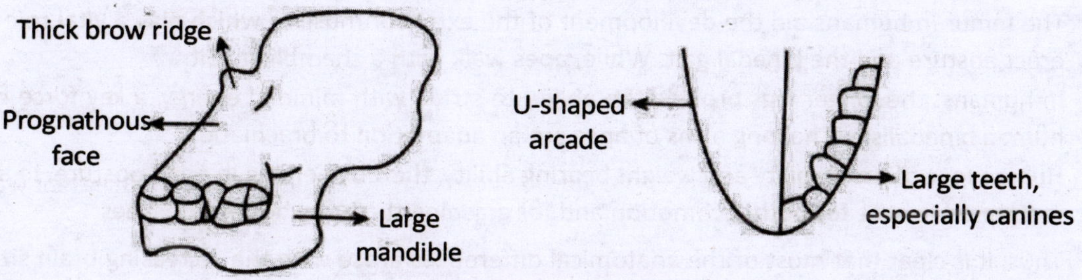

Skull and Teeth of Apes

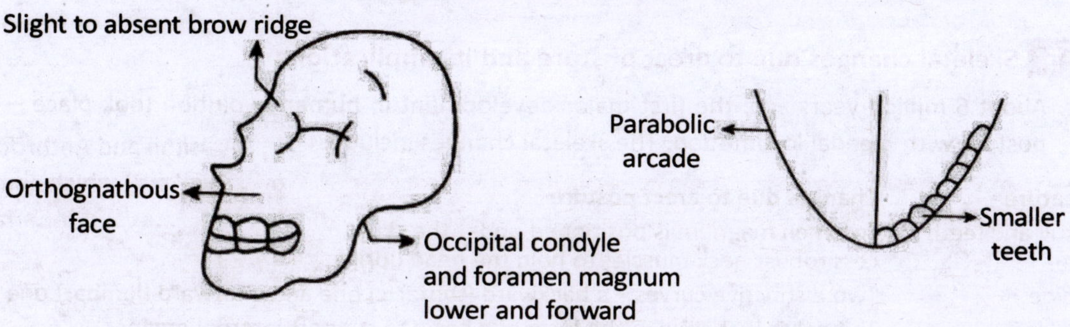

Skull and Teeth of Humans

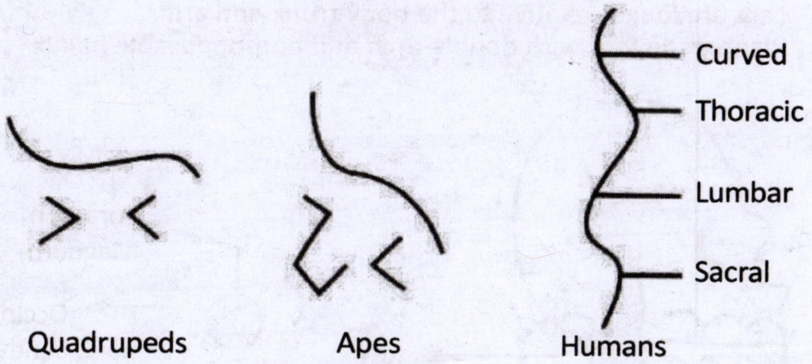

Spine in Primates

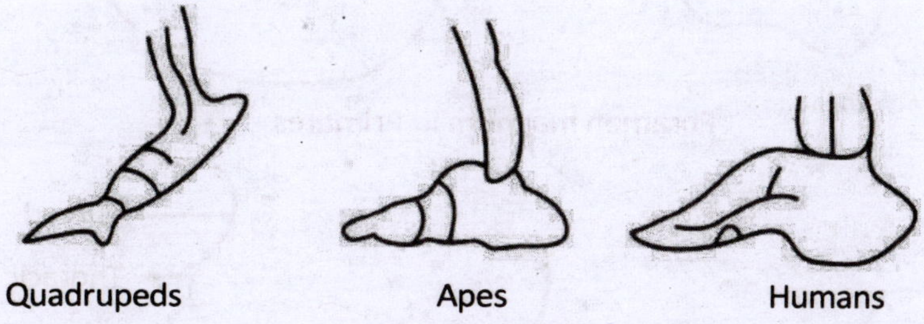

Foot in Primates

Evolutionary significance:

1. The foramen magnum's position in humans puts much of the weight of the head behind the spine. Thus, there is need of less robust neck muscles to hold the head upright.
2. The two curves, thoracic and lumbar, in humans help bring the body's centre of gravity directly above the feet. The pelvis' shape gives support to the internal organs, and the broad iliac blades stabilize weight transmission.

3. The femur in humans aid the development of the extensor muscles which play a vital role in the erect posture and the bipedal gait. While, apes walk with a shambling gait.
4. In humans, the longer legs provide the ability to stride with minimal energy, a key force behind human bipedalism. The long arms of apes are an adaptation to brachiation.
5. Human foot offers stability and weight bearing ability, thereby helping in erect posture. In apes, it is adapted for use for both locomotion and for grasping the branches on the trees.

Thus, it is clear that most of the anatomical differences arose with the increasing brain size, and development of erect posture with bipedal locomotion in human beings.

Q 5 Skeletal changes due to erect posture and its implications

Ans. About 6 million years ago, the first major development in human evolution took place – erect posture with bipedal locomotion. The skeletal changes include:

Feature	Changes due to erect posture
Skull and teeth	Foramen magnum is positioned under the skull Less robust neck muscles to hold the head upright
Spine	Two distinctive curves – a backward (thoracic) one and a forward (lumbar) one
Pelvis	The pelvis is shaped in the form of a basin to support internal organs Iliac blades are also shorter and broader, thus stabilizing weight transmission
Limbs and foot	Legs are longer relative to the body trunk and arms Plantigrade foot with double-arch and non-opposable hallux

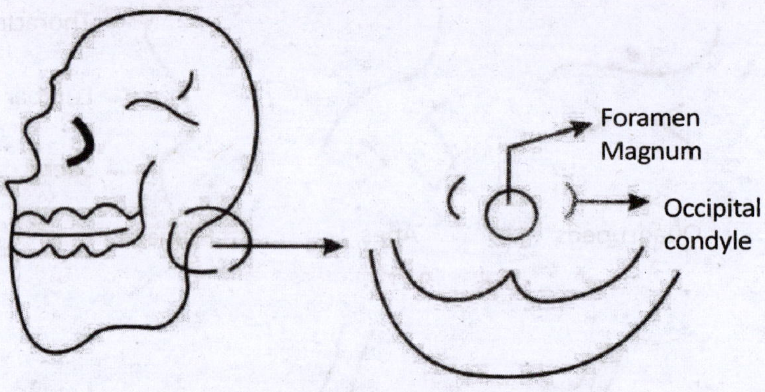

Foramen magnum in Primates

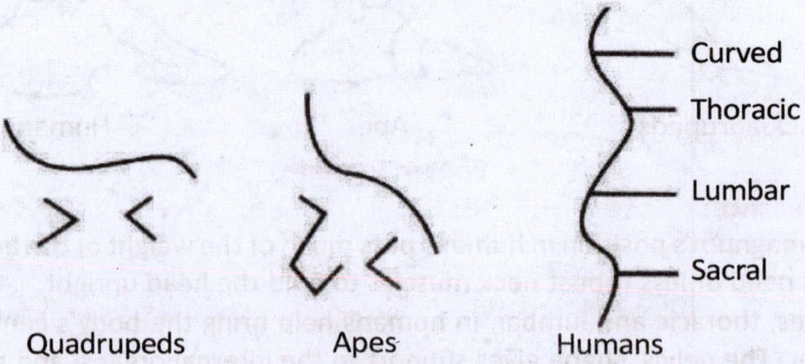

Spine in Primates

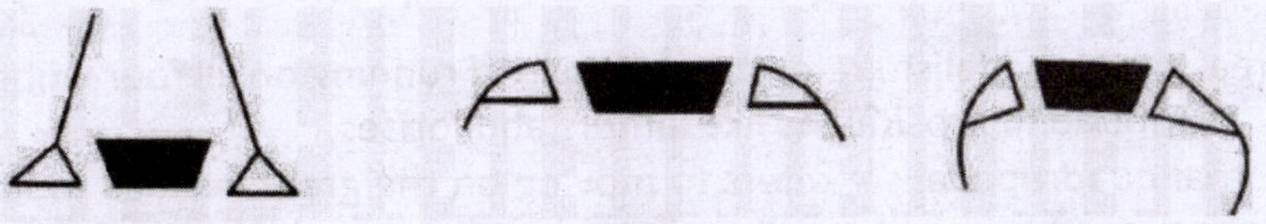

Pelvis in Primates

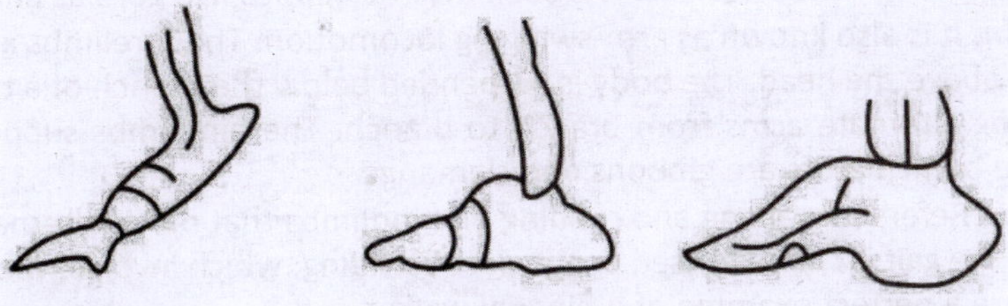

Foot in Primates

Implications:

1. More efficiently in walking than knuckle-walking apes (*Rodman and McHenry).*
2. Greater heat dissipation as lower body surface area exposed to the sun (*Pete Wheeler*)
3. Freeing of hands for other purposes like tool making.
4. Enhanced social bonding for support during the birth process, like family and marriage institutions
5. Painful berthing process due to the narrowing of the birth canal.
6. Lower back problems as more weight is supported.

As the positive implications outweighed the negative ones, natural selection worked in favour of erect posture with bipedal locomotion.

Q 6. Primate Behaviour

Ans. The main aim of primatologists is to determine how primate behaviour influences reproductive fitness and how ecological factors have shaped these behaviours.

Types:

1. **Social grooming:** It cements social bonds and keeps the body clean. Primate mothers carry children for 6–12 months.
2. **Reproductive behaviour:** Cyclical reception in apes, associated with genital swelling. Gibbons are monogamous, while chimpanzees are not.
3. **Group hunting:** the mother-infant bond is primary and promotes learning in this process: what to eat, where to find it, how to eat it, etc.
4. **Hierarchies:** clear-cut social organisation. Chimp: patrilineal; Rhesus money: matrilineal.
5. **Aggression:** competition for food, defending infants, struggle for dominance
6. **Communication:** gesture, posture, and facial expression exist.
7. **Locomotion:** vertical clinging, quadrapedalism, brachiation, bipedalism, understanding evolution and phylogeny at different time periods
   a. **Vertical clinging and leaping:** It is present among prosimians like tarsiers and lemurs. Napier and Walker considered this mode to be the basic form from which all other modes evolved. The body is held vertically at rest and pressed to the trunk or main branch of a tree. Movement from place to place is done by a leap between trunks and branches, propelling the body through rapid extension of the hindlimbs.

b. Quadrupedalism:

i. Arboreal quadrupedalism refers to walking and running on all four limbs along branches of trees. It is found in prosimians like lemurs and lorises.

ii. Terrestrial quadrupedalism refers to moving on the ground on all four limbs. It is seen in baboons, macaques, apes, etc. A variation herein is knuckle-walking, in which the forelimbs hold the fingers in a partially flexed posture that allows body weight to press down on the ground through the knuckles. It is seen in African apes like gorillas and chimpanzees.

c. Brachiation: It is also known as arm-swinging locomotion. The forelimbs are used for securing bandages above the head. The body is suspended below the branch of a tree and is propelled by swinging alternate arms from branch to branch. The hindlimbs support the body in the trees. True branchiators are gibbons and siamangs.

d. Bipedalism: Refers to walking and running on hindlimbs that move alternatively to propel the body, and the gait is characterised by the act of striding, which involves propulsive movement. Humans are a perfect example of a bipedal walker.

Evidence from anatomy, physiology, and biochemical studies shows a close affinity between chimpanzees and humans. This suggests humans evolved from knuckle-walking ancestry; some give semi-brachiation. At present, insufficient information is available to elucidate the exact phylogeny of man's bipedal gait.

Case Study

- **Chimp Nut-Smashing Techniques Explain Our Proto-Culture**

A specific type of localised chimp culture is strongly supported by a recent study by Lydia V. Luncz, Roger Mundry, and Christophe Boesch of the Max Planck Institute for Evolutionary Anthropology in Leipzig, Germany. Luncz et al.'s research, which was published in the most recent issue of Current Biology, demonstrates how various chimpanzee groups in an Ivory Coast forest use stone and wood "hammers" to split open tasty coula nuts. Additionally, different groups employ tools in their own distinctive patterns, and the best explanation for these patterns is cultural transmission. The manipulation of stone tools and the long-distance transmission of those skills as early humans taught their offspring and fellow forebears how to do so constitute the most well-studied proto-human cultural evidence. Without the brickwork, it appears that chimps are currently carrying out identical activities. Although nut-smashing isn't dancing or voting, it has certain characteristics of a cultural practise. By extension, dolphin tool use and bird song both fit this definition.

- **Chimps use 'hi' and 'bye' greetings, just like humans.**

According to a recent study, bonobos and chimpanzees both signal "hello" and "goodbye" to one another while entering and leaving social interactions. In other words, these apes, who have 99% of our DNA in common with humans, kindly meet and part ways with one another. The researchers said that until now, this behaviour has only been observed in non-human creatures. The researchers studied 1,242 ape interactions at zoos to determine whether chimpanzees and bonobos engage in these behaviours. They found that these primates frequently communicate with one another before and after encounters such as grooming or play, frequently with gestures that include gazing at and touching each other, holding hands, or butting heads.

But the researchers discovered that of the two species, bonobos were unquestionably the more courteous ones; they greeted each other more frequently than chimpanzees did. The researchers discovered that bonobos initiated joint interactions 90% of the time, compared to 69% of the time for chimpanzees, via exchanging entering signals and reciprocal gazes. In terms of departures, bonobos excelled above chimpanzees, exhibiting exit behaviours 92% of the time compared to 86% of interactions.

- **Loango chimpanzee project**

It was focused on behavioural ecology. They investigated tool use, hunting behaviour, territoriality, community, and disease in chimpanzees living in Loango National Park, Gabon. A different kind of investigation occurred when a chimpanzee was seen attacking a gorilla for the first time.

1.6

Phylogenetic status, characteristics and geographical distribution of the following:

(a) Plio-preleistocene hominids in South and East Africa—Australopithecines.

(b) Homo erectus : Africa (Paranthropus), Europe (Homo erectus (heidelbergensis), Asia (Homo erectus javanicus, Homo erectus pekinensis).

(c) Neanderthal man—La-chapelle-aux-saints (Classical type), Mt. Carmel (Progressive type).

(d) Rhodesian man.

(e) Homo sapiens—Cromagnon, Grimaldi and Chancelede.

Q 1. Australopithecines

Ans. Australopithecines were the first bipedal hominids.

Discovery:

➢ The earliest fossil find of Australopithecines was the skull of a 5 to 6-year-old child discovered by Raymond Dart from Taung in South Africa in 1924. Dart named it Australopithecus africanus (Taung's baby). However, recent research from 2013 shows that it is an infant between 2 and 3 years old.

➢ In 1994, A. Ramidus was discovered by Tim White et al. and dated to 4.5 million years old, and in 1995, Mrs. Leakey discovered A. anamensis, dated to 4 million years old. All verified fossils of Australopithecus to date have been found in Africa.

Time Span: This genus lived between 5.5 and 1.8 million years ago, during the Pleistocene epoch.

Species: Australopithecus: A. africanus, A. ramidus, A. anamensis, A. afarensis, and A. garhi Paranthropus: P. robustus, P. boisei, P. aethiopicus

Geographical Distribution:

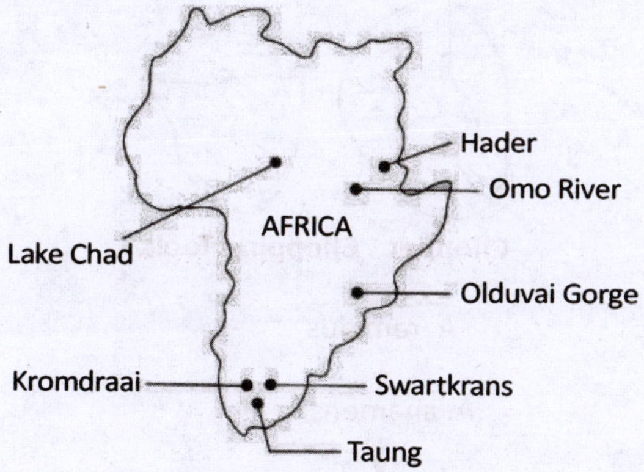

Physical Features:

1. **Cranial capacity:** 375-775 cc, indicating a brain more developed than apes
2. **Skull and Dentition:**
   a. **Forehead:** In animals in general, the face is continuous into the head without a distinct forehead. The forehead emerged in Australopithecus but was slanting backward.
   b. **Mastroid process:** an inverted pyramid-shaped structure just behind the ear emerged in Australopithecus and was fully developed in Homo erectus.
3. **Postcranial anatomy:** the appearance of the mastoid process and linea aspera are direct evidences of bipedalism. As per Lovejoy (2010), australopithecines in earlier stages had a shuffling gait.

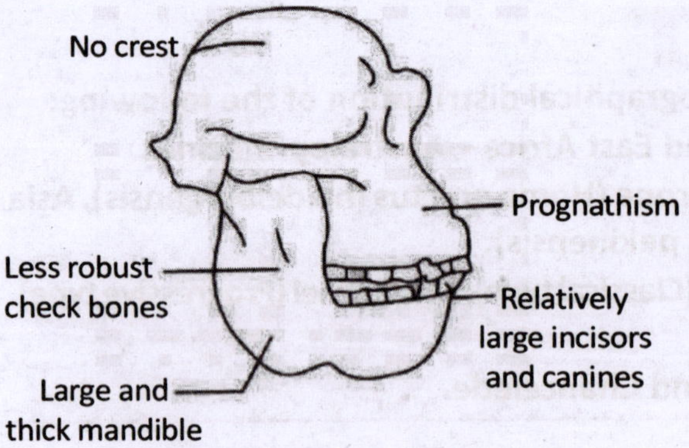

Australopithecus (gracile)

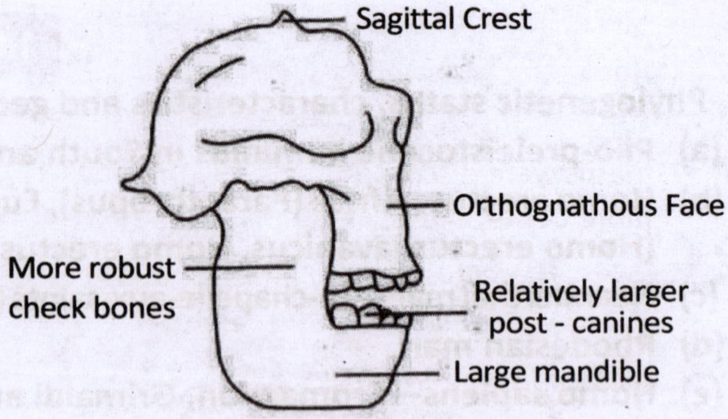

Paranthropus (robust)

A. Gracile	P. Robustus
No crest	Sagittal crest
Prognathism	Orthognathism
Less robust cheek bone	Robust cheek bone
Relatively larger canine and incisor	Relatively large premolar and molar

Cultural Features:

1. **Hunting:** In Olduvai Gorge, several small bones of animals and tools, mainly chopper-chopping, have been found.
   According to Dart, Australopithecines used the bones, teeth, and horns of bigger animals as tools for hunting small animals. This is known as osteodontokeratic culture.
2. **Marriage:** Marriage, in its primitive form, started in Australopithecines. This is evident from the fossil remains of 13 people excavated by Leakey at Hadar (Ethiopia).

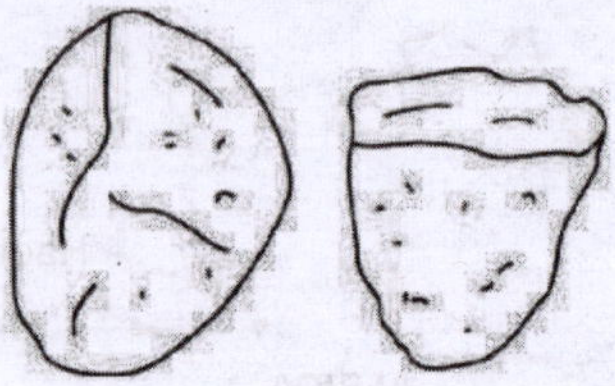

Chopper - Chopping Tools

Phylogenetic Status:

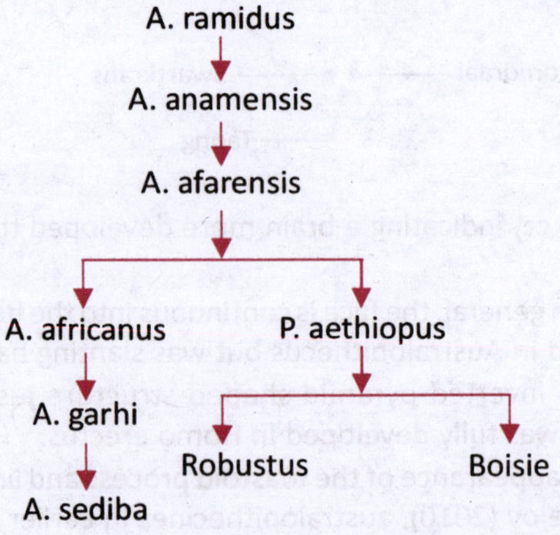

Q 2. Homo erectus

Ans. Homo erectus, meaning 'upright man', is an extinct species of the genus Homo.

Discovery: E. Dubois (1891) at Java discovered a cranium and a femur. Between 1921 and 1927, few teeths were discovered at Zhou Kou Dien in China. They were studied by D. Black. By 1937, many more bones, skulls, and teeth had been found.

Time Span: H.erectus lived between 2 million and 200,000 years ago in the Lower Palaeolithic age.

Sub-Species: H.erectus erectus (Java Man), H. erectus pekinensis (Peking Man), H. erectus heidelbergensis, and H. erectus narmadensis (Narmada Man).

Geographical Distribution:

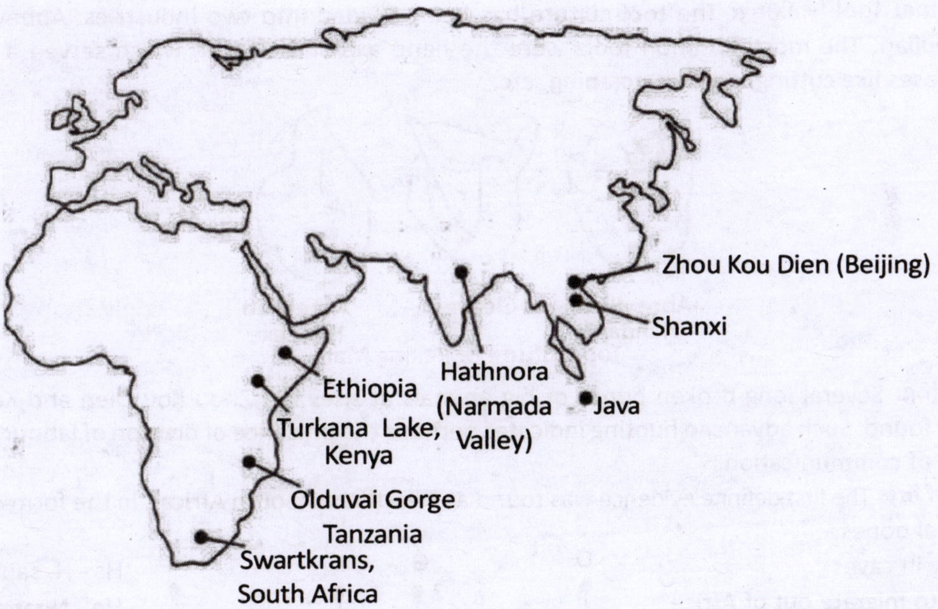

Physical Features:

1. **Cranial capacity:** 750–1260 cc, which is more than Australopithecus but less than H. sapiens on average.
2. **Dentition:** parabolic dental arcade, large teeth, and shovelled incisors
3. **Postcranial anatomy:** the mastoid process and linea aspera are present, and thus the erectus was bipedal.

Java Man	Peking man
Cranial capacity – 875 cc	Cranial capacity – 1075 cc
Large brow ridge, Thick skull bone	Smaller comparatively
Massive mandible	Less massive mandible
Parabolic dental arcade, large teeth and shovelled incisors	Parabolic and Small teeth
No chin	Slight chin
Larger, heavier and less upright comparitively	Shorter, Lighter, Upright

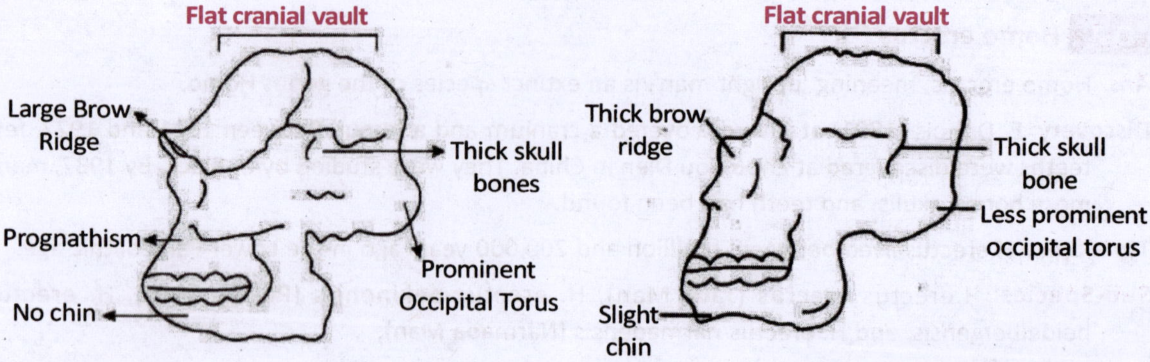

Cultural Features:

1. **Habitual Tool Making:** The tool culture has been divided into two industries: Abbevillian and Acheulian. The most common tools were the hand axe and cleaver, which served a variety of purposes like cutting, digging, scraping, etc.

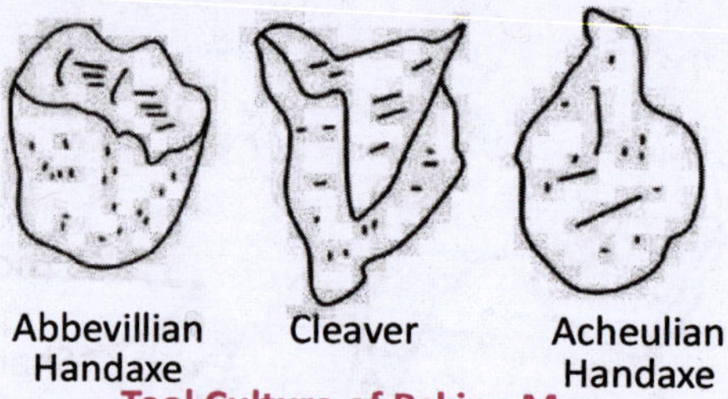

Tool Culture of Peking Man

2. **Hunting:** Several long-broken bones of big animals at sites like Zhou Kou Dien and Kenya have been found. Such advanced hunting indicates perhaps the presence of division of labour and some form of communication.
3. **Use of fire:** The first definite evidence was found at Swartkrans (South Africa), in the form of charred animal bones.
4. Living in caves
5. First to migrate out of Africa
6. Large front teeth 6 small males in Java - Omnivore diet.

Phylogenetic Status: Initially, E. Dubois, based on primitive traits like thick skull bones and a prominent brow ridge, named it Pithecanthropus erectus, meaning upright ape-man. He proclaimed it to be the missing link between apes and humans. But later, Janush, among others, based on traits like higher cranial capacity, reduced face size, and parabolic dental arcade, confirmed it to be close to modern humans. Today, it is almost unanimously placed in the genus Homo.

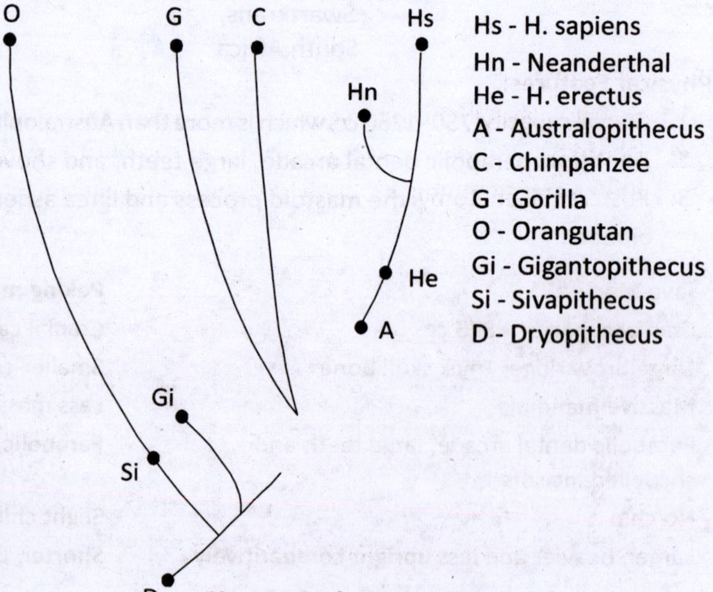

Human Evolutionary Tree

Q 3. Home heidelbergensis

Ans. Homo erectus heidelbergensis is a sub-species of the extinct Home erectus.

Discovery: In 1907, a mandible was discovered in Mauer village, near Heidelberg, Germany. It was reported in 1908 by Otto Schoetensack and was named Mauer jaw.

Time Span: The fossils date to around 600,000 to 300,000 years ago. Mauer's jaw was also the first human fossil recovered from the Middle Pleistocene of Europe.

Physical Features:

1. **Cranial capacity:** It had a large brain case with a cranial volume of roughly 1250 cc.
2. **Skull:** The cranium shows massive brow ridges and thick vault bones. The Mauer jaw is specifically described as being very large and meeassive, lacking a chin. It shows many simian features, in particular those of gibbons.

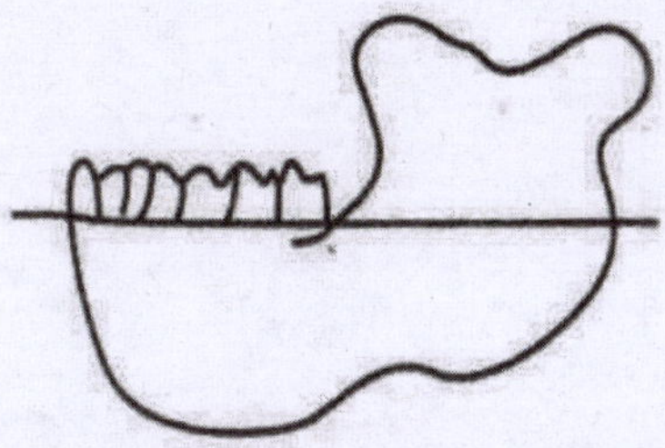

Mauer Jaw

3. **Dentition:** The size of teeth and pulp cavities is similar to that of H. sapiens.
4. **Postcranial anatomy:** It was bipedal, evident from the presence of mastoid processes and linea aspera. Also, there are no significant differences from H. sapiens in this aspect.

Cultural features: Ample evidence of tool-making, hunting, food gathering, and the use of fire has been found at sites in Germany,

Netherlands, South Africa, etc. It is widely believed that this sub-species acquired a pre-linguistic system of communication.

Phylogenetic Status: With the combination of simian and human features, *Schoetensack* concluded that Heidelbergensis represented a state between apes and humans. But today, this claim is rejected. It is believed that Heidelbergensis was the last common ancestor of H. neanderthalensis and H. sapiens. However, debate continues on whether it is a sub-species of H. erectus or an independent species of the genus Homo in itself.

Q 4. Neanderthal man

Ans. Homo neanderthalensis, meaning Neanderthal man, is an extinct species of the genus Homo.

Discovery: In 1856, fossils were found from the Neander Valley in Düsseldorf, Germany. Subsequently, William King named them H. neanderthalensis, after the valley.

Time Span: Lived between 500,000 and 50,000 years ago (Middle to Upper Pleistocene epoch).

Types:

➢ Classical type (La Chapelle-aux-Saints)

➢ Progressive type (Mt. Carmel)

Geographical Distribution: Fossils have been found from Europe, the Middle East, and Central Asia.

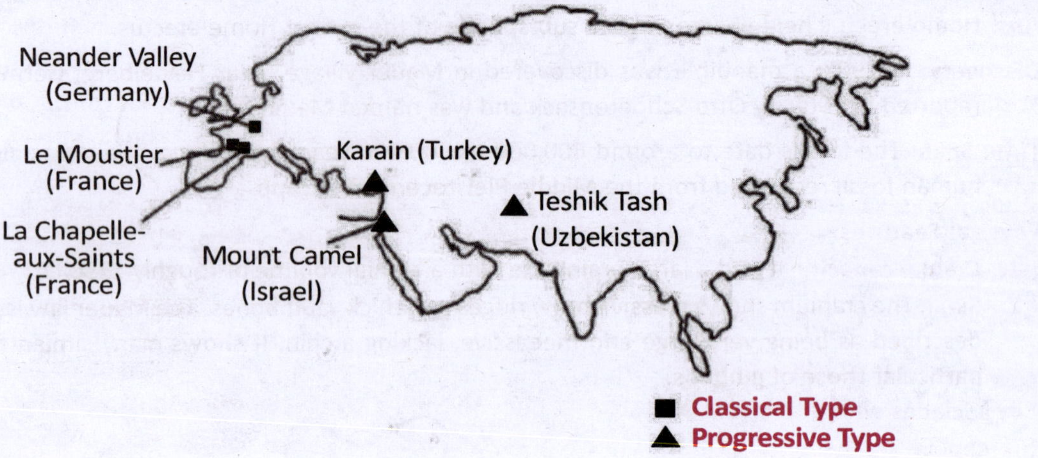

Physical Features:

1. Cranial capacity: 1700–1740 cc, indicating a large brain size.
2. Skull

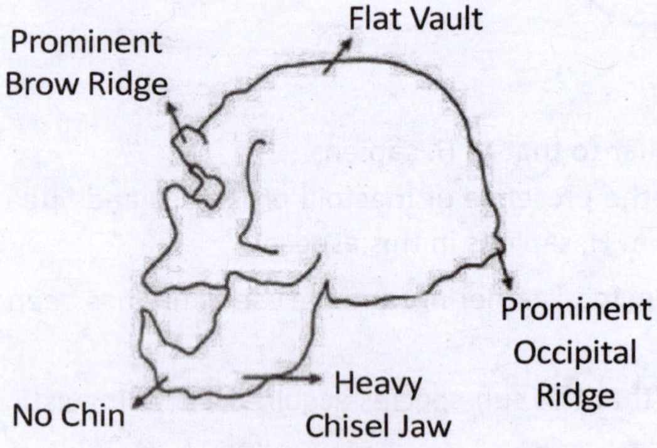

Classical Type

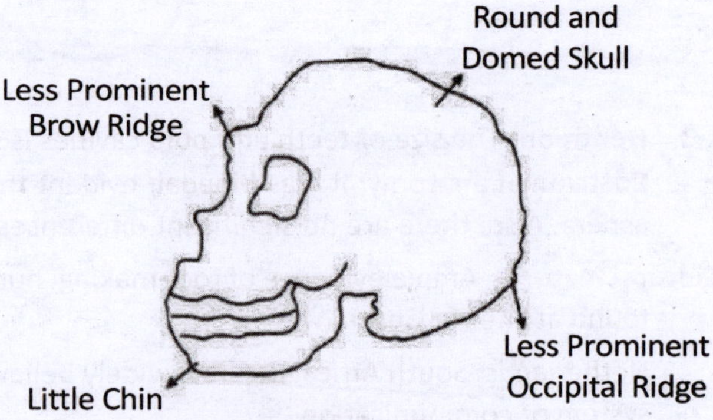

Progressive Type

3. Dentition: Both types show parabolic dental arcade, taurodontism, and dental formula (2123).
4. Postcranial anatomy: Neanderthal man shows bipedalism, evident from the presence of linea aspera in its femur. It had a short and sharp vertebral column. It was also more muscularly built than modern humans, especially the classical type. Limbs are short but stout, and ribs are strong.

Classical Neanderthal	Progressive Neanderthal
Time Span: 60,000 years ago	Time Span: 1,00,000 years ago
Cranial Capacity: 1700 cc Cranial	Capacity: 1524-1640cc for Male and 1270-1425 cc for Female
Prominent Brow ridge	Less prominent brow ridge
No chin	Little chin
Prominent occipital ridge	Less prominent occipital ridge
Flat vault	Round and domed skull

Cultural Features:

1. **Tools:** Associated with Mousterian culture, represented by flake tools such as sidescrapers and points.

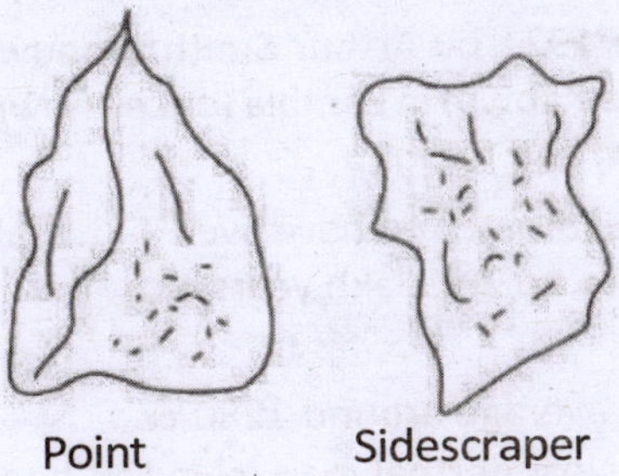

Mousterian Tool Culture

2. **Social Organisation:** They were mainly hunter-gatherers, possibly living in bands or nomadic societies with interpersonal relationships. Otherwise, La Chapelle man and Shanidar's handicap could not have survived.
3. **Rituals:** The first direct evidence of rituals in human evolution appears here in the form of burial rituals. For instance, in Teshik-Task Cave (Uzbekistan), the burials of young ones were surrounded by goat skills.

Phylogenetic Status: Prior to 2010, it was largely accepted that Neanderthals were a separate species from Homo sapiens, both having evolved from a common ancestor, H. erectus (specifically H. erectus heidelbergensis). But the findings of the Neanderthal Genome Project (2010) and gene pool studies suggest that the ancestors of modern humans may have mated with at least two groups of archaic humans: Neanderthals and Denisovans. Thus, recent studies like that of Dr. Krause (2017) argue that Neanderthals should be included within our species (that is, Homo sapiens neanderthalensis). The debate continues.

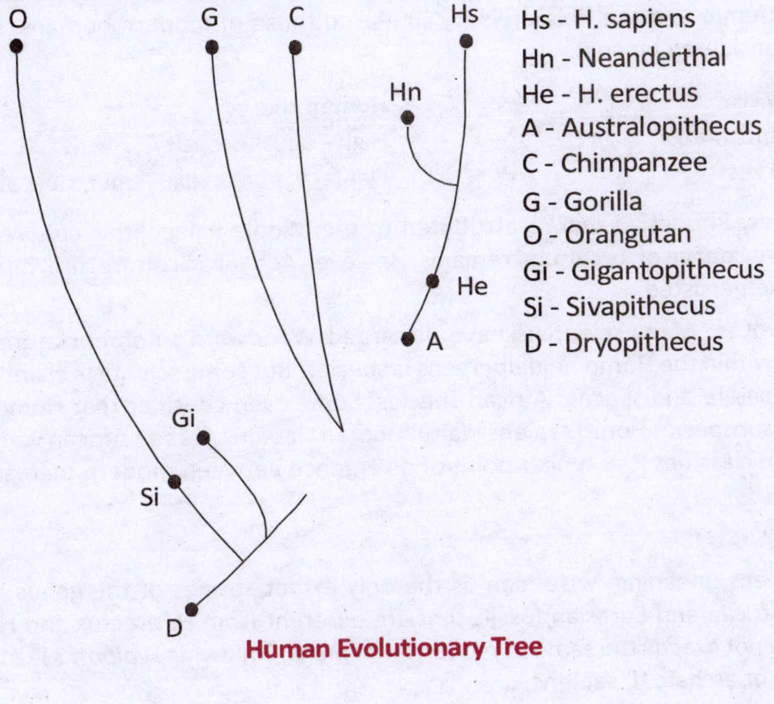

Human Evolutionary Tree

Q 5. Rhodesian Man

Ans. Rhodesian man, or Homo rhodesiensis, refers to an extinct species of the genus Homo.

Discovery: It was first described in 1921 by Arthur Smith Woodward in reference to the skull fossil found at Broken Hill (also called Kabwe) in Zambia (once known as Rhodesia). In 1941, T. Zuniglaar discovered the skull, lower jaw, and femur.

Time Span: Though uncertain, it is estimated to have lived 4–1.5 lakh years ago. Rainer Grin's study in 2020 said the skull was found to be 2.99 lakh years old.

Physical Features:

1. **Cranial capacity:** estimated to average around 1280 cc.
2. **Skull:** The skull resembles the Neanderthal man from La Chapelle-aux-Saint in many features.

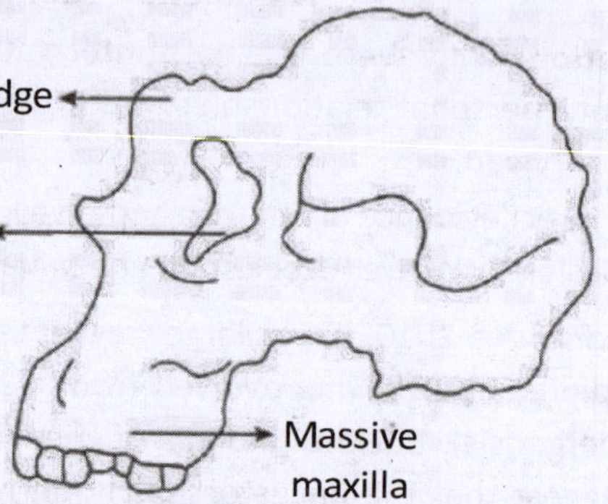

Kabwe Skull Fossil

3. **Dentition:** Teeth, in general, were like those of modern humans. Interestingly, most of the teeth were affected by caries.
4. **Postcranial anatomy:** It remains unclear whether the limb bones found belong to the Kabwe skull. The femur and the tibia are very similar to those of modern humans. Rhodesian men can thus be considered bipedal.

Erectus Like	Human Like
Heavy brow ridge	High Cranial Capacity
Sagittal keel	Flat face, human like femur, tibia and teeth

Cultural Features: Rhodesian man is attributed to the Middle Palaeolithic culture. However, there is hardly any evidence of its cultural remains. However, Acheulian culture, fire, hunting, and gathering would have persisted.

Phylogenetic Status: Many scientists have discarded Woodward's nomenclature and included this specimen within the Homo heidelbergens is species. But some scientists claim Homo rhodesiensis to be a separate and specific African species. Some even consider that Homo rhodesiensis gave rise to the subspecies Homo sapiens idaltu. Hootan classifies it as an African variety of Neanderthal. Von Bonian classifies it as a near point of divergence between modern man and Neanderthals.

Q 6 Homo sapiens

Ans. Homo sapiens, meaning 'wise man' is the only extant species of the genus Homo. There are a series of African and Eurasian fossils that are different from H. erectus and H. neanderthalensis and yet are not exactly the same as modern H. sapiens. Following *Wolpoff's* lead, these are referred to as early or archaic H. sapiens.

Geographical Distribution:

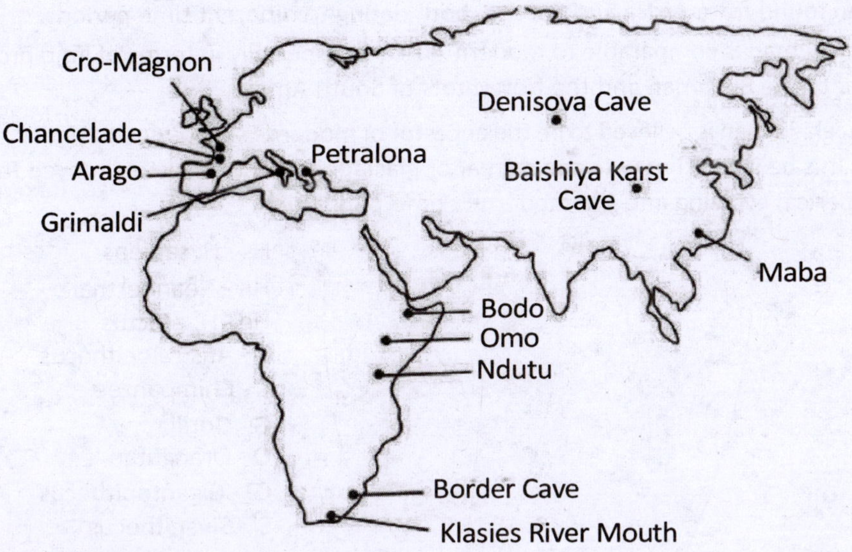

Features of early fossils:

	Cro-Magnon	Grimaldi	Chancelade
Discovery	In 1868 by Lartet, in the form of five skeletons found from a cave in CroMagnon (France)	In 1901, in the form of two skeletons found from Grimaldi (Italy)	In 1888, in the form of a male skeleton found buried in a flexed position with knees touching the jaw
Time Span	40,000-30,000 years ago	25,000 years ago	17,000-12,000 years ago
Cranial Capacity	1550-1650 cc	1250-1450 cc	1500-1700 cc
Skull	Massive skull developed Broad forehead Large cheek bone Prognathism Prominent chin	Supra orbital feebly Platyrrhine nose Small mastoid process Negroid limbs	Long and narrow High Vault Mastoid full developed Short stature
Dentition	Parabolic dental arcade, dental formula – 2,1,2,3 and small sized teeth	Same as Cro-Magnon, but with relatively larger sized teeth	
Postcranial anatomy	Longer hind limbs indicate efficient bipedalism. It had a muscular and tall built, with height estimated to be around 170-180 cm.	Hind limbs are very much longer than fore limbs, again indicating efficient bipedalism. Its height is estimated to be around 150-160 cm.	The limb bones are strong and massive, with upper limbs comparatively longer. Its height is estimated to be around 150-160 cm.
Cultural Features	Aurignacian culture of European Upper Palaeolithic Their tool kit included blade flakes and bone tools.	Aurignacian culture of European Upper Palaeolithic. Their tool kit included blade flakes and bone tools.	Magdalenian culture. Tool kit included blade and bone tools like harpoons, needles, hooks.

Phylogenetic Status: The phylogenetic status of Cro-Magnon man remains unclear, as similar fossils have been found from Africa and Europe, both dating to different time periods.

The Grimaldi man is comparable to modern Africans, especially in terms of limb proportions. It is compared to the Bushmen and the Hottentots of South Africa.

The Chancelade man is believed to be the ancestor of modern Eskimos due to similar morphological features. It is believed that with the retreat of glaciation, these ancestors moved from Europe to North America, evolving into the modern Eskimo population.

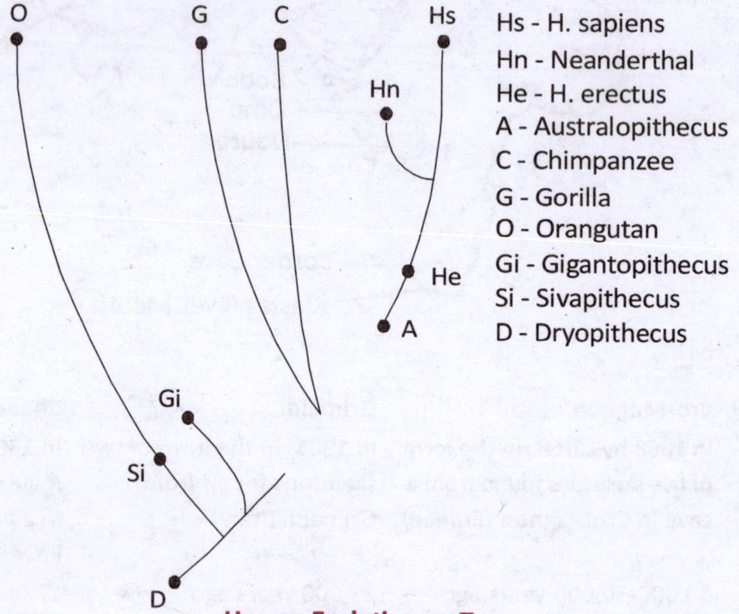

Human Evolutionary Tree

Case Study

- **Meet the 1st Neanderthal family: DNA helps 2022 Nobel Prize winner chart the family tree of our ancestors**

Our ancestors were the Neanderthals, from whom modern humans descended. They existed in the southwest and central regions of Europe between 4,000 and 40,000 years ago. Svante Paabo is the lead researcher in the current study. His discovery of Neanderthal DNA earned him the 2022 Nobel Prize in Medicine. At least twelve separate Neanderthal DNA fragments have been discovered by archaeologists. For the first time, researchers have sequenced many members of a distant Neandertal village in Siberia, including thirteen individuals who are all somehow connected. One pair of closely connected ancestors, a father and his teenage daughter, lived with a smaller family of ten to twenty individuals. The thirteen genomes allowed the worldwide team of researchers from the Max Planck Institute for Evolutionary Anthropology to get insight into the Neanderthal community's social structure.

This is the first time that Neanderthals are being evaluated on a personal level, despite the fact that researchers have previously been successful in illuminating the broad strokes of Neanderthal history. About 54,000 years ago, a Neanderthal family lived in these caverns, and during the past 14 years, their remains have been discovered there. In the river valleys that the caves overlook, ibex, horses, bison, and other animals that were migrating at the time were hunted by the Neandertals at Chagyrskaya and Okladnikov, according to researchers. In the caves, archaeologists have uncovered the bones of at least a dozen individual

Neanderthals. A few cousins of the group might be located by researchers. There were also two other family members present, either a kid and his aunt or a couple of cousins, in addition to the father and daughter. As a result, genetics now allows us to understand the Neanderthal community's social structure. Researchers found that female migration played a major role in connecting the Neanderthal tribes. They proved this by contrasting the genetic diversity of the mitochondrial DNA, which is inherited from mothers, with the genetic diversity of the Y-chromosome, which is passed down from father to son.

- **New Evidence That Neanderthals Were Carnivores**

To determine a Neanderthal's diet, researchers have examined zinc isotope ratios in tooth enamel for the first time. The tooth most likely belongs to a carnivorous Neanderthal. Other chemical traces suggest that this animal consumed the bone marrow rather than the blood of its prey. Scientists claim that the discussion is still going on. Although certain studies on the dental tartar of Iberian Peninsula residents seem to suggest that Neanderthals were big plant consumers, other studies conducted at locations outside of Iberia tend to suggest that they ate nearly exclusively meat. Researchers have now demonstrated, using a molar from a member of this species and using novel analytical techniques, that the Neanderthals at the Gabasa site in Spain appear to have been carnivores.

- **Neanderthals: how a carnivore diet may have led to their demise**

Wherever they lived, Neanderthals were primarily carnivores, according to a recent study that examined zinc from a tooth belonging to a Spanish specimen. They had a wider variety of foods, according to isotopes extracted from the remains of Homo sapiens tribes that acquired Pleistocene Eurasia from the Neanderthals at various places around Europe. The primary foods for these early humans included plants, birds, and fish. The Pleistocene was characterised by the dominance of a grassland-steppe environment in Siberia, which vanished 10,000 years ago. It had a climate that was highly unpredictable, shifting from coniferous woodlands to dry grasslands and wet tundras, which continuously changed the types and numbers of huge animals that grazed there. Therefore, these individuals would have been much more resilient if they had an omnivorous diet rather than only hunting big game.

- **Denisovan DNA: Ayta Magbukon**

According to a study that examined the genomes of close to 120 different ethnic groups in the Philippines, the Ayta Magbukon people have the highest concentration of DNA from the extinct Denisovan subspecies of humans ever discovered. The thorough investigation showed that the genome of the Ayta Magbukon Negrito has the highest percentage of Denisovan DNA. The researchers, who included Maximilian Larena of Uppsala University, were able to identify the major variations in genetic contribution using a genomic approach called masking.

- **Human species who lived 500,000 years ago named as Homo bodoensis**

Early humans and Neanderthals coexisted in the same time period as Homo bodoensis. Homo bodoensis is the name given by scientists to a recently found species of human progenitor. Scientists believe that the creature, which existed in Africa some 500,000 years ago during the Middle Pleistocene era, was the immediate ancestor of modern people. An Ethiopian skull discovered at Bodo D'ar, in the basin of the Awash River, gave rise to the term bodoensis. The Neanderthals, also known as Homo neanderthalensis, first arose in Europe at this time, while anatomically modern people, Homo sapiens, first appeared in Africa. However, due to the lack of knowledge regarding human evolution at this time, some paleoanthropologists have referred to this period as "the muddle in the middle." The study's principal investigator, Dr. Mirjana Roksandic of the University of Winnipeg in Canada, said: "Talking about human evolution during this time period became impossible due to the lack of proper terminology that acknowledges human geographic variation." The bulk of Middle Pleistocene humans from Africa and some from south-east Europe will be classified as Homo bodoensis under the new classification, whereas many people from the latter continent will be reclassified as Neanderthals.

- **Scientists find a fossil of an early hominid, Homo Naledi**

Homo naledi fossils were discovered inside the Rising Star Cave in the Cradle of Humankind World Heritage Site near Johannesburg. Homo naledi dates to the Middle Pleistocene era, 335,000–236,000 years ago. It is clearly a primitive species, existing at a time when previously we thought only modern humans were in Africa.

- **Dragon Man (Homo longi)**

An ancient human skull that may be from a different species of people has allegedly been discovered by Chinese researchers. A type of ancient human is known as a "Dragon Man," or Homo longi. The entire skull was discovered in the northeastern Chinese province of Heilongjiang, dating to the Middle Pleistocene and at least 146,000 years old. The skull was found in 1933, but because of a turbulent political climate, science did not find it until 2018 and did not give it a name until 2021. It is possible that the existing scientific consensus will need to be revised because the describers believed that modern humans were more closely connected to H. longi than to the European Neanderthals. H. longi may be a representative of the mysterious Denisovans, although this has not been proven.

H. longi shares several anatomical characteristics with other Middle Pleistocene Chinese species. The skull is low and long, the longest of any known human, with greatly inflated brow ridges, wide eye sockets, and a large mouth, just like other ancient people. The skull is the biggest human skull that has ever been discovered. The 1,420-cc brain volume is comparable to that of modern humans and Neanderthals. The nose is bulbous, possibly to aid in breathing cold air, but the face is flat, like in modern humans. H. longi might have had dark skin, hair, and eyes like other modern humans. A male under the age of 50 may have been the owner of the skull. If the "Dragon Man" is a new species, it could help close the gap between us and our distant relatives, Homo erectus, by providing fresh information on the evolution of Homo sapiens. This information is crucial because there is little agreement among scientists regarding the relationships between various human species and which animals are our closest forebears. Some palaeontologists think that Homo heidelbergensis is our closest relative. This species, which was discovered in 1908, existed between 700,000 and 200,000 years ago in Europe, pos sibly also in China, and perhaps even in some regions of Africa. There are still some unsolved issues, such as whether there was interbreeding between several human types. For example, it is thought that Neanderthals contributed nearly 1 –4 percent of the DNA in non-African modern humans.

- **Additional human species:**

The only other human species in existence today is the modern human. Although there is some disagreement over the actual number of human species, most scientists agree that there are at least 21 different types of humans. The Smithsonian National Museum of Natural History estimates that there are over 21 different types of humans.

1. Sahelanthropus tchadensis: It is thought to be the earliest member of the human ancestry. Around 7–6 million years ago, this species existed in an area of Africa that is now Chad. This species' existence is solely known through cranial material, from which scientists have deduced that it possessed both human and apelike traits and was bipedal, which may have boosted its chances of survival.
2. Orrorin tugensis: This species is the oldest early human on the family tree, and individuals from this species were around the size of a chimpanzee. It lived about 6.2–5.8 million years ago in Eastern Africa.
3. Ardipithecus kadabba, which lived in Eastern Africa between 5.8 and 5.2 million years ago, They walked on two legs and are thought to have been about the size of contemporary chimpanzees.
4. Ardipithecus ramidus was first discovered in 1994 and lived in Eastern Africa about 4.4 million years ago. It's unclear if this species had two legs.
5. Australopithecus anamensis, which existed between 4.2 and 3.8 million years ago 2016 saw the discovery of a skull from this species at a palaeontological site in Ethiopia. This skull was examined in two studies that were published in 2019, and it was shown to be older than Lucy, a different specimen of the species Australopithecus afarensis that was previously believed to be the oldest progenitor of modern humans. Additionally, according to the latest findings, Lucy and her forebears coexisted for at least 100,000 years.

6. Members of Lucy's species, Australopithecus afarensis, lived in Africa between 3.8 and 2.95 million years ago. Over the years, palaeontologists have found the remains of around 300 members of this species.
7. Kenyanthropus platyops is a species that lived there 3.5 million years ago. Given that the species lived in Africa at the same time as Lucy's species, the Smithsonian Museum speculates that their evolutionary relationship to modern humans may be closer than that of Lucy's species.
8. Australopithecus africanus, which existed in southern Africa between 3.3 and 2.1 million years ago. This species exhibited traits that were both ape-like and human-like.
9. Paranthropus aethiopicus: This species, which lived between 2.7 and 2.3 million years ago in Eastern Africa, is distinguished by its individuals' sharply projecting faces, big teeth, and robust jaws.
10. Australopithecus garhi is a species that lived in Eastern Africa around 2.5 million years ago and was distinguished by its long, muscular arms. The longer strides required for bipedal walking, according to the Smithsonian Museum, could be indicated by the arms.
11. Paranthropus boisei, which lived in Eastern Africa between 2.3 and 1.2 million years ago, was distinguished by a skull designed specifically for vigorous chewing.
12. Paranthropus robustus, which existed in Southern Africa between 1.8 and 1.2 million years ago, was distinguished by its broad, deeply concave faces.
13. Australopithecus sediba: lived in southern Africa some 1.9 million years ago. This species' individuals shared facial characteristics with later Homo specimens.
14. Homo habilis, one of the first representatives of the genus Homo, existed between 2.4 and 1.4 million years ago in Eastern and Southern Africa. However, some of the ape-like characteristics were still present in members of this species.
15. Homo erectus: inhabited Northern, Eastern, and Southern Africa as well as Western and East Asia between 1.89 million and 110,000 years ago. The most complete fossil of this species, called "Turkana Boy," is thought to be about 1.6 million years old.
16. Homo floresiensis was an ape that existed in Asia between 100,000 and 50,000 years ago. The "Hobbit" moniker refers to one of the most recently found early human species. Only one Indonesian island has so far been the location of specimens.
17. Homo heidelbergensis: inhabited Europe, parts of Asia, and Africa between 700,000 and 200,000 years ago. This was the first early human species to dwell in frigid climates, according to the Smithsonian Museum.
18. Homo neanderthalensis coexisted with Homo sapiens for a few thousand years between 400,000 and 40,000 years ago. They resided throughout Europe as well as in central and southwest Asia.
19. Homo sapiens, which is present on all continents, originated roughly 300,000 years ago.

1.7

The biological basis of Life : The Cell, DNA structure and replication, Protein Synthesis, Gene, Mutation, Chromosomes, and Cell Division.

Q 1. DNA structure and replication

Ans. DNA is a long polymer of deoxyribonucleotides. The length of DNA is usually defined as the number of nucleotides (or a pair of nucleotides referred to as base pairs) present in it. This is also a characteristic of an organism. For example, a bacteriophage known as as Æ ×174 has 5386 nucleotides; Bacteriophage lambda has 48502 base pairs (bp); Escherichia coli has 4.6×106 bp; and the haploid content of human DNA is 3.3×109 bp.

A nucleotide has three components: a nitrogenous base, a pentose sugar (ribose in the case of RNA and deoxyribose for DNA), and a phosphate group.

There are two types of nitrogenous bases: purines (adenine and guanine) and pyrimidines (cytosine, uracil, and thymine). Cytosine is common in both DNA and RNA, and thymine is present in DNA. Uracil is present in RNA at the place of thymine. A nitrogenous base is linked to the pentose sugar through a N-glycosidic linkage to form a nucleoside, such as adenosine or deoxyadenosine, guanosine or deoxyguanosine, cytidine or deoxycytidine, and uridine or deoxythymidine. When a phosphate group is linked to the 5'-OH of a nucleoside through phosphoester linkage, a corresponding nucleotide (or deoxynucleotide, depending on the type of sugar present) is formed. Two nucleotides are linked through 3'–5' phosphodiester linkage to form a dinucleotide. More nucleotides can be joined in such a manner to form a polynucleotide chain. A polymer thus formed has at one end a free phosphate moiety at the 5'-end of ribose sugar, which is referred to as the 5'-end of the polynucleotide chain. Similarly, at the other end of the polymer, the ribose has a free 3'-OH group, which is referred to as the 3'-end of the polynucleotide chain. The backbone of a polynucleotide chain is formed by sugar and phosphates. The nitrogenous bases linked to the sugar moiety project from the backbone. In RNA, every nucleotide residue has an additional OH group present at the 2'-position in the ribose. Also, in RNA, uracil is found at the place of thymine (5-methyl uracil, another chemical name for thymine).

DNA, an acidic substance present in the nucleus, was first identified by Friedrich Meischer in 1869. He named it "Nuclein'. However, due to technical limitations in isolating such a long polymer intact, the elucidation of the structure of DNA remained elusive for a very long period of time. It was only in 1953 that James Watson and Francis Crick, based on the X-ray diffraction data produced by Maurice Wilkins and Rosalind Franklin, proposed a very simple but famous double helix model for the structure of DNA. One of the hallmarks of their proposition was base pairing between the two strands of polynucleotide chains. However, this proposition was also based on the observation of Erwin Chargaff that for double-stranded DNA, the ratios between adenine and thymine and guanine and cytosine are constant and equal one. The base pairing confers a very unique property to the polynucleotide chains. They are said to be complementary to each other, and therefore, if the sequence of bases in one strand is known, then the sequence in the other strand can be predicted. Also, if each strand of DNA (let us call it parental DNA) acts as a template for the synthesis of a new strand, the two double-stranded DNA (let us call them daughter DNA) thus produced would be identical to the parental DNA molecule. Because of this, the genetic implications of the structure of DNA became very clear.

Salient features of the double-helix structure of DNA:

1. It is made of two polynucleotide chains, where the backbone is constituted by sugar phosphate and the bases project inside.
2. The two chains have anti-parallel polarity. It means that if one chain has the polarity 5'à3', the other has 3'à5'.
3. The bases in two strands are paired through hydrogen bonds (H-bonds), forming base pairs (bp). Adenine forms two hydrogen bonds with thymine from the opposite strand, and vice versa. Similarly, guanine is bonded to cytosine with three H-bonds. As a result, a purine always comes opposite a pyrimidine. This generates an approximately uniform distance between the two strands of the helix.
4. The two chains are coiled in a right-handed fashion. The pitch of the helix is 3.4 nm (a nanometer is one billionth of a metre; that is 10-9 m), and there are roughly 10 bp in each turn. Consequently, the distance between bps in a helix is approximately equal to 0.34 nm.

5. The plane of one base pair stacks over the other in a double helix. This, in addition to H-bonds, confers stability to the helical structure.

The proposition of a double helix structure for DNA and its simplicity in explaining the genetic implications became revolutionary. Very soon, Francis Crick proposed the Central dogma in molecular biology, which states that the genetic information flows from DNA to RNA to Protein.

$$\textbf{DNA} \xrightarrow{\text{transcription}} \textbf{mRNA} \xrightarrow{\text{translation}} \textbf{Protein}$$

In some viruses the flow of information is in reverse direction, that is, from RNA to DNA.

Q 2. Cell division

Ans. According to the cell theory, cells arise from preexisting cells. The process by which this occurs is called cell division. Any sexually reproducing organism starts its life cycle with a single-celled zygote. Cell division does not stop with the formation of the mature organism but continues throughout its life cycle. The stages through which a cell passes from one division to the next are called the cell cycle.

The cell cycle is divided into two phases: (i) interphase, a period of preparation for cell division; and (ii) mitosis (M phase), the actual period of cell division. Interphase is further subdivided into G1, S, and G2. The G1 phase is the period when the cell grows and carries out normal metabolism. Most of the organelle duplication also occurs during this phase.

The S phase marks the phase of DNA replication and chromosome duplication. The G2 phase is the period of cytoplasmic growth.

Mitosis is also divided into four stages: prophase, metaphase, anaphase, and telophase. Chromosome condensation occurs during prophase. Simultaneously, the centrioles move to the opposite poles. The nuclear envelope and the nucleolus disappear, and the spindle fibres start appearing. Metaphase is marked by the alignment of chromosomes at the equatorial plate. During anaphase, the centromeres divide, and the chromatids start moving towards the two opposite poles. Once the chromatids reach the two poles, the chromosomal elongation starts, and the nucleolus and nuclear membrane reappear. This stage is called the telophase. The nuclear division is then followed by the cytoplasmic division, which is called cytokinesis. Mitosis, thus, is the equational division in which the chromosome number of the parent is conserved in the daughter cell. In contrast to mitosis, meiosis occurs in diploid cells, which are destined to form gametes. It is called reduction division since it reduces the chromosome number by half while making the gametes. In sexual reproduction, when the two gametes fuse, the chromosome number is restored to the value in the parent.

Meiosis is divided into two phases: meiosis I and meiosis II. In the first meiotic division, the homologous chromosomes pair to form bivalents and undergo crossing over. Meiosis I has a long prophase, which is further divided into five phases.

These are leptotene, zygotene, pachytene, diplotene, and diakinesis. During metaphase I, the bivalents are arranged on the equatorial plate. This is followed by anaphase I, in which homologous chromosomes move to the opposite poles with both their chromatids. Each pole receives half the chromosome number of the parent cell. In telophase I, the nuclear membrane and nucleolus reappear. Meiosis II is similar to mitosis. During anaphase II, the sister chromatids separate. Thus, at the end of meiosis, four haploid cells are formed.

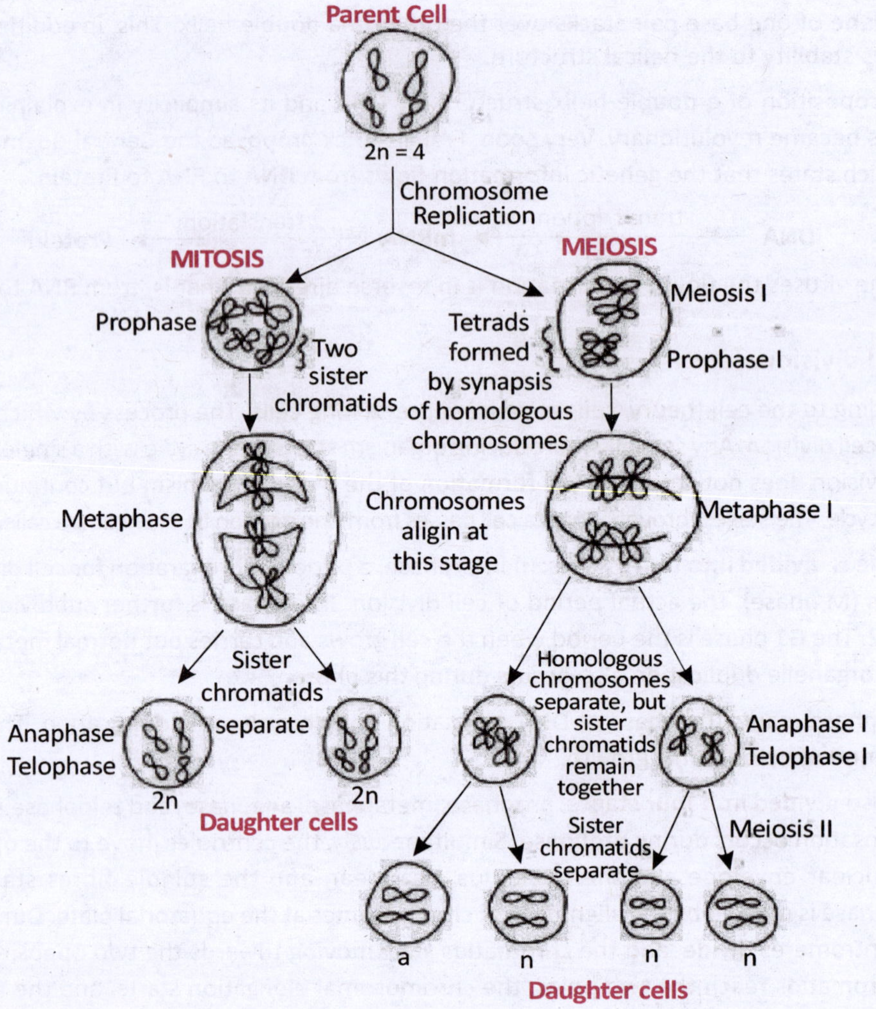

Q 3. Protein synthesis

Ans. The central dogma describes how DNA makes its own copies by DNA replication, then codes for RNA by means of transcription, and RNA codes for proteins by translation.

For the creation of a new generation, the genetic information stored in the DNA has to be transferred from one generation to another. The process begins with the replication of DNA, followed by transcription and translation. Let us have a discussion on translation, viz., protein synthesis in cells and the structure of tRNA.

DNA $\xrightarrow{\text{transcription}}$ **mRNA** $\xrightarrow{\text{translation}}$ **Protein**

The DNA is transcribed into mRNA on the basis of their complementarity. Translation is the process of converting nucleic acid information into amino acids. There is no complementarity between amino acids and mRNA. Hence, translation is not controlled by complementarity but by the genetic code. Since amino acids cannot read this genetic code, they are dependent on an adapter molecule. This adapter molecule is called tRNA (transfer RNA).

Structurally, the tRNA is an inverted L-shaped molecule that has an anticodon loop and an amino acid acceptor end. The anticodon loop makes bases complementary to the codes on the mRNA, and the amino acid end binds to the respective amino acids. Thus, it helps in protein synthesis. Each amino acid has a specific tRNA. Initiator tRNA initiates the translation, while stop codons have no tRNA.

The process by which the mRNA codes for a particular protein is known as translation. In the process, the ribosome translates the mRNA produced from DNA into a chain of specific amino acids. This chain of amino acids leads to protein synthesis.

It is a process where the expense of ATP is required, and this energy is given by the charged tRNA. The whole machinery of translation is present in the ribosomes.

The ribosomes consist of a bigger subunit and a smaller subunit. The larger subunit, in turn, consists of two molecules of tRNA that are placed close together so that a peptide bond can be developed at the expense of sufficient energy. The mRNA enters the smaller subunit, which is held by the molecules of tRNA of the complementary codon that exist in the bigger subunit. Hence, two codons are held by two molecules of tRNA placed near each other, and a peptide bond is produced among them. When this process repeats, a large chain of amino acids is synthesised. At the stop, the codon ribosome releases the amino acid chain.

Q 4. Gene and Chromosome

Ans. **Gene:** In 1909, Johanssen introduced the term gene. Before him, Mendel had used the term 'factor' for the unit of inheritance that is responsible for expressing a trait. Johanssen defined the gene as 'the elementary unit of inheritance that can be assigned to a particular trait.' Morgan's work proposes that a gene is the shortest segment of a chromosome that can be separated by crossing over.

A gene is presently defined as 'the unit of inheritance composed of a segment of DNA situated at a specific locus that carries coded information and also has the ability to undergo mutation and crossing over.'

The definition of a gene states that it is the basic physical and functional unit of heredity. Genes are structurally made up of nucleotides called DNA.

Three nucleotides together code for amino acids and a string of amino acids in a particular sequence forms a functional protein. These proteins may function as enzymes and control metabolism. Archibald Garrod studied the errors of metabolism and found that genes operate through enzymes. Beadle and Tatum in 1948 proposed the one-gene, oneenzyme hypothesis. But some enzymes require more than one polypeptide. Therefore, it is modified into the one-gene, one-polypeptide hypothesis.

Every diploid organism has two copies of genes derived from each of its parents. They are expressed in a dominant or recessive manner.

The complete set of all genes present in a cell is known as a genome. There are 3000 genes in the human genome. The largest gene in the human genome is 2400 kbp long, and the smallest gene in the human genome is 14 bp long.

Chromosome: Chromosomes are the genetic material present in all cells. They are present in the nucleus of a eukaryotic cell. They have a thread-like structure.

Each chromosome of a eukaryotic cell contains DNA and associated proteins, known as histone proteins. They are responsible for the hereditary traits that are passed from parents to offspring from one generation to the next. DNA codes for specific proteins and is responsible for variations in a species and among various organisms. Scientists have given this name to chromosomes as they are stained using specific dyes; chroma means colour and soma means body.

Humans have 23 pairs of chromosomes. This unique structure of the chromosome keeps DNA tightly packed with histone proteins to fit inside the cell, and it also helps in giving it more stability. For instance, the unwound DNA of a single cell will measure 6 feet; with this, one can understand the need for packaging inside the nucleus of each cell.

Cells must continuously repair, grow, and regenerate to replace the old cells. Cell division is important for the growth and development of an organism. We can see chromosomes clearly during cell division. Chromosomes ensure that DNA is divided equally between the daughter cells during cell division. Even a small irregularity in the process may lead to various diseases and deformities. Uncontrolled cell division results in tumour cells and causes cancer. Chromosomal aberrations like changes in structure or number can cause genetic disorders, e.g., Down's syndrome, Turner's syndrome, etc. Defective chromosomes may even lead to a certain type of leukaemia in humans.

Q 5. Molecular basis of inheritance

Ans. Nucleic acids are long polymers of nucleotides. While DNA stores genetic information, RNA mostly helps in the transfer and expression of information. Though DNA and RNA both function as genetic material, DNA, being chemically and structurally more stable, is a better genetic material. However, RNA was the first to evolve, and DNA was derived from RNA. The hallmark of the double-stranded helical structure of DNA is the hydrogen bonding between the bases on opposite strands. The rule is that adenine pairs with thymine through two H-bonds and guanine with cytosine through three H-bonds. This makes one strand complementary to the other. The DNA replicates semiconservatively; the process is guided by complementary H-bonding. A segment of DNA that codes for RNA may, in a simplistic term, be referred to as a gene. During transcription, one of the strands of DNA acts as a template to direct the synthesis of complementary RNA.

In bacteria, the transcribed mRNA is functional and hence can be directly translated. In eukaryotes, the gene is split. The coding sequences, exons, are interrupted by non-coding sequences, introns. Introns are removed, and exons are joined to produce functional RNA by splicing. The messenger RNA contains the base sequences that are read in a combination of three (to make a triplet genetic code) to code for an amino acid. The genetic code is read again on the principle of complementarity by tRNA, which acts as an adapter molecule. There are specific tRNAs for every amino acid. The tRNA binds to specific amino acids at one end and pairs through H-bonding with codes on mRNA through its anticodons. The site of translation (protein synthesis) is ribosomes, which bind to mRNA and provide a platform for joining amino acids. One of the rRNAs acts as a catalyst for peptide bond formation, which is an example of an RNA enzyme (ribozyme). Translation is a process that has evolved around RNA, indicating that life began around RNA. Since transcription and translation are energetically expensive processes, they have to be tightly regulated. Regulation of transcription is the primary step in regulating gene expression. In bacteria, more than one gene is arranged together and regulated in units called operons. The lac operon is the prototype operon in bacteria and codes for genes responsible for the metabolism of lactose. The operon is regulated by the amount of lactose in the medium where the bacteria are grown. Therefore, this regulation can also be viewed as the regulation of enzyme synthesis by its substrate.

Case Study

- **Humans Are 8% Virus—How Ancient Viral DNA in Our Genome Plays a Role in Disease and Development**

In our genomes, viral DNA sequences that were formerly part of pandemics are still active in healthy individuals. Around 8% of the human genome is made up of HERVs, or human endogenous retroviruses, which evolved from infections that our primate ancestors contracted millions of years ago. Because of the way they multiply, they end up in the human genome. These ancient retroviruses, like modern HIV, needed to splice their genetic material into the DNA of their hosts in order to reproduce. This particular viral genetic material is not typically handed down from one generation to the next. However, certain ancient retroviruses have the capacity to infect germ cells that do pass on their DNA to succeeding generations, such as eggs or sperm. These retroviruses, which over the course of millions of years evolved to specifically target germ cells, may have ramifications for how disease researchers now screen and test for illnesses.

- **Scientists Uncover the Gene Responsible for Humans' Big Brain**

A primate's brain can grow due to ARHGAP11B. It was not yet known, nevertheless, whether ARHGAP11B played a significant or insignificant part in the evolutionary expansion of the human neocortex. The ARGHAP11B gene was initially introduced into chimpanzee organoid brain ventricle-like structures to elucidate this. Would the ARGHAP11B gene lead to the expansion of the chimpanzee brain's brain stem cells, which is necessary for the neocortex to enlarge? According to our research, the gene in chimpanzee organoids produces an increase in the brain stem cells and neurons that are essential for the development of humans' remarkable mental capacities. The number of these brain stem cells decreased to that of a chimpanzee when the ARGHAP11B gene was knocked out in human brain organoids or when the function of the ARHGAP11B protein was inhibited. Thus, we were able to demonstrate that ARHGAP11B is essential for the formation of the neocortex during the course of human evolution.

1.8

(a) Principles of Prehistoric Archaeology, Chronology : Relative and Absolute Dating methods.

(b) Cultural Evolution—Broad Outlines of Prehistoric cultures:

(i) Paleolithic **(ii) Mesolithic**

(iii) Neolithic **(iv) Chalcolithic**

(v) Copper-Bronze Age **(vi) Iron Age**

Q 1. Principles of Prehistoric Archaeology

Ans. The emergence of man through the process of biological and cultural evolution is a story of a long span of time. For the archaeologist and the prehistorian who deal with the long history of man, time is the most important consideration.

In fact, chronology is one of the most fundamental issues and perhaps a characteristic of archaeology. Archaeologists use several methods to assign ages to events in the past. They are engaged in defining the states of hominid evolution, their artifactual record, and the assignment of a chronology to these stages.

Chronology is the science of measuring time and ordering things in time. According to the Dictionary of Anthropology, the word chronology means the science of computing dates or treaties showing the arrangement of events with dates. In other words, chronology is the arrangement of events, or the materials that represent them, in the order of their occurrence in time. Any study of the origins of humans must be set in a chronological context. Prehistoric archaeologists use several methods to assign ages to events of the past. Knowledge of various dating methods is therefore an essential aspect of prehistoric archaeological studies.

Types of dating: There are mainly two types of dating: i) relative and ii) absolute or chronometric dating.

1. Relative dating fixes a time frame in relation to other strata or materials and not in absolute dates in numbers. It can only define antiquity in terms of being older or younger than something else, which makes it possible to arrange a series of things in proper chronological order. But it is difficult to know the total time span involved in the intervals between things.
2. On the other hand, the absolute dating technique exhibits chronology in terms of years. It offers precise and accurate dating. There may be marginal errors that are almost negligible. Some of the common and widely applied absolute dating methods are carbon-14, potassium-argon (K-A40), thermoluminescence, dendrochronology, etc.

In the early stages of prehistoric studies, there was only relative chronology. But in the last fifty years, with the emergence of the C14 method, there has been a total change in the dating scenario.

Relative dating, however, is still applied in those areas where deposits containing organic materials cannot be dated by any absolute dating techniques.

Distinction between Relative and Absolute Dating:

1. By using relative methods, one can know whether a particular culture is younger or older than another one and thereby arrange a series of things in a sequential time frame. Unlike relative dating, absolute or chronometric dating is primarily sought to facilitate time sequence in terms of years. It provides the actual time spanned by a site sequence with a close approximation.
2. Absolute dating or chronometric dating usually demands high technology, is laboratory-based, and is hence costly. It also demands the help of sciences like geophysics, geochemistry, astronomy, nuclear physics, etc.

Q 2. Relative dating method

Ans. Relative dating fixes a time frame in relation to other strata or materials and not in absolute date in number. It can only define antiquity in terms of being older or younger than something else, which makes it possible to arrange a series of things in proper chronological order.

There are different methods:

1. **Stratigraphy:** Stratigraphy is the analysis of a series of layers that exist in the horizontal dimension and are studied in the vertical time dimension. The method is based on the basic geological principle that, among the layers, the earlier deposit lies under the later deposit.
   Therefore, whenever a stratigraphic sequence is observed during the excavation of a site, the relative ages of the cultural levels can be worked out. The stratigraphic associations of artefact types within and between archaeological sites are regarded as one of the most important methods of relative dating.
   Limitations: human interference, tectonic interference, environmental interference, etc.
2. **Typology:** An archaeological site mainly consists of artefacts and tools. The tools found on the site are classified on the basis of their form or shape, and accordingly, different categories or types are made. These are then arranged from simple to elaborate, from poorly preserved to well preserved, from crude to refined, etc. Then a relative antiquity is derived based on the presumption that simple, poorly preserved, and crude tools are older than elaborate, well preserved, and refined ones.
   Limitation: According to *Wheeler*, 'the values of typological classification are liable to be local rather than universal, but when the method is used in corroboration with the stratigraphic method, it may become very helpful'.

3. **Sequence Dating :** In 1881, a relative dating method was developed in Egypt by *Sir Flinders Petrie*. The method is based on the fact that artefacts change is predictable ways over time. Among all other artefacts, it is found that pottery changes with time and a sequence of pottery designs can thus be worked out. By detecting this trend of change, an archaeologist can trace associated cultural changes and make short-term time distinctions.
   While the excavation of graves was carried out in Egypt, *Petrie* found that the graves were associated with varied pottery. He analysed the features of pottery, such as the handles of pots, and worked out a sequence showing their change, progressing from functional entities to mere decorations. The changes on pots were then correlated with other artefacts from graves, and he finally ended with a series of numbered pottery stages that he labelled 'sequence dates'.
   This method was later applied by the great anthropologist *Kroeber* in determining the relative age of some sites in the western United States, Mexico, and Peru.
4. **Fluorine, uranium, and nitrogen analysis:** Prehistoric sites often consist of many bone remains. The basic principle of the method is that the longer a bone is placed in soil, the more fluorine will be caught in it, which can suggest a relative date. All bones, whether of animals or humans lying at the same level, exhibit a similar fluorine percentage in them. Therefore, if the quantity of fluorine remains the same in both kinds of bones, it is sure that they are of the same age.
   The bones acquired from a lower level show more fluorine in them, whereas the bones remaining from the upper level contain less fluorine. The relative ages of different bones at the same site can thus be established by measuring their fluorine contents. The method cannot provide an absolute age because the amount of fluorine differs from soil to soil, which gives a differential rate of absorption. Like fluorine, the uranium or nitrogen content of the bones can also be measured. Since fluorine and uranium levels in the bone increase with time while nitrogen levels decrease, such measurements help to place in sequence the cultural phases with which the different bones may be associated. In fact, the analysis of fluorine, uranium, or nitrogen is regarded as one of the most important techniques for relative dating. e.g., the Pildown hoax.
5. **Palaeontology:** Palaeontology, the study of fossilised remains of bones in archaeological sites, also provides relative dates. The method is based on the fact that some animals migrate or become extinct with climate change. That is climate has a direct relationship with the presence or absence of certain animals. For example, if evidence for Elephas antiques (a forest elephant) is found, one can assume a temperate climate, while the presence of E. primigenous (a steppe elephant) indicates a steppe or tundra environment with almost glacial conditions.
   Likewise, it is found that in North America, the arrival of man caused the extinction of mammals such as the mammoth, horse, camel, and several species of bison. These can be dated to approximately 6000 B.C. However, a margin of error of 1000 years might be there as all of them have not become extinct at once and some have lived in isolated areas, in which case the dating of fauna associated with other evidence is inexact and misleading.
   Smaller species of animals like rodents, birds, some molluscs, and snails are found to be more sensitive to changes in climate than larger mammals. In Northern Ireland, it has been possible to show changes in the coastal environment since the time of human occupation by studying changes in tidal-zone molluscs found in archaeological sites.
6. **Palynology:** Lennart Von Post, a Swedish scientist, was the first to develop this paleobotanical method in 1916. By this method, a microscopic analysis of pollen extracted from trees is used to identify various trees, and a pollen diagram is prepared. The pollen diagram, in which the relative frequencies of various species are plotted, helps in tracing out the changing vegetation of an area. Acid peat or bog deposits are ideal sources of animal pollen, but dry sites and clays contain enough pollen to provide a sequence. Pollens in the soil underlying or overlying archaeological sites may

be correlated with the already known regional pollen sequence, and the age of the site can thus be dated. A very good example of the application of the pollen method is the archaeological site at Choukoutien in China.

7. **Patination:** There is no precise definition for the term patination though it generally means chemical alteration of rock surfaces exposed to atmospheric conditions. The amount of patina on the stone is an index of its age and is valuable for the relative placement of the stone artefact in technological development. The chemical alterations of the stone are usually brought about by the action of iron oxides over time. The observation of the amount of patina on a stone may be used at sites where there is a long sequence and demonstrates that those tools that lie in the bottom level may have more patina than those in the upper levels. The different types of tools from the river gravels, terraces of rivers, or lakes can be differentiated in the relative amounts of patina on the basis of which of the relative ages can be assigned to the artefacts.

   Relative dating, however, is still applied in those areas where deposits containing organic materials cannot be dated by any absolute dating techniques.

   Relative dating fixes a time frame in relation to other strata or materials and not in absolute dates in numbers. But it is difficult to know the total time span involved in the intervals between things.

Q 3. Absolute Dating method

Ans. Absolute or chronometric dating is primarily sought to facilitate time sequence in terms of years. It provides the actual time spanned by a site sequence with a close approximation.

There are different methods:

1. **Carbon Dating:** Radiocarbon dating is a chemical analysis used to determine the age of organic materials based on their content of the radioisotope carbon 14. The method was developed by Willard F. Libby and a team of scientists at the University of Chicago. In 1960, Libby received the Nobel Prize for his method of using carbon-14 for age determinations in archaeology, geology, geophysics, and other branches of science. It subsequently evolved into the most powerful method of dating Holocene artefacts and geologic events up to about 50,000 years.

   By using the radiocarbon method, one can date different types of organic or inorganic materials as long as they consist of carbon. The method was actually devised to measure the amount of low-level radioactivity of carbon remaining in ancient and dead material of organic origin.

   Radiocarbon (14C) dating is the most widely accepted technique for studying the chronological relationships of archaeological complexes. Using the radiocarbon method as a source of objective information, we are able to build Stone Age chronologies as well as establish the primary chrono-cultural boundaries.

2. **Potassium-Argon (K-Ar 40) Dating:** This method is also radioactive. The earth's crust contains potassium, whose isotope K40 decays to A40 at a known rate. The ratio of potassium to argon may be measured to ascertain the date of minerals and rocks in a deposit. This method is able to cover a wide range of time, even far greater than the C-14 method, because the half life of the radioactive potassium is 1330 million years (1.36 billion years).

   The method has proved quite useful in dating some hominid fossils, as employed at the site of Olduvai Gorge in east Africa, where the remains were as old as 1.75 million years. The advantage of the method is that it works well for sites that are 500,000 years old. But the disadvantage of the method is that it can only be applied to those rocks and minerals that are rich in potassium. Therefore, the methods are restricted to areas where volcanic rocks rich in potassium are available.

3. **Thermoluminescence (TL):** The use of thermoluminescence (TL) for dating purposes was developed in the 1960s mainly at the Oxford Research Laboratory for Archaeology and the History of Art by *M. Aitken* and coworkers. Initially designed to date archaeology ceramics, it was subsequently extended to other mineral materials, such as burnt flint.

This is based on the fact that objects such as pottery that have been heated in the past can be dated by the measurement of their thermoluminescence (TL) glow. Thermoluminescence (TL) is the emitted light in the pottery that can be measured. If the ground-up pottery is reheated, it emits light. The phenomenon results from the radioactive influence of metallic elements like uranium and potassium present in the clay and surrounding soils.

The use of the thermoluminescence (TL) dating method and the results obtained could make it possible to provide a new chronological framework for archaeological and anthropological knowledge. For example, the new chronology based on thermoluminescence (TL) dating enabled the revision of some prior assumptions about the evolution of lithic industries and the nature of hominids present in the Near East at various stages of the Middle Palaeolithic.

4. **Dendrochronology :** The age of wooden objects can be determined by means of dendrochronology or tree ring analysis, which determines the calendar years of tree-ring formation and the felling dates of trees, which helps to determine the age of wooden objects with great precision. Dendrochronology has therefore become well established in the fields of archaeology, art history, and cultural heritage. The method depends on the fact that trees growing in temperate zones have clearly defined annual rings of growth. As these tree rings represent annual growth, merely by counting rings, one can count the age of the tree and hence its association.

   The dating method with the latest methodological advances helps us define the calendar year in which the tree rings were formed and interpret such dating in terms of the age of a wooden object.

5. **Palaeomagnetic Dating:** It is an important means of cross-checking the dates based on the constantly shifting nature of the earth's magnetic field, both in direction and intensity. The measurement of the earth's magnetic field in several places around the world for centuries has shown that it varies with time. A number of studies have shown that a record of past magnetic fields in the form of angles of declination and dip can be trapped in baked clay.

   When clay is heated to a certain degree, the magnetic elements of baked clay realign themselves along lines dictated by the intensity and character of the earth's magnetic field at that time. On cooling, the magnetic elements are frozen and can be recorded as long as the clay is preserved. This is called remnant magnetism.

   When records of past angles of declination and dip have been kept, it is possible to compare the values of historic records and arrive at the dates of archaeological specimens of fired clay. Fluxgate, spinner magnetometer, and superconduction magnetometer are the instruments used for measuring magnetic resonance. The method was described in detail in Great Britain by *Aitken*. It has also been used in Japan and Arizona. In India, the method is applied to date Karewa sediments in Kashmir.

   The reliability of the application of the method depends on certain conditions, such as availability of good records of changes in magnetic paths near the prehistoric sites, existence of a series of already dated baked clays in the area against which objects of unknown dates can be dated and availability of archaeological samples that are found in their place of first occurrence.

6. **Amino Acid Racemization Technique:** Amino acid racemization, a method of absolute dating applied to human fossils, was developed very recently. This is based on the fact that all living organisms have L-amino acids in their proteins, and after death, over a long period of time, all the L-amino acids except glycine undergo a change called racemization and become non-protein D-amino acids. The proportion of these D-amino acids increases with time. Thus, the age of the skeletal materials that are found in archaeological sites can be estimated by determining the amount of change or re-formation that has occurred. Amino Acid Racemization (AAR) is a useful comparative dating method with great potential, but it introduces problems of calibration and the requirement of intimate knowledge of the palaeoenvironmental conditions of the bone deposition site.

Technique	Most suitable materials	Effective dating range	Major limitations
Radiocarbon, C14	Organic materials, inorganic carbonates	20000 to 400000 yrs depending on material	Poor Sampling, contamination by younger materials, error exist around 320 yr. and applicable upto 1 lakh yr. study.
Potassium Argon, (K-Ar 40)	Volcanic rock or materials	Unlimited, coarse calibration	Availability of un weathered volcanic rock, sample preparation contamination. It needs to contain potassium necessarily. Less than 1 lakh yr. cannot be dated.
Palaeomagnetism	Intact kiln or hearth	2000 yrs	Calibration, limited applicability
Thermolumi nascence	Pottery	10000 yrs or more	Range of error, few facilities
Obsidian hydration	Obsidian artefacts	35000 yrs	Requires calibrated regional framework framework
Amino acid racemisation	Bone, marine shells	100000 yrs	Experimental stage only, few facilities
Varves	Sediments, ice, laminae	15000 yrs or more	Limited application
Dendrochronology	Tree rings	7500 yrs	Region specific Tropical climate cannot be done.

Depending upon the type of problem, accuracy required, materials available for dating, and problem of contamination, one should decide what type of technique one should use for dating. All dating techniques have their merits and demerits, and this has to be kept in mind by the archaeologist. It is essential to apply several dating methods for cross-checking the dates and building a concrete chronology.

Q 4. C-14 Dating method

Ans. Radiocarbon dating is a chemical analysis used to determine the age of organic materials based on their content of the radioisotope carbon 14. The method was developed by Willard F. Libby and a team of scientists at the University of Chicago. In 1960, Libby received the Nobel Prize for his method of using carbon-14 for age dete rminations in archaeology, geology, geophysics, and other branches of science. It subsequently evolved into the most powerful method of dating Holocene artefacts and geologic events up to about 50,000 years.

It is based on the concept that all living being absorb radio active carbon-14 (C14) and its absorption ceases at the time of death. After which C14 atoms begins to disintegrate at a known rate by which it is possible to calculate age of particular object using logarithmic scale based upon remaining C-14 in it.

It is calculated by using half life of C-14 as 5730 years about 50% of C-14 decays and converts into N-14 and subsequently in next 5730 years 25% of original amount and so on.

Thus the age of an organic substance can be calculated but there are certain limitations. Firstly after 1,00,000 year amount C-14 left is negligible, hence difficult to calculate accurate of objects for older than 1,00,000 year. Secondly with increasing radiation level in environment and contamination rate of decay could be fluctuating. Hence, it limits its accuracy.

However carbon dating is an important absolute dating method which can be used along with relative dating method to unify the facts and refine the anthropological studies.

Q 5. Palaeolithic Culture of World

Ans. Palaeolithic culture refers to the cultural debris recorded from the entire Pleistocene epoch. It is divided into three phases: the Lower (2.5 million years ago to 100,000 BCE), Middle (100,000 BCE to 36,000 BCE), and Upper (36,000 BCE to 9000 BCE) Palaeolithic.

Climate: The Pleistocene epoch witnessed four phases of glaciation and pluviation, separated by three dry phases of interglaciation and inter-pluviation.

Epoch	Period of Glaciation	Age	Arch period	Sequence of cultures
Holocene	Post glacial	10,000	Neolithic Mesolithic	
Pleistocene	Wurm 3rd inter glacial Riss 2nd inter glacial Mindel 1st interglacial Gunz	70,000 2,00,000	 Upper palaeo Middle Lower palaeo	Magdalenian Aurignacion Perigordian Mousterian Clactonian Acheulean Abbevillian Pre abbevillian

Material Culture:

Period	Material Used	Preparation Technique	Tools
Lower Palaeolithic	Quartzite	Direct hammer technique	Core tools characterized by two main industries – Abbevillian (chopper – chopping tools and crude handaxes) and Acheulian (cleavers and handaxes)
Middle Palaeolithic	Crypto-crystalline silica types	Pecking and direct hammer technique	Flake tools like scrapers and points became much frequent than core tools.
Upper Palaeolithic	Quartz and bone	Core cylinder hammer technique	Parallel –sided blade flakes and blade tools, along with bone tools.

Regional Variations:

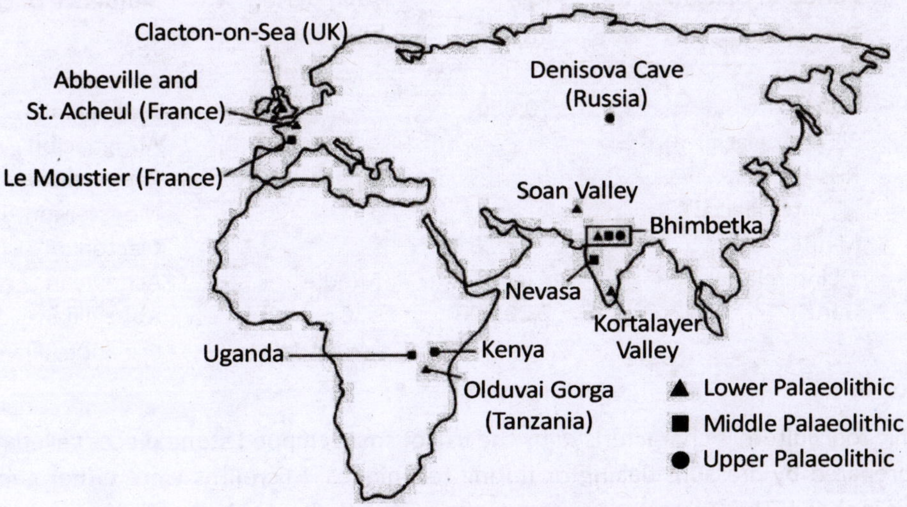

Important Palaeolithic Sites of the World

1. **Europe:** Lower Palaeolithic sites include Abbeville and St. Acheule in France. From the sites of Levallois (France) and Clacton-on-Sea (U.K.), flakes were discovered, subsequently named Levalloisian and Clactonian flakes. The Middle Palaeolithic culture is best seen at the type site of Le Mouster (France) and is thus referred to as the Mousterian culture. The upper Palaeolithic culture is divided into four stages: Perigordian, Aurignacian, Solutrean, and Magdalenian.
2. **Africa:** Olduvai Gorge (Tanzania) is among the oldest Lower Palaeolithic sites in the world. Kenya and Uganda are home to sites representing Middle and Upper Palaeolithic traditions.
3. **India:** Soan valley in the north and Madrasian industry in the south are the main Lower Palaeolithic cultures. Nevasa was the first Middle Palaeolithic site to be discovered. Belan Valley has been key in establishing a distinct Upper Palaeolithic tradition. Bhimbetka, meanwhile, shows a highly specialised Acheulian tradition.

Social life:

As can be deduced from the tools, the economy was based on hunting and gathering. Burials found with implements at certain sites indicate the start of rites and rituals. Caves and figures from the Upper Palaeolithic period, especially found in European and Asian sites, depict a developing social organisation towards the end of this period.

The Palaeolithic period represents the evolution of humans from Homo erectus (Lower Palaeolithic) to Neanderthal (Middle Palaeolithic) and finally Homo sapiens (Upper Palaeolithic). Thus, it is of immense significance in human history.

Q 6. Mesolithic Culture of World

Ans. Mesolithic culture refers to the earliest Holocene culture prior to the advent of wide-scale food production. It spans from around 10,000 to 4000 BCE.

Climate:

The glacial climatic conditions of the Palaeolithic period gave way to a warmer climate. The melting ice corresponded with the clearing up of forests and water bodies.

Epoch	Period of Glaciation	Age	Arch period	Sequence of cultures
Holocene	Post glacial	10,000	Neolithic Mesolithic	
Pleistocene	Wurm 3rd inter glacial Riss 2nd inter glacial Mindel 1st interglacial Gunz	70,000 2,00,000	 Upper palaeo Middle Lower palaeo	Magdalenian Aurignacion Perigordian Mousterian Clactonian Acheulean Abbevillian Pre abbevillian

Material Culture:

Mesolithic tool culture is characterised by the use of small chipped stone pieces called microliths. These were prepared by pressure flaking or fluting techniques. Microliths were either geometric or non-geometric in shape. They were used as composite tools, attached to arrows, harpoons, and blades.

Regional Variations:

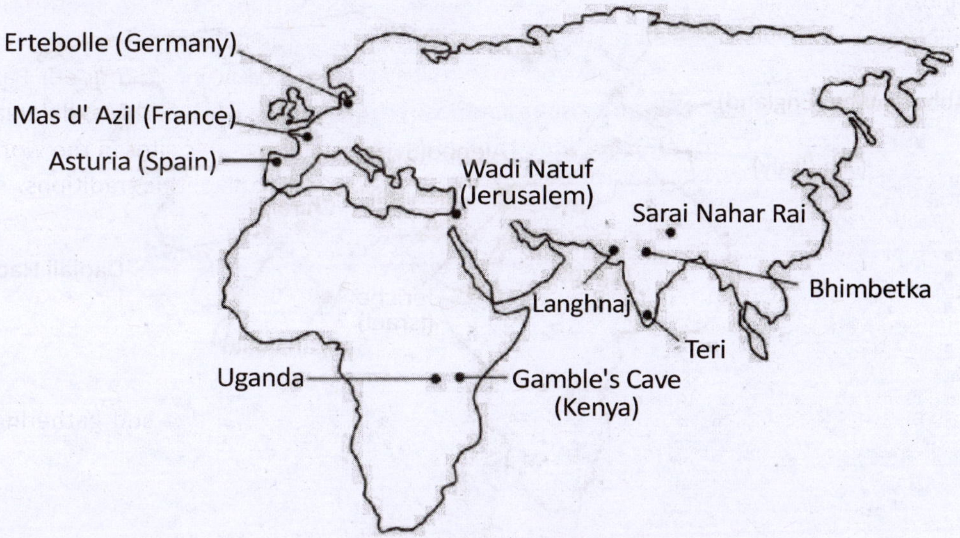

Important Mesolithic Sites of the World

1. **Europe:** The Mesolithic traditions of Europe can be divided into two phases. The first phase includes Azilian, Tardenoisian, and Asturian cultures. The second phase includes Maglemosean, Ertebolle and Campignion cultures. Ecological conditions made people habitat coastal regions and river banks.
2. **Africa:** African microlithic trends are further specialised into Elementeitan and Wilton cultures of Kenya and Magosan and Lupemban cultures of Uganda. The tools were mainly prepared on black obsidian and are accompanied by crudely baked, hand-made pottery as well.
3. **India:** Sarai Nahar Rai is the oldest Indian Mesolithic site, dated around 8000 BCE. Langhnaj, meanwhile, is one of the youngest sites, dated around 2400–2000 BCE. Most of the Indian sites show total adaptation to microliths and do not contain heavy-duty tools. Bhimbetka is rich in cave paintings dating to the Mesolithic period.
4. **Social Life:** As can be deduced from the tools and the cave paintings, the economy was based on small-game hunting, fishing, and fowling. Numerous burials found in specific postures indicate the existence of rituals. Towards the end of this period, domestication of animals and wild seed collection began.

Thus, the Mesolithic period represents a transitional phase between the Palaeolithic and Neolithic periods, with Homo sapiens on the cusp of moving into a settled and productive economy.

Q 7. Neolithic Culture of World

Ans. Neolithic culture refers to the Holocene culture marking the advent of widescale food production, and preceding the discovery of metal. It spans from around 9000-3500 BCE.

Climate: The period is marked by a warm and dry climate favourable for settlements.

Material Culture:

- Neolithic tool culture is characterised by the use of celts. Their preparation involved large, compact stones being flaked into axes or adzes, followed by grinding and polishing. These celts were attached to a wooden handle and used to clear forests and bring land under cultivation. Other tool types include ring stones and mace heads.
- Another notable feature was the development of pottery for storing food grains. It was initially hand-made and poorly fired. Wheel-made pottery began at the end of this period.

Regional Variatious:

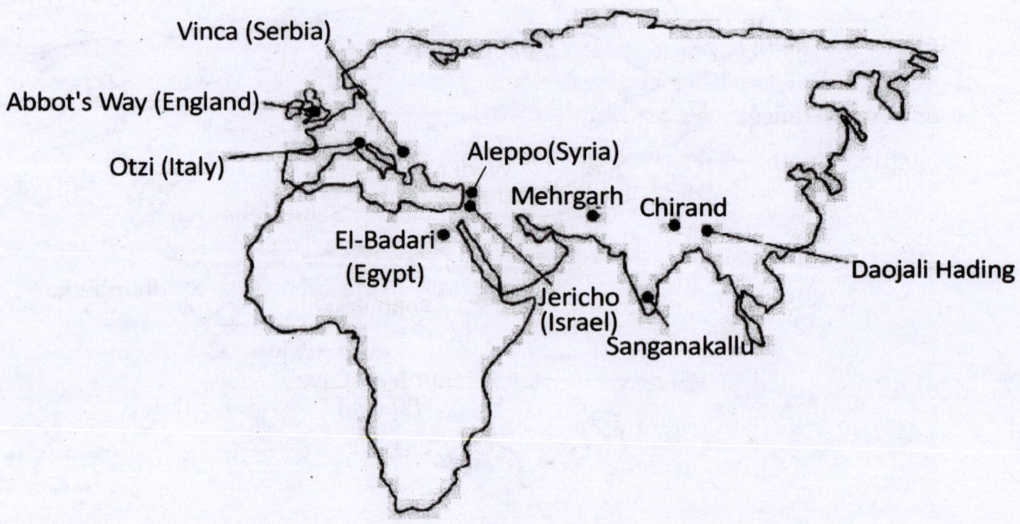

Important Neolithic Sites of the World

1. **Near East:** The oldest records of Neolithic culture in the world appear in the Fertile Crescent, dated around 10,000 BCE. The origin of agriculture is traced to the Natufian culture located in the Levant. Sites such as Aleppo (Syria) and Jericho (Israel) are home to the earliest known Neolithic settlements in the world.
2. **Europe:** The oldest records come from the river valleys in Greece and the Balkans. A number of cultures have since been reported, including Starcevo culture, linear pottery culture, and Horgen culture. Agriculture was introduced to Europe through contact with West Asia.
3. **Africa:** The Neolithic culture reached Africa from West Asia. Domestication of sheep and goats was first seen in Egypt, along the Nile Valley, around 5000 BCE. African Neolithic cultures include the Merimde and Badarian cultures.
4. **India:** The oldest Neolithic site is Mehrgarh dating to 7000 BCE. Mehrgarh represents one of the earliest evidences of farming and herding in Southeast Asia. The South Indian culture shows a mix of Neolithic and Chalcolithic traits, with a unique form of ritual seen here, that of Neolithic Ash Mounds.

Social Life:

- The economy shifted from hunting and gathering to a subsistence economy based on domesticated plants and animals. A sedentary lifestyle required a cooperative existence, and thus complex social organisations arose. Political organisation was needed to protect fields and crops and resolve conflicts over them. Also, a clear-cut presence of magio-religious practises is seen.
- Thus, the large-scale changes in such a short span of time made *V.G. Childe* term the Neolithic period the first revolution in mankind.

Q 8. Natufian Culture

Ans. Preagricultural Epipaleolithic (transitional between Upper Palaeolithic and Neolithic) culture associated with storage of crops and sedentary settlements (unusual for its time).

1. Geographical location: Levant (Jordan, Syria, Israel)
2. Discover: Dorothy Garrod
3. Time Period: 15000–11500 years old
4. Climatic Conditions: Terminal Pleistocene to the beginning of the Holocene

5. Main Sites: Eynan, el-Wad, Kebara, and Tabun
6. Salient Features:
   a. Settled Living: Larger settlement size (Natufian sites were five times larger than their predecessors). People live in circular pit houses with a permanent hearth and plastered storage structures for storing wild grains beneath their houses.
   b. Tool Technology: Microliths, Sickles, Stone Mortars, Basalt Sharpening Tools, Advanced Knowledge of Lime Plaster Production. There was a rich bone industry, including harpoons and fish hooks. Stone and bone were worked into pendants and other ornaments.
   c. Subsistence: They relied on wild grains and the hunting of wild gazelles. There was a sign of nutritional deficiency, as evidenced by the enamel and decline in stature.
   d. Burial: Common village cemetery for burial of people, indicating settled living.
   e. Evidence of increasing use of stationary resources and subsequent increases in social complexity Natufian culture is significant as it helps trace out the history of agriculture and settled living.

Q 9. Chalcolithic Culture of World

Ans. Chalcolithic culture refers to the period of human culture preceding the Bronze Age, characterised by the use of copper and stone tools. It spans from around 5500 BCE to 2000 BCE.

Climate:

The period is marked by a warm and dry climate favourable for settlements.

Material Culture:

➢ The technology was a mix of metals and stones. Metal technology is seen in the smelting of copper and the manufacturing of copper tools and weapons. The lithic technology included microliths, stone blades, and axes. Another identifying characteristic of the period is polychrome-painted pottery.

Regional Variations:

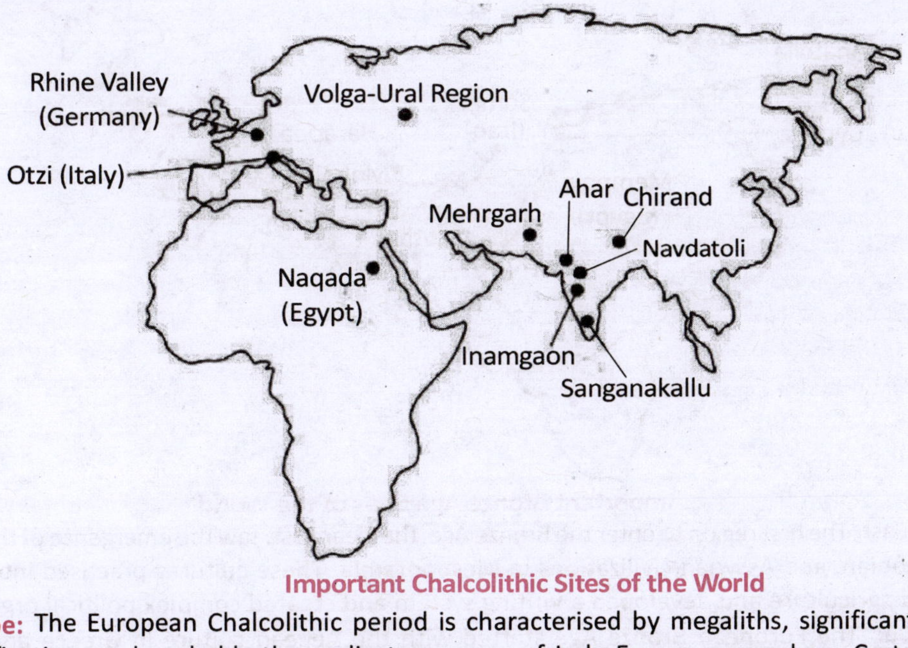

Important Chalcolithic Sites of the World

1. **Europe:** The European Chalcolithic period is characterised by megaliths, significant economic stratification, and probably the earliest presence of Indo-European speakers. Certain cultures include Yamna, Corded Ware, and Kurgan culture.

2. **Africa:** Chalcolithic culture first reached Egypt through the Naqada culture. But, for most of Africa, iron and copper smelting appeared together, and thus, there was no distinct Chalcolithic period.
3. **India:** Chalcolithic culture in India is not uniform. For convenience, it is divided into six cultural zones: Ahar-Banas, Madhya Pradesh, Gangetic Doab, Eastern, Northern Deccan, and Southern Chalcolithic. All zones are chiefly distinguished by their ceramic industries.

Social Life:

- The period saw the emergence of full-fledged villages. The economy centred on the cultivation of cereals and domesticated animals. Societies engaged in long-distance trading Mud-brick and thatched houses were common. Religious life is centred on the cults of Mother Goddess, sacred bulls, and a belief in the afterlife.
- Towards the end, copper was gradually replaced by the alloy bronze, giving rise to the Bronze Age.

Q 10. Bronze Age of World

Ans. The Bronze Age refers to the period preceding the Iron Age, characterised by bronze metallurgy as the dominant metalworking technology. It spans from around 3300 to 1000 BCE.

Climate: The period is marked by a warm and dry climate favourable for settlements.

Material Culture:

- Bronze was produced by smelting copper and alloying it with tin, arsenic, or other metals. Compared to other metals, bronze was more durable and harder, thus giving it a technological advantage.
- Stone and clay moulds were used for shaping objects such as arrow heads and axes. Molten bronze was then poured into the mould.

Regional Variations:

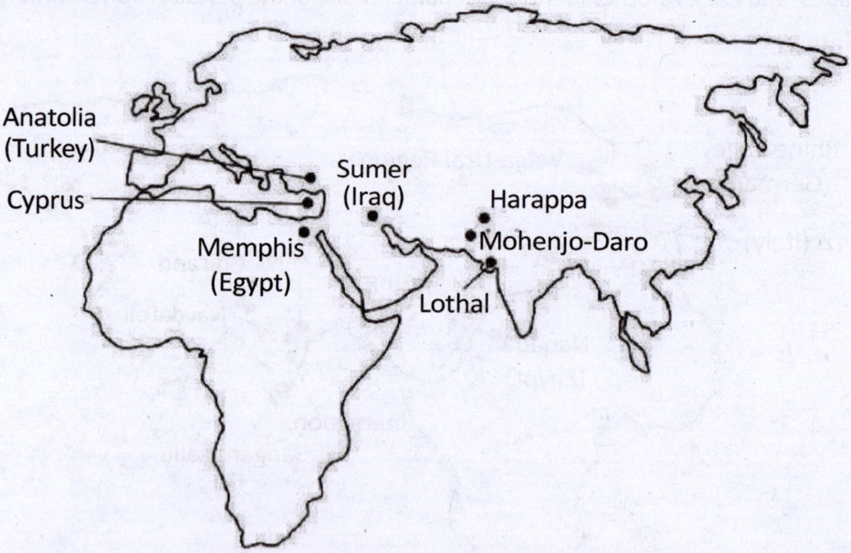

Important Bronze Age Sites of the World

1. **Near East:** The first region to enter the Bronze Age, the Near East, saw the emergence of the Sumerian, Babylonian, and Assyrian civilizations in Mesopotamia. These cultures practised intensive year-round agriculture and developed a writing system and created complex political organisations.
2. **Europe:** The European Bronze Age started with the Aegean culture in Greece and Cyprus. It subsequently spread from the Mediterranean to central and northern Europe.

3. **Africa:** Most African civilizations outside Egypt did not experience a distinct Bronze Age. The ancient Egyptian civilization thrived on the plains of the lower Nile Valley, achieving advanced levels of agricultural and architectural techniques.
4. **India:** The Indian Bronze Age is linked with the emergence of the Indus Valley civilization. The civilization had remarkable uniformity in town planning. Bronze casting was done using the lost wax technique and moulded to create tools, weapons, and sculptures. The civilization had international and maritime trade links, extending to Mesopotamia, Persia, and the Arabian Gulf.

Social Life:

- The Bronze Age marks the onset of urbanisation, supported by large agricultural surpluses. Planned towns were established to support the increasing populations. As surplus and population increased, so did the specialisation of skills and the need for long-distance trade. Writing was developed in Mesopotamia, Egypt, and the Indus Valley.
- The Bronze Age ended abruptly around 1200 B.C. Major civilizations, including Greece, Ancient Egypt and the Indus Valley fell. This is known as the Bronze Age Collapse. The Bronze Age gave way to the Iron Age, which thus began with a rural outlook again.

Q 11. Iron Age of World

Ans. The Iron Age refers to the period of human culture succeeding the Bronze Age, characterised by ferrous metallurgy as the dominant metalworking technology. It spans from around 1500–500 BCE.

Climate: The period is marked by a warm and dry climate favourable for settlements.

Material culture:

- Iron implements are found extensively, including axes, sickles, and arrowheads. These were harnessed to clear forests, work on farms, and settle permanent colonies.
- Besides them, bone objects and beads are also found. Bone objects include bangles, needles, combs, etc.

Regional Variations:

Important Iron Age Sites of the World

1. **Europe:** The European Iron Age was primarily rural and agricultural in nature. Tribes such as the Celts lived in small communities or clans. They lived in mud houses inside guarded hill forts. Weapons, implements, and utensils were elaborately designed. Few European Iron Age cultures include Hallstatt, Nordic, and Jastorf cultures.
2. **Africa:** In most of Africa, except Egypt, the Iron Age was not preceded by the Bronze Age. Iron and copper smelting appeared. African Iron Age cultures include the Akan, Chifumbaze, and Urewe.
3. **India:** The Iron Age of India is divided into Northern (Gangetic) and Southern Zones. The northern zone is characterised by the Painted Grey Ware Culture, while the southern zone is distinguished by Megalithic traditions.

Social Life:

➢ The Iron Age shows a village character with large-scale colonisation and multiple specialised craft activities. People lived in roundhouses made of mud and wood with thatched roofs. Rice, wheat, and barley were the chief crops cultivated. Sheep, cattle, and horses were the main domesticated animals.

➢ To conclude, it was the development of complex management and social order that gave rise to the Iron Age.

Case Study

- **The earliest evidence of humans decorating jewellery in Eurasia**

Mammoth tusks were first worked by Homo sapiens into pendants and mobile items like carved statuettes, occasionally embellished with geometric patterns. The oldest known punctate ivory pendant discovered in Eurasia has been reported in a new study that was conducted by scientists from the Max Planck Institute for Evolutionary Anthropology in Germany, the University of Bologna in Italy, Wroclaw University in Poland, the Polish Geological Institute-National Research Institute in Warsaw, Poland, and the Institute of Systematics and Evolution of Animals of the Polish Academy of Sciences. With a 41,500-year age, it is considered personal. This Stajnia Cave personal decoration, which dates to 41,500 years ago, can be found among the oldest Homo sapiens dispersals in Europe.

- **Scientists find evidence of humans making clothes 120,000 years ago.**

Tools and bones found in a cave in Morocco may be some of the oldest examples of recognisable human conduct. As early as 170,000 years ago, clothing may have first been worn by anatomically advanced people in Africa. The most recent research supports the hypothesis that early people may have possessed a wardrobe in some form. Hallett and colleagues describe their analysis of animal bones found during several decades' worth of excavations at Contrebandiers Cave on Morocco's Atlantic coast in a paper published in the journal iScience. Early human remains have been found inside the cave in the past.

According to Hallett, she started examining the animal bones in 2012 with the goal of reconstructing the early humans' diet and determining whether any dietary changes were connected to advancements in stone tool technology. However, 62 bones that had been used as tools were discovered by her and her colleagues in levels dated to between 120,000 and 90,000 years old. The team discovered broad, rounded end items made from bovid ribs known as spatulates; however, the purpose of many of the tools is still unknown. As they do not pierce the skin or pelt, "spatulate-shaped tools are ideal for scraping and thereby removing internal connective tissues from leathers and pelts during the hide or fur-working process," the researchers write. Bones from the sand fox, golden jackal, and wildcat revealed additional information thanks to cut marks connected to fur removal. A whale tooth that appears to have been used to flake stone was also discovered by the crew. Since whale remains have not been discovered in any Pleistocene contexts in north Africa, Hallett stated, "I wasn't expecting to find it." Hallett acknowledged that it was feasible for the bone tools to have been used to prepare leather for various purposes, but the evidence as a whole implies that early people created clothing, especially clothing containing fur.

2

Socio-Cultural

2.1

The Nature of Culture: The concept and Characteristics of culture and civilization; Ethnocentrism vis-a-vis cultural Relativism.

Q 1. Culture Vs Civilization

Ans. According to Bidney, culture is the product of agrofacts, sociofacts, manifacts, and artifacts. According to A.W. Green, when culture acquires written language, science, philosophy, proper division of labour, complex technology, and a political system, such a culture is called civilization.

Following MacIver, important points of difference between culture and civilization:

1. Civilization has precise standards of measurement, but culture does not. Products of civilization can be measured on the basis of efficiency, like an aeroplane flying faster than a bus or a power loom producing more than a hand loom. While there is no measuring rod for products of culture, some consider Bernard Shaw a better dramatist than Shakespeare.
2. Civilization is always advancing, but not culture. Like an aeroplane's improvement over a train, a train over a cart, and so on. While culture advances slowly and is often subject to regression, like our paintings, ours are not as good as those of Ajanta Caves.
3. Products of civilization can be improved by anyone, but that is not possible in the case of culture. Improvement cannot be brought about by the work of an artist—the painting Monalisa or the poems of John Keats.
4. Products of civilization can be borrowed easily, but not products of culture. Like in India, we have borrowed much from Western civilization but not much from Western culture.
5. Civilization is external and mechanical, while culture is internal and organic. Like we cannot touch belief or keep custom in museums—products of culture.
6. A product of civilization does not reflect the nature of a person, while a product of culture does. MacIver once said, "Civilization is what we have, and culture is what we are".

As per evolutionists, civilization is the apex stage of cultural development. Though there are differences, both are interdependent. These two are not only interdependent but also interactive. Example: Coins, tools, clothes, etc. are symbols of society's culture. Automobiles or radios' finishing is determined by our culture; similarly, our philosophy and novels are influenced by the printing press. Once, Ogburn said, "Both culture and civilization are two sides of the same coin".

Q 2. Cultural Relativism

Ans. The concept of cultural relativism was introduced in anthropology by Franz Boas in 1887. According to him, cultural standards are not absolute but relative to the culture in which they exist. Actually, this term was coined by Alain Locke in 1927.

Cultural relativism is a view of things in which no cultural standard is considered superior and no cultural standard is considered inferior, as this concept says that cultural standards are specific to human groups according to their own needs and circumstances, i.e., standards are culture-specific.

It also conveys that what is moral in one culture may be immoral in another, i.e., the concept of right and wrong is culture-specific. For example, Eskimo shun old kins when such kins are unable to gather for themselves. This act may seem immoral to modern industrial society, but it is moral among them due to the scarcity of resources.

Anthropologists stress this process as it helps to evaluate or understand a particular culture through the logic and meaning of that culture alone and without any prejudices.

Why cultural relativism so dear to anthropologists:

1. Promote tolerance by observing different cultures from their perspectives.
2. Understand human difference—diversity.
3. Preserve human culture and tribal languages.
4. Applied anthropology: development solution for tribal unrest makes LWE more efficient with this approach.

Elizabeth Zechenter criticised them for justifying traditional practises that violate human rights in the name of cultural uniqueness. She pointed to an example in Algeria in 1996, where two teenagers were raped and murdered because they violated a fundamental edict against attending school.

Kluckholn criticised the fact that there are certain universal human rights that need to be protected, otherwise witch hunting, head hunting (Naga tribe), genital female mutilation (Vohra community), the non-availability of LGBT+ rights, and not allowing abortion will be justified.

Paul Rosenblatt recognised the dilemma of relativism versus human rights but said that relativism can be a tool for change. Relativists' awareness of values and understanding of elites makes it easier to know what arguments would be persuasive.

Q 3. Ethnocentrism

Ans. The concept of ethnocentrism was given by W.G. Sumner in his book "Folkways". According to him, ethnocentrism is a view of things in which one's own group is considered at the centre of everything and other groups are scaled or rated with respect to one's own group. Such thinking leads to the feeling that one's own culture is best in all aspects and that others are, to varying degrees, inferior and barbaric.

History is full of examples where one group declared another as barbaric. While discussing the Revolt of 1857, British scholar Rees claimed that it was a war between civilization and barbarism. Similar is the case with Hitler's thinking regarding Jews.

Others, e.g., North Americans react negatively to child betrothal and arrange marriage but do not question their own practise of dating potential partners before selecting one. Hindus consider the custom of eating beef disgusting. It is common in the UK and US for the elderly to live alone or with non-family members.

This breeds hatred and enmity among groups, creating a barrier to inter-group unity.

Glorification of other cultures is the polar opposite. For example, young Americans may feel attracted to the Kung lifestyle. Kung share food and engage in leisure activities for a greater part of the day. But their life of moving in camps with all possessions, food, and children for 1500 miles a year may not attract.

Anthropologists highly criticise cultural relativism as this method undermines the logic and autonomy of cultures under observation.

Cultural Relativism	Ethnocentrism
Culturally sensitive. Without having pre-judgement	Cultural insensitive
Open minded	Closed minded, imposes one's superiority
Promote cooperate, respect for diversity	Obstruct cultural diffusion, cooperation between cultures
E.g. Khasas – Polyandry ↓ Hill slope – Agro production low ↓ To overcome economic cost of marriage, polyandry done. Such example as explained is unobjectionable practice from culturally relativist view point of others.	Such example as explained is derogatory practice from ethnocentric view point of others.

Similarity between Cultural Relativism (CR) and Ethnocentrism (E):

➢ Both extremists. Ethnocentrism points towards hihly intolerant behaviour and cultural relativism points towards highly tolerant behaviour.

➢ Both have negative connotations. Ethnocentrism makes racism to rise, and Cultural relativism makes traditional practises continue and violate human rights.

The middle ground is important from the point of view of an anthropologist, which is to understand their culture without needing to approve or disapprove of it.

2.2

The Nature of Society: Concept of Society; Society and Culture; Social Institution; Social groups; and Social Stratification.

Q 1. Concept of Society

Ans. Society is an association of individuals. It has a permanent population of people acting in accordance with its culture. It organises the activities of people, and the establishment of standardised behaviour is a social imperative.

Anthropologists defined society as a group of people who occupy particular territories and speak a common language not generally understood by neighbouring people. For example, Canada and the United States form a single society because they speak English and share common ideas. *MacIver and Page* said that it is a web of social relations.

From a functional point of view, society is defined as a complex of groups in reciprocal relationships interacting with one another, enabling humans to carry out their life activities and helping each other fulfil their wishes.

From a structural point of view, society is a total social heritage of folk ways, mores, institutions, habits, sentiments, and ideas.

Characters:

1. Society is a web of social relationships.
2. Society means likeness, and the sense of likeness was focused in early society on kinship.
3. Society also implies difference, as this sense of likeness doesn't include diversity or variation.
4. Interdependence is another essential element of society.
5. Cooperation is also essential to the functioning of society.

There are two major theories of relationship between man and society:

1. **Social contract theory (Hobbs, Locke):** It views society as an entity set up by man for certain ends. Individuals precede society. Individuals have reached mutual agreements and created society.
2. **Organic theory (Plato, Aristotle):** Individuals are one limb of society. They behave as cells of the body whose activity and life are meant for the sake of the whole. Individuals without society have no value, just as limbs without bodies have no value.

   Anthropologists, however, came to the conclusion that there is consensus about the necessity of society for the existence of humans, as humans are social animals.

Q 2. Society and Culture

Ans. MacIver and Page defined society as a web of social relationships that is changing. As per McGee, society is the largest indistinguishable unit of interacting individuals who share a pattern of social organisation that regulates their interaction.

E.B. Tylor, in his book "Primitive Culture" (1871), defined culture as that complex whole that includes such capabilities and habits acquired by man as a member of society.

Comparison: The first to study culture and society were the classical evolutionists, who did not differentiate between the two and used them interchangeably. With the gradual development of anthropology, in particular social anthropology in Britain and cultural anthropology in America, three main views emerged:

1. Anthropologists define culture as an all-encompassing phenomenon, encompassing social organisation, structure, and society as a whole. The leading proponent of this view was Malinowski.
2. Anthropologists who dichotomize between the two: This includes mostly British anthropologists like Radcliffe Brown, Evans-Pritchard, and S.F. Nadel. As per Radcliffe-Brown, society deals with interpersonal and intergroup relationships, while culture is the overall design of human behaviour. As per Nadel, culture is the way of life of the people, while society is an organised and interacting aggregate of individuals who follow a given way of life, that is, their culture.
3. Anthropologists who steer a middle course by accepting both as two aspects of social realities viewed from different dimensions. Culture mainly relates to action and behaviour, while society relates to relationships and grouping. The leading proponent of this view was Levi-Strauss. (Society appeared before culture.) For example, agrarian societies have cultural festivals and fairs (Baisakhi, Bihu).

   However, the debate continues about their origin, similarities, differences, and evolution.

Q 3. Institutions

Ans. Institution means the proper way of doing things. Every society has devised certain norms and procedures as guidelines to regulate the behaviour of its members. Such procedures that are adopted, established, and sanctioned by society are termed institutions. Institutions have actually organised procedures to do something. Herbert Spencer was the first scholar to use the term institutions sociologically in his book "First Principle", where he defined institutions as organs of society that fulfil various needs of their members.

Characteristics:

1. **Social in nature:** Institution is not individualistic because a single individual cannot create an institution, and the procedure followed by a single individual to do something cannot be an institution. An institution emerges through the collective efforts of a number of individuals and also when such procedures are adopted by society at large. Thus, institutions are social in nature.
2. **Universal in nature:** Institutions are universal in nature because they are found in all societies, whether simple or advanced, whereas their nature may vary from society to society.
3. **Permanent in nature:** Institutions are also permanent, but they experience change over time, whereas certain institutions are rigid in themselves. Religion and caste are two institutions which have experienced many gradual changes.
4. **Abstract in nature:** Institutions are abstract in nature, as we cannot keep marriage in a museum, we cannot bring norms into a laboratory for experimentation, and so on.
5. **Institutions have symbols:** Certain institutions also have symbols; for instance, marriage as an institution has symbols like a wedding ring, a particular type of ornament, etc. Similarly, swastik, crucifix, etc. are symbols of religion.
6. **Institutions are standardised norms:** Institutions are such norms that establish proper procedures to carry out life activities. They also manage and regulate various relationships among humans. For example, marriage, as an institution, regulates the mating relationship between husband and wife.
7. **Institutions are different from folkways:** Folkways like ways of greeting such as namaste and good morning are framed by informal agencies of society. Also, there is no set procedure to greet someone in this way, but there is another way of greeting, e.g., to salute someone, and this way of greeting is an institution because it is devised by certain organisations like the army, police, etc., and there is also a set procedure to salute someone. Therefore, Herbert Spencer also termed institutions "Super-Folkways".
8. **Institutions regulate the behaviour of individuals:** Various institutions like law, ethics, religion, etc. regulate the behaviour of individuals by checking for anti-social activities.

Types of Institutions: There are certain institutions that are essential for human beings, and such institutions are termed by Herbert Spencer as primary institutions. Some of the primary institutions are:

1. Social Institutions (Marriage, Family, Kinship, etc.)
2. Economic institutions (agriculture, trade, and any other righteous way of earning)
3. Education as an Institution
4. Political system
5. Religion
6. Expressive institution (music, literature).

Institutions later meet the different needs of human beings. It is due to institutions that various social structures are able to sustain themselves; therefore, *Herbert Spencer* calls institutions "Pillars of Society".

Q 4. Groups

Ans. A group is one in which two or more people exist in meaningful social interaction.

Different scholars using different criteria have given different classifications.

1. Cooley: Primary and Secondary
2. Sumner: In groups and out groups.

According to Cooley, the primary group is small in size and characterised by physical proximity, mutual aid, constant interaction, a sense of 'we' feeling, and companionship among its members. He further says that only social distance matters, not physical distance. E.g., family, neighbourhood families

Secondary groups were coined later by MacIver and Page, and Kinsley Davis; they lack the characteristics of primary groups and are formed for a specific purpose. E.g., trade unions, political parties.

Many functions that were previously performed by primary groups are now performed by secondary groups. Hayman proposed the concept of a reference group. It refers to a group with which one wants to be identified or is considered a role model. For example, for civil service aspirants, civil servants constitute a reference group.

Social groups are essential for:

1. Survival of human beings as they fulfil various needs.
2. Socialisation of human beings: For example, wolf children named Amola and Kamola discovered by a missionary from West Bengal lacked human activities like walking on forelimbs, drinking and eating like animals, and communicating.
3. Help heal many psychological and physical ills with the group therapy concept.

It is only through social groups that the large structures of society are built. Therefore, *Cooley* termed social groups "social bricks".

Q 5. Social Stratification

Ans. Social stratification means the division of society into various strata or hieratically arranged groups. Until about 10,000 years ago, all communities depended on food they hunted, gathered, or fished for. Egalitarianism has characterised most of human history.

Why it emerged:

1. The surplus theory of Sahlins and Lenski implies that surplus generated gets transmitted across generations.
2. Permanent investment in land or technology.
3. Population growth puts pressure on resources.
4. C.K. Mead study of Nigeria said that a reduction in the amount of available land led to the emergence of private property.

Social stratification is concerned with unequal access to three types: 1. Wealth and Economic Resources, 2. Power, 3. Prestige.

	Economic Resource	Power	Prestige	Example
Egalitarian	No	No	No	!Kung, Inuit, Australian, aborigines
Rank	No	No	Yes	Trobriand Islander, Italuk
Class/Caste	Yes	Yes	Yes	US, Canada, Greece, India

Case Study: African Americans die more often from diseases than European Americans. This is due to racial discrimination, crimes, poverty, more hypertension, and stress.

Characteristics:

1. Social stratification is characterised by the ranking of different social groups into different hierarchal statuses. For instance, Hindu society is stratified in such a way that Brahmins occupy the top position and so-called untouchables the lower one.
2. In social stratification, inequalities are institutionalised because, without inequality, there cannot be social stratification.
3. The basis of inequality may vary from time to time and from area to area. For instance, in India, inequalities are based on caste, whereas in many Western countries, inequalities are based on class.

4. Social stratification is a social phenomenon and has nothing to do with biological inequalities.
5. In social stratification, every hierarchal group is free to express a different lifestyle. Thus, every hierarchal group has its own culture.
6. Unequal access to economic resources, deprivation, exploitation, oppression of lower castes, lower classes, and commoners, slavery, hatred between different groups, prejudice, etc. become widespread phenomena.

Recent Trend: Gerhard Lenski suggested that the trend towards increasing inequality from 8,000 years ago was reversing. Inequality in industrial society is less than in pre-industrial society due to complex technology which led to delegation of power, increase in average wage of a worker and spreading of democratic ideology.

But even most industrialised societies have deep inequality, as seen by the HDI, Gini coefficient, and Oxfam report.

Future research by archaeologists, sociologists, historians, and anthropologists should provide a better understanding of the emergence of social stratification in society and how to reduce it.

2.3

Marriage: Definition and universality; Laws of marriage (endogamy, exogamy, hypergamy, hypogamy, incest taboo); Type of marriage (monogamy, polygamy, polyandry, group marriage). Functions of marriage; Marriage regulations (preferential, prescriptive and proscriptive); Marriage payments (bride wealth and dowry).

Q 1. Universal Definition of Marriage

Ans. Notes and Queries on Anthropology, a magazine published by the Royal Institute of Anthropology in its 6th edition (1951), put forth the first definition of marriage: "Marriage is union between a man and a woman such that children born to women are recognised as legitimate offspring of both the parents". But criticism arose over its structural and functional aspects. Structural: It does not cover cases of polygyny among Nagas, Mundas, and Gonds; polyandry among Todas and Nayars; polygynyandry among Khasas; women-women relations among Neurs of Sudan; or ghost marriages in British Columbia. Functional: legitimacy comes from law, and law does not exist in stateless societies. Added to it, among the Todas of Nilgiri hills, legitimacy is not decided by marriage but by purusutpini, a bow and arrow ceremony.

Westermarck, in his book "The History of Human Marriage", defined marriage as "a ritually recognised union between men and women such that spouses live together and couples have clearly recognised mutual sexual rights".

Criticism arose as rituals didn't take place among the Trobriand Islanders of Melanesia, the Kwoma of New Guinea, and the Winnebage of Africa. Also, in societies like the Tharu and Khasas of India and the Banaro of New Guinea, extramarital relations are allowed.

Kathleen Gough, after studying Nayars of Kerela, put forth the definition: "Marriage is a relationship established between a woman and one or more other persons, which provides that a child born to a woman under circumstances not prohibited by the rules of the relationship is accorded full birth status rights common to normal members of his society or social stratum".

This is the broadest definition given of marriage. But it excludes man-to-man relations among Azandes in Sudan. But social scientists do not recognise male-male marriage as it serves no purpose. Howver, Gough's definition is the most universal one.

The universality of marriage also exists due to functional aspects such as gender division of labour, prolonged infant dependency, sexual competition avoidance, postpartum feeding problems, etc.

Leach is of the opinion that although universal definition is not possible, marriage as an institution was, is, and will remain universal till the existence of human beings.

Case Study

- **The kingdom of women: the society where a man is never the boss**

The Mosuo, a long-extinct tribe of Tibetan Buddhists, live in a surprisingly modern way: women are treated as equal to men, if not superior; both can have as many or as few sexual partners as they like without being judged; extended families raise the young and take care of the elderly. The Mosuo are "condemned" as a culture of single moms from the viewpoint of an outsider, particularly one from China, where the bulk of tourists are from. Unmarried births of children are still infrequent in China. The Mosuo, however, have a different perspective; to them, marriage is an absurd idea, and a child is 'fatherless' simply because paternity isn't valued in their community. However, things are evolving.

Young residents of the Mosuo community have begun to believe that their traditional way of life is no longer relevant with the arrival of (mainly Chinese) visitors in the early 1990s, who brought paved roads, an airport, and jobs for the Mosuo people. Young Mosuo are following a different route than their parents and are enthusiastically embracing "western" marriage and family life. Few predict that Mosuo culture will be extinct in 30 years; nevertheless, after they experience the alternative, their traditional family structure can be viewed as a golden period. They were the first to set trends more than 2,000 years ago, yet they are unaware of how fortunate they are. It is a society in transition in a rapidly evolving nation. In China, the feminist movement is growing as more women fight against persistent discrimination; unmarried women over 27 are still referred to as "leftovers" in China. Can these naturally independent Mosuo men and women demonstrate to Chinese society a better way to value family? Yes, they should be proud to be single.

Q 2. Incest-taboo (Proscriptive Marriage)

Ans. Incest means the establishment of sexual activity and marriage between members of a nuclear family (mother-son, fatherdaughter, and brother-sister). Incest taboo means the avoidance of such sexual relationships. Exception: Ancient times:
Paroha (Egypt), Hawaiian Royal Family.

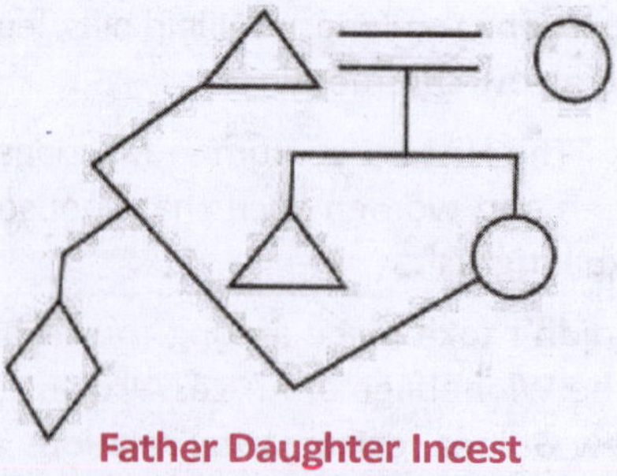

Father Daughter Incest

According to Malinowski's Family Disruption Theory, incest could lead to role confusion and conflict, a lack of authority, and ultimately chaos within the family. But this deals only with the sexual aspect and not the marriage aspect, as parents can supervise the sexual activities of children and later, in the mature stage, let them marry. Why is this not taking place?

According to Radcliffe Brown's Cooperation Theory and supported by L. Strauss, marriage outside the nuclear family enhances the kin group of individuals, and a large kin group comes in handy at times of urgencies and reduces conflict between mutually hostile groups. But this deals with only the marriage aspect and not the sexual aspect, as sexual activities could have been taking place even when married.

According to Sigmund Freud's psychoanalytic theory, incest taboo is a reaction against the unconscious, unacceptable desire of a son attracted to his mother or a daughter to her father. But such feelings cannot continue and are thereby renounced. But it does not explain brother-sister incest and is against the Westermarck hypothesis.

According to Westermarck's childhood familiarity theory, children have been familiar with each other since childhood and do not sexually attract each other. But then why do cousin marriages and marriages among neighbours take place?

According to David Aberlie's Inbreeding theory, knowledge of the harmful effects of inbreeding prompted people to prohibit incest as they could have recessive genetic disorders. But whether people at that point knew about it

Actually, no theory can explain incest-taboo existence in humans. In modern industrial societies, cases of incest, especially father-daughter incest, have been on the rise. According to NCRB (2015), 1.5% of women openly said they had committed incest. Trends are not healthy, and in modern societies, single-parent families are becoming common, an implication of the rebellion of males against incest-taboo and the reaction of females against this rebellion.

Q 3. Laws and Rules of marriage

Ans. **Needham has given classification regarding laws of marriage**

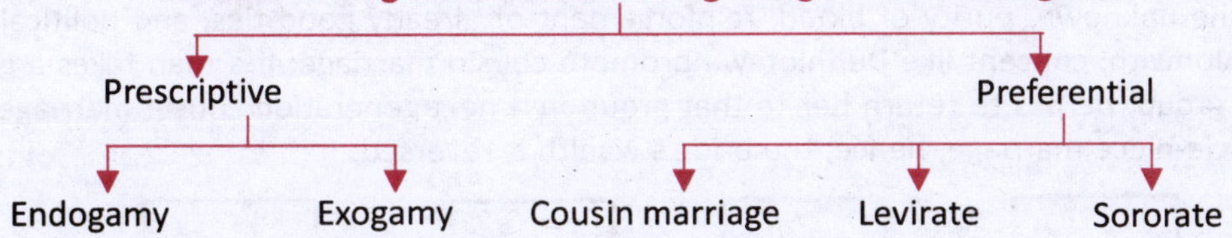

Prescriptive Marriages:

In endogamy, marriage between individuals belonging to the same group is prescribed. This group can be caste (Hindus), class (Europeans), moiety (Todas divided into Tartharol and Teivaliol), ethnic (African), deme (Bedouin), etc. The reasons behind endogamy are fear of strangers (E.B. Tylor), retention of cultural identity (Levi Strauss), purity of blood, property retention (Radcliffe Brown), and numerical strength (Robert Redfield). E.g., the Tutsi caste of Rwanda never married the hunting caste Twa.

While in exogamy, it is prescribed that a person seek a spouse from outside one's own group. In this, the group can be Gotra (Hindus), lineage, clan, village, spinda, or pravara. The reasons behind exogamy are reducing conflict between Mutually hostile groups (Levi Strauss), preventing conflicts within groups, thus promoting the stability of groups (Malinowski), and making children familiar, therefore not attracted to each other (Westermarck). E.g., Rani Khera village in India married 266 women from 200 villages.

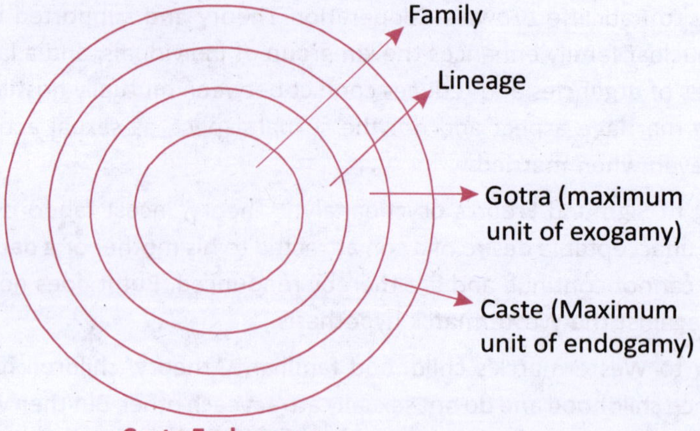

Caste Endogamy

Preferential Marriages: Marriages earlier preferred on large scale and even today by certain section of society.

Cousin marriages:

Patrilateral cross cousin	Matrilateral cross cousin	Patrilateral parallel cousin	Matrilateral parallel cousin
Ashanti of Ghana, Trobriand Islander, Kariera of Australia.	Lovedu of South Africa, Todas of Nilgiri.	Bedouins of Arab.	Kipsigis of Kenya, Bhils of Gujarat.

According to the Peoples of India Project, marriage with a mother's brother's daughter exists in 2368 communities, while marriage with a father's sister's daughter is reported in 2040 communities. Maternal uncle-niece marriages occur in 336 communities.

Cross Cousin Marriages are more common than parallel cousin marriages on a global scale, and patrilateral parallel cousin marriages are the rarest. The reasons behind cousin marriages are fear of the unknown, purity of blood, reinforcement of already good ties, and politically quite stable. Alonwith, concept like Dudhlotawa promote cousin marriage: If a man takes a girl from another group, he has to return her to that group in a next-generation cousin marriage or in a cross-uncle-niece marriage; hence, the bride's wealth is reversed.

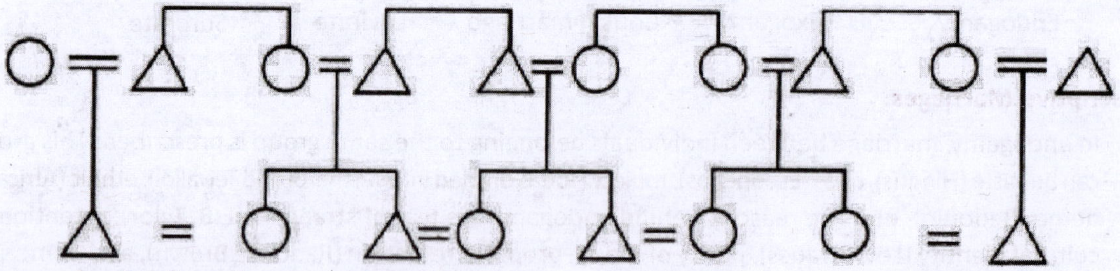

Types of Cousin Marriage

Levirate: It is such rule in which man marries wife of his deceased brother.

Examples:

Junior Levirate (younger brother marries)	Senior Levirate (elder brother marriage)
Chiricahua Apace, Kareras of Australia, Tlingit of Alaska	Chukchee of Siberia, Kuki of Manipur

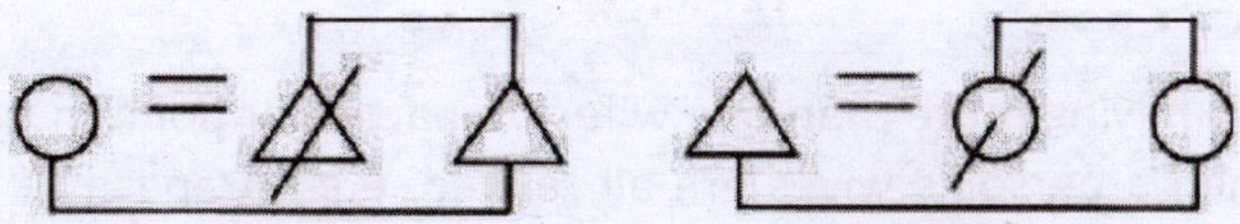

Levirate Sororate

Sororate: A girl marries the husband of her deceased or infertile sister.

- Sororal polygyny takes place among Chiracahua Apace of North America, Aruntas of Australia, Kipsigis of Kenya, etc.
- Chiricahua Apace practises both levirate and sororate. Jija-Sali and Devar-Bhabhi's joking relations in India are reflections of sorority and levitation, respectively.
- The reasons behind levirate and sororate are that they re-establish the bond of kinship that is threatened by the death of one spouse, they provide protection to the family, especially the children, and they help keep dowry or bride wealth within the family.

Hypergamy marriage means marrying or forming a sexual relationship with a person of superior sociological or educational background. Anuloma is a Sanskrit term that is used in the Manusmriti to describe a hypergamous union between a high-born man and a woman of a lower standing (by birth) relative to the respective man.

Hypogamy marriage means marrying someone of a lower social and economic class than your own. Pratiloma is a Sanskrit term used in the Manusmriti to describe a hypogamous union between a high-born woman and a man of a lower standing (by birth) relative to the respective woman.

All these rules can be enforced in societies where social bonds are strong and people's survival depends on larger kin groups, i.e., a closed system. In open societies, only nuclear families play an important role in the liv es of individuals; therefore, the only rule present in such societies is family exogamy; therefore, endogamy and preferential marriage characterise closed systems.

Q 4. Types of marriage

Ans. According to G.P. Murdock, "sexual relations can occur without economic cooperation, and there can be division of labour between men and women without sex. But marriage unites economic and sexual relations".

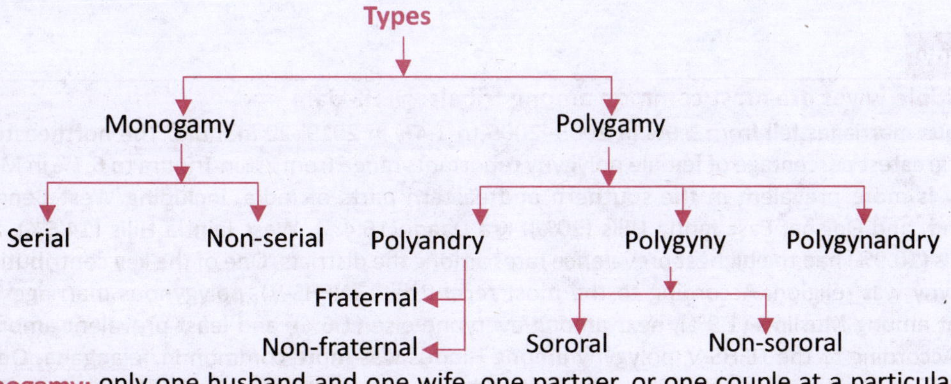

1. **Monogamy:** only one husband and one wife, one partner, or one couple at a particular point in time. Most marriages are practised throughout the world.
   a. **Serial:** After the death or divorce of one partner, the other partner has the right to marry again. e.g., mostly modern societies
   b. **Non-Serial:** After death or divorce, the other partner has no right to marry again. e.g., Andamanese, Nicobarese, and Irulas of India.

2. **Polygamy:**
   a. **Polygyny:** a man having more than one wife at a particular point in time.
      i. **Sororal:** when a person's wives are all related. e.g., Arapesh of New Guinea, Holia and Midara of Mysore.
      ii. **Non-Sororal:** If a person's wives are not related to each other, e.g., Siwai of the South Pacific, Gonds, Nagas, and Santhals of India,
   b. **Polyandry:** a female having more than one husband at a given point in time.
      i. **Fraternal:** Women's husbands are related to each other. e.g., Sinhalese of Sri Lanka, some Tibetans, Todas, and Khasas of India.
      ii. **Non-fraternal:** If women's husbands are not related to each other, e.g., Nayars of Kerala.
   c. **Polygynandry (group marriage):** D.N. Majumdar's study of Khasas in Uttarkhand revealed group marriages among multiple men and women.

Reasons for Marriage in general:

1. To satisfy biological needs and minimise sexual competition.
2. Take care of infants and their dependency
3. Division of work between male and female

Reasons for different types:

1. **Sex Ratio:** A balanced sex ratio leads to monogamy; more males lead to polyandry; more females lead to polygyny.
2. **Resources:** Rich males lead to polygyny; rich females lead to polyandry.
3. **Marriage Payment:** A high dowry leads to polygyny; a high bride price leads to polyandry.
4. **Type of Society:** Patriarchal society leads to polygyny, while matriarchal society leads to polyandry.
5. **Status:** A man's status rises with more wives, and vice versa. E.g., Nayars girls marry Namboodiri Brahmins as it is considered more prestige for girls who marry more men.
6. **Mortality rate:** Eskimos whose primary function is fishing have a higher rate of mortality as men go out fishing. It leads to polygyny.

Marriage types may vary from place to place, society to society, religion to religion, caste to caste, and class to class.

Case Study

- **Multiple wives are most common among tribals: NFHS data**

Polygynous marriages fell from 1.9% in 2005–2006 to 1.4% in 2019–20 in India. The northeastern states with the greatest percentage of female polygyny reportants range from 2% in Tripura to 6.1% in Meghalaya. Polygyny is more prevalent in the southern and eastern parts of India, including West Bengal, Bihar, Jharkhand, and Odisha. East Jantia Hills (20%), Kra Daadi (16.4%), West Jaintia Hills (14.5%), and West Khasi Hills (10.9%) had the highest prevalence rates among the districts. One of the key contributing causes of polygyny was religion. According to the most recent data (NFHS-V), polygynous marriage was most prevalent among Muslims (1.9%), next among everyone else (1.6%), and least prevalent among Hindus (1.3%). According to the NFHS-V, polygyny among Hindus was more common in Telangana, Odisha, and Tamil Nadu and less common in Jammu and Kashmir, Haryana, and Punjab. Similar to other states, Jammu and Kashmir, Maharashtra, and Haryana had lower rates of polygynous marriage among Muslims than Odisha, Assam, and West Bengal did. According to the NFHS-V, polygynous marriages were more common in Odisha and Telangana among communities other than Hindu and Muslim. The Scheduled Tribes were found to have the highest rate of polygynous marriage among the caste categories, and it decreased over time in all caste groups.

Q 5. Functions of Marriage

Ans. Marriage is a vital social institution that performs important functions without which society cannot survive and continue.

Different functions:

1. **Biological functions:**
   i. Legitimate mode of sexual gratification
   ii. Continuity of the human race and society through channelized reproduction
2. **Social functions**
   i. Providing the foundation for the establishment and propagation of families and thus society
   ii. Enculturation of the child—longest period of dependency in human infants
3. **Legal function**
   i. Legitimacy to offspring.
4. **Emotional functions**
   i. Platform for psychological and emotional cooperation between the couple and between the families of the bride and groom.
5. **Economic functions**
   i. Economic cooperation between males and females through the division of labour on the basis of sex
   ii. Economic control over a spouse's labour and property

   Thus, these functions of marriage make marriage a universal social institution.

Q 6. Marriage payments

Ans. Before, during and after marriage certain economic transactions take place between bride kin and groom kin, such transactions are marriage payments. Four types of marriage payments explained by Murdock are—

- Bride Wealth
- Dowry
- Suitor Service
- Gift Service

Groom Group	Bride Group	
	←	Bride move
	→	Bride wealth
	←	Dowry
	→	Suitor service
	↔	Gift exchange

1. **Bride Wealth:** In this, groom's kin pay to bride's kin, *i.e.*, bride and bride wealth move in opposite directions. It is a type of compensation for loss of labour, child bearing, and the social status of the bride's kin. In simple societies, brides' wealth is usually paid in kind.
   e.g., Kwakiutl: Blankets, Neurs: Cattle, Todas: Buffalo, Nagas: Paddy basket with daggers, etc.
   According to *Murdock*, it stabilises marriage. If marriage breaks down with no fault of the bride, bride wealth is not returned, and in remarriage, he will again have to pay bride wealth, so his parents pressurise him to behave properly. If she breaks due to the bride, her kin will have to pay back the bride's wealth, so they pressurise the girl to behave properly.
   It is one of the most common forms, prevalent in the largest number of simpler societies.

2. **Dowry:** It is paid in the form of cash, goods, or land. In this, both the bride and the objects move in the same direction.

   Reason: Compensation is paid to the girl at the time of marriage as she does not inherit anything; it is her share in her parental property. It's dakshina paid by the father of the girl at the time of marriage (kanyadaan).

   It is prevalent in many parts of Europe, particularly France and Italy, and also in parts of India. Dowry was paid and became part of social status and a demand-based aspect. Due to this, evils like deaths, suicides, domestic violence, etc. emerged, and India enacted the Dowry Prohibition Act, 1961, to counter them.

3. **Suitor Service:** This is a type of service transaction in which a prospective son-in-law has to provide services to prospective in-laws. In this, a man has to work for a prescribed time period for his in-laws before claiming their daughter as his bride.

   e.g., Eskimo of Alaska, Chukchee of Siberia, Bushman of the Kalahari desert, Santhal, and Gond of India.

4. **Gift Exchange**: In this system, there is an exchange of goods and services and also an exchange of women to escape the bride price and dowry.
   - Direct: Both families exchange their daughter as she attains sexual maternity.
   - Indirect: Exchange of women takes place based on prefixed agreements of tradition in some societies like Polynesia, Melanesia, etc.
   - Other types: Andamanese exchange food and items during marriage negotiations.

According to Murdock, one or another form of marriage payment is prevalent in all societies. It tells us the economic aspects of marriage and the social status of the couple. Recently, in India, many tribes that used to take bride prices are shifting to a dowry-based system.

Case Study

- **Nata Pratha: In some tribal areas of India, women's 'price' is fixed by village councils**

Indians talked about 'Bulli Bai' and 'Sulli Deals," apps that enabled fake online "auctions" of hundreds of Muslim women. But not many may know that some women are "auctioned" offline in India in the name of the centuriesold 'nata' tradition.

This custom is prevalent in some tribal belts of the country. According to the custom, a man has to pay money to have a modern-day live-in relationship with a woman of his choice after the woman's first husband breaks the marriage and passes on his wife to another man in return for money.

The "bride price" is set by the local panchayat and can be anything from a few thousand rupees to several hundred thousand, depending on the ability of the individual to pay. Men then use this money to get new spouses for themselves. Money is a terrible thing in nata, as the panchayat determines the minimum amount before a lady is permitted to do nata. Such behaviour needs to cease. To limit nata pratha, no laws exist in the nation. The police also don't record cases in accordance with this custom. The Rajasthani Bhel tribe is where this custom is most common. The educated population of the aforementioned tribe is losing interest in the Nata tradition.

Q 7. Ways of acquiring spouse in simple society

Ans. **Kathleen Gough:** "Union between women and one or more persons such that children born to women under any circumstances not prohibited by the rules of marriage will get all the rights as normal members of society and social status".

Different ways of acquiring a spouse in simpler societies:

➢ **Marriage by capture:** A man forcibly snatches a woman from her village and marries her. It symbolises valour and chivalry. For e.g., common in Naga

- **Marriage by purchase:** highly prevalent via paying bridewealth. For e.g., Tiv of Nigeria, Munda, or Oraon of India
- **Marriage by elopement:** marriage conducted in secret to overcome the high bride price. For example, the Karbis of Assam and the Tribes of Chotanagpur
- **Marriage by Service:** To avoid paying a high bride price, the groom provides service to the bride's father for 2–3 years at the bride's residence and marries her. For example, Birhor of India
- **Marriage by Intrusion:** A girl went to marry an unwilling man. She tries to convince the groom and his family, but is humiliated and tortured in return. But she persists for a long time. She is accepted as a daughter-in-law. For example, Birhor and Ho of Chotanagpur
- **Marriage by trial:** a heroic task to do, it symbolises bravery and valour. For example, Bhil of India.
- **Marriage by Consent:** Due to cultural contact with the outside world, all the arrangements are done through mutual consent.
- **Marriage on probation:** bride and groom are allowed to live together at the bride's house for some time. If they like each other and decide to marry, the elders arrange their marriage. For example, Kuki of Arunachal Pradesh
- **Premarital sex:** Premarital sex is one such practise. A nomadic tribe in the Bastar region of Chhattisgarh, Bison-Horn Maria, doesn't give primacy to premarital chastity. In fact, it values sexual comfort between lovers. British civil servant Wilfrid Grigson did a comprehensive ethnographic study of this tribe, The Maria Gonds of Bastar, which was published in 1938. In the book, he documented a marriage he once attended.
- **Live-in Relationship:** The Garasia tribe of Rajasthan and Gujarat not only allows youngsters to choose their partner but also live-in relationships. This practise is called DAPA. An annual festival, Siyawa-ka-Gaur Mela, is organised where young boys and girls come and choose the partners they wish to live with. For members of the Garasia tribe, marriage is not mandatory to live with a partner, but love.
- **Marriage and Love:** In the Garasia tribe, the bride and groom often choose each other at an annual fair, and the groom has to pay the bride's family what is termed the bride price. The Bhil, Bhilala, Pateliya, and Gond tribes of the Malwa region (central India) also celebrate an annual festival around Holi called Bhagoriya Haat (elopement fair), where boys and girls can meet and elope. Later, families negotiate the bride price, and then only decisions on marriages are made.

Marriage is a very peculiar social institution. Individual men and women alike face limitations on rights and freedom while obligations increase many fold.

2.4

Family : Definition and universality; Family, household and domestic groups; functions of family; Types of family (from the perspectives of structure, blood relation, marriage, residence and succession); Impact of urbanization, industrialization and feminist movements on family.

Q 1. Family: Definition and universality

Ans. William N. Stephans defined family as a group based on marriage, including recognition of the rights and duties of parenthood, common residence for husband, wife, and children, and reciprocal economic obligation between husband and wife.

Murdock, on the basis of his sample of 250 societies, concluded in his book "Social Structure" that either as the sole prevailing form or basic unit from which more complex familial forms are compounded exists as a distinct and strongly functional group in every society and that it universally performs four functions fundamental to human social life: sexual, economic, reproductive, and educational. Most social scientists have accepted Murdock's plea for the universality of family.

The first two so-called essential functions, sexual and reproductive, are not universal, as seen in the Nayars of Kerala, the Neur of Sudan (woman-woman), ghost marriage among British Columbians, and also among the Avunculocal community of East Africa.

Economic function is essential for the survival of society. This we realise from the Ik of Africa, who lost their source of production and society disintegrated. But it's not even universal:

1. In a large extended family, only the middle generation is the production unit.
2. In a welfare state, the state has taken over economic function through old age homes and free boarding and lodging for certain sections of society.
3. Among the Kibbutz of Israel, economic functions are never shared by families.

Thus, socialisation emerges as the sole function to explain universality. But it's not even universal:

1. In large extended families, socialisation is performed by the third generation and not by the parents.
2. In modern society, the rate of divorce is high, so single-parent households are becoming common, and children are socialised by either parent. Nancie Gonzalez's study on Livingstone found 45% of black families are female-headed and males are absent.
3. In traditional Chinese families, the whole family never contributed to socialisation.

The above discussion is based on an article by Kathleen Gough. According to her, family is not universal, neither structurally nor functionally. Only the mother-child unit is universal, and the only universal function is primary socialisation.

Along with the experiment of Kibbutizm by M. Spiro and Kolkhoj of the USSR, it was concluded that strong maternal bonds with children exist and are universal.

Q 2. Functions of family

Ans. A family is a social and economic unit consisting minimally of one or more parents and their children.

Essential functions:

1. **Sexual:** Sexual activities between husband and wife take place in a socially approved manner. It regulates sexual behaviour and sexual relations in society. Therefore, it helps to satisfy the biological needs of humans in an organised and channelled way.
2. **Reproductive:** Sexual activities between husband and wife lead to the birth of offspring who are essential for replenishing society. Families add legitimacy to the act of reproduction.
3. **Economic:** To fulfil basic needs and other materialistic needs, economic cooperation is necessary between husband and wife. It helps in the proper division of labour based on sex and age. Partners, siblings, and grandparents have crucial and different roles.
4. **Educational:** The family is responsible for converting biological beings into social beings. Many scholars termed family as first school because the first lesson regarding life is imparted to children by family members. Certain traditional occupations are also learned from family traditions.

Non-essential functions:

1. **Psychological:** Family provides psychological security by fulfilling basic needs regarding shelter, clothes, food, etc.

There is a strong feeling of belongingness among members, and they provide emotional support to each other in times of suffering. Malinowski termed family as an outlet for frustration.

2. **Status Ascribing:** In family, a child not only takes birth but also gets societal identification.
3. **Religious:** Families act as religious centres. Parents teach a number of religions virtues and practises to their offspring.
4. **Recreational:** Collective participation in festivals, visiting houses of relatives, organising family functions, family picnics, etc. are recreational functions of family.

According to *Linton,* we can trace the origin of family due to its functional aspect because there is no other institution that can perform functions as well as family.

Q 3. Types of family

Ans. According to *G.P. Murdock,* family is a social group characterised by common residence, economic cooperation, and reproduction. It includes adults of both sexes, at least two of whom have socially approved sexual relations, and one or more children, owned or adopted, of sexually cohabitating adults.

Murdock's classification put forward by him in his book "Social Structure" is considered the most appropriate classification of family on the basis of structure.

Family on basis of Structure:

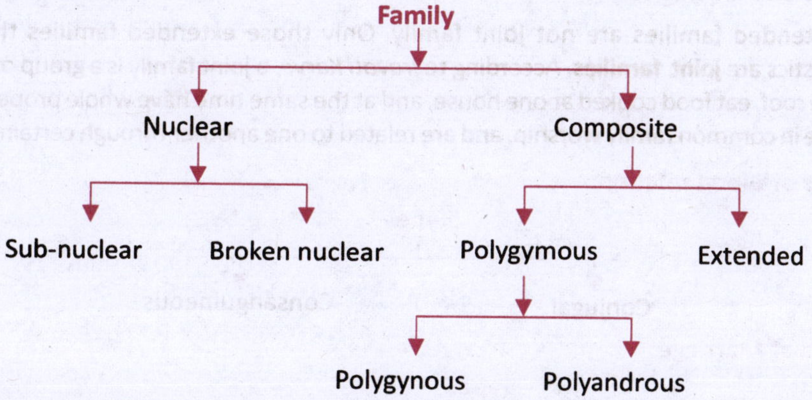

Murdock coined the term **nuclear family,** deriving from the word nucleus which is the basic unit of a cell and is composed of parents and unmarried children.

It is further divided into:

i. A sub-nuclear is one that is composed only of husband and wife without children.
ii. A broken nuclear family consists of only a single spouse with children, and the other spouse is either dead or divorced.
iii. Another type of isolated nuclear family advocated by *Talcott Parson* is the one where members of the nuclear family do not stay under one roof and are separated from one another due to certain reasons.

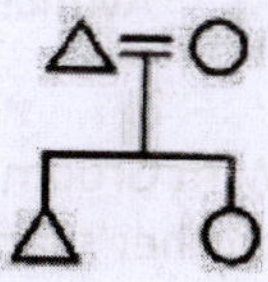
Nuclear Family

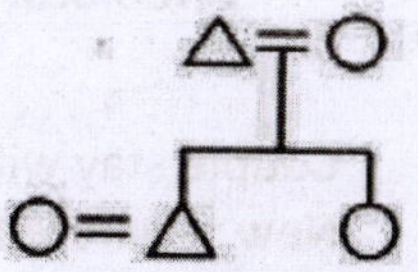
Extended Family

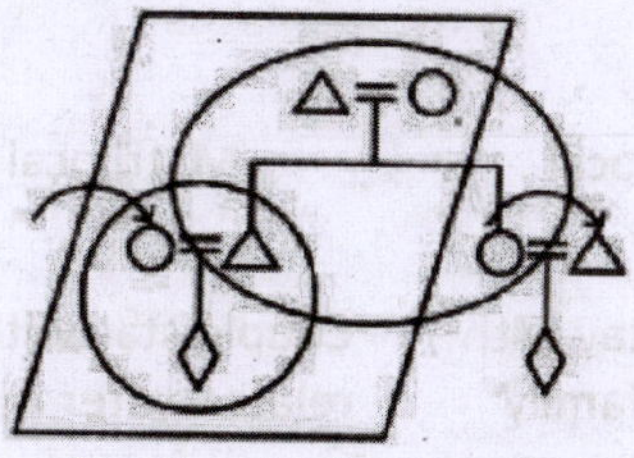
Patrilocal Joint Family

According to Murdock, a **composite family** is composed of two or more nuclear families. It is of two types: polygymous and extended families.

Polygymous family is one where a person resides with multiple spouses at one time. It is further divided into polygynous and polyandrous.

Polygynous: a man with multiple wives Eg.: Mundas, Nagas, Santhals

Polyandrous: a women with multiple husbands Eg.: Todas, Khasas, Nayars

Polygynous: Man with multiple wives

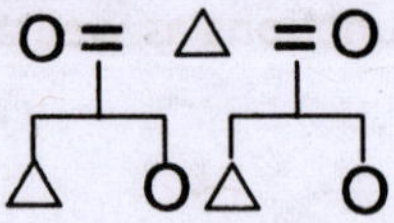

Polyandrous: Woman with multiple husbands

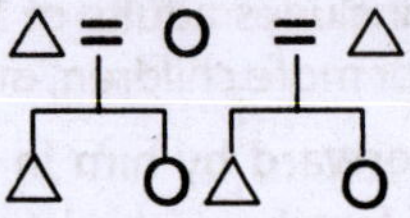

According to Murdock, when a nuclear family extends further with the marriage of offspring, it converts into an extended family.

All extended families are not joint family. Only those extended families that have certain characteristics are **joint families.** According to *Iravati Karve,* a joint family is a group of people who live under one roof, eat food cooked at one house, and at the same time have whole properties in common, participate in common family worship, and are related to one another through certain types of kindred.

Family on basis of Blood relation:

Types
- Conjugal
- Consanguineous

Family on basis of Marriage:

Types
- Monogamy
- Polygamy
  - Polyandry
  - Polygyny
  - Polygynandry

Family on basis of residence:

Types
- Patrilocal → Couple stay with groom's family after marriage
- Matrilocal → Couple stay with bride's relative after marriage
- Neolocal → Couple stay with New separate home after marriage
- Avunculocal → With Groom's mother's brother's family after marriage

Family on basis of Succession:

Types

Patrilineal family | Matrilineal family | Bilineal family

Variation in family forms:

1. **Recent increase in single-parent families due to**
   i. Males die of war, accidents, alcoholism, etc.
   ii. Higher male unemployment and fever among men than women of comparable age
   iii. High-paying employment of women (industrialised countries)
2. **Extended family is the most prevalent form due to:**
   i. Agricultural societies: prevent division of property
   ii. Mothers work outside; household care is provided by elders.
   iii. In the US, layoffs, high living costs, rising divorce rates, and an increase in the over-65 population led to a rise in extended families.
3. **Adoption:** This occurs when a family doesn't have enough kin to perform chores or inherit or when one family needs to relieve pressure on resources. As of 1990, there were more than 1 lakh legal adoptions in the US per year. Marriage types may vary from place to place, society to society, religion to religion, caste to caste, and class to class.

Q 4. Joint family

Ans. The most significant definition of joint family is given by *Iravati Karve*. According to *Karve*, joint family is a group of people who live under one roof, who eat together at one hearth, who share their whole property in common, participate in common family worship, and are related to each other through certain kinds of kindred.

Characters:

1. **Large in Size:** Joint families include more than one nuclear family and more generational depth, like grandparents, grandchildren, etc.
2. **Common roof:** Members live together under the same roof, although rooms may be separate.
3. **Common hearth:** Food for all members is collectively cooked in the same hearth.
4. **Joint property:** There is no fragmentation of property, and all lands are held on a joint basis.
5. **Common head** (Karta): It is the responsibility of the head to look after all members so that no member remains devoid of basic necessities.

Advantages:

- **Division of labour:** proper division of labour on the basis of sex and age. Due to this, no single member is overburdened with multiple tasks. It is useful, especially for agricultural activities.
- Protection and security fulfil the basic needs of all, especially handicapped people, the unemployed, orphans, etc.
- **Stability of family:** Elder members play a prominent role in solving problems both inside and outside the family.
- **Continuity of culture:** grandparents help in promoting values, moral tradition, and culture to the next generation, thereby socialising the children.
- **Economical:** goods purchased and consumed both in bulk are thus economical.

Disadvantages:

- Some members work very hard while others do nothing, thereby being termed as Home for Idlers.
- One-man authority kills individuality and leads to dependency.
- It becomes the centre of mutual bickering and quarrels, especially between mother-in-law and daughter-in-law.
- Members have favouritism while others feel like outsiders, thereby killing each other's personalities. According to Census-2011, at least in five metropolises, including Hyderabad, joint families are reviving themselves due to escalating land costs and a rise in crime rates. Similar factors are bound to lead to the revival of j oint families throughout India.

Q 5. Impact of Urbanization, Industrialization and feminist movement on family

Ans. Although family as an institution is stable, that does not mean that it is changeless, as many changes have occurred in the structure of family over time.

Factors for Stability in families:

1. **Man-woman bonding:** There is physical attraction between men and women, and this physical attraction leads to the formation of a bond in the form of marriage. After marriage, this physical attraction converts into social and cultural attraction. This social and cultural attraction further strengthens the bond of marriage. Physical attraction between men and women prevails in all ages, and after marriage, social and cultural attraction emerges between men and women in the whole history of mankind. Thus, the institution of family, due to this bonding and attraction, always remains stable. Malinowski, while working among Trobriand Islanders, observed that it is only due to social and cultural attraction that families remain stable among them. Therefore, according to him, man-woman bonding in the form of marriage and consequent social attraction are one of the basic reasons behind stability.
2. **Prolonged dependency of the human infant:** The human infant needs proper care and grooming until he attains physical and social maturity. Therefore, human infants remain dependent on their parents for a longer duration. This prolonged dependence of human infants upon their parents also leads to family stability. According to Levi Strauss, not only human infants remain dependent upon their parents, but even adults are dependent upon other members of their family. This dependency of humans upon family is also one of the major reasons for the stability of families.
3. **Importance of motherhood:** a human female gives birth to a single child at a time (multiple births are rare). In order to have more children, families must remain in existence. Radcliffe Brown is of the opinion that as legitimate offspring are born in the family, human groups, in order to acquire multiple offspring, do not let their families break down. He observed that the Andamanese allow their families to exist only because they get more and more children.
4. **Social and cultural factors:** After marriage, both husband and wife become socially and culturally bound to each other. Ralph Linton is of the opinion that there are many social and cultural barriers due to which families remain intact, and these social and cultural barriers also create cohesiveness between husband and wife. As a result, the family remains stable.
5. **Economic factor:** There are many economic factors like inheritance of property and titles due to which family has always remained stable throughout human history. Without family, proper channelization of these economic factors is not possible, and Raymond Firth is of the opinion that economic factors are among the prime factors that led to the stability of family.

Urbanisation and industrialization impact:

With the advent of industrialization, the agrarian economy was superseded by an industrial economy, and village-level traditional cottage industries came to an end. Therefore, there was no alternative but to migrate to an industrial centre. So, it was not feasible to bring all members of a joint family to such a centre. Added to that, according to Mandelbaum, a joint family is not a mobile unit and is not adaptive to posting and transfer. It is adaptive to the agrarian economy and not job culture. Also, earning members do not want to share the wages they earn with others. Also, many members prefer setting up a nuclear family to prevent clashes between achieved and ascribed status (Talcott Parsons). Industrialization leads to urbanisation. New townships emerged with modern health, education, and entertainment facilities. According to Aileen D. Ross, to reap the benefits of development, people are pulled towards urban centres.

These pull factors increased nuclear families at a mushrooming rate.

J.P. Singh, in "Eastern Anthropologist", pointed out subsequent implications:

1. Change in Habitation: different family members are living in different places.
2. Change in concept of property: individual property is more common with women as they have the right to property.
3. Change in parental attitude: Parents are unable to take care of their children and older people due to their busy lifestyles.
4. Change in profession: Now individuals are engaged in different professions and concerned with individual progress.
5. Change in women's status: women working outside the home and status arose. Even so, health conditions improved.
6. Increase in divorce rate and single-member households

J.P. Singh, after analysing NFHS-I and II, said that joint families do not make up more than 5% of all families in urban areas, and extended families do not make up more than 1/5 th of all. However, according to the 2011 Census, at least in five metropolises, including Hyderabad, joint families are reviving themselves due to escalating land costs and a rise in crime rates. Similar factors are bound to lead to the revival of the joint family throughout India (Janaki Abraham).

Yogendra Singh says that despite all the changes, the traditional worldview of the joint family still prevails in Indian society.

Feminist movement impact:

The ideology of feminism refers to reform movements that are related to the welfare and empowerment of women. It deals with the emancipation and liberation of women and gives them equal rights.

In the 21st century, feminism has become an important rights-based approach for the upliftment of women. This movement has had a profound impact on the family system, not only in India but all over the world. A precursor to it can be linked to industrialization and urbanisation.

Impact on the nuclear family:

1. Empowerment of women, due to rights like education, equality, liberty, etc., both at home and outside, is breaking traditional barriers. It is helping women get better education, nutrition, lifestyles, etc. It has become a cause of declining infant mortality rates, maternal mortality rates, etc.
2. It is helping to properly plan the expenses of the family and increase its savings, thereby providing better security and protection for children and couples in old age.
3. Katherine R. Allen: Male members accept changing gender roles and involve themselves in the socialisation of children.

4. Even in day-to-day activities, women have equal say to their counterparts.
5. Arlie Hochschild: Children are viewed as restrictions by women on their freedom; therefore, the rise of sub-nuclear families, live-in relationships, etc.

Though there are some disturbing trends as well, like an increase in divorce rates, an increase in single parents, an increase in live-in relationships, and the responsibility of looking after children shifting to crèches, daycare centres, etc. Impact on joint families:

1. The feminist movement has brought about a change in the size of the joint family, and women have migrated to towns and cities in search of education, employment, and better living conditions, resulting in a change in the traditional mindset of men towards women and subsequent empowerment of women.
2. Women have more say in the decision to form a joint family and the right to hold property, which was earlier in the hands of men.
3. Veena Das says that women in India should develop a balance between job demand and family demand.
4. Some negative aspects include discontinuity in cultural patterns that are facing the threat of extinction and conflicts due to husbands' non-cooperation.

Impact depends on the degree of feminism. If it is liberal, it has no or less effect on families. If radical, it will affect the family substantially.

Family is a function of culture. Since culture is dynamic, family is also dynamic and continuously changing.

2.5

Kinship : Consanguinity and Affinity; Principles and types of descent (Unilineal, Double, Bilateral Ambilineal); Forms of descent groups (lineage, clan, phratry, moiety and kindred); Kinship terminology (descriptive and classificatory); Descent, Filiation and Complimentary Filiation; Decent and Alliance.

Q 1. Kinship: Consanguinity and affinity

Ans. As per Abercrombie, social relationships derived from blood ties and marriages are collectively referred to as kinship.

Kinship is the study of socially recognised true or fictive biological ties. Kinship relations that are established on the basis of blood are consanguineal kinship relations and all those kin related through blood are consanguines. For example, father and son are consanguines. All those kinship relations established through marriage are affinal kinship relations and all those kins related through marriage are affines. For example, husband and wife are affines.

Actually, the concept of kinship was introduced into anthropology by Henry Morgan because according to him 'everyone has kin and is kin'. Thus, he opined that if the concept of kinship is removed from anthropology, there is nothing left to analyse. C. Levi Strauss mentions that it is only through kin that an individual is converted from a biological being to a social being. Therefore, we can say that kinship is a socio-cultural recognition of physical relations.

Types of Kins:

1. **Primary:** directly related
2. **Secondary:** related through the ego's primary kin
3. **Tertiary:** Related through the ego's secondary kin

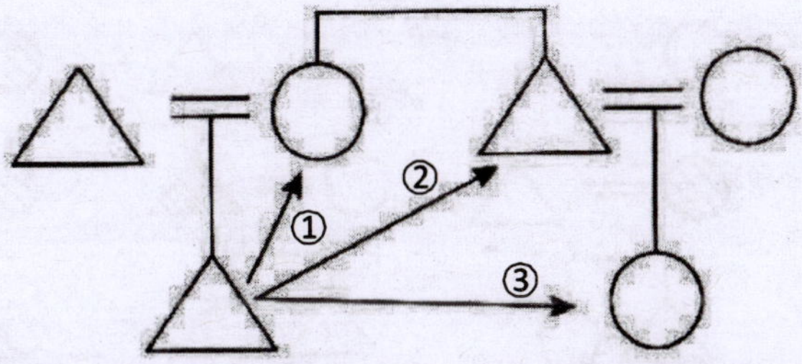

Affinal Kin ——— Consanguineal Kin

① Primary Kin ② Secondary Kin ③ Tertiary Kin

Types and Levels of Kin

Importance of kinship in anthropology:

1. **Social relations:** The laws governing marriage in a society are significantly influenced by kinship.
    - Simple communities with strong blood links frequently practise endogamy and favour laws like cousin marriages and the levirate and sororate. This is a result of their focus on reinforcing already solid kinship ties within the social group.
    - Kinship bonds outside of the nuclear family are weak in contemporary complex societies marked by individualism.
    - Only the taboos against incest and family exogamy are observed in marriage.
2. **Economic relations:** Even at the expense of profit and resource maximisation, social order must be maintained in simple societies accordi ng to rationality. As a result, kinship in this context is crucial for economic activities.
    - The Kula gift exchange among Trobriand Islanders, researched by Malinowski, serves as the best illustration. Kula is, strictly speaking, an uneconomic and irrational endeavour that involves risky, lengthy journeys to swap fami ly members' economic trinkets.
    - However, Malinowski asserts that it strengthens kinship ties and that without it, Trobriand society would fall apart.
3. **Political relations:** The foundation of law and social punishment in basic cultures is kinship. Justice's main objective isn't to punish the wicked but rather to uphold peace in order to keep family ties strong. For instance, Evans-Pritchard noted that in Nuer, conflicts between lineages are settled through mediation by the leopard skin chief, a revered elder from a neutral lineage.
4. **Religious relations:** Totemism is a good example of this. According to Durkheim, the totem is connected to the individuals by kinshiplike ties based on descent. The clan's forebears are also represented by the totem. The totem controls all interactions, both within the clan and with other clans.

Thus, kinship has been a major area of focus in socio-cultural anthropology, as evident from the work on kinship terminology, descent, and alliance theories.

Q 2. Principles and types of descent

Ans. Descent refers to inheritance and succession. The rules of inheritance direct us regarding where we can receive, with whom we can share, and to whom we can transfer. These rules are important for the proper distribution of rights and obligations within the family.

1. **Unilineal Descent:** The most common rule followed by more than 90% of all human societies, all other rules is rarely followed. According to this rule, descent is traced from either side of parentage; if male, it is patrilineal, and if female, it is matrilineal.

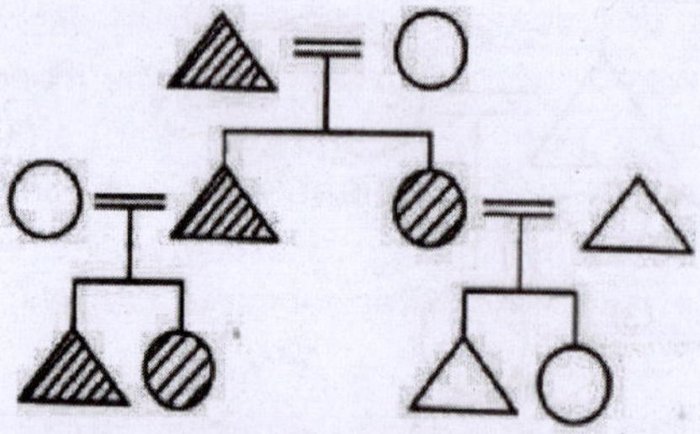

Patrilineal Descent

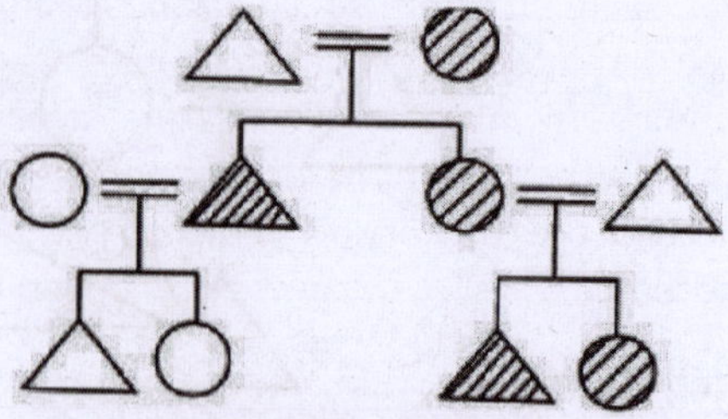

Matrilineal Descent

In patrilineal descent, descent is traced from father to son, and the strongest bond develops between father and son because males follow the rule of residential solidarity, i.e., men live at the same place throughout life. Women are considered outsiders as they have to be brought in as wives, and as daughters, they have to be married out. Daughters too share the fruits of descent, but they cannot pass on their rights to the next generation, thereby limiting the transfer of rights to males.

Examples: Tikopia of the West Pacific; Mossi of West Africa; Kupauku Papuan of New Guiana.

Conversely, in matrilineal societies, descent is traced by the daughter from her mother, who must have done it from her mother. In this sense, men do not have authority, but in practise, they do. The brother-sister combination is the strongest kinship bond. Brother is 'pater' for his sister's sons and daughter.

Example: Trobriand Islanders, Ashanti of Ghana, Chuuk of the Pacific

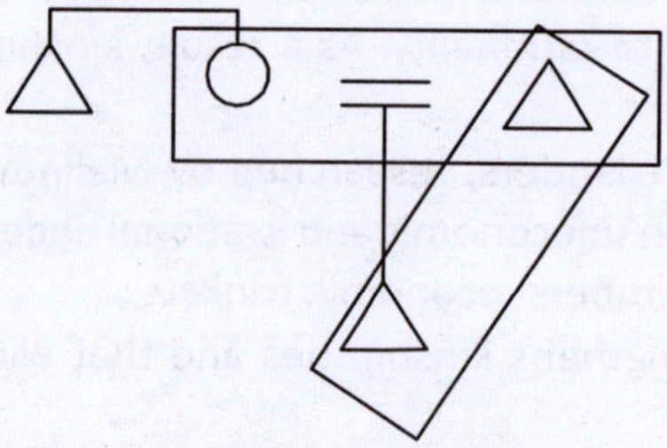

Patrilateral bonds

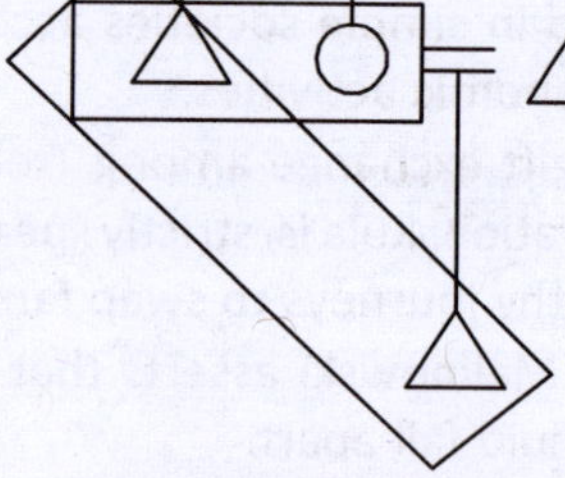

Matrilateral bond

However, it does not mean that the lineal or lateral relations of other lines are ignored. For *example*, in patrilineal society, matrilateral kin are assigned important places during rites de passage. Similarly, for patrilaterals in matrilateral societies, this is called complementary filiation.

2. **Double Descent:** Descent traced through both sides of parentage but inheriting non-overlapping elements of culture from each line of parentage.

   Example: Yako of Nigeria; Venda of Africa: rituals in matriline but resources in patriline; and Heroro: material property in matriline but religious function in patriline.

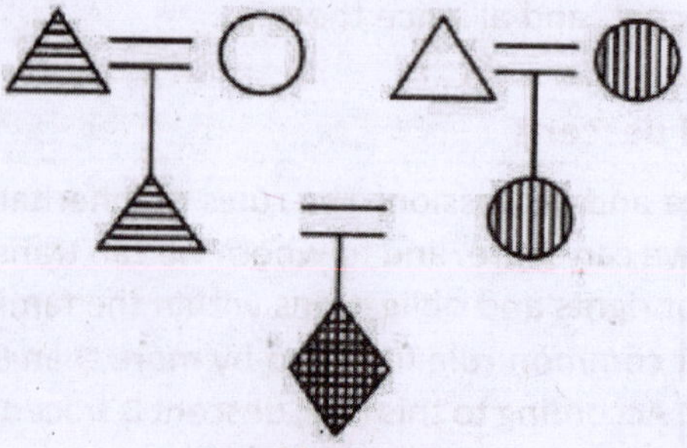

Double Descent

3. **Bilateral Descent**: Some social scientists confuse double descent with bilateral descent. Bilaterals comprise patrilaterals as well as matrilaterals, and we do not trace descent from them because descent is traced linearly, not laterally. Bilateral descent is the temporary arrangement of affiliating oneself with kin on either side of parentage almost equally and for a specific purpose. Realising that bilateral descent is not the true form of descent, in contemporary anthropological discourse, the term is replaced by "kindred". **Example: Current army based modern societies, Chipewyan of Canada.**

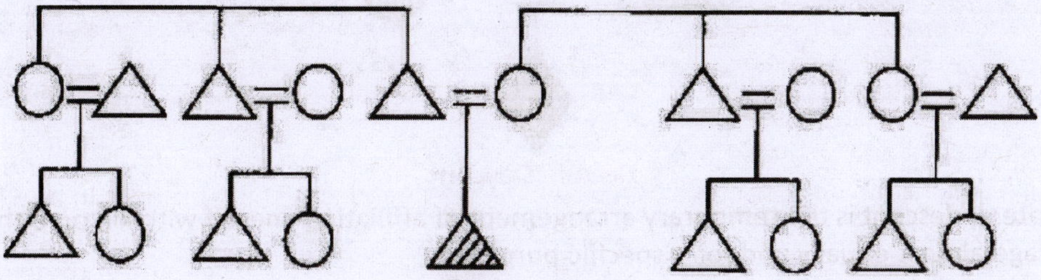

Ego

Bilateral Descent

4. **Ambilineal Descent:** According to this, it is left to the individual to trace descent from either of their parents. It is only one in which both males and females can be found in the same line of descent. **Example:** Kwakiutl of British Columbia, Samoa of Polynesia.

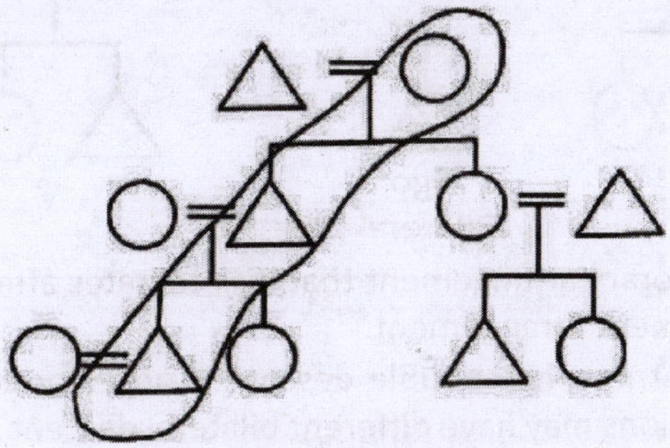

Ambilineal Descent

Factors responsible:

1. Contribution to the family economy: In a society where the nature of production activity of both men and women is the same, whoever contributes more decides the rules of descent. If men more, patrilineal descent, and if females more, matrilineal descent.
2. Prestige of profession: Among hunters and gatherers, though women contribute 2/3rd by gathering, men perform hunting, which is a dangerous profession, thereby leading to patrilineal descent.
3. Nature of division of labour: If specialisation on the basis of sex, it leads to double descent,
4. Demographic factor: a sharp decline in population without affecting resources leads to ambilineal descent.
5. A bilateral system develops in a complex political system without warfare or commercial market exchange.

The above factors represent the social-cultural needs of society; therefore, descent is a cultural rule.

Q 3. Double Vs Bilateral Descent

Ans. Descent refers to the rules of inheritance and succession. It implies from where we can receive, to whom we can share, and to whom we can transfer. Following are major areas of difference between them:

1. Double descent is that in which descent is traced from both sides of parentage while inheriting non-overlapping elements of culture from each side.

Example: Yako of Nigeria; Venda of Africa: rituals in matriline but resources in patriline; and Heroro: material property in matriline but religious function in patriline.

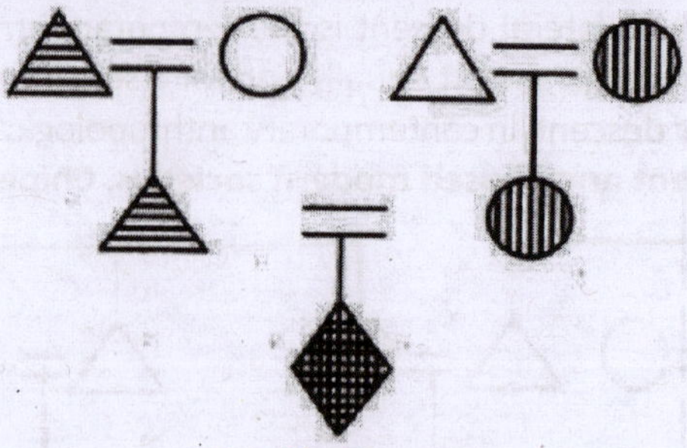

Double Descent

Bilateral descent is the temporary arrangement of affiliating oneself with kin on either side of parentage almost equally and for a specific purpose.

Example: Modern society, Chipewyan of Siberia.

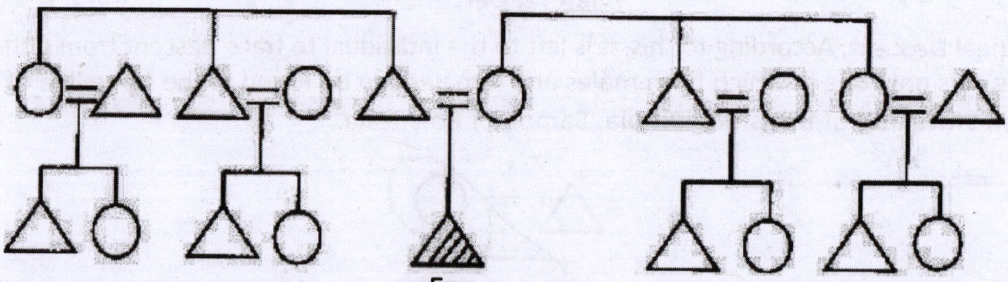

Bilateral Descent

2. Bilateral descent is a temporary arrangement that disintegrates after the death of the ego, while double descent is a permanent arrangement.
3. Bilateral descent is egocentric, while double descent is ancestor-centric. In some families, two brothers on different occasions may have different bilateral descent groups, while double descent remains the same among brothers of the same family.
4. Since descent is traced lineally and not laterally, bilateral descent is not true kind and is in contemporary discourse replaced by kindred while double descent is true form.
5. Bilateral descent serves no purpose of inheritance or succession, unlike double descent.

In some recent literature, at times bilateral descent is equated with double descent, but it is not clear why two should be the same.

Q 4. Rules of Residence

Ans. Kinship is the study of socially recognised true or fictive biological ties. The rules of residence are the rules of postmarital residence. These rules are important as they determine the post-marital life.

Following are classifications of rules of residence:

1. **Patrilocal residence:** According to this rule, couples stay with the groom's kin. In many patrilocal societies, the groom's father's family does not live alone and is a larger kin group, thereby forcing the couple to live as a separate unit within the group. If a patrilocal society follows rules of descent different from patrilineal, it is then called vivilocal. Example: Tiv of Nigeria, Tikopia of the West Pacific, Mossi of West Africa.

2. **Matrilocal residence:** This is a type of residence in which a couple stays with the bride's kin. The opposite of vivilocal is uxorilocal. Example: Trobriand Islander.
   In matrilocal residence, when a couple has to stay with the bride's mother's brother, it is called avunculocal residence. Example: Trobriand Islander.

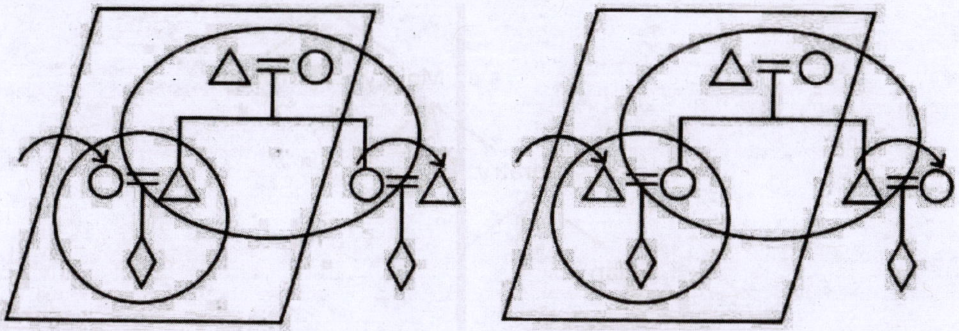

Patrilocal Residence **Matrilocal Residence**

3. **Matri-patrilocal:** An arrangement whereby newlyweds initially stay with the bride's relative but ultimately settle down near the groom's residence is called matri-patrilocal residence. Example: Dobuans of Melanesia
4. **Bi-local residence:** If a couple keeps on shifting from one kind of relative to another indefinitely. Example: Shoshone of USA
5. **Ambilocal residence:** the bi-local rule cannot be followed for long, particularly after the birth of offspring, and then the couple decides to live at either residence permanently as society has not given any direction; the rule is ambilocal. Example: Kwakiutl of British Columbia
6. **Neolocal:** A couple establishes a new household away from all types of relatives. It is the feather of modern, advanced societies.

Factors responsible for residence:

1. **Economic**
   a. **Contribution to family economy:** If in society the nature of production activity of both men and women is the same, whoever contributes more decides the residence. If males contribute more, then patrilocal, and if females contribute more, then matrilocal.
   b. **Prestige of profession:** Among hunters and gatherers, men are hunters and women are gatherers, though women contribute 2/3 of family production, yet all hunters and gatherers are patrilocal because hunting, by men, is a dangerous profession.
   c. **Type of marriage payment:** In societies practising suitor service or where bride wealth is paid in installments, matri-patrilocal residence exists.
   d. **Type of economy:** cash economy with surpluses that promote neolocal residence. Avoid interpersonal tension and the demands of kin.
2. **Political:** If, in society, men stay out for a considerable period, for example, Nayars in the Malabar Army and Trobrianders for Kula, the important function of maintaining social order falls to women, and society may become matrilocal.
3. **Warfare:** Internal warfare leads to patrilocal residence, while external warfare leads to matrilocal residence.
4. **Demographic:** If, due to some natural calamity, there is a sudden decline in population without affecting resources, society may first become bi-local and subsequently ambilocal. This occurred among the Kwakiutl, Psimshia, and Tlingit peoples of British Columbia. As above, factors represent local cultural needs of society. Therefore, residence is a cultural rule.

Q 5. Forms of descent groups

Ans. Unilineal Descent Groups (UDGs) are features of agriculturalist and other societies where state organisation lacks but maintenance of social order is important for the survival of society.

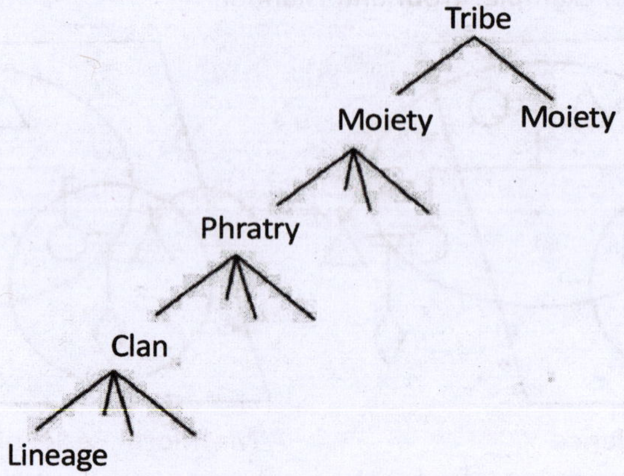

Unilineal Descent Groups

Lineage and Clan:

1. Lineage is the smallest unilineal descent group, which comprises ancestors not remote, generally 5th or 6th generation, while clan is a larger group and ancestors are remote.
2. Lineage is such an UDG in which members can trace their descent from a common known ancestor and all genealogical links between ego and ancestor are known, while clan is one in which members claim to have a common ancestor but cannot trace it and genealogical links cannot be demonstrated.
3. Excluding some Muslim communities, lineage is exogamous, while clans may be exogamous or endogamous; totemic clans are always exogamous.
4. Lineage may also be a residential (joint family) unit, while a clan lacks a common residential unit.
5. There are stronger bonds among members of a lineage than those of a clan.
6. In an Indian context, lineage may be equated with Vamsa and clan with Gotra.

Phratry:

1. The term Phratry is derived from the Greek word "Phrater," which means brother. It is a kin group of brotherhood in which several clans are combined.
2. They are found in very few societies around the world. They were reported from Hopi, Navajo, and Red Indians from the US, Muria Gond of MP, Raj Gond of AP, Ao Nagas of Nagaland, etc.
3. Based on descent, they are of two types: matriphratry and patriphratry.
4. They may or may not be exogamous; e.g., Hopi phratries are exogamous, while Crow, Red Indian phratries are endogamous.
5. They may constitute important political units; e.g., among the Aztecs of Mexico, phratries are important political units in the structure of empire.

Moieties:

1. When a whole society is divided into two unilineal descent groups, we call each group a moiety. Societies with a moiety system have a relatively smaller population than societies with clans and phratry.
2. Todas have two moieties: tartharol and teivaliol (Endogamous marriage).
3. Tlingit have two moieties: wolf and raven (Exogamous marriage).

Functions of UDG:

1. Regulating marriage: Whom to marry or not.
2. Economic: support in crisis; bride price; lawsuit

3. **Political:** The headman settles disputes of lineage and also plays a role in warfare, *e.g.,* Tiv of Nigeria.
4. **Religions:** Clans and lineages have their own religions, beliefs, and practises; e.g., the Tallensi of West Africa pacifies their ancestors.

Many societies have two or more types in combination. Some societies have lineage and clans; some have clan and phratry; and some have clan and moiety but not phratry and lineage. They help to regulate the social behaviour of individuals and common religious obligations.

Q 6. Kinship terminology

Ans. Kinship is a linguistic term used to refer to kin based on blood or alliance.

Henry Morgan, in his book "System of Consanguinity and Affinity of the Human Family", was the first to identify differences in the use of kin terms in various societies. He gave a dichotomy of classificatory and descriptive kin terms. Descriptive are those that pinpoint the relationship, e.g., father, mother. While the terms used to denote groups of relatives are classificatory (e.g., cousins, uncles).

In modern European and English societies, classificatory terms are used beyond the nuclear family; within the family, each relation is separately identified and designated. E.g. , mother and father. Many simpler societies, too, tend to be classified with certain differences vis-à-vis modern European societies. Here, descriptive terms may or may not be the rule for primary kin; many relations beyond the nuclear family may be designated by a term that, in modern European societies, is in the exclusive domain of the nuclear family. E.g., Dadi for the elderly women of the village. No society in the world uses classificatory or descriptive terms in an absolute sense.

Realising the limitation, much work has been done, and it is now universally accepted that one or more of the following factors determine the choice of kin terms between various relations (Kroeber and Lowie).

Factors:

1. Generation: Father/Son
2. Sex of relative: father or mother
3. Speaker's sex: son or daughter
4. Relative age: elder or younger brother
5. Bifurcation: Nani/Nana
6. Polarity
7. Affinity: Father/Father-in-law
8. Collaterality: Father/Uncle
9. Decendence: Alive/Dead

Today, anthropologists generally agree that kinship terminologies can be grouped into six types (Murdock):

(a) Eskimo – Extreme classificatory

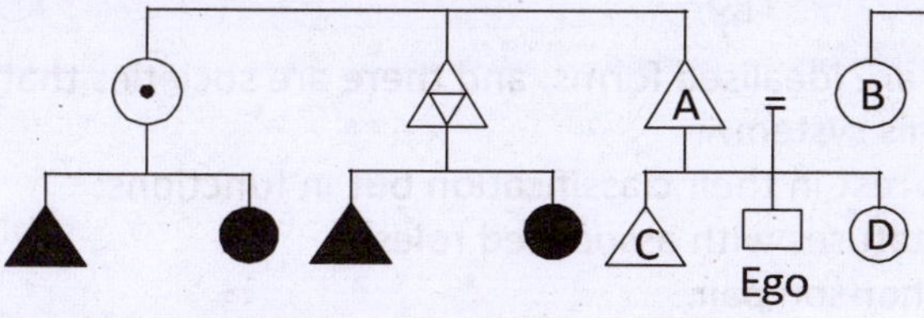

(b) Hawaiian – Feature of ambilineal societies

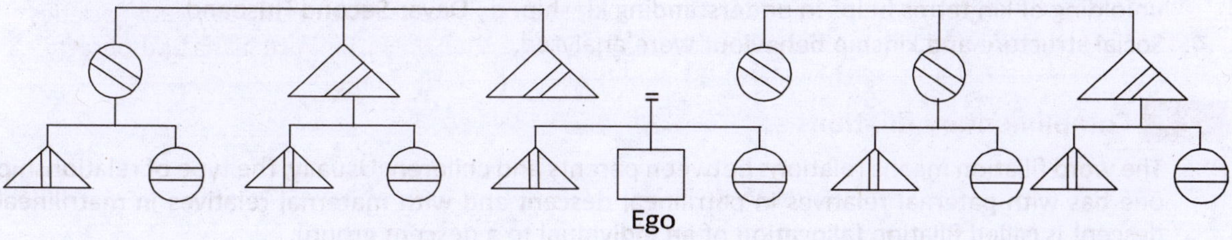

(c) Iroquois – Parallel cousin marriage prohibited

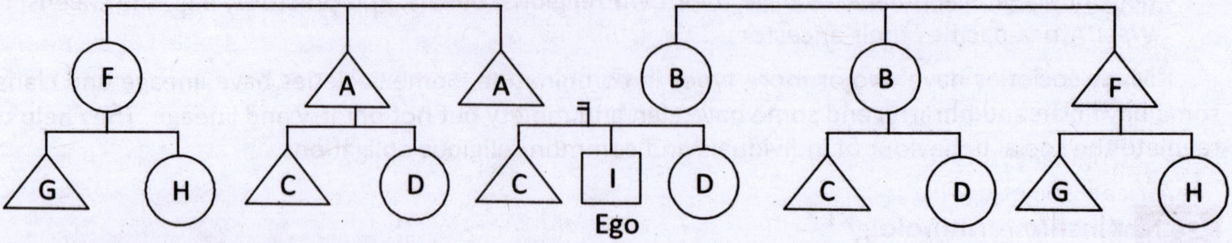

(d) Omaha – Feature of patrilineal societies

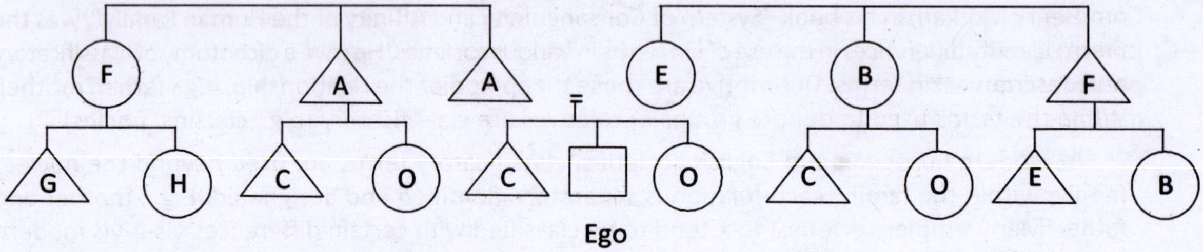

(e) Crow – Feature of matrilineal societies

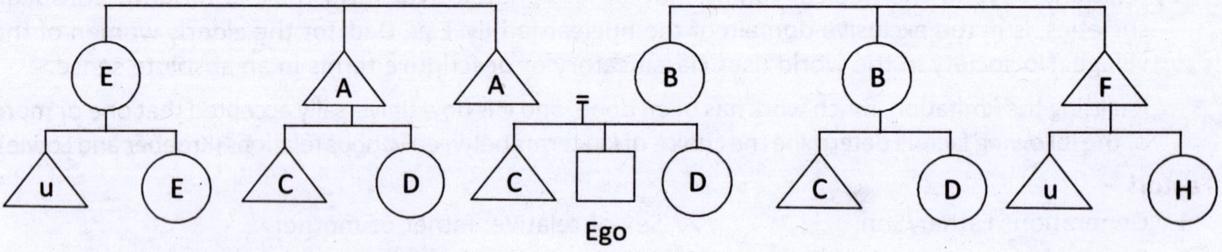

(f) Sudanese – Extreme descriptive.

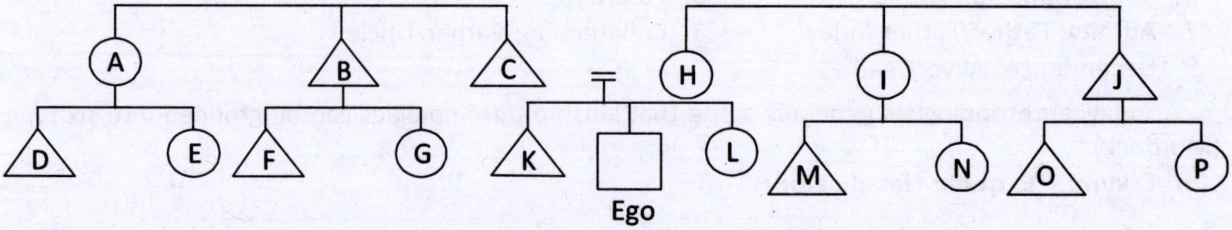

But similar is the limitation that these are idealised forms, and there are societies that have a lot of differences in their terminologies from this system.

The importance of kin terms does not rest in their classification but in functions:

1. Kin terms represent particular social statuses with associated roles.
2. Kin terms almost always occur in a father-son pair.
3. Kin terms, though they represent higher or lower social status, are more important because the unfolding of kin terms helps in understanding kinship. *g.,* Devar-Second Husband
4. Social structure and kinship behaviour were analysed.

Q 7 Complimentary filiations

Ans. The word filiation means relations between parents and children. Usually, the type of relationship one has with paternal relatives in patrilineal descent and with maternal relatives in matrilineal descent is called filiation (allocation of an individual to a descent group).

Complimentary filiations is a term used by a group of anthropologists referred to as descent theories, the foremost of whom was M. Fortes. In societies with unilineal descent groups, people also recognise kinship links with relatives who don't belong to their own descent group. For example, in a patrilineal descent group, individuals have important socially defined links with members of their mother's family—a maternal uncle or maternal grandparent.

Originally, this concept was used to describe important ethnographic characteristics of many African societies, like Tallensi of Ghana. Fortes described that Tallensi individuals saw their complimentary filiations as different from lineage links but essential to their well-being.

While lineage links have political, hierarchical, authoritarian, and obligatory features, Complementary filiation is more emotional and personal in nature. J. Goody said that while one inherited certain types of property inside a descent group, they also inherited other types of property from complimentary filiations. Complimentary filiation provides a residential society or insurance against a filiation relationship breakdown.

For example, in Patriarachal society,

Father	Mother
↓	↓
Filiation	Complimentary filiation

But the concept was criticised by Edmond Leech, who argued that complimentary filiations are not a kind of muted kinship but rather are part of affinal links.

Filiation links have a political and hierarchical character, while complimentary filiation is more emotional and personal.

Q 8. Descent and Alliance

Ans. Descent theory, although tracing its origins in the works of L.H. Morgan (Evolutionist) and Radcliffe Brown (Structural functionalist), came to light in the 1940s, when even books like "African Political System" by Fortes and Pritchard were published.

Unilineal descent group (UDG): Members of such groups behave as a single unit when dealing with legal, political, and economic matters. Thus, it was concluded that descent, in particular UDG, is the basis of stability and structure in society in the absence of state institutions and blood relations.

However, scholars criticised the fact that kinship is not organised through unilineal descent in various societies. It has minimised the importance of marriage and affinal relations in the structure of kinship.

Alliance theory: The alliance theory of kinship is given by C.L. Strauss in his book "The Elementary Structure of Kinship". The basic objective of this theory is to inquire how inter-individual relations are formed and how such inter-individual relations ultimately culminate in society. Unlike descent theory, it places affinal relations as the basis of kinship's social structure. This theory is based on the principles of reciprocity and universal incest taboo.

According to L. Strauss, inter-individual relations are established through marriage alliances. Actually, marriage alliances among different human groups take place due to incest. In other words, reciprocity, the exchange of women as wives, and the establishment of relations of affinity between different families are due to incest. According to him, the most elementary form of marriage is cross-cousin marriage (CCM), and due to CCM, the elementary structure of kinship is established.

Levi Strauss mentions two types of cross-cousin marriages: unilateral cross-cousin and bilateral cross-cousin.

Bilateral CCM: It is such a type of marriage in which the wife of a man is the mother's brother's daughter and the father's sister's daughter at the same time. Bilateral CCM was the earliest form of marriage because matrimonial alliances were initiated when men exchanged their wives as sisters.

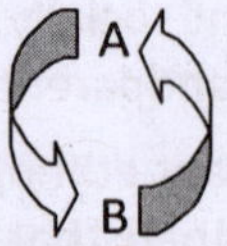

He terms such exchange as restricted exchange.

Unilateral CCM: There is another type of exchange also known as generalized exchange.

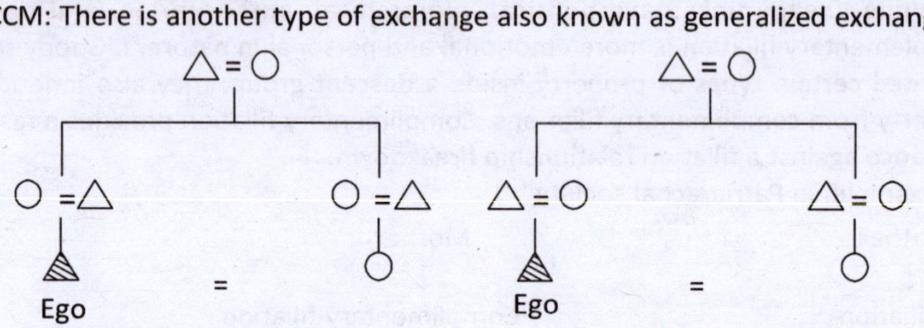

Patrilateral closs cousin Matrilateral closs cousin

Levi Strauss mentions that matrilateral C.C.M. are more numerous and significant from a solidarity point of view as they involve more families.

This alliance theory was criticised by *Needham* for using words like reciprocity and exchange with women because all such words are used for commodities, and women are not commodities. *Homans* criticised Strauss for the solidarity hypothesis and put forth the sentimental hypothesis. In patrilineal society, authority is also in the hands of the father's sister, so men are attracted to the mother's brother's children and not the father's sister's children (for sentimental reasons). This concept has minimised the role of consanguinity and residence in kinship.

In short, alliance theory signifies that the initiation of society is due to marriage alliances. But both theories taken together largely explain the concept of kinship.

3

Economic Organisation

Economic Organization: Meaning, scope and relevance of economic anthropology; Formalist and Substantivist debate; Principles governing production, distribution and exchange (reciprocity, redistribution and market), in communities, subsisting on hunting and gathering, fishing, swiddening, pastoralism, horticulture, and agriculture; globalization and indigenous economic systems.

Q 1. Meaning, Scope and Relevance of Economic Anthropology

Ans. There was no concept of economic anthropology until 1940, when two anthropologists, Herskovits and Raymond Firth, coined the term economic anthropology in their book "Economic System of Unaccessible Societies". Both of them were of the opinion that the exclusive study of the economic systems of different societies is essential to understanding the social systems of society. But real transformation with the concept of substantivism came in Polyani's "The Great Transformation".

The meaning of economic anthropology is very simple. It studies humans from an economic perspective both in time and space. Here, time means various stages of the development of the economic system in different time periods. Here, space means the prevalence of different economic systems among different human groups all over the world. According to Karl Polyani, study of economic activities with special reference to the socio-cultural life styles of humans is known as economic anthropology.

Economic Anthropology has a very broad scope. It studies the origin, development, and dissemination of different economic systems. It covers areas regarding ways employed by various human groups to procure food, means of distribution, ways of exchange, and modes of consumption. It analyses the impact of LPG reform, especially on tribal economic systems. A study of the economic systems of Neurs of Sudan, Ashanti of Ghana by Evans Pritchard, Tallensi of Ghana, and Bhils by Sahlins gives insight into tribal economics and changes due to LPG reforms, as their products are even found in international markets.

It also studies how the particular mode of production of a particular group influences the life of another group. For instance, pastoralism among Todas and agriculture among Badagas help each other survive via exchange. Another area to study is tribal markets and the contribution of Paul Bohnan in this direction, who studied what types of activities take place in these markets. It also helps as an advisor to economic planning related to tribal affairs.

In short, we can say that there is no economic aspect of humans that is not covered by economic anthropology. Thus, it is very comprehensive in its scope. Following an interdisciplinary approach, economies and economic anthropology become integrated. The best example is Amartya Sen's work on welfare economies.

Q 2. Formalist and Substantivist debate

Ans. Anthropology, while studying economics, has two schools of thought: formalist and substantiveist. According to formalists like Raymond Firth and Herskowitz, the economy of any society can be studied only through the principles of economics. While substantivists like Sahlins and Polyani argue that the economy of a simple society is not a pure economy but a social economy, i.e., the underlying basis of the economy is social,

Example: Kula Exchange, as studied by Malinowski in the village Kiriwina of Trobriand Islanders in the book "Argonauts of the Western Pacific". These island people undertake long voyages to exchange economically irrelevant red shell necklaces (Soulava) and white shell bracelets (Mwali) with their permanent partners on other islands. Economic exchanges through these voyages are few and secondary and are never undertaken with Kula partners. At all these steps, social roles score higher than economic ones. These are ritual and magical practises, as well as the ritual enforcement of preexisting bonds of friendship. Considering hazardous voyages and the meagre quantity of economic exchange, modern economists see this as an uneconomic venture, but island societies may disintegrate into small isolates, and therefore the role of Kula as a cementing agency is more important than economic exchanges.

Another example is potlatches, a feature among British Columbians in which there is mass-scale gift giving and destruction of valuables (grain, blankets). Basically, an event with the roles of display and destruction in the estimation of status It may be an anti-economic act, but studies have shown that these potlatches regulate the total social economy of an area as well as social order.

The debate can be conclusive when we discuss some principles of economics and apply them to simple societies.

1. **Principle of Maximisation:** All human beings multiply their resources. But this is not true in simple societies. For example, Carneiro studied Kuikuru of the Amazon region and concluded that Kuikuru invest 3.5 hours per day in economic pursuit, and if they worked just 0.5 hours more, they would be affluent, but they do not because they lack a sense of competition. Sahlins says: 'Tribes are not maximizers; they are optimizers'.
2. **Principle of Rationalisation:** Human beings are rational in terms of profit and loss. All their actions aim at profit, not loss. But in simpler societies, rationality demands the maintenance of social relations even at the cost of profit. *Sahlins* says: 'Money is to invest, and kinship is to rest'.

But this debate is outdated now. We follow an interdisciplinary approach to bring them together on a common platform. Economists and anthropologists are working together, thereby leading to a welfare economy. The best example is *Amartya Sen's* concept of welfare economics.

Q 3. Primitive Vs Modern Industrial Economy

Ans. The economy of simpler societies based on mutual cooperation and reciprocity is the primitive economy, while the economy of open systems driven by principles of demand, supply, and profit and loss is the modern industrial economy.

The economy is made up of four parts:

- Production
- Distribution and exchange
- Ownership
- Consumption

Anthropologists have never been much interested in the study of consumption: Ownership in the modern industrial economy has two models: communist and capitalist. In the communist model, everything belongs to people through the state, while in the capitalist model, it is individual ownership. In simple economies, traditional rights govern ownership. There is collective ownership with individual responsibilities.

The most important components are distribution and exchange. But exchange is not possible without production. Production refers to the exploitation of natural resources. It is of three types: primary, secondary, and tertiary. Secondary and tertiary production is typical of modern industrial societies. Primary activities include hunting, food gathering, fishing, pastoral heading, cultivation, mining, etc.

Of these, hunting and gathering are found only in simpler societies, while mining is a typical feature of modern industrial societies. The lives of hunters and gatherers are reminiscent of those of prehistoric times. As hunting requires continued mobility, they live in small migratory groups called bands. The band comprises 10 families with an average membership of 30–60, occupying a large territory. Examples—Eskimo (Inuit) of Alaska, Bushmen (!Kung) of the Kalahari, Raji of India, etc.

Unlike hunter-gatherers, pastoral hunters possess plenty of wealth, but mobility is restricted comparatively with intermittent settled life and greater population density. Examples: Bedouins of the African desert; Bhotia of India; Bakhtiari tribe of the Zagros Mountains Of all tribal cultivators, the vast majority are shifting cultivators. In simple societies, cultivation with primitive tools is small-scale and labour-intensive, while in modern industrial societies, agriculture is highly mechanised, capitalintensive, and intensive.

Production is not possible without the division of labour. In simple societies, it is based on age and gender; otherwise, there is no specialisation. But in modern industrial society, age and gender are not important, while resources, qualifications, and experience are, as is the tendency for extreme specialisation. Whatever the mode of production, it leads to exchange.

Types of exchange:

1. **Ceremonial** (non-commercial): a typical feature of simpler societies Example: the Kula exchange (Malinowski) and the Pig Feast of Tsembage (Roy Rapport).
2. **Commercial:** market or trade; a typical feature of modern industrial society.
3. **Mixed:** commercial items with ceremonial items; found in both societies. e.g., the purchase of ornaments, a piece of art, etc.

Today, because of globalisation and increasing cultural contact, simple economies are facing an onslaught of market forces that are compelling them to become part of modern industrial economies. All-purpose money and consumer products have entered simple economics, changing their nature for the better. Therefore, in the near future, this discussion may become only academic in nature.

Q 4. Principles governing production, distribution and exchange in communities

Ans. Karl Polyani, in his book "The Great Transformation" mentions reciprocity, redistribution, and the market as three main modes of exchange in an economy.

Different human groups produce different goods, but such goods should reach every section of society, so they are exchanged among various human groups by following different modes of exchange.

1. **Reciprocity**: Reciprocity is considered the exchange of goods and/or services between two or more individuals or groups without the use of money at its face value. According to *Sahlins,* it is of three types:
   a. Generalised reciprocity is one in which there is a one-way flow of goods and/or services. Returns are given elsewhere, and there is no question of just equivalence. It is a feature of foodgathering and hunting societies. For example, the Hazda of northern Tanzania and the Bushmen (!kung) of Kalahari desert.
   b. Balanced reciprocity is one in which one gives without bargaining and with equivalence. It has different sub-types:
      - Barter: exchange of goods in return for goods; exchange of services in return for services is known as the barter system. Exchange among the four tribes of Nilgiri:
        Todas pastoralists exchange milk and milk products with agriculturalist Badagas for agricultural produce. Similarly, with Kotas and Irulas
      - Gift exchange is a balanced, value-based barter system in which goods and services are exchanged on some special occasion, such as marriage or a birthday. It is also known as ceremonial exchange.
      - Silent trade is balanced barter in which there is no physical or verbal contact. People contact each other silently and exchange goods. E.g., Veddas and Blacksmiths of SriLanka
      - Kula system: It is a balanced, ceremonial barter system. The island people of Trobriand Island undertake long voyages to exchange Soulavo and Mwali. Economic exchanges are secondary, and the reinforcement of cultural ties is the primary concern.
   c. Negative reciprocity is when one tries to get the most by yielding nothing - by threat, cheat, or theft, for example, Kipsigis.
2. **Redistribution:** According to Karl Polyani, redistribution means the upward movement of goods towards authority and then the distribution of such goods by authority among people by following downward mobility.

   The basic objective of redistribution is to distribute goods and services by collective authority among all so that no one can remain devoid of the basic necessities of life.

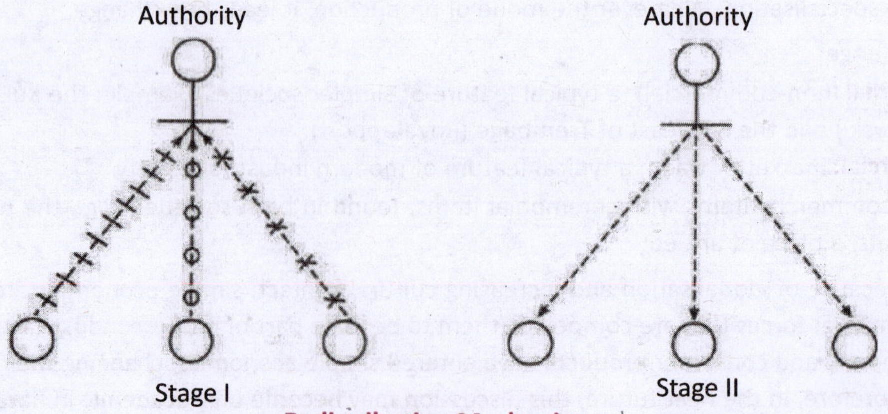

Redistribution Mechanism

Nature varies from society to society. As far as modern societies are concerned, they pay taxes in different forms. In a simpler society, as reported by *Raymond Firth*, the Tikopian Chief, who collects agricultural produce from his people without retaining it for him, redistributes it to others even from his personal production.

In Trobriand Islander, the Big Man marries the sister of the wealthiest person so that he can acquire products in dowry, but he does not retain such products for himself but redistributes them among people.

In Kwakiutl of British Columbia, redistribution takes place during potlatches when invitees present many gifts to hosts, and hosts redistribute among invitees.

3. **Market:** People visit markets to meet kinsmen. Almost each family of a neighbouring village is represented at one place, and one can easily know about relatives without visiting them personally. Authorities (local administration) can spread their message at market places; even courts may hold their sittings at market places.

   Different types of cultural activities and competitions mark the occasion in this invigorating culture. There are few buyers and few sellers, but the numbers present defy the logic of the place being called a market place. Just because socio-political functions dominate and economic exchanges are relegated to secondary activity, these markets are often called peripheral markets.

According to Karl Polyani, there are three types:

a. **Peripheral market:** In these, shops are set up, and when goods exchange, there is nothing like a market. E.g., Tiv of Nigeria

b. **Regular market:** societies that produce surplus and exchange their goods with others on a regular basis. E.g., Nilgiri Hills

c. **Regional market:** in the tribal belts of Jharkhand, M.P., the Northeast, Kenya, etc. Scientific technology is employed in production and produces in abundance. E.g., *D.P. Sinha's* study of Banari market in Chotanagpur

However, most societies of the ethnographic past are now incorporated into larger nation-states; e.g., Trobri and Islanders and other societies in Melanesia are now districts in the nation of Papua New Guinea. Selling today goes beyond nation-states. The world is now a multinational market.

Reciprocity is reserved for family members or friends who remain behind the scenes in business transactions. Redistribution occurs in the form of taxation and the use of public revenue for transfer payments to low-income families. Social stratification grew in the market economy.

Q 5. Principles governing production, distribution and exchange in hunting and gathering, fishing, swiddening, pastoralism, horticulture, and agriculture communities

Ans. Karl Polyani, in his book "The Great Transformation" mentions reciprocity, redistribution, and the market as three main modes of exchange in an economy.

Different human groups produce different goods, but such goods should reach every section of society, so they are exchanged among various human groups by following different modes of exchange.

1. **Foragers:**
   a. Foraging or food collection may be defined as a strategy whereby humans gather, hunt, scavenge, or fish to obtain their food from plants and animals found in the wild.
   b. Foragers, also known as hunter-gatherers, are not numerous in the world today. They mostly live in marginal areas of the earth—desert, arctic, and dense tropical forests.
   c. **Example:** Ngatatjara of Australia; Inupiaq of North America

d. **General features**
   i. Most live in small communities in sparsely populated territories and follow a nomadic lifestyle, forming no permanent settlements.
   ii. They don't recognise individual land rights.
   iii. They don't have different classes of people.
   iv. They don't have specialised political officials.
   v. They are less likely to face a serious food shortage or famine.
   vi. Division of labour based on age and gender: men hunt large marine and land animals and fish, while women gather wild plant foods.
   vii. Among foragers, fishing is the most common activity, followed by hunting or gathering (*Binford*). The ones more dependent on fishing are usually more permanent, unequal, and bigger, e.g., the Tlingit of Alaska and the Nimpish of British Columbia.
   viii. It was practised at one time in almost entire world.

e. In recent times, they have even started living in small, settled villages with household infrastructure, schools, and health clinics. Some earn wages, a government welfare measure, while others occasionally forage.

2. Horticulture(Swiddening):

a. The word may conjure up visions of orchids and flowers. But to anthropologists, the word means the growing of crops of all kinds with relatively simple tools and methods in the absence of permanent cultivated fields.

b. The tools used are hand-based. They are of two types: slash and burn (swidden agriculture) techniques and dependence on long-growing tree crops. Most don't rely on crops while doing fishing, hunting, or nomadism along with it.

c. **Example:** Yanomamo of Brazil; Samaon of the Pacific; Garo; Khasi; Nagas; Baigas of India.

d. **General feature**
   i. More food comes from a given area than from foragers.
   ii. Support a large, more densely populated community.
   iii. Their way of life is more sedentary than that of foragers.
   iv. They exhibit beginning of social stratification. e.g., part-time craft workers or part-time political officials.
   v. Crops don't provide protein, so hunting and fishing are important to their diet.
   vi. It was an intermediary stage before full-fledged agriculture.
   vii. 80% of them are in tropics.
   viii. Matrilineal few: Khasi of India
   ix. Polytheistic religion.

e. Change has been visible in the movement of people to towns in recent times, and state governments have prevented such cultivation.

3. Pastoralism:

a. A form of subsistence technology in which food production is based directly or indirectly on the maintenance of domesticated animals

b. **Example:** Basseri of Iran, Sammi of Scandinavia, Maldharis, and Todas of India

c. **General features**
   i. Practised mainly in grasslands (steppes, prairies, and pampas) and other semi-arid habitats without technological inputs such as irrigation.
   ii. Move frequently to find water and new pasture for your needs.

iii. Small community consisting of a group of related families.
iv. More vulnerable to famine and food shortages than foragers and horticulturists.
v. Marriage: monogamous or polygamous.
vi. **Religion:** Islam (Bakarwal of J&K), Hinduism (Todas of Tamil Nadu), and animistic beliefs

d. Recently, their grazing lands have been reduced, thereby reducing overgrazing in a small territory and increasing the risk of desertification.

4. **Agriculture:**
   a. Food production is characterised by the permanent cultivation of fields and made possible by the use of ploughs, machines, fertiliser, irrigation, water storage techniques, and other complex agricultural techniques.
   b. **Example:** rural Greece, the Mekong Delta in Vietnam, Ho, Oraon, and Bhil in India
   c. **General feature**
      i. More likely to have towns and cities.
      ii. High degree of craft specialisation, political organisation, and a large difference in wealth and power.
      iii. They work longer hours than horticulturalists.
      iv. More likely to face famine and food shortages because of production for the market (yield focus).
      v. Trade surplus, capital surplus exist.
   d. **Trend of commercialization and mechanisation of agriculture**
      i. Labour scarce
      ii. Emergence and spread of agriculture businesses
      iii. Shipped or received to other countries
      iv. In the US, less than 1% of people work on farms.
      v. In the US, Canada, and other countries, we are market foragers, collecting our food from stores.
5. **According to anthropologists,** the environment by itself has a restraining rather than determining effect on types of subsistence:
   i. No society can do agriculture in the Arctic.
   ii. Fishing is common in cold climates.
   iii. 80% of horticulture in the tropics
   iv. 75% cannot do agriculture in a tropical environment.
   v. Pastoralism in the grasslands

In recent times, technological changes have led to different strategies for food production in the same environment.

E.g., the Imperial Valley in California has a complex system of irrigation in its dryland region, thereby making it a productive region.

Q 6. Globalization and indigenous economic system

Ans. As per Anthony Giddens, globalisation refers to the gradual integration of economies and societies around the world.

Tribal economies were sort of primitive subsistence economies with exchange systems like reciprocity, redistribution, markets, etc. It was mainly barter-based, and social relations were given more importance than economic ones.

Globalisation impact: Production-based, subsistence-based economies have become unsustainable for tribal communities. This is due to the loss of natural resources and the entry of market forces into tribal land.

- **Distribution:** Market distribution mode is rising and taking over reciprocity and redistribution.
- **Ownership:** Individual ownership rising over the earlier mode of collective ownership However, there is also a bright side:
- **Production:** Commercial agriculture is rising. Products sold to MNCs and e-commerce sites like Giloy, shawls, sarees, etc.
- **Distribution:** More money in the hands of tribal members means better distribution among themselves.

Moreover, their dances like Kalbelia of Rajasthan and Warli painting of Maharashtra, got acknowledged worldwide.

Globalisation has made the formalist-substantivist debate outdated. It is increasingly important for economic anthropologists to adopt a dynamic approach in their studies to help them make better decisions.

Case Study

- **Women work harder than men**

Study carried out of farming and herding groups in the Tibetan borderlands in rural China to uncover which factors actually determine who works the hardest in a household, and why. Results published in Current Biology shed light on the gender division of work across many different kinds of society.

Study focused on rural villages from six different ethnic cultures. More than 500 people were interviewed about their dispersal status after marriage and invited wear an activity tracker (like a fitbit) to assess their workloads.

Our first finding was that women worked much harder than men, and contributed most of the fruits of this labour to their families. This was evidenced both by their own reports of how much they worked and by their activity trackers.

Women walked on average just over 12,000 steps per day, while men walked just over 9,000 steps. So men also worked hard, but less so than women. They spent more time in leisure or social activities, or just hanging around and resting.

This may be partly because women are, on average, physically weaker than men, and may thus have reduced bargaining power. But we also found that individuals (be they male or female) who disperse at marriage to live away from their kin have higher workloads than those who stay with their natal families.

So if you are female and move away from home at marriage (as most women do throughout the world), you suffer not just in terms of missing your own family but also in terms of workload. When both sexes disperse and no one lives with their natal families, both sexes work hard (as there is little help from kin) – but the woman still works harder. According to our study, perfect sex equality in workload only occurs in instances where men disperse and women do not.

These results help us to understand why women globally disperse, but men generally do not. Dispersal is especially bad for men – adding about 2,000 more steps per day to their step count, but only adding about 1,000 steps per day for women.

But things are slowly changing. As women are increasingly starting families away from both their partner's and their own family, their bargaining power is increasing. This is further boosted by their increasing levels of self-generated wealth, education and autonomy. Ultimately, these changes are leading men to take on an increasing workload in many urban, industrial or post-industrial societies.

4

Political Organization

Political Organization and Social Control: Band, tribe, chiefdom, kingdom and state; concepts of power, authority and legitimacy; social control, law and justice in simple Societies.

Q 1. State Vs Stateless Political Organization

Ans. John Beattie defined political organisation as the maintenance of orderly social relations either within a defined territory or between different social groups.

State societies, viz., primitive states or chiefdoms, monarchies, and modern states, have a centralised authority structure whereby there is a centralised head at the top. While stateless organisations are decentralized (no central authorities), acephalous (without a head), and segmentary (as divided into various segments)

Elman Service classified them into four categories: bands, tribes, chiefdoms, and states.

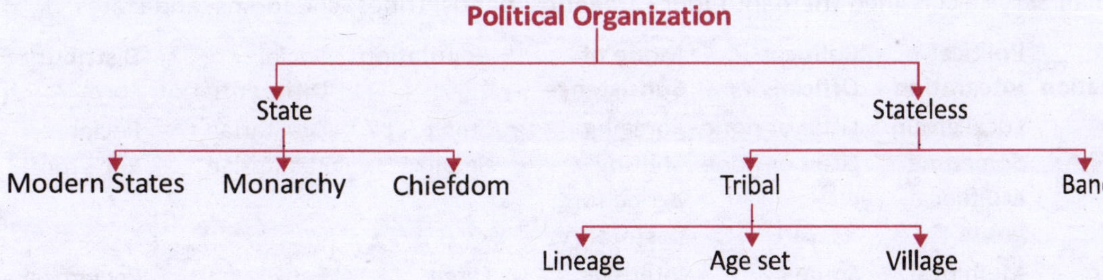

Differences:

1. **Nature:** Stateless societies are always homogenous, and states are often heterogeneous.
2. **Territory:** Bands and age-based Stateless societies lack the concept of a defined territory. Village-based and lineage-based societies do have the concept of defined territory but not defined boundaries. States have defined territories and boundaries.
3. **Locus of authority:** In band and village band stateless societies, the locus of authority is totally absent. In an ageset-based society, it is present at the top but highly diffused, while in a lineage-based society, it is well-defined at the lineage level but as a whole absent. In all state societies, authority is always present and well-defined.

4. **Power of authority:** Use of physical force is literally absent in stateless societies; use of supernatural power may be seen in age-set-based societies. While states administer through the executive class via laws and rules.
5. **Function of authority:** Maintenance of social order is the top priority of authority in stateless societies, followed by many socio-economic functions including arranging marriages, redistribution, etc. Defending the territory is the most important function of authority in a state.
6. **Types of authority:** traditional authority is the most common type of authority in stateless societies; charismatic authority too may be found, but only occasionally. All three types—traditional, legal-rational, and charismatic—can be found in state societies.

Following the processual approach, whereby all societies are moving towards the modern state, actual differences between any two political organisations may be much less.

Emergence of States (Evans Pritchard):

Band (nomadic life; no surplus)

↓

Tribal System (Marginal cultivation, pastoralism, horticulture; Little Surplus; Part time Specialization)

↓

Advanced cultivation and domestication of animals

↓

Plenty of surplus and wealth

↙ ↘

Emergence inequality and class distinction | Need of machinery to maintain peace and order

↘ ↙

Emergence of centralized authority and State

Q 2. Band, Tribe, Chiefdom and State

Ans. Different types of political systems have emerged in different time and space.

Elman Service classified them into four categories: bands, tribes, chiefdoms, and states.

Type of Organization	Political Integration	Political Officials	Mode of Subsistence	Population	Social Differentiation	Distribution Form
Band	Local group	Little or none	Foraging	Small	Egalitarian	Reciprocal
Tribe	Sometime Multilocal group	Little or none	Shifting agriculture, pastoral	Small	Egalitarian	Reciprocal
Chiefdom	Multilocal group	Some	Intensive agriculture	Large	Rank	Reciprocal and Redistribution
State	Multilocal group	Much	Intensive agriculture, manufacturing	Huge (Cities and towns)	Class and Caste	Market Exchange mainly

Dispute resolution examples:

1. **Band:**
   a. In Eskimos (Inuit), a song duel exists in which two aggrieved parties stand face-to-face and abuse each other hardly but musically. All band members gather around them and clap for both of them, but louder for the aggrieved party and less for the accused.

b. **Australian natives ritual spear-throwing:** If a wild throw of a spear from X hits Y of another band, the accused is first reprimanded by his own band members, and if Y is bent upon taking revenge, X is asked to stand at an equal distance, and Y is asked to attempt a specific number of spear throws at him.

2. **Village Based:**

a. Each village or group has some kind of elected council (each lineage is represented). But decisions taken are advisory in nature as there is no mechanism to enforce them. e.g., Pueblo of West Africa.

3. **Age-set Based:**

a. Masai: society divided into childhood, junior warriorhood, senior warriorhood, junior elderhood, and senior elderhood. Elders do not have physical force to enforce norms but use communication from supernatural power to ratify their authority.

4. **Lineage-based Societies**

a. **Neur (blood feud):** If a member of one lineage has killed a member of another lineage, the other lineage has all right to kill the man from that lineage who committed the act first. Sometimes alternate killing between times starts; a leopard skin chief is one who belongs to a neutral lineage and investigates, identifies problems, and decides compensation. He commands respect and authority for the maintenance of social order.

5. **Chiefdom:** While tribes have informal mechanisms, chiefdoms have formal mechanisms that integrate more than one community into a political unit. The position of chief is hereditary and bestows a high position on its holder.

e.g., Polynesia; the Cherokee Indian of the US's Chief has 'Mana' power.

6. **State autonomous:** Political unit with centralised decision-making over many communities and the power to govern by force, e.g., US, India, Canada

Factors Associated with Variation in Political Systems:

1. A cross-cultural study found that the greater the importance of agriculture, the larger the population that is politically unified and the greater the number and types of political officials.
2. Community size: large communities need more political officials and an administrative level of decision-making.
3. Competition: Elman Service suggested competition as a reason why society changes from band to tribal level.
4. Defensive needs: Such needs led to the switch from an informed multi-village political organisation to a formed chiefdom organisation.
5. Service said that chiefdom emerges when redistribution becomes important.
6. States emerge due to irrigation needs, the subordination of defeated groups, or trade (export or import).

Robert Carneiro estimated that in 1000 B.C.E., 1 lakh–10 lakh separate political units existed in the world. Today, they are fewer than 2000. However, the breakup of the USSR in Yugoslavia shows ethnic groups opted for autonomy. The trend towards consolidation continues in the form of European Union formation. Extrapolating it, a few investigators suggested that the entire world would be politically integrated as early as the 23rd century and no later than 4850 C.E.

Q 3. Concept of Power, Authority and Legitimacy

Ans. Power is actually based on social relationships because individuals cannot enjoy power in isolation, and people have power in relation to others.

Power + Legitimacy = Authority.

1. Burtland Russell defined power as the ability to compel the forceful behaviour of others. Authority means theexercise of power with legitimacy. A person gets work done even if against the will of another. It has physical aspect. Authority has legal aspect.
2. Power may be legitimate or illegitimate. Authority is always legitimate, as acceptance of society, the law, or any other social regulation is essential.
3. Power is unlimited, while authority is limited.
4. Power is not always duty-bound, while authority is always duty-bound.
5. Power may or may not be responsible, while authority is always responsible.
6. Power may or may not be accountable, while authority is always accountable.
7. Power is boundless and absolute, while authority is duty-bound and relative.
8. Power is not prescribed, while authority is prescribed.
9. Power can be constructive or destructive, while authority is always constructive.

   e.g., police and courts in states deriving power from laws, and in age-based societies, elders deriving powers from supernatural forces

   Legitimacy is the legality, social acceptance, rightfulness, and basis for claiming rights. Legitimacy is a universal concept. It is the law of society. It is based on social rules, beliefs, customs, traditions, etc. Legitimacy is a qualitative phenomenon, and social justice is the name of legitimacy.

Sometimes power and authority coexists simultaneously because power without authority has a limited approach, and authority without power can do nothing. Therefore, in a political system, both power and authority are essential for the proper functioning of administration.

Q 4. Social control, Law and Justice in simple societies

Ans. Law is a formal institution that maintains social order through the possibility of using power. The existence of laws entails the existence of law-enforcing agencies like the police, judiciary, etc. But law is a narrow term that can only be applied to the maintenance of social order in state societies. Thus, Radcliffe Brown gave a much wider term, 'social sanction'.

Social sanction is the response of society or a part of it towards a particular act, whereby the act is approved or disapproved. It can be divided into two types:

1. **Positive sanctions** are applied when the act of the doer is approved and socially recognised, like awards, titles, etc.
2. **Negative sanctions** are applied when the act is disapproved of by society, like mockery, about, etc. Negative sanctions are important in maintaining social order. Reciprocity is the most common and widespread threat of withdrawal of reciprocity, like wherever someone violates social norms, they are socially ostracised. Radcliffe Brown categorised negative sanction into:
   i. Organised sanction is the organised response of society as a whole. For example, a criminal is prosecuted and punished as per the law of the land.
   ii. Diffused Sanction is the sudden response of a part of society. For example, a person is socially ostracised if he or she breaks the law.

Diffused sanctions can be further divided into:

1. **Public Opinion and Mockery:** They are highly effective sanctions as they are psychological in nature; people are restrained from doing anything deviant from social norms to avoid public mockery and maintain good opinions about others.

2. **Rituals:** These include religious as well as magical sanctions. In religious sanctions, there is a concept of sin which is an act of violating God's will. People believe that even if there is none yet, there is someone who is watching everything. Simple societies don't differentiate between sin and crime. Here, the consequence of action is given more importance, while in post-industrial societies, intention is given more importance, on the basis of which civil and criminal laws are there.

In simple societies, guilt is established by two means: oath and ordeal.

1. **Oath:** It is a promise made in the name of God not to lie. This is a technique for compelling someone to admit his own guilt voluntarily. For example, the Munda of Chotanagpur takes an oath on tiger skin.
2. **Ordeal:** It is the process of determining guilt or innocence by submitting the accused to a dangerous or painful test under supernatural control. For example, accused Maler is asked to lick the red-hot sacred axe near the sacred stream three times.

Even without the use of physical force, social order is better maintained in simple societies, where maintaining social order is their top priority. Secondly, sanctions are applied through kinship, and nobody can escape kinship as they are dependent on each other.

Primitive Law	Modern Law
It is people centric. It is not prescribed.	It is prescribed by Constitution, Court, police.
It is kinship based.	It is territory based.
Expelling from society is present.	Expelling from society is absent.
Evidence proved and based	Evidence scientific-DNA.
Based on public opinion.	Based on rules and regulations.
Imprisonment absent due to lack of jail and police.	Present.
Result immediate.	Result delayed.

Peaceful Resolution of Conflicts

1. **Avoidance:** Violence can be avoided if parties to a dispute voluntarily avoid each other or are separated until emotions cool down. An anthropologist says that foragers are likely to make use of it.
2. **Community Action:** In the Inuit, an individual's failure to heed taboo or follow the suggestion of a shaman leads to expulsion from the group as they cannot accept a risk to their livelihood.
3. **Mediation:** In Neur, disputes within the community were settled with the help of a leopard skin chief.
4. **Oath and Ordeal:** Act of calling the deity to bear with us to the truth of what one says Determine guilt by submitting the accused to dangerous tests believed to be under supernatural control. E.g., scaling in Tanda, Madagascar.
5. **Adjudication by Courts:** A study by *Scaglion* in 1990 found that new courts allow women to address grievances in Papua New Guinea. In general, adjudication or enforced decisions by outside authority tend to occur in hierarchical societies with social classes and centralised power.

Violent Resolution of Conflicts:

1. **Feuding:** recurring hostility between families usually motivated by the desire to arrange offence against members of the group.
2. **Raiding:** short-term use of force to realise a limited objective, e.g., Nagas, Bedouin Arabs.
3. **Large-scale** confrontations usually occur in societies with intensive agriculture. E.g., in the military history of Dani, Massi of Kenya battled with Kalenjin over a land dispute.

Reasons for conflicts and change:

1. **Fear:** In preindustrial societies, war was done to protect against expectable but unpredictable natural hazards that would destroy food resources.

2. **Culture:** Societies with more wars have warlike activities like sports, malevolent magic, high murder rates, feuds, etc.
3. **Self-help:** Systems of individual self-help tend towards violence.
4. **Democracy:** Countries that are democratic are less likely to fight against each other.

In the UNGA Declaration of Action on Culture of Peace, it called for increased education about culture of peace, including democratisation, gender equality, sustainable development, respect for human rights, and the free flow of knowledge. Finding solutions to address resource inequity has to be part of the peace process.

The ultimate aim in all these primitive societies is to maintain social order as the top priority and apply it through the kinship system.

Case Study

- **Bacha Posh, the Afghan tradition that allows girls to access the freedom of boys**

Bacha posh is the only practise in Afghanistan's strongly patriarchal, male-dominated society that allows girls access to the more liberated male world. Women and girls are typically confined to the home. According to the custom, a girl is treated, dressed, and treated as a boy, with all the rights and responsibilities that involve. The child can engage in extracurricular activities, go to a madrassa or religious school, and, occasionally, critically for the family, work. However, a bacha posh is expected to return to typical girl gender norms once she reaches adolescence. The changeover is not always simple. The Taliban, who took control of Afghanistan in the middle of August and have made no public pronouncements on the subject, have not made it clear how they feel about the practise. With a crackdown on women's rights, the bacha posh tradition could become even more attractive for some families. The bacha posh practise may become even more appealing to some families with restrictions on women's rights. According to Thomas Barfield, an anthropology professor at Boston University and the author of several books on Afghanistan, the Taliban might not even address the issue because the practise is just temporary and the children will soon revert to female roles. The Taliban might stay out of it because it's within the family and because it's not a permanent position, according to Barfield. Albania, a country with a strong patriarchal culture, has a ritual something like this, except it is only for adults. The Albanian practise of "sworn virginity" allowed women to inherit property, work, and serve on village councils—all things that were previously off-limits to women—after taking an oath of celibacy and declaring themselves to be men.

According to Barfield, who spent around two years in the 1970s living with an Afghan nomad family that included a bacha posh, the bacha posh tradition is one of the most under-researched subjects in afghanistan in terms of gender concerns. It sort of vanishes precisely because the girls return to the traditional female role and marry. Girls who are selected to be bacha posh are typically the more brash, confident daughters. According to him, the role fits so perfectly that occasionally individuals from outside the family are unaware that it even exists. One of the few gender concerns that doesn't surface as a political or societal issue is almost undetectable, according to Barfield. Parents may want a bacha posh for a variety of reasons. The practise typically occurs in homes lacking a male because sons are traditionally valued more highly than daughters. Some see it as a status symbol, while others think it will be lucky if the next baby is a boy.

5

Religion

Religion: Anthropological approaches to the study of religion (evolutionary, psychological and functional); monotheism and polytheism; sacred and profane; myths and rituals; forms of religion in tribal and peasant Societies (animism, animatism, fetishism, naturism and totemism); religion, magic and science distinguished; magico-religious functionaries (priest, shaman, medicine man, sorcerer and witch).

Q 1. Anthropological approaches to the study of religion (evolutionary, psychological and functional)

Ans. The term religion is defined by *Durkheim* in his book "The Elementary Forms of Religious Life" as a unified system of beliefs and practises related to sacred things.

Evolutionary approach: Lubbock, in his book "The Rise of Civilization and Primitive Condition of Man", was the first anthropologist to put forth an evolutionary scheme of religion. According to him, the origin of religion took the following evolutionary course:

- ➢ Atheism: belief in the non-existence of any supernatural power
- ➢ Fetishism: the belief that certain objects like skulls, feathers, amulets, etc. contain certain supernatural powers that can be accessed by using these objects.
- ➢ Nature worship: worship various forces of nature like wind, rain, etc.
- ➢ Totemism: a mystic relationship established with certain objects, living or non-living, by which they are worshipped and not injured.
- ➢ Shamanism is a stage in which we witness the emergence of shamans, people who are considered to possess certain magical and healing powers.
- ➢ Anthromorphism: figures of humans carved and worshipped
- ➢ Monotheism: belief in a single supreme power
- ➢ Ethical monotheism: belief that a single supreme power is the creator of all ethics and norms

E.B. Tylor, in his book "Primitive Culture", mentioned that animism, i.e., belief in the soul, was the earliest form of religion. According to him, primitive man thought that something remained hidden in the body, and when such a thing escaped from the body of a person who died, primitive man named such a thing as anima (soul). Thus, they began to worship the soul. It evolved from animism to polytheism to monotheism.

Prof. Marrett provided another scheme. Animatism, the earliest form of religion, conveys that the religious life of primitive man evolved out of belief in certain ununderstandable, unindividualistic, and impersonal supernatural powers that can take abode in any object, whether living or non-living, or they can also manifest themselves in the form of many excellences as possessed by certain objects. It evolved from animatism to monotheism to polytheism.

Max Muller, in his book "The Civilization and Religion", mentions that the earliest form of religion is naturism. He remarks that during the earliest times, people were not able to understand the forces of nature. Thus, due to their ignorance, they began to worship the forces of nature, which led to the evolution of nature. Sir James Frazer, in his book "The Golden Bough: A History of Myth and Religion," mentioned that the earliest relationship between humans and superhumans was magic. Magic is the earliest belief associated with supernatural power. In magic, supernatural powers are forced to yield the desired results. Frazer remarked that a shift occurred in the thinking of primitive man when he thought that worship was necessary in order to acquire blessings, and thus a shift led to the emergence of religion.

Psychological Approach: The main advocates of the psychological approach were W. Wundt, Otto, and Freud. According to Wundt, the origin of religion was due to the emotional expression of humans towards power, which regulates the course of nature and causes human life. Due to the mental stress of humans, they began to believe that someone supernatural and supersensory existed who could control their mentality. Such an assumption of primitive man led to the establishment of a supreme power, and worship of such a supreme power established the earliest religions beliefs.

Another psychologist, Otto, was of the opinion that many emotional manifestations like fear, stress, frustration, etc., compel a simple person to believe that something is here that controls their psychological manifestation as humans. Also, a simple man became psychologically upset when he was not able to understand various forces of nature like rain, wind, etc., or the mysteries of birth and death. Thus, he thought of a certain supernatural power, and the response of primitive man towards it led to the establishment of religion.

The main authority behind this approach was Sigmund Freud; book "The Future of an Illustration". According to him, earlier there was a single human group consisting of both males and females. The eldest male in the group controls all the females. When his sons became adults, he threw them out of the group. In revenge, the sons killed their father, but later on they became psychologically upset. Then they painted a figure of their father on a flag and started worshipping him. Also, they decided not to marry women in their group. It led to the emergence of religion and incest, which were taboo. Religion is an illusion. It should be set aside in favour of science and reason.

Therapeutic Theory by Carl Jung considers religion beneficial to society. It helps in healing the mind's fear and instability (unlike Freud).

Functional Approach: According to *Malinowski*, religion is actually a tool of adaptation because it acts as an outlet for frustration. Malinowski provides a reference to the Trobriand Islanders of Melanesia. He mentions in his book "Magic, Science, and Religion" that Trobriand Islanders always remain frustrated and stressed due to fear of crop failure and sea storms. Thus, they worship many spirits to get rid of frustration. Hence, according to him, the main function of religion is to provide individuals with confidence to carry out various life activities because, under stress, they cannot act in the desired way. Another function of religion is to purge an individual of various forms of fear, frustration, and stress.

According to Radcliffe Brown, the function of religion is not individualistic but societal. Thus, the concept of sin evolved in the field of religion, and all anti-social activities were categorised as sin. Earlier, there were no formal agencies to maintain social order. Thus, religion evolved as an informal agency for the maintenance of social order and the management of public affairs. Consequently, through the concept of sin, the behaviour of individuals in society was regulated. Thus, according to him, the basic function of religion is to maintain social order. For him, society is more important than individuals. As a result, social order took precedence over individual stress and strain. Thus, Radcliffe Brown remarks that the function of religion is more important for society than for individuals. While countering Malinowski, Radcliffe Brown held that, due to religion, individuals cannot get rid of fear and frustration. But actually, religion creates fear in the minds of individuals, so that they regulate their behaviour out of fear of divine punishment. Consequently, social order is maintained.

Another advocate of this approach is *Durkheim.* Religion springs from society and serves social needs. He opined that the basic function of religion is to provide inter-group solidarity. Because worship of a similar God and participation in similar religious rituals, festivals, etc. provide a feeling of belongingness to members of a similar faith, religion is religious unity.

Among all approaches discussed above, most support the functional approach because the other two are based on assumptions, whereas the functional one seems to be practical.

Q 2. Forms of religion in tribal and peasant Societies (animism, animatism, fetishism, naturism and totemism)

Ans. Different religious beliefs prevail in tribal and peasant societies, which include animism, animatism, fetishism, naturism, and totemism.

Animism: The theory of Animism is given by E.B. Tylor in his book "Primitive Culture." Animism means belief in spirits. According to Tylor, the belief in animism emerged among primitive men due to the mystery of dreams and death.

Almost all tribes in the world are animistic, i.e., they have a belief in spirits. According to Radcliffe Brown, a number of African tribes like the Neurs, Ashanti, and Azandes have beliefs in many spirits; they believe that the spirits always surround them. The spirits are responsible for their well-being and also for their ill-health. Thus, they per form many rituals to pacify them. Durkheim reported that many tribes of Australia, particularly the Kareras, also have beliefs in many spirits; they even worship their ancestor spirits, whom they call 'Shotoro'.

Evans Pritchard mentioned that the Ashanti of Ghana are animistic, and their supreme spirit is 'Notoro'. D.N. Majumdar mentioned that Santhals, Mundas, and Hos of the Chotanagpur region have beliefs in many spirits. Primarily, they worship their ancestral spirits at their most sacred place, known as 'Majhiye Than'.

L.P. Vidyarthi said that the Malers of Rajmatal Hills, Jharkhand, also have belief in many spirits, and 'Gossaiyan' is their supreme spirit.

W.H.R. Rivers remarked that the Todas of the Nilgiri Hills believe that hills are full of different spirits, and these spirits are responsible for the multiplicity of their buffaloes and also for the well-being of buffalo.

In addition, many tribes of north-east India, like the Garo and Khasis, are also animistic because they believe in many spirits.

Animatism: The main advocate of Animatism is Prof. Marrett. According to him, many tribes all over the world have a belief in supernatural power, which is beyond the senses of humans but can take abode in any object and can also express itself in the form of many excellences. According to Marrett, Trobriand Islanders call such power "Mana" and believe that if a warrior excels in battle, it means he possesses Mana. If they find stone in the shape of a pig, they keep such stone in a "pigsty," with the assumption that stone being abnormal in shape will help in the multiplicity of pigs.

Among the Iroquois of North America, such power is known as 'Wakonda'.

Among Hopi Indians in North America, such power is known as 'Orenda'.

D.N. Majumdar reported that a number of tribes of Chotanagpur, like the Santhals, Mundas, and Hos, termed such power "Bonga'. Cycle is Bonga for them; railway engines are greater Bonga; and aeroplanes are the greatest Bonga. Majumdar further mentions that the tribes of the Chotanagpur region consider Bonga a well-wisher, so they worship everything that seems abnormal to them.

Fetishism: The term Fetishism is derived from the Latin term "fetisho" which means an object that is believed to possess certain powers and that is used to perform certain magic. Thus, magic is actually associated with fetishism. Fetishes may be objects like pieces of jewellery, skulls, feathers, amulets, vadoo dolls, etc.

S.C. Dube reported that Kamars of M.P. always keep a piece of the bone of their ox in their fields with the intention that it will help in a good yield.

L.P. Vidyarthi narrated that the Malers of Jharkhand use the skull to carry out many magic spells. Verrier Elwin, while conducting his fieldwork among the Gonds and Baigas of M.P., found that they use the feathers of different birds, particularly peacocks, to perform rituals to cure someone of disease.

Murdock mentions that a number of tribes, like the Crow Indians, Chiricahua Apace, etc., of North America also use pieces of jewellery, particularly a ring, to perform any magic, generally for the well-being of their newborns. Raymond Firth reported that Tikopians of the West Pacific use a number of objects, particularly the skull and femur, to perform many magics.

According to Malinowski, the Trobriand Islandersof Malanesia also perform many magic tricks to save their boats from sea storms, and in this process they use a number of objects like pieces of wood, bronze, and iron rods.

Naturism: The theory of naturism is given by Max Muller. According to him, earlier people were not able to understand and control the forces of nature. Thus they begin to worship such forces; this belief is known as naturism. A number of tribal groups worship many forces of nature, like the sun, moon, rain, trees, etc.

According to D.N. Majumdar, for the Santhals, Mundas, and Hos, Sun is the supreme deity, whom they termed "SingBonga".

N.K. Bose reported that for the Juangs of Orrisa, the Sun is also the supreme god, whom they call 'Dharma Raja'.

L.P. Vidyarthi found among Malers that they worship many trees and hills. Evans Pritchard said that the Neur of Sudan worshipped many forces of nature, even thunder. Hopi Indians worship the rain, many fruit-bearing trees, and even the natural lights.

Totemism: The word totemism is taken from the term "todam," which is part of the terminology of the Ojibwa (North Americantribe) and means a relative or an ancestor. Totemism is a widespread phenomenon among members of simpler societies who associate themselves with certain species of animals, plants, and even some non-living objects. They termed them "totems" and considered them their ancestors. They express their relationship with totems in a variety of ways, like by collecting periodic offerings of totems, painting images of totems on the walls and gates of their houses, wearing masks of totems, and so on. They refrain from injuring, killing, and eating their totems. The death of the totem is ceremonially mourned. Many tribal groups possess different totems; for example, Kharia has two totems: Muria (a tortoise) and Kiro (a tiger).

The Juangs of Odisha have pigeons as totems. The Crow tribe of North America and the Koya tribe of South India have crows as their totems. The Minas of Rajasthan have fish as their totem. The Todas of the Nilgiri Hills consider the buffalo their totem.

According to Radcliffe Brown, many tribes in Africa have the cobra as their totem.

Durkheim, who considered totemism the earliest form of religion, mentions that totems are symbolic representations of groups, thus necessary for group unity.

Malinowski mentioned that brotherhood among Trainband Islanders is due to the fact that they possess a common totem. Thus, we can say that the totem acts as an integrating force.

Variations in religious beliefs exist.

- Swanson found that societies with hierarchical political systems should be more likely to believe in a high God.
- Similarly, societies dependent on food production (agricultural) are more likely to have beliefs in a high Godx than food-collecting societies.

Swanson found that concern for God in moral behaviour is more likely in large, complex societies. They intervene more in societies that have inequality, live in harsh environments, or experience environmental uncertainty.

Case Study

- **Himba people's rituals of birth and death**

The date of birth of a kid is established in the Himba tribe of Namibia in southern Africa long before the child is actually born, beginning on the day he is imagined to be a young boy. When a lady determines she is going to have a kid, she lies down and takes a nap under a tree while waiting to hear the singing of the unborn child. After hearing this boy's song, return to the man who will serve as the boy's father and ask him to teach the song to the boy. Then, they sing the child's song to invite him, and they make love to literally produce the child. The village midwives and elderly women are taught this child's song by the expecting mother. As a result, when the child is born, the elderly women and those nearby sing a song to greet him. The other villagers pick up the boy's singing when he gets older. Therefore, always find someone to pick up the youngster and sing to him if he falls or gets harmed.

Similar to this, the locals will sing their song in praise of the youngster if he accomplishes something fantastic or successfully completes a rite of passage. Another chance exists in the tribe, where the villagers can sing to the young man. A person is summoned to the town square, and the residents gather in a circle around him if, at any point in his life, he commits an out-of-character crime or social act. Then they started singing. The tribe understands that antisocial behaviour can only be corrected through love and a reminder of one's identity, not via punishment. When you hear your own song, you don't need or want to do anything that would put the other person in danger. Throughout their entire lives, too. The songs are sung together in marriage. And as this boy, who is getting older, lies on his bed, preparing to pass away, the entire community knows his song and sings it for the very last time.

- **'Animism' is finding renewed interest around the world**

Worldwide support is growing for a movement known as "new animism," which attempts to establish personality rights for nonhuman species via the use of law. Environmental activists are not the only ones who use the word; new animists do as well. Even animism itself has grown popular. Some bloggers on spirituality discuss animism as a means to strengthen one's spiritual connection to nature. Religious rituals are one type of these practises, but others include environmental protection, farming methods, and demonstrations like those staged by the Standing Rock water protectors, who oppose the Dakota Access Pipeline and go by the hashtag #NoDAPL.

Since most people don't typically think of protests like the #NoDAPL as "religious," media stories frequently fail to mention the commitments to place and land that drive demonstrators. Animism has taken on a legal shape with New Zealand's 2017 act recognising the Whanganui River as a legal person, the result of decades of Maori campaigning. Additionally, it is easy to ignore the very real biological and ecological scientific knowledge of these societies when Indigenous practises are categorised as animist religion.

Q 3. Monotheism and polytheism

Ans. Monotheism is a form of religion in which only one god is worshipped. Monotheism is considered a later stage in the evolution of religion because it is considered a higher level in the religious field. It is believed that higher forms always evolve later, but there is no historical account to prove this fact.

Monotheism is of different types:

1. **Basic Monotheism:** Only one God is worshipped, who is considered supreme, the creator of the world, and also the regulator of the world. In it, the existence of any other god is totally negated. Islam and Christianity are examples of basic monotheism.
2. **Exclusive Monotheism:** In this type of monotheism, only one god is worshipped and considered supreme. It is believed that other gods don't exist, they are fake gods, or they are demons. In it, it is believed that the actual God is also the creator of various ethical codes, values, and norms. Thus, ethical monotheism is part of exclusive monotheism. e.g., Jews, Judaism
3. **Multifacet:** In this, the supremacy of one God is established, but it is believed that such a God can manifest itself in different forms. e.g., the Neurs of Sudan consider Kwoth (the spirit) as the supreme god, but they worship Kwoth in different forms. Every form of Kwoth is named differently, but when they worship different forms, they are indirectly worshipping the Kwoth. Thus, in it, one and only one God is worshipped, but it is believed that such a God can manifest in different forms.

Polytheism means belief in a number of gods. In the evolution of the religious history of humans, it is believed that polytheism was the earliest stage before monotheism. Except for Islam, Christianity, and Judaism, almost all other religions are polytheistic.

Polytheism is of different types:

1. **Henotheism** is a belief system in which one god is considered supreme but the existence of other gods is not negated. The supreme God is considered the creator of the world, and the supreme God controls the course of nature and human life. Other gods are considered minor gods. These minor gods also worship the supreme god, but every minor god has a different identity and a different name. In Henotheism, the numerical strength of the gods is limited to a few hundred.
2. **Unlimited polytheism:** In this belief system, they worship an unlimited number of gods. Every god is considered the supreme god, and every god has one name. Every god acts according to his

own will and is not under the control of any other god. Hinduism is a significant example of polytheism. Many tribal groups are polytheistic because they have different gods for villages, different gods for cattle, different gods for crops, different gods for rain, different gods for kinsmen, different gods for well-being, and so on. Every god is worshipped in a different way, every god has different responsibilities, and every god is specified by the performance of different religious activities.

Religions beliefs and practises are found in all known contemporary societies, and archaeologists think they have found signs of religions beliefs associated with Homo sapiens, who lived at least 60,000 years ago.

Q 4. Sacred and Profane

Ans. The concept of sacred and profane is given by Durkheim in his book "The Elementary Form of Religious Life", and this concept is the main theme of Durkheim's theory of religion. According to Durkheim, all human groups, on the basis of their experience, have categorised objects as sacred and profane.

According to Durkheim, sacred objects are the essence of any religion. Thus, he defined religion as a unified system of beliefs and rituals towards sacred objects.

Sacred: Durkheim narrated that sacred is holy, extraordinary, supernatural, individualistic, and impersonal. He further maintained that sacred includes every object that is put aside by humans for special religious treatments. God, a tree, a rock, a king, etc. may be sacred. But an object should be approved as sacred by the community. The sacred object may include:

1. **Gods as Sacred:** God is considered sacred; all those human groups that consider only one God sacred are monotheistic, like Muslims and Christians. All those human groups that consider a number of gods sacred are polytheistic, like Hindus.
2. **Ghosts as Sacred:** God is not only sacred, but many groups also consider ghosts and ancestral spirits sacred. Many tribal groups consider a number of ghosts sacred. Religions beliefs: Shontism (China) also has the belief that ghosts are sacred.
3. **Moral Code or Philosophical Aspect as Sacred:** Philosophical aspects or ethical codes may also be sacred. Buddhists consider the four noble truths and eight-fold path as advocated by Mahatma Buddha sacred rather than considering Mahatma Buddha as God. For them, the moral code as envisaged in the eight-fold path is important to attain salvation (Nirvana). The same is true with Taoism.
4. **Totem as Sacred:** According to Durkheim, many tribal groups also considered totems sacred. A totem may be an animal, plant, cosmic body, or non-living thing. Belief makes it sacred, as seen in the Aruntas tribe of Australia.
5. **Supernatural powers as sacred:** Except for God, ghosts, and totems, there are certain other objects that are considered sacred due to the belief that they possess supernatural powers. For instance, among many tribes, if an individual excels in battle or in hunting expeditions by using a spear, such a spear is considered sacred. Such sacred supernatural powers abode in any object, whether it is a stone, ring, or symbol like Swastik, a cross, etc.

Profane: In order to distinguish sacred objects from other objects, Durkheim put forth concepts of profane. Profane is unholy, ordinary, natural, personal, and individualistic. Durkheim also put unethical acts under the category of profane. For example, abusing the pope, showing disrespect to the priest, etc., is also profane.

Profane is always considered inferior to sacred, and sometimes it is contemplated not to touch profane objects with sacred objects. For instance, objects made of leather are not supposed to touch idols of gods and goddesses because leather is considered profane.

Through the concept of sacred and profane, Durkheim attempted to explain that one should follow various activities to approach sacred objects and to abstain from profane. According to *Eric Wolf*, Durkheim tries to prevent human groups from indulgent in profane activities and acting in a desired way to seek the blessings of sacred ones.

Criticism:

1. Jack Goody: The dichotomy of sacred and profane is not universal.
2. Evans Pritchard: It is not useful in the research field or in real-life situations.

Q 5. Myths and rituals

Ans. Myth and ritual have been two central components of religion in both traditional and modern societies.

Myth: Myth is a symbolic story, typically of undetermined origin, that seems to relate to real-world occurrences. Usually, it is a precise description of gods or superhumans who participated in remarkable occurrences in an indeterminate time that are believed to have existed outside of the realm of ordinary human experience. In Levi-Strauss' opinion, the creation of myths is the mental activity that is most similar to the unconscious mind. This is due to the mythmaking mind's independence from societal values, which distinguishes it from the kinship system and marriage laws. He therefore emphasised the importance of studying myths in order to comprehend models of the human mind. According to Malinowski, myth enriches social tradition by giving it a revered beginning and so encouraging, sustaining, and incorporating acceptable social activity.

Ritual: Ritual is the practise of ceremonial activities that have been established by custom or by a priestly decree. Religious rituals are predetermined actions that manipulate religious symbols. For the purpose of contacting and/or controlling supernatural beings, such ceremonies combine prayers, offerings, and sacrifices. Totemism, in the opinions of academics like W.R. Smith, S.J. Frazer, and E. Durkheim, is where ritual first emerged. Functionalists like Malinowski have emphasised ritual's function rather than its inception. Ritual, in their opinion, serves as an environment- and social-adaptive mechanism.

Relationship between the two: There have been three main views. Scholars like W.R. Smith and Frazer believed that every myth was derived from a particular ritual. However, scholars like Tylor saw myth as an attempt to explain the world. Thus, for them, rituals are secondary and an application of myth. Finally, scholars like Malinowski regard both as partially independent from each other. For them, not all myths grow out of rituals, and vice versa.

Case Study

- **Rituals of Renewal**

According to anthropologists, rituals give participants a sense of routine that aids in reducing anxiety.

Participants gain a sense of community and an emotional bond through coming together to carry out these collective actions, which sociologist Émile Durkheim referred to as "collective effervescence." Even though these joyful customs frequently appear to undermine social order in their exuberance, they ultimately ser ve to reaffirm it. They enable individuals to get past the past and embrace optimism for the future by establishing symbolic thresholds.

DIWALI: Harvest time is a happy time in rural communities. Hindus, Jains, Sikhs, and some Buddhists celebrate Diwali, also known as the festival of lights, throughout India and throughout the world. According to the Hindu lunisolar calendar, Diwali takes place between the middle of October and the middle of November. It serves as an indication that the new year has arrived in several parts of India. It commemorates the victory of light over darkness, good over evil, and hope over despair, and occurs on the gloomiest night of the year. At the end of the monsoon season, which irrigates the rice fields, fills the aquifers, and feeds the cows, comes Diwali. People clean their homes before lighting and decorating them with clay oil lamps (diyas) and rangoli, geometric designs created with vibrant sands, powders, rice, stones, and flowers, to mark the end of this season during the festival. Windows are left open to welcome Lakshmi, the goddess of prosperity, or other household deities when the elaborate preparations are complete. In order to frighten away evil spirits, onlookers dress to the nines and light fireworks and firecrackers in the streets. Diwali has numerous forms and regional variants, just like other traditions in multicultural Indian society. But it offers a chance for interpersonal interaction for everyone. People visit their families during the five-day holiday, exchange gifts, send cards, and enjoy sweets and other celebratory meals. even though renewal rituals have existed since the beginning of civilization, they are still important today.

The COVID-19 pandemic serves as a sobering reminder of the need for such rituals in human society. Collective celebrations offer individuals everywhere a way to put their everyday concerns aside, interact with others, and just have fun during these uncertain times. It is no accident that the town of Ayodhya in the Indian state of Uttar Pradesh hosted one of their most extravagant New Year's celebrations ever in 2021, a year when India fought to contain the pandemic. Over 900,000 oil lamps were lit during Diwali by the community, breaking the previous record and providing much-needed light and hope to the locals.

Q 6. Religion, Magic and Science distinguished

Ans. According to James Frazer and Malinowski, magic is both primitive science and primitive religion. Magic is the basis for both science and religion. Magic is present in most primitive societies, and so is religion as magic religion.

Religion	Magic	Science
Based on belief of supernatural power	Based on spirits and forces	Based on facts and logic
Religion is social practice	It is not social practice	It is research practice
Hymns, Kirtan, Bhagan with known meaning used	Spells and rites with unknown meaning are used	Laws, hypothesis are used
Religion is open and all can participate e.g., Church	It is secret and closed affair	It is open and public.
Religion is emotional attitude	Magic is also emotional	Science is not emotional
One cannot prove religion	One cannot prove magic	One can prove science
Practitioner are called as priest, father, Mulla	Practitioner are called as Shamans magician	Practitioner are called as Scientist
Religion is meant for social good	Magic is both good and bad	Science is also for good
Priest occupy lower position than God but mainstream in society	Magician regard himself superior but lives outside mainstream society	No such assumption by scientist
Belief is basis of religion	Secrecy is basis	Rationality is basis
Based on belief and not laws	Based on Illogical laws	Based on Logical laws
End in itself	Not end in itself	Not end in itself

According to Frazer, although magic is losing its importance with advancement in science and technology, it will always remain part of human life because people in the modern world also have a belief in magic. During WWII, pilots of fighter jets kept certain objects along with them because they believed that they would bring them good luck.

Although both religion and science differ from one another, neither is able to dominate the other. Both exist independently and simultaneously in almost all societies, and even the greatest scientists in the world have a belief in God, and they never discard God's existence.

Q 7. Magico-Religious functionaries (Priest, Shaman, Medicine man, Sorcerer and Witch)

Ans. Different types of magico religious functionaries exist in different societies.

Priest:

1. A religious person who is authorised to perform certain activities related to a particular organised religion is known as a priest. A priest is named differently, like Imam, Mullah, Lama, and many others.
2. A priest undergoes various trainings, like how to pray, how to meditate, and how to control the senses. Even learning the dogmas and rituals of a particular religion is part of priest training.
3. A priest is a full-time specialist; the basic function of a priest is to remain busy in religious pursuits.
4. A priest is authorised to perform certain religious rituals in order to have access to supernatural powers.
5. A priest is authorised to guide the general public about how to follow particular religious beliefs, and he also imparts religious teachings to people.
6. A priest performs many rituals related to agriculture, health, and the well-being of people.
7. Priests always perform many rites of passage at the time of one's birth, one's wedding, and also at the time of one's death.
8. Priests are symbols of sacredness and enjoy respectful status in society; it is advocated not to say anything wrong about them.
9. In some religions, both men and women can be priests, but in others, only men can become priests (Islam and Hinduism). Even in Hinduism, only Brahmins can become priests; thus, in Hinduism, priesthood is based upon birth rather than work.
10. In many religions, priests can be married or unmarried. But in many religions, priests always remain unmarried, e.g., Buddhism and Christianity.

A priest is considered a mediator between humans and superhumans in the religious field, so people mostly approach their respective priests for the performance of many religious rituals so that they can seek the blessing of God.

Shaman: The term Shaman is taken from the language "Tungus" of Central Siberia, which means spiritual medical specialist. A shaman, who may be male or female, can provide medical aid to people on earth with the help of spirituality, i.e., spirituality can help a human being with the intermediation of a shaman.

1. Shamans are masters or mistresses of spirits. They always keep good spirits and perform many activities like beating the drums, dancing in an unusual way, wearing unusual clothes, getting tattoos of many spirits, painting their bodies, etc., to entertain the spirits.
2. Shamans always help the people. It is believed that the world consists of three realms: the upper realm consists of good spirits, the middle realm consists of humans, and the lower realm consists of evil spirits. It is believed that shamans in the unconscious stage bring good spirits from the upper realm and visit the lower real m to warn the evil spirits and not harm humans in the middle realm. Shamans have the power to access the upper and lower realms.

3. In many societies, shamans are considered the main healers because it is believed that shamans have certain healing powers that they acquire from spiritual beings. Thus, shamans can help people get rid of many diseases and sufferings.
4. Shamans also perform many activities to enhance the fertility of the soil, maintain the good health of humans and cattle, bring rain, and prevent the occurrence of many disasters. A number of tribes, like the Neurs of Sudan, Chukchee of Siberia, Tapirape of Brazil, Zulu of Africa, Aruntas of Australia, Santhals, Gonds, and Todas of India, always visit Shamans at times of frustration for the cure of diseases that may be cold only.
5. People can become shamans in different ways. Among the Tapirape of Brazil, people become shamans who continuously see spirits in dreams. Among the Zulu of Africa, people are inflicted with much displeasure by spirits. Among many Indian tribes, a person who is very tall, is able to manipulate other people, and also has certain capabilities beyond his or her fellow being is declared a Shamana.
6. Like a priest in the field of religion, a shaman has a respectful personality in the field of magic. Many times, a shaman is known as a witch doctor because he wards off the effects of witchcraft and sorcery.
7. A shaman is also a mediator between this world and another.

Medicine Man:

1. Medicine man, also known as medicine person, is an indigenous head. Medicine people are acquainted with the ritualistic, medicinal, and chemical potentialities of substances that may be herbs.
2. A medicine person is generally called upon to prevent or heal the physical and emotional illness of an individual. A medicine person pretends to pull out evil substances that cause illness from a patient's body through sucking or with their hands. A medicine person motivates the patient psychologically by telling him that the evil substance is now out of his body and that he will be cured.
3. A medicine person always carries a kit consisting of feathers, stones, medicinal plants, and some other objects that he or she generally uses to heal a person. Medicine people are found in many simpler societies. Many tribes, like the Gussi of Kenya, Tiv of Nigeria, Birhor, Chenchu, and Irulas of India, totally depend on medicine people for the prevention and healing of different diseases.
4. Among the Kipsigis and Gussi of Africa, both shamans and medicine people are the same. Whereas, among others, shamans and medicine people are different. Among the Tiv of Nigeria, only men can be medicine people, whereas among others, both men and women can be medicine people.

Witch and Sorcerer: Both witches and sorcerers practise black magic. Both of them practise magic to harm someone.

1. Witches are considered to be possessors of supernatural powers, which are internal and inherited. A witch can transmit these powers to the next generation. While sorcerers can acquire powers through rigorous practises like staying in a graveyard or cremation grounds for several months, they cannot transmit their powers to the next generation.
2. Witches can cause unnatural deaths, whereas sorcerers can only inflict illness.
3. Witches don't use any objects to perform magic because they can harm someone just by sight, whereas sorcerers always use certain objects like a piece of cloth, a skull, a piece of bone, a stick, etc. to perform magic.
4. According to Evans Pritchard, among the Neur, Azandes, and Ashanti of Africa, both witches and sorcerers are different, whereas in many other societies both are the same.
5. Among the Nupes of Africa, witches are always women and sorcerers are always men. Whereas among the Gwari of Africa, both men and women can be witches and sorcerers.

6. James Frazer mentions in his book "Golden Bough" that both witches and sorcerers are part of almost all societies, and particularly sorcerers, through the laws of similarity and contact, harm a number of individuals by using voodoo dolls, pieces of cloth, nail trimmings, hair trimmings, etc.
7. In many parts of Europe, witches and sorcerers are considered agents of the devil (Satan). Thus, they are severely punished. In many parts of Africa, many unexplainable events are related to the activities of witches and sorcerers. Many tribes in Africa even associate the occurrence of HIV/ AIDS with the activity of witches and sorcerers.
8. Both Evans Pritchard and James Frazer are of the opinion that, like priests and shamans, witches and sorcerers are also part of magico-religious communities like humans in almost every part of the world.

Variation in Religious Practices: Wallace identified ways in which people around the world perform religious practices:

1. Prayers
2. Physiological experiences like being deprived of food and water, dancing till exhausted, and social isolation
3. Divination: Getting the supernatural to provide guidance E.g., Omar Moore was found among Naskapi hunters in Labrador for successful hunting.
4. Feast: Sacred meals; e.g., Australian aborigines have a totem feast once a year.
5. Sacrifice: food, drink, sex, or the life of an animal or person
6. Magic is the performance of certain rituals believed to compel supernatural powers to act in a particular way.
7. Sorcery is the use of certain materials to invoke supernatural power to harm people. For example, in New Guinea, sorcery is used to promote fertility.
8. Witchcraft: the practise of attempting to harm sorcery by supernatural powers but through emotions and thought alone, not through tangible objects. Witches in Africa, for example, have the "Mangu" power to steal the vital organs of others at night.

More complex societies tend to have more types of practitioners. If nomadic or semi-nomadic, usually a single practitioner, i.e., a shaman, If agriculture, shamans, and priests exist, If complex political integration extends beyond the community, then additional sorcerers or witches are needed. All types of practitioners exist in society: agriculture, political integration beyond the community, and social classes.

6

Anthropological Theories

Anthropological theories:

(a) Classical evolutionism (Tylor, Morgan and Frazer)
(b) Historical particularism (Boas) Diffusionism (British, German and American)
(c) Functionalism (Malinowski); Structural— Functionalism (Radcliffe-Brown)
(d) Structuralism (L'evi-Strauss and E. Leach)
(e) Culture and personality (Benedict, Mead, Linton, Kardiner and Cora-du Bois)
(f) Neo—evolutionism (Childe, White, Steward, Sahlins and Service)
(g) Cultural materialism (Harris)
(h) Symbolic and interpretive theories (Turner, Schneider and Geertz)
(i) Cognitive theories (Tyler, Conklin)
(j) Post-modernism in anthropology.

Q 1. Classical Evolutionism

Ans. Classical evolutionists considered themselves the earliest human grouping in the history of mankind. According to them, the civilised society of today evolved from the primitive societies of earlier times after passing through many different cultural stages. Every successive cultural stage was more complex than the previous one. Thus, gradually, complexity superseded simplicity, and consequently, a complex civilised society evolved out of a simpler primitive society.

Basic Postulates:

1. The direction is from simple to complex, similarity to dissimilarity and indefinite to definite. Origin: Later half of the 19th century.
2. Classical evolutionists hold that a reflection of civilised society can be seen in primitive societies; for this purpose, they compare cultural survival, both material and non-material. This methodology of these scholars is known as comparative methodology. This is the prime methodology used by classical evolutionists.
3. Classical evolutionists also got puzzled by the question of how similar discoveries or inventions took place among the human population simultaneously all over the world without having any historical relations. They solved this puzzle through the concept of cultural parallels.
4. According to them, similar inventions and discoveries were made all around the world in parallel during the same time period; they termed this ideology as cultural parallelism. Cultural parallelism conveys the evolution of or modification of cultural traits in parallel among all human populations.

5. Classical evolutionists associate the concept of cultural parallelism with the psychic unity of mankind. The psychic unity of mankind conveys the development of a similar mentality among all human populations all around the world to react and think similarly under similar environmental conditions.
6. They postulated that it was due to the psychic unity of mankind that financial institutions of society like management, family, religion, etc. emerged at the same time among all human populations. They further mentioned that the emergence of agriculture took place almost at the same time in Southeast Asia, South West Asia, and America. Similarly, the invention of writing and the printing press also took place at the same time in many parts of the world. Also, many ages, like the Stone Age, Copper Age, Bronze Age, and Iron Age, evolved almost at some point in many countries of the world.

Summarising, we can say that the basic postulate of classical evolutionists revolves around:

1. Considering primitive society as an earlier one and civilised society as an evolved one
2. Concept of cultural similarity
3. Concept of cultural parallelism
4. Concept of the psychic unity of mankind

Techniques: Secondary sources of data except for Henry Morgan's Iroquois study

Criticism:

1. They totally discard the concept of the diffusion and migration of cultural traits.
2. Critics held that during the same time period, environmental conditions were different in different parts of the world. Thus, under different environmental conditions, similar inventions or discoveries take place.
3. Many studies prove that many tribes in America and Africa became agriculturalists just after hunting and gathering, i.e., they didn't follow the stage of domestication of animals. Similarly, many tribes in India were earlier hunter-gatherers and pastoralists, and consequently, they became industrial without passing through the stage of agriculture. Thus, the sequence of economic organisation is not universal.
4. Many tribes in Africa directly followed the Iron Age after the Stone Age, i.e., they were not acquainted with the Bronze Age. Almost the same is the case with the megalithic culture of South India. Thus, this sequence is also not universal.
5. They were armchair anthropologists and worked based on secondary data provided by missionaries and travellers. These anthropologists never took pains to establish the authenticity of such data.

In spite of these criticisms, classical evolutionists still deserve credit because it was due to E.B. Tylor that anthropology was established as a distinct academic discipline. They made the earliest attempt to understand cultural evolution, and later theories were influenced by them.

Q 2. E.B. Tylor

Ans. E.B. Tylor was considered the first great anthropologist. When the department of anthropology was established at Oxford University in England in 1885, he was appointed as the first professor of anthropology.

E. B. Tylor adopted the methodology of evolution to explain the development of human culture. He was one of the greatest classical evolutionists. E.B. Tylor published his first book in 1861 entitled "Anahuac" (close to water, term used for Mexico); this book is also termed "Mexico-Mexican: Ancient and Modern".

In this book, it is mentioned that the civilised people of Mexico evolved from primitive ones. In other words, Mexico's culture has evolved from something simpler into something complex. He used the concept of similarity to justify his claim. According to time, survivals may be non-material, like customs, beliefs, and some other practises, or they may be material, which persist through habits even though they have lost their utility. He cited the example of saying "God bless you" to someone who sneezed. Tylor claimed that from the earliest times, it was believed that sneezing was an attempt by the soul to leave the body. Thus, people said, "God bless you," and even in the civilised society of today, it is considered a bad omen, and people even say, God bless you. This practise indicates that civilised people evolved from primitive ones, and this evolution brought complexity to simplicity and heterogeneity to homogeneity.

The second book by Tylor was published in 1865 and was entitled "Researches into the Early History of Mankind and the Development of Civilization". In this book, Tylor talks about cultural progress on the basis of human mentality. According to E.B. Tylor, there emerged independent inventions and independent discoveries without any historical relation, and it happened due to the psychic unity of mankind. The psychic unity of mankind comes about when, under similar environmental conditions, people residing in different parts of the world react in similar ways. Thus, among all, there evolved the institutions of marriage, family, and kinship simultaneously. Also simultaneously, people passed through the Stone Age, Copper Age, Bronze Age, and Iron Age. These similarities indicate that human mentality also progresses in a similar manner.

The most recognised book by E.B. Tylor was "Primitive Culture", 1871, in which he explained the origin of culture and the origin of religion. In this book, it will be mentioned that all humans have developed their culture in sequence, i.e., stage by stage. It evolved from savagery to barbarism to civilization. In this book, Tylor also talked about the origin of religion; he defined religion as beliefs in spiritual forces or spirits. Thus, according to him, the earliest form of religion was belief in the soul or spirits, which he termed animism. According to him, the second stage was polytheism and ultimately monotheism.

The fourth book by Tylor, "Anthropology: An Introduction to the Study of Man and Civilization", was published in 1888.

In this book, comparative methodology is explained, which conveys that he made a comparative study of different cultures and their survival. In this, he again mentioned that all civilised human populations evolved from the savages of earlier times.

Later on, he wrote an essay on 'A method to analyse the development of institutions', as published in the Journal of the 'Royal Institute of Anthropology'. In this essay, he talked about the origin and development of marriage, family, and residence. He collected data from 282 societies, ranging from small-scale hunting and gathering to large-scale civilised societies, and opined that earlier there was sexual promiscuity, which gradually evolved into polygamy and then monogamy. Initially, descent was traced through females, societies were matrilineal, and residence was matrilocal. Patrilineality and patrilocality are later developments.

E.B. Tylor used the unilinear approach to cultural evolution, indicating all cultures have evolved in a single line and simpler cultures become complex stage by stage by following unilateral evolution. e.g., savagery to barbarism to civilization; Stone Age to copper to bronze to Iron Age; sexual promiscuity to polygamy to monogamy.

Contribution other than evolution:

1. **Definition of Culture:** A complex whole of knowledge, art, norms, beliefs, laws, customs, or any other capability acquired by man as a member of society.
2. **Linked happiness** with Montesquieu's three-stage classification of society—civilised are happier than non-civilised (savagery, barbarism).
3. **Role of statistics in anthropology:** Did a comparative study of 282 societies and showed correlation between different institutions, i.e., patrilineal society associated with patriarchal residence.

Criticism:

1. Armchair anthropologist
2. Used non-scientific ethnographic data
3. Ignored social character of religion
4. Lack the emotional component of religion
5. Evans Pritchard criticised the theory of animism as the "If I Were a Horse Theory".

Q 3. Henry Morgan

Ans. Henry Morgan was the greatest classical evolutionist in America. He was the first anthropologist to study a tribal group, i.e., the Iroquois of North America, after which he wrote the book "League of Iroquois". This book was a treatise on classic people. While studying the Iroquois, he was attracted to their matrilineal descent, their family structure, their political organisation, etc. But the field that attracted the most attention was the way to refer their kin.

The Iroquois used the same term for their father and their father's brother; similarly, they used the same term for the mother and the mother's sister. The children of two sisters call themselves brothers and sisters. Similarly, the children of two brothers follow the same principle. Initially, Morgan believed that this system existed only among the Iroquois. But later, he found a save system among Ojibwa, which indicates their unity in origin.

Morgan got interested in knowing whether the same system applies to other American Indians or not, and he also hypothesised that American Indians have Asian origins. In order to prove his hypothesis, he sent questionnaires to Americans residing in different parts of the world. The data so received indicate that a similar system of kinship exists among all American Indians, and the data from Tamil Nadu revealed the prevalence of a similar system of kinship terminology. From these data, Morgan justified the claim that all American Indians had a common origin and that their ancestry was from Asia. On the basis of this data, he wrote the book "System of Consanguinity and Affinity of the Human Family", in which he mentioned that classificatory kinship terminology represents the earliest level of human culture and descriptive kinship terminology is a later development.

Afterwards, Herry Morgan also attracted his attention to the process of the origin of management and family, and he traced their origin through five stages, which are:

1. **Consanguine family:** This form represents the earliest form in the evolution of the institution of marriage and family when there was sexual promiscuity and marriages between blood relations were not prohibited.
2. **Punaluan family:** This stage represents group marriages in which a group of brothers marry a group of sisters of another family.
3. **Syndyasmian family:** During this stage of family, a man could marry only one woman, but he could establish sex relations with other women married in his family.
4. **Patriarchal family:** During this stage, the domineering male was established, and he could have many women at the same time, i.e., marriage and family were polygynous.
5. **Monogamous family:** It is the last stage in the evolution of marriage and family where a man marries a woman and vice versa.

Thus, according to him, the institution of marriage has evolved from sexual promiscuity to monogamy, and there are consequent family systems.

The most monumental work of H. Morgan was "Ancient Society". In this book, he envisioned human history through three stages: savagery, barbarism, and civilization. The first two stages had three subdivisions: Lower, middle, and upper. The three ethnic periods, along with their subdivisions and sequences of technological innovation, are given below:

	Period	Technological Development
1.	Lower Savagery	Invention of speech and subsistence of fruits & nuts
2.	Middle Savagery	Use of fire and Subsistence on Fishing
3.	Upper Savagery	Bow and Arrow
4.	Lower Barbarism	Pottery
5.	Middle Barbarism	Domestication of animals and cultivation of Maize
6.	Upper Barbarism	Iron smelting & Iron tools
7.	Civilization	Phonetic alphabets & writing

According to him, every stage has its own culture and unique lifestyle. He further mentions that lower savagery is out of existence now. Except for civilization, Morgan used technological advancement as a criterion to classify various stages of evolution.

In addition to establishing the sequence of evolution of marriages, families, and kinship technology, Morgan also provided the sequence of evolution of socio-political organisation, descent patterns, and rules of inheritance.

Morgan associated the evolution of socio-political organisation with the evolution of marriage and the family system. According to him, during the first two forms of marriage, there were promiscuous hordes. During the third stage of marriage, families emerged as organised intermarried sets of male and female siblings. Afterwards, there was the evolution of matrisibs and then patrisibs. Gradually, these siblings evolved into phratries, phratries into tribes, and tribes into confederacies. Morgan further mentions that all these socio-political organisations were based on personal relationships, which can be distinguished from a well-organised political setup, which was later developed and based upon identities and power. Such setups are townships, countries, and states.

As far as the descent pattern and rules of inheritance are concerned, Morgan holds that during the stage of sexual promiscuity, there was random mating. Thus, it is difficult to ascertain the actual father of the child, but there are no doubts regarding the mother. Thus, society is matrilineal. Matriliny emerged with savagery and lasted up to barbarism. With the emergence of earlier periods of civilization, matrilineal societies were converted into patrilineal societies when the role of men became more significant in economic pursuits.

Criticism:

1. After Morgan, a number of studies were conducted with respect to his scheme, and it was found that his scheme was faulty because, according to him, the first stage in cultural evolution was based upon nuts and fruits, but we know today that hunting and gathering have remained in existence for millions of years. Thus, these were not exclusive stages for gathering.
2. His scheme regarding fish subsistence is also not expected because fishing is a matter of local conditions. Thus, this type of subsistence can't be used as criteria to establish a cultural stage.
3. The invention of the bow and arrow doesn't indicate technological efficiency. Thus, it cannot be associated with an advanced stage of cultural evolution.
4. It was the fault of Morgan to put proto-agricultural Hawaiians under the Middle Savagery stage because they didn't possess a bow and arrow, but they evolved agriculture, were stratified, and exhibited more advancement than those who possessed a bow and arrow.
5. According to Morgan, the invention of iron came before the invention of written language. But Azetee of Mexico and the native metals were not acquainted with iron, yet they knew how to write.
6. His association of the phonetic alphabet and writing with the emergence of civilization is also challenged by many. On the grounds of Incon in Peru, an evolved state system has a complex set-up similar to civilization without knowing even a single phonetic alphabet.

7. Also, his scheme regarding the emergence of marriage and family is criticised on the ground that these two institutions didn't undergo all the levels explained by Morgan because monogamy emerged earlier in human history.
8. Another criticism is that a clear-cut application of the comparative method didn't appear in his studies.

Q 4. James Frazer

Ans. Sir James Frazer was represented as an epoch in classical anthropology, and the era of classical evolutionism came to an end with his death because he was the last surviving classical evolutionist. His famous works are "The Golden Bough", "Psyche's Task", "Taboo and Totemism", and "Totemism and Exogamy".

In the book "The Golden Bough", he talks about magic, religion, and science.

In one of the chapters of Psyche's Task, "The Devil's Advocate," he mentioned that although superstitions are evil, they have certain positive values, like compel people to show respect to authority and also prevent them from engaging in any type of violence.

In the book "Taboo and Totem", he talks about the origin and significance of taboo and why primitive societies should be studied.

In the book "Totemism and Exogamy", he talks about the origin of totemism and its relation to exogamy.

Frazer's Approach: Like other evolutionists, Frazer also employed comparative methodology to examine the origins of human culture. The comparative methodology along with the evolutionary approach helped him to live with certain general assumptions, like all men are similar because all of them have evolved from the same level. James Frazer also provided psychological interpretation of human beliefs; for instance, his theory of the origin of magic, his theory of the origin of totems, etc. is associated with psychological interpretation of the human mind.

Frazer's Evolutionary Principles: James Frazer was also interested in the progress of the human mind as it took place during different historical periods. According to him, cultural evolution, in which simpler became complex, took place due to the progress of the human mind. Consequently, mankind passed through three developmental stages: magic, religion, and science.

Frazer's opinions on Taboo and Totemism: According to Frazer, both taboo and totemism are creations of the savage mind because taboo has become essential to maintaining social order as it prohibits indulgence in anti-social activities and regulates human activities. In his work "Taboo and Totemism," he says that it is important to analyse the savage in order to comprehend the civilised because civilization is complex, whereas savagery is simple, and civilization is full of homogeneity. Thus, it seems to me that if someone attempts to understand complexity and heterogeneity, then it is necessary to familiarise themselves with simplicity and homogeneity. Also, by analysing savagery, the nature and extents of change can be evaluated as they prevail among contemporary civilised populations, so it is imperative to analyse the savage for understanding human cultural evolution. Through this statement, Frazer conveys that all civilised populations evolved from the savagery stage.

In his book, "Totemism and Exogamy", he mentions that Totemism originated due to beliefs in souls. He postulated that earlier men thought that the souls of the dead took abode in various plants and animals and may also have taken abode in certain non-living things. All those things that were possessed by dead souls became sacred to primitive men. They began to show respect towards them and also began to worship them; such objects came to be known as totems. When totems became hereditary, the totemic group also became exogamous. In this way, exogamy originated.

Frazer's view on magic, religion, and science: "The Golden Bough" is considered the most classical work of J. Frazer. Even Malino, one of the greatest anthropologists, praised this book, declaring it the most monumental work of his time. In The Golden Bough, Sir James Frazer talks about magic, religion, and science.

In this book, he mentions that earlier people were not acquainted with science, and they believed that they could control nature through two laws, which were actually their ignorance: the Law of Similarity and the Law of Contact.

The law of similarity conveys "like produces like," and magic related to it is known as imitative magic. People of earlier times thought that nature could be controlled by imitating it, i.e., if a similar cause could be created, it would yield a similar effect.

The second law conveys that "once in contact, always in contact", and the magic so produced is known as contagious magic. This law is based on the assumption that if something is in contact with one's body, it will remain so even after detachment. Therefore, if that thing harms others, then the actual owner also gets harmed. The stage of magic was the earliest stage in the evolutionary process of human culture. Later, people became frustrated when they observed that their laws were not working and that they were not able to control nature.

Now, the human mind also attempts to comprehend many mysteries. Thus, people began to believe in certain supernatural powers that are considered regulators of nature and the human mind. Their attitude towards such supernatural powers led to the origin of religions. Thus, religion constitutes the second developmental stage in the process of human cultural evolution.

Science constitutes the last and highest stage in such an evolutionary process. According to Frazer, there is a similarity between magic and science because, like magic, science is also of nature but with well-established laws.

Thus, the evolutionary approach of Sir James Frazer conveys that civilization is the last stage that emerges out of the first stage of savagery, and these stages are represented by magic, religion, and science.

Criticism:

1. No field work
2. Both religion and magic coexist as explained by Malinowski.
3. Depicted early humans and contemporary primitives as ignorant beings.

Q 5. Historical particularism (Boas)

Ans. Emerged as a reaction to classical evolutionism and extreme diffusionism. The school of historical particularism is associated with Franz Boas. Franz Boas conducted his fieldwork among the Eskimos of Alaska and the Kwakiutl of British Columbia, which was also the first fieldwork conducted by any anthropologist, after which he wrote two books: "Central Eskimos" and "Kwakiutl Text". After conducting this fieldwork, Franz Boas provided an alternative answer to why there are similarities and differences between human cultures. He concluded that every society is the outcome of its own unique historical development. Thus, similarity between cultures is due to the same origin in history, i.e., all those societies that exhibit cultural similarities exhibit historical development, but those that experience different historical developments follow different cultural setups. Thus, according to him, every society or cultural group should be viewed from its own historical perspective. This approach by Franz Boas is actually historical particularism.

As Franz Boas advocates that every society is a product of its own history, his approach to historical particularism also conveys the idea of cultural relativism, by which it is conveyed that a standard is not absolute but specific to the culture in which it exists.

As part of cultural relativism, Franz Boas conveyed that we should not categorise groups on the basis of savagery, barbity, and civility, and these derogatory terms should also be removed from the terminology. He advocated the conduct of fieldwork through participant observation in order to know the cultural setup of any group.

Franz Boas also advocated a historical approach in place of a comparative approach.

He also opined that in the course of history, many historical processes may have different causes, and he proved his point with the practise of wearing a mask by different cultural groups.

Franz Boas was of the opinion that initially the histories of small human groups that reside in particular geographical areas should be studied, and then it should be attempted to establish the similarities and differences between them. The only assumption acceptable to Franz Boas regarding similarities was similar origins in history; because he even discarded the psychic unity of mankind on the ground that mankind all over the world did not follow the same laws.

He also discarded the similarities on the basis of similar environmental conditions because his empirical studies proved that different cultures exist in similar environments and vice versa. He also discarded speculation that every human group experiences development in various fields simultaneously. Accordingly, even a particular cultural group was not able to experience all the developments at the same time; i.e., developments in social order, technology, and social life took place independently. For example, he cited that among Australian Aboriginals, technology is still poor, but even then, they have complex social organisations. In addition, he discarded speculative methods and advocated their substitution with historical methods.

Criticism:

1. Criticised for excessive and unrequired data collection and broad theories, focusing on describing culture rather than explaining why culture varied with a limited slope of method.
2. According to many later anthropologists, the works of Franz Boas had a geographical orientation because he explained the geographical setup of the Eskimo and Kwakiutl rather than their histories and cultures.
3. Franz Boas also did not advocate any general laws to explain the evolutionary process of culture.

In spite of this criticism, Franz Boas is still considered a renowned personality in the field of ethnology, particularly cultural anthropology. He is even known as the "Father of Cultural Anthropology".

Q 6. Diffusionism

Ans. Cultural diffusion is the process by which the cultural trait invented or discovered at a particular place spreads to different regions, and such a trait attains widespread recognition rather than being just localised.

Basic Postulates:

1. According to them, man was uninventive, and inventions didn't take place in different parts of the world. Inventions took place in particular places and at particular times, and then such inventions and discoveries diffused to other parts of the world.
2. Although the origin of a particular trait is not so easy to establish, its process of diffusion can be traced historically.

3. Many places during historical times acted as centres of diffusion. Initially, Egypt was considered a centric country from which agriculture, political organisation, etc. diffused to different parts. Rome is also considered a centre for cultural diffusion, particularly in Roman law. India diffused the principles of Buddhism to different countries in the world, like China, Japan, Sri Lanka, etc. Presently, America and other developed nations are exporting their cultural traits.
4. Diffusionists make it clear that the centre from where diffusion takes place may not be the creator of such cultural traits that experience diffusion. During historical times, Greeks acted as cultural migrators. During the period when India was extended up to Afghanistan, Kabul was the main centre of trading, and traders from different countries visited Kabul, where they exchanged their goods and also their cultural ideas. Thus, Kabul acted as a centre for cultural diffusion without being the creator of diffused cultural traits.

Main Conditions behind Cultural Diffusion:

1. A cultural group adopts a cultural trait from another cultural group only if such a cultural trait is beneficial to the former either socially, economically, or both.
2. Cultural traits may lose their originality and can be modified by imitators based on their own needs and circumstances.
3. In the process of cultural diffusion, diffusion always takes place from a higher cultural group to a lower cultural group or from a developed cultural group to an undeveloped cultural group.
4. During the process of diffusion, certain changes occur in the culture of the imitator group.
5. If diffusion doesn't take place, it means there is a lack of transportation, communication, or certain other barriers like water bodies, mountains, etc.

Diffusion is thought to understand culture vis-à-vis the origin and spread of cultural traits. Diffusionists criticized many concepts of evolutionists, particularly the psychic unity of mankind.

Q 7. British school of diffusionism

Ans. Elliot Smith was the founder of the British School of Diffusion. This school of thought is also known as the Pan Egyption School because the founder of this school considered Egypt to be the centre of civilization. Perry was the main supporter of Elliot Smith. Both of them are also known as Egyptologists.

Elliot Smith: His first book was "The Origin of Civilization," in which he mentioned that Egypt was the main centre of civilization. According to him, well-irrigated agriculture, pottery, ploughing, writing, etc. were invented or discovered first of all by Egyptians. They also established the institutions of law, political organisation, etc. They discovered navigation and travelled to faraway places in search of precious objects.

In this process, they also diffused their cultural traits among the population they visited, but people were weak imitators. Thus, according to him, Egypt was the only centre of culture and civilization from which cultural traits were diffused.

According to him, all those people who were beyond civilization were natural people, but when they came into contact with Egypt, they also became civilised.

Smith observed many similarities between the Egyptian complex of large stones as a symbol of the sun god and the megaliths of England, the Japanese pagodas, the Mayan pyramids, certain temples in Cambodia, and American Indian burials. These similarities compelled him to think that these structures were actually first erected by Egyptians, and through diffusion, they spread among others. All those human groups that were without megaliths or pyramids were actually not in contact with Egypt. Thus, according to him, the diffusion of all traits of culture and civilization came only from Egypt. He explained the same idea of diffusion from Egypt to other parts of the world in his second book "Diffusion of Culture"

William James Perry: He also considered Egypt to be the only cultural cradle in the world. He wrote the book "Children of the Sun," in which he mentioned that Egyptians are the children of the sun, thus they worship the sun. Sun worship is an ancient form of belief and religion. Sun worship diffused to other parts of the world from Egypt. He further mentioned that pyramids, temples, and the use of gold and silver for ornamentation are only due to the diffusion of these practises from Egypt to other parts of the world. According to him, every trait of civilization possessed by any human group is the result of its contacts, either directly or indirectly, with Egypt.

W.H.R. Rivers: He came to India in 1904 to study the Todas of the Nilgiri Hills. A monograph on 'Todas' was published in 1906, which was the most classical monograph ever presented on any Indian tribe. Until the publication of this monograph, he was not influenced by the school of diffusionism because he didn't mention anything about the diffusion of Hinduism among Todas. In 1 911, he wrote a paper entitled 'Ethnological Analysis of Culture', in which he declared that he was a diffusionist. Almost at the same time, he presented an article with a degenerative orientation entitled 'Disappearance of Useful Arts'. In this article, he mentioned that cultural traits do not always progress but can experience degeneration. In this article, he also mentions the uninventive nature of the human mind. The univentive and degenerative aspects were explained by him in his book "History of Melanesian Society".

In this book, he mentions that the inhabitants of many small islands live without canoes. But he remarked that it was not possible for them to reach these islands without canoes. Thus, their ancestors were acquainted with them, but gradually, the canoe craft guild degenerated and eventually disappeared. Through this reference, he proved the disappearance or degeneration of cultural traits. He observed five different burial practises among Australian aborigines, who otherwise constitute a homogenous group residing in the same geographical region. Austradian aborigines, according to him, are simple and uninventive, so they could not develop all these burial practises on their own. Therefore, he thought that small successive migrations took place from different regions to Australia, but only men came here, and they married local women. Under compulsion, they give up their languages and totally assimilate themselves into Australian culture. They gave up all habits except one, i.e., their burial practise, to which they were emotionally attached. Thus, there emerged a variation in burial practises.

According to River, cultural similarities can best be understood from the perspective of migration and diffusion because cultural similarities among different human groups are the result of cultural diffusion.

Criticism:

1. British diffusionists were really anti-evolutionists, and they held the unanimous opinion that inventions were rare and cultural changes among the human population were due to diffusion. It may be true that people have borrowed more than they invented, but it cannot be said that all inventions took place at a particular place and at a particular time, as advocated by these diffusionists.
2. They were so biassed in their scheme that they considered only Egypt as the cultural cradle and claimed that all human groups borrowed culture from Egypt, which is actually not the truth.
3. While providing their scheme of diffusionism, they mostly talked about the diffusion of material culture and thus ignored the process of diffusion of non-material culture.
4. Rivers claimed that ritual practise among Australian aborigines is due to the fact that migrators were emotionally attached to burial practises, thus they didn't shun them. But he failed to explain why the original settlers gave up their own burial practises, to which they might be emotionally attached.

According to Lowie, due to the biased and united approach of British diffusionists, they were the last to appear and the first to disappear from the scene of British anthropology.

Q 8. German school of diffusionism

Ans. The German diffusionists were not extreme diffusionists like their British counterparts. Although their scheme was also based on diffusion, they also talk about evolutionism.

According to them, culture originates from multiple cultural circles. Cultural traits have not originated in a particular place because cultural traits evolve differently and freely at different places, and then they are diffused or migrated to different parts of the world. However, it is not necessary that every cultural trait be diffused to every part of the world.

The German diffusionists are of the opinion that cultural traits evolve in particular cultural circles or cultural districts during different time periods, and then cultural traits are diffused from one cultural circle to another, thus revealing similarities between cultural traits in different cultural circles. According to them, the diffusion can be analysed in terms of historical facts. As they talk about cultural circles or cultural districts, this school is also known as Kulture Kriese School. Also, they put stress on understanding diffusion on the basis of historical facts; thus, this school is also known as the Culture Historic School. Ratzel, Graebner, and Schmidt were the main pioneers of the German School of diffusionism.

Ratzel: Ratzel is regarded as the founder of the German School of Diffusion. He wrote a book entitled "Volka Kunda", i.e., the history of mankind. In this book, like other diffusionists, he mentions that every human group has borrowed more and invented less. In this book, he warned that every similarity should not be considered a result of historical connection because certain cultural elements are always similar due to their similar utility. For instance , canoe sails always need paddles and arrows, and spearheads are always pointed, so all those human groups that are canoe, arrow, and spear exhibit similarity in the basic construction of material culture. But if there are similarities in certain items that go beyond their utility, then a historical connection can be established. For example, if canoe paddles as used by different groups possess certain similar engravings or spear shafts have feathers, then historical connections cannot be ruled out. He observed the arrows and spears of Africans and found that the shaft of their spears is ornamented, and their arrow heads contain certain engravings that are similar to those of Indonesians. Thus, he conclude d that diffusion has taken place either from Africa or from Indonesia.

He further remarked that, in the course of diffusion, cultural traits may be elaborated on or modified according to local conditions. He termed it the principle that items should be viewed beyond their utility perspective to establish historical connections (the criteria of form).

Graebner: Graebner was another German diffusionist. He wrote a book entitled "Methodder Ethnology" (Ethnological Methods). In his books, he mentions that two principles are enough to establish historical relations, i.e., a criterion of form or a criterion of quality. Criteria of form convey that if there is similarity between certain items that is beyond the perspective of their utility, then there is really a historical connection between such groups that exhibit these similarities. Criteria of quantity signifies that the quantity of similarities establishes the duration of historical connection, i.e., if similarities exist in a large number of items, then it can be said that there was a prolonged historical connection between such groups that exhibit the similarity.

Graebner talks about six layers of cultural circles:

1. Tasmanian culture (the earliest one)
2. Australian boomerang culture
3. Totemic Hunting Culture
4. Horticulturistic Culture
5. Melanesian Low Culture
6. Polynesian patrilineal culture

According to him, these cultures, alone or in combination, also exist in Africa and elsewhere.

Schmidt: He not only talked about historical connections but also provided a classification of cultural circles. According to him, there were four cultural circles:

1. Primitive Culture Circle
2. Primary Culture Circle
3. Secondary Culture Circle
4. Tertiary Culture Circle

According to him, primitive culture circles are characterised by hunting and gathering; primary culture circles by pastoralism; secondary culture circles by agriculture; and tertiary culture circles by the emergence of civilization.

According to him, respective cultural traits first of all appeared in the respective culture circle, and then traits diffused from that culture circle.

Criticism:

1. German diffusionists talk about cultural circles, but they don't mention the actual centres of such circles. Also, many studies were conducted, but no centre for such cultural circles was established. Also, it is not feasible to accept that diffusion took place only at 4-5 bands, as explained by Graebner.
2. German diffusionists only talk about diffusion, but they don't mention how diffusion took place or what the modes were through which such diffusion occurred.
3. German diffusionists also mention that every human genome has borrowed more than invented itself, which may not be the universal truth.

Q 9. American school of diffusionism

Ans. The American School of Diffusion was founded by Franz Boas, Clark Wissler, and A.L. Kroeber. It addressed the problem of how diffusionism takes place.

Postulates:

1. According to the American School of Diffusion, the give and take of cultural traits and cultural complexes took place through the means of transportation and communication because, due to these means, contact was established between two cultural groups. To explain diffusion, they desired a culture-area appr oach. A culturalarea is a geographical area occupied by groups whose cultures show a great degree of similarity w hen groupedtogether.
2. They were of the opinion that those human groups that reside nearby have a greater opportunity for give and take. Thus, such groups reflect more cultural similarities than those who line apart and have less opportunity for give and take.
3. American diffusionists also discarded the conception that one cultural group is more progressive than another because, according to them, every cultural group evolves according to its own adaptation and historical setup.
4. According to them, certain factors like mountains, water bodies, thick forests, etc. acted as hurdles in the process of cultural diffusion. Thus, all those human groups that are separated by these barriers have their own unique cultures, and they would experience change when contact was established between them.
5. American diffusionists were of the opinion that it was not feasible to understand the cultures of the whole world simultaneously. Thus, they classified the world into various geographical regions, with every such region known as a cultural area. Therefore, this school is also known as a cultural area school.

Franz Boas: Franz Boas was the founder of this school. But later on, due to his shift towards the study of cultural groups from a historical perspective, he was regarded as the founder of a new school of historical particularism. Clark Wissler and A.L. Kroeber, students of Franz Boas, were the main proponents of this school.

Clark Wissler: According to Wissler, the cultures of no two groups could be similar, and the similarities that exist between cultural groups of different populations are due to the diffusion of cultural traits and cultural complexes.

He further mentions that those human groups that live closer reflect more cultural similarities than those that live far away from one another. According to him, an area that reflects similar cultures is known as a culture area.

Actually, the term culture area was coined by Oil T. Mason in one of his works "Influence of Environment on Human Industries or Art". When he studied many tribes, he classified them into different geographical regions. Although this term was coined by Mason, it was scientifically applied in anthropology by Clark Wissler. According to him, natives of the new world cannot be classified on the basis of cultural traits, because that will give us food areas, textile areas, ceramic areas, etc., but if all these traits are considered simultaneously and we shift our approach from trait to complex and from individual to social, we get cultural areas. In simple terms, Wissler mentions that a culture area is an area that reflects cultural similarities within a bounded geographical region.

According to Wissler, historical relations among human populations can also be established by applying the cultural area approach. Clark Wissler put forth the concept of a culture centre. According to him, a culture centre is such a centre within a cultural area from where cultural traits and cultural complexes spread to the whole cultural area. He further maintains that those places within the cultural area that were near the cultural centre were known as cultural traits or cultural complexes earlier than those that were away from the cultural centre.

In order to understand the relative age of a cultural trait or cultural complex, he put forth the oncept of an age area. According to him, by applying the concept of age area, the relative age of a cultural trait or cultural complex can be estimated by analysing its geographical distribution. If a cultural trait or cultural complex exhibits more geographical distributions, then, according to Wissler, it is regarded as an older trait or older complex than those whose geographical distribution is limited.

A.L. Kroeber: A.L. Kroeber was another main authority in the American School of Diffusion. Kroeber put forth concepts like culture intensity, culture complex, and culture is super individual and superorganic.

According to Kroeber, culture intensity reflects the degree to which norms, customs, material objects, etc. of units are absorbed by other units. Higher cultural intensity means more imitation, and lesser intensity means less imitation.

Kroeber maintained that there are certain cultural elements that are beyond a statistical approach, and he included belief systems, philosophy, and other elements of intellectual life under such elements, which he termed sensitive indicators. According to him, sensitive indications are more diagnostic indicators of cultural intensity in comparison to other elements. If sensitive indicators of two groups also exhibit greater similarity, it indicates extreme diffusion rather than those who differ in their sensitive indicators.

A.L. Kroeber also put forth the concept of cultural climax, which is similar to Wissler's concept of culture centre. According to Kroeber, culture climax is that point from where various cultural traits and cultural complexes are diffused, and culture is able to acquire complex traits only due to culture climax.

The concepts of super individual and super organic were given by Herbert Spencer, defined by E.B. Taylor, and applied in anthropology by A.L. Kroeber. According to A.L. Kroeber, although culture is learned by an individual and can also be transmitted by an individual to next generation, culture is not the creation of a single individual; it is the creation of a number of individuals. The particular habits and behaviours of an individual cannot become part of culture unless such habits and behaviours are adopted and practised by society. Also, the habits and behaviours of a particular individual die with the death of that individual, but culture always persists because it is social in nature. Thus, Kroeber termed culture super individual. He also held the view that culture is superorganic. According to him, many plants, vegetables, fruits, etc. are organic, but when viewed culturally, they have different meanings. Therefore, culture is superorganic.

Criticism:

1. They put forth the concept of culture area thus trying to understand diffusion on the basis of geographical region. It is not easy to classify the whole world into culture areas; thus, through the concept of culture area, only the diffusion of certain areas can be estimated and not the diffusion of the whole world.
2. Wissler put forth the concept of a culture centre, and Kroeber put forth the concept of a culture climax. These concepts convey that traits and complexes are inverted or discovered only at these points and then diffused from here, which cannot be acceptable.
3. The culture area approach is also criticised on the basis that it is difficult to list down all cultural traits and cultural complexes as advocated by these diffusionists.
4. These diffusionists are also criticised on the grounds that they divided cultural areas on the basis of geographical regions, whereas some critics are of the opinion that such areas could be established on the basis of common languages, food habits, common traditions, etc.
5. It was observed later on that cultural areas, classified by these diffusionists, vary in many cultural traits and cultural complexes.

Q 10. Functionalism (Malinowski)

Ans. The functional school of thought was established by Malinowski, and he was influenced by Durkheim, experimental psychology, etc. These influences on Malinowski prompted him to think that every cultural trait has a function.

Postulates:

1. Culture is meant to fulfil certain needs.
2. Every cultural trait, cultural element, or cultural aspect has a function.
3. Cultural traits and cultural aspects are organised in the form of social institutions; every social institution has to function in an organised way to fulfil various human needs.
4. Earlier needs were not sophisticated, so culture was simple. Every sophisticated need adds a complex element to culture. Thus, complexity in culture is related to the sophistication of needs because, in order to fulfil sophisticated needs, culture has to function differently.
5. The basic function of culture is to fulfil human needs, modify human needs, and endorse human needs.
6. Culture is dynamic.

Concept of culture: According to Malinowski, culture includes artefacts, goods, technical processes, ideas, habits, values, and a social system or social structure. Malinowski includes social structure or social system within the ambit of culture because, according to him, social system or social structure cannot be understood beyond the perspective of culture.

As part of his concept of culture, he maintains that every cultural trait should not be studied individually but should be studied in relation to others because all cultural traits are interrelated and interdependent. Thus, they should be studied as an integrated whole. It is also known as Malinowski's theory of cultural integration.

Malinowski further remarks that every characteristic or trait of culture that is functionless will not be able to survive. Therefore, in order to remain in continuity, every cultural trait has to perform its respective function.

Malinowski, as part of its concept of culture, further advocates that humans, as biological and social beings, have certain needs, and it is the obligation of cultural traits to fulfil such needs, which are essential for the survival of humans. If the culture becomes functionless, both culture and humans will not be able to survive.

Theory of functionalism: Malinowski, in his book "Magic, Religion, and Science", put forth his theory of functionalism. Earlier, when he was not a functionalist but was working among Trobriand Islanders, he observed that certain cultural traits or certain institutions have prescribed functions, and such functions are also related to the physical survival of humans. Consequently, he attempted to understand the functional aspects of such traits and institutions, which ultimately led to the emergence of his theory of functionalism. According to Malinowski, magic provides confidence to human groups to perform certain activities even if they lack actual knowledge; similarly, religion also acts as an outlet for frustration, so the basic function of magic and religion is to provide emotional strength to individuals in times of frustration and stress. While illustrating Trobriand Islanders, Malinowski cited that they are experts in boat making, but they always remain under stress because storms can draw their boats. Therefore, they perform many magic tricks before going on fishing expeditions. Thus, the biological survival of Trobriand Islanders is also associated with one of their cultural aspects, magic.

While defining functionalism, Malinowski states that in every civilization, each custom, tradition, artefact, belief system, and good has a certain function to perform, and civilization is able to survive due to the functioning aspect of culture.

According to Malinowski, human beings have certain needs for food, shelter, reproduction, safety, clothing, etc., and all such needs are fulfilled through certain cultural responses. Different cultural traits are devised as functional units to fulfil the basic and derived needs of humans. Basic needs are actually biological needs, and derived needs are such needs that are created to fulfil basic needs.

Malinowski explains his functionalism through a charter of institutions. According to Malinowski, an institution is created to fulfil human needs. For instance, in order to fulfil the need for reproduction, there are institutions of marriage, family, and so on. The character of an institution signifies the basic purpose or aim of the institution.

According to charter theory, every institution or society has individuals who have certain norms or values, which prompt them to acquire material apparatus. Through material apparatus, activities take place, and such activities lead to function.

Theory of need: Malinowski explained his theory of need in his book "Scientific Theory of Culture", which was published after his death. The functional aspect of Malinowski signifies that cultural traits have to function in an organised or desired way to fulfil various human needs. In his theory of need, he properly elaborates on the different needs of humans. He classified human needs into three types:

1. Primary needs, or basic needs, or biological needs
2. Secondary needs, or derived needs, or instrumental needs
3. Tertiary needs or integrative needs

Under primary needs, he put certain biological needs like food and sex. Under instrumental needs, he puts those needs that are created to fulfil basic needs. Integrative needs are imperative for the integration of society.

According to Malinowski, for every need there is a cultural response, as he explained in the following table: primary need and consequent cultural response.

Primary Need	Cultural Response	Primary Need	Cultural Response
Metabolism	Commissariat	Movement	Activities
Reproduction	Kinship	Growth	Training
Bodily Comfort	Shelter	Health	Hygiene
Safety	Protection		

Through various cultural responses, all basic needs are fulfilled. In addition to primary and instrumental needs, Malinowski talked about integrated needs, which can create cohesiveness among members of society, strengthen solidarity between them, and create integration within society. According to Malinowski, due to integrated needs, culture responds in the form of customs, traditions, religion, mythology, etc.

Malinowski, through his theory of need, attempts to explain that it is only due to needs that various cultural traits and institutions exist. When a new need is created, culture responds in a new way, which brings about a change in culture. Also, the simplicity of need corresponds to a simple culture. But when needs become sophisticated, culture also has to respond in a sophisticated way; thus, complexities emerge in culture. Thus, he relates the dynamic nature of culture to the emergence of new needs. Simply put, he says that culture is adoptive because new needs prompt culture to adopt in a new way. Also, when need becomes absolute, then cultural traits related to it also become absolute. In order to fulfil their various needs, human beings have created secondary or artificial environments out of the natural environment. Such a secondary or artificial environment is nothing but culture. Thus, according to Malinowski, human beings fulfil their various needs through their culture.

Criticism:

1. If the needs of individuals are the same, then why do cultural variations exist?
2. Why do certain cultural patterns arise to fulfil needs that can be fulfilled by any alternative?

Q 11. Structural – Functionalism (Radcliffe Brown)

Ans Radcliffe Brown was the main pioneer of the structural-functional school. According to him, the main components of social structure are human beings; social structure itself signifies the arrangement of human beings into institutionalised and regulated relations.

Later on, in his book "Structure and Function in Primitive Society", he again defined social structure. Here, he defined social structure as human beings connected through a complex web of relationships, and due to such relationships, social structure emerged.

Radcliffe Brown's Theory of Social Structure: Radcliffe Brown first put forth the concept of social structure in 1914 while delivering a lecture on social anthropology at Birmingham. He elaborated on the concept of social structure during his presidential address to the Royal Institute of Anthropology of Great Britain in 1940. But he explained his theory of social structure in his book, "Structure and Function in Primitive Society".

According to him, structure means the arrangement of parts or components that are related to one another in particular patterns. For instance, the structure of a house reveals the arrangement of walls, roofs, windows, doors, etc. Due to the proper arrangement of all these parts of the house, the structure of the house is built. Similarly, the structure of a physical organism is also composed of many parts like tissue, cells, bones, etc. But all these parts are properly arranged. Similarly, social structure signifies the arrangement of a person in institutionalised relationships, i.e., social structure not only consists of persons but should also be arranged in terms of relationships. For instance, in a village, people are arranged into families and households, which reflect the structure of the village; furthermore, every part of the village itself reflects structure. For example, a family consists of a mother, father, and children; thus, it is a structural unit of society and has its own internal structure. As part of his theory of social structure, Redcliffe Brown put forth structural features of social life.

Elements of Social Structure: According to R. Brown, social structure has the following elements, which he explained in the form of systems:

1. **Normative System:** Every social structure has devised certain norms for its components, and every member of the social structure has to act according to such norms. Thus, social structure is normative.
2. **Positional System:** It signifies that in every social structure, each person has a status and a corresponding role. The success of social structure is based upon the proper functioning of roles by every individual with respect to their status.
3. **Sanction System:** Every social structure has devised certain sanctions, i.e., modes of response to one's acts. The effectiveness of social structures is based on criteria such as how efficient the sanction system is.
4. **System of Anticipated Response:** The anticipated response system conveys that every member of the social structure should participate in social life. Social structures act effectively if their members understand their duties as social beings and act accordingly.

Structure and Features of Social Life: According to Radcliffe Brown, the structural features of social life are as follows:

1. **Existence of Social Groups:** The social structure is reflected through the existence of social groups, which are family, clan, kingroups, etc.
2. **Existence of internal structures of social groups:** Every social group in a social structure has its own internal structure. For instance, families as social groups have their own structure, which is reflected in the presence of the father, mother, and children in the family and their respective roles towards each other.
3. **Existence of Social Divisions:** Social groups in social structures are divided on the basis of sex, caste, class, etc. For example, there is social stratification in India on the basis of caste. Similarly, there is a class division in western countries.
4. **Existence of Social Distances:** In social structures, there may be social distance between different social groups, which can be illustrated by the distance between Brahmins and Shudras among Hindus.
5. **Existence of Dyadic Relationships:** In social structure, there are also dyadic relationships, i.e., person-to-person relationships, for instance, between husband and wife, master and servant, etc.
6. **Existence of relationships between person groups and between groups:** According to Brown, in social structure, every person is related to another group. Due to these relationships, the social structure is able to sustain itself.

Structural Continuity: As part of his theory of social structure, R. Brown put forth the concept of structural continuity. According to him, as social structures are composed of human beings, they always remain in continuity. With the passage of time, social structure may change, but form remains the same. For instance, old ones die and new ones are born, but they always remain human beings as components of social structure.

Structure and Function: In his book "Structure and Function in Primitive Society", R. Brown also inter relates structure and function; he again depends on biology. According to him, a biological organism consists of many organs, and such organs create the structure of the organism. But just the presence of organs doesn't make an organism meaningful because every organ has to function properly so that an organism can survive. Also, every organ is interdependent and related to other. organs. Similarly, in social structure, there are many social groups, and every social group functions in a proper way so that social structure can remain in continuity. Also, every social group is interdependent and interrelated with every other social group. R. Brown inter relates the structure and function of society and mentions that there is a relationship between function and structure because it is due to function that structure is able to survive. E.g., Bathonga's joking relationship between the mother's brother and the sister's son is to maintain patrilineage.

Difference between functionalism and structural functionalism:

1. Malinowski took the individual as a unit and thought that social institutions came into being and persist because they fulfil the needs of an individual. These needs are both biological and psychological. That is why it is also known as bio-psychological functionalism. His approach is also called bottom-up (individual > society) because it places the primacy of the individual before society. On the other hand, Radcliffe-Brown's structure-functionalism puts society before individuals. He believed that social institutions existed because their primary function was to maintain society and social solidarity. His approach is also known as the top-down (society > individual) approach.
2. Functionalism seeks to explain social institutions from the perspective of their functions, while structural functionalism sees society as a functional interplay of different components forming an overall structure.
3. Functionalism is concerned with relations between the needs of an individual and the satisfaction of those needs through cultural and social frameworks. Structural Functionalism tends to be less concerned with individual action or need and more with the place of individuals in the social order, or indeed with the construction of the social order itself.
4. Malinowski suggested that individuals have certain biological needs and that social institutions exist to meet these needs. Radcliffe-Brown focused on social-structural needs rather than biological ones.

Criticism:

1. It leads to static analysis and analysis without space.
2. It is unable to study social conflicts.
3. M. Harris points out that techno-economic parameters are not given importance.
4. Unable to answer how any tribe has a particular system.

Q 12. Structuralism (Levi Strauss and E. Leach)

Ans. According to Levi Strauss, the basic objective of the structure of human society is to understand the structure of human society. L. Strauss remarked that it is essential to observe the innate and deep tendency behind the creation of the structure of society, and he equated such a tendency with the human mind, i.e., according to him, the basic theme of structuralism is to establish that the human mind is only responsible for the creation of social structure. Levi Strauss holds that the human mind has an unconscious tendency to categorise objects into binary opposites like 'hot vs. cold', 'good vs. bad', 'light vs. dark', 'cooked vs. raw,' etc. He states that the human mind has classified the whole world into contrasting parts and developed a logical set of relationships. The most significant contrasting pair is 'self vs. others' because, due to this contrasting pain, a person is able to understand the existence of others, and suchunderstanding leads to the creation of culture.

As part of structuralism, L. Strauss mostly dealt with the rules of marriage. According to him, it is due to the ability of the human mind to think that marriages among siblings are bad and marriages between members of different families are good that the incest taboo emerged. Thus, the prohibition of incest is not due to any ethical setup but to the creation of the human mind. Taking it further, he remarked that the human mind was also capable of thinking about how incest taboo enhanced one's kin group and how incest taboo helped human beings in their survival. He illustrated an example in this regard: Suppose a guy of group A wants to kill a guy of group B, but if that guy of group B has many sisters, then the latter will not kill his sister's husband. Through these examples, he wants to convey that incest taboo minimises inter-group rivalries as it establishes relations of affinity between different families, thus extending the kinship horizon of the group. Thus, the human mind considers marriage between siblings as bad and marriage outside the family as good.

L. Strauss, in his book "The Elementary Structure of Kinship", explained how inter-individual relations are woven and how such relations lead to the creation of the structure of society. According to him, inter-individual relations are woven only through marriage, and what happens in marriage depends on binary opposites. In this book, he further mentions that incest-taboo leads to exogamy, through which reciprocity occurs within different families, which is reflected in the exchange of women as brides between different families. This exchange and reciprocity create social relations between different families, and the arrangement of such relations is actually social. Thus, the creation of social structure through incest taboo is an outcome of the human mind.

He further mentions that rules of marriage, myths, totems, patterns of clothing, food habits, etc. are also creations of the human mind. L. Strauss also attempts to understand how the structure of society is constructed. He associated the construction of the structure of society with the construction of language. According to him, the basic unit of language is the phoneme (word). These are certain prescribed rules by which phonemes are arranged so that language can become meaningful. Thus, every structuralist, according to him, should analyse such rules. He applied the same methodology to understand the construction of society when he opined that, like words in language, every society has basic units, and like proper arrangement of words makes language meaningful, similarly, proper arrangement of units of society makes society an actual entity, but how units of society that may be persons or social groups will be arranged is unconsciously decided by the human mind. L. Strauss also studied kinship terms; he also associated language with kinship terms. According to him, like a phoneme (word), every kin term has meanin g, but every kin term is integrated with another one, and this integration of kin terms leads to the creation of kin groups, and the structure of society is nothing but the composition of kin groups. Thus, through the construction of language, he tries to make the concept of structuralism understandable.

E. LEACH: He put forth his theory of structuralism in his book "Political System of Highland Burma," which he compiled after studying the Kachin and Shan of Burma. According to Leach, many rules of marriage, religious practises, myths, totems, etc. are creations of the human mind. Like Strauss, Leach also advocates that the human mind always perceives things in binary opposition, i.e., if the human mind has to know about hot, then it should know what is cold; if the human mind considers something good, then it must know what is bad; and so on. E. Leach also considers competition and conflict as part of structuralism. According to him, sometimes social structures experience change due to competition or conflict. Among the Kachin and Shan of Burma, he observed that in order to raise their status, groups may change the rule of marriage, i.e., from monogamous to polygynous, because they claim that having more wives means having more status. Similarly, sometimes they deliberately change their myths and totems. A group may claim myth as reality or trace their ancestry to a brave mythological hero; similarly, a group may become separated from a larger group due to certain conflicts and then claim a strong animal or more valuable plant as a totem. By citing examples, he attempts to explain that although structuralism is the creation of the human mind, change in structuralism is associated with certain changing circumstances and needs, so change is not associated with the human mind.

The structuralism of L. Strauss also doesn't explain the process of cultural change because, according to him, the structure of society is the outcome of the structure of the mind, which more or less remains static. If we accept this principle, then the structure of society should also remain static, which we know is not true because there are many cultural or social changes from time to time. It was later modified by E. Leach, who explained the process of cultural change.

Criticism:

1. Many critics consider the structuralism of L. Strauss vague because, according to them, it seems to them that L. Strauss attempts to create structure himself rather than analyse already existing structures.
2. If we analyse L. Strauss structuralism, it also conveys the psychic unity of mankind because, according to Strauss, the cultural trait of every cultural group is the creation of the minds of members of such groups, but this cannot be true because processes of give and take occur during different time periods among different human groups, so one human group may borrow many traits that may be mythological totems from other groups. Thus, structuralism totally discards the concept of diffusionism, but historical accounts prove that diffusion took place among human groups from time to time.
3. L. Strauss's methodology regarding the construction of society in relation to the construction of language is also critical because, according to many critics, rules that govern the construction of language should not be the same as rules that govern the construction of society because words as units of language are not social, whereas humans as units of society are social.
4. Many cross-cultural studies have ignored the hypothesis of E. Leach.

Q.13 Ruth Benedict

Ans. Culture and Personality School worked on three aspects:

1. How culture shapes a group's personality
2. How personality develops culture
3. How culture and personality are inseparable

These three aspects of this school become clear by analysing the contributions of individual advocates for this school. Ruth Benedict deals with how personality influences culture.

Although the concept of culture pattern was known even before R. Benedict, she was the first to make an attempt to study the cultural pattern of a particular group. In her book, "Patterns of Culture", while giving her concept of culture pattern, she also talks about culture configuration. Her concept of cultural patterns runs as follows: According to her, culture can be classified into many large sections, many small sections, and many sub-sections. When subsections are arranged in a meaningful way, then sections and large sections also become meaningful. This process is known as configuration of culture, and when culture is configured by the proper arrangement of its parts, we get cultural patterns, and the number of cultural patterns forms culture as a whole.

Every culture consists of cultural traits. They are grouped in complex and complexes later form culture patterns. e.g., age of marriage is a trait; it groups with other traits into the culture complex of marriage. Other complexes like religion, economy etc. group with marriage to form a cultural pattern.

According to her, the integration of cultural patterns is due to the influence of a certain genius known as the genius of cultural patterns. She talks about two such geniuses: Apollonian and Dionysian.

The word Apollonian is derived from the sun god Apollo, who is regarded as kind, disciplined, and very cooperative. Thus, if the cultural patterns of any group reflect these traits, they are regarded as having been inf luenced by Apollonian genius. She put forth the example of Pueblo Zuni in Mexico in this regard. According to her, Pueblo Zuni are very peaceful, very kind, very disciplined, and very cooperative. They practise magic for the welfare of all. For instance, they fling large boulders down hills with the assumption that the rumbling sound of large boulders will bring rain, as does the sound of a thunder storm. Thus, here, the performance of magic is for all.

The world of Dionysius is derived from God Dionysius, who always remains in an intoxicated mood and leads a luxurious life; thus, this God is not considered disciplined, full of jealousy, in conflict with others, and also selfish. All those cultural patterns that reflect the above traits are regarded as influenced by Dionysian genius. She cited the examples of Dobu of Melanesia and Kwakiutl of British Columbia in this regard.

According to her, Dobu are very selfish, deceivers, never fulfil promises, very aggressive, and always harm others. They even practise imitative magic to harm others. Likewise, Kwakiutl are very materialistic; they always attempt to grab more wealth by hook or crook. Among them, those who possess few materials are ashamed of them; thus, maximisation of profit is their only motive. Self-assertion is also a personality trait among them. For self-assertion, they observe a ceremony known as potlatching, in which a person destroys more than he can handle.

Actually, through these examples, she attempts to explain how the personality of a group influences the culture of the concerned group because the culture of the above groups is the outcome of their personality traits.

Ruth Benedict's Study on National Character: During WWII, it became impossible to conduct fieldwork, so Ruth Benedict decided to study Japanese from a distance, and she made the study of Japanese the basis of her study. She interacted with many POWs (prisoners of war) and also analysed Japanese literature to know the national character of the Japanese. She came to know that Japanese adopted two different methods in the socialisation process. She explained in her book "Chrysanthemum and the Sword" that in Japan, from infancy to childhood, parents pay special attention to offspring with love and kindness, but when offspring are moving towards adulthood, parents leave them alone, and consequently, adults become aggressive. The title of her book properly explained this socialisation process. Chrysanthemum is the national flower of Japan, so initially parents grow their offspring so that they can blossom like Chrysanthemum, but when they become adults, parents don't cooperate with them; they have to do it on their own, thus the sword is always hanging at their neck. This process of socialisation makes them aggressive. Through this study, R. Benedict attempts to show that the aggressive nature of Japanese adults is a result of their socialisation process. She further mentions that when Japanese children are minors, their personalities reflect Apollonian genius, but when they become adults, their personalities reflect Dionysian genius.

Criticism:

1. Morris Opler, in his book "Apache Life Way", criticised Ruth Benedict on the basis that only two ideals or geniuses can influence all human groups, as there are many factors behind personality formation. Morris Opler talks about cultural themes. According to him, there are many cultural themes like inspiration, motivation, etc. that create personality.
2. Why does culture or its members have a particular personality?
3. How is personality transmitted from one generation to another?
4. Ignored concepts that don't fit in, like drunkenness among Pueblo people or self-control practise by Kwakiutl people.

Q 14. Margaret Mead

Ans. Culture and Personality School worked on three aspects:

1. How culture shapes a group's personality
2. How personality develops culture
3. How culture and personality are inseparable

These three aspects of this school become clear by analysing the contributions of individual advocates for this school. Margaret Mead deals with how culture shapes a group's personality.

Like Ruth Benedict, Margaret Mead was another lady anthropologist at this school. Her first book was "Coming of Age in Samoa", in which she attempted to explain whether rebellion among adolescents in many societies is due to biological changes that occur at the time of puberty or whether it is due to cultural circumstances.

Her second book was "Growing up in New Guinea". According to her, among them, boys and girls are groomed equally; both boys and girls are allowed to mix together; there are no restrictions on premarital and extramarital relations; both boys and girls follow social norms; and so on. Thus, among them, both boys and girls are not too aggressive towards sexuality. But in many other societies, like America, such freedom is limited, so her boys and girls develop different types of personalities.

The third book was "Sex and Temperament in Three Primitive Societies", which dealt with three societies: Arapesh, Mundugumor, and Tschambuli. By studying these three societies, she attempts to understand why different groups that reside in the same region possess different cultures and consequent personalities. According to her, Arapesh resides in such a geographical area, which is totally the same, and they have no fear of external threats. Also, their population is low and their resources are abundant; hence, they don't have to compete with others for lack of resources. Thus, their personalities are reflected in such traits as being peace-loving, cooperative, kind, not quarrelsome, not jealous, and not involving themselves in conflicts.

Another group from the same region is Mundugumor, which reflects and contrasts the personality of Arapesh. Here, both males and females are aggressive; people indulge in quarrels, conflicts, etc. due to the aggressive nature of their parents, and offspring are also aggressive. Among them, the status of a person is based upon the number of wives; having more wives means higher status. Therefore, every person attempts to grab more and more wives. Due to which there is conflict and competition among males. Among them, marriage through exchange is prevalent, where a person has to exchange his daughter for a new wife, which in these cases leads to female infanticide due to the multiplicity of wives. The multiple wives always quarrel with one another, and wives also quarrel with their husbands. There is always conflict between father and son on the issue of the exchange of a girl for a new wife. Thus, due to all these factors, the Mundugumor possess traits like being quarrelsome, jealous, aggressive, indulgent in conflicts, not so kind, etc.

The third group, which is Tschambuli, reflects another personality trait. Among them, males are suppressive, but females are aggressive because females have the choice to decide their husbands; husbands have to do all the jobs like cooking, washing clothes, etc., and wives just enjoy their lives. This culture of Tschambuli makes men submissive and women aggressive.

Through the above studies, she attempts to make it clear that it is actually culture that moulds the personality of a group. She also analysed the national character of Americans, Japanese, and Russians in her book "And keep your powder dry: An anthropologist looks at America". She found that, like Japanese, American minors are also full of love and kindness, but that certain differences in national character can be seen at a glance between American adults and Japanese adults because of their different socialisation processes. She further remarked that, in order to understand the national character, it is necessary to analyse the historical set-up of such nations rather than only contemporary aspects.

Q 15. Ralph Linton, Kardiner, and Cora Du Bois

Ans. Culture and Personality School worked on three aspects:

1. How culture shapes a group's personality
2. How personality develops culture
3. How culture and personality are inseparable

These three aspects of this school become clear by analysing the contributions of individual advocates for this school. Ralph Linton, Kardiner, and Cora Du Bois deal with how culture and personality are inseparable.

Ralph Linton: His most famous book was "The Cultural Background of Personality". In this book, he defines culture as 'the sum total of knowledge, attitudes, and natural behaviour patterns shared and transmitted by members of a particular society'.

On the basis of behaviour patterns, he classified culture into three types:

1. Real culture is the actual behaviour of members of society.
2. Ideal culture: ideological and traditional culture
3. Cultural construct: what has been written down about culture?

Linton also distinguished between cultural universals, cultural alternatives, and cultural specialists. Cultural universals signify that there are certain universal cultural traits; for instance, weaving clothes is one of these cultural universals, whereas the nature and way of making clothes may vary. Religion also conveys cultural universals. Cultural alternatives mean some people have the choice to adopt certain peculiar behaviour patterns that may not be followed by others. In some instances, one has the choice to eat food at home or at a restaurant. One has the choice either to train through trains or aeroplanes; one has the choice to follow any belief system or to follow none. The concept of cultural specialists signifies that, in every cultural group, certain individuals are specialists in carrying out certain cultural practises which is not the function of other members. For instance, scaring children is a specialty of mothers. Similarly, the performance of rituals is the specialty of the priest, and so on.

He also talks about sub-culture patterns and whole-culture patterns. Such sub-culture patterns reflect the peculiarities and uniqueness of a particular cultural group. For instance, Hindu culture is a subculture of Indian culture.

In his book, R. Linton also talks about contraculture. According to him, contra culture means a contrasting cultural pattern that is against the prevailing cultural pattern and may also pose a threat to the prevailing cultural pattern. For instance, a group of dacoits has different behaviour patterns, different norms, different activities, and different attitudes. This culture of dacoits is contraculture.

Linton was of the opinion that, on the basis of all the above cultural aspects, the personality of a group is formed, and when personality is formed, it also influences culture.

Linton also mentions that culture is a response to needs. He talks about two types of needs: biological and psychic. According to him, both needs are important for one's survival. For instance, children not only require their mother for milk or food but also for love and affection. The fulfilment of psychic needs also contributes greatly to the development of one's personality. Fulfilment of needs is due to the simultaneous response towards them, and he turned this principle into the simultaneous response principle.

Linton mentions that every society has a set pattern of socialisation during childhood and adulthood, and every society imparts almost similar customs and traditions among its members; thus, all members of a particular society exhibit an almost similar personality type, which he termed the 'Basic Personality' Type.

Kardinar: His most famous book is "The Psychological Frontier of Society". He, along with Ralph Lonton, developed the concept of the 'Basic personality' type. According to him, every individual in society almost shares similar behaviours, has a similar attitude, has undergone a similar socialisation process, and deals with similar situations. Thus, similar psychological behaviour is reflected by all members of society, and this similar psychological behaviour constitutes the basic personality type.

According to Kardinar, the institutions of society help provide information about personalities. He talks about two types of institutions: primary and secondary institutions. According to him, the basic objective of a primary institution is to carry out the socialisation process. He didn't provide any lists of primary institutions, but indirectly, he talked about family. Secondary institutions, according to him, fulfil needs and suppress frustrations that occur in the life of an individual from time to time, and such institutions are religions, myths, folklore, etc. According to Kardinar, changes in the nature of institutions also change one's personality. For instance, if a change occurs in an economic institution so that a mother has to work long hours outside the home, it will affect mother-child bonding, but if a mother has to stay for a longer duration at home; it will strengthen the emotional bond between mother and child. By citing the above reference, he attempts to illustrate that this type of relationship is also reflected in the basic personality type. The basic personality type can be understood by the Marquesans of Polynesia.

Among Marquesans, there is a scarcity of resources, so they devise ways not to get starved in the form of female infanticide. Due to female infanticides, there is an imbalance in the sex ratio, i.e., more men than women, and the alternative to this situation is polyandry, in which women have multiple husbands. Due to more husbands, women have to attend all of them. Therefore, she remains busy, and her children are neglected. Thereby, the emotional bond between mother and child is weak, and children are characterised by fearfulness, suspicion, and a lack of self-esteem. Children have been deprived of their mothers' love since infancy. Also, every husband is not able to get full attention from his wife, thus remaining devoid of her love, but he never complains of it because, since infancy, he has been devoid of love for women. The folklore and myth of the Marquesans also project females as wicked, heartless, food-sober, and cannibalistic. These folklores also create feelings of hatred towards women.

Thus, due to scarcity of resources, infanticide, polyandry, and inadequate attention towards children and husbands, the basic personalities of Marquesans are developed. According to Kardinar, every society has a different basic personality type, which is based upon different customs, traditions, behaviours, and circumstances or situations. The basic personality type also influences the culture of such a society.

Cora Du Bois: She was another renowned scholar of culture and personality. Alor is a small and obscure island in the Dutch East Indies. It lies directly north of central Timor, at the end of that long string of land fragments called the Lesser Sundas. More specifically, it is 8 degrees south of the equator and between 124 and 125 degrees longitude east of Greenwich. This places it about halfway between Java and New Guinea in an east-west line and about halfway between Australia and Celebes in a north-south line. The data that she collected from her studies was compiled into a book entitled "The People of Alora". Instead of the concept of a basic personality type, she used the term 'Model personality'.

According to her, it is the norm among the people of Alora that vegetarian food is collected by women and nonvegetarian food by men. As their economy is at a subsistence level, both father and mother have to spend more time outside the home, due to which emotional bonds between parents and children remain weak. Thus, Alorese children are full of chauvinism; they lack confidence and self-esteem. When children become adults, their relationships with their parents are strained, and they don't show any discipline towards their parents because they are not trained and groomed in a disciplined way. Even folklore and Alorases reflect the hatred of offspring towards parents.

Indiscipline, shallowness, lack of confidence, a life full of frustrations, etc. characterise the personality of Alorese. Cora du Bois termed such a personality type a 'model personality'.

According to her, every human group or society has a different model personality, which depends on different socialisation processes and behaviour patterns. Folklore and myths play a significant role in the formation of model personalities. Such model personalities are also part of the culture of the concerned group.

Q 16 Neo evolutionism

Ans. In the 19th century, classical evolutionists talked about the classical evolution of culture in terms of regularities and similarities, i.e., parallels that exist in different cultures of humans.

The evolutionists of the 20th century modified the approach and methodology of classical evolutionists with their own new methodology; thus, these evolutionists are known as neo-evolutionists. The most important ones are V.Gordon Childe, Julian Steward, Leslie White, Sahlin, and Service.

Main Theme: The neo-evolutionists were of the opinion that all the weaknesses of classical evolutionists can be solved if it is accepted that cultural evolution has not taken place in a unilinear sequence but through a parabolic curve. Parabolic Curve Theory conveys that social institutions evolve in a specific form during an early stage and then develop differently in different directions. Ultimately, such institutions moved towards their original form but in a different, more developed form. They cite examples of property ownership, nudity, and sex relations in this regard.

1. According to them, the institution of property evolved in the form of common ownership, but later on, particularly during medieval times, there evolved the concept of private ownership of property. But now again, the concept of common ownership of property has developed in the form of a state.
2. They were of the opinion that earlier there was a shortage of cloth due to which people remained naked; with the invention of clothes, gradually people began to cover their whole bodies, but again, under the compulsion of fashion, people like to remain half-naked.
3. This sequence is also applicable to sexual relationships. Earlier, there was sexual promiscuity; gradually, mating relations were regulated strictly, and monogamy evolved. But at present, there are discussions again in favour of sex freedom.

Advocators:

- **Childe:** The four-fold evolutionary scheme is based on material remains from differen archaeological periods.
- **White:** It is cultural materialism phrased in energy terms.
- **Steward:** Unilinear, universal, and multilinear culture ecology model.
- **Method:** Empirical, field work.
- **Criticism:** Functionalists said that they studied cultural traits in isolation and not as an integrated whole.

Q 17. Childe

Ans. Gordon Childe is the only pioneer of British school neo-evolutionists. He attempted to keep the theory of evolution alive. He wrote many books, but his most famous one was "Social Evolution", in which he explained the evolution of the culture of all mankind through different sequences. In this book, he narrates that the development of the culture of all mankind is influenced by three historical events: the invention of food production, urbanisation, and industrialization.

By analysing the transition that took place in the culture of all mankind, he put forth his theory of cultural evolution. Actually, he was an archaeologist, thus he propounded his theory of cultural evolution with respect to the evolution of archaeological periods and their corresponding features.

The evolution of archaeological periods and their corresponding features are tabulated below:

Archaeological stage	Way of life	Life activity
Palaeolithic	Savagery	Hunting & gathering
Neolithic	Barbarism	Domestication of animals & crop production
Copper	Higher barbarism	Smelting of copper
Bronze	Civilization	Written language & township

Like E.B. Tylor, Childe also talked about the evolution of culture in the sequence of savagery, barbarism, and civilization. But he deals with the culture of mankind as a whole, rather than specific cultures. As he proposed a general theory of the evolution of mankind, Julian Steward called him a "universal cultural evolutionist" and this theory as universal cultural evolution. While discussing his theory, Childe mentions that different human societies have passed through different historical environmental conditions. Thus, they evolved different cultural traditions. Thus, the multiplicity of cultures and diversity in cultural traditions are due to different environmental conditions, although humankind as a whole has passed through similar archaeological periods.

While discussing his theory, he also advocated that the concept of diffusion cannot be ignored because people might be able to acquire certain diffused technological skills and social features.

The theory of V. Gordon Childe was so general that it is not much arguable because no one disputes the fact that hunting and gathering preceded domestication of animals and crop production. Similarly, no one can deny the fact that the smelting of copper, bronze, and written language delayed development.

Gordon Childe mostly studied the civilizations of Europe and the Middle East. While studying these, he put forth a working model that was related to Darwinian Theory. Darwin talked about variations, heredity, and natural selection. Childe associated variation with invention, heredity with learning, and natural selection with cultural adaptability. Thus, he holds that mankind as a whole made many inventions in order to adapt properly to a culture. According to him, drastic change occurred in the development of human culture with the emergence of civilization when huntergatherers became food producers, dwellers became house dwellers, there was the emergence of mathematics to count things, there was written language to preserve traditions, and there was the smelting of copper and bronze to make portable utensils and tools.

Gordon Childe refers to human aggressiveness towards the exploitation of the environment as a factor of cultural development. According to him, during earlier times, mankind was very weak in technological skills. Thus, its aggressiveness towards the exploitation of natural resources was also weak, but with the passage of time, mankind became more skilled in technology and became more aggressive in exploiting natural resources. This aggressiveness brought about a change in culture, and such changes led to cultural development.

As V. Gordon Childe put forth a generalised methodology to explain the sequence of cultural evolution without any specification, his theory is also known as the "General Theory of Cultural Evolution".

Criticism:

1. Childe only observed the civilizations of Europe and the Middle East and didn't show interest in the study of the civilizations of other countries like China and India.
2. Childe put forth the universal cultural evolution theory and didn't mention anything about particular cultures that exhibit variations from the cultures of whole mankind during similar archaeological periods.
3. Childe totally relied upon archaeological data; he framed characteristic features of hunter and gatherer that were very much generalised because he didn't differentiate old hunters and gatherers from present time.
4. Childe also didn't mention anything regarding universally existing practises like matriarchy and sexual promiscuity without giving any reason.
5. Although Childe claimed that he had modified classical evolutionary theory and is a neo-evolutionist, his theory, particularly the sequence of three stages, i.e., savagery, barbarism, and civilization, is more or less similar to the idea as proposed by classical evolutionists.

In spite of all these criticisms, V. Gordon Childe still deserves credit for keeping the concept of classical evolution alive and also preparing the sequence of classical evolutionism on the basis of archaeological periods.

Q 18. White

Ans. Leslie White is another neo-evolutionist. Out of his many books, his two books, "The Science of Culture" and "Evolution of Culture", are very significant because both of these books reflect evolutionary ideas. The evolutionary idea of white is related to cultured materialism, which is phased in terms of energy harnessing.

According to him, the process of a socio-cultural system consists of three parts:

1. Techno-economic
2. Social
3. Ideological

He explained the techno-economic aspect of social organisation as the use of energy by employing particular technology, and to modify the economic aspects, he further held that social formation is the consequence of the use of technology in harnessing energy.

If technology improves and expands, then similarly, society expands and experiences complexities. Therefore, he associated socio-cultural evolution with technological evolution.

According to White, when more advanced technology is employed to harness more usable energy, culture experiences evolution. He put forth the law of cultural evolution or cultural development, which is that "culture evolves as the amount of energy possessed per capita per year is increased or the efficiency of instrumental mechanisms to use energy is increased".

He formulated this law as E *T = C, where E is energy, T is technology, and C is culture. This formula has three implications:

1. If energy is not increased and technology is not improved, then culture will remain unchanged.
2. If energy is increased and technology is improved, then complexities in culture will also increase, i.e., culture will evolve.
3. If energy is decreased and technology is degenerated, then culture will also experience fewer complexities, i.e., it will stop evolving.

As he associated cultural evolution with evolution in technology and the consequent harming of energy, his approach is known as the cultural material approach or cultural materialism.

He cites examples from history to justify his approach. According to him, during the period of hunting and gathering, they were not able to harness more energy, and they used the energy whatever the muscle would provide them. The pace of cultural evolution was very slow. With the advent of agriculture and animal husbandry, technology improved and the harnessing of energy increased, resulting in the evolution of agriculture and the subsequent emergence of civilization. With the advent of industries, coal began to be used as energy, so the amount of energy harnessed per capita per year increased, which marked the further evolution of culture. Lately, for defensive purposes, there has been the use of atomic energy, which led to the atomic revolution. Thus, the culture of the whole of mankind experiences many complexities. Thus, according to him, history has also witnessed that with improvement in technology and consequently more harnessing of useable energy, culture evolves. Even the emergence of civilization and its progress are related to improved technology and harnessing of more energy.

Leslie was talking about the general law of evolution, and he was also concerned with the cultural evolution of mankind rather than specific cultures. Thus, Julian Steward termed him "universal evolutionist".

Criticism:

1. According to Julian Steward, technology cannot be the sole criteria to explain the evolutionary process of culture because a number of other factors are also responsible for its evolution.
2. Leslie White is also not able to explain why some cultural groups became capable of harnessing more energy and why some cultural groups remain capable of doing so.
3. Leslie White also does not cover the aspect of cultural traits' adaptability to a particular environment because a number of cultural traits evolve as a result of their adaptability.
4. Technology is a response to cultural stimulus; thus, technology is a product of culture, not culture is a product of technology (Norman Asle).

Q 19. Julian Steward

Ans. Julian Steward is one of the main American neo-evolutionists. He wrote many books, but his most important was "The Theory of Cultural Change". In this book, he puts forth threefold classifications of the sequence of cultural evolution, which are: Unlinear evolution, universal evolution, and multilinear evolution.

Unilinear Evolution: 19th-century classical evolution talks about unilinear sequences, cultural parallels, and the psychic unity of mankind; thus, their approach is known as the unilinear evolutionary approach because it signifies that cultures of humans have passed through different successive stages equally and in continuity due to which similar forms developed into complexes and homogeneity into heterogeneity.

Julian Steward discarded the concept of unilinear evolution; E.B. Tylor, Henry Morgan, etc. were exponents of unilinear evolution.

Universal Evolution: The universal evolutionary approach deals with the evolution of the culture as a whole rather than the evolution of a particular culture or cultures. V.G. Childe and Leslie White advocated a universal evolutionary approach because they held the methodology of the general evolution of whole mankind, which according to them has evolved after passing through various stages.

Multilinear Evolution: Julian Steward was the main authority behind multilinear evolutionary approach. According to him, the cultures of different human groups and the cultures of whole mankind didn't evolve through similar stages because the cultures of different groups have evolved differently in different areas and sub-areas during different time periods by following different evolutionary stages. According to him, the cultures of those who resided in coastal areas, arid areas, forests, etc. have evolved differently because the environmental conditions of these areas are different.

He also equated cultural variations with variations in the environment. According to him, in order to adapt to different environmental conditions, humans evolved different cultural traits. Thus, cultural adaptation is also one of the main themes of the multilinear approach.

He further mentions that the environment is dynamic and experiences many changes, which consequently puts certain pressure on humans. Thus, to cope with such pressure, humans devised complex and new cultural traits, which led to cultural evolution. Thus, Julian Steward stressed the role of the environment in the process of cultural evolution.

Julian Steward mentions that all such societies that experience similar environmental conditions and use similar technology to exploit the environment exhibit certain parallels. For instance, he studied the cultures of Mexico, Mesopotamia, Egypt, China, and the Andes and found that all these cultures evolved by following the same developmental stage of pre-agriculture, and the cultures of these regions exhibit parallels because their environments were either arid or semi-arid. This hypothesis of Julian Steward was strengthened by Karl Wittfogel, who found that all such societies that resided in river valleys developed well-irrigated agriculture and also had a centralised state political system, even in ancient times. According to Wittfogel, even the political setup is influenced by the environment and technology.

Concept of cultural ecology: In his book, "Theory of Cultural Change", Julian Steward put forth his concept of cultural ecology. Cultural ecology signifies the interrelationship between humans and their environment. According to Steward, human culture is influenced by the environment and technology. Culture is changed or evolved when certain changes occur in the environment and new technology is invented or discovered to control them.

Julian Steward put forth his concept of ecology after studying the Shoshone of America. He found that their sociocultural lives are influenced by their environment. Economically, they are hunters and gatherers because they live in forests. Socially, they are nomads and thus have very few possessions because possessions became a hurdle in movement. Their population density is also very low.

He also cited the example of many African tribes that mostly remain half-nude. Many scholars declare them savages because they have no sense of clothing, but according to Stewards, their dress pattern is influenced by their environment, as they live in very hot regions, thus making their adaptability possible by wearing fewer clothes.

He also narrated that those societies that remained dependent on rainfall for agriculture devised new religious beliefs in which rain and water were sacred.

According to Steward, the technology that exploits environment is the main cultural core because culture evolves. When advanced technology is employed to exploit the environment, many changes appear in the culture. For instance, during the Palaeolithic period, the environment was very cold and the technology to exploit such an environment was primitive; therefore, people were merely hunter-gatherers, and culture was simple. Consequently, during the Mesolithic period, the environment became temperate, humans modified their technology, and consequently, culture changed as they became pastoralists, changed their attitude towards animals, made milk and milk products part of their diet, etc. During the Neolithic period, technology became more advanced in the form of the sickle and axe. Consequently, there appeared crop production, and when, in subsequent periods, agriculture became sufficient, people became civilised. But according to him, all these cultural changes among different human populations took place differently during different time periods and followed different evolutionary lines. Classifying this concept further, he said that every society cannot progress at the same pace and at the same time because progress is directly proportional to environmental and technological factors.

Thus, Steward put stress on three concepts in relation to cultural ecology:

1. The inter relationship between environments and technology should be analysed to understand the culture.
2. The approach of humans to utilising technology for exploiting natural resources should also be analysed.
3. To what extent the environment influences the behaviour patterns of a human group should also be analysed for the construction of the cultural life of the group.

Criticism:

1. Marvin Harris: Discard the multi-linear evolutionary approach as a methodology because he puts stress on cultural materialism.
2. Steward's approach also explains how many cultures evolved by following a multilinear evolutionary process.
3. Andrew Vaidya criticised Steward for his concept of cultural ecology. According to him, although there is a relationship between humans and their environment, it is not necessary that all cultural traits of human culture are due to their adaptability to environments. Thus, cultural adaptation in relation to the environment is a misconception.
4. His concept regarding cultural core, i.e., technology, is also not accepted by many on the ground that, in addition to technology, many other aspects of human life like their customs, rituals, and belief systems also play a role in dealing with environments, so only technology cannot be cultural core.

In spite, he was the first anthropologist to reflect the role of environment and technology in the formation of human culture through his concept of cultural ecology.

Q 20. Sahlins and Service

Ans. Sahlins and Service have put forth the concepts of general evolution and specific evolution in their book "Evolution and Culture". According to them, both in biological and cultural spheres, evolution can be understood in general and specific ways.

They remark that cultural diversities appear as a result of environmental conditions or some other factors, due to which many new forms evolve from old forms. They term this 'specific evolution'. On the other hand, culture progressed, and one stage evolved over time into another, i.e., a successive stage surpassed the previous stage. They termed this 'general evolution'. According to them, the culture of humans has evolved both through general and specific evolution.

The evolution stage by stage, i.e., stages of hunting and gathering, pastoral farming, agriculture, etc., as experienced by the whole of mankind is a general evolution. But changes that occur in particular cultures due to particular environments, inventions, discoveries, diffusion, etc. are specific cultural evolutions that also take place from time to time. General evolution conveys change over a long period of time, but specific evolution conveys change over a shorter period of time. Specific evolution also indicates that evolution among different human groups takes place differently and during different time periods.

For instance, according to him, perhaps the institution of marriage evolved among all mankind almost at the same time period, but specifically different cultural groups evolved different races to solemnise the marriage during different time periods. Similarly, the institution of religion may have also evolved at the same time among the whole of mankind, but cultural variations among religion groups regarding belief systems, rituals, etc. evolved by following specific evolutionary trends.

Thus, both Marshal D. Sahlins and Elman Service corroborate the theories of V. Gordon Childe, Julian Steward, and Leslie white as they also explain general evolution with reference to Gordon Childe and Leslie White and the multilinear evolution of Julian Steward through specific evolution.

Q 21. Cultural Materialism (M.Harris)

Ans. Actually, the concept of cultural materialism is associated with the name of Leslie White who, being a neoevolutionist, talked about the relation between material aspects of culture and corresponding social and cultural changes. But the approach of cultural materialism was elaborated by M. Harris in his book, "The Rise of Anthropological Theories."

Cultural materialists believe that culture changes with the material lives of people. According to Marvin Harris, technology, environment, and economic life are the main determinants of socio-cultural evolution. Further elaborating on this aspect, he narrates that when new technology is employed, the exploitation of the environment can be expanded, bringing about changes in economic life and, consequently, socio-cultural life.

M. Harris divides all the socio-cultural systems into three parts: 1. Infrastructure, 2. Structure, 3. Superstructure.

Infrastructure includes material apparatus or techniques that are employed to expand or limit the production of basic resources like food, clothes, and shelter.

Structure includes domestic economy, i.e., family structure, division of labour, gender, or sex roles. Super structure includes philosophy, religion, magic, art, etc.

According to Marvin Harris, changes in infrastructure also bring changes in structure and super structure. He mentions that every society has adopted particular material apparatus for the fulfilment of basic needs, and such material apparatus determines their socio-economic system.

He cites certain examples from an Indian perspective. According to him, when agriculture was adopted as a means of production by Indians, Then their approach and philosophy towards cows changed, and cows became sacred. Similarly, family structure and gender roles also changed.

He didn't deny the role of structure and superstructure in the evolution of culture but put more stress on infrastructure as an important tool in socio-cultural evolution.

As he viewed the evolution of socio-cultural in relation to material culture, his approach is known as cultural materialism.

Criticism:

1. According to Julian Steward, material apparatus cannot be the sole criteria to explain the evolutionary process of culture because a number of other factors are also responsible for its evolution.
2. He also does not cover the aspect of cultural traits' adaptability to a particular environment because a number of cultural traits evolve as a result of their adaptability.
3. Technology is a response to cultural stimulus; thus, technology is a product of culture, not culture is a product of technology (Norman Asle).

Q 22. Symbolic and interpretive theories (Turner, Geertz and Schneider)

Ans. Symbolic anthropology arose as a reaction to structuralism, Marxism, and materialism. Structuralism used symbols such as language, but unlike symbolic anthropology, it did not emphasise symbolism, i.e., the study of the underlying process behind the origin and meaning of symbols.

Victor Turner: Victor Turner was a British anthropologist. His works include "The Forest of Symbols" (1967) and "Social Drama and Stories about them" (1980).

Victor Turner differentiated between a sign and a symbol, calling the former an indexical relationship with the world and the latter an iconic relationship with our inner selves. Thus, Turner says, we master the world with signs, but we master ourselves with symbols.

Turner investigated symbols as operators in the social process, believing that symbolic expression of shared meanings lies at the centre of human relationships. For him, symbols produce transformation, which exerts determinable influences, inclining people and groups to action. Turner called this social drama.

He mostly talked about ritual symbolism. According to him, ritual symbolism tied members of society to societal norms, and thus social order was maintained. He cited an example of Ndimbu Ritualism to explain how particular activities act as symbols and how such symbols lead to the creation of society. Among Ndimbu, every action, every object, and every institution represent a symbol. For instance, they associate breast with an action to nourish someone; such nourishments symbolise relations between mother and child which further enhances an institution that is family, and this institution symbolises a large institution that is society. He explained the Ndimbu ritual, which is associated with the tree Mudyi, which has milky sap and is also known as the Milky Tree. When a child is born, they take the child under this tree; stretch the back of this tree, and milky sap oozes out, which they give to the child. Now this white sap of a milky tree symbolises human milk, which symbolises breasts, which symbolise mother-child bonds, which symbolise family, and which symbolises society.

Clifford Geertz: He was an American anthropologist. His works include "The Interpretation of Cultures" (1973), "Myth, Symbol, and Culture" (1974), and "The Religion of Java" (1960).

Geertz defined culture as a historically transmitted pattern of meanings embodied in symbols. Thus, for him, symbols operate as vehicles of culture. A symbol must not be studied simply in and of itself but for what it reveals about culture.

He used the concept of thick description to describe his interpretative approach. A thick description, simply put, is the interpretation of the mental thought processes and reasoning of natives as made by an ethnographer. It thus relies heavily on an emic approach to study. By analysing the whole of culture as well as its constituent parts, an ethnographer can develop a 'thick description'. The ethnographer tries to convey this interpretation to the people of his own culture. Thus, the ethnographer is a kind of selective inter-cultural translator. This is called interpretive anthropology. To illustrate the thick description, Geertz uses the difference between a 'blink' and a 'wink'. A blink is an involuntary twitch (the thin description), and a wink is a deliberate signal to a friend (the thick description).

Geertz's study on religion is based on his 1960 book, "The Religion of Java". Geertz studied Modjokuto, a town in Java where conflicts are common between Abangan (a traditional animistic religion), Santri (Muslims), and Prijaji (Hindu-Buddhists). According to Geertz, the factors responsible for the conflict are:

1. Ideological conflicts rest on a deep-felt dislike for the values of other groups.
2. The changing system of social stratification and increased social mobility tend to enforce contacts between individuals and groups formerly more or less socially segregated.

3. The sharply increased struggle for political power to fill the vacuum left by the colonial government
4. The need for scapegoats upon whom to focus tensions generated by a rapidly changing social system

Thus, he concludes that when there is religious plurality, ideological conflicts are bound to occur. These ideological conflicts are intimately tied to the respective economic and political achievements of these communities.

The major difference between Turner and Geertz lies in their respective influences. Geertz was influenced largely by the sociologist Max Weber and was concerned with how symbols operate as vehicles of culture. Turner, influenced by Emile Durkheim, was concerned with how symbols operate in social processes. Thus, while Geertz focused on the operations of culture, Turner was more interested in the operations of society.

David Schneider: Retained Levi-Strauss idea of culture as a set of relationships. He defined culture as a system of symbols and meanings. Unlike Geertz, he detached culture from everyday life. For him, regularity in behaviour is not necessarily culture, nor can culture be inferred from a regular pattern of behaviour.

Criticism:

1. Marxists believe it does not explain the system of symbolism but rather focuses too much on individual symbols.
2. Cultural ecologists consider their studies to be unscientific due to their subjective interpretations.

Despite the criticisms, symbolic anthropology has put a much-needed emphasis on the meaning of culture, thus making cultural studies more holistic and oriented towards culture bearers.

Q 23. Cognitive theories (Tyler, Conklin)

Ans. Cognitive anthropologists, since dealing with human thought process, invariably focus on the study of symbols. They consider the knowledge of the cognitive process that imparts meaning to a symbol as their achievement. Cognitive anthropology is closer to psychology because it tries to understand and explain how groups classify their thoughts.

The approach states that culture is composed of logical rules based on ideas that can be accessed in the human mind.

As per Harold Conklin, people construct their world in terms of their culture. Culture, as a cognitive system, helps them segregate the significant from the non-significant and decide the course of action. In his book, "Hanunoo Colour Categories", he studied Hanunoo of the Philippines. Their colour codes are very different from those in the West. For them, significance is placed on aspects like the wetness and dryness of colours, which are a reflection of their linguistic system (i.e., culture).

Stephen Tylor added that humans simplify their chaotic world through classification. Each culture has its own classification categories to make sense of its reality. For example, in his work, "Koya: An Outline Grammar", he found that Koyas of India had seven different categories of bamboo. Meanwhile, Western society refers to them all as simply bamboo.

Methodology: Striving to discover 'the native's point of view', they adopted an emic approach. In addition, they gave huge importance to the study of symbols, especially language.

Criticism: The approach is deemed to be too abstract. It is unclear whether the results reflect how people organise and perceive society or are just mere constructs of the investigator's mind.

Despite the criticisms, the theory has made significant advances in a relatively short period of time in understanding the human mind and people's worldviews.

Q 24. Post Modernism

Ans. The post-modernist anthropologists are Clifford, Marcus, Stephans, Foucault, and Fisher. According to them, there cannot be an objective reality because the concept of reality changes with the viewer's perception. They criticised traditional ethnographers on the basis that they fixed objectivity and then put forth their assumptions. But their assumptions cannot be considered reality because the lives of people are full of subjectivity, and their activities have different meanings in different situations and for different people. Thus, the action generated through an activity cannot be fixed as reality by the viewer because the objectivity of such reality may vary.

Post-modernism in anthropology does not accept that the assumption of an anthropologist is the only truth because truth may vary from individual to individual. For instance, it is considered objective reality that legitimate offspring are born only to wed couples, but now it is not objective reality because even children born to unwed couples who are engaged in live-in relationships are regarded as legitimate. Thus, marriage is the only institution that institutionalised reproduction, which is no longer regarded as the only reality because reproduction can be institutionalised in other ways as well.

Post-modernists even criticised Malinowski for providing data on Trobriand Islanders as an outsider. Thus, they even decline to accept all the assumptions put forth by Malinowski. The basis theme of post-modernism is that one should not accept a single reality as objective reality because reality can vary from individual to individual. It is suspicious of anthoritative definitions and the singular narrative of any event. It is divided into two camps: "sceptics," who are extremely critical, and "affirmatives," who think theory needs to be transformed.

Methods used: 1. Deconstruction, 2. Intuitive interpretation, 3. Fieldwork

Accomplishment:

1. A critical examination of ethnographic explanations
2. It leads to heightened sensitivity within anthropology to the collection of data.

Criticism:

1. Melford Spiro argues that post-modernism cannot dismiss scientific method without objective procedure.
2. Postmodernism introduced political bias in anthropology, which may undermine its legitimacy.
3. This approach can lead to anarchy in society. As in society, there should be consensus regarding certain aspects, and if everyone thinks or acts according to their own, then social order will be distrusted and society cannot function properly. Thus, to be cultural, every member of society should follow certain cultural realities.

7

Culture, Language and Communication

Culture, Language and Communication: Nature, origin and characteristics of language; verbal and non-verbal communication; social context of language use.

Q 1. Nature, origin and characteristics of Language

Ans. The word communication comes from the Latin verb "communicare", meaning to share, to make common. Communication is much broader than language.

Bernard Bloch and G.L. Trager defined language as a system of arbitrary vocal or written symbols by means of which social groups communicate. However, human languages are a large set of symbols that can be combined to produce new meanings, communicate about past and future events, apply linguistic rules for the combination of sounds, and have many kinds of discourse.

Nature:

1. **Structural Perspective:** Language is formed by the proper arrangement of phonemes (sounds in speech), morphemes (sound sequences having meaning), and syntax (words arranged to form sentences). Noam Chomsky says that language becomes understandable only due to structural aspects.
2. **Functional perspective:** It is a vehicle for the expression of functional meaning. Grierson says that it helps to communicate.
3. **Interactional perspective:** Ferguson says that it helps humans interact, develop social relations, and maintain them.

Origin: There is broad agreement that human language must have existed 50,000 years ago in the Upper Palaeolithic period.

Only unambiguous remains of language are found on written tablets, and the earliest stone tablet dates only about 5,000 years ago, so pinpointing the emergence of the earliest language remains speculative.

But there is an understanding that animal communication systems lack the open-ended power of human language, so genetic changes must have occurred in human evolution to make language possible after humans separated from apes.

1. **Tracing Origin**
   a. **Pidgin and Creole languages:** Pidgin language combines features of various languages but without basic components such as prepositions or verbs. Some pidgin languages develop further into creole languages, which have a grammar different from the source language. Some argue that creole languages throughout the world have similar grammar and may resemble early Latin.

b. **Child's Acquisition of Language:** A child is equipped from birth with the capacity to reproduce all sounds used by the world's languages and to learn any system of grammar, an ability that gives way to cultural influence around the age of 7 years.

2. **Imitation**
   a. **Ding Dong:** Language began when humans started naming objects and phenomena after a sound associated with them in real life. E.g., boom for explosion
   b. **Pooh Pooh:** The first words were developed through responses associated with emotions like laughter, pain, hunger, etc. E.g., Ha-Ha-Ha (Laughter)
   c. **Bow-Wow:** Vocabulary developed from imitation of animal noises. E.g., Moo, Hiss
   d. **Ta-Ta:** Language was generated to support hand gestures and individual movements.
3. **Necessity**
   a. **Warning:** Language evolved from human signals to alert members of a tribe of any impending danger, especially while hunting.
   b. **Lying:** Language was invented for the purpose of lying or deceiving.
   c. **Yo he ho:** Language evolved on the basis of human cooperative efforts.

Characteristics:

1. **System:** comprises phonemes and grammar
2. **Dynamic:** Changes from generation to generation
3. **Dialects:** regional variation
4. **Sociolects:** social variation
5. **Symbolic and arbitrary:** meaning to things

It led to the development of a writing system that is 6,000 years old. We are not sure when humans first developed spoken language. But enormous linguistic diversity took a long time to develop on this planet. Unfortunately, it may take a short time for that diversity to become a thing of the past.

Case Study

- **To learn Klingon or Esperanto: What invented languages can teach us**

Most languages evolve through centuries of use by various populations. However, some come from a different place: they are original creations of one person's mind. The world tongue Esperanto, the Klingon dialect from Star Trek, and the Elvish dialects from The Lord of the Rings are all well-known examples. The practise is not new; the first recorded invented language was created by the mediaeval nun Hildegard von Bingen. However, the Internet has made it possible for the small communities of people who speak and create these languages to share their languages much more widely. In the 2021 Annual Review of Anthropology, linguistic anthropologist Christine Schreyer of the University of British Columbia's Okanagan campus in Kelowna, Canada, writes about her research on invented languages and the speakers of them. But Schreyer brings another skill to the table: She's a language creator herself and has invented several languages for the movie industry: the Kryptonian language for Man of Steel, Eltarian for Power Rangers, Beama (Cro-Magnon) for Alpha, and Atlantean for Zack Snyder's Justice League.

Schreyer spoke with Knowable Magazine about her experience in this unusual world and the practical lessons that it provides for people trying to revitalise endangered natural languages. I teach a course on linguistic anthropology, in which I give my students the task of creating new languages as they learn about the parts of languages. Around the time I started doing that, Avatar came out. At the time, the Na'vi language from the film was often used in news articles to describe how quickly individuals picked up the language. My additional academic work focuses on minority or indigenous groups' language revitalization. People taking a long time to learn a language is one of our problems. In order to learn languages more quickly, I was curious what endangered-language groups could pick up from these created-language fan networks. I was interested in knowing more about the Na'vi people, including who they were, why they spoke the language, and how they went about acquiring it. Many Na'vi speakers who I interviewed stated they joined because they liked the movie and stayed for the community. They're very welcoming and inclusive communities. It doesn't matter what your race is or what your gender is, though many of these fandoms tend to be more male. But also, one of the things I saw in the Na'vi case was that individuals joined the fan community because Avatar was very tied to environmental and indigenous rights. These ideals of environmentalism are part of the language, and they picked up on that. That is part of the reason that some of them were learning the language.

The ones that are learned most widely are those intended as international auxiliary languages, like Esperanto, meant to be shared by people around the world to promote unity and world peace. It is a streamlined, very simple language that is intended to be neutral. Millions of people have learned it all across the world. It's available to learn on Duolingo!

Q 2. Non-verbal communication

Ans. The word communicate comes from the Latin verb "communicare" meaning to share or to make common. Non-verbal communication (NVC) is a process of communication that involves the sending and receiving of wordless messages. Its first scientific study was done by Charles Darwin in his work, "The Expression of the Emotions in Man and Animals" (1872).

Types:

1. **Clothing and bodily characteristics:** Elements like physique, height, weight, skin colour, gender, and clothing send non-verbal messages during interactions. Research says that taller people are perceived as more impactful while speaking.
2. **Physical Environment:** Environmental factors affect the behaviour of communicators during an interaction. These are of two types: (a) proxemics which deals with how physical space between sender and receiver influences the interpretation of the messages. (b) Chronomics which deals with the role of time. Time perceptions include punctuality, speed of speaking, willingness to listen, etc.
3. **Kinesics:** interpretation of body language, or basically non-verbal behaviour related to movements, either of the whole or part of the body. This field of research was founded by R. Birdwhistell.

   Examples:

   a. When authority figures were present, Japanese subjects more often than Americans tried to mask negative feelings with a half-smile.

   b. Moving the head up and down signals 'yes' in the US but 'no' in Greece.

   c. People raised in New York City showed engagement by responding while others were speaking. But it is considered rude in the south and southwest.

   d. Paul Ekman's studies of facial expressions related to emotions like anger, fear, joy, etc. show that these aspects of kinesics are universal. But aspects like gestures and signs vary across cultures.
4. **Paralanguage** refers to all the operational vocal features or silences that communicate meaning apart from language itself. These include tone, pitch, accent, and sounds like grunts and giggles.

Today, nonverbal communication studies range across different fields, including linguistics, semiotics, and social psychology, among others.

Q 3. Social context of Language use

Ans. The goal of ethnography of speaking, according to sociolinguistics, is to find cultural and sub-cultural patterns of speech variation in different social contexts.

Social status and speech:

1. **Class Difference:** Clifford Geertz's study of Javanese showed vocabulary division among peasants, townspeople, and aristocrats. E.g., "now" word use as 'saiki', 'saniki," and "samenika," respectively. John Fisher found higherstatus families less likely to drop the "g' from fishing or singing in a New England town than lower-status ones.
2. **Status Relationship:** Roger Brown showed that reciprocal or non-reciprocal use of the first title or name in speech reflects a difference in status between speaker and receiver.
3. **Social Aspiration:** William Labour showed that people wishing for higher status or class try to sound like them. Even seen by M.N. Srinivas in the concept of Sankritization.
4. **Gender difference**
   a. Male and female use different words for the same term in Japan, e.g., "water" is used by males as 'mizu" and by females as 'ohiya'.
   b. Robin Lakofffound that women tend to answer questions with sentences that have a rising inflection at the end. E.g., they caught a robber last night, didn't they?
   c. Labour found men to be more verbally aggressive while conversing. Tannen highlights that these are due to cultural differences between boys and girls.
   d. Everett found the Karitiana (Brazil) language doesn't indicate gender by its pronoun, thereby having a lower gender marker as compared to English.
5. **Age difference:** Young people use more slang among themselves than older ones.
6. **Multilingualism:** For many people, the ability to speak more than one language is a normal part of life. Singapore has four official languages: English, Mandarin, Tamil, and Malay. Very often, we find ourselves codeswitching, using more than one language in the course of conversing. E.g., Puerto Rico in New York City code switches with friends but speaks entirely Spanish with outsiders.
7. **Speech community:** using language in a unique and accepted way among themselves, e.g., a doctor group.

To conclude, society and language are mutually indispensable, with the latter reflected in each and every aspect of the former.

Q 4. Relationship between Language and Culture

Ans. Language is the vehicle on which culture travels from generation to generation, implying that culture is a learned trait.

Culture's influence on language

- Colours: Berlin and Kay's studies found a larger number of basic terms for colour with more technological specialisation. If language has two basic colours, then it will be black and white.
- Plants, animals: More complex societies have a larger number of terms for plants and animals than simpler societies.
- All languages have a vocabulary of almost the same size. But the vocabulary of language reflects everyday distinctions in society. Similarly, this is true for grammar. E.g., language develops the verb 'have' after a system of private property or personal resource concepts develops.

Language influence on culture

- Sapir-Whorfsuggested that language influences other aspects of culture; e.g., language is a force that affects how individuals in society perceive and conceive reality. They found that the English language conveys discreteness with regard to time and space, but Hopi doesn't. English has past, present, and future occurring at a definite time, but Hopi expresses things without time apportioned into fixed segments.
- Alexander Guiora found the Hebrew language of Israel to have more gender emphasis than the English language and the least in the Finnish language. Consistent with it, Hebrew speakers acquire the concept of gender identification the earliest and Finnish children the least.
- John Lucy found The English language has a linguistic way of indicating whatever something is, singular or plural, while the Yucatecan Mayan language doesn't. Therefore, English speakers recall the number of objects more accurately than Mayans.

However, one serious problem in testing the linguistic relativity hypothesis is that researchers need to figure out how to separate the effects of other aspects of culture from those of language. Still, more research is needed on this aspect of the relationship.

Case Study

- **Assam's Haflong Hindi, a fluent example of give and take**

Haflong Hindi, which dates to the 19th century, has Tibeto-Burman syntax with Bengali and Nepali terms. In the midst of a controversy over the Centre's decision to make the "standardised" form of the language mandatory in high schools throughout the northeast, a "nativized" form of Hindi connected to Assam's solitary hill station is attempting to hold its own. Haflong Hindi features vocabulary additions from Bengali and Nepali and adheres to Tibeto-Burman rather than Hindi grammar. It does not employ numbers like Hind does, and it has a generic plural marker. For instance, ladki (female) in Haflong Hindi is pluralized as ladkiluk or ladkilukun, as opposed to ladkiyaan in "mainland" Hindi. Similarly, a tree is referred to in Haflong Hindi as gachchhi, a Nepali loan word, rather than ped, as it is in Hindi, and the majority of sound modifications use the Bengali form.

8

Research Methods in Anthropology

Research Methods in Anthropology:

(a) Fieldwork tradition in anthropology

(b) Distinction between technique, method and methodology

(c) Tools of data collection: observation, interview, schedules, questionnaire, case study, genealogy, life-history, oral history, secondary sources of information, participatory methods.

(d) Analysis, interpretation and presentation of data.

Q 1. Fieldwork tradition in Anthropology

Ans. According to Ember and Ember, fieldwork means first-hand experience with the people being studied and is the usual means by which anthropological information is obtained.

Fieldwork is an important means for the anthropologist to explore and analyse the data and to develop theory on that basis. In this, an anthropologist goes to the field and stays with people whom he wants to study.

Cultural evolutionists are being criticised as armchair anthropologists because they were not field workers and used secondary sources of data like that of missionaries, travellers, and businessmen, except L.H. Morgan, who conducted field work, though not systematically, among Iroquois Indians. He used genealogical techniques and a questionnaire to study kinship organisation. In America, systematic field surveys began with the works of Franz Boas in Baffin Bay and British Columbia. In Britain, it was the Torris Strait Expedition in 1898–99, headed by A.C. Haddon that became the turning point. One of the scholars on this team, W.H.R. Rivers visited India and conducted fieldw work among the Todas of the Nilgiri Hills in 1906. In 1906–08, Radcliffe Brown conducted fieldwork among the Onge tribe of Andaman Island. In 1914–18, B.A. Malinowski conducted the largest fieldwork among Trobriand Islanders till that period, and that through learning their native language—participatory observation. Earlier, certain aspects of social life were studied and neglected, like political structure. Later structural-functionalists studied political systems like E.Leach, who studied the political system of Highland Burma. Margaret Mead brought improvement to the personality school by employing cameras and tape recorders to capture events, and another improvement is the use of the re-study method to show changes taking place in society. Another development in the fieldwork tradition took place when the study of peasant society was introduced via the works of Robert Redfield and the concept of the folk-urban continuum. Certain new approaches to studying new ethnographs like the emic and etic approaches came into being.

Methodology:

1. Spend a significant amount of time in the field (1 to 3 years).
2. Communicate with them in their native language.
3. Conduct an objective study of all aspects of social life.

Approaches:

1. **Synchronic and Dychronic:** The synchronic approach is based on empirical fieldwork, where first-hand information or data is collected. The synchronous approach is based on written documents.
2. **Inductive and deductive:** In inductive, the unit of research is small and conclusions are drawn at a larger scale, whereas in deductive, the unit of research is large but conclusions are drawn at a smaller scale.
3. **Textual and contextual:** Contextual is direct fieldwork, while textual is indirect fieldwork.
4. **Etic and Emic:** In Emic, the researcher presents an insider's view, while in Etic, the researcher provides an outsider's view of culture.

Importance:

1. Due to fieldwork, anthropology became an empirical study.
2. Since fieldwork leads to the collection of information, which is essential for promulgating theories, it follows that fieldwork leads to theory formulation.
3. On the basis of fieldwork, old theories were verified or some assumptions were rejected.
4. Fieldwork is the basis of applied anthropology and action anthropology.
5. The importance of fieldwork can be gleaned from the statement that 'a theory cannot develop without sound fieldwork, and a subject cannot develop without theory'.

Despite criticism for compromising on objectivity, fieldwork is the soul of anthropology. What the lab is to science, fieldwork is to anthropology.

Q 2. Distinguish between the research terms – technique, method and methodology.

Ans. Research in any discipline is built around the three concepts of technique, method, and methodology. The three are often used interchangeably but actually differ when considered closely.

Technique: It refers to the behaviour and instruments used in performing research operations such as making observations, recording data, data processing, etc.

Method: It refers to the behaviour and instruments used in selecting and constructing research techniques in order to achieve a desired goal.

Participatory observation is a method in which the researcher deploys techniques like interactional recording and questionnaires to achieve the target of the study.

Methods can be divided into three groups:

1. Data collection methods like surveys, interviews, and case studies
2. Statistical method: To establish relationships between data sets
3. Accuracy evaluation method: To validate the accuracy of the results obtained

In practise, both methods and techniques are used interchangeably. When we talk of research methods, we encompass techniques as well.

Methodology: It refers to the way to systematically solve the research problem. It is the overarching framework used for research. In it, we include the various steps generally adopted by a researcher in studying a problem and the logic behind them. It is very important for the researchers to design their methodology for a particular problem in order to decide which methods and techniques are relevant for the problem and why.

When we talk of research methodology with respect to a particular problem, we deal with the following questions:

1. Why was a research study undertaken?
2. How have research problems been defined?
3. In what way and why has the hypothesis been formulated?
4. What data is to be collected or has been collected, and with what methods and techniques?

Thus, the scope of research methodology is wider than methods and techniques.

Q 3. Participant observation

Ans. Observation refers to systematic and deliberative study through eyes of investigator.

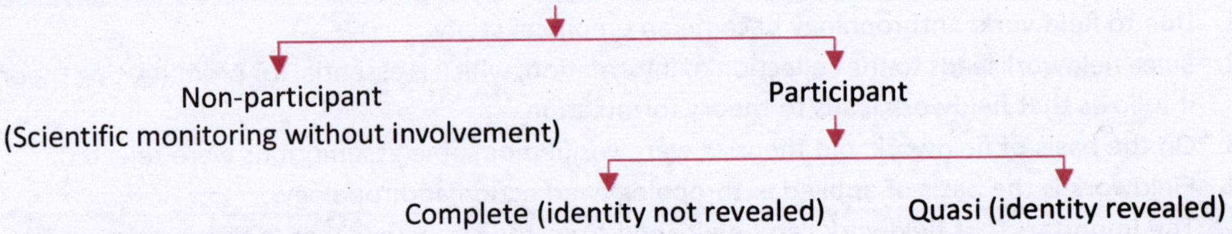

Although fieldwork existed at the time of Boas and R. Brown, the concept of participant observation was advocated by Malinowski while working among Trobriand Islanders in his book "Argonauts of the Western Pacific".

The ideal participant observation begins with the learning of their native language and knowledge about their customs, beliefs, religious practises, etc. The researcher should reside with respondents and assume the role of "friend, philosopher, and guide" for them. The researcher should maintain very intimate relationships with people and try to win the confidence of some people in the field who serve as 'key informants'.

Participant observation is of two types: "participant observer" or "observer participant" according to the nature of participation. When the observer is external at the start and afterwards involves himself in the group, he is a participant observer, and if the observer is internal to the group and practices introspection to study social reality, he is an observerparticipant.

Merits:

1. It provides fieldworkers with perfect information (deep and extensive).
2. It offers no scope for errors arising from misunderstandings of words or verbal reports.
3. The difference between ideal and real culture can be made.
4. Access to sensitive information like marriage, family, sexual, etc.

Demerits:

1. Possibility of lack of objectivity as the researcher gets too emotionally attached.
2. Too much time, manpower, and money are consumed.
3. The presence of observers distorts the behaviour of the study group.

   However, if one is able to achieve "detached attachment", one is a perfect field researcher.

In order to minimise limitations, a quasi-participant observation approach was followed, whereby the researcher regulated his participation as per the situation.

Q 4. Questionnarie and Schedule

Ans. A questionnaire refers to a device for securing answers to questions by using forms that the respondent fills up himself or herself. A schedule is a structured set of questions on a given topic that are asked personally by the interviewer or investigator.

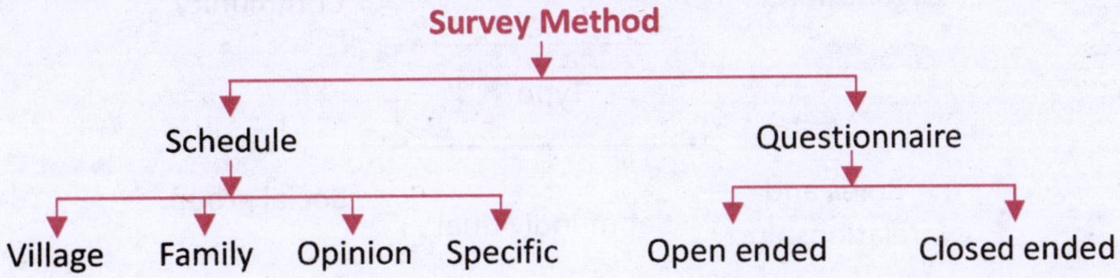

Differences:

1. The questionnaire is self-explanatory, while the schedule has to be explained by the interviewer.
2. Questionnaires are only applied to literate people, while schedules can be applied to both literate and preliterate people.
3. The questionnaire is mailed when it is not possible for schedule.
4. A questionnaire takes less time, less manpower, and less data collection ability than a schedule.
5. No alteration in question or extra information can be collected via questionnaire, unlike schedule.
6. Investigator effect is not possible in the questionnaire but is possible in the schedule.
7. The questionnaire is an indirect, non-participatory one, but the schedule is a direct, research-oriented one.
8. A questionnaire ensures anonymity and helps study problems that are highly personal, unlike schedules.

Similarity:

1. Both focus on the problem-oriental approach.
2. Both cover large respondents.

Both are survey methods, though schedule is more important than questionnaire, and both complement each other to do fieldwork.

Q 5. Case Study method

Ans. Young P.V. defined case study as a comprehensive study of a social unit, be it a person, a group of people, an institute, a community, or a family. Herbert Spencer was the first to use case studies in his ethnographic studies. Dr. William Healy, Cora du Bois, Radcliffe Brown, and Oscar Lewis are scholars who used this method.

Characters:

1. **Descriptive study:** data collected constitute a description of psychological processes and events. It is more of a qualitative method than a quantitative method. A high level of detail is provided.
2. **Narrowly focused:** often it focuses on limited aspects of a person, such as their psychopathological symptoms.
3. **Combine objective** and subjective data.
4. **Process-oriented:** case studies continue over time, e.g., the development of language in children over time.

Techniques of Case Study:

1. Observation
2. Interview
3. Secondary data
4. Document/Recorder

Source of Data: Life history, personal documents, biography, letters, interviews, etc.

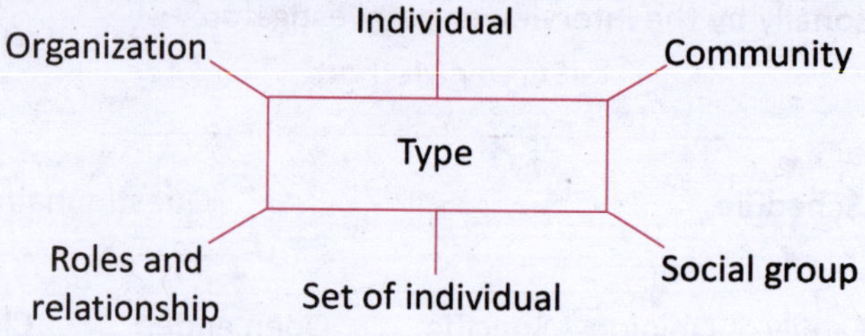

Example: Cora du Bois, "The People of Alor'.

Advantage:

1. Intensive and in-depth analysis helps to contradict enabled theory.
2. In-depth studies help stimulate new research.
3. Suitable to collect data on sensitive areas of social phenomena.
4. Details were collected regarding the habits, traits, and qualities of the unit under investigation.
5. Know the social change of different facets of a social group.
6. Understand the past of social units.
7. Useful for administrative purposes in diagnosis and therapy.

Limitation:

1. Open to error due to faulty selection of cases and inaccurate observation.
2. A chance of inaccuracy in the case history has been developed.
3. The process is more subjective.
4. The information collected is incomparable since each informant gives his or her own opinion.
5. Not possible in a large society.
6. Consume more time and expenditure.

Despite its limitations, it is one of the most useful methods of data collection and analysis.

Q 6. Genealogical Table Method

Ans. Genealogy is a wider term that links individuals who are not only genetically related but also socially related; for instance, adopted children are included in genealogy. It connects ego with his or her ancestors, alive or dead, and with relatives who are alive. It is a statement of the ways in which individuals are related to one another through common relatives and through marriage (an egocentric approach).

According to Barnes, a genealogy is prepared by an ethnographer as part of field work. For social anthropologists, it is important to have information regarding kinship and affinal groups. It was introduced by L.H. Morgan and popularised by W.H.R. Rivers.

Symbols:

Δ – Male Π – Female = – Marriage

| – Generation Ɇ – Death

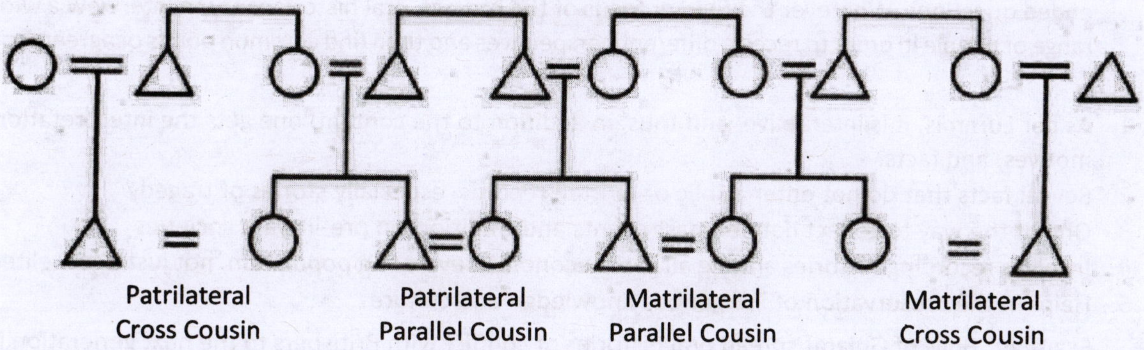

Types of Cousin Marriage

Information obtained from genealogy:

1. Demographic features: ratio of males to females, structure of families, spacing of children.
2. Information on patterns of marriage, facilities, and migration.
3. Study kinship terms on the basis of genealogy along with rules of descent.
4. Know about rites of passage.
5. Information about interpersonal behaviour between relatives.

It is now considered useful in sociological investigations.

Q 7. Life history

Ans. A life history is defined as a sequentially laid-out account of an individual's life experiences, covering all the dimensions that cumulatively make up the identity and perceptivity of a life.

Methodology: A life history requires a detailed account of every event that has happened to a person throughout the course of their life. Thus, the informant must have a sharp recall and be able to consider his or her life. It is essential that the researcher and informant have a strong rapport. The context, or culture, of which the informant is a part, as well as his or her precise place in society, must be included in life narratives in order to give them substance.

Advantages: One can comprehend the socialisation and enculturation processes by studying one's life history. The rites of passage and their effects are also clarified. Any significant event can also be documented, along with how it affected people and society as a whole.

Limitations: The informant's narrative is deeply ingrained in the constantly evolving socio-cultural content. Life histories continue to evolve as a result of these changes. Furthermore, the real-life reports could be embellished with fictional details over time. Thus, what may get recorded is 'what ought to be' rather than 'what actually is'.

However, life histories do give a good account of the state of mind and social context in which the informant is operating.

Q 8. Oral History

Ans. Oral history is concerned with the recording, preservation, and interpretation of historical information based on the personal experiences and opinions of the respondents.

It often takes the form of eyewitness evidence about past events, but it can also include myths, folklore, and songs passed down orally.

Methodology: After getting the informed consent of the respondent, oral historians prefer to ask open-ended questions. Whatever the field or focus of the project, oral historians try to interview a wide range of people in order to receive different perspectives and then find common points of agreement.

Uses:

1. As per Lummis, it is interactive, and thus, in addition to the content, one gets the interpretation, motives, and facts.
2. Reveal facts that do not enter public or written records, especially stories of tragedy.
3. One of the way to collect data on past events and traditions in pre-literate societies
4. Involves recording histories among all socio-economic levels of a population, not just a few elites.
5. Helps in the preservation of indigenous knowledge and culture.

Example: Bhils of Gujarat spread oral histories of conflict with Britishers to the next generation in the form of songs. Certain limitations include repetitive data and ethnocentrism. But these can be minimized by a well-trained interviewer.

Q 9. Secondary sources of information

Ans. Secondary data means data that has already been collected and analysed by someone else.

It may either be published data or unpublished data.

Published data:

1. Various publications of the central, state, and local governments
2. Various publications of international bodies and their organisations
3. Journals, books, magazines, and newspapers
4. Records prepared by scholars, economists, etc.
5. Public records, statistics, and historical documents

Unpublished data:

1. Diaries, letters, and unpublished biographies

Features:

1. Readily available and readymade.
2. Researcher has no original control over collection and classification.
3. Not limited in time and space.

Uses:

1. Used for reference purposes or as the sole source of information.
2. Used as a benchmark against which the findings of research may be tested.

Limitations:

1. It may reflect bias or be out of date.
2. Parts may be missing, *i.e.,* it may lack authenticity.
3. It may not be representative of a wider population, especially with older documents.

Q.10. Analysis, interpretation and presentation of data

Ans. Data includes any information or observation that is associated with a particular project, including experimental specimens, technologies, and products related to the inquiry.

Data analysis is the process of systematically applying statistical or logical techniques to describe and illustrate, condense and recap, and evaluate data. There are two types of data analysis: qualitative and quantitative. Kreuger and Newman offer similarities and differences between them.

Similarities:

1. Both involve influence.
2. Both involve public methods.
3. Both involve comparison as a central process.
4. Both strive to avoid errors and false conclusions.

Differences:

1. Qualitative data analysis is less standardised, with a wide variety of approaches, while quantitative researchers choose from a specialised, standard set of data analysis techniques.
2. The result of qualitative data analysis guides subsequent data collection and analysis, which is thus a less distinct final stage of the research process than quantitative analysis, where data analysis doesn't begin until all the data is collected and condensed.
3. Qualitative researchers create new concepts and theories, while quantitative researchers manipulate numbers in order to test hypotheses with variable constructs.

Elements of analysis: analysis involves estimating the value of an unknown parameter in the population and testing it for drawing inferences. Analysis may therefore be described as descriptive analysis or inferential analysis.

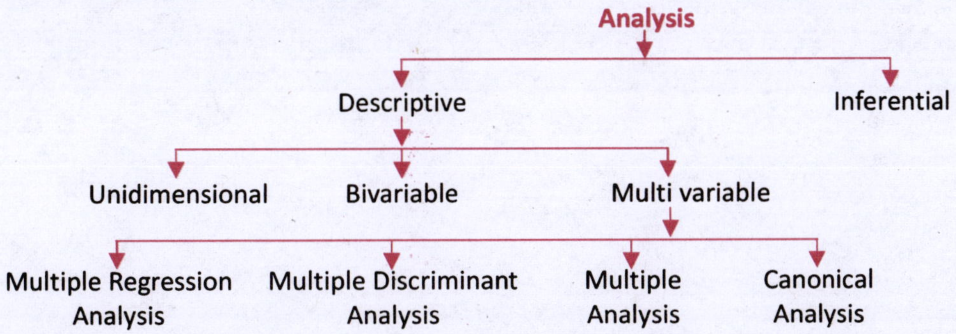

In modern times with computer facility there has been development of multivariate analysis.

Interpretation is drawing inference from collected facts after an analytical or experimental study. It is search for broader meaning of research findings. The taste of interpretation has two major aspects—

1. Effort to establish continuity in research through linking result of given study with those of another.
2. Establishment of some explanatory concepts.

One should always remember that even if data are properly collected and analyzed, wrong interpretation would lead to inaccurate conclusions.

Data afterwards **can be presented in form of:**

1. Distribution in form of frequency, percentage, and cumulative.
2. Table
3. Graphs in form of bar diagram, pie chart, and histograms.

Case Study

- **A case of rampant use of Tetanus Toxoid (TT) injection by the workers in the unorganised e-waste sector in the slums of a South Indian city**

In order to perform this study, we adopted an exploratory sequential mixed-methods technique. We performed in-depth interviews, participant observation, and casual conversations with the study respondents throughout the first phase. In the second phase of the study, 248 respondents were interviewed using an interview schedule that included both closed-ended and open-ended questions. The most prevalent health issue was job injuries, for which TT injections were regularly used as a form of treatment—even as frequently as every two months. Despite the fact that it was free in public health centres, employees opted to pay for it at nonprofit or private clinics instead.

In this situation, using TT injections denotes playing a social role in the interaction between patients and doctors. Since the public healthcare system seems to be mostly irrelevant to their demands, the phenomenon needs to be regarded as something that was jointly established by employees and healthcare providers. They are prevented from taking a break from work to recover from their injuries due to precarity in the workplace. Frequent TT injections may be considered an active choice made by the workers in the particular eco-system where the study was conducted as a coping strategy.

9

Human Genetics, Race, Ecology and Epidemiology

9.1

Human Genetics : Methods and Application : Methods for study of genetic principles in man-family study (pedigree analysis, twin study, foster child, co-twin method, cytogenetic method, chromosomal and karyo-type analysis), biochemical methods, immunological methods, D.N.A. technology and recombinant technologies.

Q 1. Meaning and scope of Human Genetics

Ans. Human genetics is the study that determines how genes among humans transmit into traits as well as patterns of inheritance from parents to children. In short terms, it is the study of the process of inheritance. The term genetics was coined by *Bateson* in 1906.

The process of inheritance was first explained by *Gregor John Mendel* in his experiments on the pea plant. He gave principles like the law of dominance, etc. He is therefore known as the Father of Genetics.

Human Genetics aims:

1. Principles of inheritance (hereditary and variations of genes)
2. Nature of inheritance
3. Variance within the population
4. Application for human welfare.

There are different branches:

1. **Classical genetics:** It studies the rules of inheritance.
2. **Molecular Genetics:** It examines the structure, organisation, transmission, and functions of genes. It determines traits (phenotypes).
3. **Cytogenetics:** It studies human chromosomes and sex chromosomes and their abnormalities and consequences.
4. **Population genetics:** It focuses on the stability and change in gene frequencies in various human populations.
5. **Biochemical Genetics:** It controls the secretion of enzymes.

Example	Genetics	Deficient enzyme	Feature
Albinism	AR	Tyrosinase	Lack of skin and hair pigment eye defect

6. **Immunogenetics:** It studies how genes control the immune system of the body. Different types of antibodies, histocompatibility (HLA), etc.
7. **Medical Genetics:** It studies transfer of diseases
8. **Eco Genetics:** It deals with the adjustment and adaptation of populations to their environment, particularly in the fields of nutritional ecology and infectious disease. For e.g., Bergmann, Allen rule
   Applications: Sports, nutrition, defence, forensics, genetic counselling, etc.
   It is a vast field that studies human variations and the transmission of traits along with physiological function. It is an inseparable part of biological anthropology. Indeed, the subdiscipline that transformed physical anthropology into biological anthropology

Q 2. Pedigree Analysis

Ans. Galton was the first person to attract the attention of others towards pedigree analysis. A pedigree is a family tree or chart made of symbols and lines that represent a patient's genetic family history. The study of the inheritance pattern of certain traits or diseases through the use of pedigrees is called pedigree analysis. The individual from which pedigree starts is called pro-band. It is done by a geneticist and a genetic counsellor.

Symbols used:

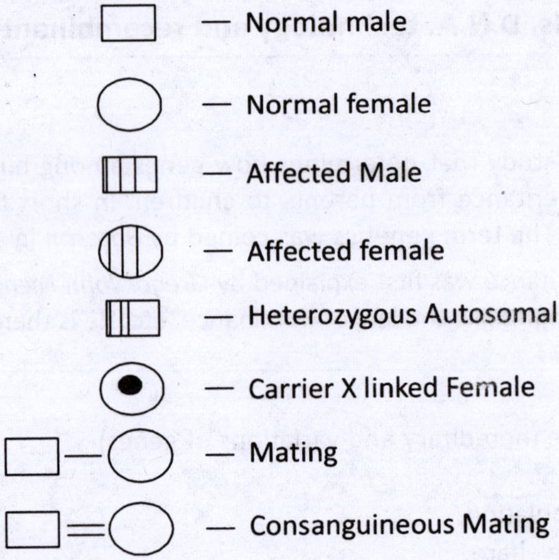

Various ways of inheriting traits:

1. **Autosomal Dominant inheritance:**

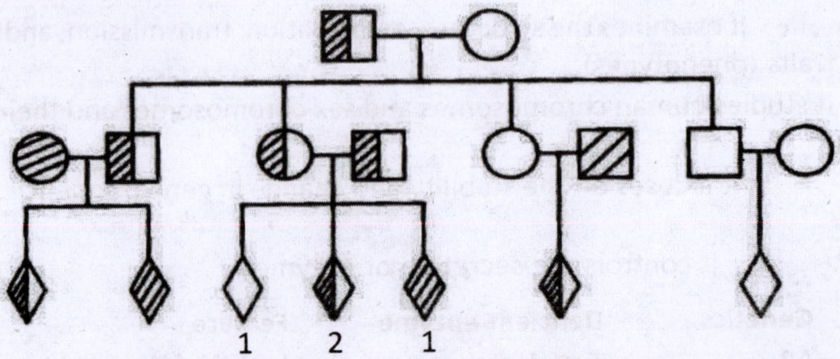

Pedigree of Autosomal Dominant Trait

- Each affected individual has an affected parent at the point in their ancestry where the mutant gene arose.
- Disorders express themselves in heterozygous conditions.
- e.g., Huntington's disease, cold urticaria.

2. Autosomal Recessive inheritance:

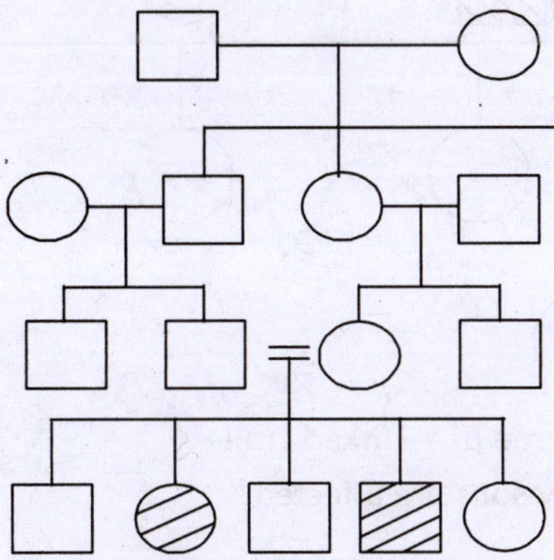

Pedigree of Autosomal Recessive Trait

- Almost never is disease present, but it comes out in cases of consanguineous marriage (1:4 ratio).
- e.g., cystic fibrosis, albinism, phenylkatonuria.

3. X-linked Recessive inheritance:

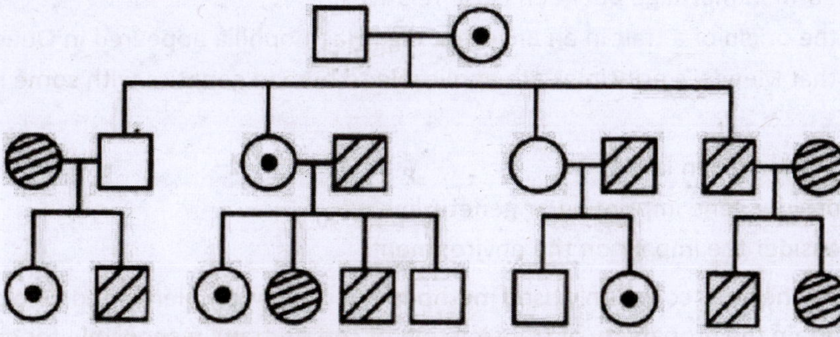

Pedigree of X-Linked Recessive Trait

- Also known as criss-cross inheritance (father to daughter to son).
- e.g., haemophilia, colour blindness

4. X-linked Dominant inheritance:

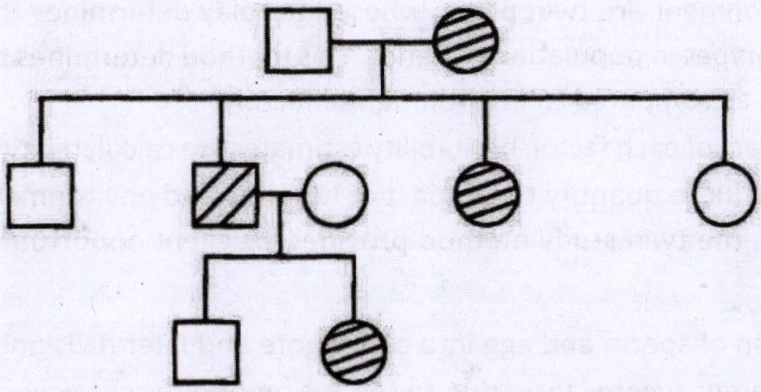

Pedigree of X-Linked Dominant Trait

- If the father is affected, the sons are unaffected, but the daughters are affected.
- e.g., Xg blood group, vitamin D rickets.

5. **Y-linked inheritance:**

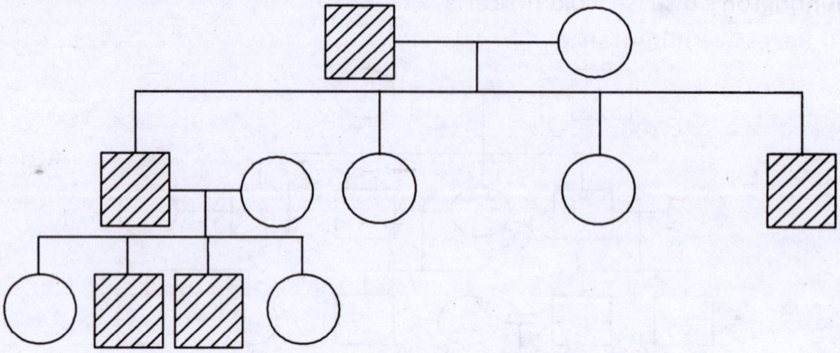

Pedigree of Y-Linked Trait

- Daughters are never affected. Only sons are affected.
- e.g., hypertrichosis (hairy ears)

Applications:

1. It is useful for genetic counsellors to advise couples about the possibility of having children with genetic defects.
2. It indicates harm in marriage between close relatives.
3. It indicates the origin of a trait in an ancestor, e.g., Haemophilia appeared in Queen Victoria.
4. It indicates that Mendel's principles are applicable to human genetics with some modifications.

Limitations:

1. Only work on Mendelian laws.
2. It doesn't consider gene imprinting or genetic linkages.
3. It doesn't consider the impact on the environment.

It is still one of the most commonly used methods and can be complemented with other methods. It is useful to ascertain the probability of transmission of certain traits responsible for chromosomal or genetic diseases.

Q 3. Twin Study Method

Ans. Heredity and environment are twin pillars whose interplay determines the stability and transfer of particular phenotypes in population genetics. This method determines the genetic contribution of a particular trait as compared to environmental factors.

To evaluate the impact of each factor, heritability estimates are calculated through the Twin Method. Ordinarily, it is difficult to quantify the impact of heredity and environment due to their complex interplay. However, the twin study method provides excellent opportunities.

Twins can be:

1. Monozygotic: Fusion of sperm and egg into one zygote and later division into two.
2. Dizygotic: Two different zygotes form due to the fusion of different eggs and sperm.

Identification of Twins by:

1. Placental method
2. Blood group/HLA method
3. DNA fingerprinting
4. Dermatoglyphics
5. Genetic marker
6. Skin Graft.

The twin study is based on the assumption that different traits developed in monozygotic (Mz) twins reared apart would be due to environmental factors. Similarly, similar traits developed in dizygotic (Dz) twins reared together would be due to environmental exposure.

One of the important measurements to find the relative contribution of heredity and environment to quantitative character is the Concordance Score of a trait. Concordance means the same phenotype in twins for a particular trait, while a different one is called disconcordance.

Heritability means how much of a given trait can be attributed to genetic variations. Concordance for traits higher in the Mz twin than the Dz twin means a strong genetic component. While high concordance rates for both Mz and Dz represent strong environmental determination.

The formula for heritability estimates is $H = \frac{Vg}{vg + ve}$

Vg : Environment component

Ve : genetic component.

There are two methods of heritability estimation:

1. Concordance—Discordance Method:

For discrete character, $H = \frac{\text{Conc Mz - Conc Dz}}{\text{100 - Conc Dz}}$

High Mz & Dz - Environmental determination

High Mz and low Dz - Genetic predisposition.

2. Rearing Studies

For continuous characters such as height $H = \frac{\text{VDzRA - V MzRA}}{\text{VDzRA}}$

V DzRA: Total variance

V MzRA: Environment Variance

If V MzRA is small (H-1), genetic character is more

If V MzRA is large (H-0), the environment character is more

A case study by *Clifford* on 4000 twins of the US Army with respect to height and weight and found that the concordance of Mz was higher than Dz, thereby proving that these traits are genetically controlled.

Limitations:

1. It has neither a specific genetic component like the nature of genes or location nor an environmental component (physical, chemical, etc.).
2. Mz twins are identical; the assumption is fallacious. Evidence shows Mz twins differ in size and vigour.
3. There can be a mistaken identity between genetic and environmental factors. E.g., Mz twins reared together but may attract the attention of different fellows in school, which might be missed.

4. Such studies do not consider inter-population variation. A character may be more genetic in one population or *vice versa*.
5. Heritability estimates of complex characters such as IQ and behaviour are difficult because of the complex interaction of heredity and environment.

Q 4. Co-Twin Study Method

Ans. Heredity and environment are twin pillars whose interplay determines the stability and transfer of particular phenotypes in population genetics. This method determines the genetic contribution of a particular trait as compared to environmental factors.

In the co-twin method, identical twins along with co-twins and fraternal twins along with co-twins are investigated together and compared. These are the types of studies in which twins are provided with different environments. Earlier, these studies were conducted only on Mz. In this study, an identical twin is separated from another identical co-twin. Due to this separation, if they still exhibit similarity in certain traits, such traits are regarded as controlled by heredity. But if there is variation, it means such traits are controlled by the environment.

Scholar *Stephens* measured the intelligence level of certain Mz. He separated them and provided them with different environments. In one environment, the twins were provided proper training, but their co-twins were not trained properly. Thus, after a lapse of time, they were again examined, and such examination revealed that those who were properly trained were enhanced in comparison to those who were not trained properly. Through this study, Stephens claims that intelligence is influenced by the environment.

In another study, he included both Mz and Dz and also studied their respective parents in order to understand the appearance of schizophrenia. In this case, he makes a pair of single Mz and single Dz twins and also their respective cotwins. Then they were provided with different environments—one stressful and another calm. Those who were raised in stressful environments also began to show signs of schizophrenia while co-twins remained normal. This study proves that schizophrenia is not exclusively controlled by heredity but may appear due to environmental factors.

Advantages of twin studies:

1. Disentangle genetic and environmental factors for a trait of interest.
2. Environmental impact on genes studied
3. Help in nutritional, growth, and developmental studies

Thus, due to co-twin studies, the nature and nurture problems can be solved, and such studies also reveal which traits can emerge or be modified due to the interaction of nature and nurture.

Q 5. Foster child Method

Ans. Heredity and environment are twin pillars whose interplay determines the stability and transfer of particular phenotypes in population genetics. This method determines the genetic contribution of a particular trait as compared to environmental factors.

A foster child study is also conducted to understand nature-nurture problems. In these types of studies, certain children are selected randomly assuming that they share similar genetical characteristics at a similar level, which may be intelligence. Then, such children are reared in different homes classified as good homes, average homes, and poor homes.

If, after rearing, they exhibit differences in level of intelligence, it means intelligence is influenced by the environment, and if not, it means intelligence is influenced by heredity.

Obsorne specified the following as a requirement for good study:

1. Place the child in early foster care here.
2. No selective placement of children
3. Adequate sample
4. No ethnic variation sources

In this regard, a study was conducted in Chicago, where around 112 children were reared in good houses, around 105 children in average houses, and around 96 children were reared in poor houses, assuming that before rearing they had similar intelligence levels. After rearing, they were examined by providing a similar test, and it came to light that all those who reared in good houses scored 75–80% in the test, in average houses scored 55–60%, and in poor houses scored

30–40%. This study indicates that intelligence is influenced by the environment or nurture.

Minnesota graded home study: A similar study was conducted in which children of managerial (higher) class were reared in houses of labour class and children of labour class were reared in homes of higher class. After a lapse of time, it was observed that the IQ levels of children of higher class remained high and those of lower class remained low. Although reared in a contrasting environment. This study proved that intelligence is also influenced by heredity.

Actually, these studies aimed at showing that there are certain traits that are neither exclusively controlled by the environment nor exclusively controlled by heredity.

We can use orphanages as an example of how this can be repaid. In orphanages, children with different genetic compositions are reared together under similar environmental conditions, and if they exhibit similarities, those are due to nurture (environment), and if they exhibit differences, those are due to nature (heredity).

Limitations:

1. Contradictory studies of Chicago and Minnesota.
2. Intelligence and behaviour have abstract interactions between genes and the environment. The ultimate factor did not get to be known.
3. Ethical issue of taking children away from parents.
4. Research bias cannot be neutralised.

Q 6. Cytogenetics/Karyotyping

Ans. A branch of genetics that is concerned with the study of the structure and function of cells, especially chromosomes, is called cytogenetics. Cytogenetics helps in revealing various genetic disorders via the analysis of chromosomes.

Normally, chromosomes cannot be seen with a light microscope, but during cell division at metaphase, they are so condensed that they can be visible at a 1000X microscope.

Systematised arrangement on the basis of length of chromosome arm, position of centromere, banding pattern, and other physical features is called karyotype analysis.

It is done by:

1. Arresting mitosis at metaphase using colchicine
2. Squashing them onto the slide so that all chromosomes come on a single plane
3. Staining (banding) with fluorescent dyes results in a pattern of bands and inter-bands all along the chromosomal length.
   a. G-banding—first nurtured by trypsin to denature the protein content, and then adds Giemsa stain. Thick bands represent A-T bonding; thin bands represent C-G bonding.
   b. Q-banding is done by the quinacrine strain. Fluorescent region: A-T bonding (thick). View by UV fluorescent telescope.
   c. C-banding: done with light acid, strong alkali, and warm saline water prior to the Giemsa stain. Colour appears at the centromere.
   d. R-banding: heat treatment prior to Giesma stain Reverse the G-method. Thin bands represent A-T bonding; thick bands represent C-G bonding.
4. Cutting them down and pairing them with partners based on the position of the centromere, size, and shape of the chromosomes.

Human Karyotype:

A: 1 to 3 —large, metacentric

B: 4 to 5 —large, submetacentric

C: 6 to 12 + X — medium, submetacentric

D: 13 to 15 —large, acrocentric

E: 16 to 18 —medium, metacentric (16); small, submetacentric (17, 18)

F: 19 to 20 — metacentric

G: 21 to 22 + Y: short, acrocentric; Y has no satellite.

These methods are useful for detecting chromosomal abnormalities of both types:

➢ **Structural abnormalities**

1. Deletion: loss of a chromosome segment; e.g., Cri du Chat syndrome (deletion of the 5 th chromosome).
2. Duplication: addition of segments to the chromosome
3. Inversion: inverted chromosome order
4. Translocation: transfer of a segment from one chromosome to another

➢ **Numerical abnormalities**

1. Turner: XO
2. Klinefelter: XXY
3. Down: Trisomy 21
4. Edward: Trisomy 18
5. Patau: Trisomy 13

➢ Another application is satellite chromosome observation. The region of the chromosome between the 2* constriction and the telomere is called the satellite. 13, 14, 15, 21, and 22 pairs are satellite chromosomes.

➢ In addition to karyotyping, cytogenetics also uses the advanced fluorescence in situ hybridization (FISH) method. FISH uses fluorescent probes that bind to only those portions of DNA with which they are complementary.

➢ This helps with spatial and temporal patterns of gene expression. It also helps in identification of diseases like Angelman syndrome and Prader-willi syndrome.

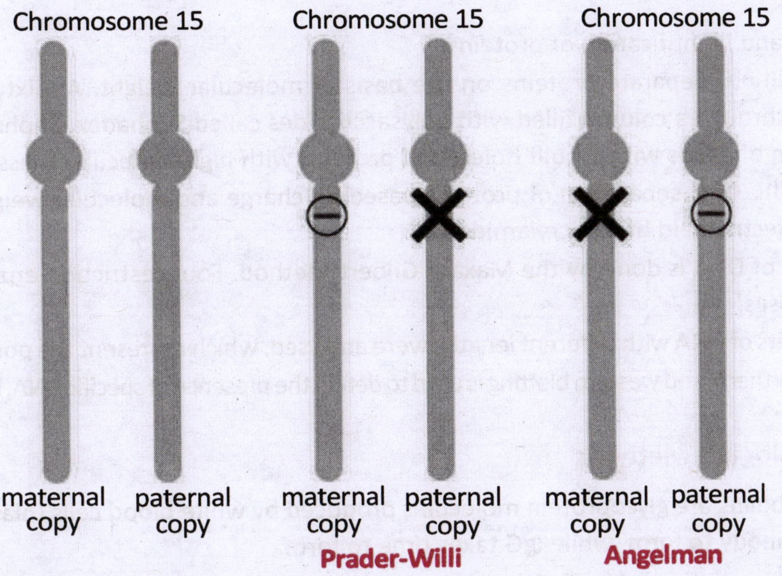

Limitation: It studies chromosomes superficially.

Gene mapping is an improvement over karyotyping for study, and further research is bound to happen.

Q 7. Biochemical Methods

Ans. Biochemical genetics combines genetics and biochemistry to elucidate the nature of metabolic pathways and their functions.

Biochemical markers in Red blood cells:

- Red Cell Antiques: Rh System, ABO Secretions
- Haemoglobins (HbS)
- Enzymes, G6DP

Biochemical methods are applied to the main chemical compounds of genetics: DNA, RNA, proteins, etc. It is mainly used to determine the activity of genes within cells.

Human activities are initiated and controlled by some sort of biochemical reaction at the cellular level. Genes control the appearance of phenotypic traits in organisms by exercising development and biochemical activity within cells.

Biochemical genetics was initiated by A. Garod in his study on hereditary diseases in 1909. He concluded that hereditary diseases are due to the impact of mutant genes, which act as blocks in metabolic systems. Thus the concept of "one mutant gene, one metabolic block" emerged. It was, however, ignored but rediscovered by Beadle and Tatum.

By proposing the "one gene, one enzyme" hypothesis, Beadle and Tatum demonstrated that genes express themselves through the synthesis of enzymes.

Usage:

1. Understand protein synthesis and human genetics.
2. It helps in understanding inter- or intra-population variation. Population affinity and diversity can be estimated from the frequency of variants of such biochemical markers.
3. It reveals the fate of inherited genetic disorders.
4. It depicts the health status of the population.

Methods:

1. Separation and identification of proteins
   a. **Gel filtration:** Separate proteins on the basis of molecular weight. A mixture of proteins is passed through a column filled with polysaccharides called Sephadex. Sephadex is present in the form of beads with inbuilt holes, and proteins with high molecular masses cannot pass.
   b. **Electropherosis:** separation of proteins based on charge and molecular weight Protein is put in the electric field of an acrylamide gel.
2. Sequencing of DNA is done by the Maxam-Gilbert Method. Four restriction enzymes cut DNA at different bases.
   Thus, four sets of DNA with different lengths were analysed, which represent the position of enzymes.
3. Southern, northern, and western blotting is used to detect the presence of specific DNA, RNA, and proteins.

Q 8. Immunological Methods

Ans. Immunoglobulins are glycoprotein molecules produced by white blood cells (plasma cells). IgM is the first antibody to form, while IgG takes time to form.

Immunological methods are used to understand and prevent certain emerging infectious agents like dengue fever, rift valley fever, West Nile fever, and certain biological weapons like anthrax and viruses like small pox, etc. The immunological methods are related to antigen-antibody interactions. The various immunological tests are the agglutination test, the antiglobulin test, and the precipitation test.

In the agglutination (serological) test, serum is taken from saliva, blood, etc. to detect antigen-antibody interaction. It was attempted to understand whether the serum of a particular individual is able to produce antibodies if a foreign element is inserted into it or not.

An antiglobulin test is generally carried out on pregnant women to understand certain prenatal conditions. This test is also carried out prior to the transfusion of blood. The serum from the blood is taken, and then it is determined whether such blood can be transferred to the patient or not.

The precipitation test is almost identical to the agglutination test. It is also based on antigen-antibody interactions. All these methods and tests are conducted to understand the immune system of human beings. Through these methods, it can be estimated that the immune system can become strong enough to fight many infections and viruses. Thus, the implications of these tests are very significant for the well-being of human beings.

Methodology:

1. Immunological methods are dependent on antigen-antibody reactions. There are five types of antibodies, namely IgA, IgG, IgM, IgE, and IgD, each made up of two heavy protein chains. If protein is treated with phenyl-isothiocynate and a mild acid, the terminal amino acid is separated, which can be analysed.
2. A technique used in immunogenetics is immunoelectrophoresis, in which different types of antibodies present in the blood are separated by using an electric gradient. Then the level of antibodies present in the blood is compared with normal levels.
3. The variation in the antibody is used in the immunological method. Some antigen is injected into the body, and antibodies are separated and purified. Such antibodies are studied, and their amino acid composition is determined. It has been found that antibodies elicited by different individuals differ in the amino-acid composition of different chains.

4. Study of HLA incompatibility and transplant rejection.
5. ABO incompatibility and clumping of the blood occur when different types are mixed because type A individuals have anti-B antibody molecules present in their blood and type B people have anti-A antibodies. Type O individuals are found to have both anti-A and anti-B antibody molecules. On the other hand, type AB individuals have no antibodies to the ABO group of antigens at all.
6. Blood group system, Rh blood group system
7. Auto-immune disorder: Crohn disease, cytokine storm in COVID-19

Application:

1. Study of the structure, function, and cellular control of immunoglobulins in the human body.
2. Immune responsiveness of an individual.
3. Histocompatibility study: The results obtained from immunological studies can be fruitfully applied for the benefit of humans.
4. Detection of immunodeficiency diseases that is hereditary in nature (e.g., IgA deficiency, severe combined immune deficiency syndrome, Wiscot-Aldrich syndrome, etc.)
5. Separation of environmental and genetic factors in the development of a trait
6. Genetic counselling for parents with traits of hereditary immunodeficiency disorder.
7. Timely treatment of immunodeficiency disorders
8. Help determine the extent to which diseases like Corona have spread.
9. Genetic profiling of people around the world by Gm, Haplo, etc.

Case Study

- **Sero-ecological studies**

The National Centre for Biological Sciences undertook research among the Bomrr clan in Nagaland to understand how and why they are immune to viruses in bats, which they interact with. They are carrying out sero-ecological studies on this human-bat interface (both have shared antibody responses to some viral families).

Q.10 Recombinant DNA Technology

Ans. DNA stands for deoxyribonucleic acid. It is mostly located in the cell nucleus, but a small amount can be found in mitochondria. Info within it locks in chemical bases (A, T, C and G).

Recombinant DNA refers to the joining together of two pieces of DNA that are not normally found together, usually involving DNA from two different species, and the technology used for this process is recombinant DNA technology.

It occurs in five steps:

1. Generation of DNA fragments using restriction endonuclease
2. Incorporation of these fragments into a suitable vector
3. Introduction of this vector into the host organism.
4. Growing host vectors in culture medium, producing clones, and preparing multiple copies of DNA fragments.
5. Selection and harvesting of clones containing relevant DNA fragments.

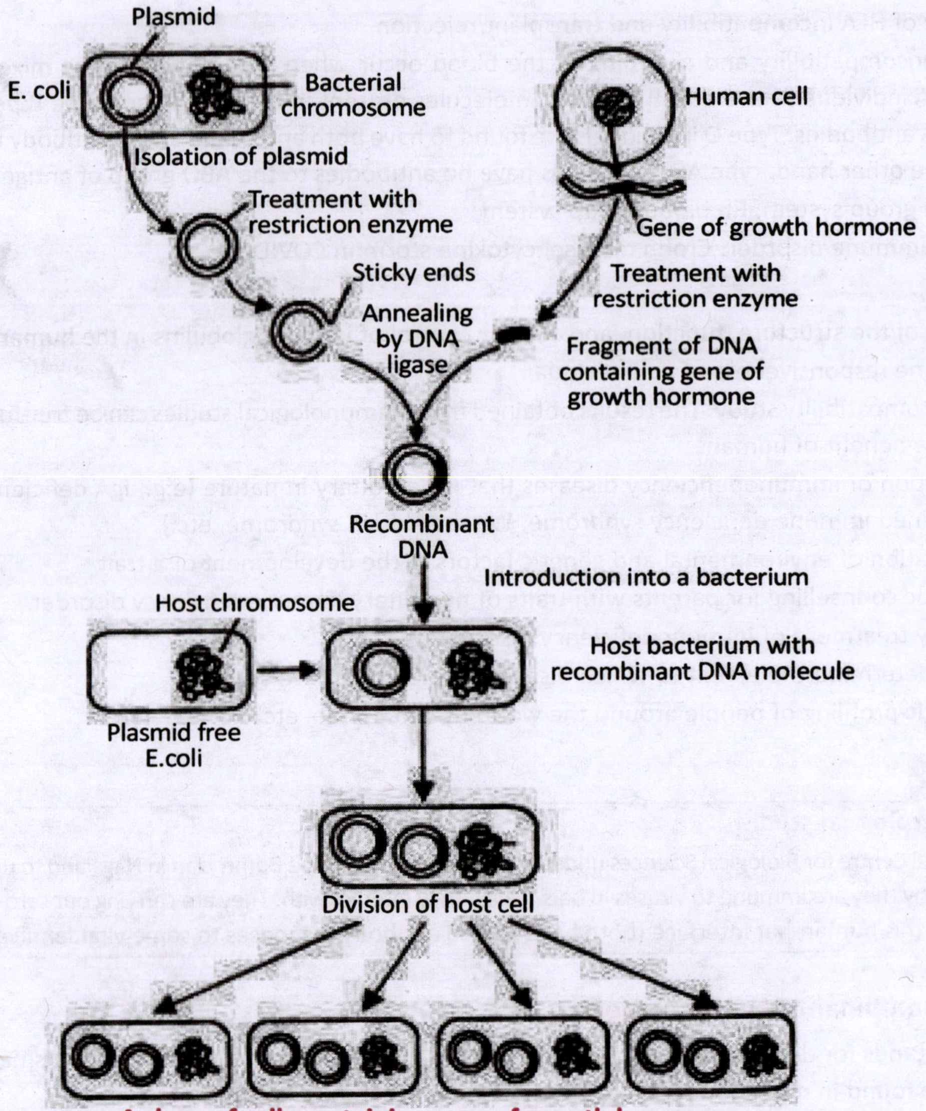

A clone of cells containing gene of growth hormone

Applications:

1. Gene mapping and structure analysis Eg., Globin gene
2. Population genetics in relation to diseases and population structure
3. Controlling genetic diseases and detecting carriers.
4. Agricultural growth like the development of BT cotton, GM mustard, etc.
5. Biosynthesis is like making insulin.
6. DNA recombinant vaccine, like the vaccine against Hepatitis B.

Concerns:

1. Cancer susceptibility is genetic.
2. Designer baby making

3. Development of bioweapons
4. Consent and awareness are lacking.
5. Patenting problem.

Great care needs to be exercised for no other reason than to allay the fear of the general public.

9.2

Mendelian genetics in man-family study, single factor, multifactor, lethal, sub-lethal and polygenic inheritance in man.

Q 1. Single Factor Gene

Ans. When single genes control one trait, alleles of the gene are clearly demarcated as dominant and recessive.

Characteristics:

1. Follow Mendel's law of inheritance.
2. Sharply defines segregation of phenotypic traits.
3. Discontinuous and discrete expression.
4. Doesn't get impacted by the environment.
5. Alleles are located at the same fixed locus.
6. Most of them are qualitative traits.

Examples:

➢ Mendel conducted experiments on the pea plant (Pisum satixum). In the monohybrid experiment, he chose plants of the same character with contrasting forms, i.e., tall and dwarf plants.

In the F1 generation, when interbred, all plants were tall, and when they were interbred in the F2 generation, the ratio of dwarf and tall was 1:3.

Gamates - T T × (t)(t)

F_1 Gen - Tt

Gamates - (T)(t) × (T)(t)

F_2 Gen - T T,Tt,Tt,tt

Among humans, there is a similar genetic trait concerning the faster and non-tasting of PTC (phenyl thio carbamide). The taster character is dominant, while the non-taster character is recessive. Now, when we conduct mating between tasters and non-tasters of PTC, similar results are the result.

➢ In the dihybrid experiment, Mendel chose two contrasting forms: the height of the plant and the shape of the seed. Firstly, all tall plants (T) and round seeds (R) are separated from all dwarf (t) and wrinkled seeds (r). Later interbred,

Gamates - (T)(T)(R)(R) × (t)(t)(r)(r)

F_1 Gen - TtRr

Gametes - (T)(R) (t)(R) (T)(r) (t)(r)

F_2 Gen -

9 (Tall&round) : 3 (Tall& wrinkled): 3 (Dwarf &round) : 1 (Dwarf and wrinkled)

In humans, similarly, tasters and nontasters of PTC, along with rollers and nonrollers of the tongue, can be experimented with. Other examples: haemophilia; ear wax (dry or sticky); free and attached earlobes; dimples; and chin fissures.

Q 2. Polygenic inheritance in Man

Ans. Certain traits are determined by the interaction of genes on several chromosomes at several places on the chromosome.

Characteristics:

1. Don't follow Mendel's law.
2. Effect of each contributing factor is cumulative.
3. Continuous and graded expression
4. Show the role of the environment.
5. Alleles of different kinds are located in different locus
6. Traits can be quantitatively measured.

Skin colour, eye colour, and intelligence are some examples.

	Typically Black		Typically fair Alpino
	A A B B C C		a a b b c c
Gametes	A B C		a b c
F1 Gen		Aa Bb Cc	
		Aa Bb Cc × Aa Bb Cc	
Gametes		(A) (B) (C)	(A) (b) (C)
		(A) (B) (c)	(a) (B) (c)
		(A) (b) (C)	(a) (B) (C)
		(a) (B) (C)	(a) (b) (c)

	ABC	ABc	AbC	aBC	Abc	aBc	abC	abc
ABC	6	5	5	5	4	4	4	3
ABc	5	4	4	4	3	3	3	2
AbC	5	4	4	4	3	3	3	2
aBC	5	4	4	4	3	3	3	2
Abc	4	3	3	3	2	2	2	1
aBc	4	3	3	3	2	2	2	1
abC	4	3	3	3	2	2	2	1
abc	3	2	2	2	1	1	1	0

6D	T. Black	1
5D	Very Dark	6
4D	Dark	15
3D	Intermediate	20
2D	Fair	15
1D	Very Fair	6
0D	Albino	1

If we draw a graph of the above squares, we get a bell-shaped graph, meaning people with an average phenotype are more

Influence of the environment: Adults are affected by nutrition. Skin colour is affected by sunlight, altitude, temperature, etc. But blood groups and haemophilia don't get affected by the environment.

Q 3. Multifactor Aspect

Ans. R.A. Fisher proposed the multiple factor hypothesis. Traits in humans are influenced by multiple genes as well as the environment. However, it is different from polygenics in that:

1. The environmental impact is greater than in polygenics.
2. It is discontinuous, i.e., it shows abrupt changes from one phenotype to another, unlike polygenes.

Example

➢ Coronary Artery Disease:

Onset is triggered by factors like obesity, high BP, a high level of LDL, type II diabetes, etc.

Factor 1, Factor 2, Factor 3 } Above threshold ⟶ Disease

Below threshold ⟶ No discase

Therefore, it shows an extreme phenotype as compared to average polygenic heritance.

➢ Blood pressure disease

➢ Onset of diabetes and schizophrenia

Hypothesis faster proved to be correct by *Nilsson Ehle* in an analysis of a graded series of seed pigmentation in wheat crosses.

Case Study

- **Genome-wide analysis of 102,084 migraine cases identifies 123 risk loci and subtype-specific risk alleles**

Over a billion people suffer from migraines globally, but little is known about their hereditary causes. 102,084 migraine cases and 771,257 controls were used in genome-wide association research, which found 123 loci, 86 of which were previously unidentified. These loci offer a chance to examine both shared and unique genetic elements between the two primary migraine subtypes, migraine with aura and migraine without aura. Using 29,679 cases with subtype information, stratification of the risk loci revealed three risk variants that seem specific for migraine with aura (in HMOX2, CACNA1A, and MPPED2), two that seem specific for migraine without aura (near SPINK2 and near FECH), and nine that increase susceptibility for migraine irrespective of subtype. The novel risk loci contain genes for calcitonin gene-related peptide (CALCA/CALCB) and serotonin 1F receptor (HTR1F), two recently discovered migraine-specific therapeutic targets.

Q 4. Lethal Inheritance

Ans. Gene: It is a sequence of nucleotides in DNA or RNA.

Genes that cause the death of an organism are called lethal genes. All these lethal genes are mutant genes; they are not present in natural genes. Depending on the time of death, they are classified as:

1. **Absolute lethal:** causes death during the prenatal stage. They are negligibly present in the human population. It can be gametic death, zygotic death or foetal death.
2. **Sub-lethal:** causes death at the post-natal stage; e.g., epiloia, haemophilia, patau, edward syndrome.
3. **Semi-lethal:** cause death after puberty, e.g., Huntington disease, thalassemia, sickle cell disease, down syndrome.

These genes are also classified into:

1. **Dominant lethal** – They kill possessor even in heterozygous condition.

Sublethal	Semi lethal
Eg. Epiloia	Eg. Huntington disease
Multiple skin tumours and death in early infancy	Express in middle age. Person suffer from muscular failure, mental retardation and ultimately death

2. **Recessive lethal** - one which express in homozygous condition only.

Semi lethal	Sub lethal
Eg. Thalassaemia	Eg. Haemophilia – X linked disorder which
Sickle cell anelemia	Express mostly in males

3. **Conditional lethal–** Genes which are normal in particular environment but lethal when environment changed.

   Eg. Erythroblastosis fetalis - Rh is not lethal in normal condition but Rh–ve mother with Rh+ baby becomes lethal for next baby.

   Eg. Phenylketonuria can be minimized by prevailing phenylkalenine free diet.

   Favism – Deficiency in G6PD. If they eat fava beans, they develop haemolytic anaemia.

4. **Incomplete Dominance –** Lethal in homozygosity but heterozygous condition beneficial under particular environment.

Eg. Sickle cell anaemia under malaria area

Hbs/Hba —— HbA/HbA

Hbs/HbA Hbs/HbA Hba/HbA HbA/HbA

Q 5. Mendelism and its application

Ans. Mendel, also called father of Genetics, carried out various experiments on garden pea plant (Pisum Sativum) for eight years in which he performed cross breeding between isolated pure plants and arrived at conclusion also known as Mendel's laws of heredity.

Monohybrid: Mendel conducted experiments on the pea plant (Pisum satixum). In the monohybrid experiment, he chose plants of the same character with contrasting forms, i.e., tall and dwarf plants.

In the F1 generation, when interbred, all plants were tall, and when they were interbred in the F2 generation, the ratio of dwarf and tall was 1 : 3.

Gamates	-	T T	× (t) (t)
F_1 Gen	-	Tt	
Gamates	-	(T) (t)	× (T) (t)
F_2 Gen	-	T T,Tt,Tt,tt	

He found all individuals in next generation (F_1) tall. When he self-fertilized F_1 generation, Genotype came 1 : 2 : 1 and Phenotype came 3 : 1.

Law of Dominance: When two parent types representing contrasting strains of single unit character are crossed, strain of one of parent is expressed absolutely in offspring while one from other parent goes unrepresented. The one that expresses is dominant one while one which does not is recessive. Mendel himself did not give it but later studies made it so.

Law of Segregation (Law of Purity of Gametes): While body cells and germ cells, prior to reduction division involved in gamete formation, contain genes of both alternative character and are hybrid in character, segregation of alternative genes take place during maturation so that only one or other gene comes to be present in any gamete. Thus, gametes are pure for any gene.

Law of Independent Assortment: It states that genes of different character located in different pairs of homologous chromosome are independent of one another in their behaviour during gamete formation and in subsequent expression in individual.

In the dihybrid experiment, Mendel chose two contrasting forms: the height of the plant and the shape of the seed. Firstly, all tall plants (T) and round seeds (R) are separated from all dwarf (t) and wrinkled seeds (r). Later interbred,

Gamates - ( ) (T) (T) (R) R × (t) (t) (r) (r)

F_1 Gen - TtRr

Gametes - (T) (R) (t) (R) (T) (r) (t) (r)

F_2 Gen - TR:Tr:tR:rr

9 (Tall&round) : 3 (Tall& wrinkled) : 3 (Dwarf &round) : 1 (Dwarf and wrinkled)

Applications:

1. **Medico-legal –** 10-15% of cases of medico-legal (paternity) disputes are solved merely with ABO blood group system. For rest, we take help of other blood group system – Rh, MNS, serum or plasma protein, dermatoglyphics.
2. **Medical application –** Study of modes of inheritance of different types of histo-incompatibility and inborn errors of metabolism with help of Mendelian principle has led to development of cure for such anomalies eg. Rh –ve incompatibility leading to erythroblastosis fetalis.
3. **Genetic counselling –** Genetic advice sought by people who have history of genetic disease. Like X-linked recessive, autosomal dominant disease etc. Pedigree analysis form core of counselling.
4. **Hybrid Varieties –** For green revolution and other agricultural revolution, hybrid varieties of seeds, vegetables etc., are being prepared via these laws usage.

Exceptions:

1. **Co-dominance:** When both alleles of a pair are fully expressed in heterozygote condition it is called co-dominance. Each allele exhibits unique pattern of expression in which both alleles express themselves e.g. AB blood type of ABO blood group, cow with white and black pattern. It goes against the law of dominance.
2. **Semi dominance/incomplete dominance:** Semi-dominant product in the heterozygote condition is intermediate between dominant and recessive alleles. E.g. in snap dragon plant, heterozygotes for colour alleles have pink flowers with dominant characters have red colour while flowers with recessive character have white colour. It goes against the law of dominance®.

3. **Suppressor Gene:** When a gene product can suppress the expression of dominant alleles then gene inheriting the expression is called suppressor gene. It goes against the law of dominance. For e.g. Proto-oncogene.
4. **Polygenic trait and Pleiotropy:** There are certain characters which are governed by more than one gene those are known as polygenic traits. For e.g. height, skin colour, eye colour etc. On the contrary, there are some genes which can govern more than one character, these are known as Pleiotropic genes. For e.g. gene for sickle cell anemia. These two phenomena go against law of gene one character.
5. **Gene Imprinting:** In case of gene imprinting, with the change in the source of alleles, the expression in offspring's also changes. For e.g. Huntington chores syndrome. It is a dominant disorder. When the allele comes from mother it express differently which can be compared with allele coming from father. This phenomenon goes against the principle of law of equivalence.
6. **Linkage:** Law of independent assortment was not universally applicable. In some cases there is marked tendency for parental combinations to remain linked and produce new combinations. It goes against the law of independent assortment.

Thus, all the laws of Mendel have exception except the law of segregation which is the universal or absolute law.

9.3

Concept of genetic polymorphism and selection, Mendelian population, Hardy-Weinberg law, causes and changes which bring down frequency - mutation, isolation, migration, selection, inbreeding and genetic drift. Consanguineous and non-consanguineous mating, genetic load, genetic effect of consanguineous and cousin marriages.

Q 1. Genetic Polymorphism and Selection

Ans. Genetic polymorphism is defined as the occurrence together in the same population of two or more than two alleles such that the frequency of the rare allele is always >1% and is maintained in the population, not merely by recurrent mutation.

Sources:

1. Mutation is the ultimate source of genetic polymorphism.
2. Natural selection operates on mutant genes.
3. Product of mutation and the flow of genetic information from neighbouring populations, i.e., migration.

Level: Genetic polymorphism can be seen at the level of

1. **DNA**
   a. Single nucleotide polymorph
   b. Variable number of tandem repeats
   c. Restricted fragmented length polymorphism
2. **Serological**
   a. Antigen A,B,O
   b. HLA
3. **Enzyme: G6PD, etc.**

Significance of Genetic Polymorphism:

1. Understand pathological entities, evolutionary past, and guidance about the biological future.
2. It produces diversity within the population.

3. Used in population diversity studies
4. Used in forensic testing

Example: study of human evolution with special reference to mitochondrial DNA and Y-chromosome polymorphism.

Relationship with Natural Selection:

1. **Stabilising Polymorphism:** When two or more versions of a gene are available. However, populations having both versions of genes are less stable than populations having either version of genes. E.g., sex polymorphism: stabilising polymorphism removes populations that are not perfectly male or female, thus showing only two discrete sexes: male and female.
2. **Transient or directional polymorphism:** when environmental demands shift in a constant direction, the frequency of alleles corresponding to favourable phenotype traits keeps increasing at the expense of others.
   Eg., moths at the time of the industrial revolution in London went from white to black, as described by Kettlewell.
3. **Balanced polymorphism:** a situation in which two different versions of a gene are maintained in a population and those carrying both are more fit than those with either one. For example, Heterozygous sickle cell anaemia (HbA - Hbs) protects against malaria, Heterozygous haemoglobin Hba/Hb-C protects against blood parasites, and Thalassemia minor (only one chain is affected) protects against malaria.

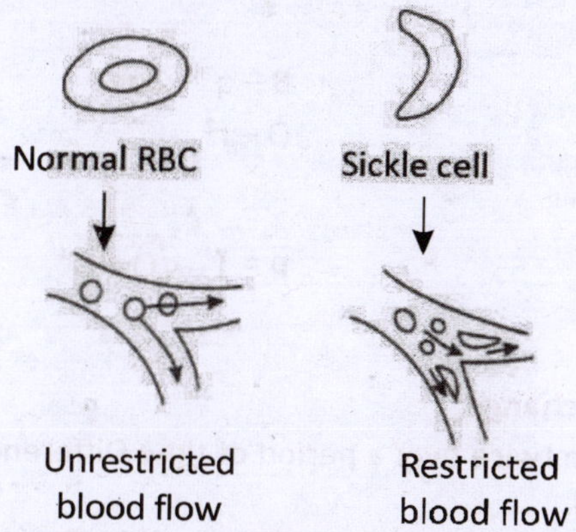

Sickling of RBCs

Under conditions when the environment is in flux, populations with different polymorphic traits can explore adaptive success.

Q 2. Hardy Weinberg law

Ans. G.H. Hardy and W. Weinberg propounded the law on the premise that, given certain conditions, the proportion of genotype and allele frequency in a population will remain constant generation after generation.

Conditions specified under which populations will not evolve:

1. The population should be infinitely large and mate at random.
2. No selection is operative.
3. Population closed, i.e., no immigration or emigration occurs.
4. No mutation is operative in alleles.

Obviously, no population can satisfy all these conditions; therefore, there is no population that can stay in genetic equilibrium.

According to the Hardy Weinberg equation: The proportion of genotype in a gene is represented as the square of the sum of allele frequencies. It means if there are two alleles of a gene in proportion to p : q, then genotype frequency will be represented by $(p + q)^2$ or $p^2 : 2pq : q^2$.

The concept serves as a baseline to predict the probability of allelic frequency in the descendant population. It has a number of applications:

1. **Know about genetic structure of population –**
   i. One gene two alleles, dominant & recessive

      Ratio – p : q.

      $p^2 : 2pq : q^2$ – genotypic frequency

      $T - p^2 + 2pq$

      $t - q^2$ $\Rightarrow q = \sqrt{t}$

      Also, $p + q = 1$ $\Rightarrow p = 1 - \sqrt{t}$

   ii. One gene three alleles as in ABO blood group where A & B dominant, O recessive.

      Frequency – p : q : r for A, B, O respectively

      $p^2 : q^2 : r^2 : 2pq : 2pr : 2qr$ – genotype frequency

      Then,

      $A - p^2 + 2pr$ $B - q^2 + 2qr$

      $AB - 2pq$ $O - r^2$

      It implies,

      $r = \sqrt{O}$ $p = 1 - \sqrt{O + B}$

      $q = \sqrt{O + A}$

2. **Direction of evolutionary change:**
   a. Studying the population twice over a period of time Differences in allele frequency represent the direction of change.
   b. Studying the total population, which is divided into different age groups—changes in allele frequency from old age to childhood represent a dish of evolutionary change.
3. Help in genetic counselling to determine the likelihood of a child being homozygous for a recessive deleterious trait.
4. Qualitative genetics: estimate the role of the environment and genetic components.
5. Invalidate the theory of genophagy.
6. Find whether the population is mendelian or not.

   However, new techniques that are more relevant, like genome mapping, have emerged.

Q 3. Causes and changes which bring down frequency-mutation, isolation, migration, selection, inbreeding and genetic drift

Ans. Mutation refers to any sudden change in genetic material; it does not arise to fulfil a need; instead, it is totally random. E.g., a change of one amino acid in the beta chain of HbA makes it HbS.

Mutation

- Somatic
- Germinal
  - Chromosomal
  - Gene/point

Types of Mutations:

1. Gene and chromosomal
2. Spontaneous and induced
3. Dominant and recessive
4. Somatic and germinal

Mutation is caused by changes in temperature, viruses (organic), chemicals, and radiation. But in humans, radiation is the main cause of mutation. But it is for **natural selection** to decide the importance of each mutation on merit and spread these mutated genes from individuals to the whole population. Natural selection operates in terms of fertility and fecundity. Greater advantage has greater fertility and fecundity and spreads faster. Natural selection operates on phenotype and not genotype.

Natural selection as the guiding force of selection was the principle contribution of *Charles Darwin* given in his book "On the Origin of Species".

Natural selection acts in different ways:

1. Normalising natural selection is when it acts to remove unwanted genes, genotypes, and phenotypes.
2. Directional natural selection: changes in the environment favouring a particular gene or genotype E.g., after industrialization, dark-coloured moths escape predation as the trunks of trees are covered with soot (compared to earlier white-coloured moths).
3. Balanced natural selection, e.g., when one allele of a pair is relatively advantageous in effect at low frequency but disadvantageous at high frequency. E.g., HbA/Hbs provides resistance against malaria.
4. It is not always heterozygotes that are bestowed with favourable selection. e.g., Erythroblastosis fetalis, in which a RH+ve heterozygote born to Rh-ve mother is selected out.

Inbreeding refers to the mating of a member of a group with another member of the same group. The extreme expression is consanguinity; it increases homozygosity, decreases heterozygosity, and consequently decreases genetic variability.

Some scientists give the example of the Great Andamanese, whose population according to the 1971 Census was reduced to 28 from about 300 a hundred years ago as they did inbreeding and possessed autosomal recessive lethal or semi-lethal genes. As inbreeding increases homozygosity, autosomal recessive will become homozygous, and as it becomes lethal, its phenotype appears and is removed through natural selection. As recessive homozygotes keep dying, the population declines in number and is eliminated in the end.

However, inbreeding is not inherently harmful:

1. Unless there is the presence of an autosomal recessive lethal gene.
2. According to Malthus, living beings in general have enormous fertility; therefore, the survivors will produce much more than those eliminated.
3. Decreased Darwinian fitness of the population: In biology, it is usually said that a smaller number of genotypes means a greater chance of elimination if the environment changes. However, for men, there is neither a study nor evidence that a reduced number of genotypes have a negative effect.
4. As continuous inbreeding over a long period of time reduces the frequency of deleterious alleles as a result of longterm effects.

Inbreeding can be harmful only in the situation where the survivor does not have enormous fertility to compensate for the loss of a recessive lethal homozygote. As human beings have sufficient fertility, the harmful effects of inbreeding in humans are only theoretical in nature. Here, we must remember that this issue concerns population genetics and not human genetics.

Inbreeding increases homozygosity, but heterozygosity reduces to half in every generation. Inbreeding leads to disruptive selection (a decrease in the number of heterozygotes). Thus, recessive diseases like albinism, retinitis pigmentosa, dwarfism, etc. increase in the short run.

Genetic drift is a random aspect of evolution that refers to fixation or elimination without the role of mutation or selection. It can be seen in the form of the founder and bottleneck effects.

Founder Effect: *Ernst Mayr* says that the establishment of a new population by a few original founders who carry a small fraction of the total genetic variation of the parental population.

When certain individuals migrate many among them and have blood group frequencies revolving around the migrant ancestor and not around the parent population, new population emerged, this is called the Founder Effect. E.g., Retinitis pigmentosa among Tristan da Cunha Island; Ellis Van Creveld among Amish; G6PD high frequency among Naga, India.

Bottleneck Effect: Catastrophe wiping out most of the population without regard to its previous fitness. It changes the proportional random distribution of alleles and even leads to the loss of alleles. E.g., cheetahs and American bison were wiped out; 2 million years ago, transition from Australopithecus to Homoerectus; the Toba Volcano in the early 2000s affected a 75,000-year-old human population, which was reduced to 10,000–30,000 individuals.

Meaningful mutation is caused by radiation, and the last six decades have seen a sharp increase in radiation due to industrialization, nuclear activity, etc. Since natural selection acts on mutation, its rate has also increased. Inbreeding, hybridization, and genetic drift are cultural factors in man. In the last 6-7 decades, due to the increase in transportation and telecommunication, inbreeding has declined while hybridization has increased, and there is not much role left for genetic drift.

Case Study

- **Researchers uncover a gene mutation linked to the development of kidney disease.**

VANGL1 deletions are associated with an increased risk of antibody-mediated kidney disease. Some genetic variants, such as those in the MYH9 and APOL1 genes, are associated with a higher chance of developing kidney disease. The development of kidney illness has now been linked to a mutation in the VANGL1 gene, according to researchers at the Australian National University (ANU). Additional research also showed that the gene aids in shielding the kidney from immunological attack. The genomes of patients with autoimmune kidney disease and Tiwi Islanders with incredibly high rates of renal illness were sequenced by the researchers. Kidney disease is considerably more likely to develop in patients with this mutation.

The Tiwi Islanders will be greatly affected by this discovery. They have the highest documented renal disease rates anywhere in the world. This mutation enables the immune system to assault the kidney when you have a systemic immunological or inflammatory disorder. This gene's natural role is to reduce the rate of inflammation. People mistakenly believe that immunological disorders like lupus randomly target the kidneys. We have truly demonstrated for the first time that the kidney has a unique mechanism for fending off or halting that attack. The latest research emphasises the developing function of VANGL1 and other PCP genes in kidney damage and repair, which may have significant therapeutic and transplant implications.

Q 4. Genetic Load

Ans. Coined originally as costs of natural selection by *J.B.S. Haldane* but renamed by *MJ Muller.* Muller discussed the harmful effects of genetic load in one of his papers, 'Our Load of Mutations'. In this paper, he mentioned that due to mutations, genetic load is increasing, and the day is not far when whole human species will become extinct due to genetic load.

Therefore, genetic load is often defined as a measure of the harmful genes present in a population or the harmful effects that such genes have on the population.

Genetic load, in strict terms, is defined as the extent to which a population departs from a perfect genetic constitution. It is also defined as a relative decrease in the average fitness of the population with respect to the fitness of all individuals in the population who have a genotype that has maximum fitness.In general, if Wmax – Maximum fitness, load inferred by $\frac{Wmax - \overline{W}}{Wmax}$ if optimum fitness is 1, genetic load equals to 1– $\overline{W}$.

Types:

1. **Mutational Load:** load, risk, or burden of death due to mutation E.g., mutations in the insulin gene cause diabetes I, mutations in the blood clotting gene cause haemophilia, and mutations in the haemoglobin gene cause sickle cell anaemia.
2. **Segregational load:** genetic risk caused when the population segregates less fit homozygotes due to the reproductive fitness of heterozygotes.
3. **Incompatibility Load:** decrease in fitness due to mother-child incompatibility, e.g., erythroblastosis fetalis.

Effect:

1. Extinction of species may occur due to a huge genetic load.
2. Increase in the incidence of diseases.
3. Induced sex-linked lethal genes may affect sex ratio in the long run.

Beneficial: However, according to some scholars, genetic load is also beneficial in some cases.

1. If the genetic load is high, death is high, but it helps in the continuation of the population where land and resources are limited.
2. A higher genetic load is successful when subjected to a new environment, and one with little or no genetic load becomes extinct when subjected to rapid environmental changes.

More mutations meant more genetic load. Natural selection has no role in the formation of genetic load, but it increases or decreases the number of such genes in a population.

Q 5. Genetic effects of Consanguineous and Cousin marriage

Ans. General mating is actually random mating, or panmixia. In random mating, every individual has an equal probability of marrying another individual of the opposite sex. But in certain societies, marriages between closely related individuals are preferred.

Consanguineous mating is defined as mating between closely related individuals who have a common ancestor two or three generations back. It is of two types: cousin marriages and uncle-niece marriages.

A non-consanguineous marriage is one that takes place between unrelated individuals. It is of two types: positive assortative mating and negative assortative mating. A positive assortative one is between individuals who exhibit phenotypical similarity with respect to colour, height, etc. Negative assortative is between individuals who exhibit different phenotypical expressions with respect to certain traits. In India, mostly positive assortative mating is preferred.

Genetic Effects: Such consanguineous and cousin marriages increase homozygosity, and the chances of a recessive lethal gene to express increases, e.g., albinism, Tay-Sachs diseases, short-finger dwarfism, retinitis pigmentosa, alkaptonuria, etc.

Case of Brother & sister marriage:

Total No. of father side $= \frac{1}{2} \times \frac{1}{2} = \frac{1}{4}$

Total No. of father side $= \frac{1}{2} \times \frac{1}{2} = \frac{1}{4}$

Total no. of F & M side $= \frac{1}{4} \times \frac{1}{4} = \frac{1}{16}$

Total probability $= \frac{\frac{1}{16}}{\frac{1}{4}} = \frac{1}{4}$ (out of four, probably one child will die)

Effects:

1. Short run: Recessive autosomal disease is lethal (Afzal & Sinha study on Ansari Muslims of Bhagalpur)
2. Long run: consanguineous marriage of much longer duration reduces the proportion of heterozygotes through natural selection and increases the proportion of normal homozygotes (Imbaraj and Rao study on Tamil Brahmins).
3. Because of the elimination of mutant alleles, populations lose diversity in their gene pools.

Such consanguineous and cousin marriages can be harmful only in the situation where the survivor does not have enormous fertility to compensate for the loss of a recessive lethal homozygote. As human beings have sufficient fertility, harmful effects on humans are only theoretical in nature.

9.4

Chromosomes and chromosomal aberrations in man, methodology.

(a) Numerical and structural aberrations (disorders).

(b) Sex chromosomal aberration- Klinefelter (XXY), Turner (XO), Super female (XXX), intersex and other syndromic disorders.

(c) Autosomal aberrations- Down syndrome, Patau, Edward and Cri-du-chat syndromes.

(d) Genetic imprints in human disease, genetic screening, genetic counseling, human DNA profiling, gene mapping and genome study.

Q 1. Numerical and Structural aberrations

Ans. Chromosomes are coloured bodies, i.e., they can be stained in a human cell. There are 46 chromosomes, which exist in 23 pairs. 22 pairs, i.e., 44 chromosomes, are known as autosomes, and 1 pair, i.e., 2 chromosomes, is known as allosomes or sex chromosomes.

CHROMOSOMAL ABERRATIONS

AUTOSOMAL

- Numerical: Down syndrome, Patau syndrome, Edward syndrome
- Structural: Cridu Chaat Syndrome

ALLOSOMAL

- Numerical: Turner, Klinfelter, Super Male, Super female
- Structural: Inter sex

Structural Aberrations:

1. **Deletion:** a segment of the chromosome is deleted.
2. **Duplication:** addition of a segment of the chromosome
3. **Inversion:** Inverted Chromosome
4. **Translocation:** transfer of chromosomal segments from one pair to another non-homologous pair

   E.g., Cri du Chaat syndrome: the patient cries like a mewing cat. One symptom is microcephaly (a small head). Another is mental retardation. It is because of the deletion of the 5th chromosome.

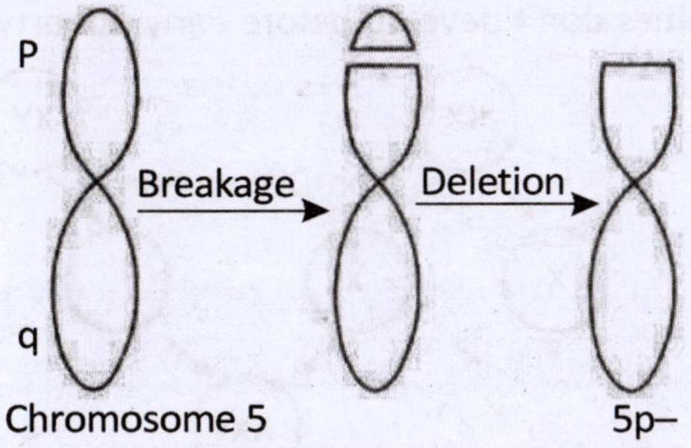

Deletion of Short Arm of Chromosome 5, Causing Cri-du-chat Syndrome

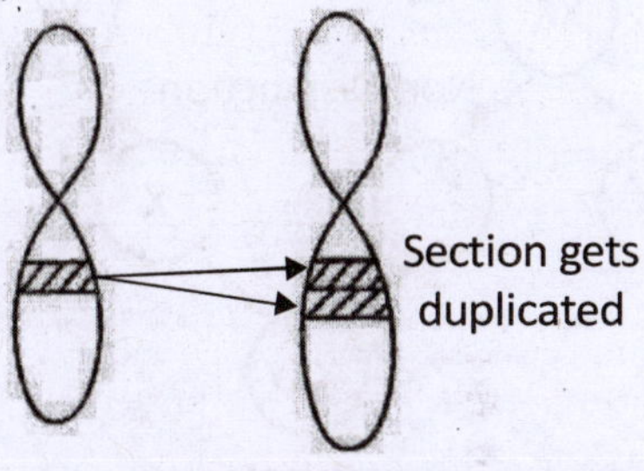

Duplicated

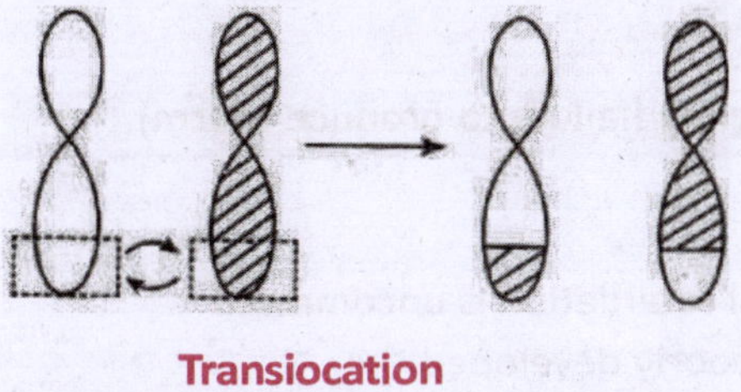

Transiocation

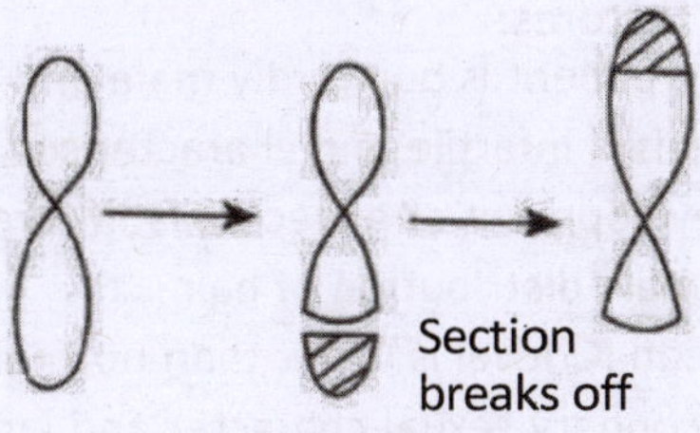

Inversion

Numerical Aberrations:

1. Trisomy of the 13 th Chromosome: Patau
2. Trisomy of the 18th Chromosome:Edward
3. Trisomy 21: Down
4. XXY: Klinfelter
5. XO:Turner

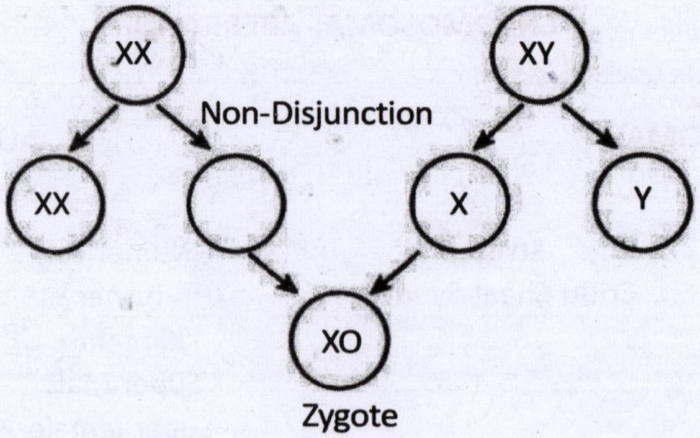

Full Monosomy X

Q 2. Klinfelter Syndrome

Ans. Klinfelter Syndrome is best defined as male hypogonadism that occurs when there are two or more X chromosomes and one or more Y chromosomes, i.e., 44 + XXY, which occurs in 82% of cases. It is one of the most common forms of genetic disease involving the sex chromosome. It occurs in 1 out of 850 live births. It occurs due to non-disjunction during gamate formation. Advanced maternal age and irradiation by either parent are also causative factors. It can rarely be diagnosed before puberty because testicular abnormalities don't develop before early puberty.

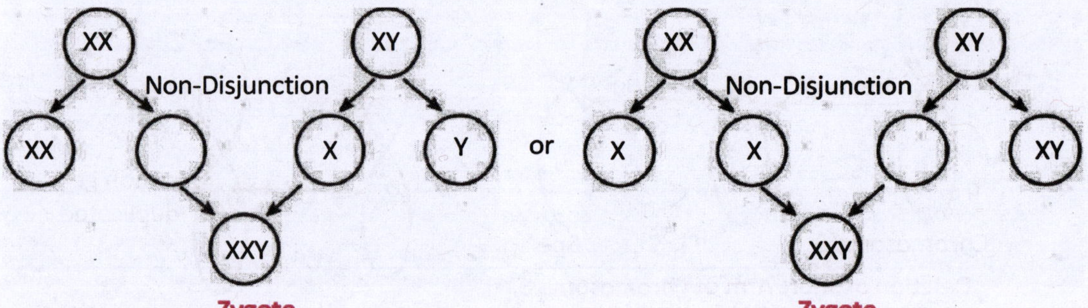

Clinical features:

1. The patient is outwardly male and long-legged.
2. Testis is infertile and characterised by azoospermia (failure to produce sperm).
3. Development of gynecomastia (breast).
4. Female distribution of hair.
5. Mean IQ level is lower than normal, but mental retardation is uncommon.
6. Secondary sexual character and language are poorly developed.

However, these patterns are not seen in all cases; the only consistent finding is hypogonadism. Klinfelter syndrome is the main cause of male infertility and morphological changes in the testis.

Detect:

1. The presence of a 1 -barr body in males indicates this syndrome.
2. By karyotype analysis.
3. By way of walking and levels of testosterone.
4. By testocular biopsy.

Treatment:

1. Testosterone replacement therapy
2. Speech and language therapy

Changes in chromosomal aberrations play no vital role in evolution since people suffering from such syndromes have low fecundity, but if the rate of the syndrome increases, it can impact evolution.

Q 3. Turner Syndrome

Ans. Turner syndrome results from complete or partial monosomy of the X-chromosome and is characterised by hypogonadism in phenotypical females. It is also referred to as X-monosomy.

The 45 X karyotype is found in 1 out of 2500 female births. In 57% of cases, an entirely absent X chromosome is present, while others have mosaics or deletions. 45,X Karyotype survives up to birth. It occurs due to non-disjunction during gamate formation.

Clinical Features:

1. Short stature.
2. Primary amenorrhea: absence of menstruation until the age of 16.
3. Absence of normal ovaries, which are replaced by thin white streaks of ovarian stroma without follicles.
4. Webbed neck.
5. Broad chest and wide-spaced nipples.
6. Intelligence is normal or slightly lower.

The absence of the second X chromosome leads to accelerated loss of oocytes, which leads to menopause occurring before menarche.

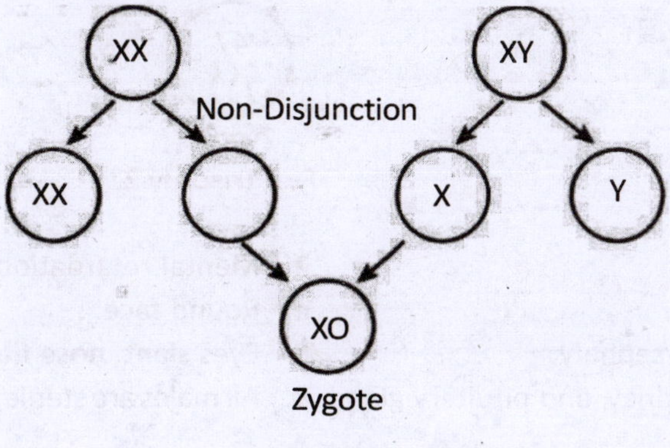

Detect:

1. Absence of the Barr Body in a female.
2. Karyotype analysis.

Treatment:

1. Steroid and estrogen therapy
2. Speech and language therapy

Changes in chromosomal aberrations play no vital role in evolution since people suffering from such syndromes have low fecundity, but if the rate of the syndrome increases, it can impact evolution.

Q 4. Down Syndrome

Ans. This syndrome is named after Landon Down. This syndrome occurs due to a trisomy of chromosome 21. It is also known as mongolism because affected people have eyelid folds and some physical features like mongoloid people.

It occurs approximately in 1 out of 700 individuals; however, its frequency in Caucasoid is 3 out of 200 live births. Aside from that, there is a direct correlation between the occurrence of the syndrome and the advanced age of the mother.

Mother Age		Frequency
30	→	1/1000
40	→	1/100
45	→	1/50

During mitosis, a process of disjunction takes place in which chromosomes separate from each other. However, in this syndrome, the 21 st chromosome pair doesn't separate from one another during the disjunction process.

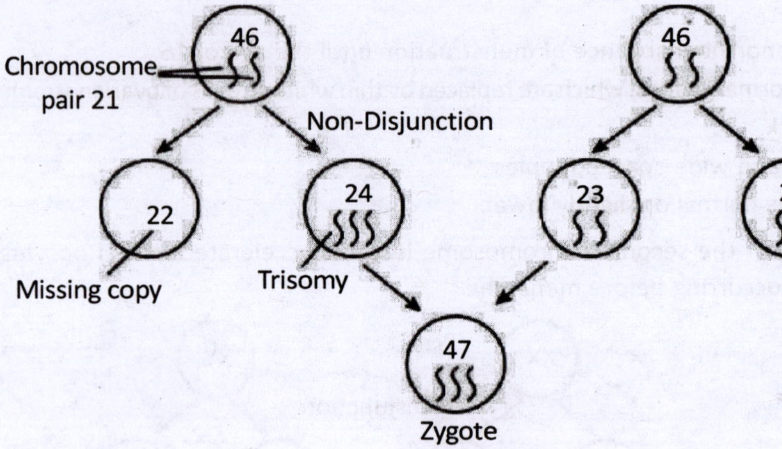

Full Trisomy 21

Clinical Features:

1. Short stature
2. Mental retardation
3. Epicanthic fold
4. Round face
5. Tendency of brachycephaly
6. Eyes slant, nose flattened
7. Deformed heart, kidney, and pituitary gland
8. All males are sterile, while females may be fertile.

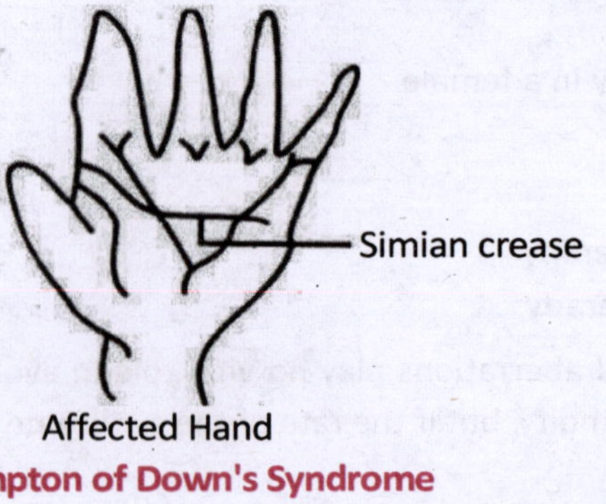

Sympton of Down's Syndrome

Diagnosis:

1. Amniocentesis
2. Chorionic villus sampling (CVS)
3. Karyotype analysis

Treatment:

1. Awareness and a genetic counsellor provide proper knowledge to the couple about the probability of its occurrence as age advances. Thereby avoiding pregnancy at a later age.
2. Cognitive-behavioural therapy and physiotherapy
3. The MTP Amendment Bill, 2020, now allows pregnancy even after 24 weeks in cases of substantial foetal abnormality.

Changes in chromosomal aberrations play no vital role in evolution since people suffering from such syndromes have low fecundity, but if the rate of the syndrome increases, it can impact evolution.

Case Study

- **Hormone therapy may boost brain function for people with Down's syndrome.**

A pilot study has revealed that regular hormone dosages may aid in improving cognitive abilities in patients with Down's syndrome. Seven Down's syndrome men were connected to a pump that delivered a dose of the gonadotropin-releasing hormone (GnRH) every two hours for a period of six months. In comparison to a control group who were not given the hormone, six out of the seven men had moderate cognitive improvements following the treatment, including in attention and the capacity to comprehend instructions.

Q 5. Edward Syndrome

Ans. This syndrome is named after Edward, who described it along with his colleagues in 1970. This syndrome occurs due to a trisomy of chromosome 18.

It occurs approximately in 1 out of every 4500 live births. There is also a relationship between the advanced age of the mother and the syndrome's chance of occurrence.

During meiosis, non-disjunction of the 18th chromosome or self-duplication at the cellular level causes this syndrome.

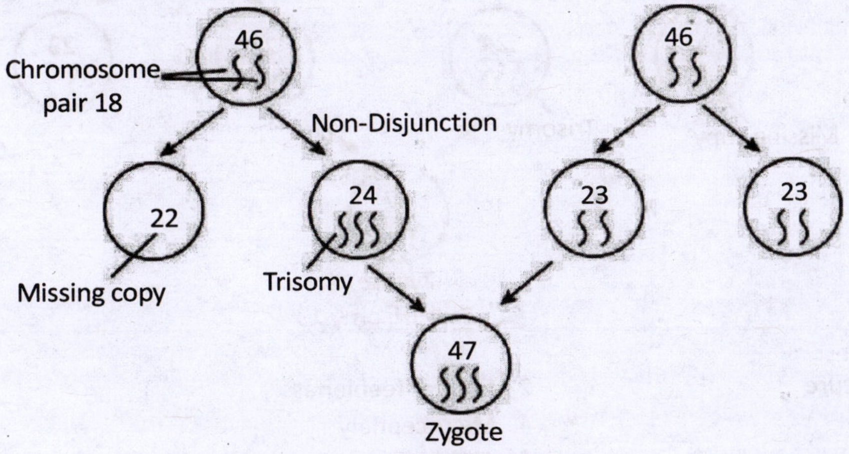

Full Trisomy 18

Clinical Features:

1. Short stature
2. Mental feebleness
3. Polydactyl
4. Microcephaly
5. Cliffed palate and lip
6. 3 rd finger overlapped on 2nd and 5th on 4th.
7. Heart diseases
8. Die young and infertile (2–3 months, exceptional 10 years).

Diagnosis:

1. Amniocentesis
2. Chorionic villus sampling (CVS)
3. Karyotype analysis

Treatment:

1. Awareness and a genetic counsellor provide proper knowledge to the couple about the probability of its occurrence as age advances. Thereby avoiding pregnancy at a later age.
2. Cognitive-behavioural therapy and physiotherapy
3. The MTP Amendment Bill, 2020, now allows pregnancy even after 24 weeks in cases of substantial foetal abnormality.

Changes in chromosomal aberrations play no vital role in evolution since people suffering from such syndromes have low fecundity, but if the rate of the syndrome increases, it can impact evolution.

Q 6. Patau Syndrome

Ans. This syndrome is named after *Patau*, who, along with his colleagues, described it around 1960. This syndrome occurs due to a trisomy of chromosome 13.

It occurs approximately among 1 out of 2200 live births. There is a relationship between the advanced age of the mother and the syndrome occurrence ratio.

During meiosis, non-disjunction of the 13 th chromosome or self-duplication at the cellular level causes it.

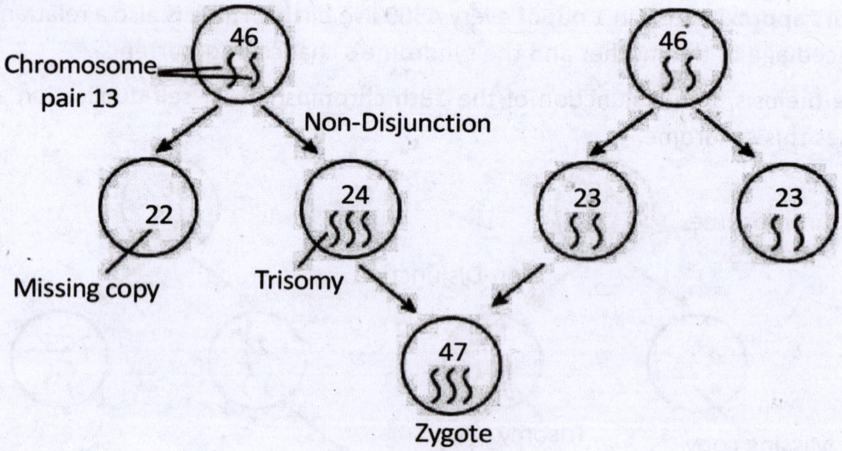

Full Trisomy 13

Clinical Features:

1. Short stature
2. Mental feebleness
3. Polydactyl
4. Microcephaly
5. Cliffed palate and lip
6. All fingers overlapped on the thumb.

7. Heart disease
8. Infertile and die young (1-2 months and exceptional 1-2 years).
9. Microphthalmia
10. Webbed neck
11. Newborns have low calcium and low Hb.

Diagnosis:

1. Amniocentesis
2. Chorionic villus sampling (CVS)
3. Karyotype analysis

Treatment:

1. Awareness and a genetic counsellor provide proper knowledge to the couple about the probability of its occurrence as age advances. Thereby avoiding pregnancy at a later age.
2. Cognitive-behavioural therapy and physiotherapy
3. The MTP Amendment Bill, 2020, now allows pregnancy even after 24 weeks in cases of substantial foetal abnormality.

Changes in chromosomal aberrations play no vital role in evolution since people suffering from such syndromes have low fecundity, but if the rate of the syndrome increases, it can impact evolution.

Q.7. Cri-du-chat Syndrome

Ans. It was first clinically detailed by Lejeune. In humans, autosomal monosomy has not been reported beyond birth. Individuals with such chromosomal complements will not survive beyond embryonic and foetal development. However, there are examples of survival with partial monosomy.

If the 5th chromosome pair is partially deleted or shortened, it is called Cri Du Chat Syndrome. In this, a small piece of the short-arm 'p' of the 5th chromosome is deleted.

Ratio: 1: 50000 live births

Life: 10–15 years in extreme cases

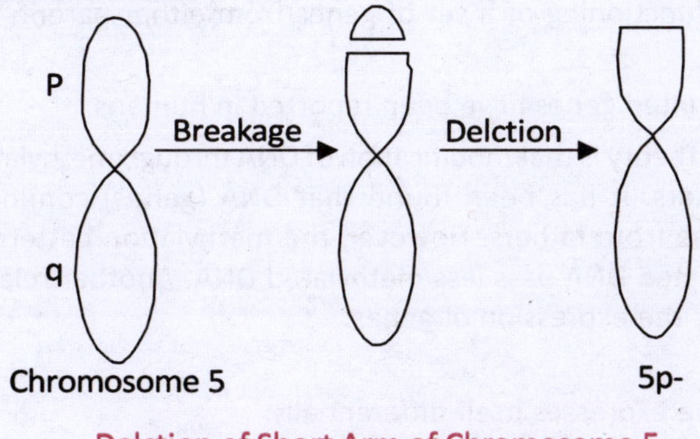

Delction of Short Arm of Chromosome 5, Causing Crl-du-chat Syndrome

Clinical Features:

1. Because the affected baby's cry resembles that of a cat, the condition is also known as cat cry syndrome.
2. Mental retardation.
3. Epicanthic fold
4. Speech, throat, eating, and drinking problems
5. Continuous saliva oozing from the mouth is also called drooming.
6. Combination of Patau, Edward, and Down syndrome symptoms.

Diagnosis:

1. Amniocentesis
2. Chorionic villus sampling (CVS)
3. Karyotype analysis

Treatment:

1. Awareness and a genetic counsellor provide proper knowledge to the couple about the probability of its occurrence as age advances. Thereby avoiding pregnancy at a later age.
2. Cognitive-behavioural therapy and physiotherapy
3. The MTP Amendment Bill, 2020, now allows pregnancy even after 24 weeks in cases of substantial foetal abnormality.

Changes in chromosomal aberrations play no vital role in evolution since people suffering from such syndromes have low fecundity, but if the rate of the syndrome increases, it can impact evolution.

Q 8. Genetic Imprinting

Ans. Genetic imprinting is an epigenetic phenomenon that causes genes to be expressed in a parent-of-origin-specific manner. It even means the suppression or inactivation of genes.

Genetic imputing occurs due to a process called epigenetics. Epigenetics suppresses the functioning of a set of genes by way of DNA methylation.

Every individual possesses one chromosome from their mother and another from their father. Every individual therefore possesses a set of maternal genes and a set of paternal genes. What the body does is keep a set of genes from either parent inactive or another set from the other parent active.

In other words, it is also defined as the differential manifestation of genetic material either at the chromosomal or allelic level, depending on the sex of the transmitting parent.

It is an exception to Mendel's law: in this case, the number of genes remains the same, but it only suppresses the functioning of a set of genes from either parent. It is not a disorder but a normal process.

In 2019, 228 imprinted genes have been reported in humans.

Causes: The most accepted theory is that modification of DNA through methylation is achieved differently by mothers and fathers. It has been found that DNA (genes) coming from mothers is more methylated than those from fathers. However, the methylation pattern changes as people who receive highly methylated DNA pass less methylated DNA. Another relationship is that the more methylation, the later the expression of genes.

Characteristics:

1. The imprinted genome expresses itself differentially.
2. It is erasable, i.e., not a permanent modification, e.g., gene imprinting in gonadal tissue.
3. It is most common in mammals and flowering plants.
4. It is species specific.
5. Genetic imprinting is not a rule. It is discovered only in some male and female genes. E.g., the gene for growth factor is imprinted on mice and not humans.

Effects: Imprinted male and female genes differ in expression severity or onset age. Age of onset of symptoms of hunting tax disease later if inherited gene from mother Heredity: glomus tumours are seen only if inherited from the father. Imprinting, along with deletions, leads to disorders. Example chromosome no. 15:

- Prader-Willi syndrome: obesity, short stature, intellectual immaturity, low production of sex chromosomes, etc.
- Angelman Syndrome: inappropriate laughing, speech delay, seizures, growth retardation

Therefore, genetic imprinting helps to know the effects of deletions in different sexes and the variation of disease according to gender. *Mcgrath et al.'s* study says that gene imprinting is important for early embryonic development.

Q 9. Genetic Screening

Ans. Genetic screening refers to the application of tests to groups of individuals for the purpose of detecting carriers of deleterious genes or chromosome rearrangements.

Goals:

1. To identify individuals with genetic diseases so that they may receive treatment to obviate the effects of mutated phenotypes.
2. To identify individuals or couples at increased risk for having offspring with genetic diseases.

Additional benefits may include the collection of epidemiological data and the expansion of our knowledge of these diseases.

Two important questions raised are:

1. Is corrective treatment available
2. How early the treatment may be administered

Tay Sach disease is associated with death and is common among Jews in Central and Eastern Europe. It can be detected at the foetal stage, and steps can be taken accordingly.

At the postnatal stage, genetic screening helps to analyse whether one is affected by a genetic disease and address it accordingly. Phenylkatonuria is one of the disorders associated with mental retardation, and if screened, it can be addressed accordingly. The most widely used test in the US related to it is the Gutherie test.

If carriers of sickle cell anaemia are identified, they can be prevented from marrying, thereby preventing further deaths.

Techniques:

1. Amniocentesis
2. Chorionic villus sampling
3. Ultrasonography
4. Foetoscopy
5. Pedigree analysis
6. PCR test
7. Karyotyping analysis

Limitations:

1. Personnel and laboratory facilities are simply not yet available to undertake widespread amniocentesis.
2. Genetic screening approaches to the treatment of genetic diseases are still limited in their applicability, and often abortion is advised, which is still not desirable.
3. Parents are still sceptical about the privacy issue and the impact of sharing genetic information with private or insurance companies.
4. A biological husband and a legal husband may be different, and the mother might not transmit this information during counselling.

Further interconnected with it is the concept of genetic counselling.

Q.10. Genetic Counselling

Ans. As per American society, human genetics is the process by which patients or their relatives who are at risk of genetic disorder are made aware of the consequences of disorder, its transmission, and ways by which disorder can be prevented.

Process involves:

1. Diagnosis of genetic disorder: screening
2. Determination of mode of inheritanc
3. Transmission of info.
4. Management of disorders, either curative or supportive

Diagnosis:

1. Pedigree Analysis
2. Hardy Weinberg's law
3. Amniocentesis
4. Chorionic villus sampling
5. Pedigree chart.

The most important step is the communication of information about the nature of inheritance, symptoms, remedies, etc. A genetic counsellor should also have knowledge of psychology, as revelations can sometimes depress the consultant.

Management of Disorder:

1. Pre-Natal: Often abortion is undertaken as it is difficult to treat it effectively except for a few, like congenital adrenal hyperplasia.
2. Post-Natal
   a. Treatment with drug: Wilson disease: pencillamine used
   b. Dietary restriction: diary products containing lactose should be avoided by patients with hereditary lactose deficiency.
   c. Gene Therapy
   d. Surgery: cleft lip, treated with plastic surgery
   e. Before mating, Eugenics was used to avoid marriage between carriers or close relatives.

Limitations:

1. Personnel and laboratory facilities are simply not yet available to undertake widespread amniocentesis.
2. Genetic screening approaches to the treatment of genetic diseases are still limited in their applicability, and often abortion is advised, which is still not desirable.
3. Parents are still sceptical about the privacy issue and the impact of sharing genetic information with private or insurance companies.
4. Biological husbands and legal husbands may be different, and mothers might not transmit this information during counselling.

Presently, the scope of genetic counselling is restricted, but with enhanced research on genetic therapy and overcoming ethical issues, it can help us cure diseases permanently at the zygote level, especially by using CRISPR-CAS9 technology.

Q.11. Gene Therapy

Ans. Replacing defective genes with normal genes to restore cost gene function, inactivating mutant genes that are functioningimproperly, or introducing new genes to fight disease is called gene therapy.

In 1990, gene therapy started mainly with the genetic engineering of genes with ADA deficiency. Another disease in which significant progress has been made is sickle cell anaemia.

Gene Therapy consists of:

1. **Gene Replacement:** Removal of defective genes and replacement with normal genes

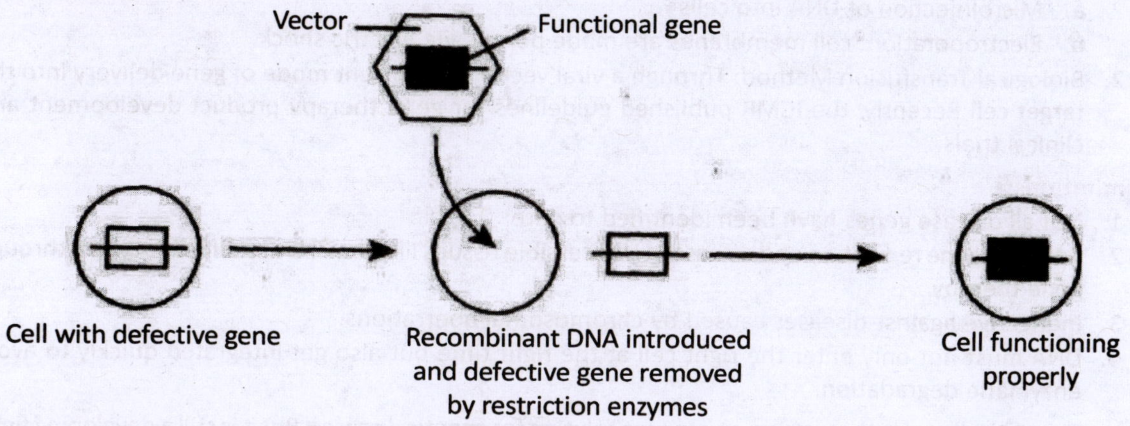

Gene Replacement

2. **Gene Targeting:** Correction of defective genes through the introduction of complementary parts

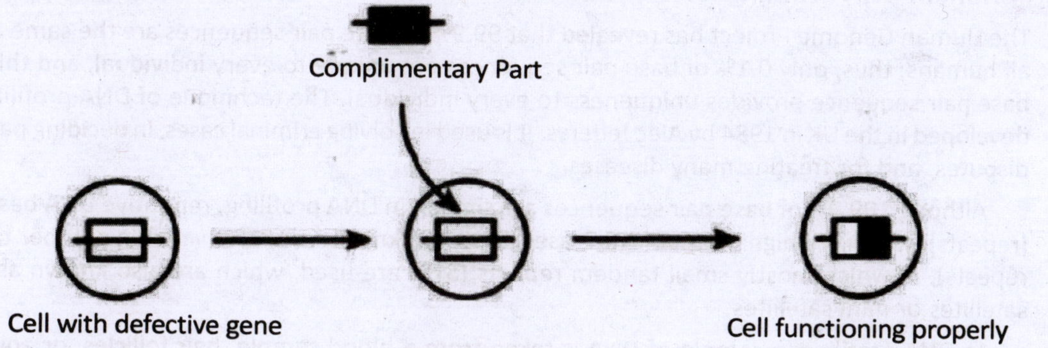

Gene Targeting

3. **Gene Augmentation:** Introduction of a few or more copies of a gene if the gene is not functioning.

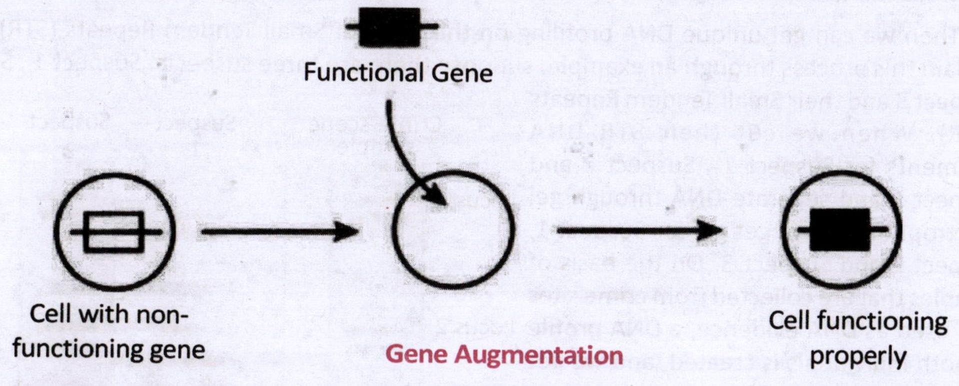

Gene Augmentation

Steps involved:

1. Identification of a gene and its mutation, i.e., defective gene
2. Cloning of a normal healthy gene version of the defected gene
3. Identification of the target cell: Insertion of a normal gene into diseased tissue
4. Insertion: cells are isolated to treat in vitro, and genetically corrected cells are transplanted to patients.

Methods of transfer:

1. Physical and chemical methods
   a. Microinjection of DNA into cells
   b. Electroporation: cell membranes are made porous via electric shock.
2. Biological Transfusion Method: Through a viral vector, an efficient mode of gene delivery into the target cell Recently, the ICMR published guidelines for gene therapy product development and clinical trials.

Limitations:

1. Not all disease genes have been identified to date.
2. Complex gene regulation and disease in inaccessible tissues like the CNS are difficult to cure through gene therapy.
3. Ineffective against diseases caused by chromosomal aberrations.
4. DNA must not only enter the right cell at the right time but also get integrated quickly to avoid enzymatic degradation.

Theoretically, gene therapy is a permanent solution for genetic diseases. But it is still a developing field.

Q.12. Human DNA profiling

Ans. The Human Genome Project has revealed that 99.9% of base pair sequences are the same among all humans; thus, only 0.1% of base pair sequences are unique to every individual, and this 0.1% base pair sequence provides uniqueness to every individual. The technique of DNA profiling was developed in the UK in 1984 by Alec Jefferys. It is used in solving criminal cases, in deciding paternity disputes, and for treating many diseases.

Although 99.9% of base pair sequences are similar, in DNA profiling, repetitive DNA base pairs (repeats), which are highly variable, are used. They are known as VNTR (variable number tandem repeats), in which mostly small tandem repeats (STR) are used, which are also known as micro satellites or mini satellites.

Process: In DNA profiling, a sample of DNA is taken from a blood sample, hair follicles, or any other tissue. DNA is then isolated, digested (fragmentation of DNA), created through PCR (polymerase chain reaction), separated through gel electrophoresis, and then blotted.

Then we can get unique DNA profiling on the basis of Small Tendem Repeats (STR). We can explain this process through an example: suppose there are three suspects: Suspect 1 , Suspect 2, Suspect 3 and their Small Tendem Repeats (STR). When we cut their STR DNA fragments for Suspect 1 , Suspect 2 and Suspect 3 and separate DNA through gel electrophoresis, we get gel for Suspect 1, Suspect 2 and Suspect 3. On the basis of samples that are collected from crime sites and used as DNA evidence, a DNA profile of both individuals is created, and we get results. From this result, it becomes clear that Suspect 2was the culprit.

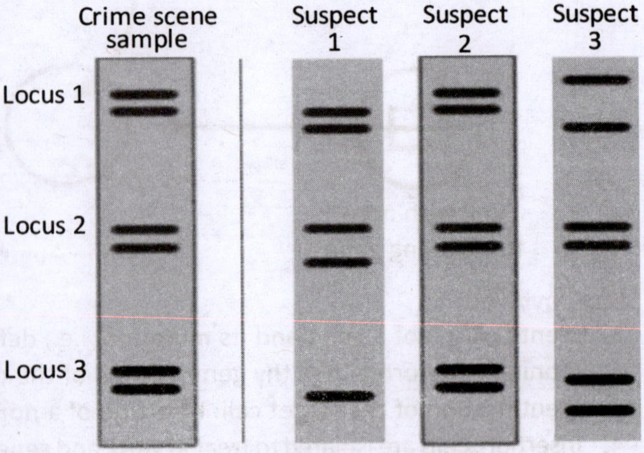

Thus, DNA profiling, also known as DNA finger printing, is very helpful in the field of criminology.

Applications:

1. Identification in criminal cases (e.g., murder, rape, etc.)
2. In cases of disputed parentage, the DNA fingerprints of the child, mother, and suspected father are compared. As a rule, the bands in the child's DNA fingerprint can be accounted for by those in the father's and mother's. The DNA fingerprint of the child is compared with that of the mother's, and the common bands are marked. The remaining 189 band in the child's fingerprint must belong to the father. In the N.D. Tiwari case, Saddam Hussain was identified by DNA profiling.
3. In medicine, DNA fingerprinting has applications in genetic counselling, tracing the frequency of donor cells in bone marrow transplants, tissue culture, cell line identification, etc. (e.g., RT-PCR test for COVID).
4. In the case of animal husbandry, proof of parentage, poaching, identification in cases of theft or loss, detection of trait markers (Basmati), etc. are the uses.
5. Missing children, cases of baby swapping in hospitals, unidentified bodies (forensic use), e.g., Suddam Hussain

Limitation:

1. Lack of awareness and privacy issues
2. Lack of availability of probes
3. With the present knowledge and understanding, it is difficult to teach the technique to the common man.
4. Presently, infrastructure is lacking in India. There are limited DNA profiling labs in India.
5. Blood transfusion and bone-narrow transplant cases: DNA profiling changes
6. DNA chimera: multiple genomes

Considering the ever-growing field of DNA profiling and analysis, it is crucial to overcome these limitations so that proper benefits can be accrued by society.

Case Study

- **Left-handed DNA was found, and it changes brain structure**

The first genetic instructions connected to left-handedness in human DNA have been discovered by scientists. The instructions also appear to have a significant impact on how the brain is built and how it works, particularly how the language-related areas of the brain work. According to researchers at Oxford University, left-handed people may have stronger verbal skills as a result. The cytoskeleton, a complex "scaffolding" that arranges the interior of body cells, is composed of instructions that underwent mutations. It has been demonstrated that similar mutations that alter the cytoskeleton in snails cause the molluscs to develop an anticlockwise, or "lefty," shell. The white matter in the brain was altering in structure, according to scans of participants in the UK Biobank study. "For the first time in humans, we have been able to establish that these handedness-associated cytoskeletal differences are actually visible in the brain," stated Prof. Douaud, who is also left-handed.

The left and right hemispheres of the brain were more connected and coordinated in areas related to language in left-handed people. The data from this study do not support the researchers' hypothesis that left-handed people have superior linguistic abilities, although they make this assumption. Additionally, the study found that left-handed people had marginally higher risks of schizophrenia and marginally lower risks of Parkinson's disease. Being left-handed is viewed as unlucky or wicked in many cultures, and this is reflected in language. "Gauche" can imply "left" or "clumsy" in French. "Right" also means "to be right" in English.

This study demonstrates that being left-handed is just a result of how the brain develops; it has nothing to do with chance or malice. And it is influenced, at least in part, by genetic variations that we have found. This advances our knowledge of what makes us human. Is this the conclusion of the tale? The best estimate places environmental factors (everything not determined by genes) at 25% of handedness and genetics at 75%. But only the first 1% of that genetic component, and only in the British population, has been discovered in this study. Therefore, much more research is required to fully comprehend the genetic basis for handedness in people all over the world, let alone the significant environmental influences, and to piece together how those influences lead to people being either left- or right-handed.

- **Ancient DNA reveals a hidden history of human adaptation.**

According to our recent study, which analysed the genetic information of more than a thousand people who lived in Europe and Asia during the previous 45,000 years and collected genetic data, humans may be just as susceptible to environmental change as other animals. We discovered evidence of more than 50 "hard sweeps," in which a rare genetic variation spread quickly through a population, most likely as a result of environmental changes that caused those without the variant to go extinct. The most notable sweep occurred in an immune system-related genomic area called MHC-III among early Anatolian farmers. While hard sweeps are frequently observed in other animals, there has not yet been much evidence of them in humans. The harsh sweeps' remnants had been obscured for the past 8,000 years by repeated population mixing.

Based on our findings, it is not always possible for humans to adjust their behaviour and create new tools and strategies in order to survive when the going gets rough. Our findings demonstrate that hard sweeps are a legitimate genetic adaptation available to humans. This implies that perhaps we don't actually differ all that much from other animal species.

Q.13. Gene Mapping

Ans. Gene mapping: mapping of all the genes of human beings or particular individuals, groups, or families.

Gene mapping makes two things clear:

1. It reveals on which chromosome a particular gene is situated.
2. Which genes are linked and which are not

Thus, gene mapping clarifies the location of a gene on a chromosome and the relative distance between different genes.

There are two kinds of maps:

1. Linkage maps clarify the relative distance between different genes on the same chromosome.
2. Morphological map clarified on which chromosome a particular gene is placed.

For instance, there are two genes, Gene A and Gene B. A linkage map clarifies whether Gene A or Gene B are linked or not, and a morphological map clarifies on which chromosome they are placed.

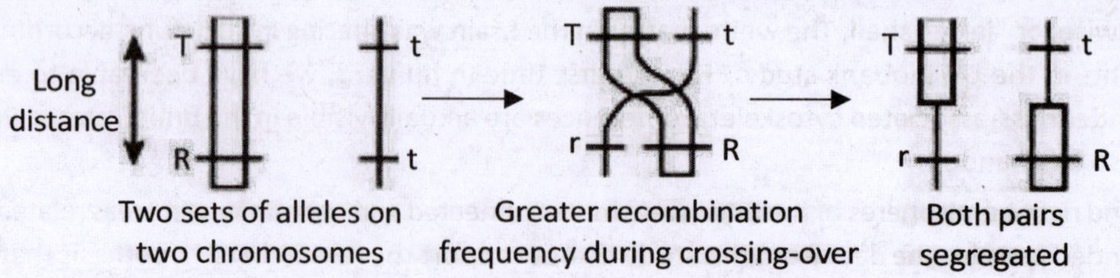

Principle of Genetic Mapping

The linkage between them is measured in map units, which indicate recombination frequency. Now suppose the distance between genes A and B is 10 map units. Thus, recombinant frequency is 10%, and if the same distance is 50 map units, recombinant frequency is 50%. Thus, as distance increased, recombination frequency also increased.

Methods for finding the position of a gene:

1. Family pedigree data by linkage mapping
2. Chromosome banding technique: Q, G, C, and R banding
3. Somatic cell hybridization: e.g., mouse and human cells produced by virus cells

Advantages of Gene Mapping:

1. If the map of normal genes is known, for instance, in a family, then any deviation in such a map in the future or for a newborn will indicate a genetic disorder. Thus, preventive measures can be taken since infancy to minimise the effects of such disorders.
2. Gene mapping has opened new frontiers for gene therapy. Due to gene mapping, the location of a gene that causes a disease like cancer can easily be ascertained, and such a gene can be targeted and modified through gene therapy.
3. With the help of gene mapping, one can understand why some people are more prone to certain infectious diseases and why some are not. The genes that are responsible for enhancing susceptibility can be targeted.
4. It can even help in the fields of forensics, human genome project, gene therapy, medicine, etc. Genes constitute the basic genetic material of humans. Thus, knowledge of all genes with respect to their position on various chromosomes is essential to a proper understanding of various genetic disorders and diseases.

Q 14. Genome Study

Ans. Simply put, the genome is divided into chromosomes; chromosomes contain genes, and genes make DNA. A genome study means deciphering the exact order of base pairs in an individual. In simple terms, the genome is the complete set of human genes, or DNA, and its study is known as the genome study.

The genome study is conducted by the Human Genome Project. According to the report on this project, there are 20,500 genes in every human cell. On the basis of gene mapping, which is part of a genome study, the location of different genes is identified. By comparing the DNA sequences of different organisms, the evolutionary trend can be ascertained. By comparing the human genome with the genome of non-human primates, the nature and degree of relationship between humans and non-human primates can be established.

Sequence Genome:

Entire Genome

↓

Fragment of DNA approximately 100-200 kb

↓

Inserting them into bacterial artificial chromosomes (BAC) Vector

↓

Positioning of BAC on individual chromosome

↓

Production of BAC clone

↓

Clones Broken into small fragments

↓

Using computer algorithms for functional analysis of each of the gene

Techniques used:

1. RT-PCR
2. Karyotyping
3. Pedigree
4. Amniocentesis

Applications:

1. Detailed knowledge of the genomes will provide new advances in medicine, biotechnology, anthropology, etc. The tracking of disease genes will be enormously facilitated. E.g., a number of companies like Myriad Genetics started offering easy ways to administer genetic tests that can show predisposition to varieties of illnesses, including breast cancer, hemostatic disorders, cystic fibrosis, liver diseases, and many others. It will also help in the determination of genes involved in complex diseases.
2. Probes for any gene will be available if needed, leading to improved diagnostic testing for disease-susceptible genes and genes directly involving the causation of specific diseases.
3. Tailor-made drugs can be prepared to accommodate the variations in enzymes and other proteins nvolved in drug action and metabolism found among individuals.
4. Etiology for cancers: Alzheimer's and other areas of clinical interest are likely to benefit from genome information, which may lead in the long run to significant advances in their management.
5. Studies of genes involved in behaviour may lead to new insights into the causation and treatment of psychological disorders.
6. Managing the vulnerability of ethnic groups to various diseases

Human Genome Mapping Project's Observations:

1. Human genome contains 3.1 billion chemical nucleotide bases.
2. Total genes: 30,000
3. Per gene, 3000 bases, but sizes vary greatly.
4. 9% nucleotide bases are the same in all people.
5. 98% of the genome is noncoding for proteins.
6. The human gene is less uniform but has a greater repeat sequence than other organisms.

Case Study

- **A Monumental Project Underway to Sequence the Genome of Every Complex Species on Earth**

There is an increase in the Earth Biogenome Project. A multinational team has set a ten-year goal of sequencing the genomes of all complex living forms on Earth (about 1.8 million described species). Phase one's objective is to sequence one genome from each of the 9,400 taxonomic families that make up the planet. One-third of these species ought to be finished by the end of 2022. The sequencing of a representative from each of the 180,000 genera will take place in phase two, and the sequencing of all the species will be finished in phase three. It is incredibly effective to compare closely and distantly related species to learn what genes do and how they are regulated. For instance, my University of Canberra colleagues and I found that Australian dragon lizards regulate sex through the chromosome neighbourhood of a sex gene rather than the DNA sequence itself in another PNAS study that was coincidentally also published on January 18. Researchers can uncover extraordinary conservation of gene function across almost a billion years by tracing the evolutionary history of genes and regulatory networks using species comparisons. For instance, the formation of human and fruit fly photoreceptors involves the same genes.

Furthermore, the BRCA1 gene, which is faulty in breast cancer, is in charge of fixing DNA nicks in both plants and mammals. For instance, my University of Canberra colleagues and I found that Australian dragon lizards regulate sex through the chromosome neighbourhood of a sex gene rather than the DNA sequence itself in another PNAS study that was coincidentally also published on January 18. Researchers can uncover extraordinary conservation of gene function across almost a billion years by tracing the evolutionary history of genes and regulatory networks using species comparisons. For instance, the formation of human and fruit fly photoreceptors involves the same genes. Furthermore, the BRCA1 gene, which is faulty in breast cancer, is in charge of fixing DNA nicks in both plants and mammals.

9.5

Race and racism, biological basis of morphological variation of non-metric and characters. Racial criteria, racial traits in relation to heredity and environment; biological basis of racial classification, racial differentiation and race crossing in man.

Q 1. Race and Racism

Ans. The concept of race has biological, social, and other dimensions.

Biological:

- **Dobzhansky:** Races are genetically distinct mendelian populations. They are neither individuals nor particular genotypes; they consist of individuals who differ genetically among themselves.
- **Montague:** Population that differs in frequency of some gene or genes, which actually exchanges or is capable of exchanging genes across boundaries and separates it from other populations of species.

Social: The American Census considers it a social concept. *Franz Boas* study of 19000 children (American) rejected the relation between intelligence quotient (IQ) and cranium size. Therefore, it is not a biological concept.

Not Valid: Livingstone, Montague, and UNESCO considers that it is not a valid concept. Replace it with the term 'ethnic group'. Livingstone used the term 'clines' in respect of races. In today's time, forensic anthropology uses 'race' as a biological concept. Otherwise, it is a value-laden concept and is replaced by the neutral team 'ethnic group'.

UNESCO declaration on races:

1. All human beings belong to one species: Homo sapiens.
2. Differences exist because of heredity or environment.
3. Changes in heredity are caused by mutation.
4. Races can't be grouped on the basis of nationality, religion, geography, culture, or linguistic factors.
5. Intelligence has no role.
6. Cultured differences have no role.
7. Pure races don't exist.
8. All humans are equal and desire equal treatment.

Racism: Racism is the ethnocentric belief that one race is biologically or culturally superior to another. Due to the concept of race, there emerged the misconception of the superiority and inferiority of races and such a misconception is termed racism.

The racists consider themselves superior and others inferior. As far as India is concerned, we can trace aspects of racism to the Rig Vedic period, when Aryans divided the society into two Varnas on the basis of colour. Actually, Aryans were fair-skinned people who considered themselves superior. As they considered the original inhabitants of India as inferior due to their dark complexion, they put them under a separate Varna i.e. Dasa.

In modern times, the misconception of racism emerged when Europeans colonised Asia and Africa. When Europeans encountered the dark-skinned original inhabitants of Asia and Africa, they considered them inferior. Due to this inferiority and superiority between races, the evil practise of slavery emerged. The racists coined the new concept of Social Darwinism by which they considered themselves the fittest to survive and also declared that they helped the unfit in their survival, which otherwise could be wiped out from the struggle for existence. Due to racism, a number of human groups have faced many exploitations, sufferings, and hardships, which have led to a feeling of hatred among various human groups. Therefore, anthropologists are against the concept of racism. According to them, no human group can be declared inferior on the basis of physical features. Juan Comas is one such anthropologist. According to him, if superiority and inferiority are decided by skin colour, then a white horse should be superior to a black horse, which is actually not the case.

Livingstone conducted many I.Q. tests among Africans and Americans, from which he observed that in many cases the I.Q. level of Africans was higher than the I.Q. level of Americans. He remarked that it is difficult to distinguish the brain of an African or American just on the basis of physical features, as intelligence level is also influenced by many external factors. Later, in his book "On the Non-Existence of Race", he narrated that although various human populations can be grouped on the basis of physical features, such grouping should be beyond the stigma of inferiority and superiority. While discussing the concept of racism, two human groups are worth mentioning: Aryans and Jews. Hitler, in order to convert Germany into a pure Aryan nation, almost eliminated the Jews, with the misconception that Jews constitute an inferior race. But Jews as a race is a misnomer because Jews constitute a cultural group and not a racial group. Due to the racist approach of Hitler, Jews have suffered a lot, as is almost always the case with many other human populations.

Cavalli-Storza et al.: There is only one human species, and no objective reason exists for splitting at any lower taxonomical level. In 2001 -02, Craig Venter and Francis Collins proved, through the Genome Project, that there are no genetic races.

Montague, in his book "Man's Most Dangerous Myth", opined that no race is superior and no race is inferior; there is no pure race; actually, there is no race.

Case Study

- **Critical Race Theory**

The critical race theory, which was developed a few decades ago, makes the assumption that a thorough examination of our socio-cultural systems is necessary in order to understand the current meaning and Social implications of the race concept, which is a prerequisite for enacting real change. It is a methodology, an approach, and a suggested selection of tools and resources for research. Apart from its racial presumptions, it "says" nothing, makes no claims, and was never intended to be taught in middle school or even high school. Derrick Bell (1930– 2011), a black legal scholar and well-known civil rights activist, and Alan Freeman (1944–) are generally recognised as the two legal scholars who founded CRT. By comprehending quantitatively how evolution drove the diversity of hair, people can better understand the significance and influence of their appearance.

However, numerous academics from various fields have actually contributed to the creation of CRT. 2000 saw the release of a sizable book edited by legal professors Richard Delgado and Jean Stefancic that included contributions by numerous authors. One crucial lesson we can learn from the current CRT controversy—as well as from much of the deluge of false information coming from many of our well-known news sources—is to be sceptical of your sources. Anthropologists are aware of how crucial history is to people. The past often shapes a culture's identity and relationships with others, making history instruction in complex societies inherently political. Nations and ethnic groups from all over the world now deal with not only how to teach history but also what history to teach.

Q 2. Racial traits in relation to heredity and environment

Ans. Ashley Montague has given a genetic definition of race as a population that differs in frequency of some genes and is actually exchanging or capable of exchanging them across whatever boundaries separate it from other populations of species.

According to the pre-Mendelian concept, race is an ethnic group that differs from all other groups with respect to certain physical features. Genetically, race is a mendelian population that differs from all such other populations with respect to certain gene frequencies.

Number of factors in race formation:

(i) **Mutation:** A sudden change in a particular gene produces a new form of an old character. This change is permanent; as soon as a mutant gene appears, it multiplies from one generation to the next. It is seen that some genes are more adaptive than others to certain conditions of life. For example, skin colour and nose form are adaptive characters with selected values, with a few exceptions, like dark-skinned people, who are concentrated in regions with the hottest climatic conditions, while light-skinned people are in colder areas. The reason is that dark colours protect the body from certain rays of the sun; on the other hand, white is the best colour for keeping the body's heat.

(ii) **Natural Selection:** In the previous example, let us assume the earliest men had light skin colour. As a result of the mutation, some more colours, like dark or yellow skin, appeared. As dark skin has some advantages over light skin in hot and moist climatic regions, this will lead to an increase in dark-skinned populations due to natural selection.

(iii) **Isolation and hybridization:** Isolation is of three types: geographical, genetic, and cultural. It leads to inbreeding, and with the course of time, heterozygosity decreases in every generation, which leads to the development of a new phenotype by homozygosity of recessive traits and results in the formation of a new racial group. On the other hand, hybridization will lead to mating between individuals of different racial groups and could result in the formation of new races. Eg, Anglo-Indians have been formed by the intermixing of Europeans and Indians.

(iv) **Migration:** It is of two types: permanent and temporary. Temporary migration has no role in race formation, while permanent migration plays a role in isolation and hybridization. Groups of people migrated in different directions from the common centre, and becoming isolated from one another leads to isolation, while mixing with another racial group leads to hybridization.

(v) **Genetic drift:** It refers to the elimination or fixation of a gene in a population by sheer chance without the role of mutation in selection. For example:- Duncan Community of Pennysylvania also migrated to the US in the mid-18th century and exhibit a much higher frequency for blood Group A as compared to ancestoral Germans as well as American neighbourhoods.

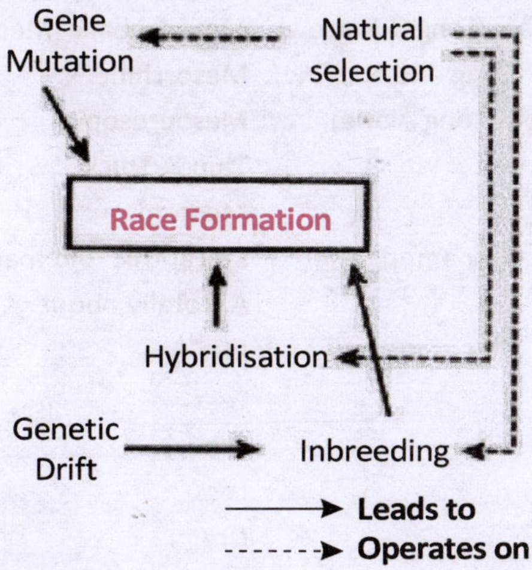

Schematic Representation of Race Formation

Role of heredity and environment on race formation: There is no role for heredity in race formation. The only function of heredity is to pass genes to subsequent generations in their present form based on what was received from the previous generation. If it continues like this, there will be no change in gene formation.

But the environment is dynamic and keeps changing whenever it changes. The heredity was to change itself to suit the change in the environment. There is interaction between heredity and environment, and environment compels heredity to change, resulting in race formation.

The five factors of race formation are environment factors. Meaningful mutations are caused by radiation, which is environmental. Natural selection itself is natural. Inbreeding, hybridization, and genetic drift are cultural factors in man, but culture itself is a man-made part of the environment. These five factors interact with heredity, resulting in race formation.

However, *Levotin* studied races by dividing the human population into seven geographical zones. He concluded that only 15% of variations can be attributed to racial differences between men, families, regions, etc. Finally, in February 2001, the first report of the Human Genome Project reported that all human beings are genetically similar by 99.99%. A genetic variation of 0.01% is not enough to create racial categories.

Q 3. Racial Criteria

Ans. As per Boyd, for criteria to work, they should be:

1. The mode of inheritance is known
2. Stable: not affected by any mutation or natural selection.
3. Discrete variable and not continuous.
4. Objective

Feature	Caucasoid	Mongoloid	Negroid
Skin colour	Leucoderms (White)	Xanthoderms (Yellow)	Melanoderms (Black)
Hair form	Cymotrichy (Wavy)	Leiotrichy (Straight)	Ulotrichy (Wooly)
Hair quantity	Abundant	Scarce	Medium
Head form cephal Index	Dolichocephalic (Long & Narrow)	Mesocephalic (Medium)	Brachycephalic (Broad)
Nose form	Leptorrhine (Long and Narrow)	Mesorrhine	Platyrrhine (Broad)
Face form	Leptoprosopic (Long Alone)	Mesoprosopic	Euryprosopic (Broad)
Lips	Thin	Thin & Thick	Thick & Everted
Ears	Small	Medium	Large
Eyes	Grey & Blue only among them.	Epicanthic fold mainly	Dark
ABO blood group	A_2 Present	A_2 totally about	
Rh factor	Rh- max	Rh+ max	
Thalasemia	Max	Less	More less
Dermatoglyphics	Loops	Whorls	Arches
Secretor gene	Most	Less	Least
Ear Wax	Wet	Dry	
PTC taster	Present mostly	Absent mostly	

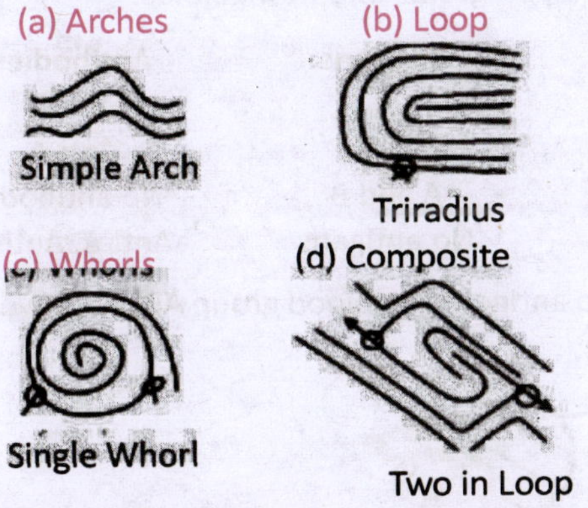

Finger Dermatoglyphics and its Types

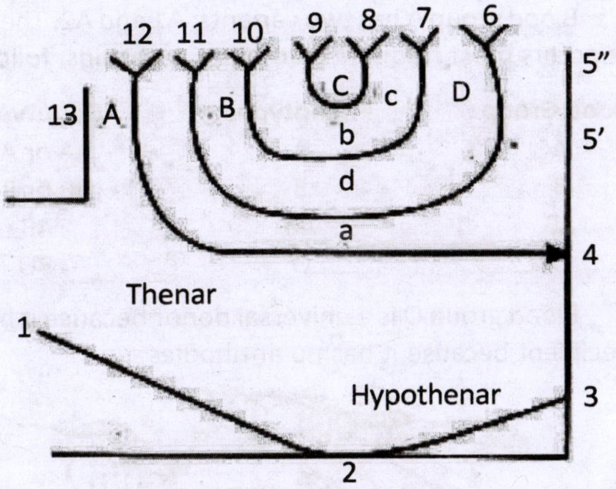

Palm Dermatoglyphics

Morphological criteria don't satisfy the above condition; genetic criteria do. However, it has been realised that it is not possible to divide the population into races because pure races don't exist among humans (UNESCO Declaration).

Case Study

- **Untangling Race from Hair**

In the same way that dark skin shields against UV radiation, tightly curled hair shields people from the sun. Tight curls give the head lofted, airy ventilation structures that allow it to breathe while also doubling as additional sun protection. She claims it was crucial for our ancestors when they transitioned to walking on two legs, and you can't accomplish that with flat hair. Perhaps more than at any other time in our history, race is a delicate topic in America now. Additionally, it has grown more contentious in public education than the ageold topic of sexuality in the curriculum. It appears that CRT is now a catch-all term for the study of American slavery and racial relations in many school districts.

9.6

Age, sex and population variation as genetic marker: ABO, Rh blood groups, HLA Hp, transferring, Gm, blood enzymes. Physiological characteristics-Hb level, body fat, pulse rate, respiratory functions and sensory perceptions in different cultural and socio-ecomomic groups.

Q 1. ABO blood groups

Ans. A genetic marker is a gene or DNA sequence with a known position on the chromosome that can be used to identify a particular trait of a human group or an individual and even classify a population. The ABO Blood Group system was discovered by *Landsteiner* in 1900–1902. There are four types of blood groups: A, B, AB, and O.

O is common in frequency of prevalence, followed by A and B. The blood group A is most prevalent in Europe and Australia. Whereas blood group B is most prevalent in Central Asia and North America. The O blood group is prevalent in Central and South America.

Blood group A has two variants: A1 and A2. The occurrence of A2 has racial significance because it occurs most frequently among Caucasoids, followed by Negroids and Mongoloids.

Blood Group	Phenotypes	Genotypes	Antigens	Antibodies
A	A	AA or AO	A	Anti-B
B	B	BB or BO	B	Anti-A
AB	AB	AB	A and B	No antibody
O	O	OO	No antigens	Anti-A, Anti-B

Blood group O is a universal donor because it has no antigen. The blood group AB is a universal recipient because it has no antibodies.

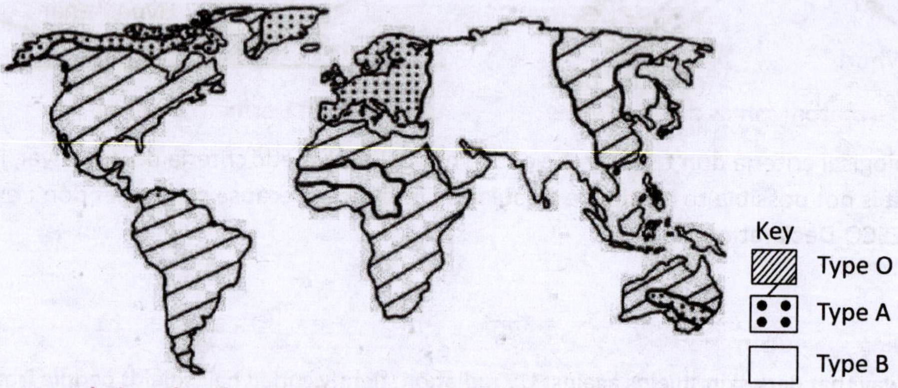

Population Classification Through ABO Blood Group System

Applications:

1. Useful and reliable genetic marker as it doesn't get affected by sex, age, or environment.
2. Used in solving paternity disputes
3. Related to certain diseases like blood group O with ulcers, A with pancreatic cancer, and B with hypertension.

Q 2 Rh blood groups

Ans. It is red blood cells (RBC) antigen. It was first discovered by Landsteiner and S. Weiner in 1940. This factor is named after the Rhesus monkey, among whom it was discovered first of all. Those individuals who possess this factor are Rh+,and those who lack it are Rh-. Suppose someone's blood group is B+; then their blood group is actually B, but concerningly, they possess this factor.

Fisher demonstrated 3 pair of allele:

$$\begin{bmatrix} C, & c \\ D, & c \\ E, & e \end{bmatrix} \rightarrow \underset{\text{Rh + ve}}{\begin{bmatrix} D, & c & e \\ D, & C & e \\ D, & c & E \\ D, & C & E \end{bmatrix}} \underset{\text{Rh - ve}}{\begin{bmatrix} d, & C & E \\ d, & c & E \\ d, & C & e \\ d, & e & e \end{bmatrix}}$$

The frequency of Rh-ve is highest among Caucasoids. The frequency of Rh+ve is highest among mongoloids and negroids at intermediate levels.

Rh-ve is absent in most of the world but is found in 15% of Europeans, especially the Basque community in Spain.

Rh+ve is found in the Mediterranean, North India, Africa, China, etc.

Different haplotypes exist like:

1. Ro among Africans
2. R1 among Meditttereans
3. R2 among Southeast Asian
4. Rz among the Veddoid tribe

Applications: Fatal conditions occur due to Rh incompatibility between couples, which is known as erythroblastosis fetalis, which is fatal for both mother and child. But now injections of anti-Rh bovine are administered to prevent this fatal condition.

Case Study

- **Country-level factors, dynamics, and ABO/Rh blood groups contributions to COVID-19 mortality**

The role of the ABO and Rh blood types was examined in this study while taking demographic, economic, and health system-related confounding factors into account. We confirmed prior findings that blood groups are associated with the severity and fatal outcome of COVID-19 by using a machine learning approach to discover that the "B+" blood group frequency is a significant determinant at all stages of the pandemic. Mark the COVID-19 severe form. Recent research suggests that the Rh blood group, which has a protective role, may be related to the severity of COVID-19. The disappearance of variables like "diabetes prevalence" or "cardiovascular death rate" coincided with the rising prevalence of B+ as adversely connected to COVID-19 fatalities.

Therefore, it's possible that in the early stages of the pandemic, severe COVID-19 was picking on groups of people who had favourable comorbidities. Individual genetics may have had a greater impact on the fatal outcome of COVID-19 in subsequent waves of the pandemic because of rising acquired immunisation, which may have protected this group of victims. Furthermore, according to recent research, both B and Rh+ were effective at preventing influenza brought on by a zoonotic or pandemic influenza virus. B also offered protection from S. pneumoniae-caused pneumonia. Additionally, there is a gradient of decreasing frequency for the B blood group from East Asia to the West. Therefore, it is plausible that an ancient viral pandemic that changed the original eastern Asian genome and exerted positive selection pressure on the B allele.

Q 3. HLA

Ans. HLA stands for Human Leucocyte Antigen. It is the locus of genes that encode proteins on the surface of cells that is responsible for the regulation of the immune system. HLA is a protein complex in our body. HLA is present on chromosome 6 in every human cell.

Broadly, three groups of alleles exist:

1. A2: High in all populations
2. A1: Present in all but high in Africans
3. Bw42: Confined to Africans

Applications:

1. Graft rejection: HLA matching decides whether a donor can donate an organ or not. It prevents the occurrence of GVHD, i.e., Graft Versus Host Disease. HLA matching also helps in engrafting, i.e., the growth and replication of the donated part in the patient.
2. HLA also protects the body against certain viral attacks because, when the body is attacked by a virus, HLA brings fragments of the virus to the surface of the concerned cell so that the immune system can destroy such cells.

A mutation in HLA causes certain autoimmune diseases. Actually, it is the function of HLA to decide which cells are body cells and which cells are foreign cells. HLA directs the immune system to fight against foreign cells, but sometimes the immune system misunderstands its own cells as foreign cells and begins to work against its own cells. It leads to certain diseases like type-1 diabetes, many types of cancer, arthritis, etc.

Thus, HLA plays a significant role as a defence against many diseases and also helps patients receive blood and other organs from donors.

Q 4. Transferrin

Ans. Transferrins are glycoproteins that bind the free-floating iron in the blood and transport the iron to different cells of the body through a process called endocytosis. Transferrin has many alleles, like Tf A, Tf B, TfC, Tf D, and TfF. TfC is most common and found among all populations of the world. TfB is found among the Nvajo Indians of South Africa. Tf D is found in Africa, Australia, New Guinea, etc. The production of transferrin is hampered when the liver is not functioning properly due to certain liver diseases, during stages of cancer (malignancy), and also when a person is suffering from severe diseases. Thus, doctors take proper care of patients by providing catalysts so that the production of transferrin cannot be minimised.

Application: Transferrin is mostly produced in the liver, and from the liver it remains attached to the RBC, from where it sticks to free-floating iron and then transports such iron throughout the body. Therefore, through transferring, the different cells of our body are able to receive the required iron.

The functioning of transferrin should also be proper because if transferrin doesn't function properly, it may lead to a lack of iron among many body cells, which leads to anaemia, or it may lead to an excess of iron in the blood, which can lead to blood poisoning.

Thus, proper production and functioning of transferrin are important for a person to remain healthy.

Q 5. Gm Factor

Ans. When our body is attacked by bacteria or viruses, we take different medicines against such an attack, but this type of treatment is extended. Therefore, our body also has an internal system to fight against diseases. Such a system is known as the immune system. The immune system consists of many components. One of such components is B-cells. B-cells produce antibodies, or immunoglobin. The immunoglobulins are Ig^A, Ig^D, Ig^E, Ig^G, and Ig^M.

IgM: This antibody is most important because it is the first antibody to be developed in the foetus. It is first expressed phenotypically. It is the largest antibody in terms of size. It is first expressed at the time of any viral or bacterial attack. It is first necessary to act against any foreign element in the body. IgM is in the shape of a 'Y'.

When IgM scatters on the body, it acts as a pentamer (imagine two fireflies diving into each other's hands). But when it works against disease-causing agents, it forms the shape of a spider. IgM antibodies are also responsible for the clumping of RBC if the recipient receives blood through transfusion that is not compatible with his or her own RBC. Therefore, the IgM of both donors and recipients is matched before any blood transfusion.

IgG: Gm factor is a variant of the IgG antibody. IgG is the only antibody that crosses the placenta, and it is secreted sometimes in milk. When there is variation in the constant region of IgG, it is treated as an antigen when it crosses the placenta to the baby's body. This variation is called the Gm factor.

If the mother has a Gm factor not possessed by her baby, the mother's IgG antibody will be attacked when the baby grows and forms its own antibody. However, a mother's antibodies, which are gained through the placenta or milk, tend to disappear after the first few years of life.

There are two types of GM factors:

1. Gm (1)+: At positions 356–358 they have aspartic acid, glutamic acid, and lucine, respectively.
2. Gm (1)-: At positions 356–358, they have amino acids like glutamic acid and methionine, respectively.

These two are produced by one locus. There have been many such loci in different individuals. It has been found that different populations have been characterised by different Gm characteristics. The Gm factor is an important genetic criterion for the differentiation of races.

Q 6. Enzymes

Ans. **Blood Enzymes**

- G6PD
  Glucose 6 Phosphate Dehydrogenase
- Adenylate Kinase

G6PD is a blood enzyme found in RBC that metabolises glucose levels in the blood. Thus, for the metabolism of glucose levels in the blood, the presence of G6PD is necessary. But certain people are deficient in G6PD and encounter G6PD deficiency. Such people are allergic to certain drugs. For instance, when they are administered an anti-malaria drug, they get hemolytic anaemia.

Certain individuals who are deficient in G6PD are also allergic to fava beans. Even the breath of fava beans leads to a disorder known as Favaism, but cases of Favaism are more prominent in Europe and Asia but are almost absent in Africa. It indicates that there is variation in the number of allergies to Fava beans among different populations in cases of G6PD deficiency. People with G6PD deficiency are found mostly around the Mediterranean Sea, the Parajas of Odisha, Sri Lanka, and some parts of Africa.

Adenylate kinase: It is a blood enzyme that acts as a catalyst to convert adenosine triphosphate (ATP) into adenosine diphosphate (ADP) and further into adenosine monophosphate (AMP).

Adenylate kinase reduces energy expenditure at the cellular level. Different cells require different amounts of energy during different activities, and this enzyme prevents the wastage of energy. A deficiency of adenylate kinase leads to hemolytic anaemia.

Q 7. Physiological characteristics-Hb level, body fat, pulse rate, respiratory functions and sensory perceptions in different cultural and socio-ecomomic groups

Ans. Different cultural and socio economic groups have different physiological characteristics:

1. **Hb Level:** It consists of the hema group and contains an iron-containing ring with a protein known as globin. It is a protein molecule in the RBC that carries O2 from the lungs to body tissue and returns CO2 to the lungs. The haemoglobin level in RBC also determines the iron-carrying capacity of the blood. The normal level of Hb in an adult male is 16 gram per deciliter. In adult females, it is 14 g/deciliter, but this level of Hb is not realised by many populations. Some scholars, like Allen, Galton, and Collinwoods, studied various populations in India and Africa and later found that the maximum level of Hb in India and Africa is 12 g/deciliter among males and 10 g/deciliter among females. Thus, according to them, most of the population of India and Africa is anaemic.

   Variations:

   - High in Arab due to an iron-rich diet (dry fruit, dates)
   - High in the agricultural community (vegetables) and low in the pastoral community (milk).
   - *Verma* studied Great Andamanese anaemia, both female and male.
   - Oraon tribe anaemia: 60–70 percent
   - igh in infants; gradually increases till age 30.

   The Hb level is also related to activity pattern, nutrition, sex, and age. The Hb level is low among those whose activity pattern is lethargic and whose nutrition is also not balanced. In comparison to males, Hb levels are low among females. Also, Hb levels mostly become low in old age. In order to remain healthy, it is necessary to maintain a proper Hb level.

2. **Body Fat:** The amount of fat is regulated both genetically and environmentally. Those parents who possess more fatty tissue generally have fatty offspring, but as far as environmental factors are concerned, the amount of fat is regulated by the climatic region. In cold regions, the amount of fat is higher because more fatty tissue generates more heat and thus keeps the body warm. But in hot climates, there is less body fat because if body fat is less, there is less generation of heat.
   The amount of body fat a person has in their lifetime varies with age. For instance, subcutaneous fat begins to lay down when the foetus is 34 weeks old, and it increases up to its peak by 9 months or by the time of birth. From birth up to the age of 8–9 years, the growth of body fat is also low because growth hormones use fat tissue to increase stature. Thus, those children who are not able to grow properly gain more body fat, and soon they become fatty. From 8–9 years up until puberty, both boys and girls gain body fat. But after puberty, mostly up to the age of 20, boys lose both trunk and limb fats, but girls, although they lose limb fats, gain trunk fats. In this way, body differentiation occurs between boys and girls. After 20 years, boys regain body fat and thus achieve perfect body structure. Although boys stop gaining fat after a certain age, girls usually continue to gain fat.
   Genetics also play a key role in controlling body fat. Significant fats prevail in the thighs and buttocks of Bushmen, while other populations in the same environment don't show the same pattern.
3. **Pulse Rate:** The pulse rate is the number of pulses per minute. The pulse rate corresponds to the heart rate. The normal pulse rate is 72 times per minute. But sometimes the pulse rate may be higher or lower. A high pulse rate, i.e., higher than 72 times per minute, leads to a condition called tachycardia, and a lower pulse rate leads to a condition called brachycardia.
   Generally, the pulse rate is higher among those who do regular exercise. To remain healthy, it is necessary to maintain a proper pulse rate.
4. **Respiratory Function:** Respiratory functions refer to the inhale and exhale processes of the lungs. Those human groups that used to live at higher altitudes have to respire more due to the presence of less oxygen in such regions. As a result of this system, their lungs and hearts have to work harder, and they usually encounter many heart and lung diseases.
   Respiratory function also alters with patterns of activity. For instance, during exercise, respiratory function is different, and during rest, respiratory function is different. The respiratory function also differs with age. For instance, respiratory function is different among adults and the elderly. Thus, respiratory function is associated with area of habitation, activity pattern, and age.
5. **Sensory Perception:** Many populations are also studied on the basis of sensory perceptions, and two main criteria regarding this are:
   - PCT taster or non-taster
   - Colour blindness: Deuteranomaly is the most common type of red-green color blindness.

   If we talk about racial groups, the frequency of PTC taster is higher among Caucasoids, and among Caucasoids, the frequency of PTC tasters is higher among females than males. The frequency of PTC non-tasters is higher among negroids, whereas mongoloids are at an intermediate level.

Red & Green colour Blindness	Male	Female
Overall	7-10%	0.5-1%
Caucasoid	8%	0.64%
Asian	5%	0.25%
African	4%	0.10%

Some individuals are not able to distinguish red and green colours from other colours. Such individuals are affected by red and green colour blindness. Such individuals are found mostly in Nigeria, Turkey, Indonesia, and some parts of Northeast India. These studies were done in India by Rao & Reedy, Veera Raju Naidu, etc.

9.7

Concepts and methods of Ecological Anthropology: Bio-cultural Adaptations—Genetic and Non-genetic factors. Man's physiological responses to environmental stresses: hot desert, cold, high altitude climate.

Q 1. Concept and methods of Ecological Anthropology

Ans: It is a multidisciplinary field that studies the dynamic interface between humans and their socio-economic and biocultural environment.

The foundation was led by Julian Steward. He emphasised four major approaches:

1. Explained culture in terms of environment
2. Culture and environment as process
3. Considered small-scale Environment
4. Ecology and multi-linear evolution

Julian Steward studied the cultural ecology approach of the Tsoshone Indians of the Basin Plateau. He discussed sociocultural patterns and how they related to technology, the environment, and the distribution of resources.

Other approaches:

1. **M. Harris:** Techno-environmental materialism, with a direct material payoff, could explain all cultural institutions.
2. **Leslie White:** Technological Determinism
3. **Roy Rapport & A. Vadya:** A New Ecological Approach Culture has been linked not only with the environment but also with the emerging science of system ecology.

Another part of ecological anthropology is the biocultural part.

Sherwood Washburn talked about the evolutionary adaptation of groups of people.

1. Variation in adaptation: cold, hot, high altitude
2. Biological factors responsible for adaptation
3. Improve further human conditions

Baker, in his book "Man in the Andes", stressed the effect of the environment on the biological traits of the human population.

Methods used

Socio cultrual:
- Field work
- Participant observation
- Etic perspective

Bio-cultural:
- Genetics
- Physiological response
- Longitudinal and cross sectional study

Significance:

1. Led to the development of more fields in anthropology like ethno-ecology, historical ecology, and socio-ecology.

2. Understand how humans adopt
3. Tourism Development: Acclamation
4. Future adaptation to climate change (Paris Deal)

Criticism:

1. Too much emphasis on homeostasis
2. Environment determination

Q 2. Man's physiological responses to hot desert climate

Ans. The ability of humans to survive in a particular environmental condition depends on physiological, biological, and cultural factors.

Humans are believed to have first appeared in Savannah-type climates, so humans have the capability to tolerate heat to a certain extent. The body temperature of humans is 370 C, and heat up to 35 0 C is tolerable. Beyond it, we have:

1. **Physiological response:**
   a. Vasodilation will take place to counter heat, as the rushing of blood will increase the tendency to match the temperature of the skin with the outside temperature.
   b. Sweating cools the body. In extreme hot deserts, young males staying for short periods may excrete 4 litres per hour. Gradually, 2 lt/hr, but on average, for longer periods, 8 lt/day.
2. **Biological response:**
   a. Bergmann Rule: Organisms of the same species will be less massive in the warm equatorial region and more massive in the polar region. E.g., Pygmies of tropical forests
   b. Allen rule: In an equitorial region, people tend to be thin and tall, i.e., have a larger surface area and less body mass. e.g., Nitolics of Africa
   c. Gloger Rule: People in hot climates possess more melanin, which prevents them from developing skin cancer. They look dark.
   d. Flat and broad nose to cool, warmer air from outside.

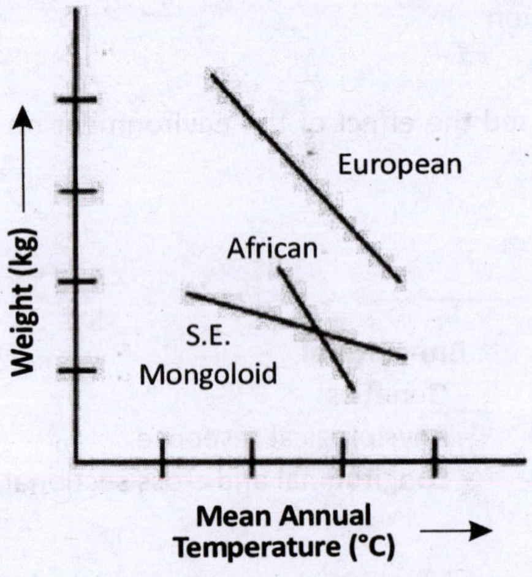

Graph 1 - Bergmann's Rule

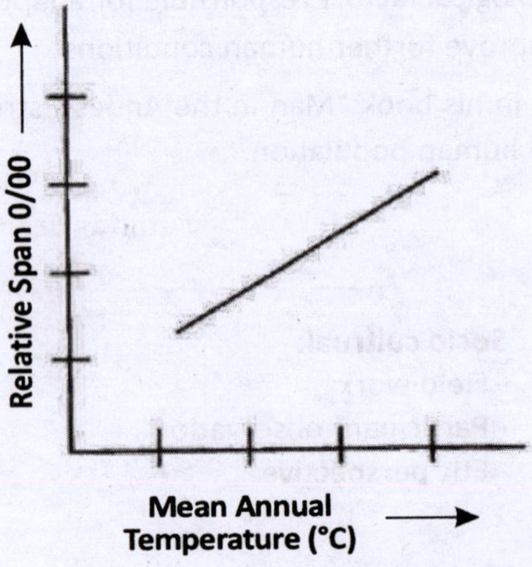

Graph 2 - Allen's Rule

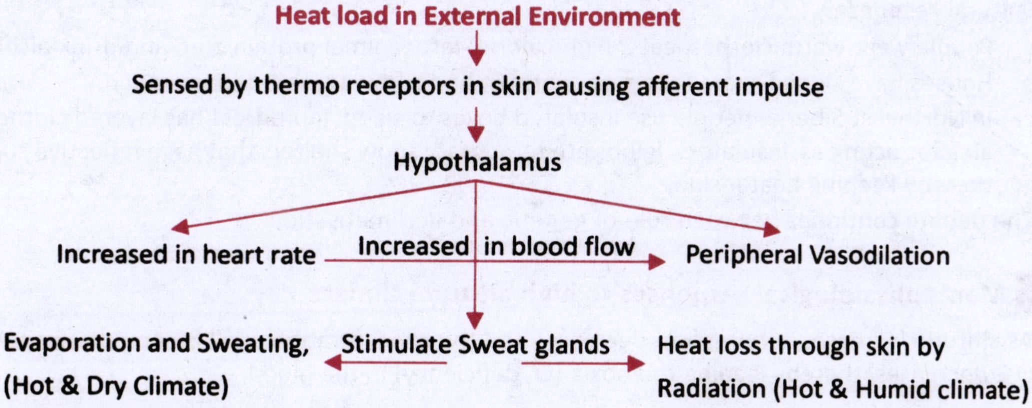

3. **Cultural response:**
   a. People tend to wear cotton clothes and consume non-alcoholic, non-fatty food.
   b. Shelter: high heat-reflective material, e.g., houses of Pueblo Indians

Animal adaptations to heat are only physiological, while humans have physiological, biological, and cultural.

Q 3. Man's physiological responses to cold climate

Ans. In this case, according to the second law of thermodynamics, heat will be lost from the body; therefore, the body will try to preserve it.

1. **Physiological response:**
   a. Vasoconstriction: warmed blood from the core of the body is shunted away from the skin, thereby reducing heat loss.
   b. Running and other activities increase metabolism, thereby making the body warm.
   c. Shivering to conserve heat
2. **Biological response:**
   a. Bergmann Rule: Organisms will be more massive in the polar region.
   b. Allen Rule: People in cold climates are short, stout, and bulkier with short appendages like hands, fingers, etc. It thereby reduces surface area and increases body mass, comparatively. As a result, less heat is released from the body.
   c. Gloger Rule: Pigmentation occurs less, thereby resulting in less melanin, and a person has a fair complexion.
   d. Long and narrow nose: air spends more time in the nose, thereby getting warmer and humid. Eskimos, for example, have thick subcutaneous fat, which acts as an insulator, protecting vital organs.
   e. Genetic cold genes for preventing frost bite.

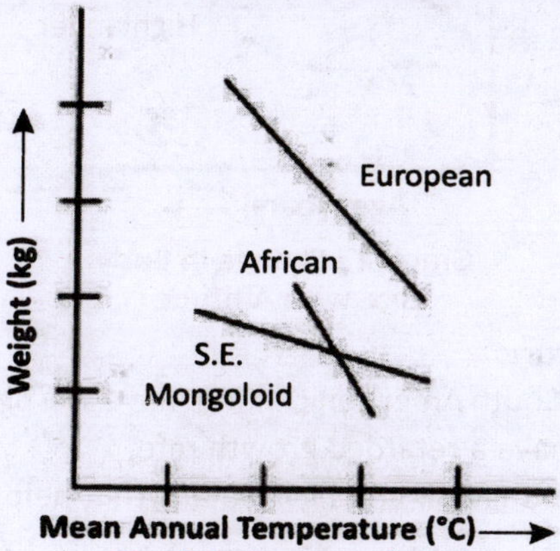

Graph 1 - Bergmann's Rule

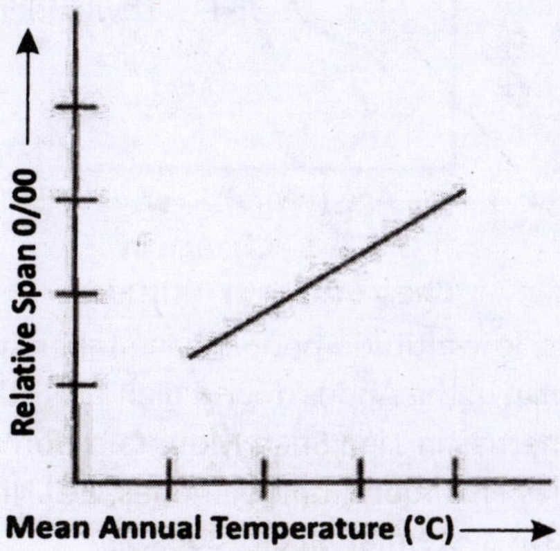

Graph 2 - Allen's Rule

3. Cultural response:

a. People wear warm clothes, eat a high-calorie, fatty animal protein diet, and drink alcohol.

b. Houses have sloped roofs to remain warmer, and snow doesn't deposit much.

c. In Northeast Siberia, people use insulated boxes to sleep. Inuit dress has layered clothes with air gaps acting as insulators. Igloos are temporary snow shelters that have reflective surfaces, thereby keeping heat inside.

The debate continues between role of genetic and acclimatisation.

Q 4. Man's physiological responses to high altitude climate

Ans. As altitude increases, air pressure decreases and the concentration of all gases, most importantly O 2 decreases, thereby leading to anoxia (O_2 deficiency) in the blood.

To overcome, there are:

1. Acclimatisation:

a. Increased breathing rate
b. Increased RBC and haemoglobin
c. Increased lung surface
d. Increased blood supply
e. Cellular acclimatisation, like in mitochondria.

2. Adaptation:

a. Increase in the number of capillaries and pulmonary ventilation.
b. Increase in chest size.
c. Small body size
d. The size and height of babies born are smaller.
e. Nose shortened and nostrils directed upwards.

3. Cultural:

a. Diet: Utilise maximum glucose. e.g., Brazilian Highlanders
b. Migrate to low altitudes during pregnancy. E.g., Quechua Indians of Peru

Studies:

➢ At all ages, high-altitude people have a great chest circumference. *Paul Baker's* studied Peru Highlanders.

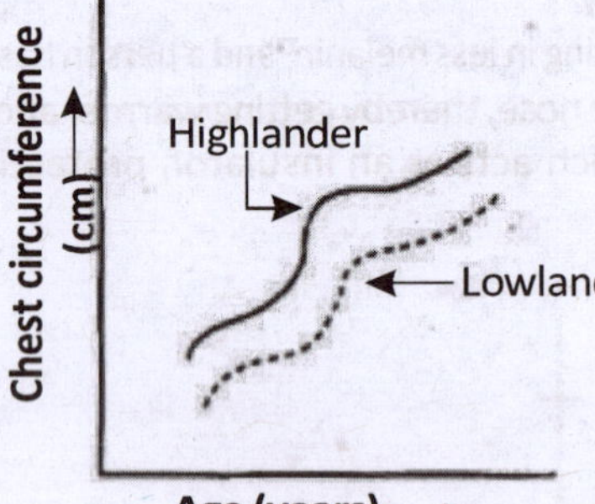

Graph 1 - Change in Chest Size with Altitude

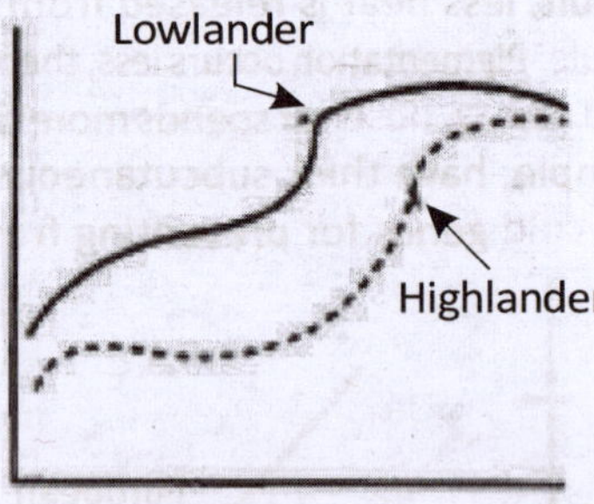

Graph 2 - Change in Body Size with Altitude

➢ At all ages, low-altitude people have taller stature.

➢ Project 'Man in the Andes' found high-altitude South American children have low physical growth.

➢ In Asia, Sherpas in Tien Shan Mountain don't have a retarded growth rate.

➢ A study has also found unique genes, EGLNI and EPASI, among Tibetans that help in the oxygen homeostasis system at all altitudes.

Case Study

- **Adapt or abandon? A Hard Choice in the Himalaya**

Jiban Mani Poudel, an anthropologist, found how sensitive mountain herding groups are to natural cues. Traditional herders in Nepal, for instance, organise their lives around natural occurrences like ngosho, the season associated with flowering plants. The transitions in nature are being altered by climate change. Tek Bahadur, a 73-year-old herder, recalled to Poudel seeing a little pond as a youth above the Wagreche pastureland in 1955; the pond has now grown into a sizable lake as a result of glacier meltwater. About 500 metres below, in the pastureland of Kromche, 68-year-old Mangal Bahadur reported prickly shrubs encroaching on the pastures. The Himalayan region's grasslands, which are essential to supporting livestock, are disappearing.

Climate change is more than just a phenomenon related to rising temperatures and glacier melt in natural science. Additionally, it is a social and cultural phenomenon. A signal for the continent could be changes in the Himalayas. These mountains, which include some of the tallest peaks in the entire globe, are a portion of the "third pole," so-called because of the enormous amounts of ice they hold. They serve as Asia's "water tower," supplying the Ganges, Indus, and Yangtze rivers, among others. People in the Himalayas are leading the way in addressing climate change, as Poudel and others are documenting. The calendars of many of these tribes follow the cycles of nature since they are so dependent on the land. To prepare for animal movement and planting, they must keep track of when snow melts or grass sprouts. Social and communal occasions like festivals and weddings are correlated to particular seasons since herders must roam with their livestock, breaking up family units for brief periods of time.

Calendar-based laws of common ownership are also used to control how livestock are moved from one pasture to another. The calendar no longer coincides with weather patterns, which makes the Lobas feel "helpless," according to anthropologist Man Bahadur Khattri. But all of these operations are hampered by global warming. For instance, less intense snowfalls have postponed the establishment of grass in meadows, which has altered the migration of herds, particularly yak herds. Growing seasons now start sooner and last less time. According to Poudel, "the agriculture calendar has shrunk by about one month." Some crops are ripe a month earlier than others, such as barley in the winter and maize in the spring. Buckwheat is one of the summer crops that is ready about a fortnight earlier. Poudel noted in the International Journal of Anthropology and Ethnology, "Global warming is not just shortening and shifting the harvesting time of crops; it is also upsetting the social life of the farmers."

9.8

Epidemiological Anthropology : Health and disease, Infectious and non-infectious diseases, Nutritional deficiency related diseases.

Q 1. Epidemiological Anthropology: Health and diseases

Ans. During the 1960s, anthropology started expanding its scope and becoming interdisciplinary. The study of health and diseases resulted in medical anthropology. Subsequently, it was realised that, at least in content, medical anthropology is quite close to epidemiology, hence combining two evolved epidemiological anthropologies.

MacMohan and Pugh define epidemiology as the study of the distribution and determinants of disease frequency in humans.

Hippocrates, a Greek physician, is known as the father of medicine and the first epidemiologist. *John Snow* is known as the "father of modern epidemiology. His identification of contaminated water as the cause of the Soho epidemic is considered a classic example of epidemiology. Today, computers, IT, and ecological approaches have altered the field of epidemiology.

Scope:

1. Population perspective: social, environmental, and psychological factors
2. Evaluate trends in diseases and risk factors.
3. Specific groups and diseases like
   - Infectious epidemiology
   - Chromic disease
   - Environmental
   - Nutritional
   - Occupational
   - Health policy
4. Insight to prevent disease outbreak.

Methods:

1. **Experimental Studies:** Sample survey, Random control trials, and Community trial
2. **Observational studies:** cohort studies, Case-control studies, and Cross-sectional studies

Epidemiological anthropology mainly considers social aspects related to diseases:

1. **Gender based:**
   a. Only in males: Y-linked disorders and diseases related to the male reproductive system e.g., prostrate cancer.
   b. Only in females: related to the female reproductive system e.g., breast cancer, cervical cancer
   c. Common in males: X-linked recessive disorder, e.g., colour blindness, haemophilia.
   d. Common in females: X-linked dominant disorder, arthritis, anaemia, and osteoporosis.
2. **Geography based:**
   a. In the equatorial region, there is a higher incidence of infectious disease as microorganisms grow faster, while in the polar region, pneumonia-like disease is caused by microorganisms that grow faster at lower temperatures.
   b. In African Hill, Plasmodium falciparum which causes malaria is common. But it grows only in normal RBC and not sickle shaped RBC. Hence, sickle cell anaemia is natural strategy in African Hill to counter malaria.
3. **Age based:**
   a. Old age: diseases like Alzheimer's and Parkinson's
   b. Middle Age: Diseases like arthritis, diabetes, osteoporosis, and mood-saving
   c. Childhood: nutrition-related issues like vitamin deficiency
4. **Class-Caste-Education-Related Low** class and low-educated people have nutrient deficiency diseases like scurvy and rickets and infectious diseases like cholera. According to a survey in Delhi, 60% of children in private schools are obese, and 50% in public schools are underweight.
5. **Religion-based:** Few, like Jainism and Buddhism, preach vegetarianism, which therefore lacks amino acids.
6. **Human density and social habits:** deforestation, unplanned housing, poor drainage, and sewage systems are responsible for the speed of communicable diseases.

Genetical analysis: Africans are more prone to frostbite bite than Eskimo. Rh incompatibility is most prone to Europeons. Blood group O: high probability of ulcers

Relevance:

1. Relationship of disease with culture and ecology
2. Assess community health.

3. Public health surveillance
4. Increase the efficacy of medicine.
5. Accurate pattern of disease by participant observation

The rise of chronic and non-infectious diseases in the 20th century due to lifestyle, which is influenced by social and cultural factors, has led to convergence between anthropology and epidemiology.

The scope is bound to increase as simpler societies have a treasure trove of knowledge, e.g., Birhor of Chattisgarh has knowledge of plant roots that can cure diabetes. The tribes of Assam Valley use the meat of snails for the treatment of jaundice.

Recent trend: Shift from infectious to non-infectious, feminization of old age and increased morbidity due to accidents.

Case Study

- **COVID-19: Pandemic or Syndemic?**

Merril Singer, an anthropologist, coined this term while researching HIV/AIDS. People who are worst hit by these infectious diseases are already suffering from other problems that are rooted in fundamental social inequalities. The same holds true in some sense for COVID-19.

- **How anthropology can bring the human element to emergency outbreak response**

Without community input, technical responses to a health emergency run the danger of failing; anthropologists can help here. West Africa experienced the greatest Ebola outbreak in history in 2014. It led to an incredible mobilisation of forces to preserve lives and halt the disease's spread throughout the rest of the world. Medical anthropologist Darryl Stellmach claims that that outbreak also marked a watershed in the way the world responded to outbreaks. For the first time, it witnessed the widespread integration of anthropology into the handling of public health emergencies. Anthropologists were able to make sure that local populations were involved in infection prevention and control strategies like contact tracing and the safe burial of Ebola patients. They filled the gap between creating technical answers and putting them into practise in a society that needed to accept responsibility for them for them to work. It is crucial to promote communication and understanding so that the intervention can be modified in a way that is suitable for the local environment. This required, for instance, changing burial practises so that families could still fulfil their social obligations to departed loved ones while maintaining infection control. The Ebola crisis followed a rising trend to incorporate medical humanities and social sciences into public health policy. It ultimately served as a benchmark for the importance of the social science perspective in an emergency.

The duties of anthropologists were debated in real-time throughout the pandemic. The "anthro-epi tandem," which Stellmach and colleagues developed at Médecins Sans Frontières (MSF), is described as "a very simple, robust little team, consisting of a field epidemiologist and a field anthropologist, offering two pairs of eyes to any problem." However, they offered two separate perspectives on the same issue, providing a nuanced viewpoint that resulted in more comprehensive, solid suggestions for how to address it. He became aware of how the global health community had perfected the technical components of outbreak response but may still make errors regarding how people would react to these efforts during that period. We are aware of how to monitor the outbreak, determine incidence rates, describe the virus, and create vaccinations; COVID-19 has shown us exactly how much we can expedite so that all the necessary "hardware" is available. But instead, "what anthropologists bring is the "software," or the understanding of human factors and how social responses can affect the technical response."

Q 2. Medical Anthropology

Ans. It is an interdisciplinary study of human health and diseases, the health care system, and bio-cultural adaptations. It aims to understand all factors that influence health, including the distribution of disease, prevention and treatment of sickness, the healing process, the social process of health management, and the cultural importance of a pluralistic medical system.

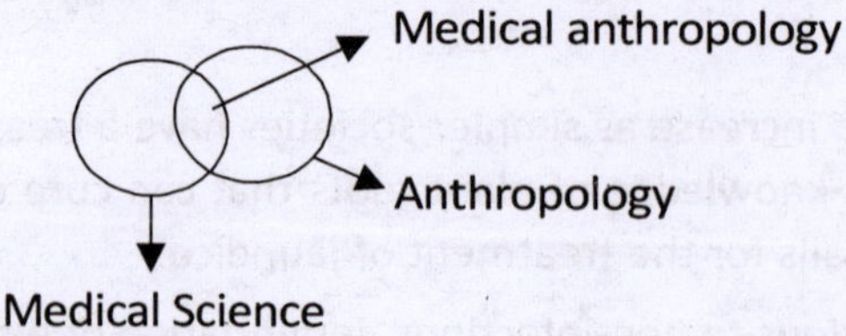

Developmental Phases: George Foster and Barbara Anderson gave four phases of development:

- 1st — Early physical anthropologist study of human execution and adaptation
- 2nd — Ethnographic interest in primitive medicine
- 3rd — Psychiatric phenomena in culture and personality school
- 4th — Anthropological work in international health

W.H.R. Rivers is considered first ethnologist of non western medical practices.

Ethnomedical analysis ← **Orientation** → Medical Ecology

↓

Applied Medical Anthropology

Scope:

Scope
- Social organization of clinical interactions
- Factors affecting health
  - Nutrition
  - Health care fertility
  - Health care policy
- Adaptation and Maladaptation
- Traditional health care system and practices
- Human behaviour and diseases
  Eg. Kuru disease among New guinea due to eating brain of dead

Case Study

Tribe	Natural product	Disease treated
Dimasa	Snail Meat	Jaundice
Khasi	Goat weed	Cuts & Wounds
	Pine needles	Cough & Asthma
	Pitcher plant	Cataract
Monpa	Clematis	Leprosy
	Leaf of Nakhrang	Goitre
	Taxus	Epilepsy
Munda, Santhal	Munzini	TB
	Satavar	Sperm Form

Q 3. Nutritional deficiency related Diseases

Ans. The body requires many different vitamins and minerals that are crucial for both body development and preventing disease. These vitamins and minerals are often referred to as micronutrients. They aren't produced naturally in the body, so you have to get them from your diet. A nutritional deficiency occurs when the body doesn't absorb or get from food the necessary amount of a nutrient. Deficiencies can lead to a variety of health problems. These can include digestion problems, skin disorders, stunted or defective bone growth, and even dementia. The amount of each nutrient you should consume depends on your age.

1. **Iron deficiency diseases:** Iron deficiency is one of the most common mineral deficiencies in the world. It may result from the following: Inadequate iron intake, common in infants, adolescent girls, and pregnant women; malabsorption (e.g., celiac disease); and chronic bleeding, including heavy menses and bleeding from GI lesions (e.g., tumours). Anaemia occurs when you have a decreased level of haemoglobin in your red blood cells (RBCs). Haemoglobin is the protein in your RBCs that is responsible for carrying oxygen to your tissues. Iron deficiency anaemia is the most common type of anaemia, and it occurs when your body doesn't have enough of the mineral iron. Your body needs iron to make haemoglobin. When there isn't enough iron in your blood stream, the rest of your body can't get the amount of oxygen it needs.
2. **Kwashiorkor:** Kwashiorkor is caused by a lack of protein in the diet. Every cell in your body contains protein. You need protein in your diet for your body to repair cells and make new ones. A healthy human body regenerates cells in this way constantly. Protein is also especially important for growth during childhood and pregnancy. If the body lacks protein, growth and normal body functions will begin to shut down, and kwashiorkor may develop. The name is derived from the Ga language of coastal Ghana, translated as "the sickness the baby gets when the new baby comes" or "the disease of the deposed child", reflecting the development of the condition in an older child who has been weaned from the breast when a younger sibling comes. Kwashiorkor is most common in countries where there is a limited supply or lack of food. It is mostly found in children and infants in sub-Saharan Africa, Southeast Asia, and Central America. A limited supply or lack of food is common in these countries during times of famine caused by natural disasters, such as droughts or floods, or political unrest. A lack of nutritional knowledge and regional dependence on low-protein diets, such as the maize-based diets of many South American countries, can also cause people to develop this condition. This condition is rare in countries where most people have access to enough food and are able to eat adequate amounts of protein.
3. **Marasmus:** Marasmus is a form of severe malnutrition. It can occur in anyone who has severe malnutrition, but it usually occurs in children. It typically occurs in developing countries. Marasmus can be life-threatening, but you can get treatment for it. The main symptom of marasmus is being underweight. Children with this condition have lost a lot of muscle mass and subcutaneous fat. Subcutaneous fat is the layer of fat just under the skin. Dry skin and brittle hair are also symptoms of marasmus.
4. **Beriberi** affects the cardiovascular and nervous systems. Symptoms: increased heart rate; severe lack of energy or constant fatigue; shortness of breath; waking at night due to shortness of breath; swelling in the legs and feet.
5. **Glossitis** refers to inflammation of the tongue. The condition causes the tongue to swell in size, change colour, and develop a different appearance on the surface.

6. **Pellagra** is marked by dementia, diarrhoea, and dermatitis, also known as "the three Ds". If left untreated, pellagra can be fatal.
7. **Pernicious anaemia** is caused by an inability to absorb the vitamin B-12 needed for your body to make enough healthy red blood cells. This type of anaemia is called "pernicious" because it was once considered a deadly disease.
8. **Scurvy** symptoms include weakness, feeling tired and sore arms and legs. Without treatment, decreased red blood cells, gum disease, changes to the hair, and bleeding from the skin may occur.
9. **Xerophthalmia:** the eyes fail to produce tears. This damage may take the form of white spots on your eyes and ulcers on your corneas.
10. **Rickets**: People with rickets may have weak and soft bones, stunted growth, and, in severe cases, skeletal deformities.
11. **Iodine deficiency:** You need a certain amount of iodine in your body in order for it to make a chemical known as thyroid hormone. Thyroid hormone controls your metabolism and other important body functions. Low levels of iodine are not the only cause of low thyroid function. But a lack of iodine can cause an abnormal enlargement of the thyroid gland, known as goitre, and other thyroid problems. In children, it can cause mental disabilities.

Vitamin	Deficiency Disease	Vitamin	Deficiency Disease
Thiamine (B1)	Beriberi	Retinol (Vitamin A)	Eye and skin diseases
Riboflavin (B2)	Glossitis	Calciferol (Vitamin D)	Rickets
Niacin (B3)	Pellagra	Tocoferol (Vitamin E)	Fertility disorders
Cyanocobalamine (B12)	Pernicious Anaemia	Phylloquinone (Vitamin K)	Blood clotting

10

Human Growth and Development

Concept of human growth and Development: Stages of growth—pre-natal, natal, infant, childhood, adolescence, maturity, senescence.

Factors affecting growth and development genetic, environmental, biochemical, nutritional, cultural and socio-economic.

Ageing and senescence. Theories and observations

Biological and chronological longevity. Human physique and somatotypes. Methodologies for growth studies.

Q 1. Stages of growth—pre-natal, natal, infant, childhood, adolescence, maturity, senescence

Ans. As per Malina, the term growth denotes an increase or decrease in size, number, or volumes of cells or tissues, while development involves qualitative change like the expansion of cells or the onset of puberty, is related to maturation, and is irreversible.

Development leads to functional specialisation, and while talking about development, there are two specific periods:

1. 5th day to 12th week: organs develop.
2. Adolescence to maturity.

There are different stages of growth and development:

1. **Prenatal Growth:** It is usually a 40-week period beginning with the last menstrual cycle and ending with childbirth.

- 5th day: Morula forms: a ball-shaped hollow formed from 16 cells. Then Blastula formed, and ultimately Gastrula fully formed.
- Until the 12th week, the velocity of growth in length is not very great. During this period, differentiation of the whole body into the head and arm (regionalization) and differentiation of cells into tissues such as the nerve and muscle (histogenesis) take place.
- Peak velocity of length is reached at about 18 weeks postmenstrual age and that of weight in the 34 th postmenstrual week.
- The majority of growth is completed by the 36th week.
- If the child is genetically tall but the uterus is small, then immediately after birth there is an increase in height to compensate for the loss.
- At birth, boys are 2cm longer and 100g heavier than girls, with the ring finger larger in boys and the index finger larger in girls.

2. **Infant:** At birth, the brain represents 10–12% of total body mass, compared to 2% of total body mass at adulthood. The brain approximates adult size by the age of 10.

- Height and the majority of body measurements follow a general curve.
- The brain develops 90% by age 5 and 95% by age 10.
- Reproductive organs grow rapidly in adolescents.
- The lymphoid tissue of the tonsils, appendix, and intestine reaches its maximum amount before adolescence and, probably under the influence of sex hormones, declines to its adult value.

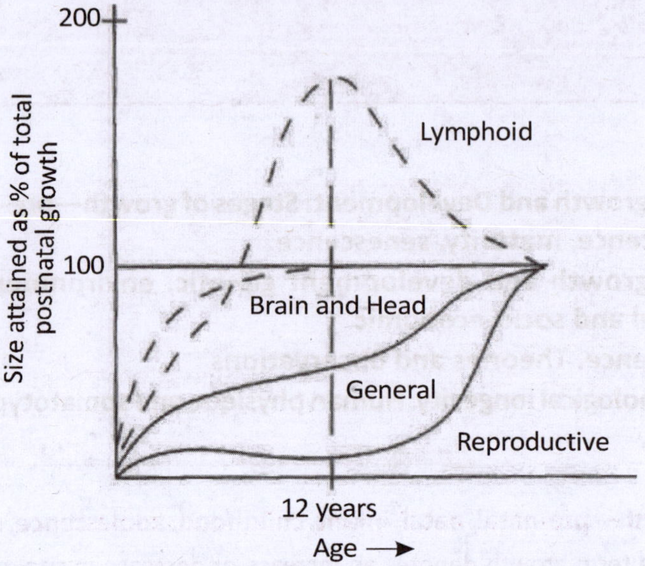

Graph 1- Growth Rate of Different Organs

3. **Adolescence:**

- Puberty begins in girls at 12 years of age and in boys at 14 years of age, generally. But a spurt in height takes place in boys for 2 years and girls for 2 years at a rate of 10 cm per year and 8 cm per year, respectively. Therefore, in absolute terms, the adult sex difference in height between boys and girls is 13cm. 2cm due to pre-puberty, 4cm due to increased spurt intensity, and 7cm due to greater leg bone elongation in the infant stage
- The greater relative width of shoulders in males and hips in females is largely due to the specific stimulation of cartilage cells by androgens in the first instance and oestrogen in the second.
- A greater length of male legs relative to trunk comes as a consequence of a longer prepubescent period of male growth.
- The male forearm is longer relative to the upper arm than the female forearm, and this difference is established at birth and increases throughout the growing period.
- The second finger is longer than the fourth finger more frequently in females than the index.
- Early maturation of females: *M. Tripathi* says that women from urban areas witness an earlier onset of menarche than those from rural areas.
- The first sign of puberty in boys is accelerated growth in the testes and scrotum. Pubic hair starts at the same time, but axillary hair usually first appears about 2 years after pubic hair. In boys, facial hair begins at the same time as axillary hair. Enlargement of the larynx in boys occurs about the time penis growth is nearing completion.
- In girls, the appearance of breast buds is the first sign of puberty. The uterus and vagina develop simultaneously with the breast.

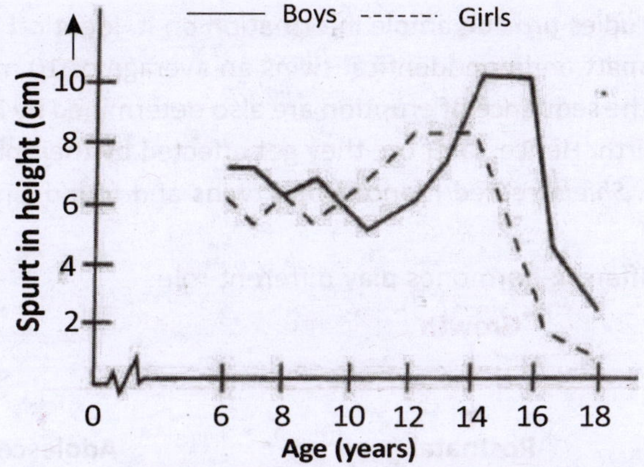

Graph - High Spurt in Boys and Girls →

4. **Post-Adolescent:** In many cases, the epiphyses of long bones close completely and cannot grow thereafter. However, the vertical column continues to grow from 20 to 30 years by apposition of bone to the top and bottom of vertebral bodies. Thus, height increases by a small amount (3-5 mm/year). From the age of 30 to 50, it remains stationary and then begins to decline.
5. **Senescence:**

➢ In this, many molecular and cellular changes occur, due to which greying of the hair, the body's inability to repair tissue, bones becoming weak, memory becoming weak, and a reduction in sitting height occur. Work on identifying genes for ageing is going on.

➢ In the present scenario, stages of growth with respect to age are changing. Adolescence and menarche age are decreasing, especially in urban areas. People in the so-called "ageing period perform work with equal efficiency as in their previous stages.

Case Study

- **When does the metabolism start to drop?**

The research results were divided into four metabolic stages and published in the journal "Nature." A baby's metabolism changes from being roughly the same as that of the mother between birth and age one to "burning calories 50% faster for their body size than an adult." A person's metabolism will continue to decrease by around 3% annually until their 20s, when it levels off into a new normal. Between the ages of 20 and 60, there were no noticeable alterations in metabolism. After age 60, metabolism will gradually decrease until it is 26% lower than it was in midlife by age 90.

- **Gastrulation**

The study's findings focused on gastrulation, which starts 14 days after fertilisation and lasts for a week. They were published in the journal "Nature". Researchers discovered a wide variety of cells, including RBCs, which are the earliest germ cells from which eggs or sperm develop. But the neuron was not located. Learning about how to convert stem cells into certain cell types from nature can be helpful.

Q 2. Factors affecting growth and development genetic, environmental, biochemical, nutritional, cultural and socioeconomic

Ans. According to Malina, an increase or decrease in size or volume is called growth, whereas qualitative change is called development. Factors affecting people can be classified into heredity and environmental factors. Heredity factors include genetic and biochemical factors, whereas environmental factors include nutritional, environmental, and socio-economiccultural factors.

1. **Genetic factor:** Twin studies provide ample information on it. Identical twins reach menarche an average of 2 months apart and non-identical twins an average of 10 months apart. The time of eruption of teeth and the sequence of eruption are also determined by heredity. All genes are not active at the time of birth. Hence, later on, they get affected by their physiological environment, which varies with age. *Shield* reared monozygotic twins and found similarities in their physical characteristics.
2. **Biochemical factor:** Different hormones play different role:

Growth

Prenatal
- HCG- Human Chorionic Gonadotropin
- Testosterone

Postnatal
- HCG- Human Growth Hormone

Adolescent

Body
- HCG - Human Growth Hormone
- Androgen
- Aldosterone
- Cortical

Sexual
- LH- Luteinizin g Hormone
- FSH - Follicle stimulating hormone

a. The human foetus secretes thyroxin at the 12th week of gestation under the influence of thyroid stimulating hormone (TSH) from the pituitary. It helps in growth and development and maintains metabolism.

b. CG: It reaches its peak in the 12th week of postmenstrual age. It causes the appearance and stimulation of leydig cells in the testes to stimulate testosterone. In the absence of a Y chromosome, at the 10th postmenstrual week, the gonad turns into an ovary.

c. HGH is secreted by the pituitary gland, but only after birth up until adolescence. It causes growth by stimulating an increase in cartilage-generating cells and making them secrete the somatomedin C hormone.

d. Testosterone causes an increase in the size of muscles.

e. A group of hormones—androgen, aldosterone, and cortical hormones secreted from the adrenal cortex— controls growth.

f. LH causes ovulation in females and secretes testosterone to grow secondary sexual characters, leydig cells, in males.

g. FSH causes the development of the ovarian follicle, secondary sexual character, and the secretion of oestrogen in females and spermatogenesis and the growth of the testis in males.

3. **Environmental Factor:**

a. According to Turner, those who reside in cold regions are shorter in stature but heavier, whereas those in hot regions are taller in stature but slender. The trunks of Highlanders are long, but their legs are shorter.

b. Season: growth of height is fastest in spring, and growth of weight is fastest in autumn. Vincert and Dierickxx found that healthy children living in Zaire near the equator grew more rapidly in the dry season than in the rainy season.

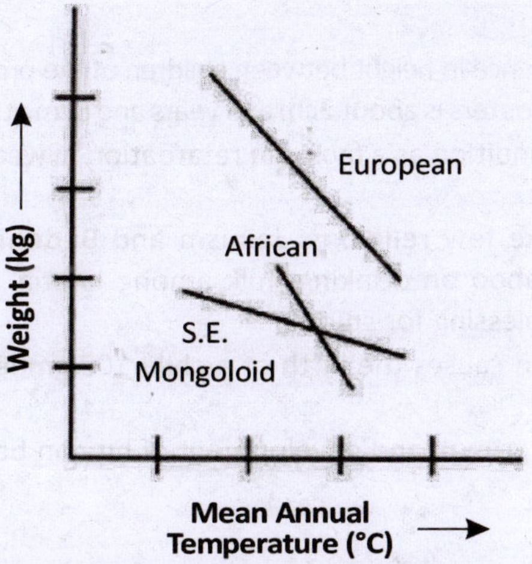

Graph 1 - Bergmann's Rule

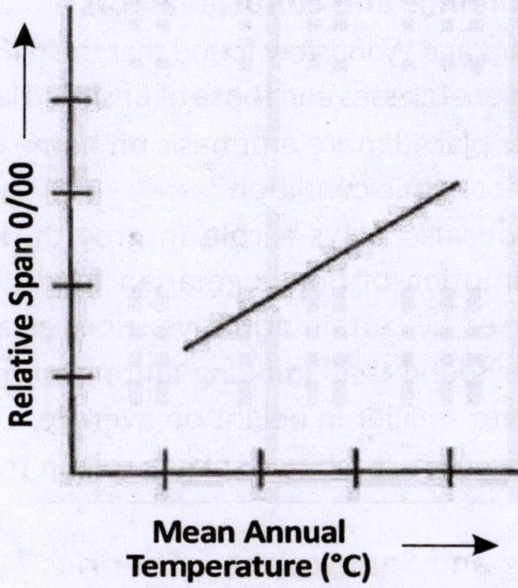

Graph 2 - Allen's Rule

4. Nutritional Factor

a. Greene studied Ecuadorian India, an Andean region with chronic iodine deficiency. Individuals without deficiency are taller (155.5 cm) than affected ones (146.2cm).

b. Malnutrition delays and slows growth. Girls are more buffered than boys against the effects of malnutrition.

c. Infections in mothers and malnutrition in mothers lead to intrauterine growth retardation.

d. Malnourished effect:

   i. Prenatal Infant Mortality Rate (IMR): 62 in the tribal area and 40 in other regions

   ii. Infant: Retarded mind

   iii. Adolescent: Delay menarche by 2 years in Kenyan girls compared to US girls.

   iv. Maturity: starts early and less growth takes place.

   v. Senescence: rapid decline and lower life expectancy

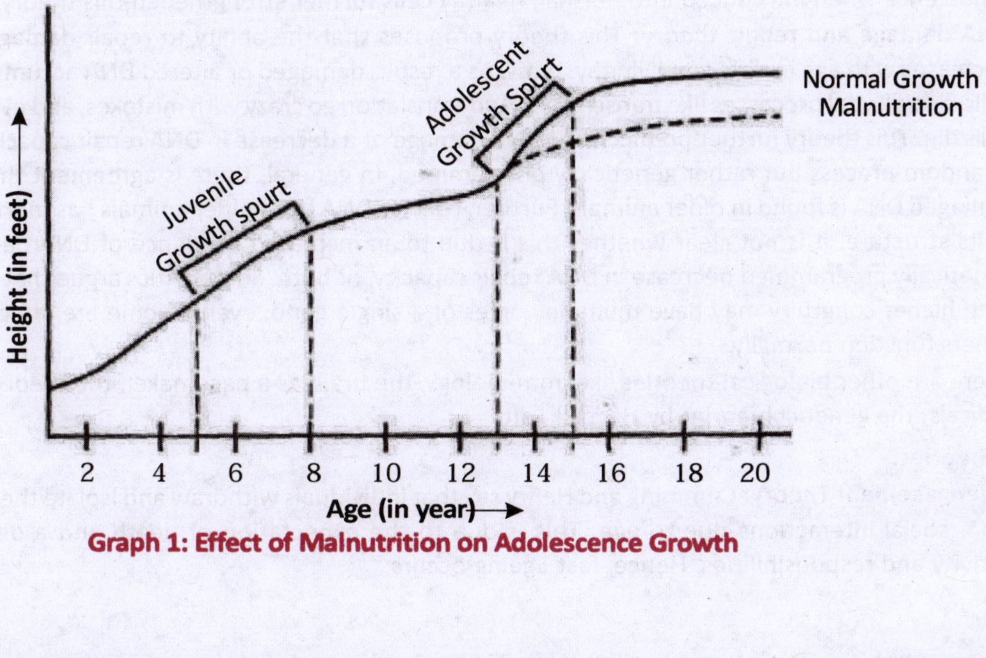

Graph 1: Effect of Malnutrition on Adolescence Growth

5. **Socio-economic and cultural factors**
   a. Topinard and Woodsrow found that the difference in height between children of the professional and managerial classes and those of unskilled labourers is about 2cm at 3 years and 5cm at adolescence.
   b. Tauner placed more emphasis on home condition as a factor in retardation in weaker sections than economic condition.
   c. Religion also plays a role in growth. Like few religions, Jainism and Buddhism prohibit consumption of non-vegetarian foods. Taboo on drinking milk among Kharia, Alcohol was preferred by certain primitive tribes as a blessing for spirits.
   d. Tauner found that smoking among women causes the birth of a child 100 gm less in weight and 1cm smaller in height on average.

   All these factors, combined, play a role in the growth and development of human beings.

Q 3. Ageing and Senescence – Theories

Ans. According to *Strechler*, senescence means various changes, both functional and physiological, that take place during the later stages of life. Ageing simply means growing old. For example, at the start of puberty, there is ageing change but not senescent change.

These are different theories:

1. **Death Gene Theory:** This theory proposes that ageing is genetically programmed through one or more harmful genes in an organism. These genes become active at a particular time in late life and alter the physiology of the organism in such a way that death results. It is also possible that these genes are active during the early years but are altered in later years, thus switching their functions. This theory therefore suggests that human life span is an inherited trait.

   Studies with twins have shown that there is considerable similarity in the age of death of monozygotic twins, whereas similarity is not apparent in dizygotic twins. Studies show that, in general, the offspring of long-lived parents have a longer life span. For example, Vilcabamba (Ecuador), Hunza in Pakistan, and Abkhazia (Soviet Georgia) live up to 100–120 years.

   Finally, the recent identification of some genes in cultured cells that are capable of inducing senescence when introduced into normal, healthy cells further strengthened this theory.
2. **DNA damage and repair theory:** This theory proposes that the ability to repair damaged DNA decreases with age in different living systems. As a result, damaged or altered DNA accumulates in cells, and all vital processes like transcription and translation go crazy with mistakes, and eventually cells die. This theory further predicts that DNA damage or a decrease in DNA repair capacity is not a random process but rather genetically programmed. In general, there is agreement that more damaged DNA is found in older animals. Further, cellular DNA from older animals has more breaks in its structure. It is not clear whether this is due to an increased incidence of DNA damage, a genetically programmed decrease in DNA repair capacity, or both. Some critics argue that animals with higher congruity may have multiple copies of a single gene, even if some are affected and others function normally.

   There are other biological theories like immunology, the brain as a pacemaker, the theory of free radicals, the geneticblueprint by Hayflick, etc.

Social Theories:

1. **Disengagement Theory:** Cumming and Henry say that individuals withdraw and isolate themselves from social interactions due to age. This is due to the expectation of death and a decline in activity and responsibilities. Hence, fast ageing occurs.

2. **Activity Theory:** Robert J. Havighurst says that fast ageing occurs when the elderly stay active and maintain social interactions.
3. **Continuity Theory:** Robert Atchley says that elders try to maintain the continuity of their lifestyle by adopting strategies connected to past experiences. Hence, fast ageing occurs.
4. **Social Clock Theory:** Expectation of behaviour occurring at a particular time according to social norms. Hence, fast ageing occurs.

Molecular damage → Impaired cell → Impair tissue/organ → Low efficiency humans → Death

Biological theories are conflicting, while social theories are not universal. No single theory can sufficiently explain ageing, and thus it remains a hot research topic in anthropology.

Q 4. Ageing and Senescence – Observations

Ans. Ageing simply means growing old. According to *Strechler*, senescence means various changes, both functional and physiological, that take place during the later stages of life.

Senescence means various changes, both functional and physiological, that take place during the later stages of life. It may start after age 30 and may not start at age 60. It has more to do with biological age than chronological age. It is subject to different factors: Nutrition level, Genetic makeup and Nature of work.

Different features involved are:

1. **Rate of Greying Hair:** Similar to any other somatic cell, hair cells wear out but at a faster pace. However, it varies with environmental factors. Recent anthropological studies conducted by Sahay among Andamanese and Gonds found that traditional nutritional methods delay the greying of hair.
2. **Skin Elasticity:** The quality of the skin is a measure of youthfulness. It is due to the faster decay of collagen molecules in the proteins of the skin. Collagen molecules are extracellular substances that form a boundary between the skin and the environment. With age, collagen decay increasesand it reduces the elasticity of the skin.
   An anthropological study by Thompson and Gluckman analysed perceptions of beauty and age. According to them, Japanese society gives higher value to age; as such people have vast experience and knowledge. It is different from American society, where artificial methods are used to look young.
3. **Hand Grip:** Strength fades with biological age.
4. **Maximum heart rate**, kidney blood flow, work rate, and breathing rate decrease with age. Skin elasticity and greying of hair do not have a relationship with death, but decreases in cardiovascular systems increase the probability of death. However, the actual reason has yet to be found.
   By 2030, India's elderly population is expected to rise to 12% from the current 8%. Anthropology can play a key role in enhancing the lives and lifestyle productivity of the elderly population.

Case Study

- **Age vs. DNA: Which has more influence on how humans age?**

Natural selection is thought to be less important for individuals once they have finished reproducing since, at that stage of life, gene variants are not passed on to offspring. According to a recent study, environmental variables and ageing itself have a greater influence on some tissue types in older people than DNA does. Even though these tissues are extremely crucial, they may also cause cancer, demonstrating a limit to what evolution can do.

Q 5. Human physique and Somatotypes

Ans. According to Sheldon, somatotypes are morpho-phenotypic ranges along constant cognizable characteristics and are functional end products of the whole genetic and developmental complex. Somatotyping refers to the study of personality by dividing people into different types on the basis of body build (physique).

The constitution of human personality is defined by a certain set of morphological and behavioural characteristics. But later in anthropological studies, behavioural characteristics are dropped as they are a reflection of enculturation, and focus is laid on physical characteristics.

Various methods were devised:

(i) Sheldon Classification: Based upon laboratory and field studies wherein he used pictures and body measurements of about 4000 undergraduate students and divided them into three types:

- **Endomorph:**
  1. Wide hips and shoulders.
  2. Short arms and legs and a large amount of mass in the trunk, thereby reducing agility.
  3. Lot of fat, especially on the upper arms and thighs.
  4. Rounded body
- **Mesomorph:**
  1. Wide and broad shoulders
  2. Muscled arms and legs
  3. Low-fat
  4. Medium hips
- **Ectomorph:**
  1. Narrow and dropped shoulders
  2. Lean arms.
  3. Little fat.
  4. Narrow hips

Sheldon, on the basis of this, tried to recommend sports based upon the 7 points given to a particular somatotype.

Endomorph	Mesomorph	Ectomorph	Type	Sports
7	1	1	Extreme Endo	Sumo wrestlers
1	7	1	Extreme Meso	Weightlifters and gymnasts
1	1	7	Extreme Ecto	High jumpers

Sheldon also associated them with diseases like endomorphic individuals having diabetes (type II) and ectomorphic individuals having TB (pulmonary TB).

Limitations:

1. Highly subjective
2. Limited range (16–20 years).
3. Only applicable to males
4. Based on the assumption that physique won't change from birth to death

ii. Heath and the Carter Method: To overcome the negatives of the Sheldon method, Heath and Carter took measurements of 10 different body parts and changed scales for three components:

- Endomorphy: 1 to 15 (relative flatness scanners)
- Mesomorphy: 1 to 12 (relative muscularity per unit height)
- Ectomorphy: 0.5 to 9 (relative linearity)

It also evaluates the physique at a given time as compared to Sheldon's unchanging somatotype.

Merits:

1. Objective method
2. Explore spatial-temporal variations
3. Applicable to females as well as males

Limitation:

1. Cannot fit all of the general population into these three.
2. Not applicable to children under six years of age.

iii. **Viola Method:** It was introduced in the 19th century and is an outdated concept right now. It is classified by length of limb, length of trunk, and circumference of body.

10 aspects of morphology reduced to 4 indices:

- Longitude: long limb relative to trunk
- Brachytype: longer trunk than limbs
- Normatype: falls between two (trunk = limb).
- Mixed: didn't fall in the above category.

With rising specialisations, somatotyping helps in selecting suitable physical activity for an individual. It evaluates the physique at the time of assessment, and it may change.

Relevance:

1. Kinanthropometry
2. Design of defence equipment
3. Ergonomics

Q 6. Methodologies for growth studies

Ans. The entire life span of man, beginning from embryo to death, is characterised by some form of positive or negative growth and development.

Reason to study growth:

1. Tanner: It is a powerful tool to monitor the health of the population.
2. Understand morphological differences among people.
3. Understand the factors and requirements of well-being.
4. Understand the interaction of nature and nurture.
5. Trends in health across the population

There are methods to study it:

1. Longitudinal Growth Study:

1. It is studied by an individual over a long period of time. It studies individuals from birth to maturity after a regular interval, say 6 months or 1 year.
2. It is an ideal and exact method, but there are plenty of problems.

Limitations:

1. After an individual goes to school, it is difficult to maintain regular contact.
2. It requires a lot of energy, time, and resources.
3. The researcher himself may not survive the required life span. It is an ideal method, but not practical.

2. Cross-Sectional Study:

1. In this, individuals of different ages are randomly selected from the population, and growth measurements are obtained. A large sample size was observed, and an average was taken.
2. It is an easy method that saves a lot of time, energy, and resources but is not accurate.

Limitations:

1. The people studied do not remember their exact date of birth.
2. Average never gives accurate results.

But it is a very good method to train young scientists and introduce them to growth studies.

3. **Semi-Longitudinal Method:** This method combines both longitudinal and cross-sectional methods. Taking a statistically significant section and studying it for a minimum of 3 to a maximum of 5 years.

So the limitations of the cross-sectional method and the many advantages of longitudinal methods are also covered. It is a practical method that is followed in growth research.

We conduct these studies in order to convert large amounts of data into graphs.

Through these methods, the role of heredity and environment in the growth of sections of the population is studied.

Techniques: 1. Anthropometric, 2. X-ray method

Measurements taken: 1. Linear, 2. Circumference, 3. Pondial

Case Study: LASI (Longitudinal Ageing Study of India) reports:

1. 75% of elders suffer from one or more chronic diseases.
2. 20% have mental health issues.
3. Self-reported cardiovascular: 28% above 45 years of age.
4. Comorbidity increases with age.

These methods will help broaden the scope of the programme of health care for elders and work to reduce noncommunicable diseases.

Q 7. Catch up Growth and Secular Growth

Ans. Catch-up growth

Ability to stabilise and return to a predetermined growth curve after being pushed off track throughout the whole period of growth. Commonly prevails due to illness, starvation, and civil wars (Syria, Yemen, and Palestine).

This is an increase in growth velocity when sufficient nutrition is available after a period of disease or starvation. It shows the plasticity of human growth and development.

Studies:

- Kulin conducted a cross-sectional survey comparing girls from three privileged schools with impoverished district schools. By the age of 18, impoverished girls had caught up with affluent girls.
- Alvear: Previously malnourished children in Chile, Peru, and Capetown show evidence of catch-up when provided nutrition, though they didn't achieve it normally.
- Adnair: There is a large potential for catch-up growth in children, even in the pre-adolescent years.

Secular Growth: Attainment of larger sizes in terms of height and weight and the acceleration of maturation over several generations are collectively labelled as secular trends.

Factors responsible:

1. Elimination of growth-inhibiting factors such as epidemics and famine
2. Favourable economic conditions such as family income and occupation
3. Genetic changes such as population admixtures

Positive trend

Taller and heavier trends:

- Hauspie and Colleague: 17 countries from Europe, Japan, and Taiwan studied. After World War II, the Japanese saw a strong secular trend with a 2.67 cm increase in height per decade.
- Boas: Europeans who migrated to the US experienced an increase in height.
- Shapiro: Japanese immigrants to Hawaii are significantly taller than their parents.

Early mature trend:

- Hulanika and Waliszko: Age at menarche reduced by 4.15 months per decade in town and village and 3 months per decade in the city of Poland from 1955 to 1978.
- Khanna and Kapoor: Increase in stature and decline in age of menarche of daughter compared to mother in Punjabi Arora families
- Maharashtrian Girls: From 1960 to 2000, there was a consistent age decline in menarche of 6 months per decade compared to 3 months in Europe and North America.
- Biswa and Kapoor: lower age of menarche of daughters compared to mothers

Negative trend:

- Shorter, lighter, and more mature due to crisis situations like war, food shortages, etc. It prevailed in Guatemala, 1974–1983; and Cuba, 1990–2005.

Neutral trend:

- Population attained potential: North European Countries.

11

Bio-Events Related to Fertility

11.1

Relevance of menarche, menopause and other bioevents to fertility. Fertility patterns and differentials.

Q 1. Relevance of menarche, menopause and other bioevents to fertility Fertility patterns and differentials

Ans. Female reproductive glands are pairs of ovary present in the abdominal cavity. Each ovary contains numerous ovarian follicles. One ovarian follicle matures per month, and this matured ovarian follicle is called a Graffian follicle. This Graffin follicle releases eggs and disintegrates afterwards into yellow-coloured solid matter called corpus luteum, which in turn produces progesterone. Fertilisation of the egg takes place in the fallopian tube, and the fertilised zygote travels down the tube and reaches the uterus.

Process:

1 → 14 → 21 → 28 (1)

1 st day of menstruation → Egg released from ovary → Reaches uterus → During this, endometrium gets separated from uterus & surrounding egg cell. Hormone called oxytocin is released which make uterus to contract.

Egg released from ovary ↓ Uterus prepare for receiving egg

The uterus may receive a fertilised or unfertilized egg. While the egg is travelling down the fallopian tube, the uterus forms endometrium as preparation for the fertilised egg. If on the 21 st day, the uterus receives an unfertilized egg, endometrium separates from the walls of the uterus and around the egg cell. The oxytocin hormone gets released, which causes the uterus to contract. So that unfertilized egg, along with unused endometrium and other material, gets expelled out. This is the process called menstruation. The first menstrual cycle is called menarche.

On the 21 st day, if the uterus receives a fertilised egg, it grows thicker and larger, supporting pregnancy for the next 9 months. At the end of 9 months, the oxytocin hormone gets released, leading to contraction of the uterus and childbirth. But when the fertilised egg reaches the uterus, oestrogen and progesterone levels increase drastically, which will block the release of the next egg from the ovary. Menstruation doesn't occur during pregnancy and is called gestational amenorrhea.

Amenorrhea also occurs before menarche, known as primary amenorrhea. If it occurs after menopause (cessation of menstruation), it is called permanent amenorrhea. If due to surgery the ovary or uterus removed, it is called surgical amenorrhea. During lactation, menstruation doesn't occur, which is called lactational amenorrhea.

The average age of menarche is 13–15 (12.9).

Prerequisite for Menarche:

1. 17% of body weight must be fat.
2. Ovulation must begin or occur no later than one year.
3. Estrogen and progesterone hormone production must begin.

Reasons for early menarche:

1. Child obesity
2. Absence of a father at home during early childhood
3. High conflict family relationships
4. Genetics: Identical twins reach menarche at 2 months apart, non-identical at 20 months.
5. Girls in urban society reach menarche earlier than rural girls (Kenya is 2 years later than US girls).

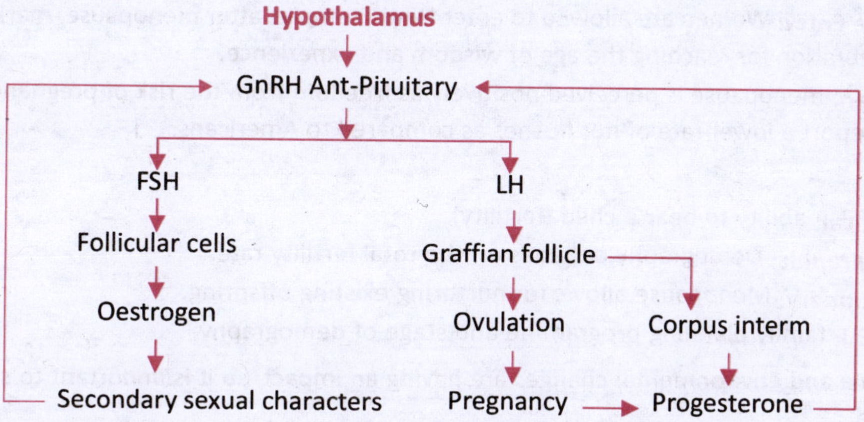

***Menopause:** Cessation of Menstruation Hypothesis*

1. **Mother Hypothesis:** Older mothers might profit more by investing resources in existing children than in giving birth to new ones. Therefore, menopause occurs.
2. **Grandmother Hypothesis:** Providing support to kin can ensure that their genetic interests are met and enhance their resources; therefore, menopause occurs.

But unlike menarche, menopause is not one single marked event but a process that takes place gradually. Pre-menopause before menopause, post-menopause after menopause, and peremenopause before and after menopause

Symptoms	Menopause Feature
• Hot flushes	• Mood swings
• Skin burning sensation	• Typically between 40-60 age
• Skin loosing elasticity	• Average age – 51 years
• Backache	• Indian age – 45 years
• Arthritis	• In western countries, mean age of menopause is higher. It may be due to nutrition, climatic & racial factor
• Migrain	• Higher in better nourished then poor

Cultural Impact of Menarche:

1. **Ritual of Learning:** In Australian aboriginal, girl is taught with ways of woman hood by other woman in tribes. She remains confined to hut for time until she marries a boy. In urban societies, sex education is given.
2. **Ritual of Transformation:** In Tiv of Nigeria, ethnic women cut four lines into the abdomen of girls during menarche, representing fertility.
3. **Religious Rituals:** In Nepal, Kuwari girls are worshipped by Hindus and some Buddhists. But on the onset of menarche, it is believed that the goddess spirit vacates her body and she returns to ordinary life.

Cultural Impact of Menopause:

1. **Temple Entry:** Women are allowed to enter Hindu temples after menopause, marking it as an act of celebration for reaching the age of wisdom and experience.
2. **In Japan,** menopause is perceived positively as freedom from the risk of pregnancy, and women even report a lower rate of hot flushes as compared to Americans.

Relevance:

1. **Biological:** ability to bear a child (fertility)
2. **Demographic:** Demography depends on the total fertility rate.
3. **Evolutionary:** Menopause allows for nurturing existing offspring.
4. **Political:** family planning programme and stage of demography

Lifestyle and environmental changes are having an impact, so it is important to study these two phenomena.

Case Study

- **Menstrual Taboo and the Fluid Feminine: Kamakhya (Sacred vs. Profane)**

The menstrual goddess Kamakhya's influence is seen as extraordinarily potent in Assamese culture. Three days are set aside each year for her followers as taboo because of the goddess' "sacredness," making the area where she resides taboo for "visiting others." This is paradoxical and intriguing because for any other typical Assamese woman, the taboo is flipped; her mobility is restricted as opposed to that of her family or society. As a result, the menstruation taboo that is placed on women is based mostly on the notion of their profanity, but the menstrual taboo of Goddess Kamakhya is based primarily on the notion of her holiness and places restrictions on her followers rather than herself. Here, the ambiguities and inconsistencies of social constructions surrounding menstruation taboos are made clear.

- **The Tuloni Biya: Sealing "Womanhood"** (Rites de passage)

Tuloni biya literally translates to "a marriage that uplifts the girl," since in Assamese, "tuloni" means "to carry up" and "biya" means "marriage." In addition to the ceremonial upliftment, tuloni unmistakably suggests a form of "social" upliftment for the young woman. It represents her initial ritual initiation into a sexual being and her social elevation to the status of a fertile, menstrual female who is therefore sexually available. The girl is made aware of her sexuality at this initiation, which is noteworthy because it also clearly signifies her shift from a non-sexual to a sexually aware individual. However, this awareness typically involves suppressing the sexuality she is becoming aware of out of shame and guilt. The tuloni, or social or ritual upliftment, is significant from a gender perspective not because it elevates the girl's social status to that of a sexual and fertile being but rather because it creates social situations that introduce the girl to a status of restraint, conditioning her to behave in specific ways.

- **Anthropologists find new ways female bones are permanently altered after giving birth.**

A group of anthropologists has discovered that reproduction permanently changes women's bones in ways that were not previously understood. Its revelation, which was based on a study of monkeys, provides new insight into how childbirth can fundamentally alter the body. To determine variations in calcium, phosphorus, oxygen, magnesium, and sodium contents in the monkeys' bones, Cerrito and her colleagues employed energydispersive X-ray analysis and electron microscopy, two techniques frequently used to determine the chemical composition of tissue samples. Their findings indicated that several of these components were present in females who gave birth at different concentrations from males and females who did not give birth. Specifically, bone produced during reproductive events included less calcium and phosphate in females who gave birth.

Q 2. Fertility patterns

Ans. Fertility patterns around the world have changed dramatically over the last few decades. Global fertility has reached unprecedented low levels, yet differences exist. According to the results of the 2015 Revision of World Population Prospects, the total fertility rate (TFR) is now 2.5 children per woman globally. This global average masks wide regional differences. Africa remains the region with the highest fertility rate of 4.7 children per woman, while Europe has the lowest rate of 1.6 children per woman. Both Asia and Latin America and the Caribbean have a total fertility rate of 2.2 children per woman.

Middle and western Africa have a high fertility rate of 5 children per woman. Eastern Asia, Eastern Europe, and Southern Europe have very low fertility rates, with fewer than 1.6 children per woman. Today, 46% of the world's population lives in countries with fewer than 2.1 children on average.

The global fertility rate is projected to decline to 2.4 children per woman by 2030 and 2.2 children per woman by 2050. In Africa, fertility is projected to decline to 3.9 children per woman by 2030 and 3.1 by 2050.

The net reproduction rate (NRR) is the average number of daughters that would be born to a woman, taking into account prevailing levels of fertility, female mortality, and sex ratio at birth. When it is one, each woman is replaced by her surviving daughter, and this implies that fertility is at replacement level.

When more boys than expected are born compared with girls, the NRR will be lower than expected for given fertility, and the long-term population growth rate will be lower as a result. This is the case in many countries in Asia.

Globally, NRR is 1.1 surviving daughters per woman. In all regions, it is at or below this level except Africa, where it is 1.9. It means that each African mother replaces herself with two daughters, which leads to fast population growth.

11.2

Demographic theories-biological, social and cultural.

Q 1. Demographic Transition

Ans. Demography is the science that deals with the study or analysis of population structure. It also studies changes in population structure and various factors that influence such changes in population:

1. **Size:** large or small
2. **Age structure:** expanding, static, or declining
3. **Sex ratio:** 1 : 1 biologically

Broadly, theories are divided into three groups:

1. Sexual related
2. Food related
3. Population density-related

Demographic transition theory falls under population density-related theory.

a. Frank Notestein:

- In the first, early stationary phase, there is a high birth rate and a high death rate, characterised by a backward society of hunters and gatherers.
- In the second phase of population growth, the death rate decreases due to medical advancement, but the birth rate remains high.
- In the last phase of late stationary growth, the birth rate and death rate both decrease, and there is no net rise in population.

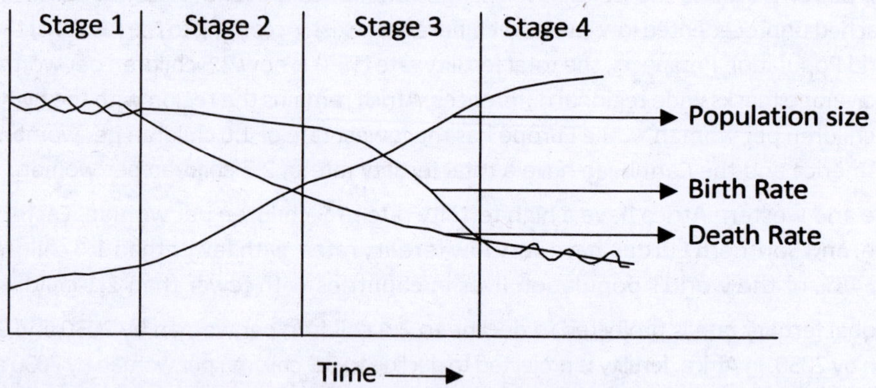

Stages of Demographic Transition

b. C.P. Blacker:

- **High stationary phase:** birth rate high and death rate high
- **Early expanding phase:** birth rate high and death rate low
- **Late expanding phase:** birth rate reducing but still high and death rate low
- **Low stationary phase:** birth rate and death rate are both low.
- In a declining phase, the birth and death rates are extremely low.

C.P. Blacker

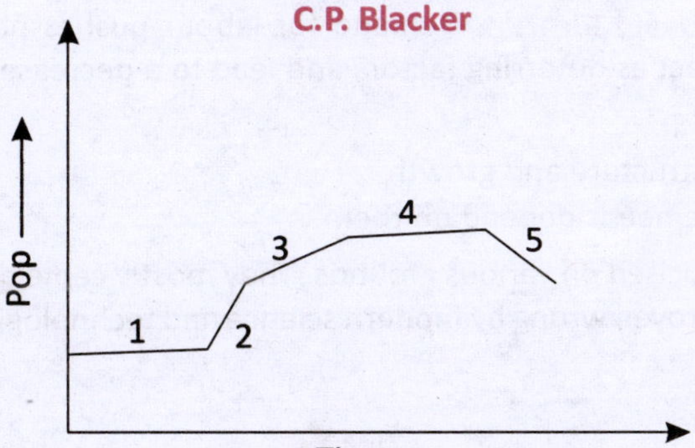

According to this theory, when society transforms from illiterate, rural, and agrarian to literate, urban, and industrialised, a particular direction of demographic change can be traced.

Criticism: Loschky and Wildcose criticised it, arguing that theory is neither productive nor its stages sequential and definite, and the role of technology in today's era is different and should not be underrated.

The theory, despite its shortcomings, provides a generalised macro-level framework that can comprehend demographic processes in a particular country.

Q 2. Demographic theories-biological, social and cultural

Ans. Demography is the science that deals with the study or analysis of population structure. It studies changes in population structure and various factors that influence such changes.

1. **Sexual Behaviour related:**
   a. Malthusian Theory: Because of the passionate behaviour of male and female sexes, our population doubles in geometric progression while food grows in arithmetic progression. This disparity leads to world hunger, thereby being called positive check by nature (miseries). Neo-Malthusians have added other factors that influence population size. Anti-malthusians consider that world hunger is not due to insufficient resources but to improper distribution.
2. **Food fertility nexus-related:**
   a. Theory of Thomas Doubleday: Doubleday maintained that a plethoric state is unfavourable to fertility while scarcity enhances fertility. He even asserted that a vegetarian diet and leanness were favourable to fertility.
   b. Theory of De Castro: Less consumption of proteins by females is the cause of high fertility. Less protein leads to fatty degeneration of the liver, making it weak. Weak livers are unable to neutralise excess oestrogen, which causes fertility to rise.
   c. Theory of Herbert Spencer: Lower forms of life have high genesis because of low individuation, while higher forms of life have low genesis because of high individuation.
3. **Density-fecundity nexus theory**
   a. Demographic transition theory: explained in the previous question
   b. Sadler theory: When density increases, privacy decreases, therefore leading to less fertility.

Other social theories:

a. **Theory of Karl Marx:** The only form of capital for the working class is manpower. People of low economic status tend to have more fertility.

b. **Classical theory of David Ricardo:** Demand for labour pushes population in the early stages. Decreases in wages act as deterring factors and lead to a decrease in population size.

Applications:

1. Analyse population structure and growth.
2. Peak rates and future needs depend on them.

Every theory gets criticised on various grounds. They mostly came during the 19 th and early 20th centuries, thereby being proven wrong by modern science and technology related to population growth and food production.

11.3

Biological and socio-ecological factors influencing fecundity, fertility, natality and mortality.

Q 1. Biological and socio-ecological factors influencing fecundity, fertility and natality

Ans. Fecundity is defined as the biological potential of giving birth to a child, while fertility is defined as the realised potential of giving birth to a child. If an individual is fertile, it definitely means she is fecund, but if she is fecund, there is no compulsion to be fertile. It is in turn related to natality, which means a measure of the birth rate of the population, i.e., the number of live births per year per 1000.

Biological factors common to both fecundity and fertility:

1. **Menarche and menopause:** Menarche starts around 13–15 and menopause at around 50–55.
2. **Contraception:** Use of vasectomy, tubecatomy, condoms, pills, etc. to prevent fertilisation
3. **Sterility:** In males, azoospermia, i.e., low sperm count, and in females, amenorrhea or constriction of the fallopian tubes, lead to sterility.
4. **Sexual intercourse** is highly probable on the 21st–28th days of the menstrual cycle.
5. **Histoincompatibility** (Rh-mother and Rh+child), chromosomal changes, and lethal and sublethal genes lead to intrauterine mortality.

Socio-economic factors for fertility:

1. **Age of Marriage:** In Kerela, marriage age is high and low TFR. In Uttar Pradesh, Bihar has a low marriage age and a high TFR.
2. **Education:** Low women's education leads to low awareness and a high fertility rate.
3. **Employment:** Women employed with low TFR, e.g., Tharus of UP, work in industries.
4. **Rural Residence:** Women in rural areas who mostly work in agricultural fields have high fertility. e.g., Sugali of Andhra Pradesh.
5. **Health:** DN Majumder did a study on the Assam Hill Tribe's high IMR and high fertility.
6. **Caste:** high caste, high education and employment, low fertility, and vice versa for lower caste.
7. **Race:** Blacks have compared higher fertility to others.
8. **Religion:** Few religions consider contraception a sin.

Socio-Economic Factors for fecundity:

1. **Nutrition:** Low nutrition levels delay the onset of menarche (e.g., Sahariya tribe of MP).
2. **Cigarette/Smoking:** Heavy smoking and alcohol consumption reduce fecundity.
3. **Occupational Pressure:** Study says that hazardous industry work reduces sperm count.
4. **Lactational in Fecundity:** Sucking depresses the hypothalamus; no LH and RSH; no follicle maturity; Low Fecundity.

With lifestyle changes like smoking, stress, etc., it becomes important to study these concepts.

Case Study

- **Blood Magic: The Anthropology of Menstruation**

By Alma Gottlieb, University of Illinois professor of anthropology, gender studies, and women's studies. Positive stance: The Yurok, a class-segregated native tribe from the northwest coast of the United States, had a group of aristocratic women who viewed their periods as a time for self-purification. This group's menstrual cycles occur at the same time each month, as they do for many women who live close to one another. They performed a number of rituals throughout their shared menstrual cycle, which they claimed was the time when they had their most intense spiritual experiences. Neutral stance: The Rungus women of Borneo take a neutral attitude towards their menstrual cycles. They don't claim it's clean or filthy, either. It's just a bodily fluid that needs to be evacuated. They don't make a big deal of it.

- **Impact of Education on Fertility**

Amarjyoti Mahanta's Evidence from a Tribal Society in Assam, India After investigating the relationship between education and fertility in tribal society using cross-sectional research on the Misings, the secondlargest scheduled tribe in the Indian state of Assam, The paper's multiple regression analysis reveals that while both a wife's and a husband's education have a regressive effect on fertility, the number of live births is dramatically reduced when a wife has a higher level of education than a husband. In order to reach the replacement level of fertility at the graduate level of education, it has been discovered that the education of females has a positive relationship with fertility up to 5.3 years of schooling and a negative relationship beyond that. Therefore, 5.3 years of education are necessary for the spouses to have a lower effect on reproduction. The report makes policy recommendations for increasing access to education, with a particular emphasis on attracting and keeping female students.

Q 2. Biological and socio-ecological factors influencing mortality

Ans. Mortality means the number of deaths in one period of time or in one place. The mortality rate is typically expressed in units of deaths per 1,000 individuals per year.

Biological factors:

1. X-linked immunoregulatory genes contribute to greater female resistance to infections.
2. Sex differences in reproductive physiology and anatomy contribute to higher female mortality from breast cancer and maternal mortality.
3. Women's endogenous sex hormones reduce women's risk of ischemic heart disease.
4. Link between genetics and male sex hormone in behaviour leading to higher deaths from accidents
5. Certain inherited genetic disorders exist among males and females.

Socio-ecological factors:

1. Poor conditions in the uterus and early childhood are associated with higher mortality, even at an advanced age.
2. Higher education is linked to higher socio-economic status, and both are linked to high longevity.
3. Advances in medicine and socio-economic status reduce mortality levels.
4. People employed in dangerous occupations increase the death rate.
5. Factors of fertility and fecundity also impact these socio-ecological aspects.

With lifestyle changes like smoking, stress, etc., it becomes important for anthropologist to study these concepts and act as action anthropologist.

12

Applications of Anthropology

Applications of Anthropology : Anthropology of sports, Nutritional anthropology, Anthropology in designing of defence and other equipments, Forensic Anthropology, Methods and principles of personal identification and reconstruction, Applied human genetics—Paternity diagnosis, genetic counselling and eugenics, DNA technology in diseases and medicine, serogenetics and cytogenetics in reproductive biology.

Q 1. Anthropology of sports

Ans. Kinanthropometry, a term given by *Bill Ross*, evaluates the physical structure of an individual in relation to gross motor function, i.e., human size, shape, proportion, composition, and maturation. The composition of body components is different in males and females and dependent upon environment, sex, socioeconomic condition, nutrition, and exercise. A sport needs not only muscle strength but also coordinated body movements. For different sports, coordinated body movements are required in different ways. This individual with certain anthropometric characteristics is supposed to perform better than others. Anthropometric studies of individuals in such cases can help select players who have better potential in particular sports than others.

1. **Somatotype and sports performance:** For classification of physique, system most followed is that of More House and Rasch.

Height	Weight	Suitable for Event
Tall	Heavy	Wrestling
	Medium	Boxing
	Light	Sprinting - Jumping
Medium	Heavy	Throwing
	Medium	Long distance seminary
	Light	Games – Hockey, Football
Short	Heavy	Weight lifting
	Medium	Gymnastic
	Light	Skating

A study by Parizkova on gymnasts proved that reversibility of body composition begins immediately after cessation of physical activity by an athlete, no matter how long the athlete remained under a heavy work load; hence, regular exercise is required.

Another study by *Robert Trivers* on why Jamaicans are fast runners showed that the symmetry of children's knees at the age of 8 predicts how fast a person runs 14 years later in life. With all sprinters, those with the most symmetrical knees have the best times.

2. **Genetics and Sports:** Initially, sports anthropometrics relied only on physique. Later on, after the discovery of the latest diagnostic tools such as ultrasound, X-rays, and CT scans, it became possible to analyse deep-seated muscles. And now, a new category of genes has been discovered that make athletes. The American Journal of Human Genetics (2003) reported a study by the Australian Institute of Sports that showed that for short-distance running, the ACTN-3 gene and the ACTN-2 gene are responsible for increasing efficiency in a large manner.
3. **Design of sports equipment:** Anthropometric studies also sometimes help redesign articles to suit indigenous groups. For example, Dr. Sachindra Narayan redesigned hockey sticks to suit certain groups in Chotanagpur, and these boys soon became National Champions in 1995. Another work was in the field of archery's stick redesigning to suit Saura Pahariya of Jharkhand, and now they excel at this sport. As they were short-statured shifting cultivators, the national standard did not suit them.
4. **Training and nutritional requirements:** In recent times, the role of sports anthropology is bound to increase with more research on genetics. A project started in Bhiwani district of Haryana, which produced India's best boxers, to understand the role of genetics in sports.

The Sports Authority of India (SAI) is taking the help of anthropologists to find talent and map it in India, and it is expected to grow further.

Q 2. Nutritional Anthropology

Ans. It is a branch of applied anthropology that studies nutrients and the nutritional status of individuals or communities.

Scope:

1. **Food intake and health:** At least 50 different nutrients are required for normal functioning of the body. Unbalanced combinations of nutrients during the period from birth to 18 years may retard growth.

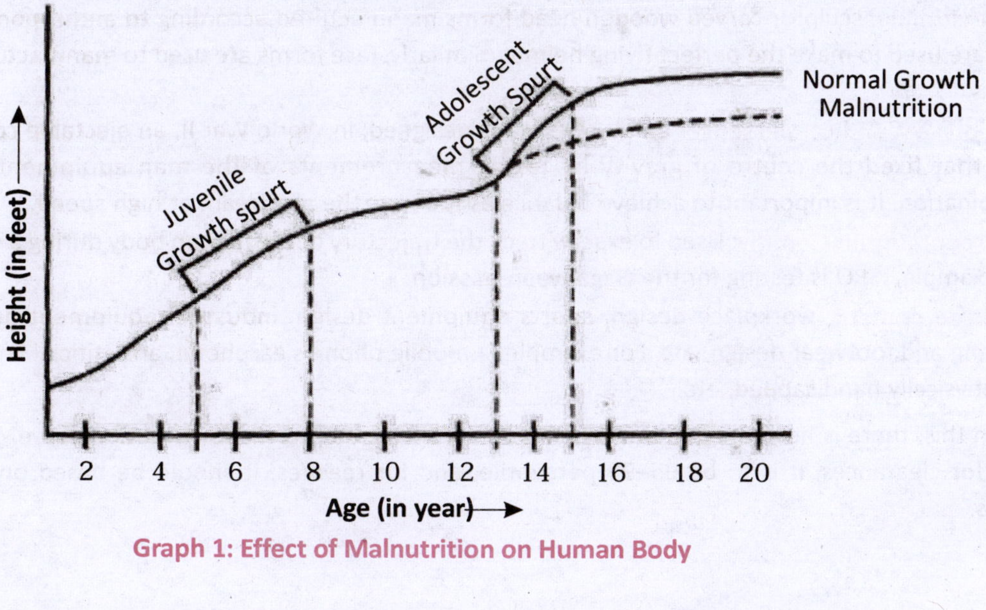

Graph 1: Effect of Malnutrition on Human Body

2. **Population Dynamics:** Malnutrition can delay the age of menarche and the early outset of menopause.
3. **Cultural ecology:** *Lee* studied !Kung and found a low level of nutritional stress due to a diverse diet.
4. **Social Epidemiology:** *Bolton* studied the Orang Asli tribe of Malaysia and found pregnant women could only eat small animals that possessed so-called weak spirits.

Methods to study: Anthropometric, biochemical, and clinical

Relevance: Strategy-making to address the problem of nutrition or obesity depends on the area. Anthropologists need to be involved, especially for making strategies in tribal areas.

With climate change-induced food crises and lifestyle changes such as obesity and the rise of noncommunicable diseases, the scope of nutritional anthropology has further increased.

Q 3. Application of anthropology in designing defence and other equipments

Ans. Physical anthropologists, as experts in human anatomy, were first involved in the design of defence equipment during World War II. The term anthropometry is concerned with the measurement of the human body, coined by Queflet. The application of human body knowledge can be helpful in designing safe, efficient, and comfortable equipment in various fields.

Applications:

1. **Gun Turret**: It is a movable enclosure containing the gunner, a pair of machine guns, and a sighting machine. In designing it, when anthropometric knowledge is used, efficiency gets improved.
2. **Cockpit and seat configuration**: Various cockpit sizes and seat configurations can be defined in both fighter and bomber flight so as to reduce cockpit fatigue in the pilot. For example, the cockpit design was changed by the Russians to sell aircraft to India as per Indian anthropometric data.
3. **Partial pressure suit**: *J.P. Henry* designed it as a one-piece, non-stretch garment with air tubes connected to it. When air pressure drops, air enters the suit from tubes and prevents muscles from swelling. An anthropologist figured out that stature and weight fields had the highest correlation with other bodily dimensions and became diagnostic dimensions for complex-fitting garments.
4. **Flight clothing:** sculptor-carved wooden head forms manufactured according to anthropometric data are used to make the perfect flying helmet. Similarly, face forms are used to manufacture O_2 masks.
5. **Ejection seat and car passenger safety**: Germans designed, in World War II, an ejectable cockpit seat that fixed the centre of gravity by taking measurements of the man-equipment seat combination. It is important to achieve balance as it enters the air stream at high speed.
6. **Anthropomorphic Dummy**: Used to exactly track the trajectory of the human body during a crash. For example, ISRO is testing for the Gaganyaan mission.
7. **Other equipment:** workplace design, sports equipment design, industrial equipment design, clothing and footwear design, etc. For example, a mobile phone's earphone, an artificial limb for the physically handicapped, etc.

But in this, there is no average man. It is the percentile of the normal distribution curve. While designing for clearances, it is to be 95–99 percentile, and for reaches, it should be based on 1 –5 percentiles.

Case Study

- **The Indian Army gives the first public view of its new uniform with digital camouflage.**

The Indian military has showcased brand-new battle gear with a digital camouflage ("digicam") pattern resembling the seven-year-old American pattern. The cloth represents the absence of the black colour palette while accentuating the earthen and olive tones on the pixelated design. Indian armed troops will no longer be compelled to tuck in their uniforms like American forces. The US Army, US Airmen in the Middle East, and Air Force Global Strike Command security forces have all adopted a modified version of the Canadian CADPAT camouflage design, which is similar to the new Indian Army Combat Uniform. The design of the new uniform for the Indian Army is widely used by troops overseas and was created to endure extreme weather conditions, explosive bursts, and varying air pressures while also supposedly making the soldiers more comfortable.

Q 4. Forensic Anthropology

Ans. According to *C.C. Shaw,* forensic anthropology is the application of physical anthropologists specialised knowledge of human sexuality, racial age, and individual variation to solve problems of medical jurisprudence. Identification of decomposed or mutilated bodies where skin has designated that no clue is available from it, and analysis of skeletal and fragmentary remains an important aspect.

Following questions get addressed:

i. **Is it human?**
   - It can be done on the basis of comparative anatomy, precipitin test of blood stain, etc.

ii. **How many people are involved?**
   - It can be assessed by an inventory of bones recovered from the site, but if the bones are in a fragmented or burned state, blood group typing may be established by the number of persons at the site.

iii. **Determination of sex:**
   - If all teeth have not erupted and the basis phenoid suture at the base of the skull has not fused, the skull belongs to a subadult, and sex identification in such cases cannot be performed.

From skull;

Skull	Female	Male
General Size	Small	Large
Architecture	Smooth and gracile	Rough and rugged
Forehead	More vertical rounded	Steeper and less rounded
Supra orbital ridge	Small to medium	Medium to large
Orbits	Less square rounded but sharp margins	Squared
Mandible	Smaller, less broad with parabolic shape	Larger with U-shape
Teeth	Small in size, lower molars 4 cusbed	Large size with T-shape

In pelvis, sub-pubic angle narrow in male and greater sciatic notch can differentiate between sexes.

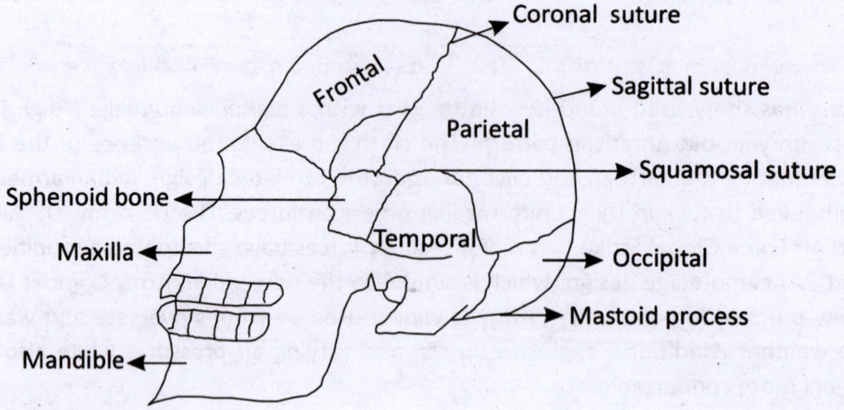

Human skull

iv. Determination of the age of bones:

1. Infants show an ossification centre at the lower end of the humerus.
2. Children show the unification of two bones of the pelvis: the pubis and the ischium.
3. Adolescents show fusion of the coracoid process with the scapula and triradial cartilage with the acetabulum.
4. Adults show fusions of epiphyses with their shafts.
5. Sternum is an indication of maturity.
6. Around 40, fusion of the xiphoid process with the sternum
7. Around 60, fusion of the manubrium with the sternum

v. Determination of age by tooth on five features:

1. Attrition (A): Wearing down
2. Periodontosis (P): loosening of the gums
3. Secondary dentine (S): formed in the pulp cavity.
4. Cementum opposition (C): Cementum at and around the tooth
5. Root transparency (T): transparency

As age increases, the value of (An + Pn + Sn + Cn + R + Tn) increases.

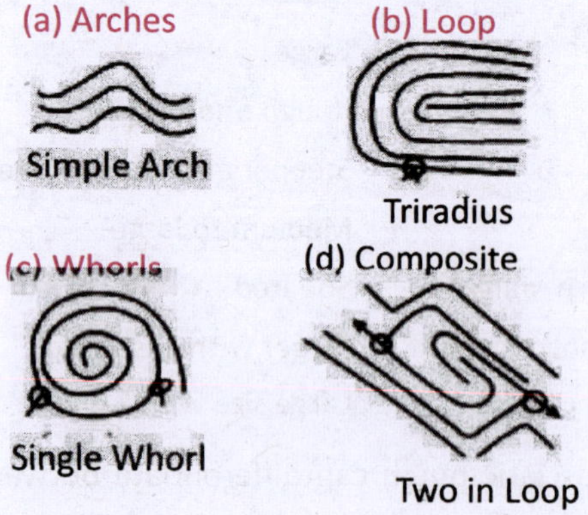

Finger Dermatoglyphics and its Types

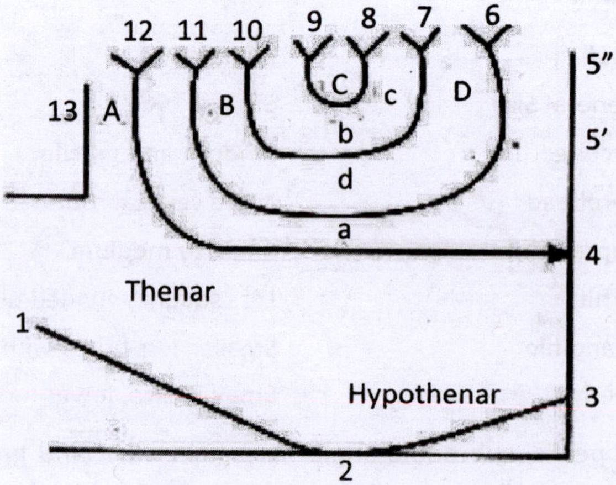

Palm Dermatoglyphics

Other areas for forensic anthropologists:

1. **Study of fingerprints:** According to *Nath*, forensic anthropologists are capable of playing a crucial role in identification. The anterior surface of our fingers bears a unique ridge, so that they leave a unique pattern of side friction where they come into contact with some surfaces. Most difficult are latents, which are not visible to the naked eye. But such can be made visible by sprinkling fine black or grey powder. Alternative chemicals like bromine, silver nitrate, tannic acid, etc. can be used. There are about 75–150 ridge characteristics on which one is required to look for navigation, like ridge ending, fork, break, lake formation, etc. The All India Forensic Science Congress has ruled that a minimum of eight characteristic patterns of ridges are essential to establishing an identity.
2. **DNA Fingerprinting:** As human beings, we share similar genes. But such genes constitute only 5% of our total DNA; in the rest of the 95% of DNA, we all have way more. This 95% DNA shows a unique arrangement of DNA bases in the sense that some bases are repeated most often. There may be a short repeat (9–40) base pair, an intermediate pair, or a large pair. It is called Variable Number Tandem Repeat (VNTR)

   Similarly, differences in DNA patterns are determined by the southern blotting technique. In this, the pattern obtained on gel after electrophoresis is plotted on filter paper, and this filter paper is used in hybridization experiments with DNA probe applications: try to match the blood stain with a sample from a particular suspect, resolve the case of disputed parenthood and identify a dead person on the basis of DNA.

Conclusion:

But the science of forensic anthropology has not been given its due place either in the university curriculum or in the fields of its practical applications. To achieve all-round progress, things must improve on both fronts: theoretical education at the university and practical utility at the laboratory in India. It is in its infancy stage, but with time, it may get proper recognition at various levels.

Case Study

- **A body found in a barrel at Lake Mead is the tip of the iceberg. Forensic anthropologists are now recovering human remains following droughts, sea-level rise, and wildfires.**

A warming climate is bringing to light objects that were buried in glaciers or submerged in lakes decades ago, including human remains. A warmer globe could lead to more discoveries being made by retreating water and ice, which is good news for forensic anthropologists who are responsible for recovering them. It also entails helping victims of climate change. Boaters on Lake Mead in Nevada made a disturbing discovery on Sunday afternoon: human remains inside a rusted barrel. According to Jennifer Byrnes, a forensic anthropologist who consults with the Clark County coroner's office, more bodies might surface given that water levels have dropped to historic lows amid a drought brought on by climate change. As the water level continues to recede, "I would anticipate that the human remains of missing persons will likely be revealed over time," Byrnes said.

Q 5. Methods and principles of personal identification and reconstruction

Ans. Personal identification involves establishing the identity of an individual, whether dead or alive. A need arises in disasters like tsunamis, earthquakes, terrorist attacks, mass murders, etc.

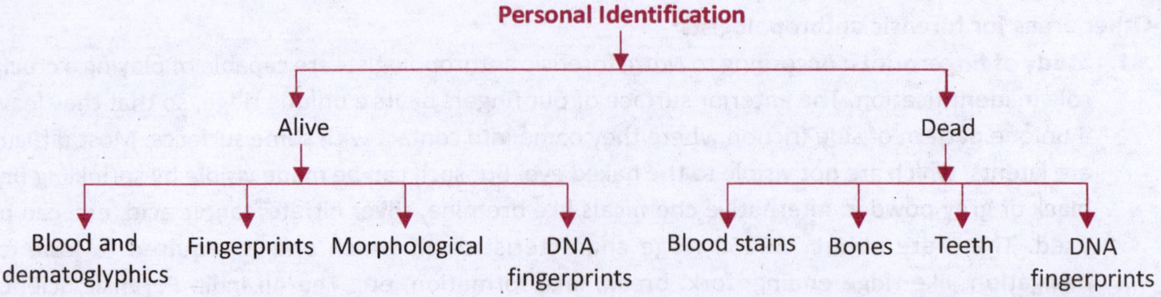

From alive:

a. **From fingerprints and DNA fingerprints:** This process is mostly followed to identify criminals who left visible, plastic, or hidden fingerprints at the site. The All India Forensic Science Congress has ruled that in order to identify a person, eight characteristics of fingerprints should match. DNA fingerprints can be used to solve cases of parental determination related to parental disputes, immigration disputes, and child rape victims.

From Dead:

a. **From blood strains:** First, it is made sure that blood belongs to human beings, and secondly, its group is ascertained so that it can be matched with the blood group profile of missing persons under investigation.

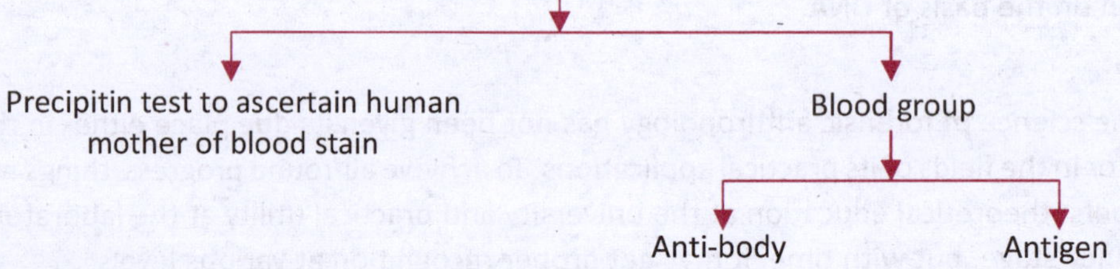

The principle followed is that blood group A has antigen A and anti-body B. B has antigen B and antibodies (anti-A and anti-AB). AB has both antigens and no antibodies. O has no antigen and two antibodies.

b. **Bones:** Bones are used to find out the height of a person so that it can be matched with the recorded height of the individual.

	Length of femur bone(F)	Constant
Male	F*2.238	+27.2 inch
Female	F*2.317	+24.17 inch

Sex by studying Bones: Female skull: small, gracile, lesser developed, small foramen magnum, etc. Age by studying bones and the fusion of epiphyses at different times.

c) **From teeth:** It helps to ascertain the age of a person. The sum of accretion, periodontosis, secondary dentine, cementum opposition, and transparency helps determine age.

Even by some known eruptions:

Lower incisor: 6 yr; Upper incisor: 8 yr; First premolar: 9 yr; Second premolar: 10 yr; Canine: 11 – 12 yr; First and second molars: 12–13 years and Third molar: 17–25 yr.

The famous Frankfurt murder case was solved on the basis of forensic odontology.

d) **DNA fingerprinting from charred bones:** the identification of Naina Sahni on the basis of charred bones recovered from a Tandoor furnace is a classical example.

It has a wide possibility of usage, but it has not received due recognition, and there is a lack of correlation between theoretical knowledge in universities and laboratory usage, especially in India. But with time, it is bound to grow. DNA fingerprinting is considered the best of all.

Conclusion:

But the science of forensic anthropology has not been given its due place either in the university curriculum or in the fields of its practical applications. To achieve all-round progress, things must improve on two fronts: theoretical education at the university and practical utility at the laboratory in India. It is in its infancy stage, but with time, it may get proper recognition at various levels.

Case Study

- **Bare bones: Research explores a new method of determining sex**

A forensic anthropologist can detect minute traits and variations in bones that are invisible to the untrained eye. An essential ability in identifying crime victims is being able to piece together the person those bones reflect with the help of this pattern of indications. Some of those minute variations are related to biological sex, which, it should be noted, differs from gender, which is a social construct. Mary St. John, a graduate student at Binghamton University, is developing a novel approach to identifying the sex of unidentified people through her research, which tracks variations in human cheekbones using quantitative measurements and software techniques.

- **Bones, brains, and bugs: Meet the Colorado forensic anthropologist who's helped crack cases for decades.**

France, 67, has been a board-certified forensic anthropologist with a base in Colorado for more than three decades. She examines bones to help identify the cause of death. She has the ability to identify a skeleton's gender and age at the time of death. She has worked in the wake of explosions, airline disasters, and the 9/11 attacks, and she assists authorities in identifying the remains of those who have been missing or long dead. She gave testimony in two well-known Colorado cold cases this year: the 1984 murder of 12-year-old Jonelle Matthews and the 2012 disappearance of 13-year-old Dylan Redwine. Both times, a significant amount of time passed before the bones of the kids were discovered. The suspect in the Redwine case was found guilty. The jury in the Matthews case was deadlocked on a murder charge. But for France, the results are irrelevant. In order to protect the integrity of the cases, France will not discuss any of the active criminal investigations she is involved in. However, those who have worked with her claim that she has a reputation for being impartial and thorough while testifying in court.

Q 6. Applied human genetics-Eugenics

Ans. Francis Galton coined the term eugenics and defined it as the study of agencies of social control that may improve the racial qualities of future generations both physically and mentally with the application of principles of genetics. As Charles Darwin propounded, undesirables are eliminated through natural selection. Thus, conscious efforts are needed to eliminate defective genes in particular environments. Even defective genes cannot sometimes stand in the best of environments, and sometimes they give an extra edge in a particular environment.

Eugenics are categorised as:

➢ **Positive Eugenics:** Increase better or more desirable germplasm.

1. Assortative Marriage: It recommends bonding between certain individuals. For example, Greek and Egyptian royal families assumed purity of blood and married among themselves.
2. Artificial insemination: In this, the germplasm of outstanding individuals was preserved for future generations.

3. **Genetic counselling:** communicating with the couple about the possibility of a deleterious impact on the child through pedigree analysis
4. **Removal of social hindrance:** Eugenics promotes intercaste, interrace, and interreligious marriages so that genetic stock improves.
5. **For fit ones:** encouraging early marriage, funding them, keeping them in a healthy environment, etc.

➢ **Negative Eugenics:** Eliminate the defective germ.

1. **Regulating Marriage:** In Cyprus, it is mandatory to have a blood test for beta-thalassemia before marriage. Unfavourable tests result in marriage only after treatment.
2. **Sterilisation** of individuals with defective genes. For example, in New Zealand and the state of California, it is voluntary.
3. **Termination** of pregnancy in cases of high chances of a child being born with serious diseases

Issues:

1. It builds racism.
2. Only the rich have access to such things.
3. It reduces variations and thereby promotes homozygosity.
4. Deliberate focus on imbibing certain characteristics like high IQ, eye colour, etc.

However, eugenics is a tool that has socio-economic ramifications as well. But at last, it is we who have to utilise this technology for our welfare through strict monitoring.

Q 7. Applied human genetics – Paternity diagnosis

Ans. Biological anthropology is a vast discipline that has been widely used in various fields to solve various problems. One such problem is paternity disputes, which arise mainly due to:

1. Exchange or theft of babies at the hospital
2. Instances of rape in which the victim becomes pregnant
3. Extramarital affair

In ascertaining it, various methods were used:

1. **Morphological Analysis:** It includes morphoscopic characters that are viewed, like eye, hair, and skin colour, and morphometric characters that can be measured, like head index, nasal index, etc.
2. **Dermatoglyphic Analysis:** Dermatoglyphic prints obtained from palms, fingers, soles, etc. It is hereditary and doesn't change with time or environment.
3. **Genetical Analysis:**
   a. **Serological Analysis:** It includes various systems like the ABO blood system, the Rh system, and the MNS. Mainly used: ABO Blood Group analysis:

Parents	Possible Child	Impossible
A × A	O, A	B, AB
O × O	O	A, B, AB
B × B	O, B	A, AB
AB × AB	AB, AB	O

   b. **Biochemical Analysis:** It includes the analysis of a wide variety of proteins and enzymatic systems present in our body, e.g., haemoglobins.
   c. **Immunological Analysis:** It includes variability variants such as GM(1) +, GM(1) -, etc. GM(1)+ parental types cannot give birth to GM(1)-type progeny. Another area is the HLA system.
   d. **Non-serological criteria** include rolling ability and tasting ability. A non-roller and non-taster parent can never give birth to roller and taster children.

4. **DNA fingerprinting:** Exact identification is done by this method by comparing the variable number tandem repeats (VNTR) of the child and parents, which can definitely detect the parentage. It was used in Deepa Murmu's case. Deepa Murmu charged government officials with her rape and an old person with being the father of her child. DNA 240 prints of all concerned were examined at the Centre for Cell and Molecular Biology, Hyderabad, and found to be true.

Q 8. DNA technology in Medicine and Disease

Ans. DNA technology involves the artificial modification of the genetic constitution of living cells by the introduction of foreign DNA through experimental techniques. DNA technology involves the study and manipulation of genetic material to serve different purposes.

R-DNA technology involves the introduction of a desired gene into the DNA of another species. This technology is based on the principle of structural and functional similarities in DNA from prokaryotes to eukaryotes to humans.

Applications:

Diagnosis:

1. Monoclonal antibodies that are formed by the fusion of tumour-causing genes and genes of lymphocytes are used in blood typing, pregnancy tests, the detection of pathogens, and the early and accurate detection of cancer.
2. DNA probes are small nucleotides used to detect the presence of complementary sequences in nucleic acid samples. Probes have been elaborated for detecting Kala Azar, malaria, sleeping sickness, encephalitis, etc. They are also used in the diagnosis of genetic diseases like thalassemia.

Treatment

1. **Monoclonal antibodies:** These are used to carry cytotoxic substances to target cells, such as cancer cells.
2. **Gene Therapy:** Treating genetic diseases by replacing an incorrect gene with a correct one that can cure genetic diseases, e.g., cystic fibrosis, ADA deficiency, etc.
3. **Hormones and enzymes:** These can be produced commercially to treat diseases. Example: insulin (diabetes), growth hormones (dwarfism), factor VIII (haemophilia).

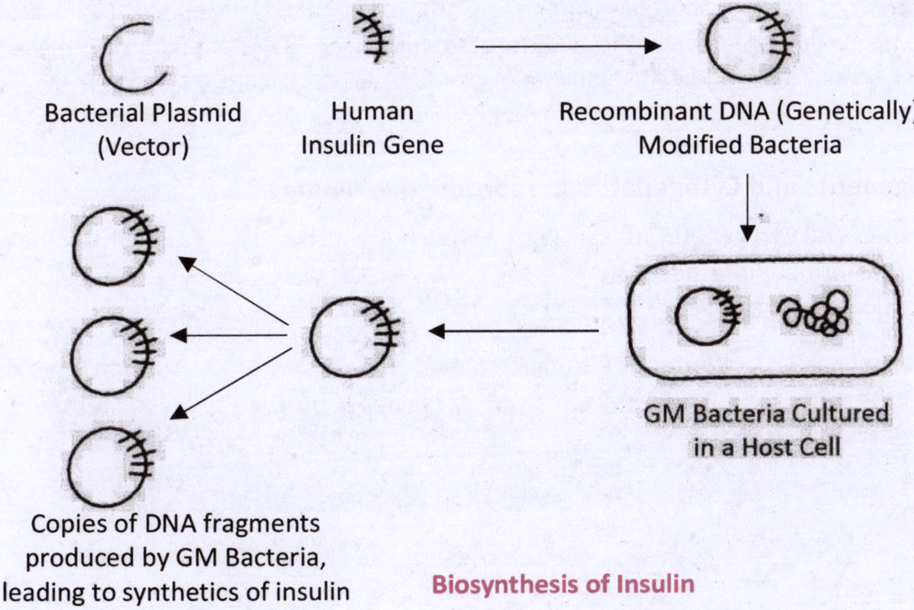

Biosynthesis of Insulin

Prevention

1. Monoclonal antibodies are likely to be used to vaccinate against malaria.
2. Recombinant DNA vaccines can be used to vaccinate against Hepatitis B, the Feline Leukaemia Virus, etc.

   Recently, CRISPR-CAS 9 has held prospects. CRISPR-CAS 9 is a type of gene editing technology that lets scientists more rapidly and accurately cut and paste genes into DNA. It is based on a targeted DNA-destroying defence system originally found in certain prokaryotes.

   In those cases, if viruses infect bacteria or archaea, CRISPR-associated enzymes would seek out and break apart infectious nucleic acid sequences identified by code, destroying any potentially deadly virus represented in the CRISPR library. This ability to identify and break genes was quickly recognised as the perfect tool for editing genes.

A protein called CAS9 is to be used in conjunction with CRISPR sequences to hunt down codes and slice into them like molecular scalpels, either to remove or replace them with new sequences.

Case Study

- **Breakthrough Using CRISPR to Target Fat Cells in the Genetic Study of Obesity**

Romanelli, Ormand MacDougald, Ph.D., and their coworkers disclose a breakthrough using CRISPR-Cas9, a technique that has revolutionised molecular biological research but whose usage in the study of adipose tissue has been difficult to come by. It is a method of gene editing that uses the Cas9 enzyme, which can split DNA strands, and a bit of RNA to direct the enzyme to a particular location in the genome for editing. The instrument has been effectively used to investigate the heart, liver, neurons, and skin cells, to mention a few; however, brown fat, a particular form of adipose cells, has never been studied. The method allowed the scientists to successfully target brown fat, a particular type of adipose tissue required to produce heat and maintain body temperature In adult mice, scientists used their adeno-associated virus CRISPR-Cas9 components to knock off the UCP1 gene, which specifies brown adipose tissue and makes it capable of producing heat. They discovered that the knockout mice could adjust to the deletion of the gene and keep their body temperature stable in cold environments, suggesting the involvement of other pathways in temperature regulation. Additionally, they were able to simultaneously delete numerous genes using this technique, which may aid in the understanding of crucial biological circuits. Although these findings are preliminary, they mark a significant advancement in our understanding of fat.

Q 9. Serogenetics and Cytogenetics in reproductive biology

Ans. Serogenetics and Cytogenetic are specialized branches which include study of serological protein and gamete formation respectively.

Axis of reproductive biology:

Hypothalamus → Anterior Pituitary → Gonads (Testes & ovary) → Gonadal Steroids (Testosterone, Estrogen)

↓

Reproductive Steroids

Male Reproductive Biology:

Hypothalamus
↓ GnRH
Anterior Pituitary
↓
FSH → Spermatogensis
LH → Leydig cell → Testosterne

Serogenetics: It includes the production of testosterone, luteinizing hormone (LH), and follicle-stimulating hormone (FSH).

Functions:

1. Testosterone: secondary sexual characters
2. LH helps in the production of testosterone.
3. FSH regulates spermatogenesis.

Cytogenetics: production of male sex cells, which are sperm. Various cells involved in spermatogenesis:

1. **Sertoli Cells:** Tall columnar cells Maturation and nourishment of the developing spermatid into sperm happen here.
2. **Leydig's Cells:** small round diploid cells outside seminiferous tubules Function: production of testosterone.
3. **Germinal cells:** source of sperm

Spermatogonia (2n) → 1° Spermatocyte (2n) → 2° Spermatocyte (n) (1 st Meiotic Division)
2° Spermatocyte (n) → Spermatid (n) (2nd Meiotic Division)
Spermatid (n) → Spermatozoa (n)

Female Reproductive Biology:

Hypothalamus
↓ GnRH
Anterior Pituitary
↓
FSH → Follicle Cell
LH → Graffian follicle → Ovulation
Follicle Cell → Graffian follicle

Serogenetics: Production of various female reproductive hormones

1. Oestrogen: female sex hormone, ovulation, secondary sex characteristics
2. Progesterone: pregnancy hormone
3. Prolactin: a milk-secreting hormone
4. Oxytocin: milk-ejecting hormone
5. Relaxin dilates the vagina during childbirth.

Cytogenetics: Production of female sex cells (i.e., ovum)

Ovular Cells	**Ovum Cells**
↓	↓
Graffian Follicle	Oogononium (2n)
↓	↓
Secondary Follicle	Primary Oocyte (2n)
↓	↓
Primary Follicle	Secondary Oocyte (n)
↓	↓
Primordial Follicle	Secondary Oocyte
↓	↓
Ovular Cell	Ovulation

Ovular Cell → Ovum ← Ovulation

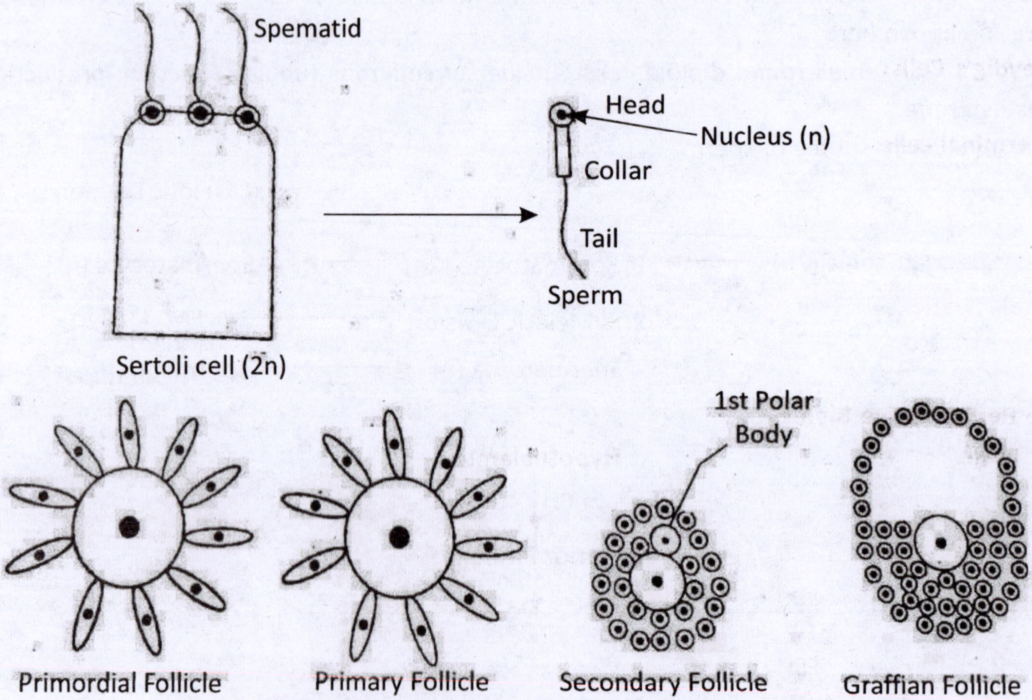

Cytogenetics of Male and female reproductive system

13

Unconventional UPSC Previous Year Questions

Q 1. Glottochronology

Ans. The study of vocabulary statistically for historical inference is called lexicostatistics. M. Swadesh proposed a method for determining the time when two related languages became independent, which is called glottochronology. Glottochronology is the method of lexicostatistics for determining degrees of relationship between languages based on counting the number of cognates in a particular set of vocabulary items.

Assumption: the common words in languages are maintained at a definite rate, i.e., some parts of the vocabulary are much less subject to change than other parts.

The basic (core) vocabulary consists of words for concepts assumed to be a necessary part of all human cultures. The semantic field represented by the lexical items includes pronouns, numerals, adjectives (e.g., big, long, small), kinship terms (mother, father), living beings (dog, louse), body parts (head, ear, eye), events and objects in nature (rain, stone, star), and common activities (see, hear, come, give).

There are several versions of Swadesh's list; the two that are most commonly used are the 100-word list and the 200-word list.

Swadesh made several further assumptions:

1. The rate of retention of vocabulary items in the basic core is constant over time.
2. The rate of loss of basic vocabulary is approximately the same in all languages. The rate of loss was determined by testing lexical loss in languages with a long series of texts (e.g., Latin and Romance languages). On the basis of these tests, there is an 80–85% loss over 1000 years.
3. If the percentage of cognates within the core vocabulary is known for any pair of languages, the length of time that has elapsed since the two languages began to diverge from a single language can be computed using a formula.

   Example: animal, four, head, I, sun

   In German: Tier, vier, Kopf, ich, Sonne.

   The first and third words are unrelated; thus, there is 60% agreement between English and German.

Next step: compare this percentage with the rate of loss.

At least three problems have to be considered before glottochronology can be accepted as a valid technique:

1. Is the list representative?
2. Are the words contained in the list really the common core shared by all languages?
3. Is it a fact that the items on the list are not culture-bound?

Criticisms of glottochronology:

1. The existence of a basic vocabulary is culture-bound; e.g., in the cultures of South Asia, some items referring to natural objects (such as the sun) are not part of the core vocabulary.
2. Duplication of elements in the core vocabulary in some languages, e.g., in Navaho
3. The rate of retention is not constant from language to language; e.g., the rate of loss in English is slower than the rate of loss in the Gipsy dialect of Armenian.
4. Recognition of true cognates is often difficult. As far as the phonetic shape of words is concerned, there are two possibilities:
   a. Either true cognates may not be recognisable because of sound changes (e.g., English tooth = German Zahn).
   b. Chance similarities may be interpreted as evidence for the presence of the true cognate pair (e.g., Latin habere and German haben (Gmc *khaben) both mean 'to have' but are not cognates).
   Result: overestimation of cognates results in underestimation of time depth, and vice versa.

Lexicostatistics applied to determine the oldest relationships among language families.

1. Pedersen proposed a proto-language from which Indo-European, Hamito-Semitic, Uralic, Altaic, and possibly other language families have descended: NOSTRATIC.
2. Dolgopolsky proposed a "mathematically rigorous procedure" to examine the Nostratic hypothesis. He made a list of 15 items assumed to be essential in every language.

Difficulties with the list:

Taboo words: the word tongue has several forms in IE languages.

1st and 2nd person markers may not be stable, as there are languages where they don't even occur (e.g., Japanese, Chinese).

The verbal negative may be replaced, e.g., in French.

French ne (< Latin non) was originally the only negative and was placed before the verb. Later, it became reinforced by the word pas'step' after the verb, which was added for emphasis: "not a step" (compare English not at all). Over the centuries, the emphatic negative became the norm: Je ne sais pas. Eventually, the reinforcement pas came to be thought of as the main negative, and this has led to the omission of ne in casual speech: Je sais pas.

Conclusion:

When considering the rate of retention after six millennia, the number of maintained cognates is comparable to that of items similar by chance.

Q 2. William Ogburn and cultural lag

Ans. The term cultural lag was developed and coined in 1922 by William F. Ogburn, a sociologist most notable for his published work "Social Change with Respect to Culture and Original Nature." According to Ogburn, material items such as tools and developing technologies were advancing at an observably faster rate than social norms and ways of life. Because social norms can be said to resist societal changes (or advancements), they develop at a much slower rate of progression. By contrast, an understanding or reliance on new technology may therefore not be received quickly because pre-existing social beliefs are accepted as standard or as "the correct way" of using it. Ogburn's theory of cultural lag is used to describe how conflict is created when innovation and progress surpass adaptation to new ideas.

Ogburn later expanded on cultural lag theory in the 1964 publication "On Culture and Change," where he examined 25 studies to measure societal change against technological change in the areas of social evolution, social trends, and short-term changes as a result of scientific advancement. Later published works by writers James W. Woodward, Alvin Toffler, and Brinkman develop the theory under more current technological standards, examine its relevance, and present findings in a more accessible and exemplifiable manner.

According to William F. Ogburn (1966), the elements of nonmaterial culture are more resistant to change than material culture. He refers to the term 'cultural lag' to refer to the maladjustment in which nonmaterial culture fails to adjust to the rapidly changing material conditions. For example, it is more difficult to adapt to a Western culture and accept foreign ideas than to accept foreign technology. We accept technology much faster as it makes our lives much easier, but we are unable to change our ways of life accordingly. In a fast-changing society, cultural lag is very prominent, as a change in one aspect will bring stress and strain to other parts. There is a time lag before the other part of the culture catches up and restores equilibrium in society.

Ogburn posited four stages of technical development:

1. **Invention:** The process by which new forms of technology are created
2. **Accumulation:** growth of technology due to the fact that invention of new things outplaces the process by which old inventions become obsolete.
3. **Diffusion:** Spread of an idea from one cultural group to another
4. **Adjustment:** The process by which non-technical aspects of culture respond to invention. Any retardation of the adjustment process leads to cultural lag.

Causes of cultural lag:

1. **Ideology:** Non-material culture is influenced by ideology. For example, changes in religious beliefs are slow and few.
2. **Technology:** Techniques change fast but vary from society to society.
3. **Psychological dogmatism:** Humans commonly respect old concepts, dogmas, and mores. It's considered convenient to follow the path of our ancestors.

For example, automobiles were introduced long before we could sufficiently broaden our streets, which were suitable for horse-drawn carriages, and enforce strict traffic rules in order to avoid motor accidents. There is, thus, a gap between the material aspects of a culture, represented by the automobile, and the non-material aspects, represented by broader streets and appropriate traffic rules.

The above illustration indicates that cultural lag appears when technological innovations move faster than social innovations. But many instances may be cited in which the leading factor of social change, which leads to cultural lag, has been political or social-psychological. Thus, a country may adopt a parliamentary form of democracy as an instrument of political action.

But, in the initial stages, this form of government may not be very effective because of the failure of the people to develop habits of thought, attitudes, and temperaments that are so necessary for making the best use of this machinery. The initial failure of democracy in some of the newly independent countries in Asia and Africa is partly due to this reason.

We may also think of some striking forms of cultural lag that emerge from the development of non-technological innovations. For instance, the progressive income tax, that is, income tax assessed at a progressive rate, may be regarded as a definite social innovation that is non-technological in character.

Since the amounts of money involved are often quite large in the case of some people, the inducement to find some dishonest method of escaping from part or all of the payment becomes great. The higher the rates of taxation, the greater the inducement to evasion of taxes.

The cultural lag in this case is the time interval between the innovation of progressive income taxation and the development (which is not yet completely achieved) of adequate social controls to prevent tax evasion and to maintain honest tax payments.

Cultural lag sometimes disturbs the balance of society and brings 'anomie'. Anomie is a concept coined by Emile Durkheim that refers to a condition in which the normative order of society is broken down. In this situation, there may be a slight contradiction and confusion or a serious deterioration and disintegration in society.

Limitations of the Concept of Cultural Lag:

1. According to Mueller, cultural lag is artificial and imaginary.
2. According to James W. Woodward and R.M. MacIver:
   a. The Ogburn distinction between material and nonmaterial culture is not clear. Again, it is not necessary that non-material culture should invariably lag behind material culture.
   b. The term cultural lag has been employed for all disequilibriums occurring in the process of social change.
   c. This word of cultural change should be used in the context of those objects, in whose case the encouraging as well as the restraining objects are similar and possess a common standard of evaluation.

In spite of the above limitations, Ogburn's theory of cultural lag is very useful in understanding cultural processes and changes.

Q 3. Jane Goodall contribution in studying primate behaviour

Ans. Jane Goodall is an English primatologist, ethologist, and conservationist best known for conducting her long-term study (forty-five years) of chimpanzee social and family life in Tanzania. She has a Ph.D. in ethology from Cambridge University. She worked as director of the Jane Goodall Institute in Gombe Stream National Park in Tanzania.

Louis Leakey, a British palaeoanthropologist and archaeologist known for his excavations in Olduvai Gorge, believed that studying other primates anatomy and behaviour would help scientists understand early hominid societies. Under him, Jane Goodall started the Gombe chimp observation in 1960. It is the world's longest-running continuous wildlife research project, as she was completely accepted by the chimpanzee group she set out to study in almost two years. Her works on it include "In the Shadow of Man (1971)" and "The Chimpanzees of Gombe: Patterns of Behaviour (1986)".

Method of her study: Jane used the simple method of observation of chimpanzee groups and imitated the animals, writing down copious notes in a field journal. She named each animal she studied instead of assigning it a number.

Important contributions of Jane Goodall to primates behaviour:

1. **Eating Habits:** The first main contribution from her was on eating habits when she discovered that chimpanzees are omnivorous, not vegetarian as had been supposed. On several occasions, she observed the chimps hunting and eating small mammals.
2. **Tool Making:** The second and most important observation from her in the field of primatology was the discovery of tool making in chimpanzees. She discovered that some chimps employed modified twigs or grass to "fish" for termites from termite mounds. The termites would grab onto the blade of grass or twig with their mandibles, and the chimpanzees would then just pull the grass out and eat the termites. At that time, only humans were thought to use tools, and tool-making was considered the defining difference between humans and other animals. This discovery convinced several scientists to reconsider their definition of being human. As Leaky said on her discovery, "Now we must redefine 'tool,' redefine'man' or accept chimpanzees as humans."
3. **Cooperative Hunting:** Another characteristic of the chimpanzees that Jane Goodall discovered was their cooperative hunting of red colobus monkeys.
4. **Complex social system:** The use of tools with cooperative hunting practices led to the next discovery of the complex social system existing within the chimpanzee groups. Jane's work has documented unique personalities displayed by each chimpanzee with a complex social system, acts of warfare between rival groups, murder, brutality, and even cannibalism in competition for food, sex, or territory, or under emotions of jealousy, fear, or revenge. Their behaviour proved as dark and troubling as that seen in humans. At the same time, they displayed ritualised behaviours of mutual sharing, including the use of the social embrace to comfort an animal in mourning. They display altruism through the adoption of orphaned chimpanzees by others in the band.
5. **Primitive Language:** Another main argument made by her through the study is that the chimpanzees show the beginnings of a primitive language system that includes more than 120 sounds with specific meanings.

Criticism of her work:

1. Some scientists have criticised the book for Jane's habit of naming the animals she observed.
2. Some other primatologists have criticised Goodall's methods, especially her use of bananas in feeding stations to attract chimps. They claim that the food causes higher levels of aggression and conflict, distorting normal behavior. But other research has shown similar levels of conflict without feeding stations.

Also, some other primatologists consider it a successful balance between scientific documentation and exciting story-telling. It introduced the public to the serious scientific work being done on primates behaviour. Since then, other researchers have observed chimpanzees using more than half a dozen tools for assorted purposes, as well as other animals like birds and dolphins using the tools.

Q 4. Natufian Culture

Ans. Preagricultural Epipaleolithic (transitional between Upper Palaeolithic and Neolithic) culture associated with storage of crops and sedentary settlements (unusual for its time).

1. **Geographical location:** Levant (Jordan, Syria, Israel)
2. **Discover:** *Dorothy Garrod*
3. **Time Period:** 15000–11500 years old
4. **Climatic Conditions:** Terminal Pleistocene to the beginning of the Holocene
5. **Main Sites:** Eynan, el-Wad, Kebara, and Tabun

6. **Salient Features:**
   a. **Settled Living:** Larger settlement size (Natufian sites were five times larger than their predecessors). People live in circular pit houses with a permanent hearth and plastered storage structures for storing wild grains beneath their houses.
   b. **Tool Technology:** Microliths, Sickles, Stone Mortars, Basalt Sharpening Tools, Advanced Knowledge of Lime Plaster Production. There was a rich bone industry, including harpoons and fish hooks. Stone and bone were worked into pendants and other ornaments.
   c. **Subsistence:** They relied on wild grains and the hunting of wild gazelles. There was a sign of nutritional deficiency, as evidenced by the enamel and decline in stature.
   d. **Burial:** Common village cemetery for burial of people, indicating settled living.
   e. Evidence of increasing use of stationary resources and subsequent increases in social complexity Natufian culture is significant as it helps trace out the history of agriculture and settled living.

Q 5. Experiential Ethnography

Ans. Experiential ethnography is an anthropological approach that emphasises the active participation and immersion of the researcher in the culture or context they are studying. This approach allows the anthropologist to gain a deeper understanding of the community's beliefs, values, and traditions and the ways in which they shape the everyday experiences of its members. It is particularly useful for understanding indigenous and marginalised communities, whose perspectives are often overlooked in mainstream research.

Malinowski's immersive fieldwork in the Trobriand Islands set a precedent for participant observation and experiential research.

Basic premises:

1. **Direct Participation:** Researchers actively engage in the experiences, activities, and practices of the culture they are studying. This often involves living within the community for an extended period.
2. **Immersive Observation:** The researcher not only observes but also experiences the daily life and rituals of the community, gaining a firsthand understanding of the culture.
3. **Language Acquisition:** Learning the language of the community is a fundamental aspect of experiential ethnography. This allows the researcher to communicate with and understand the people more deeply.
4. **Empathetic Perspective:** Immersion fosters a deep empathy and understanding of the people being studied, enabling the researcher to see the world from their point of view.
5. **Thick Description:** Researchers aim to provide detailed, context-rich descriptions of the culture, its practices, and the experiences of its members. This contributes to a nuanced understanding.
6. **Holistic Insight:** Experiential ethnography aims to provide a holistic and insider's perspective on the culture, going beyond surface observations to uncover hidden nuances and meanings.
7. **Cultural Reflexivity:** Researchers reflect on their own experiences and biases as part of the research process, acknowledging their impact on the study.

Methodology: Anthropologists associated with Bronislaw Malinowski, Margaret Mead, Clifford Geertz, etc.

Extensive fieldwork by Clifford Geertz in Indonesia and Morocco involved immersing himself in the local cultures to understand their religious practices, rituals, and symbolic systems. Geertz's concept of "thick description' emphasises the importance of interpreting cultural practices within their cultural context and serves as a guiding principle for experiential ethnography.

This method encourages researchers to directly engage in the experiences, activities, and practices of the culture. By participating in these experiences, researchers aim to gain a deeper and more empathetic understanding of the people they are studying. It can help civil servants better appreciate the complexities of the societies they serve and implement policies that are sensitive to their needs and aspirations.

Q 6. Victor Turner and Liminality

Ans. Liminality is a concept that refers to the state of being in between two distinct social, cultural, or psychological states. It is often described as a threshold or transitional stage where an individual or group experiences a period of ambiguity, uncertainty, and disorientation.

Clifford Geertz defined liminality as a state of 'betwixt and between', where individuals or groups are associated with a threshold of change or transition. In his work, "Rituals and Social Change: A Javanese Example", Geertz studied the rituals of Javanese villages and showed how liminal periods, such as weddings and funerals, serve as mechanisms for social change and transformations.

Victor Turner, a British symbolic anthropologist, expanded it and introduced the concept of liminal space in his book "The Forest of Symbols" on the basis of his study of the Ndembu tribe of Zambia. He defined it as a space that is neither here nor there. He argued that liminal spaces are places of transformation, where individuals or groups can break free from their social roles and engage in creative, imaginative, and transformative activities.

He was influenced by Arnold von Jennep, who had first introduced this idea while analysing rites of passage. He divided it into three stages: preliminary, liminal, and post-liminal. Limen, in Latin, means threshold. Rites of passage are symbolic ways of changing the status of members of a society. The symbol becomes associated with human interests, purposes, ends, and means. For example, puberty marks the transition from girl to woman. What is expected of a girl is different from what is expected of a woman. The stage before is called pre-liminal, and the stage after is called post-liminal.

Basic premises:

1. Liminality refers to the transitional or in-between phase in a rite of passage or a cultural ritual.
2. During this period, individuals or groups experience a sense of ambiguity, where the old social norms and identities are suspended, and they have the potential to undergo a transformation.
3. Liminality is often characterised by a sense of communitas, where people temporarily set aside their usual roles and hierarchies, fostering a sense of equality and solidarity.

Relevance: Its relevance lies in its ability to help us understand various aspects of human behaviour, cultural dynamics, and social change.

1. **Rituals and Rites of Passage:** Turner's concept is widely applied in the study of rituals and rites of passage, where individuals or groups go through liminal phases. It helps us understand how these transitional periods serve to transform individuals and their roles in society.
2. **Cultural Change and Transformation:** Liminality is used to explain how societies and cultures undergo change and transformation. It provides insights into how new cultural norms and values emerge during transitional phases.
3. **Identity and Belonging:** The concept of liminality is relevant in exploring issues of identity and belonging, especially in multicultural and diverse societies. It helps us understand how individuals navigate their identities during periods of cultural transition.
4. **Social Movements and Revolutions:** Liminality can be applied to analyse social movements and revolutions, where traditional social structures are challenged and transformed during moments of crisis and change.

5. **Migration and Diaspora Studies:** It is relevant in understanding the experiences of migrants and diaspora communities, as they often find themselves in a liminal state between their home culture and the culture of their destination.
6. **Psychological and personal transformations:** The concept of liminality is used to explore individual experiences of personal change and transformation, such as during major life events or periods of self-discovery.

   Liminality is a complex and multifaceted concept that is relevant in various fields of study.

Q 7. Erving Goffman's concept of total institutions

Ans. Total institution is defined as a place of work and residence where a great number of similarly situated people, cut off from the wider community for a considerable time, together lead an enclosed, formally administered round of life, i.e., their needs are under bureaucratic control. This includes boarding schools, orphanages, prisons, juvenile detention centres, and military branches. As a concept, total institutions were first coined by American sociologist Erving Goffman in his 1961 work "Asylums: Essays on the Social Situation of Mental Patients and Other Inmates.".

According to Goffman, the total institutions are established for resocialization, the radical alteration of residents' personalities by deliberately manipulating their environment. This resocialization is a two-part process in which:

A. First, the staff of the institution tries to erode the residents' identities and independence.

B. Next, resocialization involves the systematic attempt to build a different personality or self. This resocialization involves a system of reward and punishment. E.g., as a total institution, the military resocializes new recruits into the military to operate as soldiers.

Based on it, Goffman divided the total number of institutions into five different types:

1. Institutions established to care for harmless or incapable people, including orphanages, poor houses, and nursing homes
2. Institutions established to care for people that are incapable of looking after themselves and are also a threat to the community, including leprosarium, mental hospitals, and tuberculosis sanitariums.
3. Institutions organised to protect the community against perceived intentional dangers, with the welfare of the sequestered people not the immediate issue, include concentration camps, prisoner of war camps, penitentiaries, and jails.
4. Institutions purportedly established to pursue some task, including colonial compounds, work camps, boarding schools, and ships
5. Institutions designed as retreats from the world while also often serving as training stations for the religious, including convents, abbeys, and monasteries.

The four Common Characteristics of the total institutions identified by Goffman to understand their functioning includes:

a. **Totalistic features:** Total institutions are tightly scheduled and administered by a single authority. It helps them remove the barriers that typically separate key spheres of life, including home, leisure, and work, by bringing them all together in one place with all the same participants.

b. **Inmate world:** When entering a total institution, whatever the type, a person goes through a "mortification process" that strips them of the individual and collective identities they had "on the outside" and gives them a new identity that makes them a part of the "inmate world" inside the institution. e.g., in prisons, by taking their clothing and personal possessions and replacing those items with standard-issue items that are the property of the institution. Usually, the new identity is a stigmatised one that lowers the person's status relative to the outside world and to those who enforce the rules of the institution.

c. **Privilege system:** In order to foster obedience, the total institutions have strict rules for behaviour that are imposed on those contained within them. At the same time, they have a privilege system that provides rewards and special privileges for good behavior. This system is designed to foster obedience to the authority of the institution and discourage breaking the rules.

d. **Adaptation alignments:** These are the ways designed for people to adapt to their new environment once they enter it.

Some criticisms or issues raised: With the rise of new communication mechanisms and other technological innovations, the distinctions between total institutions are getting diluted. According to Susie Scott, with modernity, new organisational forms have emerged. These institutions use subtler mechanisms of social control with more positive meanings and motivations. E.g., the spiritual and yoga/vipassana centres working across the world where members voluntarily commit themselves Many of them join these institutions willingly to attain new identities and work towards self-improvement.

Similarly, many secret societies or virtual groups have emerged to serve these purposes. Based on it, Scott introduced three critical discussions on total institutions:

1. Goffman overemphasises the coercive identity erasure in total institutions while overlooking the subtle processes of negotiation, legitimation, and mutual surveillance through which power operates in the interaction order.
2. Methodological flaws and questions of representativeness: "Institutions vary in their degrees of totality, just as inmates vary in their degree of commitment to them."
3. The nature of total institutions has changed since Goffman conducted his research in the 1960s, especially those establishments linked to (mental) health care, even though some totalizing momentum still exists there. Despite all these changes, we still have asymmetric organisational power configurations. They support subjective, organisational, and societal conditions, helping in the emergence and persistence of oppressive or total institutions. The narrow goals of efficiency and effectiveness set by management lead to abusive employment practices, even in private organisations.

Q 8. Arjun Appadurai's conceptualization of global economy

Ans. Arjun Appadurai (born 1949) is an Indian-American anthropologist recognised as a major theorist in globalisation studies. Appadurai was born in 1949 into a Tamil family in Mumbai (Bombay), India, and was educated in India. He graduated from St. Xavier's High School, Fort, Mumbai, and earned his Intermediate Arts degree from Elphinstone College, Mumbai, before moving to the United States. He then received his B.A. from Brandeis University in 1970. He was formerly a professor at the University of Chicago, where he received his M.A. (1973) and Ph.D. (1976) in anthropology.

In his anthropological work, he discusses the importance of the modernity of nation-states and globalization. He is the former University of Chicago professor of anthropology and South Asian Languages and Civilizations, Humanities Dean of the University of Chicago, director of the city centre and globalisation at Yale University, and the Education and Human Development Studies professor at NYU Steinhardt School of Culture.

Some of his most important works include Worship and Conflict under Colonial Rule (1981), Disjuncture and Difference in the Global Cultural Economy (1990), of which an expanded version is found in Modernity at Large (1996), and Fear of Small Numbers (2006).

The concept of global cultural flows was introduced by anthropologist Arjun Appadurai in his essay "Disjuncture and Difference in the Global Cultural Economy" (1990), in which he argues that people ought to reconsider the binary oppositions that were imposed through colonialism, such as those of 'global' vs. 'local', south vs. north, and metropolitan vs. non-metropolitan. He instead proposes that "flows" or "scapes" move through the world, carrying capital, images, people, information, technologies, and ideas.

The five dimensions of global cultural flow include:

1. ethnoscapes - flow of people Human migrations;
2. technoscapes - flow and configurations of technology;
3. financescapes - flow of money and global Business networks;
4. mediascapes - flow of cultural industry networks; and
5. ideoscapes - flow of ideas, images, and their nexuses.

As these flows travel through national boundaries, they form different combinations and interdependencies, mutate, and divide cultural ideas into "nation" and "state."

Appadurai further states that, despite disjunctures having always existed between the flows of people, machinery, money, ideas, and images, the world is at a crossroads where this is happening to a greater extent; he thus points to the importance of studying the "scapes." These disjunctures also contribute to the central idea of deterritorialization, which Appadurai describes as the main force affecting globalisation in the sense that people from different countries and socioeconomic backgrounds are mixing with one another, namely, the lower classes of some countries integrating into wealthier societies via the workforce. Subsequently, these people reproduce their ethnic culture, but in a deterritorialized context.

Appadurai claims that global flows occur in and through the growing disjunctures between the scapes. The Olympic Games, for instance, organise financescapes (regional, national, and international business networks come in to invest in the host city) and mediascapes (the opening and closing ceremonies showcase national cultures), as well as ideoscapes (images of the host city and country, their history, and customs circulate worldwide to attract tourists) and ethnoscapes (migrations of business networks and localities that are removed from parts of the city to make space for Olympic venues). Finanscapes can become in disjunction with ethnoscapes as networks of global social movements often protest against human rights violations that take place during the Games. As a result, ideoscapes clash with ethnoscapes as city brands and narratives are disrupted by these demonstrations and subsequent negative press.

Dr. Arjun Appadurai conducted multisited fieldwork in Mumbai, India, examining the effects of globalisation on urban life. His research focused on the influence of global media, consumer culture, and transnational migration on the formation of urban identities and social dynamics. Appadurai's book "Modernity at Large" provided insights into the ways in which globalisation reshapes cultural practices and identities in contemporary urban contexts.

Bibliography

- Naresh Kumar Vaid . *An Introduction to Social Cultural Anthropology*. 3rd ed., Palaka Prakashan.
- P.Nath. *PHYSICAL ANTHROPOLOGY*. 4th ed., Higher Pub.
- V.S. Upadhyay, and Gaya Panday. *History of Anthropological Thought*. 1st ed., Concept Publishing company.
- D.K. Bhattacharya. *An Outline of Indian Prehistory*. 8th ed., Palaka Prakashan.
- Akshat Jain IAS. *Anthropology Demystified*. 1st ed., Jice Publications.
- Dr Sudhir Kumar. *Anthropology Test Series Material*.
- Vaid's ICS. *Study Material for Anthropology*.
- Laurels institute. *Study Material for Anthropology*.
- "Chimp Nut-Smashing Techniques Explain Our Proto-Culture." *Chimp Nut-Smashing Techniques Explain Our Proto-Culture*, www.vice.com/en/article/yppqvk/proto-tech-and-proto-culture-in-our-proto-cousins.
- @LiveScience. "Chimps Use 'hi' and 'bye' Greetings, Just Like Humans." *livescience.com*, 14 Aug. 2021, www.livescience.com/chimp-bonobos-greetings.html.
- "Meet the 1st Neanderthal Family: DNA Helps 2022 Nobel Winner Chart Family Tree of Our Ancestors." *India Today*, 20 Oct. 2022, www.indiatoday.in/science/story/ancient-dna-helps-2022-nobel-winner-chart-1st-family-tree-of-our-neanderthal-ancestors-2287615-2022-10-20.
- "Human Species Who Lived 500,000 Years Ago Named as Homo Bodoensis." *The Guardian*, 28 Oct. 2021, www.theguardian.com/science/2021/oct/28/human-species-homo-bodoensis-who-lived-500000-years-ago-is-named.
- "Explained: China's Dragon Man, and Where It Fits in the Evolutionary Tree of Modern Humans." *The Indian Express*, 26 June 2021, indianexpress.com/article/explained/explained-chinas-dragon-man-its-significance-and-where-it-fits-in-the-evolutionary-tree-of-modern-humans-7377216.
- "New Research Indicates That Hydrogen Sulphide Suppresses HIV Infection." *New Research Indicates That Hydrogen Sulphide Suppresses HIV Infection-the Hindu*, 7 Dec. 2021, www.thehindu.com/news/cities /bangalore/new-research-finds-that-hydrogen-sulphide-suppresses-hiv-infection/article37879366.ece.
- Davis, Nicola. "Scientists Find Evidence of Humans Making Clothes 120,000 Years Ago." *The Guardian*, 16 Sept. 2021, www.theguardian.com/science/2021/sep/16/scientists-find-evidence-of-humans-making-clothes-120000-years-ago.
- "The Kingdom of Women: The Society Where a Man Is Never the Boss | Family | the Guardian." *The Kingdom of Women: The Society Where a Man Is Never the Boss | Family | the Guardian*, amp-the guardian -com.cdn.ampproject.org/v/s/amp.theguardian.com/lifeandstyle/2017/apr/01/the-kingdom-of-women-the-tibetan-tribe-where-a-man-is-never-the-boss?amp_js_v=a6&amp_gsa=1&usq p=mq331AQKKAFQ ArABIIACAw%3D%3D#aoh=16418755340175&referrer=https%3A%2F%2Fwww.google.com&amp_tf=From%20%251%24s&ampshare=https%3A%2F%2Fwww.theguardian.com%2Flifeandstyle%2F2017%2Fapr%2F01%2Fthe-kingdom-of-women-the-tibetan-tribe-where-a-man-is-never-the-boss.
- Special to Gulf News, Adil Khan. "'Nata Pratha': In Some Tribal Areas of India, Women's 'Price' Is Fixed by Village Councils." *'Nata Pratha': In Some Tribal Areas of India, Women's 'Price' Is Fixed by Village Councils | India – Gulf News*, 20 Feb. 2022, gulfnews.com/world/asia/india/nata-pratha-in-some-tribal-areas-of-india-womens-price-is-fixed-by-village-councils-1.85888402.
- "Bacha Posh, the Afghan Tradition That Allows Girls to Access the Freedom of Boys." *India Today*, www.indiatoday.in/world/story/bacha-posh-the-afghan-tradition-that-allows-girls-to-access-the-freedom-of-boys-1900796-2022-01-17.
- "Himba People Rituals of Birth and Death." *Exploring Africa*, 28 Feb. 2017, www.exploring-africa.com/en/namibia/himba-people/himba-people-rituals-birth-and-death.
- Sapiens. "Five New Year's Rituals of Renewal." *SAPIENS*, 3 Jan. 2022, www.sapiens.org/culture/renewal-rituals.

- Knowable Magazine, Bob Holmes. "To Learn Klingon or Esperanto: What Invented Languages Can Teach Us." *Ars Technica*, 1 Jan. 2022, arstechnica.com/science/2022/01/to-learn-klingon-or-esperanto-what-invented-languages-can-teach-us.
- "Assam's Haflong Hindi, a Fluent Example of Give and Take." *Assam's Haflong Hindi, a Fluent Example of Give and Take - the Hindu*, 4 May 2022, www.thehindu.com/news/national/other-states/haflong-hindi-tries-to-hold-its-own-in-assam/article65381104.ece.
- SAPNA MISHRA, et al. "Coping With Precarious Work: A Case of Rampant Use of Tetanus Toxoid Injection by Workers in Unorganized E-waste Sector in Slums Ofa South Indian City." *Indian Anthropological Society*.
- Hautakangas, Heidi, et al. "Genome-wide Analysis of 102,084 Migraine Cases Identifies 123 Risk Loci and Subtype-specific Risk Alleles - Nature Genetics." *Nature*, 3 Feb. 2022, https://doi.org/10.1038/s41588-021-00990-0.
- Jackson, Christina. "Researchers Uncover a Gene Mutation Linked to the Development of Kidney Disease." *GEN - Genetic Engineering and Biotechnology News*, 22 Dec. 2021, www.genengnews.com/news/researchers-uncover-a-gene-mutation-linked-to-the-development-of-kidney-disease.
- "Left-handed DNA Found - and It Changes Brain Structure." *BBC News*, www.bbc.com/news/health-49579810.
- "Monumental Project Underway to Sequence the Genome of Every Complex Species on Earth." *SciTechDaily*, 29 Jan. 2022, scitechdaily.com/monumental-project-underway-to-sequence-the-genome-of-every-complex-species-on-earth.
- Sapiens. "Untangling Race From Hair." *SAPIENS*, 9 Mar. 2022, www.sapiens.org/biology/hair-race-evolution.
- Padma, T. V. "Adapt or Abandon? A Hard Choice in the Himalaya – the Wire Science." *Adapt or Abandon? A Hard Choice in the Himalaya – the Wire Science*, 4 Nov. 2021, science.thewire.in/environment/adapt-or-abandon-a-hard-choice-in-the-himalaya.
- "How Anthropology Can Bring the Human Element to Emergency Outbreak Response." *How Anthropology Can Bring the Human Element to Emergency Outbreak Response | Gavi, the Vaccine Alliance*, 8 June 2023, www.gavi.org/vaccineswork/how-anthropology-can-bring-human-element-emergency-outbreak-response.
- "When Does Metabolism Start to Drop? It's Much Later Than You Might Think, Study Shows." *The Kansas City Star*, 17 Aug. 2021, www.kansascity.com/news/nation-world/national/article253549369.html.
- "Our DNA May Have Less Influence on How We Age Than Initially Thought." *Our DNA May Have Less Influence on How We Age Than Initially Thought*, www.medicalnewstoday.com/articles/age-vs-dna-which-has-more-influence-on-how-humans-age.
- Maitrayee Patar. "Tuloni: Experiences and Negotiations Around Womanhood in Assamese Society." *Indian Sociological Society*, vol. 3 (1), Apr. 2019, pp. 65–88.
- Amarjyoti Mahanta. "Impact of Education on Fertility: Evidence From a Tribal Society in Assam, India." *International Journal of Population Research*, 2016.
- "Army Day 2022: Indian Army Gives First Public View of New Uniform With Digital Camouflage." *Republic World*, 15 Jan. 2022, www.republicworld.com/india-news/general-news/army-day-2022-indian-army-gives-first-public-view-of-new-uniform-with-digital-camouflage-articleshow.html.
- "Body Found in a Barrel at Lake Mead Is the Tip of the Iceberg. Forensic Anthropologists Are Now Recovering Human Remains Following Droughts, Sea-level Rise, and Wildfires." *Business Insider*, 5 May 2022, www.businessinsider.in/science/news/body-found-in-a-barrel-at-lake-mead-is-the-tip-of-the-iceberg-forensic-anthropologists-are-now-recovering-human-remains-following-droughts-sea-level-rise-and-wildfires-/articleshow/91357368.cms.
- "Research Explores a New Method of Determining Sex - Binghamton News." *News - Binghamton University*, 24 Feb. 2022, www.binghamton.edu/news/story/3493/bare-bones-research-explores-a-new-method-of-determining-sex.
- Bradbury, Shelly. "Bones, Brains and Bugs: Meet the Colorado Forensic Anthropologist Who's Helped Crack Cases for Decades." *The Denver Post*, 2 Jan. 2022, www.denverpost.com/2022/01/02/forensic-anthropologist-diane-france-colorado-bones.
- Network, Good News. "Breakthrough Using CRISPR to Target Fat Cells in Genetic Study of Obesity." *Good News Network*, 8 Jan. 2022, www.goodnewsnetwork.org/breakthrough-using-crispr-to-target-fat-cells-in-genetic-study-of-obesity.

ANTHROPOLOGY EXEMPLIFIED

PAPER-II

TOPICS

1

Evolution of Indian Civilization and Archaeology

1.1

Evolution of the Indian Culture and Civilization—Prehistoric (Palaeolithic, Mesolithic, Neolithic and Neolithic-Chalcolithic), Protohistoric (Indus Civilization). Pre-Harappan, Harappan and post- Harappan cultures. Contributions of the tribal cultures to Indian civilization.

Q 1. Age System

Ans. C.J. Thomson has given three time period divisions: Stone Age, Bronze Age, and Iron Age. John Lubbock in 1865 further divided the Stone Age into Palaeolithic, Mesolithic, and Neolithic.

Period	Tools	Economy	Housing	Society	Religion
Palaeolithic	Natural tools–stone, copper hand axe, harpoon, spear etc.	Hunting & gathering (H&G).	Mobility lifestyle–caves, huts, mostly by riverside.	Band of Hunting and Gathering.	Evidence for belief in after life first appeared in Upper Palaeolithic. Marked by burial ritual and ancestor worship. Shamans, priest appears in prehistory.
Mesolithic	Harpoon, bow & arrow, fishing baskets, boats.	Wild seeds used for domestic planting, intensive H&G.	Temporary villages appear for economic activities.	Tribes & Band.	
Neolithic	Polished stone tools –Hoe, plough, yoke, chisel, earthen ware.	Domestication of plants & animals.	Permanent settlement startedsss.	Chiefdom.	Polytheism, sometimes presided over by mother goddess, shamanism.
Copper	Copper tools.	Civilisation including craft, trade.	Urban centres, political communities.	City states.	Ethnic gods, state religion.
Bronze	Bronze tools.				
Iron	Iron tools.	Trade & taxes.	Large cities, towns.	Large kingdoms.	One or more religion sanctioned by state.

Epoch	Period of Glaciations	Age	Archaeological Period	Sequence of Cultures
Holocene	Post glacial	10,000	Neolithic Mesolithic	
Pleistocene	Wurm 3rd inter glacial Riss 2nd inter glacial Mindel 1st interglacial Gunz	70,000 2,00,000	Upper Palaeolithic Middle Palaeolithic Lower Palaeolithic	Magdalenian Aurignacion Perigordian Mousterian Clactonian Acheulean Abbevillian Pre Abbevillian

Q 2. Palaeolithic culture of India

Ans. The cultural remains from the entire Pleistocene era are referred to as Palaeolithic culture. The lower Palaeolithic (2.5 million years ago to 100,000 BCE), Middle Palaeolithic (100,000 BCE to 36,000 BCE), and Upper Palaeolithic (36,000 BCE to 9000 BCE) are its three periods.

Climate: The hilly areas of the north saw multiple glacial and interglacial periods. In the meantime, Peninsular India's river valleys saw successive inter-pluvial and pluvial periods.

Material Culture

Period	Material Used	Preparation Technique	Tools
Lower Palaeolithic	Quartzite	Direct hammer technique	Core tools characterized by two main industries– Abbevillian (chopper–chopping tools and crude handaxes) and Acheulian (cleavers and handaxes)
Middle Palaeolithic	Crypto-crystalline silica types	Pecking and direct hammer technique	Flake tools like scrapers and points became much frequent than core tools.
Upper Palaeolithic	Quartz and bone	Core cylinder hammer technique	Parallel–sided blade flakes and blade tools, along with bone tools.

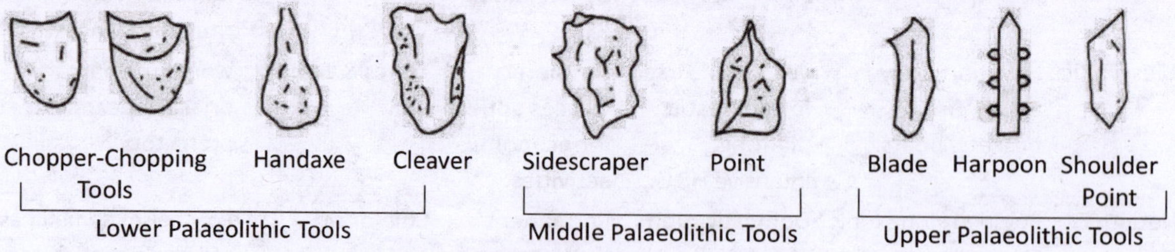

Palaeolithic Tools

Regional Variations: The non–uniform Palaeolithic climate in the sub-continent gave rise to regional variations, as shown through the following sites:

1. **Soan Valley (Lower Palaeolithic):** De Terra and Paterson (1935) excavated it. It demonstrates the incrementa l improvement of tools from high to lower terraces, integrating with Chauntra, another zone that had implements.

2. **Madrasian Culture (Lower Palaeolithic):** It is dominated by handaxes and cleavers that have been thinned out using the Vall process. The existence of hafting on these instruments, according to H.D. Sankalia, would be among the world's oldest cases ever discovered if confirmed.
3. **Nevasa (Middle Palaeolithic):** Nevasa, which was unearthed by H.D. Sankalia in 1956, produced a number of Levallois based flake tools made of jasper.
4. **Muchchatla & Chintamani Gavi (Upper Palaeolithic):** The richest Upper Palaeolithic bone industry in India was discovered by Murthy in 1970. Shouldered points, scrapers, and barbs can all be found here among the common bone tools.
5. **Bhimbetka:** It was found in 1957 by V.S. Wakankar. V.N. Misra excavated one of its biggest cave shelters, III F-23, between 1973 and 1976. This shelter is one of the few Indian sites to have produced all three phases of the Palaeolithic period, and it has produced eight cultural formations.

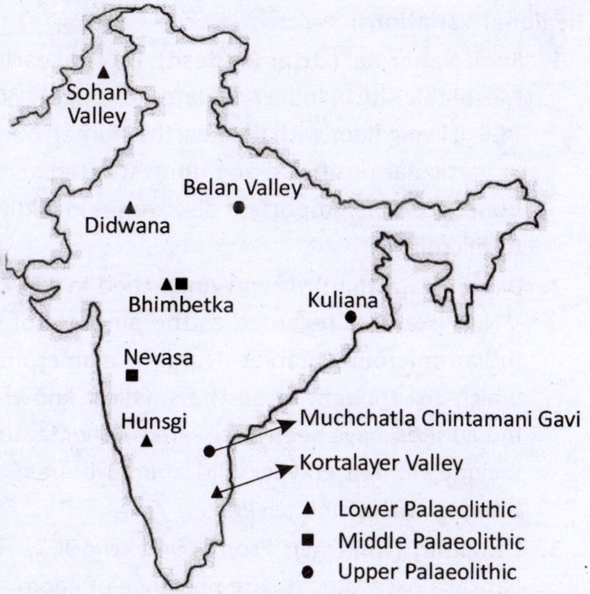

Palaeolithic Sites of India

Social Life: Hunting and gathering were the main sources of income, as can be seen from the tools. Burials discovered with tools suggest ritual activity. The Upper Palaeolithic period's figures and cave art show a developing societal structure towards the conclusion of this time. It can be said that the Palaeolithic in India is neither chronologically homogenous nor culturally uniform.

Q 3. Mesolithic culture of India

Ans. The earliest Holocene civilization that existed before industrialised food production is known as Mesolithic culture. In the case of India, it covers the period from 9,000 to 2,000 BCE.

Climate: A warmer climate replaced the glacial climate of the Palaeolithic epoch. Forests and water bodies were cleared in time for the ice to melt.

Material Culture: Microliths, which are tiny fragments of chipped stone, were a common component of Mesolithic tool cultures. These were made using fluting or pressure flaking techniques. Microliths could be either geometrically shaped or not. They were mounted to arrows, harpoons, and blades to be used as composite tools.

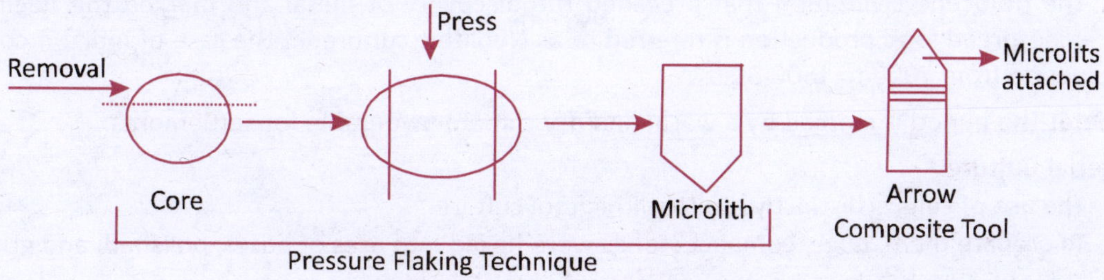

Mesolithic Tool Tradition

Regional Variations:

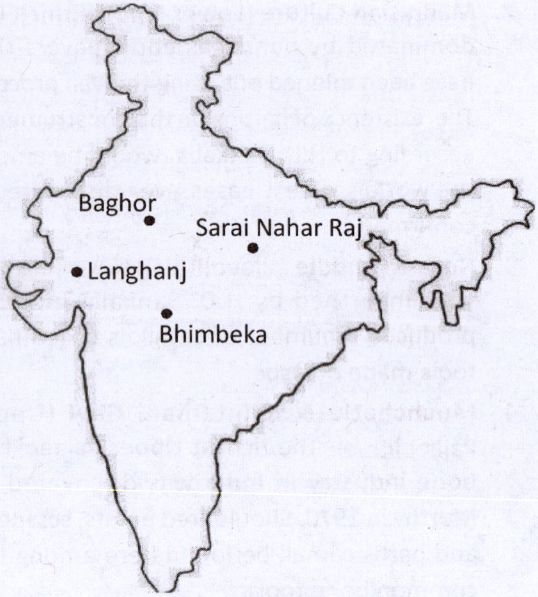

Mesolithic Sites of India

1. **Sarai Nahar Rai (Uttar Pradesh):** It is the earliest Mesolithic site in India and dates to roughly 8000 BCE. A living floor with fire hearths, human burials in particular positions, and domesticated animal bones are other important discoveries in addition to microliths.
2. **Bagor (Rajasthan):** It was unearthed in 1967 by V.N. Misra. It is regarded as the pinnacle of the Indian microlith market. Numerous microliths, which are thought to be the smallest known at Indian sites, have been discovered. Other features include human graves, wild animal bones, and flooring with stone pavers.
3. **Langhnaj (Gujarat):** From 1944 to 1963, H.D. Sankalia excavated it. The presence of geometric microliths is evident. Human skeletons discovered buried in a crouched position suggest ritualistic activity. Bones from both domestic and wild animals are present, indicating some degree of pastoralism.
4. **Bhimbetka (Maharashtra):** It was found in 1957 by V.S. Wakankar. V.N. Misra excavated one of its biggest cave shelters, designated III F - 23, between 1973 and 1976. Eight cultural formations have been found at this shelter, the first three of which date to the Mesolithic era. There is an extensive geometric microlith industry. Additionally, a number of shelters have reported seeing cave drawings.
5. **Teri (Tamil Nadu):** There are eleven sites in this group that are similar to Sri Lankan microliths, particularly in the style of bifacially pre ssure flaked points.

Social life: The economy was based on smallgame hunting, fishing, and fowling, as inferred from the implements and the cave paintings. The discovery of numerous burials in particular positions suggests the existence of rituals. The taming of animals and the gathering of wild seeds started towards the end of this time. Since Homo sapiens was on the verge of settling down and developing a thriving economy, the Mesolithic period served as a transitional stage between the Palaeolithic and Neolithic periods.

Q 4. Neolithic culture of India

Ans. The Holocene civilization that preceded the discovery of metal and marked the beginning of widespread food production is referred to as Neolithic culture. In the case of India, it covers the period from 7000 to 1500 BCE.

Climate: The period is marked by a warm and dry climate favourable for settlements.

Material Culture

➢ The use of celts is distinctive to Neolithic tool culture.

➢ To prepare them, huge, compact stones were flaked into axes or adzes, polished, and grinded.

➢ These wooden handles with attached celts were used to clear forests and prepare the ground for farming.

- Mace heads and ring stones are examples of other kinds of tool.
- The invention of earthenware for the storage of food grains was another noteworthy achievement.
- It was poorly fired when it was first constructed by hand.
- At the end of this time, pottery production on wheels started.

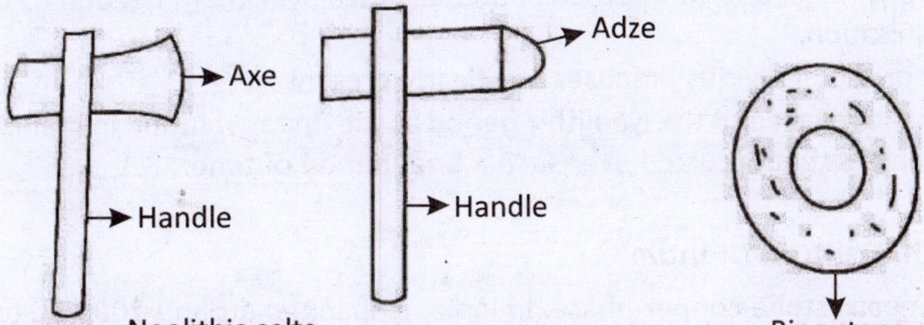

Neolithic Tool Types

Regional Variations:

1. **Burzahom (Jammu and Kashmir):** The Archaeological Survey of India excavated it in-depth (1960–1971). Numerous bone and celt tools, as well as handmade coarse pottery, have been discovered.
2. **Mehrgarh (Pakistan):** The excavation was done by Jarriage (1974–1986). One of the earliest farming and herding sites in South Asia is Mehrgarh, which dates to around 7000 BCE and has traces of wheat, barley, and livestock. Mehrgarh is considered a forerunner of the Indus Valley Civilization because of characteristics including correctly constructed towns, pottery manufactured on wheels, and trade-based goods.

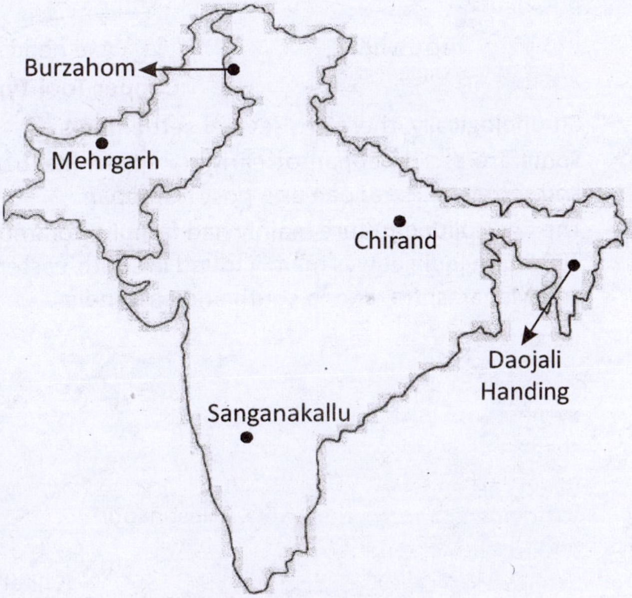

Neolithic Sites of India

3. **Chirand (Bihar):** Chirand exhibits a higher frequency of bone and antler tools than celts, in contrast to most Neolithic sites. Additionally, Chirand is also known for its terracotta artefacts, particularly its serpent-related sculptures.
4. **Deojali Hading (Assam):** It was unearthed in 1967 by T.C. Sharma. The Neolithic Celts discovered here feature border grinding that is distinct and are shouldered at butt ends.
5. **South Neolithic/Neolithic-Chalcolithic culture:** Tekkalakota, Sanganakallu, and Piklihal are South Indian sites that exhibit a combination of Neolithic and Chalcolit hic characteristics. Neolithic ash mounds, which are essentially burned piles of cow dung, are distinctive characteristic and may have be en used in special rite.

Social Life

- Hunting and gathering gave way to a subsistence economy based on tamed plants and animals.
- Complex social organisations developed as a result of the cooperative existence demanded by a sedentary lifestyle.
- Fields and crops needed to be protected, and disputes over them needed to be settled through political organisation.
- Additionally, magico-religious practises are clearly present.
- Thus, V.G. Childe referred to the Neolithic period as the first revolution in mankind because of the profound change s that occurred over such a brief period of time.

Q 5. Chalcolithic culture of India

Ans. Chalcolithic means stone copper phase. In India, it spanned around 2000 BC to 700 BC. The first metal age of India is called the Chalcolithic Age, which saw the use of copper along with stone. It was also called the Stone–Copper Age. Along with the use of copper and stone, these people also used low-grade bronze to make tools and weapons.

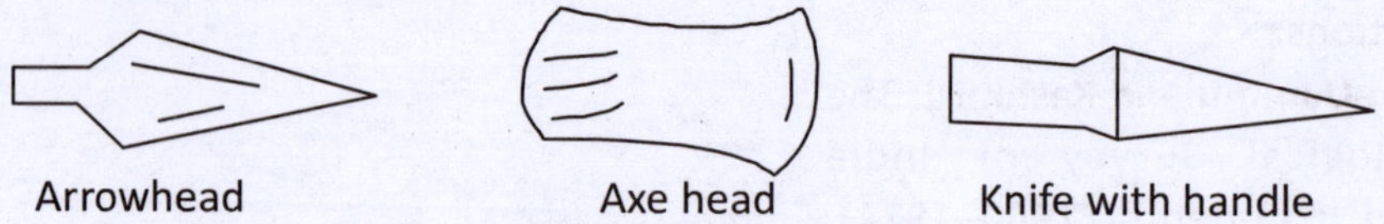

Copper Tool Types

- Chronologically, there are several settlements.
- Some are pre-Harappan or early Harappan (Kalibangan in Rajasthan and Banawali in Haryana), and some are Harappan and post-Harappan.
- The Chalcolithic culture mainly had farming communities, and they existed between 2000 BC and 700 BC. In India, it was mainly found in south-eastern Rajasthan, western part of Madhya Pradesh and Maharashtra, and in south and east India.

Chalcolithic Sites of India

Excavations revealed a five-fold sequence of culture:

1. Kayatha culture (ca. 2450–2000 BC)
2. Ahar Culture (ca. 1950–1700 BC)
3. Malwa Culture (ca. 1700-1400 BC)
4. Early Historic (ca. 600 BC–200 BC)
5. Vunga–Kusana–Gupta (Ca. 200 BC–600 BC)

The chalcolithic cultures such as Ahar, Kayatha, Malwa, Jorwe, ochre-coloured pottery, and painted grey are discussed below:

1. **Kayatha culture:** This Chalcolithic culture was named after the type site, Kayatha, in Ujjain district, Madhya Pradesh. Over forty settlements of the Kayatha culture have been discovered so far in the Malwa region of Madhya Pradesh, most of them located on the tributaries of the Chambal River. The characteristic forms of ceramics include chocolate-slipped ware, also known as kayatha ware. The types are bowls, high- and short necked storage jars with a globular profile, and basins. Similarities are evident with the sturdy painted pottery found at some pre-Harappan sites.
2. **The Ahar culture** is also known as the Banas culture; the latter term is derived from the name of the valley in which most of the sites of this culture are located. It is among the earliest Chalcolithic cultures in India. This is seen from the calibrated radiocarbon dates available from many of the sites. The culture has been named after the type site, Ahar, in District Udaipur, Rajasthan, which was excavated in 1961–62 by H.D. Sankalia of Deccan College, Pune. This region is rich in mineral deposits, and archaeologists postulate from available evidence that this region also supplied copper to the Harappan sites.
3. **The Malwa culture** is the most predominant Chalcolithic culture in central India, with a wide distribution of sites almost all over the Malwa region. It was first among the Neolithic and Chalcolithic cultures identified in the excavations at Maheshwar, on the Narmada River. Maheshwar was identified with the ancient Mahishmati of the Puranas. Navdatoli on the opposite bank also revealed great potential and was subsequently excavated. Other excavated sites of this culture are Nagda, Kayatha, Eran, etc. The decline of the Malwa culture has been placed around 1400 BC, which was considered along with that of the Ahar culture as well. Dhavalikar suggests climatic deterioration for the end of these cultures.
4. **Jorwe Culture:** It is the most important and characteristic chalcolithic culture of Maharashtra, extending almost all over the present state, excepting the coastal strip on the west and Vidarbha in the north-east. The culture is named after the type site of Jorwe in Ahmadnagar District, Gujrat. The culture was discovered in 1950. In regions such as Prakash in the Tapi valley, Daimabad in the Pravara Godavari valley, and Inamgaon in the Bhima valley, large centres of this culture were found. This is a notable feature of Jorwe culture. Although over 200 sites of this culture have been documented so far, only a few sites have been subjected to large-scale excavations. Inamgaon and Daimabad are two excavated sites. In understanding the settlement pattern of the Jorwe, 38 Neolithic and Chalcolithic Culture sites' ecological differences between different regions have been highlighted (Dhavalikar, 1997).
5. **The OCP, or Ochre-coloured Pottery Culture,** is named after a ceramic type that is extremely rolled and fragile. It has a wash of red ochre that is easily washed off, hence its name. It was first recognised by B. Lal in 1951 in a small excavation at Bisauli and Rajpur Parsu, the two sites in Uttar Pradesh where copper hoards were found earlier. Jodhpura is the only site where the habitational deposit of the OCP has been found in the form of wellmade floors, mud huts, hearths, terracotta human male figurines, and bull figurines. This shows that the OCP people led a sedentary existence, similar to many early farming communities of this period. Remains of domesticated animals like cattle and evidence of cultivated crops like rice and barley further provide information on their subsistence practises.

6. **Painted Grey Ware (PGW):** Painted Grey Ware (PGW) is a very fine, smooth, and even-coloured grey pottery with a thin fabric. It was made out of well-worked, very high-quality clay. Designs, mostly simple geometric patterns, were painted on the pots in black. The uniform colour and texture of the pots indicate very sophisticated firing techniques. The main concentration of sites is around the Indo-Gangetic divide, Sutlej basin, and upper Ganga plains.

Social life:

- People of the Chalcolithic Age survived on hunting, fishing, and farming. Cotton was produced in black cotton soil.
- Traces of rice cultivation are also found. This shows that their food included fish and rice. Eastern India produced rice, and Western India produced barley. The major crops cultivated were barley and wheat, lentils, bajra, jowar, ragi millets, green peas, and green and black gram.
- The use of bricks was extensive during the Chalcolithic people of Harappa, but there are no traces of burnt (baked) bricks. People buried the dead on the floors of their houses in the north-south direction, along with pots and copper objects.

Q 6. Pre Harappan Culture

Ans. The Pre-Harappan period refers to Chalcolithic culture, which is believed to be the historical antecedent to the Harappan Civilization. It is said to be dated around 3300–2500 BCE.

In the Indian subcontinent, chalcolithic cultures first appeared close to Mehrgarh in Balochistan and later extended to Amri, Kot-Diji, and other locations in the Indus Valley. From there, it advanced and established farming villages in Kalibangan and Banawali to the east.

Common features:

1. A modest settlement with mudbrick houses and microliths that include primitive pottery.
2. Despite the appearance of metal, subsequent phases demonstrate the persistence of microliths. Ceramics place a strong emphasis on vibrant ornamentation.
3. Over time, secular structures that show the maintenance of a sizable population emerge. Black-on-red bichrome ceramics have taken the place of multicoloured ceramics. Still made of mudbricks, but now smaller and raised.

   Some of these farming tribes, particularly those from Mehrgarh, relocated to the Indus flood plains, picked up bronze technology, and started the urban or mature phase of the Indus Valley Civilization (IVC), according to experts.

This knowledge has contributed to the establishment of the entire IVC, from early settled village life to the metropolitan metropolis.

Q 7. Harappan Culture

Ans. The existence of this civilization was reported by Charles Masson in 1826, and this civilization was properly discovered and excavated by officials of ASI, particularly John Marhsall, Cunningham, D.R. Sahni, etc. Initially, it was termed Indo-Sumerian Civilization, but now, on the recommendation of Sir John Marshall, the name has changed to Harappan Civilization.

There is large-scale controversy regarding the period of existence, but most scholars assign the date 3800–1750 B.C. to it. Its remains were discovered in many cities like Harappa, Mohenjodaro, Lothal, Kalibangan, Surkotda, etc.

This civilization engulfed a large area and spread over 12,99,600 sq. km. Manda in Jammu was its northernmost point, Daimabad in Maharashtra was its southernmost point, Sutkagendor near Karachi was its westernmost point, and Alamgirpur in UP was its easternmost point.

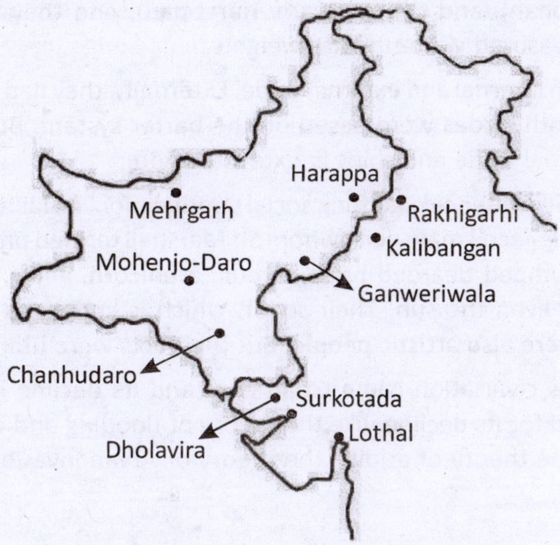

Sites of the Indus Valley Civilisation

The most distinctive characteristic of this civilization was its town planning. People built well-planned cities by following the grid system, by which cities were divided into square and rectangular blocks. The drainage system was also very efficient, like the water management system, which is evident from the discovery of many street drains and water reservoirs.

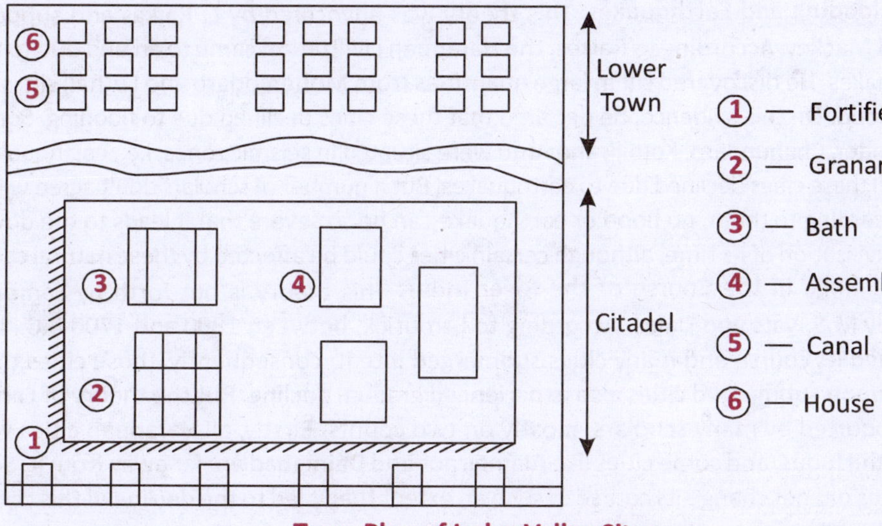

Town Plan of Indus Valley Sites

Harappan cities were administered by a centralised authority. The government's system was based on oligarchy and dominated by merchants. This civilization was also characterised by an efficient economic system. Agriculture was the main occupation, and they produced many crops, particularly wheat and barley. They were also the first to produce cotton. The Greeks called cotton

Sindhon. They also domesticated many animals like buffalo, bulls, goats, etc. They were also expert craftsmen, and many industries flourished at that time, like the textile industry, pottery making (black and red), brick making, jewellery making, and tool making. Tools were made out of stones, bronze (mature Harappan), and copper (early Harappan), and they were not acquainted with iron. Weights were measured via terracotta weights.

They practised both internal and external trade. Externally, they had trade relations, particularly with Mesopotamia; both trades were based on the barter system. Bullock carts were means of transportation in internal trade and ships in external trade.

We also have certain evidence regarding social stratification. As far as religious life is concerned, they worshipped a three-faced male deity whom Sir Marshall termed proto-shiva. They worshipped Mother Goddess, a humped bearded priest, a bull, a unicorn, goats, a peepal tree, fire, water, pigeons, and perhaps even the sun. Their script, which is known as pictographic script, is still undeciphered. They were also artistic people, but their acts were utilitarian in nature.

Around 1750 B.C., this civilization came to an end, and its decline is still a mystery. Different theories have been assigned for its decline, like the theory of flooding and earthquakes, the change in course of the river Indus, the theory of aridity, the theory of Aryan invasion, the theory of ecological imbalance, etc.

Q 8. Decline of Harappan Culture

Ans. The existence of this civilization was reported by Charles Masson in 1826, and this civilization was properly discovered and excavated by officials of ASI, particularly John Marhsall, Cunningham, D.R. Sahni, etc. Different scholars put forth their respective theories regarding its decline. Some of these theories are discussed below:

1. **Theory of Flooding and Earthquakes:** This theory was advocated by L. Raikas and supported by S.R. Rao and Mackey. According to Raikes, the Harappan civilization came to an end due to flooding and earthquakes. He discovered silt in large quantities from Mohenjodaro and Lothal; silt is actually part of the flood. On this evidence, he declared that these cities declined due to flooding. Some cities like Sutkagendor, Chahundaro, Kotdiji, and Amri were situated in seismic zones, i.e., earthquake-prone zones, and all these cities declined due to earthquakes. But a number of scholars don't agree with Raikes because, according to them, no flood or earthquake can be so severe that it leads to the downfall of the largest civilization of its time, although certain cities could be affected by these natural calamities.
2. **Theory of Change in the Course of the River Indus:** This theory is put forth by Lambrick and supported by M.S. Vats and Dales. According to Lambrick, between 1800 and 1700 B.C., the river Indus changed its course and many cities submerged into it; consequently, those cities that were dependent upon submerged cities also experienced gradual decline. But the theory of Lambrick is also not supported by many scholars, mostly on two counts. Firstly, all Harappan cities were not situated on the Indus, and some cities like Alamgirpur and Daimabad are far away from it. Secondly, the river Indus did not change its course to such an extent that it led to the decline of this civilization; hence, this theory is also not considered authentic.
3. **Theory of Aridity:** This theory is given by Aggarwal and Sood. According to them, around 1800 B.C., arid conditions were enhanced, which led to conditions of drought and starvation. It became difficult for animals and humans to survive as even many natural bodies dried up. But Aggarwal and Sood based their theory on their findings from France and Australia, not from India. As in India, no such condition even occurred in that region.

Although the river Ghaggar-Hakra (Saraswati) dried up, only adjoining cities got affected, not the whole civilization. Therefore, this theory has also been rejected by many historians.

4. **Theory of Aryan Invasion:** This theory is advocated by Wheeler. According to him, the Harappan civilization declined due to the Aryan invasion. He put forth evidence of skeletons with cut marks, as discovered in Mohenjodaro. According to him, massacres took place in many other cities, like Mohanjodaro. Also, there is mention of the term Hariupiya in the Rig Veda, which is situated on the river Ravi. It is mentioned in the Rigveda that Aryans, with the help of Indra, whom they termed Purandhar, destroyed this city. The term Hariyupiya sounds very much like Harappa, and it further authenticates the theory of Wheeler that Harappan civilization came to an end due to the Aryan Invasion. But the majority of historians dispute this theory on the grounds that recorded references indicate that Aryans entered India around 1500 B.C., whereas Harappa cities declined around 1750 B.C.; thus, how could Aryans be responsible for the destruction of Harappa cities who came 250 years after the decline of this civilization? They also put a question mark on why the Aryans destroyed Harappan cities because they could kill the people and occupy their houses. But it was not the case. Many scholars agree that Aryans were not invaders but only immigrants. Therefore, Wheeler's theory is not considered relevant.

5. **Theory of ecological imbalance:** This theory is given by Fair Service. According to him, the population of Harappan cities increased enormously over time, whereas resources did not increase at the same pace, resulting in an ecological imbalance. Due to this, Harappans abandoned their cities and migrated southward and eastward. Gradually, these abundant cities became deserted. But their theory is also not without flaws.

   As many historians are of the opinion that ecological imbalance could not take place simultaneously in all Harappan cities, it may be the case with certain cities. Thus, this theory is also rejected. No single theory can explain the decline of the Harappan civilization, and if we consider all theories collectively, we can understand, up to a certain extent, the downfall of this great civilization.

Q 9. Post Harappan Culture in India

Ans. The post Harappan period marks the civilization that emerged around 1900 BCE onwards, following the decline of the mature Harappan civilization.

Most of the urban Harappan towns were abandoned as a result of the decline. In Western UP, Haryana, and East Punjab, numerous regional cultures have arisen. These have varied degrees of Harappan cultural influence.

Features: The time frame denotes the township's decline. Many of the locations have a mostly rural feel. There have been some mudbrick buildings discovered, although they are not comparable to those from the earlier era. Three associated civilizations are used to characterise the pottery and ceramics:

1. Jhukar and Jahangar, the first buff-coloured pottery, are staples of Sindhi culture, followed by grey or black pottery.
2. Redware from Gujarat's Rangpur culture with a thick slip.
3. Reddish earthenware from Punjab's Cemetery-H culture with black motifs.

However, the pottery found here is poorly fired and coarse, in contrast to the wheel-made pottery of the mature period.

Although the ceramic content exhibits new shape types such as carinated and coconut-shaped jars, the method and quality of the decorating are also worse. The Harappan citadel mound's (cemetery H culture) citadel mound has also shown a novel aspect of urn burials. It could be an indication of an outside invasion. Finally, the extensive trade of the Harappans appears to have broken down, as resources like marine shells are no longer discovered. As a result, the illustrious Harappan civilization came to an end during the post-Harappan phase.

Q 10. Iron Age Culture in India

Ans. The term Iron Age refers to the stage of human development that followed the Bronze Age, and it is distinguished by ferrous metallurgy as the dominated metalworking technology. It runs roughly from 1500 to 500 BCE.

Climate: The period is marked by a warm and dry climate, favourable for settlements.

Material culture: Numerous iron tools, including axes, sickles, and arrowheads, have been discovered. To clear woods, labour on farms, and establish permanent settlements, these were harnessed. In addition to these, beads and bone artefacts were discovered. Bangles, combs, needles, and other things are made of bone.

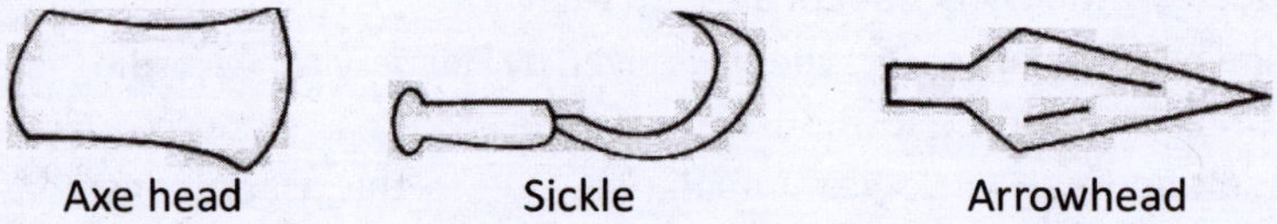

Iron Tool Types

Regional Variations: Iron Age of India can be divided into Northern (Gangetic region) and Southern zones.

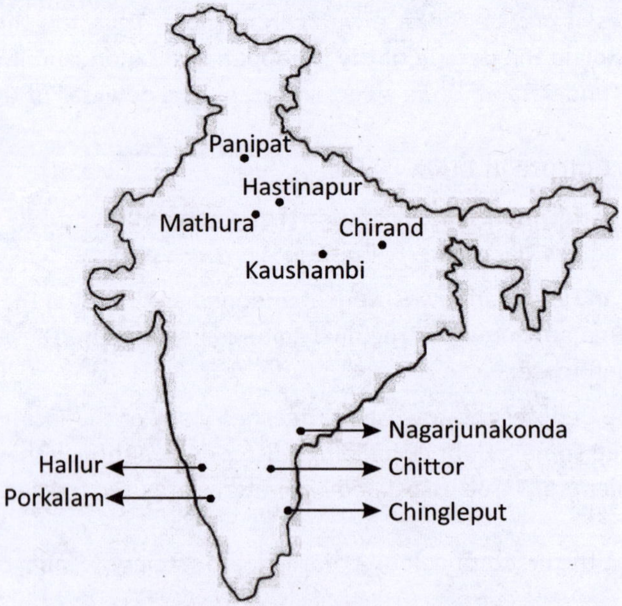

Iron Age sites of India

1. **Northern Zone:** The Painted Grey Ware is what makes this place stand out the most. It features a very fine clay fabric that is very well levitated. It is evenly burned by heating in well-oxygenated container, demonstrating a high level of technology. However, the range of shapes is limited to straight-sided bowls, platters, and lotas. There are hardly any broad black lines used as adornment.

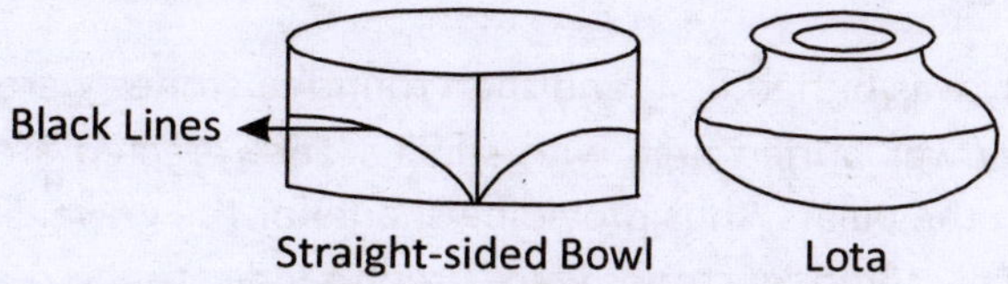

Painted Grey Ware

2. **Southern Zone:** Here, the Megalithic civilization correlates to the Iron Age. Megaliths, according to R.E.M. Wheeler, are structures made of massive, unkempt stone blocks that are associated with burials and serve funerary or religious purposes.

   All of the burials that have been located so far may be categorised and black and redware pottery has been disco vered.

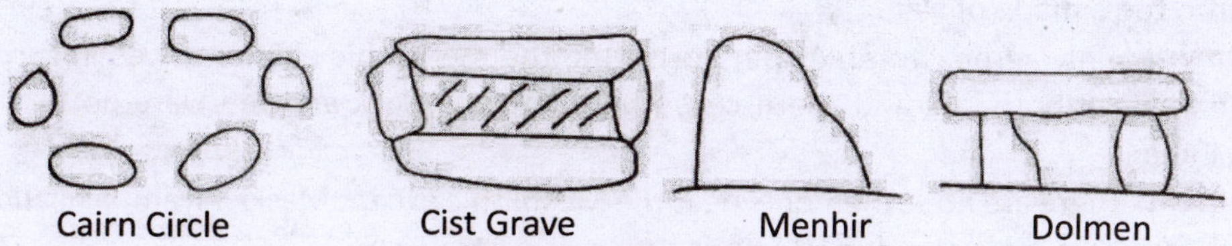

Types of Megaliths

Social Life

- The Iron Age depicts a village with widespread colonisation and numerous specific craft industries.
- Mud homes with thatched roofs were the norm. The three main crops that were grown were rice, wheat, and barley.
- The principal domesticated animals were sheep, cattle, and horses.
- To conclude, the Iron Age was a result of the growth of a sophisticated social structure.

Q 11. Megalithic Culture in South India

Ans. The megalithic culture of South India is associated with the Iron Age, dated around 1500–500 BCE. Megaliths refer to the huge memorials or burial bones erected by people. Though it began in the Neolithic and continued into the Chalcolithic, it is still found today and is thus referred to as a living tradition.

Important Sites: According to R.K. Mohanty and V. Selvakumar, around 2200 megalithic sites can be found in South India.

- South India: Maski, Piyampalli, Brahmagiri, Nagarjunakonda
- North India: Allahabad, Almora, Burzohom, Assam, and Meghalaya
- Current prevalence: Gond, Munda, Khasis

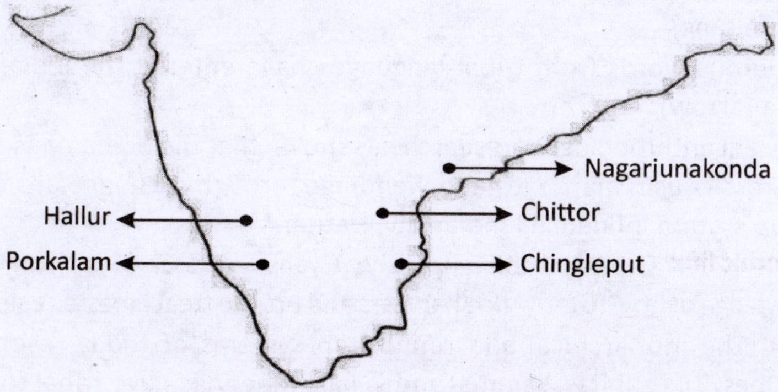

Few Megalithic Sites of South India

Burial Types:

1. **Cairn Circle:** The body was buried first, and then rounded stones were fixed around the grave.
2. **Cist Graves:** The body was buried first, with small stones erected around it. Larger stone slabs were made to rest on the pillars, thus providing shade for the grave.
3. **Menhirs:** Large and tall memorial stones were used to indicate the presence of a grave.
4. **Dolmen:** The body was placed on a slab of stone, covered from all sides with a flat stone slab resting on the four legs of stone erected at the corners of the body.

Features:

1. **Tools:** In India, megaliths belong to the Iron Age. Iron spearheads and arrow heads found on the Hallur plateau date to 1200 BC. As per D. K. Chakraborty, Naikund and Piyampalli in south India have iron tools made of slag.
2. **Economy:** Mainly agropastoral. As per Korisetter, the megalithic economy was in surplus. As per Mukund Kajale, both rabi and kharif crops were known. Black and red ware pottery is found in South India.
3. **Settlement:** There are no settlements near the Mesolithic except Maski, Piyampalli, and Tekalghat. Lashnik says that it may be due to semi-settling or pastoralism.
4. **Society:** Ranked and patriarchal belief in life after death.

Megaliths are found in various shapes, sizes, and types in tribes like

1. **Gond:** Erect a menhir, or wooden pillar, for the spirits to protect them and not harm them. It will help them bring rain.
2. **Muriya:** It is wood-made, and they apply turmeric soil over it. They even sacrifice buffalo and offer rice to make the spirits happy.
3. **Sawaras:** Grow seeds in front of pillars and sacrifice animals before sowing to promote fertility.
4. **Mottu:** Anthropomorphic headless status found.

Haimendorfstudied Nagas and found that these stones show the status of individuals who are dead. Megaliths can be seen in the form of cultures' survival and parallels among various communities.

Q 12. Discuss the contributions of tribal cultures to Indian Civilisation

Ans. Historical documents, ethno-archaeological evidence, and literary works shed light on the contribution of tribal cultures to Indian civilization. The contribution can be seen as follows:

1. **Ethnic complexities:** As a result of the cultural exchange between the Vedic people and the local tribes, these groups were assimilated into the Aryan race. The tribalization of Aryans also took place at the same time.
2. **Language:** Numerous words from tribal languages have entered the Indian language, such as bala (hair), bana (arrow), etc.
3. **To social life:** Recent anthropological research has shown that the Brahamans appropriated Gond's gotra system. Cross-cousin marriages and weddings through exchange are two other ways that the tribal kinship system influenced Indian civilization.
4. **To techno-economic life:** The Asur tribe taught the Aryans how to use iron. Similar to this, tribes pass down their knowledge of how to grow rice harvests and how to treat illnesses using magic and religion.
5. **To political life:** The monarchical and republican systems of today resemble the system of chiefdoms of tribes. The sabhas, samitis, and village meetings have tribal roots as well.

6. **To religion:** the interplay of little and great traditions led to the processes of universalization and parochialization. For instance, *Marriot* says that Hindu festivals like Lakshmi Puja were a result of the universalization of tribal festivals like Saurati Puja.
7. **Art:** Tribal mythology, music, and healing practises found their way into Indian society. For instance, the veena is a musical instrument that evolved from the aboriginal memerajan. Ayurveda uses indigenous treatments like ashwagandha and other plants.

Tribal cultures have so much contributed to Indian civilization, making it a complete and composite civilization.

Q.13. Pre historic Rock Art in India

Ans. The rock art represents the earliest evidence of the aesthetic taste and expression of man in India. It can be seen in the form of rock painting (petrographs) and/or engraving (petroglyphs).

The rock paintings in India were first discovered by *A. Carlyle* on the walls and ceilings of rock shelters in Distt.

Mirzapur (U.P.) in 1867–68. Since then, more than one hundred and fifty rock art sites have come to light. These are spread all over the Indian subcontinent, from the Himalayas in the north to Kerala in the south.

Their major concentration, however, is in Madhya Pradesh and central U.P. (the south Mirzapur region). Almost three-fourths of the total rock art sites in India are situated in the sandstone hills of the Vindhyas in central India.

This is primarily due to its unique geo-environmental set-up, which favoured the evolution of early human culture on the Central Indian plateau. Therefore, the mountainous regions of the Vindhya and Satpura ranges, which confine the Central Narmada Valley, where Stone Age man flourished, have the largest number of rock art sites.

Inferences: It may be pointed out that the prehistoric paintings normally project males as more conquering and domineering than women. While some scholars believe that these paintings may have been the medium to express and explain thoughts and planning, perhaps on hunting tactics, before the advent of the language, many others relate them to prehistoric man's magico-ritual urge and suggest that painted rock shelters might have been the places for performing scared rituals.

K.L. Kamat observed that many of them were not planned or organised nicely; they had not taken the trouble even to erase the older paintings and drawings. There are several overlaps between layers of sketches. We can separate them through colour and style differences. Most probably, these were created as a means of escape from suffering and as devotion to a supernatural entity since there are red, green, and white colours in all hues and varieties used to decorate the dead.

Case study of Bhimbhetka: Bhimbetka rock art site is in the Raisen District of Madhya Pradesh. From a distance, the site appears to be a massive fortified segmented ridge. The rocky terrain is covered by dense forest at the southern edge of the Vindhyan hills. Bhimbetka finds its first mention in Indian Archaeological Records (1888) as a Buddhist site, but its painted rock shelters were first discovered in 1957–58 by an archaeologist, Dr. Vishnu Wakankar of Ujjain. Without being much aware of the paintings, the local villagers used to assemble on the hilltop for the annual Shivaratri fair in the month of March.

Features: The rock shelter complex of Bhimbetka exhibits the earliest pictorial traces of prehistoric man's life in the Indian Sub-Continent. It is a natural art gallery complex of prehistoric man and a land of archaeological treasures, serving as an invaluable historical chronicle since the Palaeolithic through the Mesolithic until early history. Bhimbetka rock shelter was also inhabited by Middle to Upper Palaeolithic man, as is evident from stone tools, and for its quantum and quality of rock paintings as well as for its surroundings still inhabited by primitive tribes who continue with Stone Age traditions, it was declared an important World Heritage Site by UNESCO in 2003.

The paintings at Bhimbetka are found on the walls, ceiling, and hollows in the shelters. They are made in red and white colours and less commonly in green, yellow, and black colours derived from minerals in the rocks and earth. According to Yasodhra Mathpal and Somnath Chakravarty, there are about 6214 rock art motifs in Bhimbetka, predominated by zoomorphs (animal art) and a combination of them with human figures (anthropomorphs). A series of hunting scenes of archers are remarkable in Bhimbetka, representing inter-group conflicts and probably clashes within the group as well. The paintings of the later period have human figures and designs in geometric patterns, as well as other ritualistic or religious symbols and conch shell inscriptions.

Subject matter:

- The subject matter of prehistoric art consists primarily of wild animals and hunting scenes. A great variety of animals are depicted, and these include deer, nilgai, wild buffalo, boar, rhino, tiger, etc. At some sites, such as Bhimbetka, fish is a common theme.
- There are paintings of dance scenes and horse-riding warriors with umbrella-like head gear, scenes of honey collection and fishing, hunting of the wild boar, etc.
- There are depictions of musical instruments such as horns, pipes, drums, and tom-toms. We can also notice palm prints, thumb impressions, hand stencils, and finger markings.
- On the whole, they bear similarities with the subsistence patterns of the surrounding contemporary marginal cultivators and food-gatherers.
- It is pointed out that in the earliest paintings, animals were shown alone, but gradually human figures came to be associated with them. The humans are mostly drawn in a conventional manner and are stick-shaped.

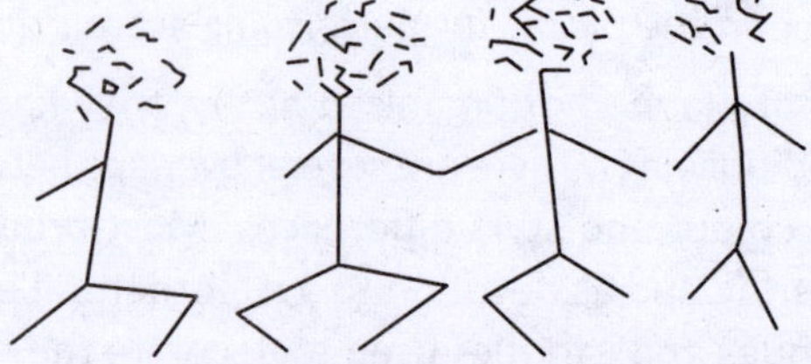

Walking Hand In Hand

Group Hunting Scene

It appears that mineral nodules were diluted with water and then mixed with animal fat, plant juice, or glue to make pigments. Paintings are basically monochromic and are drawn on natural rock surfaces without any preparation of the background, such as smoothing or plastering. Brushes made of twigs or animal hair was used.

Summing up, prehistoric rock art is a window to the minds of prehistoric humans and has helped a lot in understanding prehistoric humans.

Case Study

- **India hosted the youngest populations of 'Acheulean' human ancestors.**

The study, published in the journal Scientific Reports, shows the presence of Acheulean populations until about 177,000 years ago, shortly before the earliest expansions of Homo sapiens across Asia. The longest-lasting toolmaking tradition in prehistory, known as the Acheulean, was characterised by distinctive oval and pear-shaped stone handaxes and cleavers associated with Homo erectus and derived species such as Homo heidelbergensis.

This supports evidence from across the region indicating that India hosted the youngest populations using Acheulean toolkits across the world.

- **Palaeolithic cave paintings found in a corner of the NCR could be among the oldest.**

In a mountainous and wooded area of Haryana, archaeologists have found cave paintings that they believe date back to the Upper Palaeolithic, making them possibly the earliest cave artworks in the nation. The team came across cave paintings that included depictions of people, animals, plants, and geometric shapes. Some of the paintings have faded with time, while others are still clearly visible. Additionally, it came across open-air ritual sites and rock art. The bulk of them are on the ceilings of the rock shelters, although some can be seen in the open. According to Bhattacharyya, the age of the Mangar cave art is between 20,000 and 40,000 years old, although this may be verified through archaeological dating. Additionally, experts compare the cave art to other cave art and art from other digs using qualitative approaches.

- **A fossil of the earth's oldest-known mammal, Dickinsonia, was found in Madhya Pradesh.**

On the roof of the Bhimbetka Rock Shelters, three fossils of the 550-million-year-old "Dickinsonia," the earliest known living creature, have just been found. It provides more evidence for similar paleoenvironments and supports the idea that Gondwanaland was assembled around 550 Ma.

- **Prehistoric rock paintings were found in Telangana; history enthusiasts believe they date back 10k–30k years.**

The members of Kotha Telangana Charitha Brundam found the Mesolithic-era rock art site, which is situated on a small hillock on private land. They afterwards confirmed and cross-checked the paintings with academic publications and published books. The rock paintings were uncovered for the first time in the area, according to archaeologist Dr. E. Shivanagi Reddy. The list of Telangana rock art sites will now include a new location.

These rock-art locations provide the earliest records of hunter-gatherer experiences in human history.

Information dissemination for the future was the goal. This persisted from the Mesolithic epoch through the Neolithic and Iron Ages.

- **Two human skeletons from the Indus Valley era were found in Rakhigarhi**

The results of a scientific analysis of DNA samples taken from two human bones found at a Harappanera city site in Haryana may reveal information about the ancestry and dietary habits of people who lived in the Rakhigarhi region thousands of years ago. At mound number 7, which the Archaeological Survey of India has dubbed RGR 7, the remains of two women were discovered. This mound is thought to be close to 5,000 years old. As part of Harappan Civilization's grave practises, pots and other artefacts were also discovered buried nearby in a pit, according to ASI authorities.

- **Discovery of a new archaeological site in Haryana's Sandhai village and a brief look at the Harappan site of Bhirrana**

A few days ago, news outlets reported the discovery of a 1,600-year-old archaeological site in the Yamunanagar region of Haryana, close to the Sandhai hamlet, that had connections to prehistoric settlements along the Saraswati river. According to reports, archaeologists have discovered "continued habitation" evidence and what appears to be a temple site at a location that stood on the Saraswati river's banks during the ancient and early mediaeval eras.

The State of Haryana as the Cradle of India's Civilization:

One such location is Bhirrana, or Birhana, a small village located along the seasonal Ghaggar (Saraswati) river's channels in Fatehabaḍ District, Haryana. According to estimates, the Bhirrana site, which dates from 7570 to 6200 BCE, is the oldest Saraswati-Indus Valley Civilization site. Pottery, textiles, copper tools, arrowheads, spearheads, beads made of steatite, faience, terracotta, and shell, bracelets made of copper and terracotta, and other artefacts were discovered at this site. Wheat and barley grains that had been burned were also found in the sediments. The most intriguing discovery at this location is a graffiti-engraved female dancing girl that is a replica of the renowned "Dancing Girl" from Mohenjo-daro. Samples taken from the earliest levels at the Bhirrana site had C14 dates determined in the Birbal Sahni Institute of Paleobotany (Dikshit & Mani 2012), which led to the creation of a new chronology for Bhirrana:

- Period I (Pre-Harappan): 7500–6000 BCE
- Period IIA (Early Harappan): 6000–4500 BCE
- Period IIB (Late Early Harappan): 4500–3000 BCE
- Period III (Mature Harappan): 3000–1800 BCE

The Chalcolithic site of Bhirrana in Haryana, next to the Saraswati River (today known as the Ghaggar River), was reclassified by this new chronology as being contemporaneous with or even earlier than the Neolithic Mehrgarh site in Pakistan. When comparing the two sites, Bhirrana exhibits a more pronounced cultural continuity from the earliest to the mature Harappan age than Mehrgarh (Dr. B.R. Mani).

- **A New Study Suggests Indus Valley People Spoke Ancestral Dravidian Language**

According to a study that appeared in the journal Nature, the IVC may have had a sizable Dravidian-speaking population. the term for "elephant" used by people of the Indus Valley Civilization (IVC) and in bronze-age Mesopotamia. The languages used in the area where the IVC is located today are divided into different groups. These languages include Iranian Baluchi, Dari, Pashto, and Wakhi; Indo-Aryan languages including Punjabi, Sindhi, Hindi, Marwari, and Gujarati; Dardic Shina, Khowar, and Kohistani; Nuristani in northeastern Afghanistan; and Dravidian Brahui.

In his study, Mukhopadhyay claims that the words for "elephant" ('pri', 'pru') in bronze age Mesopotamia and the word for "ivory" ('pîru') recorded in Old Persian documents dating to the sixth century BC were originally borrowed from 'plu,' the Proto-Dravidian word for "elephant.

1.2

Palaeo Anthropological Evidences from India with special reference to Siwaliks and Narmada basin (Ramapithecus, Sivapithecus and Narmada Man).

Q 1. Sivapithecus

Ans. Sivapithecus is best known from later Miocene deposits in Greece, Turkey, and Indo-Pakistan.

Included with it is another group of fossils called Ramapithecus, once thought to be distinct but now recognised as belonging to the same group.

The name Sivapithecus has priority over Ramapithecus because it was established in the scientific literature first, so this is the name used. Their names were derived from the Indian gods Rama and Siva, as the first fossils of this group were found in India.

Time Period: The earliest Sivapithecus remains found so far are about 17 million years old, and the most recent are about 8 million years old.

Geographical distribution:

1. The first fossils of this group were found in India, but the most significant recent finds have come from Pakistan and Turkey.
2. From the latter, there is a very large collection dating back as far as 13 million years, which provides both the earliest record of hominoids living outside Africa and the first record of Sivapithecus.

Geographical distribution in the Indian Subcontinent:

1. The Sivapithecus specimens are identified from four regions in the Siwalik hills:
   a. Potwar plateau of Pakistan
   b. Ramnagar in India
   c. Hari Talyanagar in India
   d. Churia in Nepal
2. Most Potwar plateau specimens come from three precisely dated intervals separated by temporal gaps of approximately 0.7 to 1.0 million years ago.
3. As far as the Siwalik group of India is concerned, most specimens are found at Hari Talyanagar and a few near Ramnagar.

Characteristic features:

1. Sivapithecus shares with the orang-utan several features of the skull and face that are almost certainly derived from Hominoidea, some of which are uniquely shared to the exclusion of all other simian primates. These include:
   a. Concave face
   b. Absence of bony sinus in the brow area of the skull
   c. Narrow bony partition between eyes
   d. Vertically elongated orbits
   e. Smooth nasal floor
   f. Enlarged central incisors
2. The forelimbs of Sivapithecus are monkey-like, implying quadrupedal walking and climbing.

Species: Currently, three species are generally recognised:

1. **Sivapithecus Indicus:** Date from 12.5 million to 10.5 million years ago.
2. **Sivapithecus Sivalensis:** dates from 9.5 million to 8.5 million years ago.
3. **Sivapithecus Parvada:** dates to 10 million years ago.

Phylogenetic Status:

1. The fossil remains discovered in Europe and Asia suggests that Drypoithecus gave rise to at least three genera between 10 and 15 million years ago.
2. These three genera are Sivapithecus, Gigantopithecus, and Ramapithecus.
3. The first two genera have large faces, as large as those of modern chimpanzees and gorillas. However, Ramapithecus had a small face, which shows similarities to later hominids.
4. Simons and Pilbeam reviewed fossil discoveries in 1965 and suggested that all varied forms of fossil remains actually belong to only two species. They indicated Sivapithecus as one species form, which was basically apelike, and thus it can be considered an ape ancestor, and Ramapithecus, which possesses a number of hominid characters and is thus regarded as an early hominid ancestor.

5. Simons & Pilbeam and Andrews and Cronin in 1982 suggested that the two forms, Sivapithecus and Ramapithecus, are actually one single species group with the males and females of a sexually dimorphic species group.
6. The discoveries from Yunnan strongly suggest that the two species evolved there. One of the major pieces of evidence from Yunnan is a large creature with larger dental features, sexual dimorphism, large canine dimorphism, and height.
7. Comparatively, the other creature is smaller and possesses smaller dental features, is sexually dimorphic, has smaller canine dimorphism, has large canine heights, and has areas with more omnivorous dentition. Thus, it is assumed that we would not deny that it is an adaptive radiation of pre-human form.

Relationship with Orangutans:

1. Recent finds of Sivapithecus (including Ramapithecus) provide strong evidence for shared ancestry with orangutans.
2. This relationship is indicated by many characters of the face, nose, and palate that are uniquely shared by orangutans and Sivapithecus while absent in other primates.
3. According to *Andrews & Stringer*, it was previously thought that Ramapithecus was an early hominid, ancestral to humans, but since the orangutan shares ancestors with this group, it is only distantly related to humans.

Such findings, especially in India, have given a great impetus to the palaeontology of India and put India on the world map of prehistory.

Q 2. Ramapithecus

Ans. Ramapithecus is the great ape of India.

Location: Shiwalik Hills, Fort Ternan, Kenya, Greece, Turkey, Hungry, etc.

Associated with humans:

1. Lewis (1934): Based on dental and jaw remains, he considered it a human ancestor.
2. Supported by Leaky (remains from Fort Ternam, Kenya)
   a. Reason for support: Simons: Reduced canines of Ramapithecus could have been a substitute for the use of tools.
3. It was believed that Ramapithecus diverged from the common ape human line some 14–12 mya ago and was in the direct lineage of human ancestry.
4. Further research by Pilbeam: more fossils recovered Ramapithecus-Miocene radiation complex of Dryopithecus leading to orang-utan

Criticism:

1. More fossils were recovered; Ramapithecus had more non-hominid traits and more similarity to orang-utans.
2. Wilson and Sarich's albumin analysis demonstrates that the human-ape split occurred 8–6 million years ago instead of 14–12 million years ago.

Present status:

1. Palaeontologists today lump Ramapithecus and Sivapithecus together.
2. Ramapithecus is considered to be the female counterpart of Sivapithecus.

Ramapithecus vs. Sivapithecus:

1. The teeth of Ramapithecus and Sivapithecus are difficult to distinguish when in isolated form, except on the basis of size.
2. The front teeth, especially the upper central incisors of Sivapithecus, are often quite large, while the canine is fairly good-sized.
3. The most distinctive aspect of Sivapithecus dentition is seen in the back tooth row, where molars are large, flatwearing, and thickly enamelled. The facial remains of some of them have concave profiles and projecting incisors.
4. However, the Ramapithecus teeth are smaller and show less canine dimorphism than Sivapithecus, though they are larger than the Pliocene hominid Australopithecus afarensis.
5. Sivapithecus was slightly larger than Ramapithecus; it was only a small-to-medium-sized ape about the size of a modern chimpanzee.

Q 3. Narmada Man

Ans. Narmada man, or Homo erectus narmadensis, is a sub-species of the extinct Homo erectus.

Discovery: In 1982, Dr. Arun Sonakia found fossilised calvaria (skull cap) in Hathnora village in the Narmada valley of Madhya Pradesh. It was named Narmada Man. In 1997, the discovery of a right clavicle in the same region was announced. Dr. A.R. Sankhyan described it as being a part of the Narmada man.

Time span: It has been dated to be at least 400,000 years old, thus belonging to the Lower Palaeolithic period.

Physical Features:

1. Cranial Capacity: Within the span of H. sapiens, it is estimated to be between 1150 and 1400 c.c.
2. Post-cranial anatomy: According to *Dr. Sankhyan*, the clavicle should belong to a 25–30-year-old female who is the size of a stocky adult pygmy.

Cultural Features: Along with other stone tools, primarily handaxes and cleavers typical of Acheulian civilization, the fossil was discovered. This suggests routine toolmaking. The discovery of numerous broken animal bones nearby indicates that the Narmada man was a hunter.

Phylogenetic Status:

➢ Due to its connection to the Lower Palaeolithic culture, Dr. Sonakia identified it as H. erectus narmadensis.

➢ Due to its large cranium, Dr. Marie-Antoinette de Lumley classified it as an "evolved H. erectus." It is also allegedly a part of the prehistoric H. sapiens, according to certain archaeologists. Recently, many have favoured it as H. heidelbergenesis.

Evolutionary Significance:

➢ The sole known skeleton remains of a human being from the Lower Palaeolithic of the Indian subcontinent are those of Narmada Man.

➢ Dr. Sankhyan (2017) said that it is possible to hypothesise that the Narmada valley included common progenitors of the Holocene shortbodied populations of the Indian mainland, including the pygmies, based on the discovery of the Narmada man.

The 'Out of Africa' theory, which depicts that modern humans originated in South Asia, is in agreement with this fin ding, which is also backed by recent genetic investigations.

1.3

Ethno-archaeology in India: The concept of ethno-archaeology; Survivals and Parallels among the hunting, foraging, fishing, pastoral and peasant communities including arts and crafts producing communities.

Q 1. The concept of Ethno-Archaeology

Ans. According to *Stanislawski*, ethnoarchaeology means the direct observation field study of the form, manufacture, distribution, and use of artefacts and their institutional setting and social units among living, now industrial people for the purpose of constructing models to aid archaeology analogy.

Orme defined it as the study of a living community from the point of view of archaeology evidence to link behaviour and material results.

- Ethnoarchaeology is a recent development in the field of archaeology. Archaeologists study the material remains like tools, weapons, and other artefacts left behind by prehistoric people, but earlier they faced a problem interpreting the use and functioning of such material remains. Therefore, they developed a new methodology known as ethnoarchaeology.
- Ethnoarchaeology combines both ethnography and archaeology because the archaeologists themselves conduct ethnographic studies of various ethnic groups in order to create analogies between the life activities of the contemporary ethnic groups and those of pre-historic societies.
- Ethnoarchaeology employed Induct historical methods by which the activities of present ethnic groups are observed to reconstruct the life activities of contemporary ethnic groups and pre-historic societies. Ethnoarchaeology enriches our knowledge by analysing the contemporary ethnic groups to see how the people of prehistoric times made their tools and what their functions were. Similar is the case with other life activities.
- When Spencer and Gillin visited the Australian aboriginal (indigenous tribes), they observed that Australian tribes made paintings of animals hunted by them, which is a ritual among them. This ritualistic significance of rock art became possible due to ethnic reality, i.e., they interpreted from this ethnic reality that people during pre-historic times might have been creating paintings of animals for the same purpose. They put forth the interpretative model of activity reconstruction and the concept of possibilism.
- Ethnoarchaeology also depends on projected reality (imaginative reality) rather than empirical reality (factual reality).
- The real foundation of ethnoarchaeology was laid by Lowie Robert Binford and his wife Shelly Binford, who used archaeology from an anthropological point of view when they studied the Eskimo's scattering of bones in their campus area.
- Afterwards, Richard Lee studied Bushman of Kalahari desert (!Kung) and found that their belongings were very scanty due to their frequent nomadism, and from this, he interpreted the activity reconstruction of Palaeolithic people, who also had a few belongings due to their frequent nomadism.

Methods:

1. Logical Positivism
2. Quantitative data analysis
3. Interpretative Analysis
4. Hypothetico-deductive model
5. Catchment area analysis
6. Site formation analysis

Type of analogy:

1. Direct historical method: based on continuity from prehistoric to ethnographic.
2. General Comparative Method: Based on correlation between artefacts and behaviours associated with them on a cross-cultural basis.

As far as India is concerned, at Tekkalakota, we discovered circular huts of 3 m in diameter from the Neolithic Period. Now it is a question of how one would sleep in such a small hut. But when a contemporary ethnic group, the Chenchus, was studied, we got the answer to this question. Chenchus also construct circular huts of 3 m diameter. They never sleep within these huts; they sleep outside and only cook food within the huts, i.e., huts are not sleeping areas but areas for cooking and storing other objects. From this observation, ethnoarchaeologists conclude that the Neolithic circular huts had the same function.

Tool-making techniques of Lower Palaeolithic culture, like percussion techniques and hammer techniques, are interpreted with the help of contemporary society's knowledge.

Ethnoarchaeology also reflects the significance of symbiotic relationships that prevailed between various human groups during the later Neolithic and Chalcolithic periods, due to which civilization emerged. Summing up, we can say that ethnoarchaeology tries to interpret the activities of pre-historic societies by studying contemporary groups through the Activity Reconstruction Methodology and through analogies.

Criticism:

1. Projected reality and not empirical reality.
2. Choosing an analogy is subjective and different for different cultures, like the Palaeolithic and Neolithic.

Q 2. Survivals And parallels among the hunting, foraging, fishing, pastoral and peasant communities including art and crafts producing communities

Ans. The importance of knowledge of contemporary societies to interpret pre-historic and proto-historic societies is the main tenant of ethnoarchaeology. Since the 1960s, it has been in circulation as a methodology to interpret the material and non-material cultures of pre-historic and proto-historic societies by analysing the material and nonmaterial cultures of contemporary ethnic groups. For ethnoarchaeologists, India is a prime source of study because of its cultural diversity, subsistence and settlement strategies, and persistence of many traditions, including traditional arts and crafts.

Ethnoarchaeologists observed many contemporary hunting and gathering tribes, fishing, pastoral, and peasant communities, including art and craft-producing communities in India. To assess their archaeological importance, various types of studies are conducted by Murthy, Raja, Nagaraja, Saraswati, Roy and Prasad, Jaiswal, Roud, etc.

Murty, Raja Nagaraja Rao, minutely observed the hunting and gathering tribes of India, particularly those of South India like the Chenchus, Kurumbas, Irulas, etc. Different tribes are studied to judge their subsistence resources, mobility patterns, technology, and settlement.

The natural environment in which these tribes live now is different from the natural environment of Palaeolithic hunters and gatherers because the latter had a wider area to search for resources, hunt large animals, and consume a variety of plants, but now, due to the expansion of habitation areas and consequent deforestation, the contemporary hunting and gathering communities depend upon certain different types of plants and animals. Thus, they demonstrate the slightest survival and parallels with regard to subsistence resources, but like Palaeolithic hunters and gatherers, they are still nomads and use many implements.

Similar to those used by Palaeolithic hunters and gatherers. Hunters and gatherers also have different sociocultural setups now because they have maintained symbiotic relationships with other surrounding communities for the lack of many essential goods. But such symbiotic relationships didn't exist during Palaeolithic times.

Saraswati studied a number of fishing communities in Maharashtra, Kerala, Tamil Nadu, and the Northeast region. He found that the number of fish hooks used by them is similar to those bone-fish hooks discovered from Langhnaj, Burzahom, Gufkral, Birbhanpur, Sanganakallu, Tekkalakota, etc., which reflect the survivals and parallels of the Mesolithic and Neolithic periods. From Tekkalkotta, many circular huts of 3 m diameter are discovered. Presently, similar types of huts have been discovered among the Chenchus, which they use to cook food and store other materials. They never sleep inside these huts. In a similar manner, the Neolithic people of Tekkalkotle would have used these huts for similar purposes.

Roy and Prasad studied many pastoral communities both in North and South India and found that communities like Todas in the Nilgiri Hills have symbiotic relations with other communities, and perhaps the same type of symbiotic relationships prevailed between pastoral communities of the Mesolithic and Neolithic periods with others, indicating that during these periods there was the emergence of social division on the basis of occupation.

Jaswal studied the peasant communities, particularly shifting cultivators, of the N-Eastern Region in Assam and the Garo Hills. He found that these communities used axes and hoes in cultivation, although their axes and hoes were of metal. However, they exhibited many similarities in size and shape with stone axes and hoes of the Neolithic period. Their peasant communities also polished their metal axes in the same manner as Neolithic people polished their stone axes. By observing the cultivation patterns of these contemporary ethnic groups, the ethnoarchaeologist interpreted the cultivation patterns of the Neolithic period and revealed that perhaps Neolithic people also sowed the seeds just before the onset of the rainy season. This cropping pattern reflects survival and parallelism.

Jaswal also studied certain craft-producing communities in North India, like potters, metal casters, weavers, etc. He claimed that these craft-producing communities are descendents of pre-historic and proto-historic potters.

Roud studied a number of potter communities in New Delhi and found that the techniques and decorative patterns that they used in their pots were similar to those of pre-Harappan and Harappan times. Like Harappans, they also used red and black colours to decorate a number of decorative pots like vases, perforated jairs, etc.

Nagaraja Rao studied a pottery community in Pattnam, and the pots made by them reflect similarities with Neolithic and Harappan pots. By observing the techniques used by these communities to make the pottery, he concluded that similar techniques were used by the Neolithic and Harappans to make their pottery and claimed that pottery reflected the survival and parallels of craft production.

As far as art is concerned, many ethnic groups make a number of art forms on rocks (rock art), pottery, gates, ceilings, and walls of their houses that have similarities with the ancient art forms. From the above discussion, it becomes clear that India has rich data for ethnoarchaeology to interpret the ancient past by observing the survivals and parallels of contemporary ethnic groups.

2

Demographic Profile of India

Demographic Profile of India—Ethnic and linguistic elements in the Indian population and their distribution. Indian population—factors influencing its structure and growth.

Q 1. Linguistic elements in Indian population

Ans. G.A. Grierson contributed a lot to analysing the linguistic diversity in India. It was due to his efforts that the Linguistic Survey of India (LSI) was set up in 1898, and he was appointed the first superintendent of this survey. The LSI conducted many surveys regarding the languages spoken in India.

On the basis of this survey, Grierson wrote a book entitled "Linguistic Survey in India," in which he mentioned that 179 major languages are spoken here. But now more than 200 languages are spoken in India. Out of these, 23 are spoken by 97% of the total population, and among these, 22 are in the 8th schedule. India is known for the variety of languages spoken by different human groups.

The languages spoken in India are classified into four families:

A. Indo-Aryan Family: 73%
B. Dravidian Family: 25%
C. Austro Family: 1.3%
D. Sino-Tibetan Family: 0.7%

1. **Indo-Aryan Family:** The languages of this family are spoken by the majority in India. Hindi is the main language of this family, which is spoken in UP, Bihar, MP, Rajasthan, Haryana, HP, J&K, Delhi, etc. Urdu is another language of this family that is spoken in addition to Hindi in the above region; Urdu is also spoken in J&K along with Dogri and Kashmiri. Punjabi is another language of this family, which is mostly spoken in Punjab but also in parts of J&K or Delhi. Gujarati and Sindhi are other languages of this family that are spoken in Gujarat. Rajasthani, which is spoken in Rajasthan, is also a member of this family. Bhojpuri, which is mostly spoken in Bihar and also in UP and MP, is also part of this family. Another language of this family is Marathi, which is spoken in Maharashtra. Konkani, which is spoken in Goa, is also part of the Indo-Aryan family. Some other languages of this family are Assamese, Bengali, and Oriya, which are spoken in Assam, West Bengal, and Odisha, respectively. Sanskrit is one of the prime languages of this family, but it is not spoken exclusively in any part of the country, and this language is only used while performing religious rituals.
2. **Dravidian family:** The languages of the Dravidian family are spoken in South India, some parts of Central India, and the Chotanagpur region. Tamil, which is considered the oldest classical language and is spoken in Tamil Nadu, is one of the prime languages of this family. Telugu, which is spoken in Andhra Pradesh and Telangana, also belongs to this family group. Kannada and Tulu, which are spoken in Karnataka, are also part of this family group. Malayalam, which is spoken in Kerela, is

also part of the Dravidian family. Other languages of this family are Gondi and Oraoni, which are spoken among Gonds of Central India and Oraon of the Chotanagpur region, respectively. Another language of this family is Kurukh, which is spoken by mainly tribal groups in Jharkhand and Assam.

3. **Austro-Asiatic Family:** The languages of this family are spoken in Jaintia and the Khasi hills of Meghalaya, in Nicobar, in Santhal Pargana, Jharkhand, etc. The most significant language of this family is Khasi, which is spoken in Jaintia and the Khasi hills of Meghalaya. Mon-Khmer, which is spoken by Khasi, is another language of this family. Nicobari, which is spoken on Nicobar Island, also belongs to this family group. Other languages of this family are Santhali, Jharkhandi, and Mundari, which are mostly spoken in the Chotanagpur region.
4. **Sino-Tibetan Family:** The languages of this family are spoken in the north-eastern Himalayan and subhimalayan regions of India. Two major languages of this family are Ladakhi and Balti, which are spoken in the Ladakh region of J&K. Kinnauri and Lahauli are other languages of this family that are spoken in Kinnaur and the Lahul Spiti region of H.P. Kushar and Mizo, which are spoken in Mizoram, are also part of this family group. Meithei and Manipuri, which are spoken in Manipur, are also members of this family group. Khamti, spoken in Assam and also in Arunachal Pradesh in addition to Arunachali, is also a member of this family. The Naga language spoken in Nagaland is also part of this family. Two other languages of this family are Andamanese and Garo, spoken on Andaman Island and in the Garo Hills of Meghalaya, respectively.

Importance of Linguistic Diversity: The Yuelu proclamation made by UNESCO in 2018 in China says that protection and promotion of linguistic diversity help to improve social inclusion and partnerships, reduce gender and social inequality between different native speakers, enhance social inclusion, and protect intangible cultural heritage.

Language and Social Context: India's languages reflect intricate levels of social hierarchy and caste. Individuals, in their speech, speak a variety of styles appropriate to social situations. In general, the higher the speaker's status, the more speech focus is at his disposal. Speech thereby reflects social contest and the standing of speakers.

Disadvantage of Linguistic Diversity:

1. Regionalism: Hindi and non-Hindi conflict
2. Secessionism: Southern States, Nagaland
3. Conflict on a linguistic basis: Maharashtra and Karnataka border dispute
4. More importance given to linguistic identity is harmful for national unity.

However, largely, it has acted as a uniting and integrative face of national identity alongside the growth of common languages like Persia, English, Hindustani, and Sanskrit, which acted as bridges between different groups in time and space.

Case Study

- **The 8th Schedule's inclusion of Tulu and other tribal languages**

There are approximately 18,46,427 native speakers of the Dravidian language Tulu in Karnataka and Kerela.
They outnumber Manipuri and Sanskrit (8th schedule) speakers combined in size.
Having the eighth schedule in place would help you gain Sahitya Academic Accreditation.
Members will write the All India Service exam in Tulu and speak it in the legislative and state legislatures.
It will assist in bringing about the equality of opportunity and position outlined in the preamble.
Like other tribal languages, Bhili has 1,043,13,637 speakers, Gondi has 29,84,453 speakers, and Garo has 11,45,323 speakers.
The same is true for Ho, Khasi, Oraon, and Khandhesi.

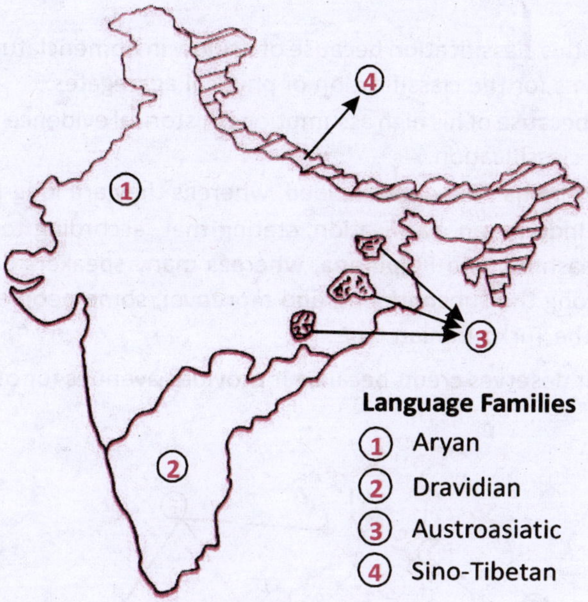

Linguistic Classification of India

Q 2. Ethnic elements in Indian population by Risley

Ans. The paucity of skeletal remains in historic times is the main reason for the gap in knowledge about racial history. Herbert Hope Risley was the first scholar to attempt racial classification. Risley was a British ethnographer. In 1890, he attempted racial classification in India and conducted studies on the basis of anthropomorphic technique. He published a report in 1915 in "The People of India". Risley classified the Indian population into seven racial types:

Risley Classification:

Character	TurkoIr-anian	Indo-Aryan	Scythio Dravidian	Aryo Dravidian	Mongolo Dravidianan	Mongoli	Dravidian
Head	Round and Broad	Long	Medium to Broad	Long with tendency toward medium	Broad	Broad	Long
Nose	Long & moderately narrow	Narrow & long	Medium	Medium to broad	Medium with broad tendency	Fine to broad	Broad
Eyes	Occasionally grey but mostly dark	Dark	Brown	Dark brown	Light brown	Epicanthic fold	Dark
Skin colour	Fair	Fair	Fair	Light brown to dark	Dark	Dark with yellow is tinge	Dark
Stature	Above average	Tall	Medium	Below average sometime	Medium with short	Below average	Short
Hair	Abundant on face	Abundant facial	Scanty	Medium	Plentiful	Scanty	Curly
Represen-ted by	Baluchs & Afghans	Rajput, Rajasthan Punjab, Kashmir	Gujarat & Coorg	UP, Bihar, Ceylon	Lower Bengal & Odisha	Assam, Nepal, Burma	Ceylon to Ganges covering whole South-Eastern India

Criticism:

1. Max Muller criticised this classification because of its flow in nomenclature, where Risley persisted in using linguistic terms for the classification of physical aggregates.
2. Others criticised him because of his high assumptions; historical evidence is scanty, and arithmetical errors are high in his classification.
3. Risley classified Turko-Iranian as round-headed, whereas they are long-headed.
4. S.N. Dutta criticised Indo-Aryan clarification, stating that, according to Risley, the Turko-Iranian group is in Punjab, Kashmir, and Rajputana, whereas many speakers of the Aryan language are widely distributed along the subcontinent, and moreover, some people in the Kashmir valley do resemble people of the Turko-Iranian type.

In spite of criticism, it deserves credit because it provides avenues for other scholars to study the racial element in India.

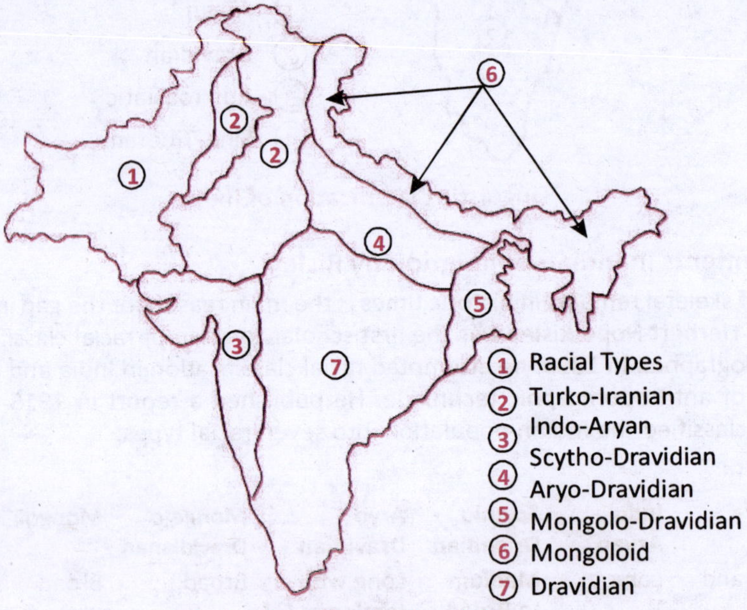

Ethnic Classification by Risley

Q 3. Ethnic elements in Indian population by Guha

Ans. B.S. Guha classified the Indian population based on his investigation during 1930–33. It is an acceptable, recognised, and sound scientific study. Guha listed six main races with nine subtypes:

1. **Negrito:** It constitutes the earliest racial element of India. Negrito of the Indian subcontinent belongs to Negroid Stock, which is found in Africa, Melanesia, Australia, etc. Negrito racial strains are found among types of Rajmahal Hills, Kadars, Irulas, and Paniyans in South India.

   Features:
   - Head - Long, medium or broad
   - Lips - Everted and thick
   - Skin - Dark colour
   - Stature - Short

2. **Proto Australoid:** It forms second oldest racial element in subcontinent. True representatives are Bhils, Kols of Central and Western India, Chenchus, Bagadas and Yeruvas of South India; Oraons, Santhal and Mundas of Chotanagpur.

Features:

- Head - Long
- Skin - Dark brown to black
- Hair - Wavy & curly
- Nose - Broad & flat
- Stature - Short

3. **Mongoloid:** Northeast acted as gateway for them to enter India. Features are epicanthic fold, scanty facial & body hair.

Features	Palaeo (Long Headed)	Palaeo (Broad headed)	Tibeto Mongoloid
Skin/Eye/ Stature	Dark to brown skin, Not prominent epicanthic fold	Short to medium stature Prominent epicanthic fold	Tall stature
Represented by	Burma frontier, Assam and sub Himalayan region	Chakmas of Chittagong hill	Lepchas of Calimpong

4. **Mediterranean:**

Character	Palaeo	Mediterranean	Oriental
Nose	Small and borad	Narrow	Long and convex
Hair	Scanty facial	Plenty Facial	Medium
Skin colour	Dark complexion	Dark to olive complexion	Brown
Represented by	Tamil Brahmin, Nairs and Telegu Brahmin of South India	Namboodiri Brahmin, Brahmin of Allahabad and Bengal, Maratha ladies of Indore	Bania of Rajputana and Chettris of Punjab

5. **Western Brachycephals:**

Features	Alpinoids	Dinaric	Armenoid
Stature	Medium	Tall	Short
Nose	Prominent	Long and convex	Narrow and aquiline
Skin	Light	Dark	Tawny white
Represented by	Bania of Gujarat and kayastha of Bengal	Coorgs, Bengal Brahmin, Kanarese Brahmin of Mysore	Parsis of Bombay

6. **Nordics:** Entered India through now from central & Turkey Scattered all over India, especially now region prominently among Red Kaffirs, Khalash of Rampur and Pathan of Bijapur.

Features:

- Head - Long
- Nose - Straight that is high bridged
- Eyes - Blue or grey
- Complexion - Reddish white

Criticism:

1. Guha was opposed because he showed the foreign origins of many Indian races. He did not believe in the evolution of many races in India.
2. Undue importance to the Negrito element in India. Primitive tribes lack the predominance of the B -blood group, which is found in Negrito. Protoaustroloids are the ones most accepted as the oldest known element in India.

However, Guha's classification is widely accepted for understanding ethnic elements in the Indian population.

Among the conclusions, the most important is that brachycephals (broad head) dominate the Indian population, which has received the maximum approval of scholars in this field.

India is a melting pot of races (Majumdar). Racial tribes in India cannot be put under any type or category.

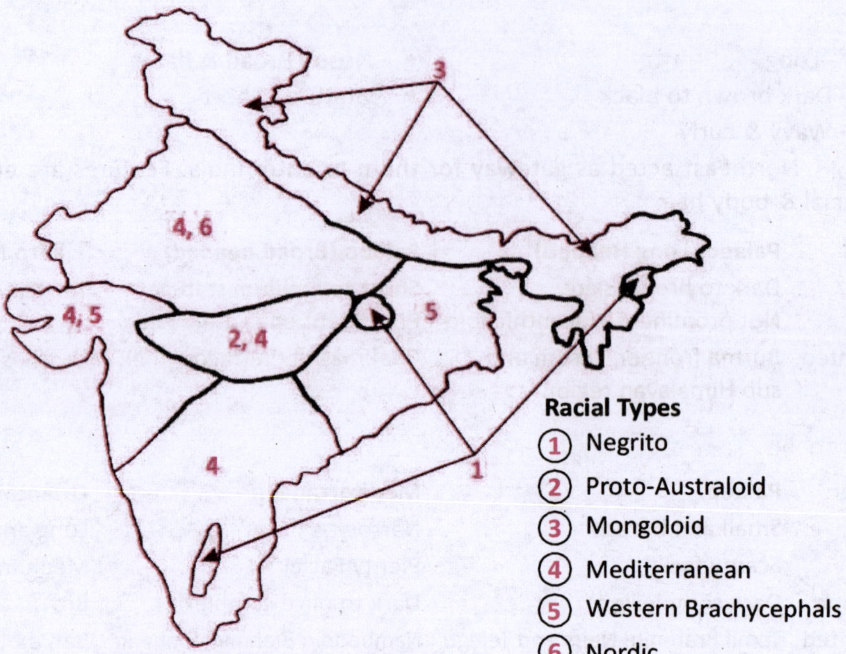

Ethnic Classification by Guha

Q 4. Indian population—factors influencing its structure and growth

Ans. The Indian population is around 1.21 billion, according to the 2011 Census. The population growth rate in India has been slowing in recent decades, from an annual growth rate of 2.2% in 1971 –81 to 1.6% in 2011 –16. Slowdown is visible even in high population growth states like UP and Bihar, while population growth is below 1% in southern states like WB, Punjab, HP, and Maharashtra.

Factors influencing its structure and growth in India:

1. **Decline in the mortality rate**
   a. Elimination of famines
   b. Control of epidemics E.g., small pox, cholera, TB, malaria, chicken pox
   c. Better sanitation and hygiene; supply of pure drinking water
2. **High Birth Rate**
   a. **Economic**
      i. Predominance of agriculture: intensive agriculture, high labour demand (40–50% population in the agri-sector)
      ii. Slow urbanisation and the dominance of villages (Around 69% of villages, 2011 Census)
      iii. Poverty: labour is viewed as a valuable economic asset. According to the 2011 census, 21% of the population lives below the poverty line.
   b. **Social**
      i. Near universality of marriage
      ii. Lower marriage age
      iii. Religious and social superstitions e.g., the demand of a male child
      iv. Joint family system
      v. Lack of education: use of contraceptives increases with increasing education.

3. **National population policy:**
   a. Reduce the IMR to below 30 per 1,000 births.
   b. Reduce MMR to below 100 per 10,000 births.
   c. Achieve universal immunisation.
   d. Achieve 80% institutional delivery.
   e. 100% registration of birth, death, marriage, and pregnancy

Consequences of overpopulation:

1. Low per capita income
2. Inadequate food production
3. Growing unemployment and underemployment
4. Low standard of living, education, medical, and housing facilities
5. Low level of capital formation
6. Environmental degradation

Remedies for Population Explosion:

1. **Economic Measures**
   a. Expansion of the industrial sector
   b. Creation of employment opportunities in urban and rural areas
   c. Equitable distribution of income and removal of poverty
2. **Social Measure**
   a. Improving status and education among women.
   b. Raising the minimum marriage age
   c. Addressing religious superstitions
3. **Family planning programme**
   a. National population policy, 2000: achieve TFR 2.1 (2025); stable population by 2045
   b. Prenatal Diagnostic Technique Act, 1994

Anthropological help to control population: Morris Opler, in a paper named 'Cultural context and population control programme in villages in India, 'talked about population control. Kinslay Davis has talked about intercourse variables to reduce population growth.

The population explosion is a multidimensional concept that needs to be included in a multidimensional approach.

- **Vital Stats: National Family Health Survey 5**

In this note, we look at the findings for the 17 states on indicators related to: (i) population, (ii) health and nutrition, (iii) access to infrastructure, and (iv) gender.

1. **Population:** The usage of family planning techniques has increased across the board, with the exception of Mizoram. The two states with the biggest increases in the usage of family planning techniques are Goa (42% point) and Bihar (32% point). The total fertility rate (TFR) has consequently decreased in the majority of states. In NFHS-5, Bihar's TFR dropped from 3.4 to 3. A TFR below the replacement level rate of 2.1 is present in all other medium and large states in the survey (i.e., those with a population of more than 1 crore). For seven (of the 17) states, the sex ratio at birth for infants born within the previous five years is less than 950. The number of female births per 1,000 male births is known as the sex ratio at birth. The ratio in three states is less than 900 (Goa: 838; Himachal Pradesh: 875; Telangana: 894). Seven states have seen a decrease in the ratio. Goa (from 966 to 838) and Kerala (from 1,047 to 951) saw the largest drops. The highest sex ratio at birth is 1,028 in just Tripura.

2. **Health and Nutrition:** Over 90% of births over the previous five years occurred in institutions in seven states. In Kerala, institutional births accounted for almost all births. In Nagaland, institutional births accounted for just 46% of all births. In eight of the 17 states, the average out-of-pocket cost for a delivery at a public health facility increased. Be aware that in West Bengal, institutional births grew from 75% to 92%, although the average cost of deliveries decreased by Rs 5,236 per delivery (66% of the cost in 2015-16). While infant mortality rates have decreased nationwide, childhood malnutrition is on the rise. IMR has essentially decreased in every state. One of the biggest reductions in IMR was noticed in Assam, decreasing from 48 to 32 deaths per 1,000 live births. The IMR (deaths per 1,000 live births) is still high in Bihar. The nutritional status of kids under the age of five is, nevertheless, getting poorer. In 11 of the 17 states, the prevalence of stunting or chronic malnutrition—defined as a low height relative to age—has grown. In 13 of the 17 states, the percentage of severely wasted children has grown. In 11 of the 17 states, the percentage of kids who are underweight has gone up (low weight for age). At least 40% of children under the age of five in Gujarat and Bihar are underweight. The prevalence of obesity is increasing for both men and women nationwide. The ratio of males to females between the ages of 15 and 49 who are overweight or obese has increased across nearly all states (except Gujarat and Maharashtra). In Andhra Pradesh, Goa, Karnataka, Telangana, Kerala, and Himachal Pradesh, nearly one-third of men and women (between 15 and 49 years of age) are overweight or obese.
3. **Access to infrastructure:** In all states, the percentage of women who own a cell phone has increased. In contrast, just approximately 50% of women in Andhra Pradesh, Bihar, Gujarat, and West Bengal own and use a cell phone. The survey calculated the percentage of male and female respondents (15–49 years old) who have ever used the internet. Men were more likely than women to use the internet overall, with some states, such as Telangana, Gujarat, and Andhra Pradesh, having a gap of more than 25% points. Less than 25% of women in Andhra Pradesh, Bihar, and Tripura use the internet. In all states, a greater percentage of homes now have access to improved drinking water sources and electricity. Additionally, households with better sanitary facilities have increased across all states. 99% of households in Kerala have an improved sanitation facility, while only 49% of households in Bihar do. In a similar vein, homes using clean fuel for cooking have become more prevalent in almost all states. Comparing Telangana to NFHS-4, there has been an almost 25% improvement in access to better sanitation facilities and clean cooking fuel. In each of the 17 states, a greater percentage of women now have savings or bank accounts. The largest increases in this regard can be found in Bihar (51%-point) and Manipur (39%-point). Almost 80% of women currently have a savings or bank account in all 17 states, with the exception of Gujarat (70%) and Nagaland (64%). However, in nine of the 17 states, the percentage of women who own a home or piece of land (including joint ownership) has decreased. Assam, Tripura, and Maharashtra all experienced significant declines in women owning houses or land.
4. **Gender-related indicators:** In this section, we look at indicators on: (i) use of hygienic methods of protection during menstrual periods among women between 15 and 24 years of age; and (ii) spousal violence among married women.

The percentage of women (15–24 years old) who use hygienic measures of protection throughout their menstrual cycle was measured by the survey. This has gotten worse in practically every state. West Bengal and Bihar experienced the highest increases, totaling 28%. In Bihar (59%), Assam (66%), and Gujarat (66%), it is still low. The prevalence of gender-based violence is still significant and has even risen in several states. In five states, the percentage of married women (aged 18 to 49) who have ever experienced marital violence has increased. From 21% to 44% in Karnataka, it has doubled. In the Indian states of Karnataka (44%), Bihar (40%), Manipur (40%), and Telangana (37%), more than a third of married women experience spousal abuse.

3

The Indian Social System

3.1

The structure and nature of traditional Indian social system – Varnashram, Purushartha, Karma, Rina and Rebirth.

Q 1. Relevance of Purusarthas

Ans. The word Purusartha is derived from two terms: pursha, meaning human being, and artha, meaning objectives of life. According to this theory, there are four purusarthas: Dharma, Artha, Kama, and Moksha. Dharma signifies behaviour in accordance with social order, which sustains society and the universe. Artha refers to the attainment of worldly prosperity in terms of wealth and power. Kama refers to the instinctive an d emotional life of man and provides for the satisfaction of sexual and aesthetic urges. Moksha represents the end of life and the realisation of inner spirituality in man.

Dharma is derived from the root 'dhr," which means to uphold, to support, and to nourish. V.P. Kane explains dharma as the rights and duties of man as man and his duties and privileges as a member of Aryan communities. It even means duties, rights, and functions as a member of a caste, as well as the rights and obligations of every man as a student or householder. Dharma is a centripetal force in man, society, and the universe. N.A. Nikam says that dharma is a means to an end and that dharma has only instrumental value, which is interesting.

Artha: Righteous and honest pursuits of economic activities are oriented towards (i) the acquisition of wealth, (ii) non-appropriation, and (iii) non-stealing. However, one has to guard against overindulging in material things.

Kama: Raghavan says that Kama provides the source from which all springs activate. It supplies energy to innovate and create something. It provides rasas, which give birth to architecture, painting, music, and poetry.

Moksha: N.A. Nikam says that Moksha is realisation in which the 'knower of Brahma becomes Brahma' (Brahmavid Brahmaive Bhavati). According to Hindu Dharamshastras, Dharma is foremost because without Dharma, Artha and Kama lead to social anarchy; therefore, attainment of wealth and enjoyment of sense can maintain social order only if Dharma is followed. However, Kautilya maintains that artha is foremost because, without attainment of wealth, sensual pleasure and a feeling of spirituality cannot take place.

Louis Dumont has given the correct perspective to this anology of human functions in society. Dharma implies duty and leads to moral universalism; Artha is profit that implies rational action in our economic theory extended to polities; and Kama refers to the pleasure of life. The concept of purusarthas is integrated with the concept of ashrams and gets concrete expression in ashrams. Ashramas are stages of life that provide training and an environment for realising the ideals of our lives. According to this scheme, life is divided into four stages: Brahmacharya, Grihastha, Vanaprastha, and Sanyasa. These Purusharthas and Ashramas are regulators of life. Most of these values are ideological-motivational phenomena.

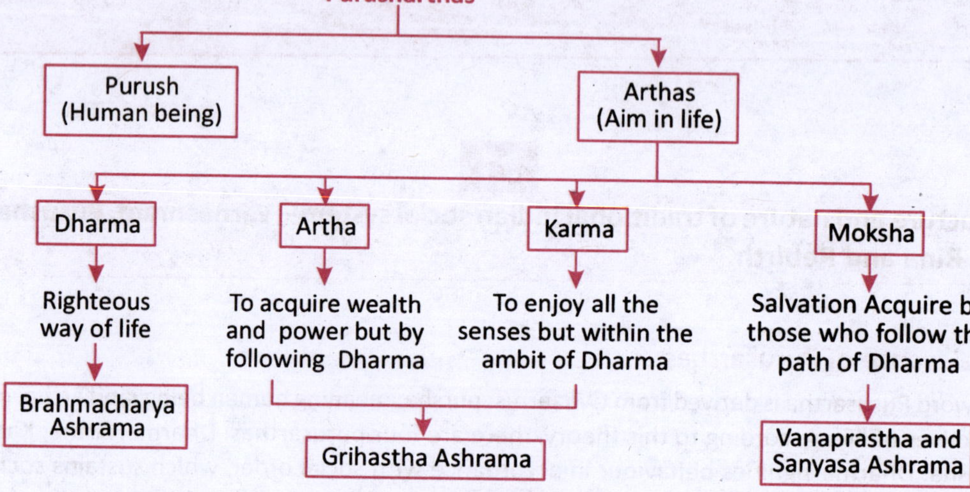

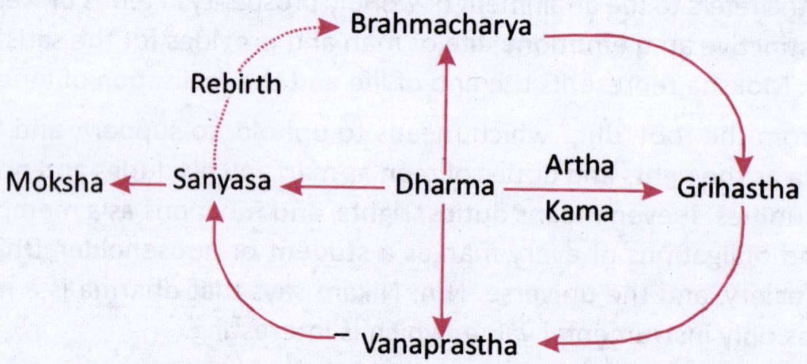

Relation between Purusharthas and Ashramas

Ideally speaking, the schemes of Ashramas and Purusarthas can resolve most of the world's problems. In Brahamcharya, channelization of thought and controlling the ego can save us from crimes related to sex and ego clashes. In Grihastha, Pitra Rina, responsible for reproduction, helps in the continuation of society. Through Atithi Rina, hunger-related crime can be regulated, and through Bhutha Rina, the environment can be protected. In Sanyasa, knowledge gained previously is spread and leads to the advancement of culture.

Current Relevance: But today, Brahamcharya starts, but when it ends, no one knows. Grihastha starts and it never ends. In terms of Purushartha, Dharma was the regulator among Trivarga, and Moksha was objective. Today, nobody talks about Moksha; Dharma is used only as a reference category, while Artha and Kama have become dominant. That is why crime around the world has been on the rise.

Q 2. Relevance of Ashramas

Ans. Ashramas are stages of life that provide training and an environment for realising the ideals of our lives. According to this scheme, life is divided into four stages: Brahmacharya, Grihastha, Vanaprastha, and Sanyasa. The first stage of life begins with the Upanayana ceremony, and thereby he is said to be reborn (Dwija). After this, the individual has to stay in Gurukul, live a simple life without desire, obey the orders of the Guru, pass hurdles put forth, and at the end, pay Guru Dakshina. It leads to the attainment of knowledge, control over the senses at adolescent times, and keeping the ego under control. Each stage lasts for 25 years.

The next Ashrama, Grihastha, begins with the solemnization of marriage. This prime function is to initiate the process of reproduction, acquire wealth, and do charity. One has to pay Rinas: Deva Rina by reciting the Vedas, Pitr Rina by reproduction, Guru Rina to the guru, and Atithi Rina by the reception of guests. In Brahamcharya Ashrama, only Dharma plays a role, while in Grihastha, Kama and Artha come along.

Next is Vanaprastha, which prepares one for the final stage, in which total detachment is to take place. He acts as an asset for society via advising younger generation. In Sanyasa Ashrama moksha can be attained only by complete detachment. It is detachment from family but not from society.

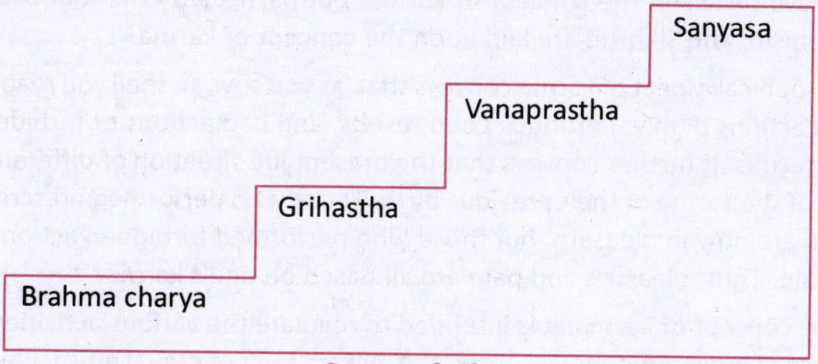

Stages of Life

The concept of Purusarthas is integrated with the concept of Ashramas. According to this theory, there are four purusarthas: Dharma, Artha, Kama, and Moksha. Dharma signifies behaviour in accordance with social order, which sustains society and the universe. Artha refers to the attainment of worldly prosperity in terms of wealth and power. Kama refers to the instinctive and emotional life of man and provides for the satisfaction of sexual and aesthetic urges. Moksha represents the end of life and the realisation of inner spirituality in man.

These Purusharthas and Ashramas are regulators of life. Most of these values are ideological-motivational phenomena.

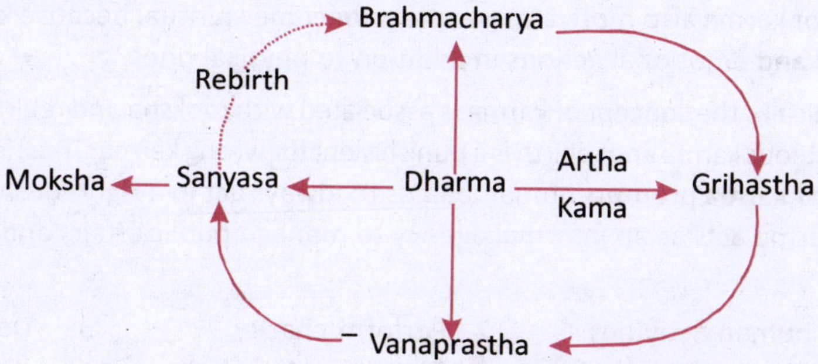

Relation between Purusharthas and Ashramas

Ideally speaking, the schemes of Ashramas and Purusarthas can resolve most of the world's problems. In Brahamcharya, channelization of thought and controlling the ego can save us from crimes related to sex and ego clashes. In Grihastha, Pitra Rina, responsible for reproduction, helps in the continuation of society. Through Atithi Rina, hunger-related crime can be regulated, and through Bhutha Rina, the environment can be protected. In Sanyasa, knowledge gained previously is spread and leads to the advancement of culture.

Current Relevance: But today, Brahamcharya starts, but when it ends, no one knows. Grihastha starts and it never ends. In terms of Purushartha, Dharma was the regulator among Trivarga, and Moksha was objective. Today, nobody talks about Moksha; Dharma is used only as a reference category, while Artha and Kama have become dominant. That is why crime around the world has been on the rise.

Q. 3. Karma

Ans. The word karma is derived from the Sanskrit word 'kar' which means all life activities. The concept of karma deals with all the good and bad actions of an individual. It is action and the consequence of action. Every action has a result, and one cannot escape from the philosophy of karma. Almost all religions have beliefs in the concept of karma, but particularly the foundations of Hinduism, Jainism, Buddhism, and Sikhism are laid upon the concept of karma.

The philosophical aspect of karma conveys that 'as you sow, so shall you reap' i.e., good actions or prescribed actions (Puniya) produce good results, and bad actions or forbidden actions (Paap) produce bad results. It further conveys that the present life situation of different human beings is the outcome of the karma of their previous birth. Those who performed prescribed actions in this previous birth are now in pleasure, but those who performed forbidden actions in their previous birth are in pain. Thus, pleasure and pain are all based on one's karma.

Due to the concept of karma, it is intended to regulate the various activities of human beings for the purpose of maintaining social order. N.A. Nikam talks of casual efficacy, artha-kriya-karitva, which says that good actions produce good effects instantaneously and bad actions produce bad effects instantaneously; the future is influenced by the present order.
Radhakrishnana says that there is no doctrine as reliable as karma theory.
In the Bhagwad Gita, Krishna talks about karma at every moment of life, with five factors involved:

- Centre from which one is to work
- Doer
- Instrumentation of the doer
- Effort
- Fate

Due to the concept of karma, people do many charity works, which are also significant for society. The concept of karma also motivates people to become spiritual because karma is also associated with spiritual and emotional actions in addition to physical ones.

Philosophically, the concept of karma is associated with moksha and rebirth because moksha is an award for righteous karma and rebirth is a punishment for wrong karma. Thus, in order to attain moksha, the concept of karma prompts human beings to always act in a righteous way, but practically, the concept of karma acts as an informal agency to manage public affairs and maintain public order.

Benefits:

1. Regulate human activities.
2. Perform charity.
3. Do spirituality.
4. Maintain public order.
5. Division of labour.

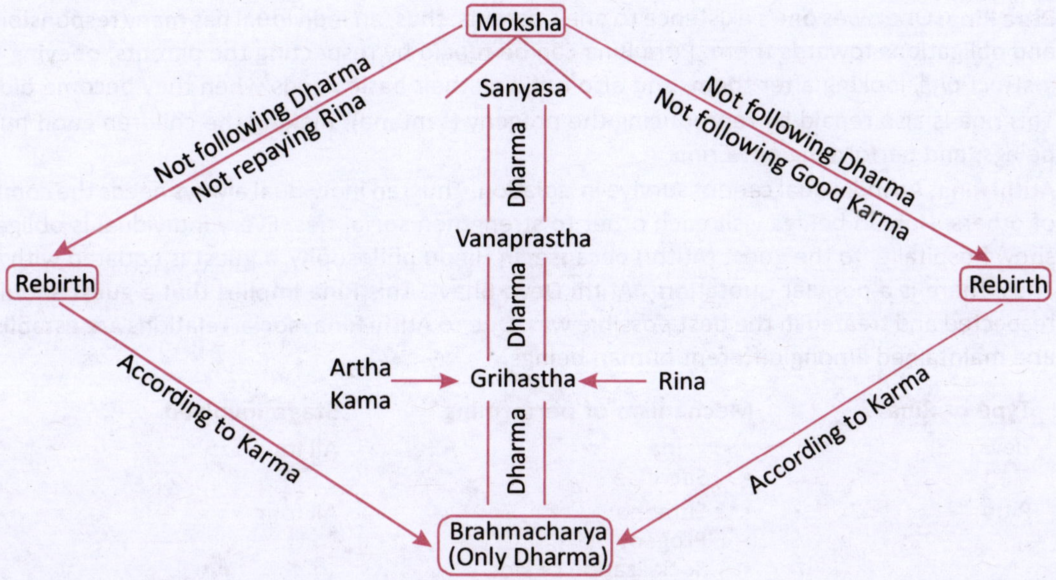

However, it is often misunderstood as belief in fate or faith in fatalism. They claim it retards moral progress and has anti-social implications. It induces a lack of concern for sufferings as it is often interested in terms of action in past lives.

But several modern interpretations believe that it is a rational concept devoid of mysterious or divine force. On the contrary, it preaches purusharthas and a sense of morality and does well in present life as well as in life to come.

Present relevance: Every object seen in the utility prospectus after the industrial revolution.People believe in 'this life' rather than 'that life ' therefore declining the role of these theories.

Q 4. Rina

Ans. The concept of Rina is an important part of the Hindu social system. To maintain the social order, every individual is socialised in such a way that he can understand his responsibilities towards his kin, friends, and society at large. Such responsibilities and obligations are Rinas. In order to attain moksha, every individual has to repay the rina that every individual is born with.

Shatapatha Brahmana mentioned 4 types of Rinas:

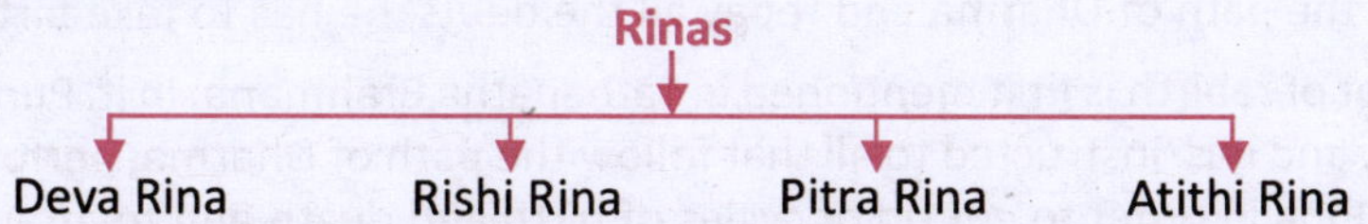

a. **Deva Rina:** Deva Rina implies obligations towards god and goddess. This rina can be repaid by recitation of the Vedas, by conducting sacrifices, and by showing reverence in various ways to different gods and goddesses. This rina implies that one should be religious and spiritual.

b. **Rishi Rina:** This rina is for gurus and teachers who have enlightened individuals, due to which an individual gets rid of many ignorances. Rishi Rina can be repaid by showing respect to the teachers, offering them Guru Dakshina, and following the path instructed by various teachers and gurus. This Rina implicates that an individual should imply the knowledge so gained by the teachers for becoming a good human being and also impact the same ethics and morality on the other members of society.

c. **Pitra Rina:** One owes one's existence to one's parents; thus, an individual has many responsibilities and obligations towards them. Pitra Rina can be repaid by respecting the parents, obeying their instructions, looking after them, and also fulfilling their basic needs when they become old. This rina is also repaid by reproducing the progeny (santana), making the children good human beings, and performing pitra rina.

d. **Atithi Rina:** An individual cannot survive in isolation. Thus, an individual always needs the company of others. Human beings visit each other to strengthen social ties. Every individual is obliged to show hospitality to the guest (Atithi) because, in Hindu philosophy, a guest is equated with God. Thus, there is a popular quotation: "Atithi Devo Bhav". This Rina implies that a guest should be respected and treated in the best possible way. Due to Atithi Rina, social relations are established and maintained among different human beings.

Type of Rina	Mechanism of performing	Stage involved
Deva	• Yajna • Sacrifice	All four
Pitra	• Shradha • Progeny • Socialization of kids • Care of perents	All four
Guru	• Scriptures • Respect	All four, Brahmacharya mainly
Atithi	• Atithi Devo Bhav	Grihastha and Vanaprastha

The basic theme of Rina is to channelize the various activities of humans and make them responsible individuals so that they can fulfil their obligations for the betterment of their families and their society.

Q 5. Rebirth

Ans. The concepts of Karma and Rina are woven around the concept of rebirth. The concept of rebirth (Punarjanam) is based on the philosophical aspect that the soul is immortal because it remains in existence even after the death of someone. Now it is based on one's karma whether one's soul (Atma) will again merge with the prime soul (Paramatma) or not.

It is generally believed that one who doesn't perform good actions or good karma and doesn't repay the Rina has to take rebirth because they cannot attain moksha. Actually, the supreme power provides another opportunity to the soul by putting it into another body to perform the prescribed actions and to repay the rina so that such a soul can ultimately merge with the supreme soul. Until an individual doesn't follow the path of Dharma and repay all the debts, he has to take birth again and again.

The concept of rebirth is first mentioned in Sathapatha Brahmana. In it, Punarjanam is equated with the curse, and it is instructed to all that follow the path of Dharma, perform the good deeds, and repay the Rina in order to get rid of cycles of birth and death and to attain moksha.

According to R.N. Saxena, in the Samakhya tradition, the final goal of yoga is for discipline to reach Moksha. Two stages are clearly marked in it. In the first, he remains content with savikalpa Samadhi, a superconscious ecstasy in which dualism exists, and in the second, he escapes from life through nirvikalpa Samadhi. Therefore, moksha doesn't mean the total negation of the worldly existence of pursha.

Practically, through the concept of rebirth, it is intended that no one indulge in anti-social activities or escape from one's obligations because this concept conveys that if one is wrong and doesn't fulfil obligations, then one has to take the rebirth, but if one lives a righteous way of life full of morality, then one can attain moksha.

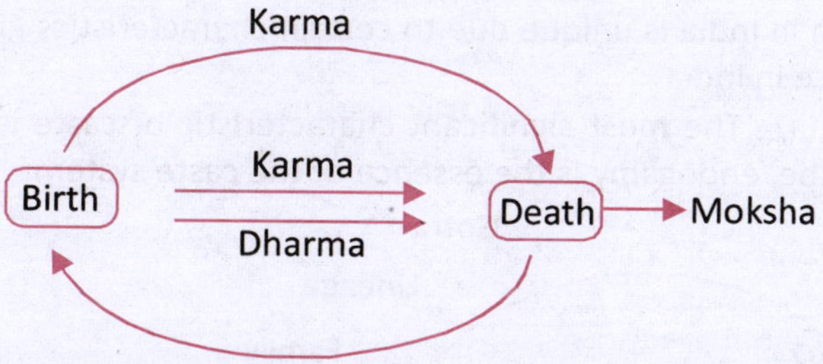

Present relevance: Due to modern education, transport, and communication, urbanisation, a monetized economy, etc., these values have gotten diluted to a great extent in cities and metropolitan areas. However, it is still a prevalent way of life in rural India.

3.2

Caste system in India— Structure and characteristics Varna and caste, Theories of origin of caste system, Dominant caste, Caste mobility, Future of caste system, Jajmani system. Tribe-case continuum.

Q 1. Caste system in India – Structure and Characteristics

Ans. The term 'caste' has been derived from the Portuguese term "casta" which means "bred," "social group," or "pure stock, which in turn is derived from the Latin term "castus" meaning clean or pure. It is believed to have originated around 2 B.C. but was largely in place by 500 A.D.

According to Hutton, caste is an endogamous group whose membership is hereditary, whose members occupy traditional professions, and whose members impose restrictions on their social intercourse with members of other groups.

According to M.N. Srinivas, a caste is an indigenous, hereditary, and localised group that has an association with a traditional occupation.

The structure of the caste system is advocated in Brahmanical texts. The caste system is a hierarchical, ranked, closed, and endogamous phenomenon. It is also attributed. The ranking in the caste system is based on the amount of purity associated with its members. Those who are considered pure are at the top of the caste hierarchy, and those who are considered impure are at the bottom.

In caste structure, the Brahmins who occupy the top position enjoy many privileges, whereas the so-called untouchables who are at the bottom are deprived of many rights.

The structure of the caste system divides society into many groups, and every group is endogamous in itself.

The structure of the caste system is so rigid that mobility up and down is totally absent, i.e., in this structure, the slot of every caste is fixed, and even processes like Sanskritization cannot bring about a change in the structure of the caste system.

The caste system is a unique institution, almost absent in other parts of the world.

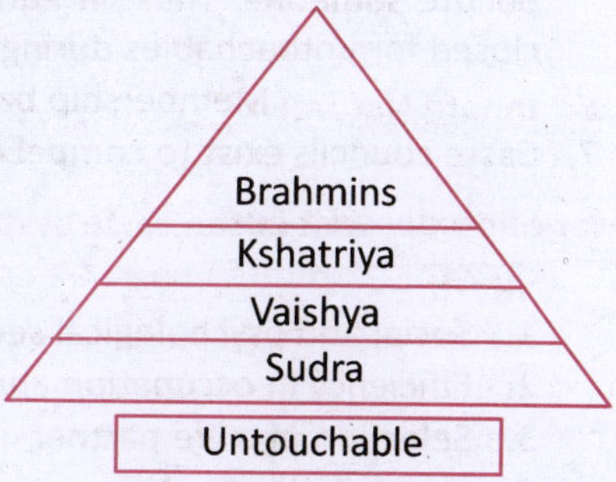

Hindu Caste System

The caste system in India is unique due to certain characteristics given by *G.S. Ghurye* in his book "Caste and Race in India":

1. **Endogamous in nature:** The most significant characteristic of caste is its endogamous nature. According to S.C. Dube, endogamy is the essence of the caste system.

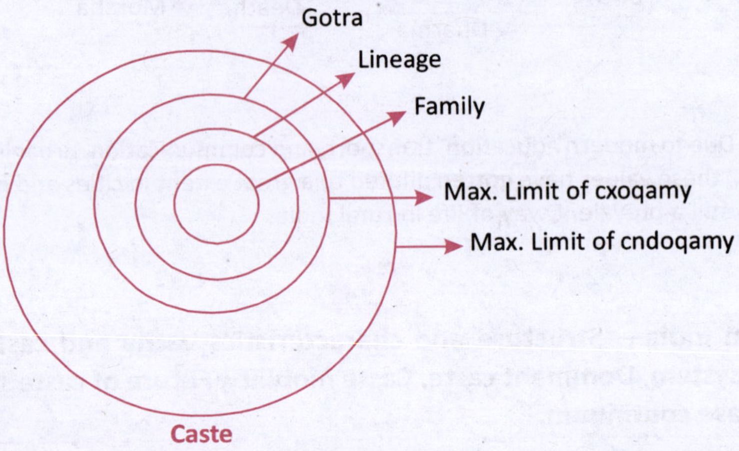

2. **Association with traditional occupation:** Every caste is also characterised by its association with a particular traditional occupation. Occupational mobility in the caste system doesn't occur.
3. **Restriction on feeding and social intercourse:** The caste system also imposes certain restrictions upon its members regarding feeding habits, like who will accept which kind of food and from whom. E.g., in North India, a Brahmin can accept pacca food (cooked food in ghee or oil) from members of a lower caste, but he can accept kaccha food (uncooked food or food cooked in water) only from members of his own caste. Whereas in South India, Brahmins can only accept food from other Brahmins. Interaction between members of higher and lower castes is also prohibited. The members of the higher caste also denied maintaining social relations with members of the lower caste.
4. **Social and religious hierarchy:** The caste system is also characterised by social and religious hierarchy, in which certain castes are at the top and others are at the bottom. Those at the bottom are declared impure, and untouchability is practised with them. Also, certain castes enjoy more religious privileges, like their priests, but certain caste members are even denied entry to temples.
5. **Social disabilities:** The caste system is also characterised by the association of social disabilities with certain caste groups. The so-called untouchables have to face many such social disabilities, like having members of higher castes maintain distance from them. E.g., in Kerela, Nayars can approach Namboodri Brahmins but cannot touch them. Similarly, Tiyan has to keep certain steps from Brahmins. The so-called untouchables are not allowed to draw water from public wells or visit certain places. In some areas, they are considered unseeable, and their shadow can also pollute someone. Thus, in Pune, during the time of Peshwas, the gate of the royal palace was closed for untouchables during certain hours when the shadow was long.
6. **Innate Nature:** Membership based on birth.
7. Caste councils exist to compel obedience.

Merit and demerit in the caste system:

Merit:

1. Social and psychological security
2. Efficiency in occupation and the security of occupational security
3. Selection of a life partner
4. Controlled behaviour
5. Decision of labour

Demerit:

1. Hindu rate of economic development because of lack of mobility
2. Exploitation and oppression of lower castes
3. Religious conversion due to a higher caste system
4. Detrimental to democracy and national unity
5. Hamper social communication between segments of society.

The structure of the caste system is an integral part of the Hindu social system up to such an extent that M.N. Srinivas once said, "The caste system in India will retain the same structure of higher and lower castes from generation to generation, and the present situation reveals that its elimination from India seems impossible". One may borrow Harold Gould's observation that in rural areas, caste still persists in its traditional form as hierarchical, integrated, occupationally and ritually specialised, endogenous social strata. In urban areas, caste persists in the form of a complex network of interest groups preserved through endogamy and legitimised by religion.

Q 2. Varna and Caste

Ans. M.N. Srinivas says that the Varna model has produced a wrong and distorted image of caste. The Varna model was more of an idealised or designed form of social stratification than an actual one. The Jati model has always been ethnographic and empirical. He even described Varna as book view and Jati as field view.

Louis Dumont, in his book "Homo Hierarchius," says that Varna is a Vedic concept while Jati is post-vedic. Both Varna and caste are two types of social stratification in Indian society. Most of the time, they are used interchangeably to mean other things, but there are certain differences between them, which are:

1. Varna is only four in number, whereas castes are innumerable: During the Vedic and post-Vedic periods, Indian society was divided into four varnas: Brahmin, Kshatriya, Vaishya, and Shudras. But it is not easy to ascertain the numerical strength of caste, and it is generally claimed by some that around four thousand castes and subcastes prevail in India.
2. Varna is based upon occupation, whereas caste is based upon birth. During Vedic and post-Vedic periods, Varna was associated with occupations like Brahmins, who were teachers and preachers, and Kshatriya, who were warriors, whereas an individual became a member of a caste only if he or she was born in such a group.
3. Varna is not so rigid, whereas caste is very rigid. Varna didn't impose certain restrictions regarding food, social relations, and occupational mobility upon its members, whereas caste imposes all such restrictions upon its members.
4. Varna is an open system, whereas caste is closed. During the Vedic and post-Vedic periods, one could change one's Varna. E.g., Vishwamitra was born in Kshatriya Varna, but he changed his Varna to Brahmin. Parshurama, a Dronacharya, was born in Brahmin Varna but changed his Varna to Kshatriya. Ved Vyasa was born into a family of fisherman who were shudras, but he adopted Brahmin Varna and became the composer of the Mahabharata. But a change in one's caste cannot occur. A person always remains a member of the same caste from the day of birth up to the day of death. Inter-Varna marriages are also allowed. E.g., Agasthya, who was a Brahmin, married a Kshatriya girl, Lopamurdra, but inter-caste marriages were not allowed.

5. Varna has divine sanction but not caste: The theory of Chaturvarna signifies that every Varna has originated from different body parts of Pursha (Brahma's Supreme Soul). Also, Lord Krishna mentions in the Bhagwat Gita that he himself has created the Varnas on the basis of gunas (qualities). However, caste has no divine sanction.
6. Untouchability doesn't exist within the Varna system, while it does at the lowest level in the caste system. Mutual repulsion exists in the caste system, unlike the Varna system.
7. Dignity of labour exists in Varna, while oppression of labour exists in the caste system. Gandhi considered the caste system exploitative, not the Varna system.

Even today, we use the termVarna but it doesn't exist. They are things of the past, but caste is still an integral part of the Hindu social system.

Q 3. Theories of origin of Caste system

Ans. Hutton defined a caste as an endogamous group whose membership is hereditary, whose members occupy a traditional profession, and which places certain restrictions upon its members regarding social intercourse with members of other groups.

Different scholars have put forth different theories regarding the origin of the caste system:

1. **Varna Theory:** The main sources of Varna theory regarding the origin of the caste system are our religious texts, because the earliest reference to the Varna system is found in the Purshasukta hymn in the Xth Mandala of the Rig Veda. In this hymn, it is mentioned that the Rigvedic society was divided into four varnas: Brahmins, Kshatriyas, Vaishyas, and Shudras.The supporters of the Varna theory of the origin of the caste system advocate that the caste system directly originated from the Varna system. Although the earlier Varna system had nothing to do with the caste system, with the passage of time, Varnas became hereditary and closed in themselves. Then Varna eventually evolved into various castes.
2. **Occupational theory**: This theory was given by Nesfield. According to him, earlier, different human groups began to practise different occupations, and those individuals who professed the same occupation became members of the same occupational group. With the passage of time, such an occupational group became indigenous, and the occupation also became hereditary. The purity and impurity associated with different caste groups are also derived from their respective occupations. Certain occupations were considered pure occupations, like teaching and preaching, whereas certain occupations like scavenging, sweeping, shoemaking, barbering, etc. were considered impure occupations. Thus, those who occupied pure professions were declared members of pure groups, whereas those who professed impure occupations were declared members of impure groups. Due to this concept of purity and impurity, the members of pure groups began to mention their distance from members of impure groups, due to which the practise of untouchability emerged. Thus, Nesfield narrated that when occupational groups became endogamous, when the occupations became hereditary, and when the practise of untouchability became part of occupational groups, such groups evolved into caste groups. Hence, he mentioned that function alone is responsible for the emergence of caste groups. He further remarked that even the names of different castes are derived from their traditional occupations, like Sonar, Lohar, and Dhobi.
3. **Religious theory**: The main advocates of this theory are Hocart and Senart. According to them, earlier, the human groups began to worship different deities and also presented different types of food items before them. Gradually, the religious groups, in order to retain the purity of faith, began to practise endogamy, and such religious groups also became hereditary. With the passage of time, certain religious groups began to maintain distance from others. As a result, untouchability

became part of those religious groups, and eventually those groups evolved into caste groups. Even today, different caste groups worship particular deities, like various incarnations of Vishnu worshipped by Brahmins, goddess Kali worshipped by Rajputs, Lord Vishakarma worshipped by carpenters, and so on.

4. **Theory of cultural integration:** This theory is put forth by Sartchandra Roy. According to him, earlier, at the time of cultural diffusion, different individuals adopted different cultural traits, and all those individuals who adopted similar cultural traits integrated themselves into a similar cultural group. As the cultural traits exhibited variations from one another, similarly, such cultural groups also differ from one another. Gradually, the cultural groups, in order to retain the purity of the culture, become endogamous as well. As offspring began to adopt the cultures of their parents, cultural groups also became hereditary. Due to the variations in cultural standards, untouchability also emerged among the cultural groups. Eventually, such cultural groups evolved into caste groups. Even today, different caste groups possess different cultures.
5. **Guna or sociological theory:** This division is based on the inherent qualities of a person. Guna can be Satvik, Rajas, or Tamas. Satvik has pure elements: Rajas elements of activity and a drive for self-benefit, and Tamas elements of darkness and destruction.

Criticism:

1. The Varna theory is a mythological one.
2. Occupational and religious groups don't have facts and evidence.
3. Satvik Guna is not solely found in higher castes.

No single theory can explain the exact reason behind the emergence of caste. Multiple factor theory, taking various aspects together, best explains the origin of the caste system.

Q 4. Dominant Caste

Ans. The concept of dominant caste was given by M.N. Srinivas while working at a village in Rampura, Karnataka. For a caste to be dominant, it should have a sizable amount of arable land locally available, have strength in numbers, and usually occupy a high place in the local hierarchy. New factors affecting dominance have emerged in the last 8–9 decades: Western education, jobs in administration, and urban sources of income. With globalisation, universal adult franchise, and panchayati raj, village-level dominance is not enough to make caste dominant, while regional dominance is important.

According to M.N. Srinivas, dominant caste of region always act as model for Sanskritization because members of other caste attempt to imitate life style of dominant caste in order to become equal to them. Thereby this concept helps to understand social mobility and change via Sanskritization. Each locally dominant caste has its own modelBrahmin, Kshatriya or Vaishya model of Sanskritization. Eg. Thakurs of UP make Brahmin cook food except kulguru.

Dominant caste plays an important role in the economic development of region. Eg. Jats of Haryana, Jatt of Punjab acted positively to green-revolution & paved way for agricultural revolution in North India. Contrary, Konkani, dominant caste of Konkan region acted negatively towards railways for many decades and postponed the development of region.

Similarly dominant caste has important role play in politics. "Casteization of politics" started after independence when Congress created caste combination KHAM (Kshatriga, Harijan, Adivasi, Muslims). Another phenomenon named "Politicisation of caste" has become dominant in India which illustrated in form of formation of Bahujan Samaj Party (BSP) by Kanshi Ram. Dominant caste influence in India in politics can be seen in Haryana where no party can win without considering Jats as their vote-bank.

State	Dominant Caste	State	Dominant Caste
Karnataka	Lingayats & Vokkaligas	Gujarat	Patidar
Andhra	Reddy & Kamma	Kerela	Nayars

Dominant caste is an important concept to explain the ground reality of the Indian social system. But S.C. Dube criticised and said that only a few numbers of dominant individuals occupy most of the power positions, and therefore it is dominant individuals and not dominant caste. While D.N. Majmudar in Chhor ka Ek Gaon reveals that dominant caste is a dynamic concept, particularly in villages and regions inhabited by both tribals and nontribals, A.C. Mayer says that a particular lineage may be dominant and not the entire caste.

M.N. Srinivas countered it by saying that dominant individuals owe their dominance to the fact that they are part of a dominant caste, and dominance can be complete only when it spreads over a substantial region.

Ghanshyam Shah pointed out the formation of caste associations, an important innovation introduced by the dominant group of the dominant caste to maintain harmony among various economic states within the caste structure, e.g., Gujarat Kshatriya Sabha.

With the implementation of schemes through democratic institutions and resource distribution, the dominant caste as a collective whole is definitely exercising power.

Case Study

- **Dominant caste: Jats of Haryana**

Due to the state's delineation, their numerical strength outweighed that of other castes. The Green Revolution and the rise of the economy's power coincided, and political power resulted from the population's size. Even though they are all tied to their economic status, the Jats and other agricultural castes' generally higher levels of education and greater political articulation, as well as the historic leadership of the former in Haryana's predominately rural society, seem to have further enhanced their political standing (Singh 1979). The "trilogy" of M.N. Srinivas is completed by the Jats' grip over the political establishment.

The Panchayati Raj changes caused Jats to perceive a danger to the long-term dominance they had attained. Jats were primarily located in the state's rural districts, and the new changes immediately affected them. The drive towards the Khap Panchayats was motivated by the Jats' fear of losing their supremacy, which has persisted since the creation of the state.

The SEZ Act of 2005 and the boom in the reality industry between 2005 and 2007 dealt another blow to the Jat hegemony. The land that was owned by the villages was sold to the real giants shortly after the real estate bubble of 2005–2007. In northern India, the land that provided the Jats with their power was slipping because it was being sold to investors for more money. Sonipat, Gurgaon, and Faridabad serve as examples of such places. The Jats' power was largely based on the land they controlled because the Green Revolution brought them significant financial rewards. The source of power that the Jats enjoyed due to their land was also fading away.

However, because of the wealth from real estate and the political clout that the group possessed, the Jats continued to dominate in rural areas. The majority-Jat communities are referred to as Jat villages and are a part of the Khap, a long-standing institution. According to Gupta (1997), a Khap is a permanent clanbased entity made up of villages where residents are from the same clan. Through their attire, the Khap Panchayats often demonstrate regional dominance, and they frequently lend that dominance other forms of support. generations, members of lower castes claim high positions. For example, Patidars of Gujarat and Coorgs got mobility.

Q 5. Caste Mobility

Ans. Caste is based on birth. A person always remains a member of some caste from birth to death. But castes can experience positional mobility. When we talk about caste mobility, it means a caste can experience both upward and downward mobility. But such a shift is only positional and not structural, i.e., the structure of the caste system remains the same.

Upward Mobility: The various factors of upward mobility are:

1. **Mobility through Warfare:** According to K.M. Pannikar, from the 5th century B.C. on, almost all ruling powers actually belonged to lower castes. But they acquired the status of a higher caste after defeating certain superior groups. He cited the example of the Mauryas, saying that the Mauryas were actually shudras, but when they defeated Nandas, they experienced mobility and attained the status of Kshatriyas. M.N. Srinivas put forth the example of Raja Shivaji. According to him, Raja Shivaji belongs to a lower caste, but after defeating powerful Mughals, he attained the status of a Kshatriya.
2. **Mobility through serving ruling classes:** Many Jati people who served either Hindu or non-Hindu rulers attained the status of higher caste in due course of time. For example, Kayastha belongs to a lower caste and was a scribe. Under the Mughals and British, they attained the status of Brahmins.
3. **Mobility through Census:** Censuses from 1891 –1931 were mostly caste-based. During the census, many lower castes recorded themselves as higher castes. For example, Kurmi cultivators in Bihar historically belonged to a lower caste, but census reports declared them members of a higher caste. Similarly, historically , the Teli caste was also a lower caste, but after census reports, it was considered an upper caste.
4. **Mobility through Sanskritization:** Sanskritization is a process that conveys imitation of life styles like food habits, dress patterns, rituals, etc. of the upper caste by members of the lower caste. In this attempt, after 2-3.
5. **Mobility through Westernisation**: Due to the contact of many lower caste members with the British, they are able to raise their position because they adopt western education and western clothing and give up their traditional occupation. A number of lower caste groups in India are enjoying higher positions due to Westernisation.
6. **Mobility through Constitutional Provisions**: Our government has provided many constitutional provisions to members of lower castes, like reservation in educational institutions, reservation in government jobs, etc., due to which they are able to attain higher positions in society. For example, Mahars of Maharashtra and Kamas of Andhra Pradesh got mobility.

Downward Mobility: It conveys the mobility of caste towards a lower position. Downward mobility occurs due to two main factors:

1. **Reap the fruits of reservation**: A number of upper castes are now protesting that they should be considered for reservation as they occupy a low position in society. For example, Jats of Haryana, Marathas of Maharashtra, and Patils of Gujarat belong to the upper caste but now claim a low position in society.
2. **Tribalization**: A number of caste people have also come into contact with tribals and now declare themselves as members of tribal society. For example, many caste people in Bastar now become tribes. Similarly, Gurjars of Rajasthan, who are actually caste people but now declare themselves tribes.

Thus, in Indian Hindu society, caste mobility has been taking place since ancient times. But during ancient and mediaeval times, this mobility was in an upward direction, but now it is mostly in a downward direction. Moreover, the concept of horizontal solidarity among castes takes place at the expense of mobility.

Case Study

The Kapu community's agitation in Andhra Pradesh is for political dominance and economic mobility. There is a demand for quotas from them. They have fear from below, i.e., mobility of Schedule caste and other backward castes, and fear from above, uninterrupted hegemony of Kamma and Reddy.

Q 6. Future of Caste system

Ans. The future of caste system is a burning debate everywhere now-a-days. There are different opinions regarding this issue.

According to D.N. Majumdar, Kuppuswamy, Opler, etc., the caste is changing very fast and is also weakening at a great pace. Thus, the future of the caste system is threatened, and we can expect a caste-less Hindu society in the coming years. But scholars like S.C. Dube, Andre Bettile, T.C. Das, Ghurye, etc. hold the view that caste is changing gradually and very slowly. Although the caste system of today is not the same as it was a half-century ago.Yet, it still exists in India and will remain so in the future. Thus, there is no threat to the caste system.

M.N. Srinivas, in his version of 'The future of the caste system' deals with two important questions:

1. Should castes exist in India tomorrow?
2. Are they going to exist in India tomorrow?

Answering the first question, he mentioned that Hindus cannot imagine their society without the caste system because the caste system has been in existence in India since ancient times. Thus, Hindus are accustomed to the caste system. Caste provides a social base and identity for an individual. The rank (ascribed) is also based on the caste system. All the kin of an individual belong to one's caste. Thus, caste should exist in the future in India. While dealing with the second question, he maintained that the economic aspect of caste is weakened, i.e., due to occupational mobility, every caste now has equal opportunity to occupy any profession. But politically, the caste system is strengthened because political parties consider the caste system a vote bank. In the largest democracy in the world, elections are contested on the basis of caste. The political parties provide tickets to such candidates whose caste dominates a particular constituency. Now, there have emerged caste lobbies; such lobbies influence members tomorrow. In India, these are caste-based reservations. All those who avail themselves of such reservations never want the elimination of caste systems. This reservation on the basis of caste strengthened this traditional institution of Indian society. Even no political party has the courage to withdraw caste-based reservations, even for those who are economically well off now. Thus, due to the efforts of those castes to avail reservation, the caste system will always exist in India. Further, some practises like caste endogamy and the social and religious privileges of certain higher castes also safeguard the future of the caste system in India.

A.M. Shah, in his article 'Caste in the 21st Century,' says that caste as a system is more or less dead but individual castes are flourishing. It has won approval in people's minds. Caste is no longer a system of ideas and values; rather, it is a matter of interpretation. Caste has now become a state of mind. Regarding the future of the caste system, many intellectuals of modern times hold different opinions:

1. **Caste should be abolished:** Progressivists, leftists, etc. hold the opinion that caste should be abolished in India because it is due to the caste system that many members of certain castes have to face exploitation. Even today, they are considered untouchables and face many social and economic

disabilities. Thus, in a modern democratic setup, every caste should enjoy equality, but the caste system is undemocratic because different castes have unequal status. It hampers the development of society and, ultimately, the development of a nation. Thus, in the future there should be no caste.

2. **Caste should be reinstated:** Traditionalists hold the view that castes of today have undergone many changes and no longer remain culturally homogenous, which is against the philosophical aspect of the Hindu caste system. Therefore, in the future, the Indian caste system should be reinstated in its traditional form.
3. **Caste system should be modified:** Many intellectuals are of the opinion that Hindu society without caste cannot be imagined, so caste will remain part and parcel of Hindu society in the future. But situations and conditions have changed now that doesn't favour the existence of caste in its traditional form. Thus, the caste system should be modified so that there should not be any untouchability even in the mind of someone, and there should not be certain disabilities associated with certain castes. But caste endogamy and caste cultural homogeneity can prevail. Thus, future India should be viewed as having a modified caste system.

Harold Gould was of the opinion that many social scientists who were working to understand the caste system revealed that there is no threat to the future of the caste system in India because it will always prevail here, although with less rigidity and more modifications.

Case Study

- **Inter-caste marriages in the Vaishnava monastery of Assam**

In the Gosain households that live inside the Sattra institution, inter-caste marriages with family approval are uncommon. According to Wilson (1959), the sects uphold specific behavioural patterns to protect their sect ideals from outside influences, and group endogamy is a key strategy for this insulation in the sects. Intercaste marriage is viewed in this setting as a betrayal of the sectarian cause, and as a result, the newlyweds must endure numerous levels of punishment for defiling the pious reputation of the higher caste family. The biggest issues arise when a boy from an upper caste marries a lady from a lower caste. According to social anthropologist Nur Yalman, female sexuality poses a concern because it could endanger their lineage by importing impure or low-caste blood (Chakravarty, 1993). Nur Yalman relates the sexual purity of women to the purity of the caste. As a result, in this spectrum of stigmatising and othering the couples, the wives suffer more than their husbands, and when the exclusionary treatment of the Gosains is examined, it can be concluded that despite joining the sectarian group, these women experience a form of internal religious exclusion.

Therefore, these are essentially newly created pseudo-brahminical norms and practises in sattras from the post-Sankaradeva era that are directly at odds with the socialist ideology of the Bhakti Movement and the concept of sect. Strong casteism and superiority complexes are said to be the two fundamental pillars of Brahminical ideology, according to Mayur Bora (2013). Although the monasteries do not exhibit the rigidity of the brahminical caste system, they nevertheless maintain a sense of caste superiority. Caste exogamy continues to be criticised and denigrated, which is a sign that this opposing mindset has persisted to this day. Ambedkar (1916) asserts that Hindus will scarcely choose inter-caste marriage as long as casteism exists in India in light of such ominous repercussions.

Q 7. Jajmani System

Ans. In village India, there is functional interdependence among various castes. Actually, every caste has a particular occupation. As a result, each caste helps other castes survive. Such occupational interdependence or functional interdependence among castes is known as the Jajmani system. The term Jajmani system was coined by Willian H. Wiser in his book "The Hindu Jajmani System," which he published in 1936 after conducting his study at village Karimpur in U.P.

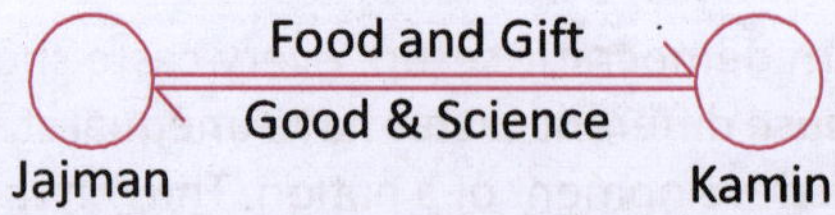

According to him, in the Jajmani system, on one side there are serving castes, and on the other side there are landowning castes. The former are known as kamin, and the latter as jajman.

Wiser showed a system of exchange of goods and services among the 24 castes of the village. He mentions that the Jajmani system is based upon the principle of reciprocity because the serving castes, like barbers, potters, carpenters, washermen, goldsmiths, blacksmiths, etc., provide their services to Jajman, and Jajman in return pays food grains to kamin. The payment is made not at the time when the job is finished but at the time of harvest.

David Mandelbaum says that Jajmani operates at the family level. Rajput families have Jajmani ties with barber and carpenter families.

According to *Harold Gould, the* Jajmani system is a relation of superordinate with subordinate in the form of Jajman and Kamin, respectively.

According to Ishawaran, in the Jajmani system, every caste has a role to play, and such roles may be social, economic, or even moral. It is due to these roles that every caste is able to survive in village India.

Although the Jajmani system is village-based, it also develops inter-village relations because a single village may not be self-sufficient with respect to all occupational castes, so sometimes villages seek kamins from other villages.

Similarly, a particular serving caste may not get a job year-round within a particular village, so such a caste provides its service to other villages as well.

Jajmani System as Egalitarian: According to Pauline Koleanda, Harold Gould, Ram Ahuja, etc., the Jajmani system is an egalitarian system because there is distribution of all occupational benefits to every caste and also distribution of food grains among all, whether one is producing himself or not. It is a cooperative, open system rather than a feudal, closed system. It is based on a barter system and is not a forced one.

In this system, everyone gets something. In this system, social relations are developed between the upper and lower classes in addition to economic elections.

Jajmani system as exploitative: According to *Lewis, the* Jajmani system is an exploitative system because the superior exploits the subordinate. He observed that in many villages in U.P., serving castes provide their services to higher castes, but higher castes don't pay them anything in return. In the Jajmani system, serving castes are known as Kamin, which is a derogatory term.

Sometimes an individual of a serving caste also borrows money from his respective Jajman, and when he is not able to repay that, he has to work like bonded labour, and this bonded labour sometimes becomes hereditary. The Jajmani system is also permanent and hereditary, based on the principle that the son of Kamin will be Kamin.

Change in the Jajmani System: The Jajmani system has now changed a lot and is almost on the verge of extinction. Various factors responsible for change in the Jajmani system are:

1. Due to improved means of transportation, links have been established between villages and markets. Now, producers who also produce cash crops think that it is better to sell the produce in the market rather than pay to serve caste. The serving caste now sells their labour on the market.

2. The Minimum Wages Act makes it compulsory to pay wages in cash rather than in kind, which weakens the Jajmani system because in the Jajmani system there were no monetary aspects.
3. There is also occupational mobility due to the fact that a particular caste is not occupying its traditional profession, i.e., the occupation is not hereditary.
4. Political mobilisation of Schedule Caste and Backward Caste via reservation also weakens the Jajmani system.
5. The abolition of the zamindari system, adoption of land reforms, and transfer of land to landless serving castes further weaken the Jajmani system.
6. It is also threatened by scientific innovations like safety razors and shaving at home. There are washing machines; therefore, there is no need for a washer and so many other substitutes now.
7. Modern education, which creates awareness, also plays a role in the disintegration of the Jajmani system. As a result of the above factors, the Jajmani system is now just a ritualistic system, and even if it prevails in certain Indian villages, it is weakening very fast because it has lost its utility.

It can be seen in the form of cultural survival in urban centres, where working castes like sweepers and washers, despite getting cash for service, also get clothes and other things on festival days.

Q 8. Tribe – Caste continuum

Ans. Robert Redfield, while working among Mexican communities, put forth the term 'folk-urban continuum' in his book "The Folk Culture of Yucatan," where a clear line of demarcation between folk and urban was not found. Much before it, Indian ethnographers were grappling with the problem of discriminating against tribe and caste. More academic regions were applied by J.H. Hutton in census operations. If a group was shown to be clearly Hindu in religious belief, it was caste; if animist, then tribal. Andre Beteille has observed differences between caste and tribe as

i) relative isolation of tribe compared to caste;
ii) language or dialect of tribes different from major Indian languages;
iii) animistic belief in tribes distinct from Hinduism practises.

However, the work of *F.G. Bailey* stands apart. In his paper 'Tribe and Caste in India', he mentioned that both tribe and caste should be viewed collectively rather than in isolation because there is constant interaction taking place between them. However, Bailey argued that caste society is organic and hierarchical, while tribal society is segmentary and egalitarian. He makes distinctions not in terms of total behaviour but in relation to the political and economic system.

Another serious attempt by Surajit Sinha in Bastar found that the supernaturalism of the lowest caste has similarities with that of tribes.

Until the 19th century, most tribes had limited contact with Hindu society. Yet interaction with caste groups has taken place, as seen below:

At Certain Level

Totally Isolated
- Great Andamanese
- Onge
- Jarawa

Partially Isolated
- Raji
- Baige
- Chenchu

Cultural Contact
- Santhal
- Munda
- Ho
- Gonds

Totally Assimilated
- Meena

The tribe-caste continuum can also be understood as the interaction of great and little traditions. Reference to tribes like Khasa and Bhil in the Ramayana and Mahabharata shows contact and interaction.

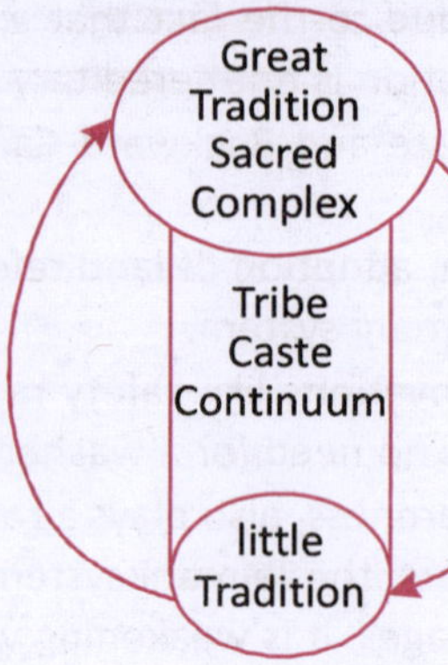

Case Study

1. **Tribal Reddis of AP, S.C. Dube:** The family of the chief of tribal reddis, during colonial rule, stopped eating beef, adopted the idea of purity and pollution, and performed other rituals performed by neighbouring Kshatriyas. Hence, Raj Reddis of the Kshatriya category emerged out of Tribal Reddis.
2. **Bhumij of WB, Surjit Sinha:** Out of the tribe, few became vegetarian, gave up drinking, and observed a strict diet under the advice of the preacher. This group claimed them to be Kshatriya and created the association 'Bhumij Kshatriya Mahasabha'. But after independence, when the policy of reservation was considered for ST, they went back to their original status and renamed the association 'Adivasi Bhumij Kshatriya Mahasabha'.

   This explains that the Hindu caste system is open to the lower end, and two stages are followed to enter the Hindu fold:

   a. Undergo socio-economic adjustment, like some change in occupation and livelihood.

   b. Imbibe the values of purity and pollution, such as vegetarianism.
3. **Badagas of Nilgiri, Paul Hackings:** In the 16th century, Badagas was a caste in Mysore (the agriculturalist caste). At some point, they moved into the forest in search of better land, settled over time, and started marrying among themselves in geographical and cultural isolation. At the end, a new tribe named the Badagas emerged.
4. **Sachidanand Paper on 'Tribe Caste Continuum:** A Study of Gond in Bihar': On the basis of 20 basic characteristics of Hindus, Gonds had 13.

Hence, the tribe-caste continuum is a two-way process that refers to the inner dynamics of the Indian social system. This knowledge can enable the effective design of development programmes that preserve cultural autonomy and understand regional dynamics.

Case Study

- **Kharchi Puja: A Synthesis of Tribal and Hindu Culture**

While being influenced by Brahmanical Hindus, this Tripuran celebration is linked to the local tribal deities. The odd thing about this celebration is that, although the ceremonies are carried out in accordance with Hindu traditions, there isn't a single deity in the Hindu religion whose body is absent, unfinished, or just partially present during this festival. Instead, only the heads of these deities are worshipped. The shattered head image is not supported by Brahmanical iconography as a ritual object, yet the Hindus of Tripura have accepted these fourteen head images as popular deities. This serves as one of the useful illustrations of the "Tribe Caste Continuum."

3.3

Sacred Complex and Nature-Man-Spirit Complex

Q 1. Sacred Complex

Ans. L.P. Vidyarthi defines sacred complex as a center of civilization where pilgrims from different regions of India and from different levels of culture interact.

The concept of sacred complex is given by L.P. Vidyarthi in his book "Sacred Complex of Hindu Gaya" after studying Hindu Gaya, Bihar. A sacred complex is an intricate and interdependent grouping of sacred geography, sacred performance, and sacred specialists. The sacred complexes of Hindu places of pilgrimage reflect levels of continuity, compromise, and combination between great and little traditions.

Components of Sacred complex

Sacred Geography: The sacred parts of Gaya constitute a heterogeneous complex of hundreds of sacred objects and places located within sacred grounds (Kshetra). Kshetra is divided into zones, segments, and clusters of sacred centres. A sacred centre is important because rites are performed here, and it may be an idol in a temple, a tree, etc. Each centre has its own importance and may vary in spread at the local, district, state, and universal levels.

Sacred Performance: There are many sacred performances at Hindu Gaya like prayers, offering prasad, floral offering etc. But the most significant performance is the final rites for ancestral spirits performed here—Gaya Shraddha—so that the ancestral soul attains Moksha.

Sacred Specialist: Various types of sacred specialists are connected, on the one hand, with sacred centres and Gaya itself and, on the other hand, with sacrificers.

The most specialised group are the Gayawal caste of Brahmin priests, who hold a monopoly over Gaya Shraddha.

All four aspects of Gayawal priesthood—folk, Sanskrit, feudalistic, and proletarian continue to exist among Gayawal.

This concept is useful to understand:

1. Cultural complexity and heterogeneity
2. Importance of pilgrim centres
3. Spread and survival of culture
4. Integration of culture
5. Great and Little Tradition: Change and Continuity in Indian Civilization
6. Communicate with the supernatural to attain moksha.
7. Promote acts, literature, etc.

The sacred specialist of the place of pilgrimage maintains a distinct style of life and transmits elements of great tradition to the rural population of India. They are even in the process of modification and transformation as a result of the general development of the large universe of Hindu civilization.

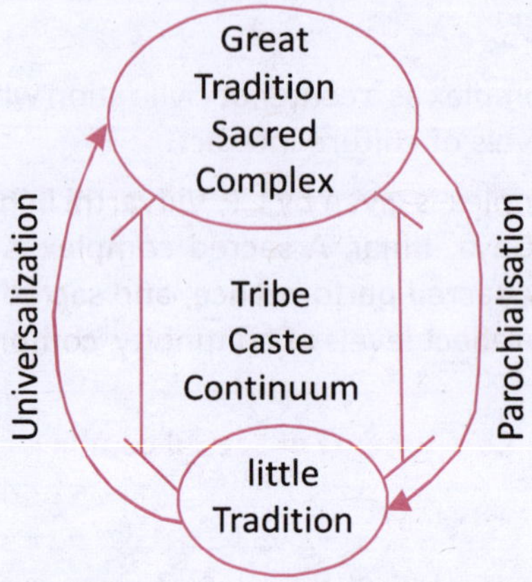

Saraswati found that unlike at Mecca or Jerusalem, where they hold a common concept of sacred and participate equally in sacred performance, it doesn't seem to be true to Hindu places of pilgrimage, yet they integrate diverse cultural traditions into a common bond of civilization.

Saraswati did prominent work like 'The Holy Circuit of Nimsar', 'The Temple Organisation in Goa', etc. In his study of Kashi, he concluded that although the Sacred Complex of Kashi may appear to be predominantly a Brahmin complex, it is indeed a complex of a much bigger organisation of traditions known as Indian Civilization, where the Brahmanical temple of Viseshwara and the non-Brahmanical shrine of Agiyabeer co-exist. The textually learned Karmakandi and the illiterate, untouchable 'Domto' conduct sacred performances together, and a Nastic Brahmin touches the feet of an Awadhoot who eats carcasses. Among others is Jha's sacred complex of Ratanpur, Mahapatra's Lingaraj temple, etc.

The concept of sacred complexes has become a very popular theoretical model for studying traditional cities and places of pilgrimage in Indian civilization.

Case Study

- **Kashi and Tamil Sangamam**

The programme's goal is to honour, affirm, and rediscover the long-standing ties between Tamil Nadu and Kashi, two of the most significant and venerable centres of learning in the nation. The curriculum intends to give individuals from all walks of life, such as academics, students, philosophers, traders, artisans, and artists from the two regions, the chance to come together, exchange their knowledge, cultures, and best practises, and learn from one another's experiences.

Our culture and civilization have always been centred in Kashi and Tamil Nadu. Tamil and Sanskrit are two of the oldest languages ever spoken. "In Kashi, we have Baba Vishwanath, and in Tamil Nadu, we have the blessings of Lord Rameshwaram," t he prime minister exclaimed. Shiva permeates Kashi and Tamil Nadu alike. The Prime Minister noted that Tamil Nadu and Kashi have always been sources of art, whether it is music, l iterature, or visual art.

Q 2. Nature-Man-Spirit Complex

Ans. Nature, man, and spirit are associated with development anthropology. Based on the cultural ecology approach of Julian Steward, it can serve socioeconomic purposes. The concept of nature-man-spirit complex is given by L.P. Vidyarthi after studying the Malers of Rajmahal Hills in Jharkhand in his book "The Maler". L.P. Vidyarthi holds that nature (Khallu cultivation), man (social organisation), and spirit (Gossaiyan) together form an interacting complex, and the social life of Malers revolves around the forest.

They depend upon forests for food, timber, housing, fodder, and medicine; they practise Khallu cultivation; and they are fond of Mahua drink brewed from trees. During marriage, couples take a round of trees instead of fire altars. Lack of privacy in small huts leads them to have sexual activity at feasts. Similarly, Malers worship spirits, and foremost among them is Gossaiyan. They govern both good and bad spirits. It serves as a bridge between Malers and the supernatural. This develops in forests, and they perform many rituals to pacify Gossain. Therefore, the lives of Malers depend upon forests and spirits, and they never create imbalance in this complex.

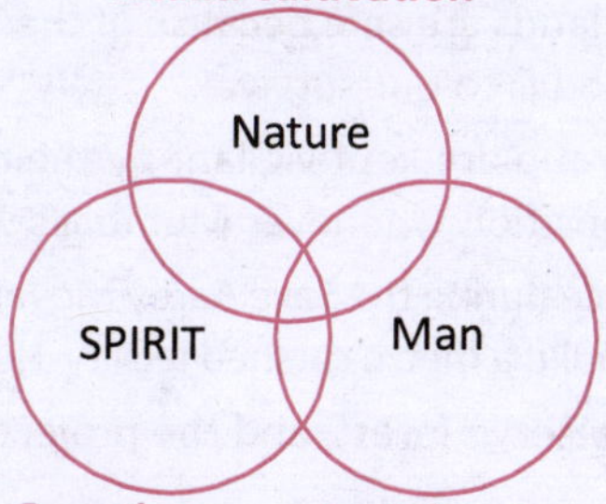

According to L.P. Vidyarthi's observation of Malers, they look at any government scheme with suspicion.

Exploitation of Paharia during British rule, prevalence of and increase in bribery and corruption among locals, and imposition of schemes without consultation of Malers led towards this type of thinking. According to PK Singh, the content of the nature-man-spirit complex may change through time; 'e' (environment) and 'q' (god) are decreasing, while the values of 't' (technology) and 'r' (dependence on man) are increasing, but the whole complex remains constant (e*q*r*t = k (constant)). If these variables are known, the level of a given culture's future course can be predicted

It helps in understanding the adaptation of socio-cultural institutions to local environmental conditions.

It even shows that little traditions are not only resilient and capable of perpetuating themselves but may reject great traditions without getting overawed by them.

Concept of L.P. Vidyarthi can be a useful tool of advice for various agencies while formulating and implementing development projects among tribal societies or while rehabilitating them. If the nature-man-spirit complex of PVTG gets disturbed, projects formulated for PVTG may backfire, e.g., Dongria Kondhs against the Niyamgiri Hill project.

Harris had given the concept of Man-Nature-Culture in cultural ecology; Vidyathi has reduced the scope of that concept by replacing culture with spirit.

Case Study

- **Tribal women making rakhis with seeds of indigenous trees under the Vruksha Bandhan Project**

As part of the Vrushka Bandhan Project, 1100 Aurangabad tribal women make Rakhis for Raksha Bandhan using the seeds of local trees, providing a distinctive contribution to expanding the forest cover and halting climate change. The project, based on Gauadharitparamparagatkheti, aims to safeguard tribal tribes' traditional ecological knowledge against the harmful effects of chemical agriculture. The concept of making rakhis from local seeds was first conceived by the 1100 members of the Mahila Kissan Manch.

- **India's Leopard God, Waghoba, Aids Wildlife Conservation in the Country**

The Adivasis of Mumbai are indigenous groups that include members of the Warlis, Kolis, Dubbas, and other tribes. They have a strong bond with the natural world.

They primarily reside in and near forested areas like the Sanjay Gandhi National Park and the neighbouring Aare y Milk Colony in Mumbai's little hamlets known as padas. These residents seldom complain, despite the fact that leopards roam freely there. They actually take satisfaction in coexisting with predators.

The Adivasis of Mumbai revere Hirwa Dev, the "Green God," who grants us access to the natural resources nece ssary to sustain our existence. We also offer prayers to the leopard or tiger god, or Waghoba.

He reigns as the Forest King. Our woodlands are safe because of the Waghoba's strength and bravery. And we are all aware of how important wood is to our survival.

Bhoir and the members of his tribal group are kept vigilant by their strong bonds with the forest and its leopards. The Adivasis stand up in opposition whenever Mumbai's woods are in danger.

Many of them were detained by the police during the Save Aarey Movement as they demonstrated against the removal of trees from Aarey in order to build a metro carshed facility. However, their objections weren't in vain.

An area of Aarey was designated as a reserve forest, and the project had to be relocated.

3.4

Impact of Buddhism, Jainism, Islam and Christianity on Indian Society

Q 1. Impact of Buddhism on Indian Society

Ans. Buddhism emerged around the 6th century B.C. Buddhism contributed a lot to Indian society, and its impact can be explained through the following headings:

Religious Impact: Buddhism is the simplest religion. It attacks the dominance of the priestly class, rituals, and many sacrifices, particularly animal sacrifice. Buddhism is based on morality and ethical values. It is based upon the principle that everyone can attain a solution by following a righteous way of life, even without performing complicated rituals.

Buddhism is against many dogmas of Brahmanism, thus it brought many changes in earlier religious belief; hence, Brahmanism also became simpler up to a certain extent and discarded animal sacrifice.

In earlier Hinduism, idols were not worshipped because the practise of idol worship was initiated by Buddhists when they created idols of Buddha at the Gandhara School of Art under the patronage of Kanishka. Buddhists also constructed stupas, and by imitating them, Hindus constructed temples. Thus, idol worship and temple building, two main components of Hindu religion, are contributions of Buddhism.

Social Impacts: Buddhism attacked the caste system. It opened the gate for all and preached that everyone can follow the belief irrespective of one's caste; it promotes equality among all. Many Buddhists opened hospitals, even for animals, and sarais for resting. Doing charity is another Buddhist principle. Buddhists also advocated morality and stood against social evils like intoxication and prostitution.

Economic Impact: The earliest Buddhist text, Sutta pitaka, advocated the promotion of agriculture. This text also mentions that animals are just like one's friends and should not be slaughtered. Thus, due to the impact of Buddhism, the cattle wealth of the country increased and agriculture flourished.

Political Impact: Buddhism places stress on national integration and non-violence. It was under the influence of Buddhism that Ashoka gave up his policy of war and adopted the principle of love. The impact of Buddhist thoughts is also reflected in foreign policy—Panchsheel and non-alignment. It is also reflected in Gandhi's policy of nonviolence. Buddhism is a missionary religion, so many missionaries were sent, particularly by Ashoka and Kanishka, to different countries like China, Japan, Sri Lanka, Jawa, Burma, etc. Foreign countries consider India a holy land and the source of their religion. Initial religious relations between India and other countries culminated in economic and political relations. The national flag of India contains a chakra, and the national emblem of India is a contribution of Buddhism.

On literature: Buddhism also contributed in the field of literature. Buddha preached in Pali, which was the language of the masses. Thus, people come to know about many religious aspects; the Tripitakas and Jatakas were translated into many languages. Many Buddhists, like Amarsingh wrote Amarksha, Ashwaghosha wrote Buddhacharitra, and Nagarjuna wrote on Ayurveda, which enriched the local literature of India.

Educational Impact: Buddhism also contributed a lot in the field of education. The famous universities of ancient times like Nalanda, Vikramshila, and Taxila were actually Buddhist viharas that later developed into universities. Students, even from foreign countries, came to these universities to acquire education.

On art: Buddhism also has a profound impact in the field of art. Buddhists constructed many stupas, like the Sanchi Stupa. They created pillars like the Sarnath pillar. They were the first to construct cave temples like Kanheri, Karle, Nashik, etc. Kanishka patronised the Gandhara School of Art. It produced the earliest image of Lord Buddha, in which Buddha was projected as the most handsome god and equated to the Greek god Apollo. Buddhists also contributed in the field of painting, like Ajanta painting and Bagh painting (M.P.).

From the above discussion, it becomes clear that there is no field of Indian society that has remained untouched by the impact of Buddhism. It made Indian society more logical and promoted rational thinking among the people. It taught people not to take things for granted but to argue for and judge them on their merit. It exercised great humanising and philanthropic influence on Indian society.

Case Study

- **Global Buddhist Summit 2023**

In New Delhi, the two-day Global Buddhist Summit 2023 came to a successful conclusion. There has been widespread agreement that the following fundamentals need to be emphasised and worked on in order to serve as inspiration and direction in light of the Buddha's teachings of peace, wellbeing, harmony, and compassion for universal peace: In the current world situation, the human species has a great desire to be free from conflict, ill will, greed, selfishness, and uncertainty. Both in our daily lives and on a worldwide scale, peace and harmony are desperately needed. The best resources for interfaith discussion, religious harmony, and world peace are the texts, doctrines, and philosophy of the Buddha Dhamma. Environment Sustainability: We recognise that environmental degradation is one of the most pressing challenges facing humanity today. We affirm our commitment to protect the environment and promote sustainable development. We urge governments and individuals to take action to reduce carbon emissions, protect biodiversity, and preserve natural resources for future generations.

We realise that contentment and inner serenity are the sources of genuine happiness. We urge people to practise mindfulness, compassion, and wisdom since these qualities are crucial for fostering happiness and wellbeing. We acknowledge the relevance of Buddhist pilgrimage as a living tradition that fosters spiritual development, cross-cultural understanding, and societal harmony. We demand that governments uphold the Buddhist religion's holiest sites, safeguard them from harm, and work to ensure that all people can visit them.

Recommendations: A paradigm shift in how people view nature is urgently needed. Members of the Sangha, Buddhist leaders, scholars, followers, and institutions can all contribute significantly and effectively to resolving this complex situation by drawing on the Buddha's teachings for the wellbeing of all sentient beings. The biennial Global Buddhist Summit's continuation is one such crucial step in this direction. The contemporary system of university education predates Nalanda, one of the most important centres of Dhamma instruction for over 700 years between the 5th and 12th centuries AD. It was renowned for cultivating moral character and teaching values. Instilling these ideals in young people is necessary to transform society into "Vasudeva Kutumbakam."

Q 2. Impact of Jainism on Indian society

Ans. Mahavira Jain believed to have lived between 599-527 B.C. The ethical idealism of Jainism occupies a central place in the description of its impact on Indian society. It has strengthened ethical life and moral virtues. Jainism stands for austerity to shut down the influx of evil. Jainism appeared almost along with Buddhism; thus, like Buddhism, it also had an impact on Indian society, which is:

1. **Religious Impact:**
   a. Mahavira Jain, the founder of Jainism, put stress on fasting. He even advocated salvation through starvation, thus fasting became part of Indian society due to the contribution of Jainism. Mahavira Jain also put stress on right meditation; thus, this feature of Hinduism is considered to be taken from Jainism.
   b. Like Buddhism, Jainism also attacked the priestly class and many irrelevant rituals. Thus, it is also a simpler religion. It preaches that anyone can become its follower.
2. **Social Impact:**
   a. Jainism was also against the caste system. It placed stress on ethics, values, and morality.
   b. It provides equality for women. It was also against many social evils, particularly prostitution and intoxication.
3. **Economic Impact:** Jainism promotes urban culture. Mahavira Jain was against the practise of agriculture, so under his influence, a class of merchants emerged. Even today, the majority of Jain is merchants and practise trade and commerce.
4. **Impact on language:** Mahavira Jain discarded Sanskrit and preached his principles in Ardha-magadhi, the language of the masses. This language also contributed to the development of Marathi and Kannada.
5. **Public services:** Maravira Jain put stress on charity, and many Dharamashalas and Goshalas are opened by many Jaina followers.

6. Impact on Architecture:

a. Like Buddhists, Jains also erected many stupas, and one of such is Kankali Tila in Mathura. They also constructed many caves, like the Tiger Cave of Udaigiri (Orrisa) and Indra Sabha at Ellora. They also constructed many cave temples, like Hathigumpha at Udaigiri. Some other temples are at Khajuraho and Mount Abu. All these Jain buildings enriched the architecture of Indian society.

b. Thus, like Buddhism, Jainism also has an impact on almost every aspect of Indian society. It still exists in Indian society despite a number of distortions from earlier times.

Case Study

- **150th Birth Anniversary of Shri Vijay Vallabh Surishwar**

The Saardh Janm Shatabdi Mahamahotsav (150th Birth Anniversary Celebrations of Jainacharya Shree Vijay Vallabh Surishwer in 2022) was celebrated by the Ministry of Culture under the auspices of Azadi ka Amrit Mahotsav and in collaboration with Shri Aatm Vallabh Jain Smarak Nidhi. The Prime Minister made a statement about the current geopolitical situation in the world, saying, "Today the world is experiencing the crisis of war, terror, and violence and looking for inspiration and encouragement to break out of this vicious circle." Shri Modi emphasised that in this situation, the strength of modern India combined with old traditions and philosophy is proving to be a great source of hope for the rest of the globe. The path outlined by Acharya Shri Vijay Vallabh Surishwar and the teachings of Jain gurus, he continued, are the answers to the world's problems. According to PM, "Acharya Ji lived a life of nonviolence, seclusion, and renunciation and made constant attempts to spread confidence in people towards these concepts. He emphasised how Acharya Ji's commitment to harmony and peace was evident even through the atrocities of partition. Acharya Shri was forced to break his Chaturmas fast as a result. The Prime Minister drew comparisons to Mahatma Gandhi, who followed the Acharyas' recommended path of "aparigraha" during the liberation campaign. "Aparigraha is not just renunciation but also controlling all kinds of attachment," he remarked.

The celebration honoured the teachings and life of Guru Vallabh Ji. In addition to guiding his followers towards spiritual enlightenment, he went above and beyond the typical demanding life of a Jain saint by taking it upon himself to better the masses through social reforms, education, and an inclusive and participatory approach to address pressing challenges and problems. His parents were Shri Deep Chand Ji and Smt. Icchya Bai, and he was born in Vadodara in 1870 AD. He discovered joy and calm in hearing the sermons of Jain saints, and these inclinations caused him to become a saint at the young age of 17.

Q 3. Impact of Islam on Indian society

Ans. The word Islam means surrendering oneself to God. The impact is mainly felt due to its humanistic concepts like fraternity, justice, charity, etc. India remains under Islamic rule for a long time. Thus, Indian society experienced Islamic influence in various fields:

1. **Religious impact:** Islam advocates the concept of monotheism, i.e., belief in one God, which provides equality to all. Islam doesn't create any priestly class; it is a simple and practical religion without any dogmas or irrelevant rituals. A number of members of depressed castes embraced Islam in order to save themselves from the clutches of the caste system. Sufi tradition emphasises Sul-i-kul, i.e., peace for all.
2. **Political impact:** As Islam advocated equality for all, the right to equality before the law as enshrined in our constitution is believed to be due to the impact of Islam. The Hindu Marriage Act, which provides more say to women in dissolution of marriage, and the Hindu Succession Act, by which a girl can claim her share in the parental property, is believed to be influenced by Islamic social ideology.

3. **Impact on Music:** Even though Islam doesn't recognise music, the contribution of Islam towards the evolution of Ghazal, Thumri, Qawwali, Sherwani, etc. was associated with Islamic scholars, and Indians absorb these musical forms with gratitude. The invention of Veena, Sarangi, etc. is also associated with Islam. The classical dance form of India, Kathak, is also an outcome of Hindu and Muslim efforts.
4. **Impact in the medical field:** Muslims, particularly Arabs, introduced in India a unique method of treatment that they learned from the Greeks, i.e., the Unani system. The Ministry of AYUSH has given due importance to the Unani system.
5. **Impact in the fields of literature, architecture, and dress pattern:**
   a. A significant language, i.e., Urdu, is a creation of Islam. Although this language was created in India by the efforts of both Hindus and Muslims, Muslims were the first to recognise it and make it the official language of India. We use many Urdu words regularly, like Kurta, Kagaz, Bandook, Chaprasi, Naukar, Sipahi, Charkha, Kalam, etc.
   b. In the field of architecture, domes and minarets introduced by Muslims became part of every religious building of Hindus and Sikhs. Nath (nose ring), which is an important part of jewellery among Hindu women, is also taken from Islamic fashion.
   c. B.S. Upadhaya said that no country in the world can boast a greater or equal number of Muslim monuments than those built in India in terms of variety or beauty.

We should recognise and cherish our composite culture and rededicate ourselves to its maintenance in the face of assaults on these values both by Hindu and Muslim reactionaries and fundamentalist.

Case Study

- **Islam in India's soft power**

Long before Joseph S. Nye invented the phrase, nations were using soft power in the course of their foreign policy and diplomacy. When visiting Abu Dhabi, Saudi Arabia, and Indonesia, nations whose mosques are revered as national landmarks, Prime Minister Modi visited them. These trips were out of politeness for the visiting head of state. A very serious speech he delivered on March 17, 2016, in New Delhi, served as the opening address for the World Sufi Forum. Then he politely accepted that India's cultural legacy includes Sufism and Islam.

"Our country arose as one of the most vigorous hubs of Sufism, just as India became a key hub of Islamic civilization. Even though it continued to have a strong foundation in the Hadis and the Holy Quran, Sufism came to represent Islam in India. India's openness and plurality fostered the growth of Sufism. It participated in her spiritual tradition and developed an Indian ethos.

People who are only interested in short-term political benefits ignore the reality that India integrated Islam and transformed it from its Wahabi character into something more positive. The Sufi school of Islam and India's Barelvi and Deobandi theology schools gave it a new and larger interpretation. The spread of Islam to Southeast Asia, where it is a more moderate religion than the radicalised one wreaking havoc in West Asia, was also largely facilitated by India.

In order to fight the radical Jihadi trend that conceptually supports terrorism, India can take the lead in embra cing Islam and displaying its more moderate Sufi interpretation.

The Islamic tourism industry has a lot of potential for growth in India.

Q 4. Impact of Christianity on Indian society

Ans. It is generally believed that Saint Thomas introduced Christianity to India around 2000 years ago. But its influence was not felt until the arrival of Europeans in India. Christianity, particularly Christian missionaries, influenced various aspects of Indian society, particularly after the Charter Act of 1813:

1. **Contribution to education:**
   a. The activities of Christian missionaries in India also involve the establishment of high-quality schools in various parts of the country. They opened schools for girls and also promoted education among dalits. Even today, many missionary schools are operating in the country. Along with education, missionaries also brought with them a printing press, which helped in the dissemination of literature of all kinds. Christian missionaries were pioneers in the promotion of English and other modern vernacular languages. *R.L. Rawat mentioned* in his book "The History of Indian Education" that India will remain indebted to Christian missionaries for the production of text books, dictionaries, and grammar.
2. **Contribution of fixed languages, literature, and journalism**:
   a. Christian missionaries also contributed a lot in the fields of language, literature, and journalism. A missionary named Constanzio improved many Tamil alphabets to make them suitable for printing presses. French missionary Francis Mary began to work on Hindustani as early as 1680, and the Hindi language is an outcome of Hindustani. Another missionary, Kellogg, brought together almost a dozen dialects to create the language that is now known as Hindi. He also produced the Hindi language in 1893, which is still in circulation.
   b. William Carey and his colleagues were responsible for producing the first journal, periodical, and newspaper in English in India. One of their papers, 'Friends of India,' lived on and is now published under the name 'Statesman' from Calcutta and New Delhi.
   c. J.L. Nehru, in his book "Discovery of India," gives credit to Christian missionaries for decreasing the dominant influence of Sanskrit and Persian on language, literature, and journalism.
3. **Contribution in the field of medicine:**
   a. Another contribution of missionaries is in the medical field. They opened many hospitals in different parts of the country, and two of such hospitals are internationally known today: Christians Missionaries College (CMC) Ludhiana, established by Missionary E. Brown, and CMC Vellore. They also established many medical institutions for TB patients and for those who suffered from leprosy. Many public health centres were opened for the disabled. The first hospital for the deaf was opened by an order of nuns in Bombay. They also distributed free medicals and provided free treatment as part of charity to the unprivileged.
4. **Social reforms:**
   a. From the very beginning, Christian missionaries were surprised by the prevalence of many social evils in India, like the killing of lepers, the Sati system, child marriage, child sacrifice, etc. It was due to the efforts of missionary William Carey that Lord Wellesley declared child sacrifice an act of murder and put a complete ban on it in 1802.
   b. The first issue of 'Friends of India' contained a detailed discussion against the Sati system. The missionary William Carey launched a campaign against the Sati system. In 1814, Raja Ram Mohan Roy joined such an agitation. Due to their efforts, Lord William Bentick prohibited the practise of Sati in 1829.
   c. Christian missionaries were also against the practise of untouchability and the caste system; thus, due to their efforts, the Caste Disability Removal Act was passed in 1870.
   d. They were also against child marriage, and consequently, the Child Marriage Restraint Act was passed in 1860. They also advocated widow remarriage, and the Widow Remarriage Act of 1856 was the outcome of their contribution.

5. Impact on economic life:

a. Christian missionaries also worked in the field of rural development. They introduced new agriculture techniques to help the family enhance their productivity. In order to promote knowledge among them, they established an agriculture college in Allahabad. Missionaries from the Basel Mission introduced for the first time in India cheap terracotta tiles as building material in Indian villages.

6. Impact on the political field:

a. Missionaries advocated aspects like the right of conversion from one religion to another. Moreover, the ideas of liberty, equality, and fraternity have emerged due to Christian influence. All these rights were accepted by the constituent assembly and became part of our constitution. The ideas of secularism and humanitarianism are also influenced by Christian missionaries.

7. Impact on the religious field:

a. Christian missionaries always advocated universal brotherhood. Many ST, SC, OBC, and many more converted to Christianity.

b. Many religious movements in India were influenced by Christian missionaries. Under the influence of Christianity, many Indians gave up dysfunctional traditions and customs and followed new ones.

According to Victor D'Souza, Christianity has been an important factor in modernization and economic development through the social values it has legitimised in India.

Case Study

- **Impact of Christianity on Naga culture**

The Nagas underwent new transformations that broadened their perspectives. The populace lost their bearings and started to experience an identity crisis that they had never experienced before. The operations of the British colonists and missionaries laid the groundwork for modernization, which resulted in the development of Naga society's economy as a self-sufficient entity. The first missionaries to forbid performing tribal dances, singing tribal songs, and engaging in other indigenous practises were American Baptist missionaries.

In order to make Nagas "civilised," it was necessary to remove from their brains their previous behaviours, which they regarded as "heathen." On the other hand, their lack of understanding of tribal culture Inculturation is seen by the church as a vital component of religious life. Bishop Stephen Fernando stated, "We Catholics have always permitted the principles so dear to Pandit Nehru to approach the tribal people with love, to preserve what is good in them, not to destroy their dances, songs, and joy, and at the same time to give them the advantage of civilization".

4

Emergence, Growth and Development in India

Emergence, Growth and Development in India— Contributions of the 18th, 19th and early 20th Century scholar administrators. Contributions of Indian anthropologists to tribal and caste studies.

Q 1. Emergence, Growth and Development of Anthropology in India

Ans. Anthropology is a young discipline in India. The emergence, growth, and development of anthropology in India are classified into the following four phases:

Phase-I: Formative Phase (1784–1919): The establishment of the Asiatic Society of Bengal in 1784 initiated the first scientific studies of nature and man in India. Prof. D.N. Majumdar found the beginning of anthropology in India with the establishment of the Asiatic Society of Bengal by Sir William Jones. This organisation conducted many surveys and studies among Indian tribes and also published many journals and papers. The most significant journal of this society was 'Man in India'. By this time, many administrators like Campbell, Lantham, and Risley had shown an interest in the study of Indian tribes, and they had published some general books on them. The first Indian who was inspired by the work of these administrators was S.C. Roy. He conducted many studies among the tribes of Chotanagpur like the Oraons, Hos, Birhors, Kharias, etc. Later on, Hutton calls S.C. Roy the "father of Indian ethnology." With the entry of S.C. Roy, Indian anthropology appeared on the world map.

Constructive Phase (1920–1949): The growth of Indian anthropology entered a second phase with the introduction of social anthropology at the P.G. level at Calcutta University in 1920, and K.P. Chattopadhaya was the first professor of social anthropology. The first generation of anthropologists produced by Calcutta University includes D.N. Majumdar, T.C. Das, Biswas, B.S. Guha, and S.S. Sarkar, who emerged as renowned anthropologists in the whole world. The year 1938 was a turning point in Indian anthropology when the Joint Session of the Indian Science Congress Association and the British Association was held, in which a number of anthropologists like D.N. Majumdar and M.N. Srinivas also produced certain remarkable outstanding works like D.N. Majumdar's changing Hos of Singhbhum and M.N. Srinivas's Marriage and Family in Mysore. D.N. Majumdar's research in Bengal, Orissa, and U.P. further led to the growth of Indian anthropology.

In 1945, the research institute Anthropological Survey of India was established by B.S. Guha, which emerged as the biggest research organisation of its kind in the whole world. The establishment of this institute further developed Indian anthropology. This period also saw the entry of Verrier Elwin, who totally involved himself in the study of the tribes of Central India. Some of his works are "The Baigas", "The Agarias", "Muria Murder and Suicide", "Muria and their

Ghotul" and "Religions of Indian Tribes," are regarded as classics in the literature of Indian anthropology. Meanwhile, C.V.F. Haimendorfalso worked in Hyderabad. His two works, "The Chenchus" and "The Reddis of Bison Hill," are worth mentioning. Due to the efforts, particularly of V. Elwin, the horizons of Indian anthropology were further broadened.

Analytical Phase: During this phase, the study of Indian villages became fashionable. A number of American anthropologists, like Morris Opler, Oscar Lewis, and Mandelbaum, and a number of their students, came to India to study Indian villages. Many Indian anthropologists like D.N. Majumdar, M.N. Srinivas, and S.C. Dube also carried out studies of Indian villages. Some American anthropologists like Robert Redfield, Milton Singer, and Mckim Marriot also conducted their studies in Indian villages to understand dimensions of Indian civilization.

During this time, religious studies also became popular. D.N. Majumdar put forth the concept of Bongaism, and M.N. Srinivas published a book entitled "Religion and Society among Coorgs". L.P. Vidyarthi put forth the concept of the sacred complex to understand the role of religious places in the formation of Indian civilization. Also by this time, many anthropologists had become interested in the applied aspects of anthropology, and they initiated the process of applying anthropological knowledge to solve many problems and bring welfare to people. The applied aspect of Indian anthropology established it as a developed discipline.

Evaluative Phase (1990 onward): This is a recent phase in the development of Indian anthropology. Now, anthropologists are interested in the study of their own societies. They are employing new methodologies, collecting new data, providing new theories, and modifying older ones. Due to the efforts of contemporary anthropologists like R.S. Mann, A.C. Danda, Makhan Jha, etc., Indian anthropology will attain new heights in the coming future.

Issues:

1. Still following colonial anthropologists' footsteps and not evolving own identity.
2. Lack of contemporary studies on issues like Article 370 removal impact and saffron wave impact in India.
3. Lack of R&D support to universities.
4. The government doesn't involve tribal research institute academicians in policy formulation for tribal.

Suggestions:

1. Studies on contemporary issues like urbanisation, pollution, the saffron wave, etc.
2. Develop sui generis models like ethnoscience.
3. R&D support and action anthropology at the front.
4. Interaction between Indian American, German, and British anthropologists.

Q 2. S.C. Roy (1871-1942)

Ans. Sarat Chandra Roy has been adorned with many great titles by Indian and world anthropologists, such as' Father of Indian ethnology', 'First Indian ethnographer', 'First Indian anthropologist', etc.

His deep interest in tribal affairs, though he was a lawyer by practise, resulted in the publication of a book entitled "Munda and Their Country" (1912). This book is the first monograph written on an Indian tribe by an Indian writer. It is because of this fact that he is regarded as the first Indian ethnologist, ethnographer, or Indian anthropologist.

Contribution to Tribal Cultures: His next book deals with Oraon, entitled "The Oraons of Chotanagpur", which throws light on the social organisation of Oraons. He was the first person to shed light on the functions of a youth dormitory. He also gave a detailed description of village panchayats and the praha system. Another book dealt with Oraons' religious and magical beliefs. The last monograph that Roy wrote in collaboration with his son was on Kharia and gave a comparative description of all three divisions of Kharia: Dudh Kharia, Dhelki Kharia, and Hill Kharia.

Studies in Physical Anthropology and Prehistoric Anthropology: In various tribal monographs, like Mundas and Oraons, he also gave details about their physical characteristics. S.C. Roy's main contribution in the field of prehistoric anthropology is digging up the Asura site and discovering stones, copper, and bronze tool sets.

Anthropology of Caste: He tried to explain the origin of the caste system, and for this he included in his sweep not only ancient Hindu literature but also ethnographic literature on caste and tribes in various parts of the country. He made a fine distinction between different areas with regard to caste rigidity and the way it affected the lives of people.

Study of Folklore: S.C. Roy made a strong plea for the study of folklore by anthropologists. According to him, folklore throws a flood of light on the early intellectual evolution of human society, and for this reason, he regarded folklore as the prehistory of the human mind.

Applied Anthropology: Roy was consulted by police officers in 1921 about a notice circulating in Chotangpur. He advised them that it was just a notice for a meeting of Parha and nothing related to subverting the British government. Another issue related to the flag in the Oraon area was solved by S.C. Roy. Oraon believed that the emblem of the flag endowed the village with extraordinary power. He solved the problem by making a flag with the symbol of an aeroplane and persuaded the villagers to adopt it as it was superior to the railway train flag of another village.

To promote further anthropological research, he started the journal 'Man in India' in 1921. He was an inspirational figure for next-generation anthropologists like N.K. Bose and D.N. Majumdar. Indian anthropology is forever indebted to his scholarship and vision.

Q.3. L.K. Anantha Krishna Iyer (1861-1937)

Ans. Diwan Bahadur Lakshminarayanapuram Krishna Ananthakrishna Iyer was a great pioneer in anthropology and ethnology, and his extensive field studies made him a renowned figure amongst his contemporaries. Born in 1861 (Kerela), he worked as a college teacher, but his interest in human society studies led him to be appointed superintendent of ethnography for Cochin princely and get it published as "Tribes and Castes of Cochin" in two volumes. The first volume gave a descriptive account of hill tribes, jungle tribes, and other low castes, while the second volume deals with higher groups such as Namboodiri, Kshatriya, Brahmin, etc.

His works revolve around life cycle studies, seeing caste and tribe as isolated entities rather than seeing linkages with neighbouring entities. He was keen to record changes occurring in various aspects of tribal life while documenting facts about tribal customs and institutions. He could not even ignore the exploitative changes that occur among tribes. As in the case of Kadars, he stated that their frequent contact with people of the plains has deprived them of simple habits and modified their lives.

He modified Risley's format (27 points) for census operations and ethnographic surveys into a 14-point format. In his book, "Cochin Tribes and Castes", he included their introduction, origin and tradition, marriage and customs, physical and mental characteristics, etc.

When anthropologists restricted themselves to the study of preliterate communities, they attempted to study literate communities such as Namboodiri, Nayars, Syrian Christians, etc. He rejected the traditional way of collecting information. During his field studies, he used to interact with people in their natural environment. He emphasised the importance of participant observation.

He was elected President of the Ethnology Section (now the Anthropology and Archaeological Section) of the first Indian Science Congress held in Kolkata in 1914. He joined the first Department of Anthropology to open at Calcutta University. He toured Europe extensively and delivered lectures in Indian ethnography in Paris, Vienna, Berlin, etc.

His best works include the book "Anthropology of Syrian Christians" and Lectures on Ethnography. Author of five books and a dozen papers, he died in 1937 in Chennai.

Q 4. N.K. Bose (1901-1972)

Ans. Nirmal Kumar Bose was a bachelor in geology; his interest in temple architecture turned him towards a master's in anthropology. He worked in various positions, such as research fellow and assistant lecturer in anthropology at Calcutta University. He worked as Director of the Anthropological Survey of India and Advisor to the Government of India on Tribal Affairs during 1959–64. Post-retirement, he accompanied a study team to Assam Hill Districts and reported on educational problems in NEFA in 1966. He was awarded the Padma Shri for his contribution.

His most famous books were "Cultural Anthropology", "Culture and Society in India", "Excavations in Mayurbhanj" and "Problems of National Integration". He wrote many articles in various journals and was editor of the first anthropological journal, 'Man in India' since 1951.

He was deeply influenced by Boas, Kroeber, Marx, Malinowski, and others. He applied the diffusion study of the distribution of cultural traits to his study of temple architecture. His Cultural Anthropology takes a functional approach to defining the nature of culture as an adaptive device, organised around the soul of culture or the body of beliefs and sentiments central to culture.

Contribution:

Caste System: Bose rejected the concept of pure and impure. He proposed that the persistence of the caste system can be found in the economic and cultural security provided by non-competitive, hereditary, vocation-based productive organisations in an ideal pattern of rural society. He proposed further that caste as an economic system and as a regulator of social life has disintegrated at different rates in different religions in India.

Tribal Studies: After brief study work at Juang, Odisha, he highlighted changes in tribal economies, the absorption of tribals into Hindu culture, and the root of the tribal separatist movement. He observed in his book "Tribal Life in India" that differences between rural folk and urban classes is greater than those between peasants and tribals.

Structure of Indian Civilization: Bose highlighted many dimensions of Indian social structure and local processes such as tribal enclaves and their absorption, self-sufficiency in village communities and links with fairs, pilgrimage centres, etc., and the impact of British rule on economy and caste. He opines that traditional systems can be studied to solve contemporary problems.

Pattern of Unity: Bose proposed a pyramidal imaginary of the unity of Indian civilization, with difference at the material level and narrowing at the ideological level. He draws a contrast with European civilization, where repeated wars led to a spirit of nationalism, while India had central pluralism in relatively peaceful conditions.

Pre-Historic Archaeology: His field research at Mayurbhanj, along with that of Dharani Sen, was designed to establish stratigraphic sequence between different types of tools recovered by excavation.

Gandhism: Participating in national involvement, he published books on Gandhian thought like "My Days with Gandhi" and "Selection from Gandhi".

He was a great nationalist and social worker, inspired by *Gandhi*. In 1960, he was awarded the Padma Shri. He wrote profusely in Bengali and helped popularise anthropology by making it more relevant to contemporary society.

Q 5. D.N. Majumdar (1903-1960)

Ans. *Dhirendra Nath Majumdar* occupies a unique place in Indian anthropology. To many, he was a father figure, patriarch, and institution within himself. Born in 1903 in Patna, he obtained a master's in anthropology from Calcutta University. He went to Cambridge to write his doctoral thesis on 'Culture contact and acculturation among Ho of Kolhan' to get his PhD. He had a specialisation in social anthropology and was the first head of the department of anthropology at Lucknow University.

Tribal Studies: Being strongly influenced by *Malinowski*, he followed a functionalist approach to studying culture. He found tribes like Ho affected by external pressure. He didn't support the Tribal Reserve Area but instead believed in tribal integration.

The book titled "Tribes in Transition: A Study in Culture Pattern" is the first scientific study of the impact of modern civilization upon Indian tribal people (influenced by *Ruth Benedict*). His knowledge of tribes like the Ho of Chotanagpur and the Khasa of Jounsar Barwar was amazing. Along with *Elwin*, he initiated problem-oriented ethnography. He brought the journal 'Eastern Anthropologist'.

Rural Studies: He played an important role in encouraging village studies in India. He presented a model of an anthropological village study in a book titled "Caste and Communications in Indian Village". He stated that anthropologists and even sociologists can play an important role in studying and exploring problems of backward classes and assessing the impact of CDP (Community Development Programme) on the lives of people at village level.

Physical Anthropology: He was a member of the Census Board to collect blood and anthropometric data in U.P., Bengal, and Gujarat; Ho of Singhbhum; Gond of M.P., etc. He used several formulas to extrapolate and draw conclusions from the data. Among Central Indian tribes like Ho, Santhal, Khasas, and Birhor, he uses anthropometry to study the pattern of child growth among natives and migrants. He followed the method of cultural personality school while they studied the personalities of Japanese migrants in America. He extended his study of criminal behaviour right from childhood. He defined race in his book "Races and Cultures of India" and claimed India was a melting pot of races.

Ecological Anthropology: He proposed the concept of MARC (Man Area Resource and Cooperation). It has resulted in the development of concepts like the Nature-Man-Spirit Complex by *L.P. Vidyarthi*. Archaeological Anthro pology: He studied 600-year-old human and horse skeletons from Uttarkhand.

He was the first complete Indian anthropologist due to his work in all fields like socio-cultural, biological, archaeological, and linguistic.

Q 6. H.H. Risley (1851-1911)

Ans. Sir Herbert Hope Risley was a British civil servant, anthropologist, and linguist who published widely on the customs and social structure of Indian society.

After qualifying for civil service in 1871, he worked as an assistant magistrate in Western Bengal. It was here he became interested in studying the tribal culture of Midnapore District.

In 1885, Risley was tasked with studying the ethnographic survey of Bengal, whose results he published in 1891 in an article titled 'The Study of Ethnology in India'.

Risley is well known for his role as architect of the 1901 census of India and his subsequent publication, "The People of India" (1908). He viewed Indian society as fundamentally structured by caste. He proposed the theory of the caste system as a racial hierarchy of classification.

Risley was greatly influenced by works adhering to the evolutionary paradigm of social Darwinism (Tylor, Spencer, and Topinard). He used the anthropometry method borrowed from Topinard for classification. The definite characteristics, like the nasal index and cephalic index, were taken into account.

He argued that strict endogamy and geographical isolation provided conditions for discrete physical traits. The creation of the caste system started with the contact between Aryans and Dravidians. Aryans followed strict hypergamy, and thus two races remained distinct, and caste was devised as a way to prevent racial miscegenation.

The legacy of Risley's work still continues in India, where the colonial understanding of caste as a rigid hierarchy has provided the basis for affirmative action since Independence.

Q 7. B.S. Guha (1894-1961)

Ans. Biraja Sankar Guha came from a non-anthropological background. Student of philosophy, but inspired by Prof. Dixon, he went to Harward to do a master's and PhD in anthropology. He worked under Hootan and did his Ph.D. thesis on "The Racial Basis of the Caste System in India".

He came back to India and joined Calcutta University's Department of Anthropology. The big break came in 1927, when the government created an anthropologist post in the Zoological Survey of India. In 1936, he founded the Indian Anthropological Institute in Calcutta. He presided over the section on anthropology and archaeology at the Indian Science Congress in 1938.

Due to his efforts, an organisation called the "Anthropological Survey of India" was carved out of the Zoological Survey of India in 1946. He was its first director.

He worked to make Indian anthropology a holistic discipline consisting of ethnology, physical anthropology, prehistory, and linguistics, maintaining close affinity with allied sciences like psychology, zoology, paleobotany, etc.

Though he was not a prolific writer, his efforts led to the formation of the Indian Museum in Calcutta and the Tribal Research Institute in Ranchi.

Q 8. S.C. Dube (1922-1966)

Ans. Shyama Charan Dube is a well-known anthropologist in India. His works were multidisciplinary in nature. He did a master's in political science and got inclined towards political anthropology. His first book, "The Kamar", is a full-length monograph of the tribe Kamar of M.P. (PhD Thesis). His book, "Indian Village" deals with the total study of village Shamirpet in the region of Telangana. It considers the historical, geographical, and political perspectives as well as the economic, religious, and social practises of village Shamirpet.

For him, the fundamental principle of caste ranking is the concept of ritual purity and pollution. In the case of shamirpet, it is determined based on traditions of prescribed daily rituals, food eaten, occupation allowed, and myths. Thus, the main criteria for caste ranking in villages are rituals and not economics.

In his paper, 'Dominant caste and village leadership', he disagrees with *M.N. Srinivas* and finds political power concentrated in a few individuals rather than diffused in general.

In his paper, 'The Restive Students: Strands and Themes in Contemporary Youth Culture', he objects to the use of the term Indian students or contemporary youth as an undifferentiated mass. He identifies sub-cultures among contemporary youth.

Dube studied the diffusion of IUCDs (intrauterine contraceptive devices), which were introduced as family planning devices. He suggested the need for improvement in research using scales to measure variables.

In his book "India's changing villages" based on fieldwork in villages in UP, he dealt with changes brought to villages by the introduction of the Community Development Scheme.

Dube followed a structural-functional approach in village studies, thus interlinking various elements of social structure at the individual level as well as at a higher level to bring about solidarity and consensus among villages.

The theme of development and modernization has been uppermost in his last two decades, and he has written works related to it in the form of "Contemporary India and its Modernization".

Q 9. L.P. Vidyathi (1931-1985)

Ans. *Lalita Prasad Vidyarthi* was born in 1931 in a village near Patna. He earned a Masters in Anthropology from Lucknow University and a PhD from Chicago University. He worked under famous anthropologists like *Majumdar, Sol Tax, and Robert Redfield* in Chicago. He was head of the department of anthropology at Ranchi University.

Sacred Complex: L.P. Vidyarthi conducted an extensive study of the sacred city of Gaya and developed the concept of a sacred complex in his book "Sacred Complex in Hindu Gaya". He suggests that three components, i.e., sacred geography, sacred performance, and sacred specialists, collectively constitute the sacred complex. The sacred complex presents a picture of national unity and denotes an integrated pattern as it serves as a merging point of different traditions, castes, and cultures.

Nature-Man-Spirit Complex: He studied Sauria Paharia and the Maler Tribe so as to describe the phenomenon of the Nature-Man-Spirit Complex. He basically employed a methodological framework to examine tribal lifestyles from the focal points of ecological setting (nature), social institutions (man), and the spiritual world (spirit).

Tribal and folklore study: His book titled "Cultural Contours of Tribal Bihar" throws light on various aspects of the social institutions of the tribes of Chotanagpur. The book titled "Tribal Culture of India," authored along with *B.K.*

Roy Burman, provides information on folk art, the course of life, matrilineal relationships, and even polyandry in India.

Action and applied anthropology: In 1967, a task force was appointed under him by the Planning Commission on the eve of the 5th five-year plan to study the effects of various kinds of planning on tribal populations. He was able to formulate a plan for the tribe that suited him. This was included in his work "Applied Anthropology in India".

His case study on the Hatia industrial complex showed cultural change due to industrialization. He classified Bihar tribes into different types like hunters and gatherers, cultivators, artisans, etc. He headed the task force on the development of tribal areas, which was instrumental in the formation of the Tribal Sub-Plan (TSP).

When the 10th International Congress of Anthropological and Ethnological Science was held in India in 1978, the first time it was held in an Asian country, it was chaired by L.P. Vidyarthi.

Q 10. M.N. Srinivas (1916-1999)

Ans. Mysore Narasimhachar Srinivas was born in 1916 in Mysore. He obtained a PhD in sociology (1945) from Bombay University. He conducted fieldwork in Coorg, Rampura, etc. He studied issues like national integration, dowry, and industrialization effects, but his most crucial works are Sankritization and Dominant Caste. Sanskritization and Westernisation: He introduced the concept of Sanskritization in his book "Religion and Society among Coorgs of South India" to shed light on the process of social change occurring among low-caste Hindus in an upward direction. The process involves a change in dietary habits from non-vegetarianism to vegetarianism, the wearing of sacred thread, and a change in one's occupational habit. Sanskritization brought changes within the framework of Indian tradition, whereas Westernisation was a change resulting from contact with British socioeconomic and cultural innovations. Westernisation is a process that includes all cultural changes and institutional reforms inflicted upon Indian society as they came into political and cultural proximity with British rule and governance, e.g., the abolition of Sati. But the structural features of India were strong and intact despite technological and economic reform.

Village study: He considered villages a microcosm of Indian society and civilization. It is a village that retains its traditional composition. He viewed villages as a vertical entity consisting of several horizontal layers, one of which is caste. In his book "Remembered Village", he talks about social and economic reforms taken in Rampura. Dominant caste: In his paper 'Dominant caste in Rampura,' he defined caste as having numerical strength, economic power through land, political power, and a high place in the local hierarchy. It plays a vital role in the settlement of disputes, even in non-dominant caste matters.

Vertical and horizontal caste solidarity: He said that some common cultural elements are shared by all castes residing in a locality from highest to lowest, like common dialect and common belief. This is vertical solidarity. On the other hand, Brahmins of North, South, and Central India have common Sanskritic elements irrespective of region and language. He proclaimed that the caste system is dying, but caste is not. He was awarded the Padma Bhushan for his contribution to the social sciences.

Criticism: His concept of village is overburdened with the caste system. He didn't give a macro-understanding of Indian villages. His focus on a single village left little scope for generalisation. S.C. Dube criticised that rather than dominant castes, there are only dominant individuals. Cognitive thinkers say that the mental processes behind structure and function need to be analysed. D.N. Majumdar says that certain castes don't follow higher castes; rather, they remain content with their rituals.

However, he was a pioneer in the field of village studies in India. His studies sparked the interest of American anthropologists in India.

Q 11. Verrier Elwin (1902-1964)

Ans. He was a British missionary, but on his visit to India, he was converted to an anthropologist. Influenced by Gandhi, he said to think like a tribal to uplift tribal. He was influenced by Pandit J.L. Nehru, Sardar Patel, and Rabindranath Tagore. His love for social work led him to raise objections with the church, thereby making him resign from the post of missionary.

While conducting field work among Baigas, he found that Baigas were being destroyed by landlords and missionaries. He proposed that tribal people should be left alone instead of being acculturated. This gave him the reputation of being a person who advocated separate 'reserved national parks' for tribes. He called such national parks as Tribal Reserve Areas.

He worked to study youth dormitory (Ghotul) among Murias. It is an integral part of Gond tribal life in the Bastar region of Chattisgarh. It has an elder facilitator and young, unmarried boys and girls as members. The members are taught lessons of cleanliness, discipline, and hard work. They are also taught the idea of public service. No major social activity could happen without the participation of Ghotul members.

Elwin wrote "A Philosophy for NEFA" in collaboration with J.L. Nehru. He supported the integration perspective and developed the idea that tribes should be allowed to develop their own rules, customs, and beliefs; thereby, the concept of Tribal Panchsheel emerged.

Among the Gond, he opened Asharam, a training school for teachers with a curriculum suited to the Gond way of life. He established hospitals and homes for people affected by leprosy. Due to such efforts, he was worshipped as 'God' by Gond.

He was one of the most influential foreign anthropologists in post-independent India.

Q 12. Iravati Karve (1905-1970)

Ans. Iravati Karve is often claimed to be the first woman anthropologist in India. She obtained her PhD in anthropology in Germany, where she carried out a comparative analysis of the human skull among diverse racial groups. Later, she established the anthropology department at Pune University and served as head of Deccan College.

Famous works: "Kinship organisation in India", "Group relations in village communities", "Yuganta", "Bhils of West Khandesh", etc.

Biological: She worked on biological, ethnohistorical, and paleoanthropological issues. She advocated the concept of using 'caste' as a unit for socio-biological studies. Comparing Marathi and Bengali doesn't serve a purpose, while we need to study endogamous groups as they maintain genetic capital as a group. She studied morphological characters like eyes, hair, skin, dematoglyphics, etc.

Her book "Kinship Organisation in India" revolves around the unfolding languages, caste system, and family structure in India.

Her book "Group Relations in Village Community" tests the hypothesis of interpersonal and enter group relations affected by factors of kinship and locality in villages in Maharashtra.

Her work on "Yuganta" was based on the main character of Mahabharat and won the Sahitya Academy Award.

She did archaeological work in Langhnaj along with H.D. Sankalia.

Though she worked extensively, Nandini Sundar claimed she was not that successful due to functionalist social anthropological growth at the time, and scholars under her didn't take it forward. Karve has knowledge of both social and biological anthropology, along with writing in both English and Marathi.

Q 13. H.D. Sankalia (1908-1989)

Ans. Hasmukh Dhirajlal Sankalia did a bachelor's in Sankrit and a master's in Indian history and Buddhist studies. He was an Indian archaeologist who specialised in protohistoric and ancient history. He was influenced by F.E. Zeuner (an ecological archaeologist). He wrote a book titled "The Arctic Home in the Vedas". He pioneered archaeological excavation with several significant discoveries from the prehistoric period.

Deccan College: As Prof. in Proto and Ancient Indian History, he started systemic surveys of monuments in and around Pune with his pupils. It resulted in his paper on the megaliths of Bhavsari and the temple of Pur in the Yadava period.

Kolhapur: Excavated in 1945–46 along with M.G. Dikshit. His detailed study of the Godavari River and its tributaries revealed much about the flake tool industry.

Nevasa: In 1954–55, he excavated this site and found middle Palaeolithic tools (a flake tool). He also proved Robert Bruce Foote's assumption that the Basalt area did not have human habitation wrong.

Navdatoli: In 1957–58, he found the largest of all excavations belonging to the Chalcolithic period. It was dated around the 2nd millennium BC, which explained the gap between the Indus Valley civilization and the Vedic period.

He found a cultural pattern depicting a mixture of Iranian and Indo-Aryan cultures.

Langhnaj: He excavated a site at the banks of the Sabarmati in Gujarat. It is an important Mesolithic site where animal and crude pot burials are found. 90% of microliths are made from waste material. Other Mesolithic tools are also found.

Stratigraphical studies: Environmental dimensions like gravel deposits from wet and dry climates are also found. His major works include calling for the replacement of Palaeo-Meso-Neo terminology with Early, Middle, Late, and New Stone Age.

He was awarded the Padma Bhushan for his Indian archaeology work.

Q 14. C.V.F. Haimendorf (1909-1995)

Ans. Christopher von Furer Haimendorfwas an Austrian ethnologist. He was influenced by Malinowski, William Schmidt of the German Diffusion School, the Golden Archaeological Researcher, etc. His famous books are "The Naked Naga", "The Chenchus", "The Reddis of Bison Hills," etc. His famous monographs are Ao Naga, Konyak Naga, Chenchus, and Sherpas.

Initially, he began his work in Nagasaki. He was accompanied by J.S. Mill, who was a political agent. He wrote a travelogue in 1938 titled "The Naked Naga". It was a very subjective account of Konyak Naga.

Later, he conducted archaeological excavations in the North East and studied the evolution of material culture in the region using a historical and museum approach.

It was way back in the 1940s that the need for education among tribal people in Adilabad district of erstwhile Nizam's Hyderabad received attention. The Gond education scheme was launched by Haiemendorf, who had come to this part to study their problems. He was appointed by Nizam as an advisor on tribe and backward. He set up many educational institutions and engaged in tribal development. By 1951, it had produced 95 teachers, five village officers, one revenue inspector, five clerks, and seven forest guards, indicating success on a grand scale. The accession of Hyderabad to the Indian Union later led to the same change in education policies. Nevertheless, no initiative of any successive government was as successful as one given by Haiemendorf, which had tribal teaching tribal.

He studied cultural and social change in Chenchu. They substituted their traditional economic subsistence from hunting and gathering for travel guides for the Lord Mallikharjuna Temple of Srisalam.

He was the forerunner of concepts like Sanskritization, in which he highlighted the imitation of the lifestyle of mainstream caste groups by tribals.

He proposed an isolationist approach to tribal development. He highlighted that due to outsider contact, Gonds are being deprived of their land and becoming poorer with each passing day, while Apatanis are comparatively isolated due to difficult terrain. This has resulted in the faster development of Apatanis.

His curiosity in tribal and linguistic studies won the hearts of tribal people, especially in Gond. Even they dedicated a poem to Haimendorf, which was translated as 'Happy we are', when he returned to study culture change among Gond.

Q 15. A. Aiyappan (1905-1988)

Ans. Ayinapalli Aiyappan joined Utkal University in 1958 as professor of anthropology after retirement from service as head of the Madras Museum. He introduced museology as a paper in the anthropology curriculum.

- He got involved in the planning of tribal welfare and activated the Tribal Research Bureau.
- He rechristened the Orissa Museum with the addition of anthropological galleries.
- He was keen to see anthropology flourish in the educational centres of Orissa.
- He followed the ideas of cultural relativism of Franz Boas.
- He followed Malinowski and stressed fieldwork. For his monograph "The Social and Physical Anthropology of Nayadis", he visited Nayadi (Malabar) households for research.
- He worked on a report on the socio-economic condition of the Aborigine tribes of Madras.
- Other work: social revolution in Kerela Village
- The archaeology study includes the Arikamedu site.
- His work on wide topics and his enlightenment journey are beacons of inspiration for many young minds.

Q 16. B.K. Royburman (1922-2012)

Ans. Bikram Keshari Royburman, described accurately as the 'Walking Encyclopaedia' by S. C. Dube, was an anthropologist, social worker, and humanist. Born in Sylhet, now in Bangladesh, in 1922, he died in 2012. He has a degree and a PhD in anthropology. He did doctoral work on the Totos of the Jalpaiguri-Bhutan Border.

He worked as a lecturer at Seth College, Silchur, and retired as a professor of anthropology at Visva Bharati, Shanti Niketan. He even held the positions of Deputy Registrar General of the Census, President of the Indian Social Science Congress, Chief editor of the journal 'Indian Anthropologist'etc.

The concept of cultural and social change in Indian society is explained through various ideas like bisociation, transociation, polysociation, metasociation, paleosociation, neosociation, and desociation. Concept of a bridge and buffer community in northeast India, Concepts of infranationalism and proto-nationalism emerged.

Different types of growth set-ups of tribes in India were studied, like tribes in pre-growth set-ups, tribes in rudimentary growth set-ups, tribes in truncated growth set-ups, tribes in unbalanced growth set-ups, tribes in balanced growth set-ups, tribes in dynamic growth set-ups, etc.

Proactive political anthropologist: As an activist, he tried to bring Naga and Kuki together in Manipur. He even set up the Institute of People's Action on land donated by the Kabui Nagas of Manipur.

He contributed to understanding the processes of acculturation, tribal movements, and ethnic identity.

Case Study

- **Professor Vinay Kumar Srivastava: A Life Full of Academic Humility**

Notwithstanding that death is a natural sequel to birth, life and death being two sides of the same coin, it is strange that relatively few anthropologists have concerned themselves directly and specifically with the sociocultural and cross-cultural perspectives of death and the dying. (V.K. Srivastava & K. Srivastava, EPW, 1997) Professor Vinay Kumar Srivastava (V.K.S.) was a talented writer who covered a wide range of subjects during the course of his nearly five-decade academic career. The field of Indian anthropology has lost a dazzling light, a luminary, a learned scholar, an ethnographic whiz, an unusually brilliant brainiac, and above all, a fine human being who was always thinking about others like a genuine anthropologist when V.K.S. died away on December 23, 2020. The author has known him for almost five decades and cannot think of even one instance in which he ever showed hostility or animosity towards anyone. This is not to say that he didn't have any animosity for people, but he never expressed it, even when they tried to take advantage of him. Typical of an ethnographer, he would always keep his displeasure close to his heart.

V.K.S. was a brilliant student; for him, life was nothing less than a field study, and he was always interested in learning about other people. Along with his extraordinary memory, this trait made him well-liked not only among anthropologists but also in the fields of physical, biological, educational, managerial, and clinical sciences. He had a strong love for social anthropology and was intensely focused. Despite having a master's degree in sociology, he was completely committed to social anthropology.

He was born into a relatively typical middle-class household that lived in his maternal grandparents' home in Peepal Mahadev, in the walled city of Delhi. He began as a pretty ordinary student and finished his education at Daryaganj's Anglo-Sanskrit Victoria Jubilee Higher Secondary School. He received an average grade from his school board, a 55% mark that was just about good enough to get him into the B.Sc. (Honours) anthropology programme. He responded to Dr. Abhimanyu Sharma's letter to the editor, in which Sharma said that only women and rejected people choose to study anthropology, in a much later reply. He became a brilliant scholar of genius after joining the Department of Anthropology, a fact he acknowledged in many of his publications.

He began studying at the Department of Anthropology in 1969, and in 1974, he graduated with a master's degree in anthropology with a focus on physical anthropology. He travelled to Ranchi for his undergrad fieldwork and the highlands of Himachal Pradesh for his master's fieldwork. He decided to pursue a second master's degree in sociology from the Delhi School of Economics after receiving first-class honours in both his undergraduate and graduate studies. He was highly affected by Professor Andre Beteille while studying sociology and became a lifelong friend of Beteille.

In actuality, V.K.S. intended to pursue his PhD under Beteille by researching lower levels of bureaucracy in Delhi, but this strangely did not come to pass, thus he was forced to go outside to Kings College for his doctorate. He was hired as a sociology lecturer at the prestigious Hindu College of Delhi University after earning his M.A. in Sociology in 1976 while once again graduating first in his class. At Hindu College, he enrolled on September 15, 1976. In the presence of his senior colleague, P. D. Khera, he introduced fieldwork as a crucial element of sociology courses for undergrads. He enrolled in the M.Phil. curriculum of Delhi University's Chinese and Japanese Department while he was a professor at Hindu College. His M.Phil. in Chinese sociology was completed in 1983.

Though he taught sociology at Hindu College, his relationships with Surinder Nath, Anil Mahajan, the author, and S. L. Malik were particularly strong because he preferred to conduct anthropological research and write anthropological papers. With two more co-authors, Surinder Nath and Anil Mahajan, he published his first work, "Estimation of Maximum Breathing Capacity from Height and Age-Group among Migrant Male Nepalese," in the Proceedings of the Third Annual Conference of Human Genetics (Abstract No. 110). He co-authored the article 'On Scheduled Castes and Tribes' with P. C. Joshi, which he presented at the Ethnographic and Folk Culture Society Conference in 1978. He collaborated with Surinder Nath on four papers titled 'On Segmental Growth' with Surinder Nath (Abstract No. 1055); 'Sex Chromatin Patterns' with H. K. Kumbnani (Abstract No.2027); 'Paradigm of Integrated Anthropology' and 'Social Anthropology Re-considered' with Anil Mahajan (Abstract Nos. 1515 and 1374, respectively) for the Xth ICAES, which was held in 1978.

With Surinder Nath, S. L. Malik, and P. K. Ghosh, he co-founded the scholarly magazine Spectra of Anthropological Progress while he was a sociology professor at Hindu College. There weren't many books or issues of this periodical. It is best recognised for starting a discussion on the "Crisis in Anthropology," a highly praised project. Because of his affinity for anthropology, he applied for a lectureship in social anthropology and was accepted, at which point he joined the Department of Anthropology.

His chances of being promoted to reading were hampered because he accepted a teaching position immediately after receiving his master's degree in sociology and did not engage in a doctoral programme. He had little prospect of getting a doctorate under Professor Beteille. He attended the interview for the Commonwealth Scholarship provided by the British government and was chosen to pursue a doctorate there. On September 28, 1988, V.K.S. entered Kings College to begin his doctoral studies. Professor Caroline Humphrey, who oversaw his research at Cambridge, was interested in the study of nomadism and the Jain religion. V.K.S. completed his doctoral work among the Bikaner, Rajasthan, and Raika cattle breeders. His doctoral viva voce took place on January 18, 1994, and as a typical Indian academic, V.K.S. respectfully supported three scholars in particular: J. D. Mehra, Gopala Sarana, and Andre Beteille. Only an Indian could comprehend such a respectful approach towards the seniors, since he was not only respectful of them but also nearly devoted to them. He was not only respectful of his seniors, but he also showed kindness and encouragement to his juniors. His professionalism required him to share freely with his coworkers and to grow in humility. He loved giving talks and was overjoyed whenever non-anthropological bodies invited him to do so.

He once told me about his experience lecturing primarily to unani medicine students at Jamia Hamdard University. He assured me that since anthropology is what I know best, I should of course talk about the subject. He was a genuine representative of social anthropology, particularly its fieldwork and methodology. In his most recent webinar lectures on multiculturalism, he fervently argued that the younger generation should start taking on problems and meaningfully contributing to anthropology scholarship by asking for assistance from the more experienced researchers. He also believed that literary anthropology should be given serious consideration. He finished as a meticulous professional.

He mentored many Ph.D. and M.Phil. students while he was a faculty member at Delhi University, in addition to assisting master's students with their dissertations. Though he had students working on a wide range of subjects, medical anthropology was one of his preferred areas for Ph.D. and M.Phil. students. Many of his former pupils now work as instructors at Sagar, Delhi University, IGNOU, and private institutions. He always thought that students should have complete liberty and that a supervisor's job was to inspire and direct. Although he was the last teacher to require student authorship, he has done substantial copyediting for his students' writings. He virtually always rewrote the papers for his students without demanding authorship numerous times.

He held that in order to cultivate new ideas, a researcher must work tirelessly and devotedly. As a researcher, V.K.S. considered the pursuit of truth to be the pinnacle of all pursuits. J. D. Mehra taught him how to be descriptive, and Andre Beteille and Abhimanyu Sharma taught him how to be thorough. J. D. Mehra was an excellent speaker who had the ability to hold the class transfixed for extended periods of time. But in contrast to Mehra, who, in V.K.S.'s opinion, would primarily teach English, V.K.S. would thoroughly examine the subject from beginning to end, supporting his lecture with relevant references and precise quotations that he had surprisingly memorised. V.K.S. had the capacity to produce scholarly draughts even before he was exposed to Cambridge's intellectual and scholastic culture.

In one of his early papers, which was published in Indian Anthropologist, he provided a superb anthropological account of the Angami Naga Khel Gate. His writings covered nearly every pertinent topic in social anthropology, from conceptual exploration of terms like peasant society, tribe, death, witchcraft, and genealogy to writing on subjects like the future of anthropology, teaching of anthropology, pastoralism, tribal development, qualitative research, ecological movements, and Gandhian ideas. His publications ranged from charisma to renunciation. He nearly became an expert at writing in-depth book reviews and affecting obituaries.

- **Stanley Ann Dunham**

Stanley Ann Dunham (November 29, 1942 – November 7, 1995) was an American anthropologist who specialised in the economic anthropology and rural development of Indonesia. She was the mother of Barack Obama, the 44th president of the United States.

Born in Wichita, Kansas, Stanley Dunham studied at East-West Centre and at the University of Hawaii at Mnoa in Honolulu, where she attained a Bachelor of Arts degree in anthropology (1967) and later received Master of Arts (1974) and PhD (1992) degrees, also in anthropology. She also attended the University of Washington in Seattle from 1961 to 1962. Interested in craftsmanship, weaving, and the role of women in cottage industries, Dunham's research focused on women's work on the island of Java and blacksmithing in Indonesia. To address the problem of poverty in rural villages, she created microcredit programmes while working as a consultant for the United States Agency for International Development. Dunham was also employed by the Ford Foundation in Jakarta, and she consulted with the Asian Development Bank in Gujranwala, Pakistan. Towards the latter part of her life, she worked with Bank Rakyat Indonesia, where she helped apply her research to the largest microfinance programme in the world.

5

Indian Village, Minorities, and Processes of Socio-Cultural Change in Indian Society

5.1

Indian Village—Significance of village study in India; Indian village as a social system; Traditional and changing patterns of settlement and inter-caste relations; Agrarian relations in Indian villages; Impact of globalization on Indian villages.

Q 1. Significance of village study in India

Ans. Credit goes *to Robert Redfield* and his students from Chicago for turning attention towards village studies. In India, in the 1930s, the work of *William Wiser* in Karimpur village in his books "Hindu Jajmani System" and "Behind the Mud Walls" was significant as it was based on intensive field work in villages. Post-independence, an explosion of interest in village studies by *Morris Opler, Oscar Levis, Mckim Marriot, and David Mandelbaum,* along with British anthropologists such as *F.G. Bailey and A.C. Mayer,* did excellent work. In the late 1950s, *M.N. Srinivas's India's* Changing Village, S.C. Dube's Indian Village, and D.N. Majumdar's Caste and Communication in Indian Village were significant ones.

Significance:

1. **Important for planning and reconstruction:** According to *M.N. Srinivas*, by studying Indian villages, one can enrich one's knowledge regarding various issues and problems faced by inhabitants of such villages. Such knowledge can help in rural reconstruction because one can understand how fields such as education, health, land consolidation, and housing can be improved in such villages. The Ford Foundation even appointed *Morris Opler* to help the planning commission plan rural reconstruction because *Morris Opler* has firsthand data about various issues and problems in Indian villages. Therefore, village studies in India are significant for bringing development to such villages.
2. **It is important to understand social reality:** According to *M.N. Srinivas and S.C. Dube*, many traditions and traditional institutions in their real form still exist in Indian villages. By studying Indian villages, one can understand the nature, functioning, and needs of such traditions or traditional institutions. One can observe traditional ways of solemnising marriage, performing rituals, and even performing last rites in Indian villages. By understanding all such traditions, one can analyse the changes that have occurred in our institutions. The study of Indian villages also establishes the real culture of almost all human groups. Once upon a time, all were inhabitants of villages because urbanisation and migration are recent phenomena. *Iravati Karve,* in her book "Group Relations in Village Communities," talked about collecting quantitative and qualitative data to test the structure of interpersonal and intergroup relations affected by factors of kinship, caste, and locality.

3. **Enrich knowledge of other disciplines:** Village studies not only help sociologists and social anthropologists but also enrich the knowledge of economists, political scientists, and historians. The economists come to know how agriculture production can be enhanced, how villages can be connected to markets, and how such changes can be helpful to both villages and the country. Political scientists also come to know how political awareness can be created among villagers, how their political participation can be ensured, and which political processes can help them.
4. **Tracing the impact of globalisation and modernization:** *Simpson* (2016), after analysing different village studies, has noted that new conflicts between agriculture and non-agriculture ways of rural life have emerged due to the marked economy, modern education, and improved access to civic amenities. Caste hegemony and joint families persist, but the Jajmani system is on the decline. Cumulatively, the frames of reference for villagers have changed as Sanskritization is no longer a major attraction. Finally, the conceptual distinction between villages and cities appears to be fading in some key respects, largely due to migration.

Debate regarding the relevance of village studies in India:

➢ **Gupta (2005):** "Village is no longer a site where the future can be planned, and village is shrinking as a sociological reality, though it still exists as a geographical space". For him, one can observe the declining importance of villages in India's national culture. Also, in contemporary political debates in India, rural character is absent at all.

➢ **Singh:** The traditional nation of village studies as a rural-urban continuum has become unviable due to changes like rural economies, migration, information technology, and globalisation. Shah observes that the rural sector is, of course, shrinking but is still huge and occupies a crucial place in the national economy, politics, and society.

Criticism:

1. S.C. Dube says that they use western models in village studies.
2. Lack of comprehensive study.
3. Lack of practical utility.

With rising suicides among farmers in villages, it is required that villages be studied more. In conclusion, one can argue that we need interdisciplinary research on villages in India where the focus needs to be not only on application but also on theorization.

Q 2. Indian village as social system

Ans. Talcott Parson explains the social system as a plurality of social actors engaged in more or less stable interaction according to shared cultural norms and meanings.

Features of the social system:

1. Plurality of individual actors.
2. Every social system must have certain aims and objectives.
3. There should be some order and pattern.
4. Unity between constituents of the social system based on functional relationships.
5. Adjustment between constituents.
6. Most important aspect of a social system is maintenance. It is based on socialisation and social control. The Indian village as a social system revolves around the following institutions:

1. **Family and kinship:**
   a. In social interactions, family collectivity is prioritised, and feelings of individualism and personal freedom are severely constrained. Joint families are therefore more common than nuclear families and are the cultural ideal.

b. Because of the extensive kin network, marriage laws are closely adhered to. *Irawati Karve* (1965) noted that whereas cross-cousin marriages are strongly encouraged in South Indian villages, village and gotra exogamy have rigid norms in North Indian villages.

2. Caste system:

a. The caste system creates hierarchically ordered groups within society. Each group has its own set of standards and guidelines, as well as limitations on how they can engage with other groups. Indian villages' social, economic, political, and religious lives are governed by the caste system. The dominant caste and the Jajmani system are the two most obvious caste-related manifestations.

b. According to *M.N. Srinivas' 1959* research paper, Dominant Caste in Rampura (1959), a caste must possess a sizable portion of the region's arable land, be well represented among its members, and hold a prominent position in the local social order in order to be considered dominant. The dominant castes are in charge of political and economic processes and are frequently used as models for the Sanskritization of lower castes.

3. Agrarian class structure: The land revenue system under colonial rule gave rise to class structures in Indian villages. As per *Daniel Thorner*, there are three classes:

i. **Proprietors:** These are landowners from the upper caste who employ labourers and peasants to work their fields. Typically, they are members of the dominant caste.

ii. **Working peasants:** These are the small-sized landowners who often work as tenants on bigger farms. They come from middle-level cultivator and artisan castes.

iii. **Labourers:** These are the landless groups that live primarily by working on others lands. Generally, they come from the traditionally landless castes, or the Scheduled Castes.

We found that interactions were taking place between individuals. Villages are based on caste and agrarian class structures. There is a functional relationship between them. However, adjustment is taking place under the current form of market economy within family, caste, and class structures. Along with this, social order continues to be maintained through caste panchayats and even nuclear families. Since all features of a social system are found in Indian Village, it can be concluded that it represents a social system.

Q 3. Traditional and changing patterns of settlement and inter caste relations

Ans. Historically, until the 19th century, Indian villages were more isolated and self-contained. There used to be a fixed division of labour and a particular structure of settlement. Due to current changes in transportation, communication, economic, and political empowerment of disadvantaged groups, changes are visible in the division of labour, the Jajmani system, and settlement patterns.

Patterns of settlement:

1. **Nucleated or clustered settlement:** This is the kind of rural settlement that is most prevalent. Houses are concentrated or densely populated in one location. The general residential area is distinct from and set apart from the nearby farmland. These communities are typically found in the Northeastern States and on lush alluvial plains. For security or defence purposes, individuals would occasionally live in small communities, like in Nagaland and the Bundelkhand region of central India. Water scarcity in Rajasthan has made compact settlement necessary for making the best use of the water resources that are now accessible.
2. **Linear settlement:** There is a scattering of houses, each with its own compound around it. However, it is difficult to physically distinguish between one village and another. In Kerala, Konkan, and the Bengali delta lands, this style of settlement is seen.
3. **Scattered or dispersed settlement:** In secluded jungles or on tiny hills with farms or pastures on the slopes, this type of settlement pattern takes the form of solitary huts or small hamlets of huts.

The severely fractured structure of the terrain frequently contributes to considerable settlement dispersion. This kind of settlement is found in the hilly regions of Meghalaya, Uttaranchal, Himachal Pradesh, J&K, etc.

The caste - stratified system has played a huge role in the settlement pattern of Indian villages. Social distance is maintained between the upper and lower castes. For instance, *Beteille* studied Tanjore village and found that caste status declines from the north to the south of the village, with the untouchables living on the outskirts.

Changes:

1. The population explosion has led to the expansion of nucleated settlements. Due to the growing pressure on agriculture, previously uncultivated areas have been brought under cultivation. New nucleated settlements have emerged around such lands.
2. Linear settlements have emerged in those areas where infrastructure projects such as new roads, highways, and canal and river-linking projects have been constructed.
3. Urbanisation has led to increased connectivity from rural areas to nearby urban centres. Rural folk have migrated to urban centres for better economic opportunities. Those who have successfully achieved have tried to bring in their immediate families as well.
4. Money plays a greater role in occupying land, whether central or peripheral.

Though it has declined to a certain level due to monetary factors, the rural settlement pattern continues to be mainly influenced by the caste system.

Q 4. Agrarian relations in Indian villages

Ans. Agrarian society may be accepted as any form of society, especially traditional society, primarily based on agricultural production and associated crafts rather than industrial production (Collin's Dictionary of Sociology). Andre Betelle says that agrarian relations in Indian villages revolve around two aspects: (i) technological arrangement and (ii) social arrangement. Technological arrangement refers to ecological conditions and agricultural technology, while social arrangement refers to land ownership and control, power structure, land tenure, and other social dimensions.

Caste in Agrarian Relations: This is primarily seen through the Jajmani system. Yogendra Singh has defined it as a system based on reciprocity in inter-caste relationships between Jajman and Kamin.

Class in Agrarian Relations: The land revenue system under colonial rule gave rise to class structures in Indian villages. As per Daniel Thorner, there are three classes:

1. **Proprietors (maalik):** These are the upper caste landowners who have peasants and labourers working on their fields. They generally belong to the dominant caste, like the Jats in North India.
2. **Working peasants (kisan):** These are the small-sized landowners who often work as tenants on bigger farms. They come from middle-level cultivator and artisan castes.
3. **Labourers (mazdur):** These are the landless groups that live primarily by working on others lands. Generally, they come from the traditionally landless castes, or the Scheduled Castes.

The growing penetration of the market economy in rural India has led to the decline of the Jajmani system. *A.R. Desai* has identified four major trends of change in village India:

1. Rapid transformation of agrarian society from subsistence to market economy.
2. Rapid transformation was followed by the introduction of modern technology.
3. Abolition of intermediaries such as Zamindars and Biswedars,
4. Emergence of associations and institutions having linkages with urban and national organisations. Surplus generation, consumption lifestyles, and commodification are new normal in village life.

Features of change:

1. The new market economy created a new class of rich peasants, big traders, petty officials, etc.
2. It promoted a large number of new facilities, especially those related to credit.
3. Entry of improved implements such as fractions, water pumps, etc.
4. Polarisation of peasants into rich landowning classes and extremely poor landless labour
5. Differential capacity to generate income led to a tendency towards a nuclear family.

However, there is agrarian distress and a rise in suicides. *A.K. Vasavi* said that commercial agriculture in semi-arid areas is leading to new ecological, economic, and social crises. *Susan George* says that the loss of staple grain in a specific region without a substantial alternative economic base indicates a threat to food security and hence the fragility of the local community.

Q 5. Impact of Globalization on Indian villages

Ans. Globalisation is defined as the intensification of worldwide social relations linking distant localities in such a way that local happenings are shaped by events occurring miles away and vice versa. Indian villages are characterised by a triangle of joint family, caste, and agrarian structures.

Impact:

1. **Caste System:** Judge and Bal's (2008) study found that 97% of respondents in rural India still perceived caste endogamy as an important means of preserving traditions. Caste is embedded in the minds of people. According to Thorat, improvements in capital assets like land, entrepreneurship, access to health facilities, etc. happened; however, if we remove the impact of reservation, inequalities have further widened between Dalits and nonDalits (51% below the poverty line, 2011 data on Dalits).
2. **Agrarian Structure:** According to P.C. Joshi, there is rise of a new agriculturalist class, replacing feudal ones with capitalist ones. Even the decline of the Jajmani system has taken place. In the words of AM Shah, "greater Sanskritization" is taking place in this newly globalised world along with the rise of westernisation and modernization.
3. **Family Structure:** David Mandelbaum sees a decline in joint family structure in India. The study of K.S. Singh also supports the same, i.e., the shift from Gemeinshaft to Gesellshaft.
4. **Agricultural:** shift towards cash crops, diversification of crops (S. Swaminathan), increasing suicidal tendency (A.K. Vasavi), and rise in individualism.
5. **Women:** A study by *Jaiswal* found that in rural areas, women's participation in the work force rose from 22% in 1991 to 26% in 2001; however, women as main workers declined from 16% to 14.7% while marginal workers increased by 5%. There is a rise in the feminization of labour in low-paid jobs. Globalisation has enormous opportunities to make villages prosperous but requires a proper policy framework and participatory governance.

Case Study

- **Gaon Connection: The State of Rural India Report 2020**

The State of Rural India: Report 2020, published today by Gaon Connection, India's largest rural media platform, is a special report that gives a summary of significant events that will occur in rural India in 2020. This annual report, which is broken down into 12 main categories, is a one-stop source of information about rural India in 2020. It covers everything from the lack of immunisation services in the villages due to COVID- 19 to increased hunger in BPL households and how cyclones uprooted the lives of the rural poor. The "State of Rural India: Report 2020" includes over 40 field reports from Gaon Connection from all over the nation in addition to giving a general review of the significant events that will affect rural India in 2020.

For instance, the chapter on Adivasis addresses the effects of COVID19 on tribal communities, the Forest Rights Act of 2006, and how education for indigenous children is impacted. Along with that, it includes firsthand accounts of the Chopan nomadic group in Jammu and Kashmir, a poultry project run by tribal women in Palghar, Maharashtra, land disputes in tribal areas, and youths from the Santhal tribe in Jharkhand who use DSLR cameras and the Internet to document their cultural legacy. Similar to this, the Water chapter offers firsthand testimonies from Guwahati, Assam, on the Bharalu River, the effects of sand mining, the resurgence of rivers in Chhattisgarh as a result of the Narwa Vikas Yojana, etc.

The Health chapter includes reports on how villagers in northeastern states struggled to access healthcare during the nationwide lockdown, the critical role ASHA workers played in disseminating information about coronavirus precautions, and patient monitoring, in addition to assessing the impact of COVID-19 on rural India. The Disaster Chapter offers details on the major catastrophes that impacted rural India in 2020. These include the Assam oil well fire in Baghjan that burned for more than five months and caused numerous displaced people; the floods in Bihar, Assam, and Uttar Pradesh; and deaths from lightning. The COVID-19 pandemic's effects on artists across the nation, including puppeteers, folk singers, and shehnai players, are documented under the Art & Culture topic. It features a favourable account of a seasoned artist who is utilising the Phad art form to raise awareness about the pandemic in Rajasthan.

5.2

Linguistic and Religious Minorities and their social, political and economic status.

Q 1. Linguistic minorities and their social, political and economic status

Ans. Language is one of the greatest glories and achievements of mankind. According to the Report of the Commissioner of Linguistic Minorities in India (1988), "linguistic minority means a population having a distinct language or script of their own and whose mother tongue is different from the principle language of the state". In TMA Pai v. Union of India Case, linguistic minority is defined with reference to the state as a unit. Examples: Koro, Dimasa, Gond, Mohali, etc.

Constitutional rights accorded to linguistic minorities:

1. **Article 347:** The President, if he or she is satisfied that a substantial proportion of a state's population desires a particular language to be recognised, may direct the language to be officially recognised in that state.
2. **Article 350A:** Every state and local authority should provide adequate facilities for instruction in the mother tongue at the primary stage of education to children of linguistic minorities, and the President may issue such directions to any state for securing the provision of such facilities.
3. **Article 350B:** There shall be a Special Officer for Linguistic Minorities, whose duty will be to investigate all matters relating to the safeguards provided for linguistic minorities and report to the President upon those matters.

Problems Faced:

1. **Loss of languages:** As per PLSI, 220 languages have been lost in the past 50 years, and around 400 more are at risk of dying in the next 50 years. Tribal languages are the most vulnerable due to a lack of script and competition from other languages.
2. **Ineffective Implementation of Constitutional Safeguards:** A dearth of teachers and educational material, combined with failure to develop a script for many minority languages, has led to an unsatisfactory impact of safeguards like Article 350A.
3. **Discriminatory State Policies:** The Centre is unable to protect the linguistic minorities against the state's discrimination, such as Bengali in Assam and Kannada in A.P. Though official recognition is granted, discriminatory policies continue, e.g., Urdu in U.P. and Bihar and Maithili in North Bihar.

4. **Discrimination in daily life:** Linguistic minorities are at a disadvantage in terms of education, jobs, and administrative facilities. This pushes them to abandon their mother tongue and adopt a more influential language.
5. **Politicisation of language:** C.V.F. Haimendorfhas stressed that the tendency of political leaders to perceive minority languages as an obstruction to national integration creates a hostile atmosphere for minorities.
6. **Problems of tribal language:** Lack of script, lack of textbooks, and lack of teachers

Steps taken:

1. **Project Samhati:** The ST and SC Development Department of the Odisha State government has already started working on a project called 'Samhati' to address the language issues faced by tribal students in early grades or elementary classes. The Scheduled Castes and Scheduled Tribes Research and Training Institute (SCSTRTI) along with the Academy of Tribal Language and Culture (ATLC), Bhubaneswar, are implementing the project.
2. **Scheme for Protection and Preservation of Endangered Languages of India (SPPEL) 2021:** Under this scheme, the Central Institute of Indian Languages (CIIL), Mysore, works on the protection, preservation, and documentation of all the mother tongues and languages of India spoken by less than 10,000 people, which are called endangered languages. In the first phase of the scheme, 117 endangered languages and mother tongues have been chosen from all over India for study and documentation on a priority basis.
3. **National Education Policy (NEP) 2020:** The policy has emphasised mother tongue, local language, or regional language as the medium of instruction at least till Grade 5, but preferably till Grade 8 and beyond. NEP recommends setting up an Indian Institute of Translation and Interpretation (IITI), a National Institute for Pali, Persian, and Prakrit, strengthening Sanskrit and all language departments in HEIs, and using mother tongue or local language as a medium of instruction in more HEI programmes.

Ranganath Mishra's recommendation:

1. The term linguistic minority should be defined clearly for operational purposes with examples of linguistic minorities.
2. Criteria for identifying the backwardness of a linguistic minority must be the same as those for identifying backward classes.
3. Welfare measures must be taken based on the fact that they are socially and economically backward.
4. Each state must provide a comprehensive multilingual profile of its population.
5. The census commissioner must provide data on those with fewer than 10,000 speakers.
6. In schools with a sizeable linguistic minority, preference is given to teachers knowing that language. Enhance the skills of linguistic minorities.

Cultural pluralism has been the essence of Indian civilization. India's destiny lies in pluralism and unityIndian civilization. India's destiny lies in pluralism and unity. Among the determining criteria of any civil society, the one that matters is the way minorities and women are treated in it.

Q 2. Religious minorities and their social, political and economic status

Ans. India is a nation of pluralism, but there are socio-cultural differences. Six religious minorities, viz. Muslims, Christians, Buddhists, Jains, Sikhs, and Zoroastrians, have been notified as minority communities under Section 2(c) of the National Commission for Minorities Act, 1992. It is not defined in the Indian Constitution, but special provisions exist for them:

1. **Article 29(1):** Any section of citizens having a distinct language, script, or culture shall have the right to conserve the same.

2. **Article 29(2):** No citizen shall be denied admission into any educational institution maintained by or receiving aid from the state on grounds only of religion, race, caste, language, or any of them.
3. **Article 30(1):** All minorities shall have the right to establish and administer educational institutions of their choice.
4. **Article 30(2):** The state shall not, in granting aid to educational institutions, discriminate against any educational institution on the ground that it is under the management of a minority.
5. **Articles 25, 26, 27, and 28** deal with religious rights.

Feature	Muslim	Christian	Sikh	Buddhist	Jain
Population % (Census 2011)	14.2	2.3	1.7	0.7	0.4
Social status	There are two major denominations amongst Indian Muslims - Sunni and Shia. The caste system prevails among Muslims as well a three-fold hierarchy of Ashraf (the noble noble), Ajlaf (the lowly) and Arzal (the degraded). The personal laws are strictly administered by their religious groups.	Several denominations exist among the Indian Christians such as the Syrian Christians, Latin/ Roman Catholics, Protestants, Dalit Christians and tribal Christians. The caste mentality prevails within the Christians as well with Dalit and tribal Christians discrimination by the higher caste Christians. Even the Church sometimes discriminates against them. Women tend to enjoy more freedom than their counterparts in other religious groups.	Based on the unity of god, Sikhism rejects the principle of caste and embraces universal brotherhood. However, caste ideology persists in the community. There are several castes, primary of which are the land-owning caste such as the Jat Sikhs, the commercial castes like Arora, Khatri and Bhatia Sikhs, and the Balmiki/ Mazhabi Sikhs comprising mainly of the Dalit groups. Sanskritisation is visible in the youth whereby the non-Jats imitate the Jats to achieve mobility.	An overwhelming majority of Buddhists are converts from other religions, especially Hindu Dalits, who were influenced by Dr. B.R. Ambedkar. As such, these Dalit converts continue to face residual discrimination from Hindi groups. The Buddhists of the Himalayan regions are believed to be the original Buddhists. In these traditional Buddhist communities, the monks enjoy the highest position in the social order.	70% of Jain population resides in urban localities. Ideally, there are no formal restrictions or hierarchy attached to the Jain society. But Jains continue to follow a caste hierarchy similar to Hindus. Most of them identify themselves as Vaishyas.
Literacy rate% (Census 2011)	68.54	84.53	75.39	81.29	94.88
Sex Ratio against 1000 males	951	1023	903	965	954

Political Status	Organized from pre independence times via organization like Muslim league, Muslim conference etc. However, after partition, Congress has tried to represent interest of all communities. But they have some parties working for their interests like National conference, All India Majlis-eIttehadul Muslimeen.	Christians are not organised into political parties due to thei smallr size and fragmentation into denominations, as well as their secular mindset and rejection of communal politics.	In 1966, the Punjabi Suba movement resulted in the trifurcation of Punjab into Punjab, Haryana and Himachal Punjab The political associations formed then have continued to function and stand for Sikh interests. The most prominent such association has been the Akali Dal, which is quite active on the regional political front.	Buddhist are not organised into political parties due to their small size and fragmentation into denomination.	Jains are not organised into political parties due to their small size and fragmentation into denomination.
Economic status	As per multi dimensional poverty Index 2018 released by UNDP, every third Muslim is multidimensionally poor. 33% Muslim multidimensionally poor. Majority of them are engaged in traditional and low paying professions or as small and marginal farmer, landless labour etc.	The upper caste Christians are engaged in both traditional and non-traditional, service -oriented jobs, especially in the fields of education and health. However, the Dalit converts are often engaged in low-paying occupations.	Partition resulted in the loss of acres of fertile and to Pakistan. However, land reforms and later the Green Revolution transformed the Sikhs as the most agriculturally prosperous community of India. In urban areas, they are mostly engaged in trade and commerce. Sikhs have also historically been well-represented in the defence forces.	Buddhists are mostly engaged in their traditional occupations. Some have entered public and private job. Dalit converts like the Mahars have benefitted from the new found educational opportunities, and thus even gained entry at senior levels of administration.	Jains are mostly engaged in trade and commerce. Some are big bussinessmen who actively participate in social and religious affairs.

Steps taken by Government: The government has implemented various schemes for the welfare and upliftment of every section of society, including minorities. The schemes being implemented include Pradhan Mantri Jan Arogya Yojana (PMJAY), Pradhan Mantri Mudra Yojana (PMMY), Pradhan Mantri Kisan Samman Nidhi (PM KISAN), Pradhan Mantri Ujjwala Yojana (PMUY), Pradhan Mantri Awas Yojana (PMAY), Beti Bachao Beti Padhao Yojana, etc.

Further, the Ministry of Minority Affairs has adopted a multi-pronged strategy by way of the implementation of various schemes that aim at educational empowerment, employment-oriented skill development, infrastructure support, etc. for the upliftment of living standards of economically weaker and downtrodden sections of all notified minorities (Muslims, Sikhs, Christians, Buddhists, Parsis, and Jains), irrespective of their further classifications. The further details of these schemes are as follows:

Educational Empowerment Schemes:

1. **Pre-Matric Scholarship Scheme**, Post-Matric Scholarship Scheme, and Merit-Cum-Means-Based Scholarship
   Scheme: For educational empowerment of students through Direct Benefit Transfer (DBT) mode
2. **Maulana Azad National Fellowship Scheme:** Provide fellowships in the form of financial assistance.
3. **Naya Savera:** Free Coaching and Allied Scheme: The scheme aims to provide free coaching to students and candidates belonging to minority communities for qualifying in entrance examinations for technical and medical professional courses and various competitive examinations.
4. **Padho Pardesh:** Scheme of interest subsidy to students of minority communities on educational loans for overseas higher studies

Employment-oriented schemes:

5. **Seekho Aur Kamao:** a skill development scheme for youth in the 14–35 age group aiming at providing employment and employment opportunities, improving the employability of existing workers, school dropouts, etc.
6. **USTTAD** (Upgrading Skills and Training in Traditional Arts and Crafts for Development) Hunar Haat is being organised across the country to provide employment opportunities and markets to artisans and craftsmen.
7. **Nai Manzil:** A scheme for formal school education and skilling of school dropouts
8. **Nai Roshni:** Leadership development of women belonging to minority communities

Infrastructure Development Programme:

9. **Pradhan Mantri Jan Vikas Karyakram** (PMJVK) is being implemented to provide basic infrastructure in deprived areas of the country. Since inception, under PMJVK, 42 Degree Colleges, 180 Residential Schools, 3,062 School Buildings, 43,838 Additional Class Rooms/ACR Blocks, 15,545 Teaching Aid & Smart Classrooms, 1,376 Hostels, 24 Working Women Hostels, 232 ITI Buildings, 55 Polytechnics, 21 Skill Centres, 5,382 Health Projects, 01 Unani Medical College, 81,503 Drinking Water Supply Projects, 40,795 Anganwadi Centres, 408 Sadhbhav Mandaps, 01 Sadbhav Kendra, 168 Common Service Centres, 609 Market Sheds, 09 Hunar Hubs, 9,330 Sanitation/Toilet projects, 76 Sports Facilities, etc. have been sanctioned.

Q 3. Problems of Religious minorities and Way ahead

Ans. India is a nation of pluralism, but there are socio-cultural differences. Six religious minorities, viz. Muslims, Christians, Buddhists, Jains, Sikhs, and Zoroastrians, have been notified as minority communities under Section 2(c) of the National Commission for Minorities Act, 1992.

Problems faced by minorities:

1. **Problem of Identity:** Historical experiences of partition and the British Policy of Divide and Rule created division between Muslims and other communities. Recently, the rise of ISIS, Al-Qaeda, and JeM has strengthened social stigma. According to Emile Durkheim's labelling theory, they are labelled as antinational, thereby being denied jobs, hostels, etc.
2. **Problem of Security:** Riots have erupted in the form of anti-Sikh riots in 1984, Godhra riots in 2002, Kandhamal riots in 2008, Muzzafarnagar riots in 2013, and Bhima Koregaon riots in 2018.

3. **Problem of Forceful Conversions:** The growing aggressiveness of fringe Hindu elements has led to an increase in attacks on Christians and the church in past years. These elements have justified their attacks in the name of Ghar Wapsi, i.e., an attempt to bring Christian converts back to the Hindu fold. Vested political interests have lent their support to such elements.
4. **Underrepresentation:** The Sachar Report (2006) identified one key problem as the underrepresentation of Muslims in the legislature, executive, and bureaucracy.
5. **The wounds of partition and the 1984** anti-Sikh riots linger in the community. They have resulted in separatist demands from certain fringe elements, who advocate for a separate country of Khalistan. Another issue has been the politicisation of the water sharing issue, with sections in Punjab unhappy over sharing the waters of their rivers with neighbouring states.
6. **Population decline:** There is a fear of the declining population of the Buddhists, Jain, and Parsis. States like Karnataka have witnessed a decline in Buddhist and Jain populations in the past decade.
7. **Problem of Perception:** According to the India Governance (NGO) Survey, Muslims feel disenchanted with the communal politics of the government. 74% believed that they were marginalised while making policy.

Sachar Committee Report on Muslims:

1. **Education:**
   a. The literacy rate among Muslims is 59%, compared to the national average of 64%.
   b. Mean years of schooling are lower for Muslims compared to the average Mean years of schooling for all children.
   c. Less than 4% of Muslims graduate, compared to 7% of the population aged 20 and above.
   d. Schools beyond the primary level are few in Muslim localities.
   e. Lack of hostel facilities is a uniting factor, especially for girls.
2. **Economic:**
   a. Self-employment is the main source of income.
   b. The share of Muslims in street vending is the highest.
   c. The percentage of women Muslim workers undertaking work within hours is much larger at 70% compared to 51% of all workers.
   d. Muslims are, by and large, engaged in the unorganised sector.
3. **Skill Development:**
   a. A rehabilitation package for innovative reskilling and upgrading occupational structure in the wake of liberalisation is seen as an urgent need.
4. **Poverty and Development:**
   a. About 38% of Muslims in urban areas and 27% in rural areas live as BPL.
   b. Muslim-concentrated villages are not well served by pucca roads.
   c. 40% of large villages with substantial Muslim concentrations don't have any medical facilities.
5. **Social Condition:**
   a. Muslims show an increasingly better sex ratio compared to other socio-religious communities.
   b. A large decline in fertility is seen in all religious groups, including Muslims.

Recommendations:

Sachar Committee:

1. High-quality school in Muslim-dominated areas.
2. Access to credit via priority sector lending (PSL) for Muslims
3. A-grade officers for Waqf councils

Ranganath Mishra Committee:

4. For identifying backward classes, there is no distinction between the majority and minority communities.
5. A comprehensive law detailing all aspects of educational rights is needed to enforce Article 30. Even Madarsa's modernization scheme needs to be revised.
6. The National Minority Development and Finance Corporation should be made effective.
7. Reservations for minorities in jobs
8. National committee of NHRC, NCW, NCBC, NCST, Waqf Council, etc. for monitoring all

Case Study

- **SC pleads for identification of minorities at the state level**

Several petitions challenging the constitutionality of the National Minority Commission Act of 1992 and the National Commission for Minority Educational Institutes Act of 2004 are being heard by a bench of justices as they relate to the identification of minorities. One of the petitions asserts that Hindus are a minority in 10 states and asks for guidance on formulating rules for identifying minorities at the state level.

- **SC Quota for Dalit Muslims and Christians**

The Supreme Court is currently hearing a case requesting that Dalit Muslims and Christians be included in the list of Scheduled Castes. The Supreme Court reviewed a 2007 report by the Justice Ranganath Mishra Commission for Religious and Linguistic Minorities, which suggested Dalit converts to Christianity and Islam be granted Scheduled Caste (SC) reservation. The government recently established a new Commission, rejecting the Mishra report, under the leadership of a former Chief Justice of India, K.G. Balakrishnan,and gave it two years to produce a report on the issue of granting SC status to "new persons who have historically belonged to the Scheduled Castes but have converted to religions other than Hinduism, Buddhism, and Sikhism." The Centre said that "Dalits who converted to Christianity or Islam to overcome the burdens of caste cannot claim reservation benefits enjoyed by those who chose to stay back in the Hindu religious system" as justification for rejecting the report.

- **Karnataka: Reservation for Muslims under the OBC category**

Lingayats and Vokkaligas have received the 4% backward class quota that had been set aside for Muslims in the state. The Chinnappa Reddy report's recommendations served as the foundation for the earlier introduction of the Muslim quota for the backward classes. Muslims can now only request reservations if they fall inside the 10% quota for the Economically Weaker Section (EWS). The government has implemented these reforms in response to the Backward Classes Commission's findings.

The 10% EWS quota can be utilised, according to the commission, to "accommodate new demands" from "various backward classes for increased reservation." The Karnataka government was informed by the Supreme Court that a reading of its ruling repealing the 4 percent quota for Muslims in the state "appears to suggest that prima facie, the foundation of its decision-making process is highly shaky and flawed, but no stay.

5.3

Indigenous and exogenous processes of socio-cultural change in Indian society: Sanskritization, Westernization, Modernization; Inter-play of little and great traditions; Panchayati Raj and social change; Media and Social change.

Q 1. Sanskritization

Ans. Robert Redfield introduced village studies into anthropology just before WWII. M.N. Srinivas was the pioneer of these studies in India. Srinivas studied Coorgs (in a book named "Religion and Society among Coorgs of South India"), where he found that lower castes, in order to raise their status in the local caste hierarchy, would imitate Brahmins. He called this process "Brahminization." Subsequently, he found that it may not necessarily be Brahmins but any dominant caste, preferably a dwija, and he changed it into Sanskritization (a book named "Social Change in Modern India"). It is social mobility within the framework of the caste system.

Today, it is defined as the process by which a low Hindu caste or tribal group of any other group changes its customs, rituals, ideology, and way of life in the direction of a high, frequently 'twice-born' caste. Sanskritization means not only the adoption of new customs and habits but also exposure to new ideas and values that have found expression in the vast body of Sanskrit literature. Karma, Dharma, Maya, Paap, and Moksha are examples of some common Sanskritic ideas, and when people become sanskritized, these words occur frequently in their talks.

According to Srinivas, there are two prerequisites for Sanskritization:

1. Wealth generation
2. Political power and patronage

Case study:

1. **Village Bisipara, studied by F.G. Bailey:** Local cultivators known as Chasa, after acquiring wealth, land, etc., started changing their lifestyle and traditions, thereby adopting the rituals and customs of Kshatriyas. They won panchayat and ward elections. Bailey concluded that they acquired capital, symbolic equivalence, and were able to convince themselves that they were originally Kshatriyas by fulfilling all conditions.
2. **Jatavs of Agra, by Owen M. Lynch:** Jatavs were shoemakers. After acquiring wealth, they started claiming Kshatriya status. But due to their untouchable status, they were denied ritual idioms. They ultimately entered politics, i.e., adopted political idioms for upward mobility.

Social change in Modern India, 1956, makes it clear that Jati mobility is not only permitted but not uncommon as well. Srinivas admits that Sanskritization is not one concept but a concept of concepts. There are three maj or models: the Brahmin, Kshatriya, and Vaishya models. Each model has two submodels: ritual and secular.

E.g., the ritual model is mainly followed in South India by adopting ritual thread, tilak on the forehead. Srinivas admits that Sanskritization is a pan-India concept. It applies only locally, as the lower caste follows the locally dominant caste because there is no all-India dominant caste. Srinivas further admits that it explains positional change but not structural change. Moreover, it is a time-consuming process. It takes two to three generations.

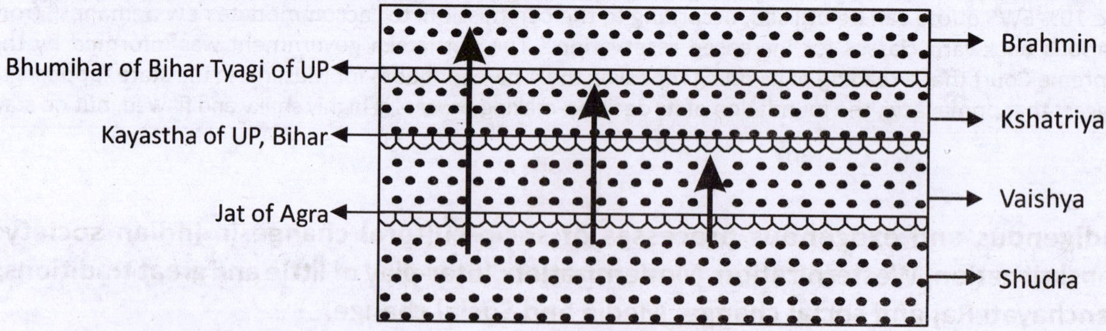

Positional Change

According to David Mandelbum, Sanskritization has served as a safety valve for the caste system. He says that caste status is ascribed and there is no scope for mobility. When there is no mobility, the only option available for lower castes is to walk out of the caste system. But this did not happen except when Mahars took to Buddhism. Mendelbaum said sanskritization is like a carrot. It keeps the tension of the caste system at a manageable level. However, Sanskritization gives some rays of hope. Thus, it acts as a safety valve. Sanskritization may result in erosion of women's autonomy in areas like choosing a partner, change in family structure towards an orthodox joint family, stronger caste organisations, etc.

According to AM Shah in his research paper 'Sanskritization Revisited', he explains that upper castes are no longer the sole agents of Sanskritization for lower castes; a number of non-caste structures and institutions have become agents of this process, such that there is 'Greater Sanskritization' as a whole.

Criticism:

1. J.F. Stall advocated that M.N. Srinivas should have used a different term than Sanskritization to explain it.
2. S.K. Srivastava in Punjab observed that local Brahmins adopted the lifestyle of Jats. He calls it deSanskritization.
3. D.N. Majumdar remarks that this process is not universal, as in Mohhan village in UP, lower castes feel proud of their culture and don't imitate upper castes.
4. It is nothing new, as is Muzzafer Sharief's reference group concept.
5. There is a rise in downward mobility.
6. Yogendra Singh: Globalisation brings social mobility.
7. SC Dube: Sanskritic sources provide not one model but many, among them fundamentally opposed ideas.

However, today in independent India, ST, ST, and OBC have been given special provisions in the constitution, so Sanskritization is not attractive to them. Besides, due to the political system, various castes at one level are joining hands to act as pressure groups to gain maximum benefit from the system. Therefore, today, horizontal solidarity is more important than vertical mobility.

Q 2. Westernization

Ans. The concept of Westernization is given by M.N. Srinivas. It is defined by him as changes that have taken place in India's society and culture due to contact with the British for more than 150 years. Here, change means change in technology, institution, and ideology.

Westernisation was initially taken up by higher classes and castes and started percolating downward. It changed our dress pattern, with machine-based products replacing handmade products, language, and hair style. It brought about changes at the level of the individual or the family and created social currents affecting wider society. It led to serious institutional and social reforms at various levels. A uniform judicial system, modern education, improved means of transport and communication, the spread of mass media, and a democratic system are results of Westernisation.

According to M.N. Srinivas, three levels of Westernisation exist:

1. **Primary:** Those who received western education and got services like Bureaucrats.
2. **Secondary:** litigants in court, patients in hospitals
3. **Tertiary:** rural folks (limited) and general spread of western traits

Impact:

1. Rationalisation of the ritual sphere
2. Change of belief system of marriage age, widow marriage
3. Western education grew.
4. Jajmani's system weakened.
5. Communication spread Sanskritization.
6. Rise of nationalism.
7. Social mobility.
8. Institutional structure set up: Parliament, bureaucracy

Yogendra Singh talk about impact

- Expansion of eduction
- Industralization and Urbanizaton
- Increased network of Communicaton
- Nationalism growth
- Humanism and rationalism
- Cultural conflict with endogenous traditions

Westernisation and Sanskritization: According to M.N. Srinivas, the process of westernisation also boosts the process of Sanskritization as members of the upper caste westernise and give up caste tradition, creating a vacuum that is filled by lower castes. Also, modern education and improved means of transport and communication, which are products of Westernisation, further accelerate Sanskritization. e.g., Harikatha, the Vedas have now spread wider.

But there are serious differences between them:

1. Sanskritization, unlike Westernisation, prohibits the consumption of non-vegetarian food and liquor.
2. Sanskritization, unlike Westernisation, is against widow remarriage and divorce but favours child marriage.
3. Sanskritization has a sacred outlook, but Westernisation has a secular outlook.
4. Sanskritization puts a check on the freedom of women, whereas Westernisation promotes the freedom of women.
5. Sanskritization put upward mobility in the framework of caste by process of imitation, whereas Westernisation put upward mobility outside the framework of caste by process of development.

Criticism:

1. Under the influence of the West, people are giving up their traditional practises, and even traditional culture is not transmitted to the present generation; therefore, the correct term is DeSanskritization (Yoginder Singh).
2. M.N. Srinivas ignored the impact of America, Russia, and German culture, plus the impact of East Asian countries like Japan and Korea, on Indian culture.
3. It does not account for social change as a transformation of structural and cultural types. Today, based on our values enshrined in our constitution, we bring about changes and correct term for it is 'Modernization'.

Q 3. Modernization

Ans. According to Eisenstadt, modernization is a process of change towards social, economic, and political systems developed in Western Europe and North America in the 17th and 18th centuries. Later, it spread to Asia, Africa, and South America in the 19th and 20th centuries. It also refers to the interactive processes of economic growth and social change.

Daniel Lerner (1964) has given five dimensions of modernization:

Dimension	Components
Technological	Modern science and technology, different sources of energy
Economic	Occupational mobility, specialisation, consumerism
Political	Political participation, individualism, rights
Social	Urbanisation, literacy, modern education
Psychological	Rationalism, cosmopolitanism

As per Lerner, empathy, mobility, and high participation constitute the core of a modernised personality As per M.N. Srinivas, modernization is one of the three core processes behind social change in India.

S.C. Dube has remarked that modernization, unlike westernisation, is value-neutral. It shows an apparent concern for cultural sensitivities. There is no standard model or fixed path for its attainment. Developing societies can adopt a model of their choice and chalk out their own path for its realisation. India has chosen democracy and secularism as the basis, built on modern science and technology.

Thus, S.C. Dube, in his 1974 work, "Contemporary India and its Modernization", has commented that modernity has entered Indian character and society, but it has done so through assimilation, not replacement.

Q 4. Inter-play of little and great traditions

Ans. According to Shils, tradition is anything that is transmitted from past to present.

The process of social change in India has been studied and analysed with the help of the concept of traditions and its social organisation. The concept of little tradition and great tradition emanates from the work of Robert Redfield in his book "Peasant Society and Culture", which he compiled after studying Mexican communities.

According to Robert Redfield, little tradition is the tradition of the illiterate, peasantry class, and "unreflective many", which is considered superstitious, unorganised, noncoded, and has oral transmission. Whereas great tradition is the tradition of the educated, elite, and "reflective few", which is considered a set of beliefs properly organised, codified, and transmitted from generation to generation through text.

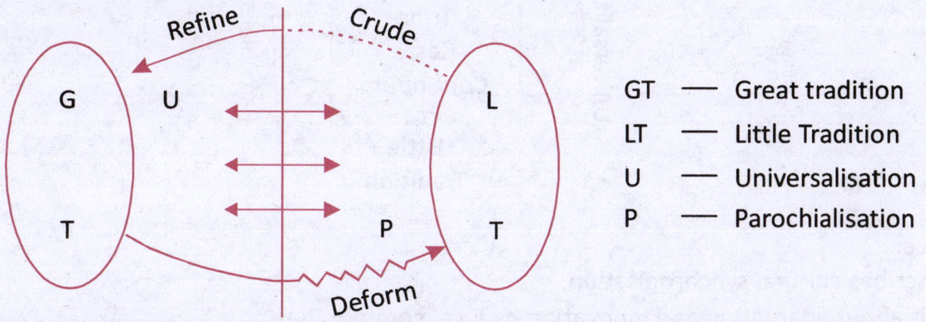

The Redfield frame of analysis has been applied to study the Indian reality of social change by Milton Singer, McKim Marriott, etc.

Milton Singer formulated a series of statements about cultural change in India: In a primary civilization like India, cultural continuity with the past is so great that even acceptance of 'modernising' and 'progressing' ideologies doesn't result in linear social and cultural change, but many result in 'traditionalizing' of apparently 'modern innovations'.

According to Sachidananda, interaction between two people has led to fusion and interpretation. Modernising processes and traditional forms don't necessarily clash; instead, what we come across is the 'modernization of tradition'.

View has been supported by McKim Marriott in his studies. He characterises the modes of interaction between "little" and "great" traditions in Indian villages as "parochialization" and "universalization" on the basis of his study in Kishengarh village. Parochialization takes place when great traditions percolate downward and become part of little traditions, thereby losing their original form.

(Great) Tradition Govardhan Puja Navratri Festival

← Parochialisation →

(Little) Gobardhan Puja Navratha Devi

Universalization takes place when elements of little tradition circulate upward to the level of great tradition.

(Great) Tradition Laxmi Puja Rakshabandhan

← Universalisation →

(Little) Saurati Devi Worship Salino festival

In practice, since universalization and parochialisation have both proceeded for a long time, we are ordinarily unable to trace the course of either process with certainty or to decide whether the present configuration of religion's contents is the result of one or the other of these two processes.

Interaction between Little and Great Tradition takes place at the sacred complex in the form of universalization and parochialisation. Even in the tribe-caste continuum, there is a look at change and continuity, which are features of the Little and Great Traditions.

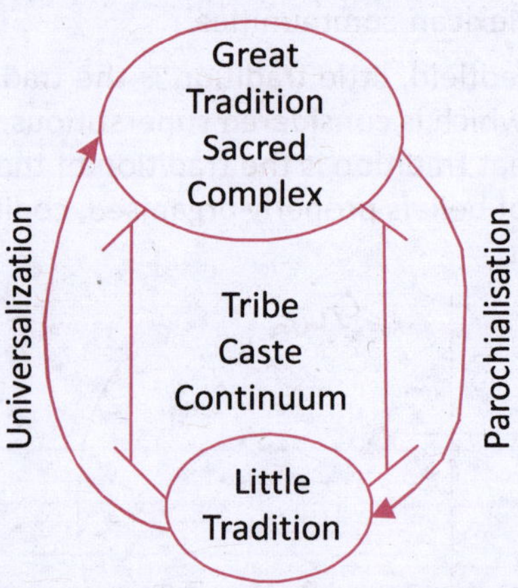

Significance:

1. It describes cultural synchronisation.
2. It tells about adaptation and innovation by local communities.
3. It helps to know that change and continuity are taking place.
4. Mostly parochialisation takes place; hence, local traditions are lost more often.

Criticism:

1. A foreign anthropologist without knowledge of Indian culture has made errors. Phonetic similarities between Gobardhan and Govardhan led to a serious error of interpretation.
2. It talks only about the Hindu social system.
3. It analyses only culture and not structure.
4. Without historical knowledge and exact origin studies, the dichotomy of universalization and parochialisation has no meaning.
5. Yogendra Singh: "Mere focus upon the orthogenetic process of cultural change makes it limited in scope.
6. These two processes show two directional flows between Little Tradition and Great Tradition, but ideally the flow should be circular.

7. S.C. Dube, in contrast, has presented a multipolar model:
   - Classical Tradition: emerged from religious texts.
   - Local Tradition: emerged from grass root level.
   - Regional Tradition: emerged from a particular region.
   - Western Tradition: emerged from Westernisation
   - New emergent nation tradition: emerged from national movement.
   - Subcultural tradition of caste groups: emerged from a special section of society.

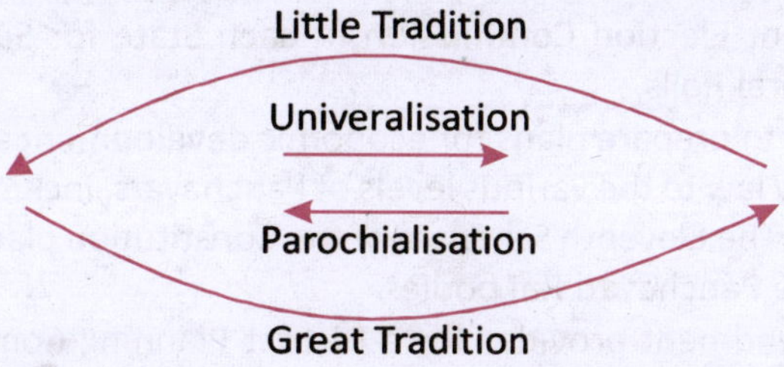

Despite criticism, this concept helps to analyse Indian civilization's richness and legacy. It becomes even more crucial in the current era of globalisation.

Case Study

- **Ethno-geography of the sun goddess festival, Chhatha, in the Bhojpur region, India: From locality to universality.**

The Indian festival of Surya Shashthi, also known as Chhatha Puja (literally, "worshipping the sun goddess"), honours the Sun God as Mother and is a prime example of an intangible cultural heritage that has endured since the distant past. Other ancient cultures have been observed to have comparable customs. Although there was undoubtedly a long history of sun worship in ancient India, there are no ties between the current Chhatha Puja and that practise. However, both rites document the goals of family prosperity and procreation. Chhatha Puja is largely a regional celebration from Bihar that migrant Biharis have brought to other regions of India, particularly urban and commercial centres like Delhi and Mumbai.

The locality has become universal via this process in terms of scope, fervour, and density of devoted participants, but the underlying message of reawakening the man-nature bond and bolstering ecological cosmology has not changed. People congregate on the banks of the River Ganga to worship, give ceremonial sacrifices to the Sun God, and bathe in the river's holy water during Chhatha Puja celebrations. This displays the birth of the fire element of the terrestrial world, the liquid element of nature, and human cognitive thought. A very intricate event known for its stunning display of vibrant costumes, music, singing, and costly ceremonies prepared and celebrated with the help of Brahmin priests is Chhatha Puja.

Q 5. Panchayat Raj & Social Change

Ans. The history of local self-government in India goes back to ancient times in the form of village panchayats, samities, and sabhas. The 73rd Amendment Act of 1992 formally introduced the Panchayat Raj system in India, which is an important mechanism for decentralising power and materialising people's participation.

Salient features:

1. **Basic units:** Gram Sabhas (village) and Ward Committees (municipalities), comprising all the adult members registered as voters.
2. **Article 243B:** Three-tier system of panchayats at the village, intermediate block/taluk/mandal, and district levels, except in states with a population below 20 lakhs.

3. **Article 243C (2):** Seats at all levels to be filled by direct elections. Seats reserved for Scheduled Castes (SCs) and Scheduled Tribes (STs) and chairpersons of the Panchayats at all levels shall also be reserved for SCs and STs in proportion to their population.
4. **Article 243D:** One-third of the total number of seats to be reserved for women One-third of the seats reserved for SCs and STs are reserved for women. One-third of the offices of chairpersons at all levels are reserved for women.
5. **Article 243E:** A uniform five-year term and elections to constitute new bodies to be completed before the expiry of the term In the event of dissolution, elections are mandatory within six months.
6. **Article 243K:** Independent Election Commission in each State for Superintendence, Direction, and Control of the Electoral Rolls.
7. **Article 243G:** Panchayats to prepare plans for economic development and social justice in respect of subjects as devolved by law to the various levels of Panchayats, including the subjects illustrated in the Eleventh Schedule. The Eleventh Schedule of the Constitution places as many as 29 functions within the purview of the Panchayati Raj bodies.
8. **Article 243ZD:** 74th Amendment provides for a District Planning Committee to consolidate the plans prepared by panchayats and municipalities.
9. **Article 243H:** Budgetary allocation from state governments, share of revenue from certain taxes, collection and retention of the revenue it raises, central government programmes and grants, Union Finance Commission grants.
10. **Article 243I:** Establish a Finance Commission in each state to determine the principles on the basis of which adequate financial resources would be ensured for panchayats and municipalities.

According to an *A.C. Nielson* survey for the Ministry of PRI, panchayats are strongly taking up social issues:

1. Child marriage is checked up to 72% due to intervention by elected representatives.
2. Alcoholism was reduced by 26%.
3. Domestic Violence: Male Pardhan sorted out about 79% of cases.
4. 8 out of 10 Pardhans took the initiative to increase school enrollment through an awareness programme.
5. 67% of Pradhans participated in health-related awareness programmes.
6. Developmental Issues: Water, Sanitation, and Roads are addressed.
7. Participation of local bodies in the developmental process: diverse planning and economic development

However, various studies showed that PRI have issues:

1. A village study in Rajasthan showed the concept of Sarpanch Pati and the patronage of dominant castes.
2. Dominant castes are powerful, like in Haryana, where Jaat holds more than 50% of the seats and tries to impose Khap panchayat orders.
3. Issue of 3F: Funds, Functions, and Functionaries
4. In Murshidabad District, Bengal, women were forced to clean their heads for not following orders and Panchayati Raj institutions supported them with silence.
5. Lack of public awareness about the role of the Gram Sabha
6. Lack of political will.

Panchayats have helped increase the participation of hitherto excluded sections of the population, such as tribals and lower castes. Elections increased women's participation in public life. It helped to develop the idea of grassroots democracy as a necessary condition for strengthening democracy at the state and national levels.

Way Ahead:

1. The recommendations of the 6th report of the 2nd Administrative Reform Commission (ARC) can be implemented for a better and more effective functioning of the Panchayati Raj institutions.
2. Genuine fiscal federalism—fiscal autonomy accompanied by fiscal accountability—can provide a long-term solution.
3. The 2nd ARC had recommended that there should be a clear demarcation of the functions of each tier of government.
4. The 2nd ARC also recommended that state governments encourage local bodies to outsource specific functions to public or private agencies, as may be appropriate, through enabling guidelines and support.
5. Comprehensive and holistic training requires expertise and resources from various subject-specific training institutes. This can be best achieved by the "networking' of institutions concerned with various subjects such as financial management, rural development, disaster management, and general management.
6. Audit committees may be constituted by the state governments at the district level to exercise oversight of the integrity of financial information, the adequacy of internal controls, compliance with the applicable laws, and the ethical conduct of all persons involved in local bodies.

Case Study

- **Ibrahimpur village: participatory governance model**

Residents of the village had regular Gramme Sabha meetings to discuss their needs and potential solutions to problems. Based on their participatory planning, they offer top-notch service delivery, including safe drinking water with low costs, 100% sanitation, efficient water conservation, the provision of organic manure, a village free of mosquitoes, solar lights for village homes, a ban on single-use plastics, and the installation of an "Any Time Water Machine" that enables residents to fill 20-litre cans at least twice or three times per day.

On the social front, the village met its goals for 100% immunisation coverage, 100% institutional delivery, proper implementation of midday meals, modern classroom facilities for digital and online learning, and the provision of 60 dairy animals at discounted prices to residents. The hamlet has received recognition for its efforts through a number of accolades, including the Best Gramme Panchayat Award and the Nirmal Puraskar Award.

Q 6. Media and social change

Ans. Social change means alterations that occur in social structure and social relationships. Alterations that occur in norms, values, and cultural products fall under this category. Mass media has an important role in contemporary democratic society as the main channel of communication. Therefore, according to cultural selection theory, any selection of message in mass media will have profound consequences for the entire society. It includes print media like newspapers, electronic media like TV and radio, new media like Twitter, over-the-top platforms, etc.

Interlinkages:

1. **Social message delivery for awareness and change**:
   a. Films framed to deal with the dreadful realities of caste systems in India, like 'Achhut Kanya' and 'Aarakshan'. In 'Matrubhoomi', the director scrutinises the influence of female feticide and female infanticide on gender equilibrium. The film 'Black' depicted a relationship between a blind-deaf girl and a teacher who has Alzheimer's disease.
   b. TV shows like 'Balika Vadhu' highlighted the issues of child marriage and widow remarriage. 'Satyamev Jayate' episodes like Nagdevwadi's water harvesting and others had a profound impact on the minds of viewers.
   c. The press reports but needs to analyse events for change.

2. **Acted as a governance tool:**
    a. Swachh Bharat campaigns and the polio campaign on TV ads by Amitabh Bachchan have led to some behavioural change.
    b. 'My Gov' initiatives also produced a new forum for connecting government and people.
    c. Twitter now-a-days has become another useful tool for spreading correct information and removing rumours.
    d. S.C. Dube conducted a survey on awareness of rural development progress and found that awareness levels are higher about Govt. of India ads like 'Jago Grahak Jago'.
    e. Kisan TV increased farmers' awareness.
3. **Structural changes:**
    a. It has increased consumerism among both rural and urban Indians.
    b. It helps in the restructuring of Indian conservative villages towards a rational and open mindset.
    c. It is considered one of the reasons for the increase in nuclear families, the reduction in caste arrogance, and the turning towards class society.

Limitations:

1. Some channels or papers have a single agenda and single political support and are biassed. They have less coverage in rural areas.
2. Sensitivities of people, urban and rural, are played with and shown in a degraded manner for TRP.
3. It hampers cultural relativism and promotes the Western model.

Case Study

- **Mobile Gram Vaani**

Access to mainstream media is difficult for the great majority of people living in rural India. According to UNSD (2017), 80% of rural areas are not connected to online services, and according to NSSO (2015), 30% of rural residents are not proficient readers. The content that reaches these communities is frequently removed from its context by local users. By offering an interactive, voice-based platform that meets the needs of disadvantaged populations in developing nations like India, Mobile Vaani was founded to close this information gap. In order to assist e-governance and e-commerce initiatives, Mobile Vaani distributes usergenerated media content via mobile devices.

The curriculum was specifically designed for low-literacy groups in India who lacked regular access to print media or the internet. In order to inform listeners of local news and events, provide a system to ensure the delivery of public services, and link rural areas to partner goods and services, Gram Vaani developed Mobile Vaani in 2012. Callers choose information that interests them from a succession of interactive voice response (IVR) menus when they call into a free voice messaging system. More than 2 million different callers have logged on to the virtual platform so far. Community members in media-scarce areas have a way to receive local news and details about programmes that will help them live better lives thanks to Mobile Vaani.

- **UNICEF's Community Radio**

A project in Jharkhand's East Singhbhum district has given locals the opportunity to ponder, talk about, write about, and create their own radio broadcast on topics that are important to them. They feel more in control and are forced to collaborate. Then, community radio and village planning are completely compatible.

6

Tribal Situation, Problems of Tribal Communities, and Impact of Development and Forest Policy on Tribes

6.1

Tribal situation in India: Bio-genetic variability, linguistic and socio-economic characteristics of the tribal populations and their distribution

Q 1. Tribal Definition and features

Ans. Ralph Linton: Tribe is a group of bands occupying contiguous territory and having a feeling of unity deriving from similarities in culture, frequent contact, and a certain community of interest.

B.K. Royburman: Tribe refers to a stage of social formation in an evolutionary scheme of technology, knowledge, capacity, and control of nature, the method of transmission of the same, perception of man's relationship with man, and the scale and nature of the organisation of a social group.

Tribal Features:

1. **Population:** 8.6% of the Indian population (2011 census).
2. **Race:** divided into 3 major ethnic groups: Mongoloid, Negroid, and Proto-Australoid.
3. **Language:** linguistically divided into Dravidian, Austro-Asiatic, and Tibeto-Chinese.
4. **Geographical location:** spread all over India. Concentrated in the north-east, central India, and even the Andaman and Nicobar Islands.
5. **Socio-economic:** Form of society: patriarchal or matriarchal. Form of marriage: polygamy or monogamy Kinship-based society. Economy: non-monetized, technologically backward, primitive agriculture, featuring barter and ceremonial exchange, etc.
6. **Religion:** belief in the supernatural, fetishism, animism, animatism, totemism, etc.
7. As per 2011 Census, Madhya Pradesh has the highest tribal population in India. While, the state and UT of India with the highest percentage of the tribal population to its total population is Mizoram (94.4 %) and Lakshadweep (94.8 %). However, the state which has a minimum ratio of Scheduled tribes is Uttar Pradesh (0.6%)."

In the Indian context, Majumdar and Madan have stated certain tribal facts:

1. In tribal India, a tribe is definitely a territorial group; a tribe has traditional territory, and emigrants always refer to it as their home.
2. All members of a tribe are not kin to each other, but Indian tribes' kin operate as strong, associative, regulative, and integrating principles.

3. Members of Indian tribes speak one common language, either their own or that of their neighbours. They are politically under state control but have panchayats.
4. Other distinguishing features—dormatories, peculiar cultures regarding birth, marriage, and death, and peculiar religious beliefs—distinguish them from even low caste groups.
5. B.K. Burman classified tribes as follows:
   a. Incorporate Hindu Social Order: Bhil, Bhumij
   b. Positive towards Hindu Social Order: Santhal, Munda
   c. Negative towards the Hindu social order: Naga, Mizo
   d. Indifferent towards the Hindu Social Order: Arunachal tribe

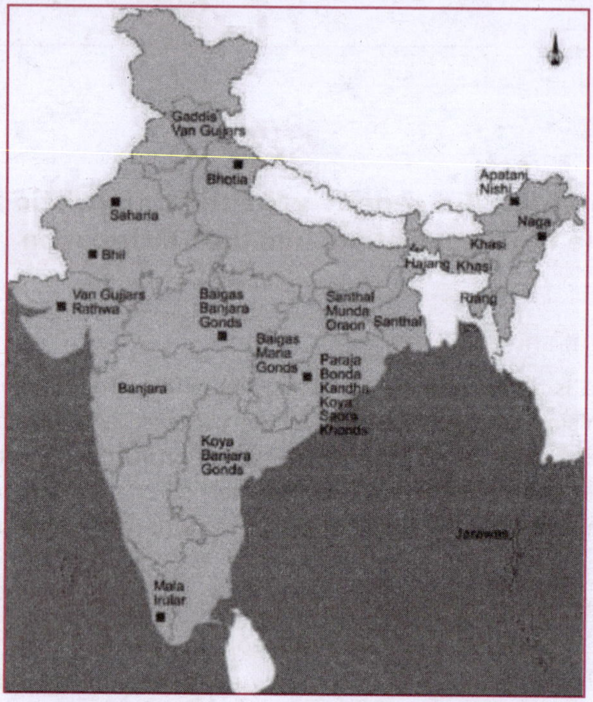

Q 2. Bio-genetic variability of tribal population and their distribution

Ans. *D.N. Majumdar* has described the complexity of the problem of classifying tribal people in India on the basis of racial affinities when he says that fixing racial origin or affinity is one of the most complicated tasks that have to be faced by Indian anthropologists. There is practically no direct evidence of ethnic stocks that inhabited different parts of India in prehistoric times. Therefore, all reconstruction has to be based on conjecture.

Numerous classifications of the racial elements of tribal India based on their physical traits have been made by various anthropologists. This classification was in debate when, in the 19th century, *De Quatrefages* expressed his opinion about the presence of the Negrito element in the Indian subcontinent. *Guha* was suppo rtive of it and even claimed Negrito to be the original inhabitants of India, while *Risley* believed Dravidians to be the first inhabitants of India. Anthropologists like *Sarkar and Majumdar* believed Australoid elements to be autochthones of India. The best representatives of Australoid racial elements are tribes in South India, namely

Irula, Kurumba of the Nilgiri area, Chenchu of Hyderbad, Kadar of Cochin, Paniyan of Malabar, and Central India tribes like Oraon, Gond, and Khond. Physical features such as short stature, dark skin colour, dolichocephalic head, wavy hair, and platyrrhine nose.

H.H. Risley also classified tribes in Assam under the mongoloid type, characterised by a broad head, a fine to broad nose, below-average stature, epicanthic folds in the eyes, dark skin with a yellowish tinge, and scanty body hair. On the other hand, Paniyans of South India and Santhals of Chotanagpur fall under the Dravidian type with features like a long head, a broad nose, dark eyes, dark skin, and curly hair. They are true aborigines, according to him.

The presence of the Negrito element was strongly advocated by *B.S. Guha*. According to him, tribes such as Kadars, Irulas, and Paniyans belong to it, with small, round, medium, and long heads, a flat and broad nose, short stature, dark skin, woolly hair, etc. On the other hand, tribes such as Chenchu, Bhil, Santhal, and Oraon are proto-Australoid with dolichocephalic heads, platyrrhine nose with depressed roots, short stature, dark brown skin, wavy and curly hair, etc. Further, the mongoloid element comprises Palaeo-mongoloid and Tibeto-mongoloid. The long head among palaeo-mongoloids is represented by Sema Naga (Assam), who has a medium nose and medium stature. Broad Head exists among the Chakmas and Maghs of Chittagong. The true representative is Lepchas of Kalimpong. Tibetan mongoloids have a broad head, a long face, tall stature, and light brown skin, as represented by Tibetans of Bhutan and Sikkim.

Despite the above scheme, racial tribes cannot be strictly put under any category; India has been a melting pot of races. Generalised types don't account for all tribes. Thus, the Todas of Nilgiri are without a racial label as yet. Sociological and linguistic research is underway, but it has yet to reveal any new aspect of the racial composition of tribal India. It is established that race crossing has been taking place since the prehistoric past. And as such, there is no so-called pure race, and all are more or less admixture groups (Das).

Negrito Element in India

Diverse ethnic Negrito people live in remote areas of Australasia. De Quatrefages voiced his opinion regarding the Negrito elements in India as early as the 19th century. This idea that some tribes in Central and South India belong to the Negrito element was endorsed by anthropologists like Guha and Hutton.

Guha said that the Negrito were the original inhabitants of India and authentic indigenous people. He noticed that Kadars in South India had the so-called Negrito characteristic, or frizzy head hair. To buttress his claims, Ehrenfels produced a few images of Kadars with woolly hair.

However, an anthropologist named Sarkar concluded in 1959 that there was no Negrito element in India after discovering characteristics including the ABO blood type, dermatoglyphics, anthropometry, and hair form of the Kadars. Kadars and Paniyans may both be classified as Australoid tribes because they resemble other Australoid tribes of South India extremely closely. Guha mentioned two examples, but no real Negrito skeleton remains have yet been discovered in India. Majumdar also rejected the notion that Negrito was one of India's first settlers.

Q 3. Bio-morphological variation among tribes of North-East India

Ans. Biomorphology is a branch of biology that studies the form and structure of organisms and their structural features. In anthropology, it relates to racial variations in external appearance. India is a mosaic of numerous cultures. The people of India have been living under heterogenous and diversified cultural complexities.

According to *Guha, the* Northeast region acted as a gateway for Mongoloid to enter India at different times.

Prominent features:

- Obliquely eye set with an epicanthic fold.
- Scanty facial and body hair
- Prominent cheekbones with a flat face.

It is divided into two groups:

Features	Palaeo Mongoloid		Tibeto Mongoloid
	Long head	**Broad head**	
Skin	Dark to light brown	Dark	Light brown
Hair	Dark, straight	Dark, straight	Dark straight
Head	Long	Broad	Broad and massive
Face	Short and flat	Medium	Long and flat
Nose	Medium	Medium	Long to medium
Stature	Medium	Medium	Tall
Represented by	Assam (Sema, Nagas)	Lepchas, Chakma	Tibetans and Bhutan & Sikkim

However, this classification was criticised for showing all racial elements in India to be of foreign origin. According to Das Gupta, no one is a pure race in India; it is one or more aggregates of similar racial and genetic compositions.

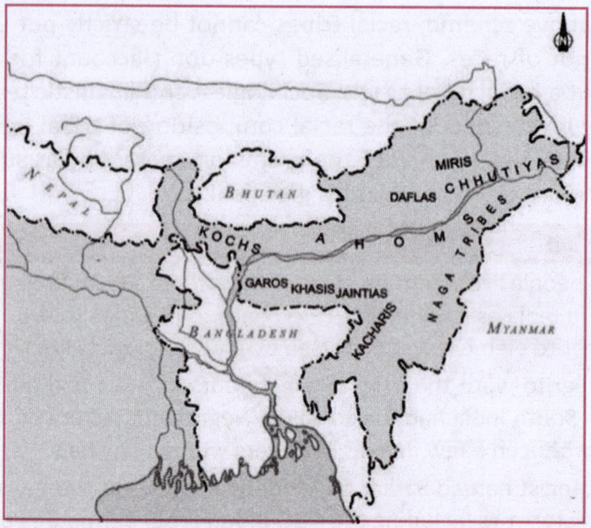

Q 4. Linguistic Characteristics of tribal population and their distribution

Ans. D.N. Majumdar opines that so far as tribal languages are concerned, Aryan speech comes into play only as a consequence of cultural contact, since almost all of our tribal people have pre-Aryan or non-Aryan racial affinities and origins.

Major classifications:

1. **Austric:** The branches of Austro-Asiatic are Munda and Mon-Khmer. Mon-Khmer is represented by Khasi in Meghalaya and Nicobarese in Andaman and Nicobar Island. Munda language comprises 14 tribal languages spoken in Santhal and Chotanagpur regions of Jharkhand, Mayurbhanj in Orrisa, Betul in Maharashtra, etc.

   Languages spoken among tribes like Asur, Birhor, Juang, Kharia, etc.

2. **Dravidian:** The distribution of this language is less diverse but is spoken by a large chunk of the Indian mainland. Based on the *Caldwell* study, there are two sub-divisions: Dravida language: Gondi, Tamil, Kui, Kurukh, Malayalam, Toda, Tulu, and Kota and Andhra language: Telegu, Kolami. With respect to tribals, Gondi speakers comprise the largest group among these. In Central India, Kui is spoken by Kondh (Orrisa), Malti is spoken by tribes of Rajmahal Hill, and Kurukh is spoken by Oraon.
3. **Indo-Aryan:** Tribal communities belonging to this are the Bhils of Rajasthan, the Warli of Maharashtra, and the Hajong of Meghalaya. Banjaras and Pardhis, nomadic tribes in the south with a history of migration from Rajasthan, speak this only.
4. **Tibeto-Burman:** It has further branches:
   - Tibeto-Himalayan further division:
   - Himalayan: Lepcha, Toto, and Reang
   - Bhotia: Ladakhi, Lahauli, Sherpas
   - Arunachal: Mishing, Adi, and Miri

Assam-Burmese further division

- Bodo: Garo, Tripuri
- Kachin: Singpho
- Naga: Ao, Angami, Rengma, and Sumi
- Kuki-chin: Manipuri, Lushai

But multilingualism is an important feature among tribal groups, influencing not only the nature of tribal languages but also socio-cultural transactions. E.g., an Oraon can speak Hindi, Nagpuri, Sadri, and even the indigenous languages of a neighbouring tribe beside Kurukhi.

In general, tribal languages are accorded lower status in comparison to other languages. *V. Elwin* study among Bonda Highlanders found that Bonda used Mundari for daily conversation but Oriya for market transactions and magical or religious recitations. Bonda believes that Oriya is a superior language and that superior entities should be addressed in a superior language. This linguistic process cannot be detached from social life, where notions of class and status influence tribal language.

One area of concern recently has been declining tribal languages. The People's Linguistic Survey of India has estimated that about 220 languages have disappeared in the last half century. While speakers of certain languages have increased, tribes have been subject to social changes, so retaining original languages has become a formidable task. Examples of extinct languages: Majhi in Sikkim, Mohali in Eastern India, Koro in Arunachal, Sidi in Gujarat, Dimasa in Assam, etc.

Effort Needed:

1. A linguistic survey of tribal languages should be done periodically so that they will be properly documented and the people speaking vulnerable languages can be protected.
2. A linguistic survey conducted by the Bhasha Research Institute in Gujarat is a good step in that direction.
3. Protection of primarily vulnerable tribal groups (PVGTs) who are on the verge of extinction

Q 5. Socio-Economic Characteristics of tribes and their distribution

Ans. Tribal economies show what *Majumdar* called "marginal economies"—a group of people practising different types of occupations at one time for livelihood, e.g., collecting fruits, roots, and honey, along with hunting. Usually, tribes have neither internal social differentiation nor specialisation in functions.

Characteristics:

1. **Small Economy:** The production and transaction of goods and services take place within a small community in a limited geographical area.

2. **Reciprocal Exchange:** The exchange of goods and services is carried out on a reciprocal basis through gifts and barter. The motive of profit is absent.
3. **No Surplus:** The manufacture of consumer goods necessary for bare sustenance is usual.
4. **Division of Labour:** Age and sex form the basic criteria for division of labour instead of specialisation.
5. **Simple Technology:** Tools are either made by the user or by local artisans living in the neighbourhood.
6. **Importance of Family and Kinship:** Families in tribal areas form units of both production and consumption.

Kinship acts as a cooperative unit: Thuruwald presented a scheme of classification on economic life like herdsman, homogeneous hunter, etc., but Majumdar rejected it as it indicated the nature of economic difficulty experienced by tribal populations. A more lucid and clear-cut classification by L.P. Vidyarthi has divided the tribes of India into eight cultural types on the basis of economy:

1. **Forest Hunting:** Mainly dependent on hunting wild animals and collecting wild fruits, roots, etc., these seminomadic tribes are found all over India except in the western parts. Examples: Raji of UP, Birhor, Hill Kharia of Bihar, Juang of Odisha, Chenchu of Andhra Pradesh, Kurumba of Kerala, etc.
2. **Shifting Cultivators:** They practise shifting or slash-and-burn cultivation on hill slopes. Such a hilly tract may have to be abandoned after three successive cultivation seasons as the soil loses fertility. Examples: Garo, Khasi of Meghalaya, Naga of Nagaland, along with tribes of Assam, Arunachal Pradesh, Mizoram, etc., Juang of Odisha, Gond and Birhor of M.P., etc.
3. **Plain agriculture type:** Agriculture in its simple form, *e.g.,* ploughing with the help of animal buffaloes, is practised by the majority of tribes in India. Examples: Mundas, Santhals, Oraon, Ho, Khasi, Jaintia, etc.
4. **Pastoral type:** Few tribes are totally committed to cattle herding and live on milk and dairy products. Examples: Todas of the Nilgiri Hills and Bakarwal of J&K.
5. **Artisan type:** Specialise in simple crafts like tool making, carpentry, and ironsmithing. Examples: Asurs of Bihar; Kollam of Maharashtra.
6. **Folk Artist Type:** Some tribes specialise in aerobatics, charming, dancing, etc. Examples: Irulas of T.N. (catch snake), Nats of U.P. (drama), Munduptu of Odisha (acrobats).
7. **Manual labour type:** Agriculturalists work in fields, while non-agriculturalists work in industries in Chhattisgarh, Jharkhand, Odisha, M.P., etc.
8. **White collar and trade type:** Engaged in government and semi-government jobs. Examples: Meena of Rajasthan; Khasi; Mizo; Naga of N-E. Thus, tribes today display great diversity in economic livelihood due to modernization and cultural contacts.

Q 6. Tribal Situation in North East (N-E) India

Ans. India's Northeast is one of the most culturally diverse regions in the world. N-E India is known as the "seven sisters, namely Arunachal Pradesh, Assam, Nagaland, Manipur, Mizoram, Tripura, and Meghalaya.

1. Assam: Boro, Kachari, Mikir, Dimasa, Hajong
2. Arunachal: Adi, Dafla, Aka, Singhpo
3. Nagaland: Sema, Angami, and Rengma
4. Manipur: Naga, Kuki
5. Mizoram: Lusai, Garo, Kuki
6. Tripura: Chakma, Lusai, Santhal, Garo, Khasi, and Kuki.
7. Meghalaya: Garo, Khasi, and Jaintia

Features:

1. Ethnic: The people of Northeast India are broadly divided into two groups: Indid and Mongoloid. Indids comprise Hindu castes and Muslims, which are Caucasoid in origin. However, tribals are Mongoloid in origin with features like yellow skin, an epicanthic fold, a broad face, black or dark brown eyes, and scanty hair.
2. Tribes of the Northeast constitute around 15% of the total population of India.
3. Language belongs to Sino-Tibetan.
4. The tribal economy mainly depends on agriculture.
5. Clan relationships regulate social behaviour. Endogamous unity of tribe and exogamous unity of clan.
6. Patrilineal Exception: Garo of Meghalaya is matrilineal. In Khasi, marriage is forbidden in the mother and father clans.
7. Political Structure:
   a. Council of elders looks after matters. E.g., Lushias, Ao, Naga
   b. Village headman: post-hereditary E.g. Khasis.
   c. Chieftainship among Naga and Khasi.
8. Different festivals like Baishagu among the Bodo Tribe, Harni Garba among the Dimasa tribe, the bamboo dance of Mizoram, etc.

Certain issues exist, like outside migrants, secessionist tendencies, inter-tribal rivalry, and inadequate development.

But the government has taken steps like the formation of the N-E Ministry, Kaladan projects, and the critical guideline of earmarking at least 10% of budget allocation for specific programmes for the development of the N-E region and Sikkim.

Q 7. Denotified tribe

Ans. Denotified tribes are communities that were notified as being born criminals under the Criminal Tribes Act 1871 by the British government. Once a tribe was notified as criminal, its members were required to register with the local magistrate, failing which they would be charged with a crime under the Indian Penal Code. The British government enacted the notorious Criminal Tribes Act in 1871 in view of a strong tribal rebellion against the British Empire. The Criminal Tribes Act was repealed in 1949 and thus denotified the tribal communities.

The Indian government replaced it with the Habitual Offenders Act in 1952. It mandates the police investigate a suspect's criminal tendencies and whether their occupation is conducive to a settled way of life. The denotified tribes were reclassified as habitual offenders in 1959.

Historical Problems: They have been stigmatised as crime-prone and subjected to highhanded treatment. They were also exploited by the representatives of law and order as well as by the general population. The communities are largely politically quiet. The various forest laws have deprived the traditional rights of grazing, hunting, gathering, and shifting cultivation in specific areas. They lack basic amenities like shelter, electricity, latrines, etc. They do not place their demands concretely before the government as they lack vocal leadership and also lack the patronage of a national leader.

Status: Most DNTs are spread across the Scheduled Castes (SC), Scheduled Tribes (ST), and Other Backward Classes (OBC) categories. It is estimated that there are about 801 denotified, nomadic, and semi-nomadic tribes in the country, comprising a population of approximately 13.5 crore people. Yet many are not covered in any of the SC, ST, or OBC categories and thus remain outside the reach of affirmative action. They are hard to reach, less visible, and therefore frequently left out.

Case study:

1. Bhargava studied the Bawarias of north India. They justified crime as they received inspiration from God or spirits. Every child, women and men alike, learns to hide things, do burglaries, thefts, etc.
2. Kanjars of M.P. and Maharashtra are so hardened from childhood that even third-degree methods have little effect on them. The father beat his son mercilessly and kept him tied and without food for days, just to toughen and harden them.

Issues:

1. Shilu Ao Report: Denial of benefits to members of denotified communities as given to ST.
2. Abolition of all criminal settlements without any serious effort on the part of the government to rehabilitate them.
3. The absence of public sympathy is the greatest hindrance to their settlement.

Government-constituted commissions:

1. The National Commission for De-notified, Nomadic, and Semi-Nomadic Tribes (NCDNT) was constituted in 2006. Objective: Prepare a state-wise list of castes belonging to denotified and nomadic tribes and suggest appropriate measures.
2. The Renke Commission estimated their population based on the 2001 Census.
3. DWBDNC was constituted in 2019 under the Societies Registration Act. DWNDNC is the Development and Welfare Board for De-notified, Nomadic, and Semi-Nomadic Communities (DWBDNC). The Ministry of Social Justice and Empowerment was given the authority to implement welfare programmes.
4. NITI Aayog has set up a committee to complete the process of identifying the de-notified, nomadic, and seminomadic communities (DNCs).

Idate Commission Report (2018):

1. A constitutional amendment to include DNTs under a separate third schedule after SCs and STs.
2. Giving them protection under the SC/ST (Prevention of Atrocities) Act, 1989.
3. Repeal of the Habitual Offenders Act to purge the historical stigma attached.
4. Promotion of their traditional skills such as juggling and acrobatics, along with revisions in anti-beggar laws that ban such skills.
5. Systematic population count of DNTs in the 2021 Census to enable targeted policies and action.

It is high time that the DNTs are recognised as equal citizens of the country and get to share the benefits of the nation's development.

Q 8. Art in Tribal India

Ans. In simple terms, tribal art is the visual art and material culture of indigenous people. It refers to the subject and craftsmanship of artefacts from tribal culture.

India is marked by a rich traditional heritage of tribal art. Since the days of the remote past, diversified art and cultural forms generated by the tribals of India have continued their creative magnificence. E.g., Bhimbetka caves, Belan Valley (*A.C. Carlleyle*).

Dr. Majumdar opined that tribal artistic life is reflected in mainly three arts:

1. Oral literature: myths, tales, song verse, etc.
2. Music and dance: folk dances, folk music
3. Art and dancing.

It excludes folk handicrafts and acrobatics.

Folklore is the oral literature of simpler societies and is perpetuated by oral traditions. In many tribes, there is an institution of youth dormitories. Unmarried youth assemble here before going to the Lord and tell stories, solve puzzles, sing, dance, etc. *Herskovitz* systematised folklore study in anthropology: catastrophe, incest, sibling rivalry, and the slaying of monsters.

Folk music and dance are composites that are dominant characteristics of their culture. It is done in the form of moral songs, thoughtful songs, teaching philosophy of life, etc., e.g., the Bihu dance or the Karma dance of the hand.

Folk handicrafts include Warli paintings of Maharashtra, Pattachitra paintings of Odisha, Madhubani paintings of Bihar, Kalam art of Kerela, etc., Bhimbetka paintings, etc. It has two dimensions: home art and cave art.

Case study: Dr. Amit Soni studied the performing arts culture of the Baiga tribe in Central India. He found that Baiga dance and songs are custodians of their fast-vanishing cultural traditions. Male dance troupes like Baiga Nritya Dal perform dances for income. However, certain dance traditions, like Parghouni Hathi, are fast disappearing from Baiga marriages.

TRIFED has taken steps to promote tribal products:

1. **Aadishilp:** National Tribal Craft Expo to showcase tribal heritage by individuals, SHGs, and organisations.Tribal artisans got to directly interact with people to get feedback.
2. **Aadichitra:** Tribal paintings displayed and sold like Warli, Pithora, etc.
3. **Octave:** It is a dance festival of the Northeast region where tribal out and festival are displayed alongside.

With the effort of the government, tribal culture progressed considerably, while at the same time globalisation led to the emergence of a synthetic, homogenous macroculture.

Case Study

- **Tribal art commodification: archiving India's indigenous tattoos**

Rural-Urban dichotomy: With some shared design aspects, tattoo traditions vary across states and regions. The Apatani tribe of Arunachal Pradesh used to tattoo its female members. The Konyaks of Nagaland, who practised headhunting, used to tattoo their faces to represent their combat prowess. In Gujarat, the Rabaris and Bharwads tribes were renowned for their intricate Trajva tattoos, which served as a symbol of strength and beauty. These are just a few of the tattoo customs that characterise India's thriving tribal culture. However, it is odd to notice that today's tattooing culture, which was once an integral part of rural life, appears to have migrated away from its original setting under the excuse that it is "outdated" and unrelated to contemporary interests. Now is an intriguing time because rural India is gradually giving up getting tattoos while urban India is seeing a spike in tattoo popularity. This is ironic in some respects because the country's urbanisation was one of the main factors in the demise of traditional practises.

Straddling the past and the present: Even though the extent of India's tattoo traditions may not be well known, we still have access to some limited but valuable sources, such as the tattoos on the skin of our elderly relatives, antiquated photographs that document the passage of time, or "even anecdotal stories of that kasav (turtle) or that bicchu (scorpion). Few contemporary tattoo artists, like Shomil, are returning to the old methods and aesthetics of tattooing because of a rising respect for their heritage.

Moranngam Khaling, also known as Mo Naga, a tattoo artist from Manipur who has been working to preserve the tattoo traditions of Northeastern tribal cultures, and photographer Shatabdi Chakrabarti, who has been capturing various tattoo practises in India for more than ten years, are two artists who have inspired him. He aspires to preserve, gather, and make accessible what is left of this antiquated art form through the India Ink Archive. Indian tattoo traditions are deeply ingrained in our skin and memory, and the India Ink Archive is a rich repository of tales and a pictorial record of them.

6.2

Problems of the tribal Communities: Land alienation, poverty, indebtedness, low literacy, poor educational facilities, unemployment, under-employment, health and nutrition

Q 1. Land alienation

Ans. Forests and tribes have been living harmoniously and symbiotically for several thousand years. While forests fulfilled all needs of tribal people, tribal people, for their part, protected forests. This relationship continued until the advent of the British, who created roads deep into tribal areas and called them "roads to development". On these roads, government officials, foresters, moneylenders, contractors, missionaries, and others entered tribal areas, and these roads turned out to be "roads to exploitation" for tribals. Land alienation is one of the consequences of the above-mentioned factor.

Hasnain has enlisted the following causes: Most tribal cultivators have uneconomic holdings. Their holdings, which appear larger in size, are nullified by poor quality of soil, poor technique of cultivation, and an ever-increasing burden of debt, which prepare the trap for poor tribals to surrender their land. This trap is further strengthened by wasteful expenditure on the part of tribal members on non-essential items. Tribals do not have good experience with state financial institutions, which demand guarantees for repayment of loans while money is readily available from money lenders who charge a high rate of interest.

Xaxa report has enlisted causes: Land alienation takes place due to development-induced displacement caused by the acquisition of land by the state without a "land for land' provision for rehabilitation. Community land of tribal communities recorded as government land creation of national parks and wildlife sanctuaries are some other ways in which land alienation took place, according to the Xaxa report.

- According to the survey, the Korwa tribe of MP and the Tharu tribe of UP were victims of land alienation due to money lenders Miyan and new Punjabi settlers in their areas, respectively. Both have the same modus operandi, i.e., advancing loans unconditionally and providing cheap liquor to tribals.
- In Narmada Bachao Andolan, 56% of tribals were displaced, and promises have not yet been fulfilled.
- 1961 -2011 (Census) study: % ST cultivators declined by 35 points, and % ST labour increased by 25 points.

Government Steps:

- PESA Act, 1996
- FRA, 2006
- Land Acquisition Act, 2013
- Andhra Pradesh Scheduled Areas Land Transfer Regulation, 1959
- M.P. Resettlement of Displaced Land Holders (Land Acquisition) Act, 1954

Xaxa Committee Recommendations to Prevent Land Alienation:

1. In pursuance of PESA, 1996, the land transfer and tenancy laws of all Schedule V areas should be amended to ensure Gram Sabha participation in identification, investigation, and restoration of lands to tribal people.
2. Plenary powers could be given to the Gram Sabha to fight cases of tribal land alienation collectively.
3. Provisions in the AP Act, where immovable property of tribal people is mortgaged to a bank and property is to be sold only in case of default to a tribal cooperative society exclusively formed by tribal people, can be replicated in other schedule areas.
4. A suitable amendment in all laws that time limit be prescribed for restoring tribal land and regular monitoring of tribal cases for restoration of tribal land are required.

5. According to Schedule Area and ST recommendations of 1961, the Deputy Collector or Commissioner should have power to suo moto or at the instance of an aggrieved tribal land holder within 12 years to institute enquiring and restore land.
6. Mining in their land is carried out by themselves, as in Andhra Pradesh, through cooperatives.
7. Forest rights are covered under FRA; however, common property resources such as government land and panchayat land are not covered by any legislation. This needs to be rectified.
8. Ultimately, it is the duty of the state government to ensure that all officials and lower-level functionaries do not conspire to take away tribal people's land. Regular monitoring at the state and centre levels for the disposal of cases and proactive efforts for the restoration of tribal land are required.

National policy for tribal land alienation:

1. Land records are to be displayed at the panchayat.
2. Tribal members should have access to land records.
3. Ease of credit availability.

Conclusion: Tribals, being simple folk, are often exploited to forgo their most important resource land to non-tribals. Therefore, certain above-mentioned steps need to be taken at the earliest to tackle the problem via political will and integrity on the part of the administration.

Case Study

- **Land Alienation and Rural Development in Northeast India, by Walter Fernandes**

According to the research, disputes and land alienation stem from the type of modernization that tribal tribes in north-east India are undergoing, which is the foundation for current rural development. Alternatives that enable the people to control their development must be created. To ensure that every rural resident in the area has access to the right to a life with dignity under Article 21, it must include not only agriculture in its restricted form but also education, health care, and rural infrastructure. It calls for a development perspective that is people-centred rather than corporate sector-focused.

- **Frequent floods in the Brahmaputra are eating away at Assam's tribal lands.**

The Mising, like other indigenous groups around the world, are highly dependent on natural resources and have few employment opportunities; thus, they frequently experience the brunt of the harsh weather that has become more frequent as global temperatures increase. Families in Besemora are constantly uprooted by the rising Brahmaputra, which forces them to move to an area of land that is becoming less and less available and strains their ability to support themselves. According to a 2018 study by India's Department of Science and Technology, Assam was the Himalayan state that was most susceptible to the negative effects of climate change. It brought attention to a number of issues, such as Assam's low per capita income, the prevalence of crop insurance, and the lack of irrigated land, which forces farmers to depend on regular rainfall to water their fields.

A Mising tribal member who has lived beside the Brahmaputra and its tributaries for many generations recalls feeling proud of their ability to understand how one of the planet's longest river systems behaves. However, society is perplexed right now by how unpredictable it is.

Q 2. Indebtness

Ans. Earliest record of tribals are seen in Kautilya's Arthashastra where tribals have been mentioned as Vanya Jati. Till the end of medieval period, rulers never interfered with tribal way of life. British exploited minerals and forests inhabited by tribals and as consequence brought miseries for them. Indebtness is one of problem initiated during British time.

Surveys conducted by the working group on cooperation for backward classes appointed by the Ministry of Tribal Affairs headed by *Bhargava, the* study group on relief indebtedness (1975), etc. have concluded that the overwhelming majority of tribals in different parts of the country were under heavy debt, indebtedness outgrew the repaying capacity of debtors, and agricultural needs constituted only half of the debt incurred.

Hasnain has enlisted causes of indebtedness:

1. Loss of tribal rights over land and forests
2. Poor and primitive modes of agriculture
3. Extravagant spending on marriages, deaths, and festivals
4. Fatalist attitude and a locally oriented world view

Consequences:

1. Loss of freedom and utilisation of their labour power by creditors
2. Alienation of land and its acquisition by creditors
3. Sale of girls and prostitution
4. Chronic venereal diseases

Tribals who failed to clear debt usually worked as "bonded labour," and yet the account books of moneylenders never give them a clean chit. The worst-hit tribes by this menace are the Jaunsaris of Tarai region and the Koltas of U.P. The bonded labour system is called Palemod in Maharashtra and the Dadan System in Tripura.

Government Steps:

- PESA Act, 1996
- FRA
- AP Scheduled Area Moneylender Regulations
- Assam Moneylender Regulation, etc.

However, continued exploitation of tribals by greedy moneylenders is taking place.

Xaxa Committee recommendations to prevent indebtedness:

1. Covering uncovered tribal areas by cooperative banking institutions
2. Making laws on money lending in tribal areas more stringent and examining the adequacy of legislation in its relevance to tribals
3. Making administration at block, tehsil, and other levels effective to bring culprits to book for violating provisions of the law
4. Political will and commitment on the part of those who are supposed to be protectors of tribal interests.
5. We need to establish agro-based institutions and related labour-intensive industries in tribal areas.
6. To make use of the land available, they should be motivated to practise organic farming and eco-forestry.
7. Microwatershed management should be given priority to enhance agro-productivity.

Conclusion: All it needs is political will, commitment, honesty, and integrity on the part of those who are supposed to be protectors of tribal interests.

Case Study

- **Child marriage rears its ugly head in Rajasthan**

Over the years, India has made significant progress in lowering the prevalence of child marriage, but the financial hardship brought on by the COVID-19 pandemic is likely to reverse the progress accomplished so far. The latest allegations of the sale of girls from the Banjaras tribal clan on stamp paper to settle debts in the desert state of Rajasthan, where social malaise is culturally pervasive, highlight how vulnerable the girl child is in families that use her as a way to get by financially.

Q 3. Low literacy / Poor Educational facilities

Ans. Like other sectors of socio-economic life, tribal people are at different levels of educational development, but, on the whole, formal education has had very little impact on tribal life. In light of past efforts, it is not shocking that prior to 1950, there was no direct programme for the education of tribals. The census figure of 1931 disclosed that only 0.7% of tribal people were literate.

In the states of Bihar, Chattisgarh, Odisha, and MP, the majority of tribes have a literacy percentage lower than that of tribes in India, while tribes in the Northeast, like Khasi, Jaintia, Mizo, etc., have crossed the national literacy average. Due to Sarva Shiksha Abhiyan (SSA), RMSA, RUSA, Midday Meal, and Residential Schools, data showed a 14.6% point increase in ST women's literacy compared to 10% for non-ST/SC women, and 9.4% in ST men compared to 4.8 among non-ST/SC men (2011 Census).

But still, a literacy gap of 14% exists between ST and non-ST due to factors like

1. **Ecology:** The main problem for tribes living in hilly, forested, and inaccessible areas is a lack of school. Even if they are available, they have to cover large distances to reach school and are usually run by a single teacher. Even the psychological issue of the same toilet for both sexes.
2. **Social:** Widespread feeling that education makes their boys and girls defiant and isolates them from the rest of society. Formal education is not considered necessary by members of tribal societies to discharge their social obligations. Koyas in AP consider the difference between education and social life. They consider it a source of alienation for the child's parents. The Ghasiya tribal children of UP are prejudiced and forced to sit backward and have a separate midday meal.
3. **Economy:** Nomadic communities are so mobile and their children are trained from very childhood in the profession of community that they hardly get time for and realise the importance of education. The role of children in collecting forest produce in those communities that practise shifting cultivation is well known. Settled agriculturalist tribals are more conscious of the utility of education than the other two. Srivastava says that poverty and a lack of food make education a luxury they cannot afford.
4. **Administration:** Problems of non-tribal teachers' different attitudes towards tribals, lack of incentive for teachers to work, tribals not being taught in their mother tongue, and low actual attendance impede and signify the failure of administration. ASER reports that 93% of students in Class V cannot read Class II books.

Government steps:

- Article 21A makes education a fundamental right.
- Proportionate reservation for ST in universities and colleges
- Schemes: pre-matric, post-matric scholarship, Samagra Shiksha, residential schools, etc.

S.N. Rath (1981) has given a few suggestions:

1. A balance should be struck to evolve a system of curricula where tribal schools should have supplementary curricula adapted to local conditions. Include local folk-dance culture, curriculum, and storytelling, painting, movies, and dance promotions in the curriculum.
2. Supplementary curriculum should be biassed towards craft and should inculcate a sense of dignity in labour, qualities of cooperation, and social discipline.
3. Scheme worked out through which schoolchildren shall link up school and teacher with their parents and tribal activities. Separate codes of conduct for teaching staff, especially for those serving in tribal areas for longer periods.
4. Tribal teachers shall be appointed in tribal areas; special teaching aids to retain students; job-oriented courses along with education in school; and more hostels or nearby residential schools in the vicinity shall be opened up.

Conclusion: The new NEP emphasizes on the use of the mother tongue. It recommends that the region's mother tongue is used to impart teaching in primary classes. If various NGOs and local media play an important role in creating awareness among the tribals, then they can bask in the auroral radiance of economic development.

Case Study

- **Digital literacy in tribal villages**

Each of the 14 villages in the Palghar district of Maharashtra has a computer kiosk that has been set up to teach young e-sevaks how to access the government's e-governance website, from signing up for Aadhar to taking advantage of government programmes. 1,875 tribal residents from 31 villages in Palghar have access to their land records thanks to the Pukar initiative, which is a necessary first step towards securing an exemption from eviction. In the Indian tribal community of Tandalwadi, researchers met six young women who had completed more than two years of e-sewale training. They are now trailblazers who keep an eye on other e-sexless users, assist villagers in forming cooperatives, encourage women to vote, educate about even constitutional provisions, etc.

- **GOAL**

Facebook recently introduced the 'Going Online as Leaders' (GOAL) initiative, which aims to train tribal girls from all around India to become young digital leaders in their villages.

- **Pathshalas' making change in tribals' lives**

Children from Primary Vulnerable Tribal Groups (PVTG) in Jharkhand continue their education with the aid of "Pathshala Change Makers" (PCM), who have been recruited by the state government during times of lockdown when schools and other educational facilities are shuttered. In their daily interactions, the Pathshala Change Makers offer support to the community. The initiative aims to increase interest in reading and writing among children from vulnerable primary tribal groups in order to boost their foundational education by the time they register for school.

Up to 140 PVTG Pathshalas are operated by the Udaan project, which benefits almost 3,000 PVTG students, in the state's ten most underprivileged districts. The process of enrolling these kids continues, with a goal of adding about 100 additional PVTG Pathshalas this year. There are over 73,000 PVTG households that are subsisting on very little money. Most of these groups live in isolated forest locations and have their own distinct social and cultural identities. They rely on non-timber forest products, livestock husbandry, hunting, and livelihoods based in the forest. The Jharkhand State Livelihood Promotion Society (JSLPS) began an intervention plan called "PVTG Pathshala" under the special project Udaan, a comprehensive and sustainable development of PVTGs in the year 2020, to tackle the crisis amid the COVID-19 pandemic. In addition to instructing, the Pathshala Change Makers are also engaged in raising widespread awareness among parents of children for whom education is never a top concern.

- **Artificial intelligence (AI) curriculum**

A deal between the Ministry of Tribal Affairs and Microsoft said that tribal children attending Eklavya Model Residential Schools (EMRS) and Ashram Schools across the nation would have access to an artificial intelligence (AI) curriculum in both English and Hindi. Teachers would also receive training on how to use programmes like Office 365 and others for educational purposes. The programme started out by implementing itself in 250 schools all around the nation.

- **Project Samhati**

The Odisha State government's ST and SC Development Department has already begun work on a project called "Samhati" to solve the language difficulties that tribal pupils encounter in the primary grades or in elemen tary school.The project is being carried out by the Scheduled Castes and Scheduled Tribes Research and Training Institute (SCSTRTI) and the Academy of Tribal Language and Culture (ATLC), Bhubaneswar.

- **Shaala Sangwari**

A project that was begun in the district of Kabirdham in Chattisgarh intends to employ educated Baiga tribal youth by having them instruct the young people in their neighbourhood's elementary and middle schools. District Mineral Foundation (DMF) funding was used to fund the project. Earlier, it was difficult for specific administrations to locate teachers to work in these locations due to the distance and challenging geographic topography. As an alternative to allocating DMF monies to infrastructure initiatives, other significant mining companies could follow its lead.

Q 4. Tribal Health

Ans. ST constitutes 8.6% of the total population in India (2011 Census). The mortality indicator for the ST population has certainly improved during the past decade, but they are still worse off than the general population. Infant and child mortality rates among ST are double the national average. Nutrition status also reveals a sad picture: 53% of boys and 50% of girls in pre-school age were underweight.

The Dhebar Commission has given four principal reasons:

1. **Need for correct approach:** The plan does not take into account different belief systems, different disease burdens, and different health care needs, as well as difficulties in delivering health care in geographically scattered areas.
2. **Problem of personnel:** Lack of health care human resources willing, trained, and equipped to work in scheduled areas. There is a shortage of doctors, nurses, technicians, and managers in the public health care system.
3. **Inadequacy of communication:** Due to the inaccessibility of tribal areas, mobile dispensaries and health centres can be more purposeful than static ones. The language barrier between tribe and doctor is another issue.
4. **Rules about supply of medicine:** Difference in condition between plain and tribal areas needs different rules regarding stocks of medicine, but this is often not taken into account.

A few other factors and cases:

1. Tribes like Toda became obese due to an affluent lifestyle and leaving traditional work.
2. Drug addiction is another serious health problem among tribes. The Singpho tribe of Arunachal Pradesh is a case in point.
3. Hypertension, diabetes, and cancer among Nicobarese and Great Andamanese are due to the breaking of the traditional balanced lives of tribals.
4. Due to poverty, the Sugalis of AP and Karnataka sold their girls to outsiders and forced girls into prostitution.
5. Jaduguda of Jharkhand worked in uranium mines; tribes like Korba lived in high pollution; tribes near Pong Dam suffered repeated malaria.
6. A study by Bardhan and others in 1989 among Bhils in MP found that they have strong traditional beliefs and seek treatment only when all other options have been exhausted. They believe in their own magic man or medicine man.
7. Sexually transmitted diseases are high among the polyandrous Jaunsari tribe and Santhals.
8. Prevalence of water-borne diseases: diarrhoea, cholera, and mineral deficiency like goitre.

Government Steps: Ayushmann Bharat and the Jan Arogya Yojana, Integrated Child Development Scheme (ICDS), Tribal Subplan (TSP), etc.

Redesign based on Xaxa recommendations:

1. The first principle is participation—the views of tribal people must be given due place in health care programmes.

2. The second principle is area-specific and tribe-sensitive local planning.
3. Intersectoral coordination in various sectors like literacy, income, sanitation, food security, and gender sensitivity is required.
4. Spreading health literacy by way of educational methods, folk methods, media, etc.
5. A sensitive way of including traditional healers and dais in health care must be explored.
6. At least 15% of the total TSP budget should be committed to the tribal health sector.
7. The availability and consumption of tobacco and drugs should be severely controlled.
8. Separate medical colleges opened in schedule district sectors reserved for ST candidates to be selected from schedule areas.

Comprehensive tribal health policy at the national level will surely address the issues and challenges of tribes and their health-related practises. The tribe's indigenous knowledge about medicine (ethnomedicine) needs to be combined with the modern scientific ways of medicine.

Case Study

- **Bonda Tribal Way**

Because of its customs prohibiting the use of mosquito nets or contemporary medications, the vulnerable and primitive Bonda tribe used to lose a significant number of individuals to malaria every year until a decade ago. But during the past year, the tribe of less than 10,000 individuals, which enjoys keeping the outside world at bay, has overcome its dislike for shots and needles to write one of the success stories of Odisha's battle against COVID. Despite the fact that the number of COVID patients in Odisha has been increasing daily, not a single member of the tribe has been infected thus far during the third wave of the epidemic. Almost all Bonda community members who qualify have received two doses of the COVID vaccine.

- **COVID Teeka Sang Surakshit Van, Dhan aur Uddyam**

The "COVID Teeka Sang Surakshit Van, Dhan aur Uddyam" programme has been started by TRIFED under the Ministry of Tribals for 10.5 crore tribal community members across the country in order to save lives, earn a living, and stay safe from Corona. The indigenous people stand to gain a lot from this initiative. The three crucial Js—Jeevan (life), Jeevika (livelihood), and Jaagrookta (awareness)—will be highlighted in the campaign.

- **Country's first report on tribal health**

Some of the report's findings demand significant, immediate attention. The life expectancy for tribal people is likely to be "over-estimated" since child deaths are "under reported" among tribals, even though the life expectancy at birth for Scheduled Tribes (ST) in India is 63.9 years as opposed to 67 years for the general population. The report, which addresses different facets of tribal health, notes that over 50% of adolescent ST females between the ages of 15 and 19 are "underweight" or have a body mass index (BMI) of "less than 18.5". Tribal women still deliver at home in the highest percentage of all population groups—27%. This may be partially due to the unpleasant demeanour of health professionals, communication barriers, and a lack of faith in an unfamiliar system. Only the Federally Administered Area in Pakistan had a higher infant death rate among indigenous communities than ST in India. Despite a significant improvement in which the tribal infant mortality rate was cut in half during a 26-year period, from 1988 to 2014, the rate of reduction in the tribal IMR fell over the subsequent ten years, from 2004 to 2014, after peaking in 2004.

Important suggestions: One important suggestion is to launch the Tribal Health Mission while allowing tribal members to have a say in how it is structured and designed. The appointment of 1,000 tribal health officers (THOs) is another suggestion. " Tribal healthcare is currently underfunded and of poor quality. According to the IAS cadre, a district THO and one THO for each of the country's 809 blocks must be selected. Additionally, a tribal health council and directorate should be established as a framework to enhance care delivery. To ensure "strict adherence" to the Tribal Sub-Plan's guidelines, the Central and State Ministries of Health must allocate more money for public health services in tribal areas, up to a total of Rs 15,676 crore, in proportion to the ST population and ensure that 70 percent of this is spent on primary healthcare.

- **Giri Poshana is the war waged against hunger**

A programme launched as a pilot project in 2019 to address nutritional deficiencies among tribal people has the potential to improve the nutritional intake of the chosen tribal population and has also grown to serve as a financial support system for Adivasi women employed in the food processing sector. The "Giri Poshana" initiative of the central government is being carried out through a merger of the Tribal Welfare and Women and Child Welfare departments, with assistance from ICRISAT in terms of technology, operations, and science. The project's goal was to provide the targeted beneficiaries with three ready-to-eat food items—such as peanut sesame chikki, peanut-fried gramme chikki, and jowar bites—and three ready-to-cook food items—such as multi-grain cereal, jowar meal, and multi-grain sweet meal—that were created and developed by ICRISAT. This year, the food is being manufactured at nutri-food processing facilities with FSSAI licences that are run by tribal women-led Joint Liability Groups (JLGs). Through backward integration, raw materials are acquired from tribal farmers' FPOs. All supply chain participants profit from it, from production to processing to consumption.

Q 5. Tribal Shifting Cultivation

Ans. Shifting cultivation is an age-old institution among Indian tribes. This, in principle, means cultivating a plot of land for a temporary period and then leaving a plot of land uncultivated for a temporary period. It consists of clearing forest slopes, burning fallen trees and bushes, and broadcasting seed in ash-covered soil.

This is known by different regional names in India. It is called 'Jhum' among the tribes of Assam, Meghalaya, Mizoram, Tripura, and Arunachal; 'Bewar' in MP; 'Podu' in AP, etc. It is acute in the states of Andhra Pradesh, the North East, Bihar, and Orrisa. It has become a regular cult among the Baigas of MP and Odisha.

There are two different views. Scholars like Nicholsan and M.L. Bor considered that the damage done to forests by shifting cultivation was serious. While M.D. Chaturvedi and S.H. Howard said that this practise is an organic response to certain geophysical conditions. They considered that if a period of rest is given between fellings, there is little damage from soil erosion.

Theoretically, it is now legally prohibited except in a few pockets of MP and the N-E region, where it is still practised with the permission of competent authorities.

Despite its disadvantages, it cannot be ignored that nearly 10% of the Indian tribal population depends on it, and they cannot be deprived of their land, livelihood, and way of life.

The 1901 Planning Commission report on tribal development programmes gave suggestions:

1. Set up demonstration farms.
2. Distribute agriculture implements, manure, fertiliser, and HYV seeds.
3. Promote credit facilities.

The 1961 Report of the Schedule Area and ST Commission gave suggestions:

1. Total replacement will be a long-term process. The proper course is to regulate it, experiment with it, improve it, and try other workable alternatives.
2. Shifting cultivation areas should be converted into terrace cultivation where hill slopes permit and the soil is deep enough.
3. Establishment of agricultural colonies to shift towards settled cultivation.

Conclusion: Shifting cultivation, or resource-based subsistence farming, is no longer relevant because of the large population and its growing demands. The system is destabilised by long cultivation and short fallow periods. There is a need to transform shifting cultivation into sustainable cultivation.

Case Study

- **SALT Approach in Northeast India**

Sloping Agriculture Land Technology, or SALT, could assist farmers in generating a stable income. Contrary to shifting cultivation, practising it won't result in any pollution. It promotes the best possible use of land resources because it is a climate-smart solution. The lives of farmers in South and Southeast Asia have changed as a result of this strategy. It is ideal for sloping terrain with significant soil loss. In order to control the loss of soil during rainstorms, the method entails the construction of vegetative barriers.

The crops are produced on the strips in between the hedgerows, which are grown along the contours. These hedgerows typically consist of nitrogen-fixing plants that support soil nitrogen levels and require maintenance to increase agricultural output productivity. To give the soil nutrients, animal dung is used. Overall, this approach is less labour-intensive and more sustainable. Reduced deforestation, lower CO2 emissions, and assistance in achieving a sustainable way of life are all advantages.

Q 6. Tribal Housing

Ans. The problem of housing for tribal people has to be viewed from the aspects of (a) shelter, (b) sanitation, (c) aesthetic taste, and (d) comparative cost.

Variation in climate coupled with differences in the economic condition of tribes and the type of architecture pose a number of problems. Chotanagpur plateau, Khasi hills, Maikala, and Nilgiri hills are home to different tribes with pleasant climates. While the Brahmaputra Valley of Assam has oppressive heat, high mountain ranges have a severe cold climate. Housing is designed to keep out heat or resist cold, depending on the local climate.

Housing sense, coupled with utility and artistic nature, is another aspect of housing among tribal people. The Garo, Mishmi, Naga, and Reang tribes of N-E are famous for beautiful houses combining utility and artistic value. The same is the case with Gond (MP), Koya (AP), Oraon, and Santhal of Bihar, etc.

However, not all tribals are so lucky. Particularly in the plains, some are all landless and homeless, and their plight is miscreable. e.g., the Yenadi tribe of Andhra Pradesh makes use of vacant land on both sides of the PWD road and canals for housing purposes until they are driven away.

Difficulties in resolving tribal housing issues—

- An architect who has never seen a tribal house or tribe draws a plan for them.
- The Forest Department does not allow them to obtain timber for house building or repairing.

Study of the Planning Commission on Tribal Development (1969) recommended:

1. The formulation of a housing scheme for tribals should make a distinction between plain tribals and hilly tribals, and that housing should conform to local needs, tastes, and traditions.
2. Selection of the site and house construction proceeded with due observance of tribal rights and rituals.

It must be kept in mind that even an extensive house is useless for a tribal if he feels uncomfortable in unfamiliar surroundings. The approach of the nature-man-spirit complex needs to be applied while formulating housing plans.

Case Study

- **Anthropological Survey of India builds tribal hut replicas to promote unique heritage**

From a Shompen hut made of jungle supari leaves with a cage for wild pigs built underneath it to a Jarawa tribe's distinctive beehive-shaped hut to a Nicobarese hut made of local cane stems covered in thick dry grasses, each provides a glimpse into tribal communities' daily lives that the majority of Indians will never experience. The Anthropological Survey of India (AnSI) has rebuilt the huts of various communities at its several regional centres in a first-of-its-kind effort to display the heritage of tribal people, notably those of Particularly Vulnerable Tribal Groups (PVTGs). These huts have been built in front of five AnSI regional centres after consultation with the surrounding neighbourhoods. Huts offer a unique look into the lives of these groups, which live in remote areas and are not easily accessible to outsiders. Huts are authentic in design and made of the same materials as the indigenous people. They also feature objects that they use. For instance, the traditional Jarawa hut, or chadda, is furnished with traditional baskets, bows, and arrows, as well as other items. When there is a food shortage, tribal members can eat the pandamus fruit paste that is kept in the Shompen hut. Living on the Andaman and Nicobar Islands are the Jarawa and Shompen communities, both of which are PVTGs. Despite estimates that Shompen people n umberfewer than 300, there are about 500 members of the Jarawa tribe.

Q 7. Employment-related issues faced by the tribes of India

Ans. The traditional economic livelihoods of tribes were aligned with their natural surroundings and aimed at meeting basic subsistence needs. However, tribes have been forced to enter the job market due to the forces of modernization, where they have been victims of unemployment and underemployment.

Key Statistics: As per the Ministry of Tribal Affairs Report 2017, 80% of the ST workforce is engaged in the primary sector, and 44% of these are employed as agricultural labourers. Further, 21% of ST households are engaged in casual labour, the highest among all groups. It is thus no surprise that ST households have the lowest annual income of all groups, not even half of that of the general population.

Exception—N-E, where the "education first' idiom helped their development.

Causes:

1. Poor agricultural productivity.
2. Exploitation by outsiders.
3. Displacement and failed rehabilitation.
4. Low level of skill standards.
5. Low awareness about legal rights.

Dr. B.D. Sharma talked about five levels of depreciation:

1. Non-recognition of rights over resources and restrictions on their use.
2. Alienation of workers from the means of production.
3. Denial of the due installment of labour.
4. Bartering of liberty.
5. Psychological state of accepting depreciation, destitution, and the demise of self-respect and dignity.

Government Steps:

- Since 1989, both the National Rural Employment Programme (1980) and the Rural Landless Employment Guarantee Programme (RLEGP) have merged into the Jawahar Rozgar Yojana
- ST Finance and Development Corporation
- TRIFED
- MGNREGA

Xaxa committee recommendations:

1. Organisation of tribal groups into self-help groups or cooperatives.
2. Employment generation by promoting agro-based and labour-intensive industries.
3. Promote modes of farming that are aligned with the tribal way, like organic farming and eco-forestry.
4. TRIFED should expand the reach of its programmes, especially the Tribes India brand used to market tribal products.
5. The vacancies in the reserved jobs for STs in the public sector should be filled.
6. Strict regulation of moneylending in tribal areas and firm action against bonded labour
7. Recognition of tribal claims over land and forest produce under the Forest Rights Act, 2006, and prevention of illegal land alienation.

Case Study

- **Tech for Tribals' programme to connect tribals with global markets**

With a focus on entrepreneurial development, soft skills, IT, and business development through SHGs functioning under Van Dhan Vikas Kendras (VDVKs), the Tech for Tribals initiative seeks to improve tribals on all levels. IIT Kanpur is creating course material for tribal and rural entrepreneurship in value addition and processing of forest products as part of the Tech for Tribals programme.

- **MoU between TRIFED and Big Basket**

The Memorandum of Understanding (MoU) for the promotion and sale of organic, natural Van Dhan, and TRIFOOD products was signed by TRIFED and Big Basket. The tribal people hold a strong belief in "Mera Van, Mera Dhan, and Mera Udhyam" and possess hidden abilities and a huge potential for producing top-notch goods. The COVID-19 and the limits have hurt the tribal market's feelings, which was also a source of employment and income. Their potential may now reach a wider market, facilitating improved price discovery and enabling them to make a good living.

- **Amazon India launched Karigar Mela.**

The inauguration of Karigar Mela, an online outlet for traditional tribal and regional Indian handicrafts, was announced by Amazon India on Monday in collaboration with Tribes India. Customers will be able to access and shop from a selection of more than 1.2 lakh distinctive traditional tribal and local Indian handicrafts and handloom options as part of the campaign. Pattichitra, bidri, dhokra, ikkat, blue art ceramics, etc. are a few examples of distinctive art.

- **Under the police's initiative, 300 tribal youths in Naxal-hit Gadchiroli got jobs in different fields.**

At the job fair hosted by the police department, 300 tribal youngsters from the Maharashta district of Gadchiroli, which has been impacted by the Naxals, received appointment letters for employment in a variety of industries, including hospitality and cars. 101 male and female candidates in all received kits to launch their own enterprises after receiving instruction in two- and four-wheeler repair, pickle- and papad-making, and fast-food products. In addition, 95 more male and female candidates who underwent training in vegetable gardening on Thursday received certificates as part of the curriculum. The police department, along with its collaborators, provided training and opened doors to employment or self-employment for 70 candidates in the beauty salon industry, 60 in fisheries, 293 in poultry, 35 in tailoring, 35 in photography, 114 in vegetable cultivation, 235 in two- and fourwheeler repair, 254 in hospitality, 196 in automobile training, 1,143 nursing attendants, and other sectors.

- **Covid-hit Dhokra tribal craft in Odisha:**

Non-ferrous metal casting, also known as dokra or dhokra, has been practised in India for more than 4,000 years and is still in use today. The dancing girl of Mohenjo-daro is one of the oldest lost wax items that is currently known. The COVID-19 pandemic has significantly changed tribal traditions, particularly in rural tribal interiors.

The COVID-19 problem has been wreaking havoc on artists since it first appeared in 2020. To make matters worse, thousands of craftsmen, labourers, and weavers in Odisha were devastated by the second and third waves of the COVID epidemic, endangering the livelihood of over 3000 odd employees who depended on them. The production and sales cycles were completely severed because the majority of their items were in the non-essential category, and they were unable to sell them during the COVID-induced lockdown.

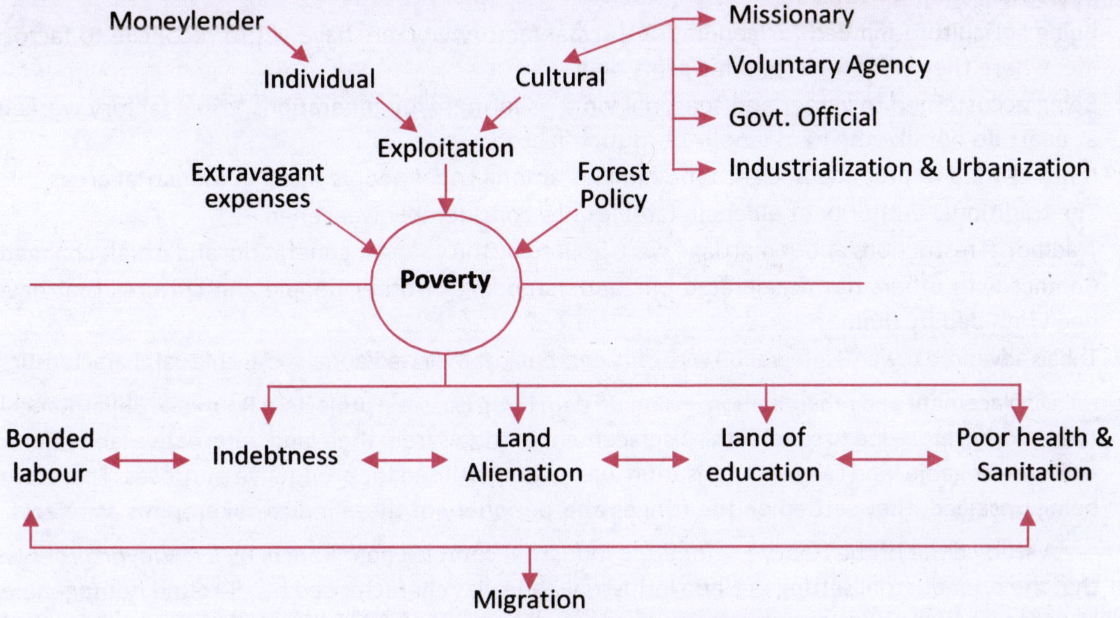

Interlinkages among Tribal Problems

6.3

Developmental projects and their impact on tribal displacement and problems of rehabilitation. Development of forest policy and tribals. Impact of urbanisation and industrialization on tribal populations.

Q 1. Impact of industrialization and urbanisation on tribal populations.

Ans. Abject poverty and ruthless exploitation have been the plight of tribals everywhere, and Indian tribals are no exception. Ironically, the regions where our tribals live are some of the richest in terms of natural bounty. They contain vast forest wealth and deposits of minerals. Rourkela, Bhilai, Ranchi, Hirakud, etc. are some of the milestones on the economic and industrial map of modern India. 80% of the natural resources required for industries are located in 18% of the total area of the country, where mostly tribal populations reside.

The natural corollary of development should have been the economic upliftment of the concerned tribal population.

But this did not happen. They were deprived of their lands under statutory conditions and were paid a meagre amount in cash as compensation, which they frittered away on drinking and celebrating tribal rituals. Since no steps were taken before hand to train youths in the crafts required in industrial projects, they became losers from all angles.

A case study done at Patratu Thermal Plant by *Rajendra Singh* showed that there was a marked decline in the traditional occupation of agriculture and that opportunities for villagers in industries came as semi-skilled and unskilled labourers.

Das and Banerji's (1964) study in Bengal has enumerated the following changes with industrialization for tribals:

1. Being agriculture-minded for generations, tribal factory workers have yet to reconcile to factory life, where they work for economic gains only.
2. Being accustomed to lighter and seasonal work as farmers for generations, tribal factory workers at heart do not like the hard labour of routine factory work.
3. It has tended to produce nuclear-type families among tribal people living in industrial areas.
4. The traditional authority of elders in families has considerably weakened.
5. Traditional restrictions about marriage were flouted by the younger generation, and rituals changed.
6. Contact with others has accelerated our understanding of other people and cultures that have been imbibed by them.
7. Tribals advanced towards integration with outsiders but lost their traditional social-cultural characteristics.

Displacement and rehabilitation—Hirakud dam in Orrisa, steel projects in Rourkela, Bhilai, Ranchi, Jamshedpur, etc.—led to substantial displacement of tribals from their land. Alternative land offered was non-irrigable, and cash compensation was seldom utilised for productive purposes. Therefore, being unskilled, they settled on the fringes and periphery of these industrial empires as rejects.

A study done of the Heavy Engineering industrial complex near Ranchi by *L.P. Vidyarthi* shows that the preindustrial setting of Hatia Industrial Zone was characterised by all-round homogeneity in terms of landscape, population, economy, and general style of life. With industrialization, it suffered a complete breakdown, and local villagers had to abandon their place or get assimilated into the industrial way of life.

This social disruption could have been minimised if the integration of tribal policy had been termed a programme of industrialization. *Das Gupta* threw light on the Ho tribe in South Bihar, in the background of the Jhinkpani cement factory. He observed that industrialization has accelerated the pace of education in general among tribals. They have accommodated modern medicine and scientific medicine along with traditional magical treatments. Industrial employment has brought Ho to a new level of solidarity higher than the traditional pattern because they have to confront many outside groups.

Conclusion: But if this policy of integration is not applied, tribals are transformed into members of cosmopolitan society without education, equipment, or resources. It creates a crisis of identity. *Dr. B.D. Sharma* has said that India must redefine her vision of development to facilitate and not deny tribal people the right to disulfide life. For this, an anthropological approach is needed.

Case Study

- **A Tale of Two Villages: How Dhinkia and Nuagaon Have Fared Differently Between Two Steel Projects**

Two of the eight impacted villages in the Jagatsinghpur district, Dhinkia and Nuagaon, found themselves on opposing sides in 2005 when the Odisha government struck a deal with South Korean steelmaker Posco Intl. Corp. to build up its massive project. Dhinkia was against Posco, but Nuagaon's rulers were in favour. Posco withdrew from the project in 2017, and just recently, the government of Odisha resumed its land acquisition campaign, but for a different project by Jindal Steel Works (JSW) Ltd. in the same region. The JSW project is still being opposed by the inhabitants of Dhinkia, and Nuagaon is also not in favour of it.

What has changed in the last ten years?

By supporting Posco, the residents of Nuagaon experienced more economic hardship. They failed to establish alternate sources of income and lost their betel vineyards due to land acquisition. They also lost compensation money to chit fund companies. On the other hand, Dhinkia prospered because its residents were able to prevent the government from destroying their betel vineyards and preserve their means of subsistence. Under the leadership of the Posco Pratirodh Sangram Samiti (PPSS), the villagers opposed the project. Over 700 family members in Dhinkia became the focus of the uprising. Women guarded the bamboo barricades that were placed around the area to prevent entry by administrative and law enforcement personnel.

To supposedly lessen the impact of the anti-Posco movement, the state administration was forced to reduce the production capacity to eight MTPA and the area to 2,700 acres in 2011. Dhinkia was not included on the list of impacted villages. The district administration was able to complete the land acquisition disassembly of more than 1,100 vines across the remaining seven villages in two phases (2011 and 2013) despite protests and the deployment of police force, proving that the method had some success. However, the community appeared to gain from the government's ostensibly punitive isolation of Dhinkia. Dhinkia's exclusion turned out to be a godsend, as the village thrived over time and became one of the largest betel leaf production hubs in Odisha. Every month, the village sends more than two million betel leaves, valued at around Rs 20 lakh, to locations throughout India, mostly Mumbai, Ahmedabad, and Kolkata, where they are used to wrap the intoxicating mixture known as "paan" and enjoyed by millions of Indians. There were only about 500 betel vines in Dhinkia when the anti-Posco movement began; today, there are 2,000. According to the locals, 85% of families in Dhinkia now have their own vines, up from 35% prior to the start of the anti-Posco movement. Every day in Dhinkia, at least 200 workers find work in the betel vines.

Contrarily, in Nuagaon, a Gramme Panchayat consisting of a single hamlet and home to almost 10,000 people, hopelessness is overt. The majority of the villagers regret having welcomed Posco. Many of the communities impacted by the project—many of whom were once proud grape owners themselves—now rely on Dhinkia for a living. That explains in detail why the Nuagaon locals are opposed to JSW's plans. The JSW project is larger than Posco's and requires about 3,000 acres of land. It includes a 12 MTPA steel mill, a 10 MTPA cement plant, and a 900 MW power plant.

Most of the Nuagaon people spoke out against the JSW project during the public hearing for it in November 2021. After their negative experience with Posco, it is obvious that the majority of residents in Nugagaon do not want any new projects. People are terrified, but they also recognise that the destruction of Dhinkia's betel bushes by JSW will have an impact on their way of life. Most people look towards an uncertain future.

Q 2. Developmental projects and their impact on tribal displacement and problems of rehabilitation.

Ans. Post-independence, in aggressive pursuit of industrialization and modernization of the economy, India's development strategy accepted the maxim that "big is beautiful". Bhakra Nangal Dam was the first to come up, which Nehru described as the "temple" of modern India. Many such small and big temples came up in quick succession in several parts. A development paradigm of this kind caused massive displacement; over 20 million people were displaced from their habitat, and about 40% of those displaced belonged to tribal populations (Sah, 1995).

Causes of displacement:

1. Industrialization: 5-year plans
2. Irrigation Projects: Koel Karo Dam, Subarnarekha Dam, Narmada Dam
3. Urbanisation: urban towns and cities like the NCR region
4. Energy Projects: Nuclear Plants Like Kudankulum
5. Forest Reserve: Nagarhole Wildlife Sanctuary (Karnataka)

6. Mining: Vedanta and Posco in Odisha
7. Railway roads, military installation—Netarhet Pilot Firing Test Range Project in Palamau district

Case Study:

1. **Sone Bhadra Projects or Rihand Dam (UP):** According to *Saksena & Sen*, 85% of oustees were landless, hence not paid any compensation with respect to the Land Acquisition Act, 1894, and only 11% got regular jobs. Displaced people were resettled as communities with complete disregard for social structures.
2. **Koel Karo Project (Bihar):** About 1.5 lakh people (90% tribals) were displaced. Tribals who lived on vital plants, herbs, and shrubs as food, medicine, and timber were distressed by displacement. The life expectancy of a project is merely 20 years.
3. **Narmada Case (Sardar Sarovar Project):** A burning example of people's protest against development by the government. Recently, in 2019, the Gujarat Government got permission to shut the gates of the Sardar Sarovar Project. It poses a threat to 244 villages and 40,000 families, mostly in the MP. Many project-affected people have not been rehabilitated, and the government has not done anything concrete for them, says *Medha Patkar.*

***Michael Cernea,* who has researched development-induced displacement and rehabilitation, has identified eight interlinked risks with displacement:**

1. Landlessness is due to land acquisition by projects and the inadequacy of cash compensation to replace lost land.
2. Joblessness as a consequence of displacement and a lack of alternative employment
3. Homelessness due to loss of shelter
4. Marginalisation after displacement in the event of the oustee's inability to revert back to an earlier standard of living.
5. Morbidity due to malnutrition and adverse health conditions
6. Food insecurity is due to the loss of traditional resources and the non-availability of food items.
7. Loss of access to common property for landless, asset-less displaced people in terms of forest produce and grazing land
8. Social disintegration due to the breakdown of social networks.

   According to the Lokayan Bulletin, dismantled production systems, desecrated ancestral sacred zones, disorganised social networks, weakened self-management and social control, disrupted tracks, etc. are consequences of displacement.

Positive Impact of Displacement:

1. Integration: Tribals emigrating to towns and cities became aware of their civil rights.
2. Demand is rising for tribal products like honey, fruits, and tribal art like Warli paintings.

Interlinked with displacement is rehabilitation: The National Policy for Tribals stipulates that displacement of tribals is to be kept to a minimum and undertaken only when all other possibilities are exhausted. It gives certain guidelines:

1. Each ST family having land in an earlier settlement shall be given land against land (a minimum of 2 hectares).
2. Tribes having fishing rights in their original habitat shall be granted fishing rights in other reserves.
3. Tribal people are to be resettled close to their natural habitat by treating all people as one group to retain ethnic, linguistic, and social cultural identities.
4. Free land is given to social and religious congregations.
5. If resettlement is away from the district, higher monetary benefits are given.
6. All basic amenities—roads, electricity, drainage, education, health care, etc.—shall be provided at the new site.

Problems of rehabilitation:

1. Only some states, like MP, Maharashtra, and Odisha, have rehabilitation policies. The National Rehabilitation and Resettlement Policy of 2007 fall short of expectations, and the Land Acquisition Act of 2013 is diluted. LAAR just reduces gross injustice, rights, and complex systems into monetary compensation.
2. The definition of "outsider" includes those who lost their houses, not those who lost their livelihoods like carpenters. Most of the land taken away is in the Common Property Resource (CPR).
3. The alternative land given is generally not productive for agriculture.
4. Rehabilitation has no time frame.
5. Bureaucratic apathy adds to the agony of tribals.
6. The literacy rate is low, and as a result, one cannot hope to get jobs in the new project (Fernandes).
7. Rehabilitation is carried out with the help of the police, thereby inducing involuntary resettlement of a forced nature.
8. Only economic domains like land, money, houses, etc. were considered after long struggles, thereby ignoring social domains like social relations, social organisation, etc.
9. An ethnocentric view of rehabilitating officials does not help in any way with those living in despair and cultural shock.

Suggestions for rehabilitation:

1. B.D. Sharma, former Chairperson of the National SC and ST Commission, suggests that there is a need to prepare tribals to benefit from industries by training and inculcating entrepreneurship.
2. Industry needs to understand, appreciate, and build the socioeconomic tribal milieu around industrial units.
3. The Forest Rights Act of 2006 and the PESA Act should be referred to to protect the interests of tribes.
4. Smitu Kothari: Commitment has to be given not just for resettlement but for rehabilitation, which should be an entitlement and not an act of reluctant generosity.

Holistic care of the needs of tribal people needs to be kept at the centre, and protections given to tribal people in the Constitution need to be adhered to in executing developmental projects.

Case Study

- **Tribal communities suffer when evicted in the name of conservation**

In order to safeguard tigers in the Kanha Tiger Reserve, some 450 households from the native Baiga and Gond populations were forced to leave in 2014. As promised by the government, many impacted families did not get compensation or benefits for rehabilitation. Forced evictions wipe out Baiga villages that have spent decades meticulously managing the tiger's habitats. The tribal groups were the best at conservation but did not engage in poaching. Similar to this, the authorities forcibly removed about 40,000 people from protected zones in 2017 while demolishing about 8,000 homes. For instance, in April 2017, the SC ordered the demolition of more than 148 homes and the eviction of 156 residents from the Thatkola and Sargodu Forest Reserves in Karnataka.

Global Case:

Thousands of tribal communities were disproportionately impacted by the Chad-Cameroon Pipeline Project. This project is a prime illustration of the destruction of cultural sites and forced relocation. Because the government immediately rejected many evicted tribal households' claims to their ancestral lands, they were not even given consideration for the compensation plan.

- **Loktak Lake: The Human and Environmental Costs of Hydropower—Meitei Tribe**

An example of a dam's long-term effects on the environment and nearby inhabitants is seen in Manipur. Locals and environmentalists claim that a recent hydropower project is slowly destroying the lake's ecosystem, severely impacting the Meitei tribe's way of life, and endangering the Loktak area of Manipur.

These issues are largely attributable to the construction of the Ithai barrage, a hydroelectric dam, across the lake's main draining outlet in 1983. The lake's natural flushing cycle, which kept the waters clear and the phumdis healthy, was damaged by this. Loktak is a case study of the impact dams can have on people. People who are not impacted by dams can never comprehend this. Many Loktak residents have not received compensation. The effects persist even after people have been made whole and given new opportunities. It transmits through generations.

- **No Means No: Kinnaur Tribals Oppose Hydropower Plant to Protect Fragile Ecology**

Kinnauras starts a campaign against the Satluj-based Jangi Thopan Powari Hydroelectricity Project, which would generate 804 MW of power. The tribal people, known as Kinnauras in the border area of Himachal Pradesh, have issued a resounding "No means no" call in opposition to the proposed 804 megawatt (MW) Jangi Thopan Powari Hydroelectricity Project. The group of young Kinnauras has sought a complete halt to the development of the hydroelectric projects under the umbrella of several tribal groupings, which also include Kyang, which in the local dialect means "spark."

- **A Success Story in Participatory R&R**

One of Orissa's participatory resettlement and rehabilitation (R&R) success stories is the World Bank-financed Upper Indravati Hydroelectric Project (UIHP). There are several ways to assess an R&R's effectiveness, including the Michael Cernea-developed Impoverishment Risks Analysis Model. What the RRU could do to ensure that the R&R process was finished was mostly the result of a few specific circumstances. They included the political will and dedication of the government at the highest levels; a dedicated bureaucracy, notably at the level of the RRU; civic involvement engaging Agragamee; and the collaboration between the government, its RRU, and the World Bank through frequent supervision missions.

- **Salient Features of the National Policy on Rehabilitation and Resettlement, 2007**

1. The policy gives rehabilitation and resettlement statutory status for the first time. The rehabilitation must be done before the displacement.
2. The benefits of the policy shall be available to all affected persons and families whose land, property, or livelihood are adversely affected by land acquisition or by involuntary displacement.
3. Benefits include—
    - Land-for-land compensation
    - Skill development support and preference in project jobs for one person per nuclear family
    - Rehabilitation grant in lieu of land or job
    - Comprehensive infrastructural facilities and amenities in the resettlement area
    - Life-time monthly pension to the vulnerable persons
4. Provision for post-implementation social audits, along with a strong grievance redressal mechanism.
5. Mandatory Social Assessment (SIA) in case of displacement of 400 or more families in plain or hilly areas.
6. Special provisions for STs and SCs, such as preference in land allocation and higher monetary benefits.

- **Salient features of the Land Acquisition Act, 2013**

1. Allows the acquisition of private land for public purposes, including several purposes such as infrastructure, development, and housing projects.
2. Consent of 80% of displaced people is required in cases of acquisition for private companies and 70% for public-private partnerships.
3. Involves the participation of local Panchayati Raj institutions prior to the start of any acquisition proceeding. Further, social impact assessment (SIA) is mandated.
4. Compensation is based on market value, which is two times market value for urban areas and four times market value in rural areas.
5. Rehabilitation and resettlement are necessary for all affected families, with their entitlements duly described.
6. Multi-crop land is to be acquired only as a last resort. States have to impose limits on such land that can be acquired and cultivate an equivalent area of land elsewhere.
7. Provision for return if the land is unutilized for five years.

Q 3. Development of forest policy and tribals

Ans. Tribals and forests lived in a symbiotic relationship. Forests are closely associated with tribal economies and cultures. They depend on forests for food, fuel, wood, herbal medicine, fodder, and agricultural implements. Their cultural and magico-religious beliefs have been rotating around forests (totems). Thus, tribal people were able to achieve such harmony, which has always been a matter of discussion for non-tribals.

First Forest Act, 1865: This was the first attempt in the direction of regulating the collection of forest produce by forest dwellers. In this process, the socially regulated practises of local people were restrained by law.

Forest Act, 1878: Control over forests was further tightened by prohibiting acts such as trespassing on cattle and declaring certain activities as offences, imposing imprisonment or fines for such offences.

First Forest Policy, 1894: The regulations and restrictions were justified by the cardinal principle, which says that the "rights and privileges" of individuals must be limited in the public interest. With this stroke, the colonial administration took over vast forests in the name of the people and set out to exploit them.

In continuation of the above measures, the Indian Forest Act of 1927 was passed. According to this, no person can claim the right to private property in forest land merely because he has domiciled there or because his forefathers lived there for centuries. Further, it directs notification to individual private property alone, not to rights in common property among tribes. Further, any forest officer without a warrant could arrest any person against whom reasonable suspicion exists of a motive to pilfer forest wealth, and his act would be punishable by imprisonment for one month or upward.

After independence, India formulated its first national forest policy in 1952. It belied all hopes of just and generous treatment of tribal people. It followed British's lines, where tribal people had virtually no statutory rights but enjoyed only certain "concessions," such as the right to take water for agriculture, the digging of wells for agriculture, free grazing in open forests, the collection of dead wood for domestic use, etc.

The Dhebar Commission, appointed in 1960, said that the traditional rights of tribals were no longer recognised as rights. In 1894, they became rights and privileges, and in 1952, they became rights and concessions. Now they are considered concessions only. The emphasis in the 1952 policy to raise revenue from forests locally and the involvement of contractors in forest operations proved disastrous for tribals.

The grim situation was revised in 1988 by a new forest policy. It stated that the principal aim of forest policy must be to ensure environmental stability and the maintenance of ecological balance. The derivation of economic benefit became subordinate to the principal aim.

Further, it takes into consideration the symbiotic relationship between tribals and forests. It envisages that all agencies responsible for forest management, including forest corporations, should closely associate tribal groups in the protection, regeneration, and development of forests. This policy also allowed tribals to collect fuel wood, fodder, and MFP from forests. It emphasised the needs of forest dwellers for the first time since forest administration began.

But the Forest Conservation Act of 1980 was in contravention of the National Forest Policy of 1988. Under it, the state government cannot, without the sanction of the centre, assign by way of lease any forest land to any person, agency, or organisation not owned, controlled, or managed by the government.

In 2006, the ST and other traditional forest dwellers (recognition of forest rights) Act, also known as the Forest Rights Act, was passed. It is claimed that it will redress historical injustices committed against forest dwellers. Under it, tribal people enjoy rights like:

1. Right to hold and live on forest land.
2. Right to ownership and access to collect and dispose of minor forest produce (MFP)
3. Other community rights of use or entitlements, such as fish, grazing, and traditional seasonal resource access, are given to nomadic tribes.
4. Right to protect, regenerate, or conserve any community forest resource that they have been traditionally protecting for sustainable use.

Therefore, it recognised tribal rights over forests and community participation in forest conservation.

Impact of such policies:

1. Original inhabitants of forest were made aliens or intruders on State property.
2. Revenue from forest exploitation increased year after year.
3. Dislocation of traditional habitat of tribal ruining their culture.
4. Lost consciousness of tribal that jungle was his security.
5. Reduced tree cover, increased floods and erosion.

Remedies (B.K. Roy Burman Approach):

1. Expand social forestry and joint forest management.
2. Scrutiny of forest-based industries.
3. Replace contractor with co-operatives.
4. Forest village formation.
5. Tribal involvement in policy making and improve.

Conclusion: Forest policy must fulfil three needs: ecological security, food and fruit, fuel, fodder, and other tribal needs. It must ensure justice to people (tribal and non-tribal), justice to nature, and justice to the coming generation.

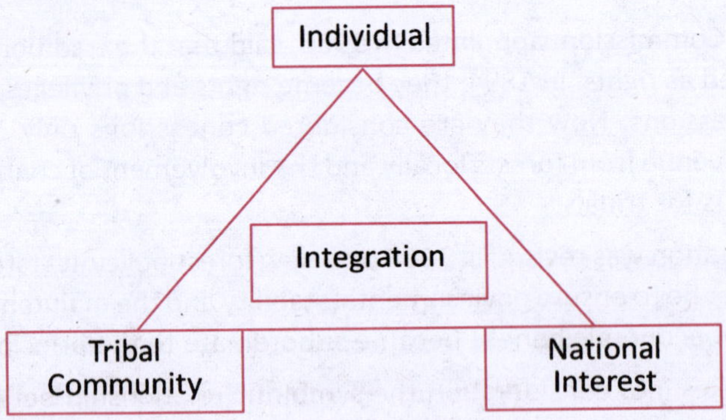

Case Study

- **Forest Conservation Rules infringe upon the Land Rights of Tribes:**

Forest (Conservation) Rules, 2022:

1. It is conferred by Section 4 of the Forest (Conservation) Act, 1980, and in supersession of the Forest (Conservation) Rules, 2003.
2. On monitoring: Constitute an advisory committee, a regional empowered committee, and a screening committee at the state or UT.

3. Integrated Regional Office:It will examine all the linear projects (e.g., roads, highways, etc.) involving land up to 40 hectares and the use of forest land up to 0.7 canopy density.
4. Time frame: A fixed time for quicker review of each project
5. Responsibility to states:States are given the responsibility of settling the forest rights of forest dwellers (Forest Rights Act, 2006) and allowing diversion of forest land.
6. Allows compensatory afforestation (CA) in other states:If the state already has over two-thirds of its area under green cover or over one-third of its area under forest cover, then CA could be taken in other states or UTs where the cover is less than 20%.

Concerns:

- **Favour of Corporations:** Corporations and other business entities can easily coerce tribal groups into giving them the approval they need or suppressing any objections they may have. Another danger is the establishment of plantations for private commercial use, which would deny the locals access to land that was intended for them in the first place.
- Tribals utilise the revenue forest area for livelihood needs, endangering biodiversity. The new rules permit private parties to plant crops on the site, which may result in monoculture cultivation and reduce biodiversity.
- **Relaxed clearance process:** As a result of the relaxed clearance procedure, developers no longer have to get all necessary clearances at once in order to divert land use. A portion of the land may be approved before work begins, and clearance may be obtained later. A clause like that would promote illicit activity and confusion, and the law's obligation to get locals' permission can be disregarded.
- The Forest (Conservation) Act of 1980 requires governments to get the free, prior, and informed agreement of forest residents before approving a project on their customary lands, and these new regulations will only uproot what little compliance there was with the Forest Right Act in forest diversion. Since it is now the obligation of state governments to acquire approval from Scheduled Tribes and other people that live near forests before trees are cut, this action will result in a serious breach of the Forest Right Act.
- New rules will simplify and shorten the process of diverting forest land for development projects and make land available for compensatory afforestation easier, thus "facilitating corporate looters to gain access and control of forest lands."

  Approaching the Gram Sabha after the final approval is granted will only make its role irrelevant and the rights holders under the Forest Rights Act redundant.

Q 4. Forest Rights Act, 2006

Ans. Under persistent pressure and advocacy for tribal rights, the Forest Rights Act, 2006, was enacted to recognise and vest forest rights to forest dwelling Scheduled Tribes and other traditional forest dwellers who have been residing in forests for generations but whose rights could not be recorded.

Salient Features: The Act seeks to undo the historical injustice towards tribes by recognising four types of rights:

1. Title rights: ownership of land being framed is subject to a maximum limit of four hectares.
2. Use rights: over minor forest produce and grazing areas.
3. Relief and development rights: rehabilitation in cases of illegal eviction or forced displacement
4. Forest management rights: protect forest resources and wildlife

The claims over forest lands are processed through a three-tier system, with the Gram Sabha as the first tier to process claims. This involvement of the Gram Sabha facilitates a human touch that enables tribal people to file claims properly. An appeal mechanism is in place in the event of a rejection of claims.

Implementation Status: As of April 2019, around 42.3 lakh claims had been received, with 40.8 lakh being individual claims and others being community claims. 19.6 million titles have been distributed, implying an acceptance rate of around 46%. Nearly 41% of all claims have been rejected nationwide. In total, forest rights have been granted for only 15% of the minimum potential forest area where rights can be recognised.

Issues:

1. The Xaxa report 2014 has pointed out that rejections are not communicated to the claimants, and their right to appeal is neither explained to them nor its exercise is facilitated.
2. In many states, rejections are being decided by forest guards or patwaris at the first level, which is wrong as only the Gram Sabha can reject the claims. These officials can only provide recommendations in the Gram Sabha.
3. Refusal by authorities to accept evidence except government documents, despite provision for oral and physical evidence.
4. Some states make additional demands, like satellite imagery for evidence, that are not part of the Act.
5. Rejection of community claims in sanctuaries and protected areas.
6. Low levels of awareness and information dissemination about the provisions of the Act

Mungekar Committee Recommendations:

1. Implement the FRA Act in letter and spirit.
2. Move away from a concession-based approach to a rights-based approach.
3. Involvement of forest rights holders in the management of natural resources should be built into all efforts.
4. Mechanisms similar to CACP should be in place for the pricing of MFPs and then MSPs for MFPs.

The need is to holistically train the officials and authorities in charge to function with an anthropological approach,exhibiting the required empathy and dedication to exhaustively implement the act.

Case Study

- **Ensure patta and effective implementation of the Forest Rights Act for tribal people.**

According to a study conducted in the hilly regions of Kadambur and Bargur, providing jobs locally, distributing patta for landowners' holdings, and effectively implementing the Forest Rights Act (FRA) of 2006 will stop tribal people from leaving their homes in pursuit of work. A project named "A Study on Rainfed Agriculture: An Instrument for Creation of Gainful Employment and Cornerstone for Counter Migration" was given to N. Mani, Professor and Head of the Department of Economics at the Erode Arts and Science College. The team saw 286 households in Kadambur and 156 families in Bargur who had moved to the plains for work but were forced to return because of the pandemic.

According to the report, tribal people lack patta but have the right to use revenue-producing poramboke land. They are unable to obtain loans or subsidies without a title deed, and their crops are not protected by insurance policies. Tribal people are unable to cover the losses resulting from inadequate rainfall that causes crop failure since the lands are rain-fed. Families underline the importance of having patta for their tiny farms because they were compelled to borrow money at excessive interest rates. To stop them from migrating, it would be important to acknowledge them as farmers.

- **Salient features of the Draft National Forest Policy, 2018**

1. Target of 33% of India's geographical area under forest and tree cover. In the hills and mountains region, the policy goal is to maintain 2/3 of the area under tree and forest cover to prevent soil erosion and land degradation and ensure the stability of fragile ecosystems.
2. Restrict schemes and projects that interfere with forests. Stabilise an ecologically sensitive catchment area with suitable soil and water conservation measures and plant trees, bamboo, etc.

3. The Compensatory Afforestation Fund will be a major source of funds for taking up afforestation and rehabilitation work. Funds from other national sectors like mills, railways, coal, power, and rural development are needed to link greening with other activities.
4. Setting up of two national-level bodies
   - National Community Forest Management (NCFM) Mission
   - National Board of Forestry (NBF) for better management of the country's forests
5. Development of public-private participation models for undertaking afforestation and reforestation activities in degraded forest areas and forest areas available with the Forest Development Corporation It will increase productivity through protection.
6. Harmonise between laws and policies like the FRA.
7. Safeguard the ecosystem from forest fires.
8. Climate change concerns will be factored into all forest and wildlife area management plans and community ecosystem management plans. Integrate the REDD+ strategy into forest management.
9. Stimulate growth in the forest-based industry sector.
10. Policy support for forest certification.

- **Salient features of Joint Forest Management (JFM)**

1. Under this programme, local communities are involved in the management and restoration of degraded forests.
2. The major purpose of the JFM is to protect the forests from encroachments, grazing, theft, and fire and also to improve the forests in accordance with an approved Joint Forest Management Plan.
3. In return, the members of these communities are entitled to intermediary benefits like those that nontimber forests produce.

Q 5. Globalization on tribals

Ans. Globalisation is the free movement of goods, services, capital, people, and information technology across national boundaries. It is the process of transforming regional or local phenomena into global phenomena.

The development policies initiated as part of the LPG programme (liberalisation, privatisation, and globalisation) not only altered the tribal relationship with the environment but also altered ownership of land and usage.

A case study done by *Priyanka Nial* on KBK (Koraput, Bolangir, and Kalahandi) district found that due to globalisation, tribal culture became popular, like the Sambalpuri and Gumura dances. Songs like Rangabati and Warli paintings became famous worldwide.

Better education facilities, more employment options like MFP sales by TRIFED, the cure of diseases like malaria, more awareness generation related to agricultural practises, the health of women during pregnancy, etc. prospered after LPG reforms.

There has been a rise in digital literacy, which is empowering tribals like the PUKAR initiative in Maharashtra. The Apatani tribe of A.P. and the Shillong tribes show a remarkable degree of modernization.

However, indigenous people throughout the world sit on the frontlines of globalisation's expansion; they occupy the last private place on earth where resources are available. It is most sought after by global corporations, pushing tribals off their land.

A study done by P. Sahu in Odisha found:

1. Displacement of 16 million people in 1500 major irrigation projects, out of which 40% were tribal.
2. Extinction of primitive tribal culture
3. Intellectual property rights are endangering or withering away among primitive communities.
4. PSUs like BALCO, which are in the tribal belt, have been privatised.

Another study by B. Ezhilarasu found that laws related to Schedule Areas like the Forest Act, Environment Protection Act, and Land Acquisition Act are under threat of dilution or repeal so as to favour corporations.

B.D. Sharma View: If globalisation were superimposed on poorly educated and poorly trained tribal people with poor systems of infrastructure and governance, it would not lead to growth or reduce poverty. A new development model needs to be created where responsibility for social development is equally shared by both the government and private players, individually and collectively.

Case Study

- **Andhra Pradesh and Globalisation**

The World Bank's structural adjustment programme will be implemented there for the first time by a state in Asia. Revenues are to be generated from profitable industries like the sale of alcoholic beverages under the state's new economic plans. Tribal women who objected to the liquor mafia setting up shops in their villages were violently "punished" for doing so. In order to promote tribal development, the state government is moving forward with its liberalisation policies in these isolated tribal regions by inviting foreign companies and nonresident Indians to enter the tourism, mining, film, agro-based, and other industries. The new economic policies for tribal people have a significant impact on the lives of adivasis, whose rights to access to natural resources, opportunities for livelihood, primary healthcare, protection from atrocities and violations of human rights, and the right to maintain their traditional and customary practises are all seriously threatened as a result of the policy and legal changes. The pressure on the Fifth Schedule is currently the biggest danger facing the Adivasi population in the nation. In a globalised environment, the market, not the community, is the key player. Strong international lobbies exerted pressure on the governments. These result in the handover of resource management from adivasis to private and international sector entities.

Q 6. Climate Change and tribal

Ans. Climate change, according to the IPCC, refers to changes in the state of the climate that can be identified by changes in the mean or variability of its properties and that persist for an extended period, typically decades or longer. It is often claimed to be anthropogenic climate change.

Indigenous people are among the poorest of the poor and thus the most threatened segment of the population in terms of social, economic, and environmental vulnerability.

A research paper published by *Hemant Prakash Minj* analysed the impact of climate change on tribal societies in Jharkhand.

1. The economy of tribal societies is mainly based on agriculture and forestry. Where rains fail, agriculture is first affected because of a shortage of water. NSSO-55th round data reveals around 10% of households in Jharkhand face seasonal food insecurity, which will rise further.
2. A high level of vulnerability due to climate change forces them to migrate. This makes them more vulnerable to discrimination and exploitation.
3. The social vulnerability of climate change can affect health, education, and access to political power, which is already in shambles.
4. Gender inequality, which is a key factor in the deprivation suffered by indigenous women, is exacerbated by climate change. Food insecurity forces women to eat last and least, making them more susceptible to illness and disease.

However, indigenous people can play a role in advancing understanding of climate change and developing comprehensive climate adaptation strategies.

The role of anthropology and indigenous people in reducing climate change:

1. **Ethnographic method usage:** Understanding of local or community-based culture that stems from the placebased scale of much anthropological research. Anthropologists have learned that local people have a strong awareness of their climate and observe or respond to changes. For example, Inupiat residents of Alaska have identified a cyclical pattern of coastal erosion, and their understanding of how quickly and in which direction wind and wave energy reaches the coast can help communities prone to flooding.
2. **Temporal depth:** Consideration of long historical scales derived from archaeological research can complement ethnographic field work. E.g., the REDD+ project can be evaluated against projects in past centuries or during Roman times.
3. **Holism:** It sees cultural systems integrating with social, economic, political, and environmental systems. In this way, climate change interacts with other factors.
   - E.g., tribal farmers in MP, Maharashtra, turned to bewar and penda forms of cultivation to cope with climate change's impact, but the government acted on rooting out these farm practises.
   - E.g., Australian Aborigines knowledge of bush fire control: "mosaic cool fire burning technique," i.e., a small patch of low intensity fire lit during a cool month to burn bush undergrowth, reducing the number of inflammable materials.

The American Anthropological Association came out with the report 'Changing the Atmosphere: Anthropology and Climate Change," which recommended local-level adaptations across all temporal scales and at regional scales needed to adapt and how anthropologists contribute knowledge bases that put contemporary events and prospective future patterns in a long-term and comparative perspective across time and cultures. We work with physical and natural scientists to put people into the equation.

In this context, Adi Darshan, or a discussion on tribal philosophies organised by the Jharkhand government, is a step in the right direction.

Case Study

- **In Odisha, an Adivasi community is using traditional farming to fight climate change.**

Subsistence living has been negatively impacted by climate change. The fertile topsoil from the hillsides is washed away by prolonged rainfall. Modern agricultural methods have had an impact on the Bonda farmers' traditional farming methods; from mixed cropping systems concentrated on millet, they have gradually switched to paddy, which has impacted the availability of their staple meal.

However, Bonda women are turning back to growing their own native millet species, including the climatically hardy finger (ragi), foxtail (kakum or kangni), barnyard (sanwa), proso (chena), and pearl (bajra) millets, which guarantee the community's food and nutritional security. In addition to the institutional impetus provided by the Odisha Millets Mission, such as guaranteed purchase and higher prices, awareness about millets cultivation through improved farming techniques to address dietary and climatic challenges is being raised by Bonda youth volunteers and local non-governmental organisations.

7

Problems of SC, ST, OBC, Social Change and Contemporary Tribal Societies, Ethnicity and Unrest among Tribes

7.1

Problems of exploitation and deprivation of Scheduled Castes, Scheduled Tribes and Other Backward Classes. Constitutional safeguards for Scheduled Tribes and Scheduled Castes.

Q 1. Problems, Constitutional Safeguards and ST

Ans. Article 366 (25) of the Constitution of India defines scheduled tribes as "such tribes or tribal communities or parts of or groups within such tribes or tribal communities as are deemed under Article 342 to be scheduled tribes for the purposes of this constitution".

Constitutional Provisions for ST:

Protective Provisions:

1. **Article 15(4):** Nothing in this article or in clause (2) of Article 29 shall prevent the state from making any special provision for the advancement of any socially and educationally backward classes of citizens or for the Scheduled Castes and the Scheduled Tribes.
2. **Article 16(4):** Nothing in this article shall prevent the State from making any provision for the reservation of appointments or posts in favour of any backward class of citizens that, in the opinion of the State, is not adequately represented in the services under the State.
3. **Article 19(5):** Nothing in subclauses (d) and (e) of the said clause shall affect the operation of any existing law in so far as it imposes, or prevents the State from making any law imposing, reasonable restrictions on the exercise of any of the rights conferred by the said subclauses either in the interests of the general public or for the protection of the interests of any Scheduled Tribe.
4. **Article 29(1):** "Any section of the citizens residing in the territory of India or any part thereof having a distinct language, script, or culture of its own shall have the right to conserve the same.
5. **Article 38(1):** "The State shall strive to promote the welfare of the people by securing and protecting as effectively as it may a social order in which justice, social, economic, and political, shall inform all the institutions of the national life.
6. **Article 46:** "The State shall promote with special care the educational and economic interests of the weaker sections of the people, and, in particular, of the Scheduled Castes and the Scheduled Tribes, and shall protect them from social injustice and all forms of exploitation.
7. **Article 244:** The provisions of the Fifth Schedule shall apply to the administration and control of the Scheduled Areas and Scheduled Tribes in any state other than the States of Assam, Meghalaya, Tripura, and Mizoram.

Development Provisions:

8. **Article 164(1):** Provided that in the States of Bihar, Madhya Pradesh, and Orissa, there shall be a Minister in charge of tribal welfare who may in addition be in charge of the welfare of the Scheduled Castes and backward classes or any other work.
9. **Article 275(1):** Grant-in-aid to States to meet the cost of such schemes of development as may be undertaken for them for promoting the welfare of ST or level of Schedule areas
10. **Article 338A:** The National Commission for Scheduled Tribes (NCST) was established by amending Article 338 and inserting a new Article 338A in the Constitution through the Constitution (89th Amendment) Act, 2003. By this amendment, the erstwhile National Commission for Scheduled Castes and Scheduled Tribes was replaced by two separate Commissions namely- (i) the National Commission for Scheduled Castes (NCSC), and (ii) the National Commission for Scheduled Tribes (NCST) w.e.f. 19 February, 2004.
11. **Article 339(1):** The President may at any time and shall, at the expiration of ten years from the commencement of this Constitution, by order appoint a commission to report on the administration of the Scheduled Areas and the welfare of these Scheduled Tribes in the States.
12. **Article 371:** Special Provisions with Respect to Tribal Areas and Hill Areas of Nagaland (371A), Assam (371B), and Manipur (371C)

Political Safeguards:

13. **Articles 330 and 332:** Reservation of seats for SC and ST in the Lok Sabha and State Legislative Assembly, respectively
14. **Articles 243D and 243T:** Reservation of seats for SC and ST in proportion to population in panchayats and municipalities, respectively.

Legislative Provisions:

- SC and ST Act, 1989
- PESA, 1996
- FRA, 2006

Implementation of Constitutional Provisions (Law Ministry Report):

1. Atrocities against ST and SC remain unabated even 50 years after untouchability was abolished by the Constitution.
2. The representation of SC and ST in Group 'A' and Group 'B' posts in the Central Government is inadequate. In the case of ST, inadequacy exists even in Group 'C' and Group 'D' posts.
3. Article 29 gives the right to protect language, culture, and script, but schools extended to tribes have been made in the language of the dominant community.
4. Even after Article 275(1), the Union Government delays devolution of funds to the State Government.
5. The Governor's reports to the President on Schedule Areas, according to the Xaxa Committee, are irregular and casual in nature.
6. Even after the Right to Equality under Article 14, Ghasiya community students were made to sit separately in classrooms.

Problems:

1. Literacy – Gap in literacy level between ST and General population is still high at 14%, despite large number of central schemes.
2. Health – Child mortality rate is double national average, 35.8% among ST compared to 18.4% among General.
3. Poor – From 1993-94 to 2004-06, gap between tribal poor and all poor increased from 15.83 to 20.49%. Recently, ST (BPL) in 2011 -12 were 45.3% in rural while 25.9% overall poor in rural (Gap–19.6%) and in urban, 24.1% ST poor while 13.9% overall urban poor (Gap–10.4%).

4. According to the Annual Employment-Unemployment Survey, 2015-16 by the Ministry of Labour & Employment, only 46% of ST workers aged about 15 years and above got engaged in any kind of work for 12 months. The tribal population below the poverty line in rural areas in 2011 -12 stood at 45.3%, which went as high as 63.5% in Odisha and 61.6% in Maharashtra.

2nd ARC Recommendation (Capacity Building for conflict resolution):

1. Authorities involved in determining inclusion and exclusion of tribes in list of ST should adopt mechanism of consultation with major States and those with tribal populations.
2. National plan of action for comprehensive development which would serve as roadmap for welfare of tribes should be prepared and implemented.
3. Convergence of regulatory and development programme in tribal areas.
4. The government should select policy, revenue, and forest officials who have the training and zeal to work in tribal areas.
5. PESA is in harmony with the Mines and Mineral Act of 1957, the Forest Conservation Act of 1980, the National Water Policy, the National Mineral Policy, etc.
6. Reiterated the importance of the annual reports of the governor under the Fifth Schedule of the Constitution.
7. Overhaul and systematic reorganisation of existing land records with free access to information about land holdings.

Q 2. Problems, Constitutional Safeguards and SC

Ans. The community is called Schedule Caste, and their oppression has historical beginnings. It can be traced back to later Vedic times, when its rigid form took place. The first reference to untouchability, which is a defining feature of SC, was found in Rig Vedic writings. It refers to the birth of outcastes resulting from inter-marriage between Aryans and non-Aryans. Chatur Varma is seen as an example of Aryan stratification. Studies found this in Muslims as well— Ashrafs and Ajlafs. These untouchable castes in India were officially recognised as 'depressed castes' in 1932. Gandhiji used the term Harijan (people of God) for them. This was replaced by Schedule Caste in 1938.

There is no precise definition of SC in our Constitution. It is mentioned in Article 366(24) that all such castes whose names are included in the schedule prepared under Article 341 are defined as SC. The president is empowered to add or delete it. SCs are found all over India except in certain states in the Northeast, Andaman and Nicobar, Lakshadweep, etc.

The two most important guiding principles provided in the Constitution are:

1. **Article 38:** State shall strive to promote welfare of people by securing and protecting as effectively as it may social order in which justice, social, economic and political shall inform all institutions of national life.
2. **Article 46:** State shall promote with special care educational and economic interest of weaker section of society and in particular SC and ST and shall protect them from social injustice and all forms of exploitation.

Constitutional Provisions for SC:

Social Safeguards:

3. **Article 17:** Abolition of Untouchability Untouchability is abolished, and its practise in any form is forbidden. The enforcement of any disability arising out of untouchability shall be an offence punishable in accordance with the law.
4. **Article 23(1):** Traffic in human beings and beggars and other similar forms of forced labour are prohibited, and any contravention of this provision shall be an offence punishable in accordance with law.

5. **Article 25(2)(b):** Nothing in this article shall affect the operation of any existing law or prevent the state from making any law providing for social welfare and reform or the throwing open of Hindu religious institutions of a public character to all classes and sections of Hindus. Explanation I: The wearing and carrying of kirpans shall be deemed to be included in the profession of the Sikh religion. Explanation II: In subclause (b) of the clause, reference to Hindus shall be construed as including a reference to persons professing the Sikh, Jaina, or Buddhist religion, and the reference to Hindu religious institutions shall be construed accordingly.
6. **Article 16(4):** Nothing in this article shall prevent the State from making any provision for the reservation of appointments or posts in favour of any backward class of citizens that, in the opinion of the State, is not adequately represented in the services under the State.
7. **Article 338:** National Commission for SC

Educational Safeguards:

8. **Article 15(4):** Nothing in this article or in clause (2) of Article 29 shall prevent the state from making any special provision for the advancement of any socially and educationally backward classes of citizens or for the Scheduled Castes and the Scheduled Tribes.

Political Safeguards:

9. **Articles 330 and 332:** Reservation of seats for SC and ST in the House of People and Legislative Assembly of State, respectively.
10. **Articles 243D and 243T:** Reservation of seats for SC and ST in proportion to population in panchayats and municipalities, respectively.

Legislative Measures:

- Under Section 8 of the Representation to People Act (RPA), a person convicted of an offence under this Act is disqualified from contesting elections to Parliament and state legislation for six years.
- POCRA, 1955 [Protection of Civil Rights Act] — The practice of untouchability is made punishable. Offence made cognizable and non-compoundable.
- SC and ST (Prevention of Atrocities) Act, 1989— The law has a defined list of offences against SC and ST, including being forced to eat or drink offensive or inedible substances, dumping excrement on his premises, parading naked, etc. The offence is cognizable. Minimum punishment of six months. Special Courts for Hearing Travel and maintenance expenses to witness Public officials neglecting duty related to SC and ST will be punished with imprisonment for a term of 6 months to 1 year. Legal aid to people subjected to atrocities.

Amendments brought in 2015: New offences were added, like abusing SC/ST in public by caste name, garlanding SC/ST with footwear, compelling them to do manual scavenging, etc. Added duties of a public servant: register an FIR, read out the complaint of the victim before giving him a copy. A new chapter dealing with the rights of victims and witnesses is added.

Certain socio-economic measures:

- National SC Finance and Development Corporation: Works for the upliftment of SC through employmentoriented schemes.
- SC sub-plan: ensure the flow of financial and physical benefits from all sectors of development for the benefit of SC.
- Special Central Assistance to a Special Component Plan for SC: assist SC families to improve income through various schemes
- The Prohibition of Employment as Manual Scavengers and Rehabilitation Act, 2013 prohibits employment as a manual scavenger.

Why need of Safeguard: The 2nd ARC says that members of SC are among the poorest in the country and most discriminated against. This discrimination manifests itself in the form of socio-economic exploitation, denial of civil rights, social ostracism, and even violence against them.

Majumdar identified problems in SC under three headings:

1. **Social Front:** They occupy lower social status due to ritual impurity and are hence regarded as untouchables. M.N. Srinivas, Majumdar & Madan, and S.C. Dube, through their field studies, brought out discriminations due to untouchability such as:
   a. Denial of education, both religious and secular and literacy rate gap of 7% between SC and general category students.
   b. Denial of ownership of land (land alienation)
   c. Prohibition on the use of precious metals (productive assets).
   d. Restriction on occupations (forced labour).
   e. Restriction or denial of the services of the priest.
   f. Lack of a minimum wage.
   g. Child labour.

   SECC data reveals that 73% of rural SC households fall into the category of deprived.
2. **Economic Front:** Untouchability led to a system of uncontrolled economic exploitation. SCs are restricted to menial jobs such as sweeping and scavenging. Census 2011 says that there are 8 lakh manual scavengers.
3. **Political Front:** SCs were never allowed to participate in panchayats, at least till independence. The introduction of reservation and democracy led to change. SC is now in a better position of awareness of political rights compared to ST. On several occasions, they fought for their rights. Later movements of globalisation and liberalisation led to mixed responses. A sociological perspective points to the reduced economic status of SC in rural areas due to industrialization, the entry of MNCs, and the establishment of SEZs, which led to the loss of land and depopulation.

Case Study:

- **Dalit vs. Vanniars, Dharmapuri district, T.N. - M**obility beyond the village has enabled Dalit youth to challenge traditional caste obligations. Refusal of Dalit youth and women to perform menial labour as new rural-to-rural and rural-to-urban mobility and the entry of Dalit youth in the service sector led to this change.

Strengthen constitutional provisions:

NCRWC made recommendations

1. In Article 46, it should be added: "And it shall be the right of weaker sections of people, and in particular SC and ST, that the state and all institutions created by, promoted by, or assisted by the state shall at all times function fully and in accordance with this right".
2. Remove the clause "consistently with maintenance of efficacy of administration" from Article 335.
3. Existing clause 4 of Article 16, to be renumbered as clause 5, which is at present worded permissibly, shall be made mandatory, thus making renumbered Article 16(5) sources of reservation for backward classes.
4. Clause (4) of Article 15 is made mandatory.
5. Entries to be included in List 3:
   a. Development, welfare, and protection of SC and ST
   b. development, welfare, and protection of BC
   c. Development, welfare, and protection of women

2nd ARC in the report titled "Capacity Building for Conflict Resolution": Though the SC and ST (Prevention of Atrocities) Acts have become the main instruments for preventing harassment in SC, the conviction rate under both Acts has been low.

Recommendations:

1. The government should adopt a multipronged administrative strategy to ensure that constitutional, legal, and administrative provisions are implemented in letter and spirit.
2. For speedy disposal of discrimination in subordinate courts, internal mechanisms were set up under the control of High Court judges to review cases.
3. Positive duty on public authorities to promote harmony and prevent discrimination against SC and ST.
4. Identification of vulnerable areas by the district administration and spreading awareness about the law
5. Rehabilitation of victims and counselling.
6. The corporate sector, NGOs, and local governments are actively involved in the development and protection of SC.

Case Study

- **Interlinking Discrimination, Poverty, and Social Exclusion of Scheduled Castes in Rural India by Jayashree Ambewadikar**

Combining social and economic reforms to increase capacity for addressing SC concerns has had a relatively limited impact on society. This is seen in terms of the types of work people do for a living, employment rates, literacy rates, and poverty rates, which also include access to health and education services as well as security and protection denial. Since India's planning involves issues of an economic, social, political, administrative, and international nature, social policy has been betrayed and has only produced illusions of security. Self-respect, possibilities for capacity development, social mobility, and change must all be taken into account in the way that the state approaches social policy. However, it has been noted that social policies fall short of bridging the gap between theory and practise because they are unable to account for the complicated social reality. The SCs in the villages have experienced social isolation, prejudice, and poverty, and these factors are interconnected; their poverty is a result of the discrimination that has been committed against them, notably in the economic sector. Therefore, discrimination has also prevented or excluded them from participating in a number of other facets of life. Similar to how racism and poverty together have prevented them from participating in community life, gaining access to public resources, and advancing socially.

- **14 Dalits locked up and tortured in Karnataka**

One of the workers, a pregnant woman, was subjected to such severe torture that she started bleeding and miscarried. The case has sparked debate over the state's practise of treating members of vulnerable communities inhumanely. According to data from the state government, a total of 2,327 murders, exploitations, and other crimes involving members of the SC/ST community were registered in Karnataka between April 1, 2020, and March 31, 2021. According to information from the National Crime Records Bureau, there was an increase of more than 54% from the prior year, when 1,504 similar cases were reported.

Q 3. Discuss constitutional safeguards and welfare of OBC

Ans. Collective terms for castes that are educationally or socially backward, as given under Article 15, are known as OBC. (Non-Dwija, non-Scheduled Castes not listed in constitutional order are OBC.) Most of them are small peasants, e.g., Yadavas and Kurmis of UP.

These communities are identified by the president under Article 340 of the Constitution. The president appointed a commission initially in 1953, headed by *Kaka Saheb Kalelkar*; however, recommendations were not implemented.

2nd Backward Classes Commission, headed by *B.P. Mandal.*

It recommended:

1. 27% of posts in public services are for OBC.
2. Welfare programmes for OBC are the same as for SC and ST.
3. Radical land reforms to free up small landholders from dependence on rich peasants.
4. Set up small-scale industries and special educational schemes for OBC.

Mandal Commission used various criteria to identify:

1. **Social:** caste or class considered socially backward by others. caste or class, which are mainly dependent on manual labour for their livelihood.
2. **Educational:** caste or class where the number of children in the age range of 5–15 who have never attended school is at least more than 25% above the state average.
3. **Economic:** caste or class where the average value of family assets is at least 25% below the state average. Recently, the government appointed a commission headed by *Justice G. Rohini* for the sub-categorization of OBC.

Constitutional Provisions for OBC:

1. **Article 15(4):** Nothing shall prevent the state from making provisions for the advancement of socially and economically backward classes of citizens, whether SC or ST.
2. **Article 15(5):** Allow the state to make special provisions for backward classes or SC or ST for admissions in private educational institutions, aided or unaided.
3. **Article 16(4):** Allow the state to reserve vacancies in public service for any backward class of state that is not adequately represented in public service.
4. **Article 338B:** National Commission for the Backward Class (NCBC) is given constitutional status like the NCSC and NCST with adequate powers.

Welfare Measures for OBC:

➢ **Assistance for skill development of OBC (NGO Scheme):** involve voluntary organisations and the National Backward Classes Finance and Development Corporation (NBCFDC) to improve the educational and socio-economic conditions of OBC with a view to upgrading their skills.

➢ **Pre-matric scholarship to OBC:** a centrally sponsored scheme to motivate children of OBC studying at the pre-matric stage

➢ **Post-matric scholarship to OBC students:** 100% centrally sponsored scheme to give financial assistance to OBC students studying post-matric to enable them to complete their education.

➢ National Fellowship for OBC students in obtaining quality higher education like PhDs, construction of hostels for OBC boys and girls, free coaching for OBC students, etc.

➢ Term Loan Scheme of NBCFDC— Saksham—Term Loan for Young Professionals Belonging to Backward Classes of the Target Group.

➢ **Shilp Sampada:** Upgrade the technical and entrepreneurial skills of the backward classes by providing training and financial assistance under a term loan for self-employment in traditional crafts, etc.

➢ **Microfinance Scheme of NBCFDC:** Mahila Samriddhi Yojana for Women

OBC Issues/Discrimination:

1. **Social Front:** They occupy a lower social status. Denial of ownership of education, land, etc.
2. **Economic Front:** OBC were restricted to menial jobs such as carpenter, goldsmith, barber, manual labour, sweeping, etc. at least till independence. The Jajmani system prevailed, which led to their exploitation. Lack of minimum wages.

3. **Political Front:** Historically, OBC were given the least representation in panchayats, at least till independence. The introduction of reservation and democracy led to change.
4. **Downward Mobility:** In the Ram Singh Case, the SC rejected the inclusion of Jat caste in the OBC list. SC said that the decision to include or exclude should be based on contemporary data.

Recently, Dharmendra Pramar, holding an M.Com. and B.Ed. degrees and employed at a cooperative bank, was thrashed for riding a horse in a Madhya Pradesh village (Agar Malwa district) during a marriage procession. He said that Rajputs (the dominant community) in the village were upset with their rise in society.

Case Study

- **105th Constitutional Amendment Act**

The bill has been enacted by Parliament to amend the Constitution in a way that can help state governments more effectively identify disadvantaged and excluded communities. The bill aims to clarify certain aspects of the one hundred and second Constitutional Amendment Bill in an effort to allow states and UTs the authority to create their own separate lists of socially and educationally underprivileged groups. It modifies Article 342 A (clauses 1 and 2) and introduces a different clause, 342 A (3), that expressly empowers states to keep their separate lists. It would also change Articles 366(26c) (which demonstrates socioeconomically or academically backward classes) and 338B (9), allowing states to inform socially and educationally backward classes (SEBC) promptly rather than proceeding through the NCBC (National Commission for Backward Classes). According to the Amendment Bill, the president's authority over the "state list" would be fully removed, and the state legislature would be notified. As a result, the proposed bill circumvents the Supreme Court's decision and restores state governments' responsibility to preserve a unique state list of backward classes.

Need of Constitution 127th Amendment Bill: The 102nd constitutional amendment (insert Articles 338B and 342A after Article 342) was related to giving constitutional status to the National Commission of Backward Classes, and the interpretation of this constitutional amendment effectively struck a blow to the authority of state governments in identifying backward classes and providing them with reservation benefits. The Supreme Court's Maratha reservation verdict concluded that the President would decide which groups would be put on the separate state OBC list based on the NCBC's suggestions.

- **Reservation for EWS:**

A 5-judge bench of the Supreme Court has upheld the validity of the 103 rd Constitutional Amendment Act (Janhit Abhiyan v. Union of India). The Act has introduced a 10% reservation for the economically disadvantaged (EWS) in education and public employment. Provisions of the 103 rd Constitution Amendment Act do not breach the basic structure of the Constitution:

(a) Permitting the state to make special provisions, including reservations, based on economic criteria The majority opinion held that while economically weaker sections (EWS) of the citizens are not declared as socially and economically backward classes (SEBCs) for the purpose of Article 15(4) of the Constitution, separate reservations are not barred by the Constitution (like provisions under free and compulsory primary education). Hence, it is not violative of the basic structure.

(b) Excluding the SEBCs, OBCs, SCs, and STs from the scope of EWS Reservation: Article 16(4) is exhaustive for reservation in favour of backward classes, but the section is not exhaustive of the concept of reservation. The provisions of the Amendment Act have introduced another affirmative action that is separate and distinct. Hence, it is not violative of the basic structure.

(c) Breach of 50% ceiling for reservations: In the present judgement, the SC held that the 50% ceiling is for backward classes and that it "overstretched to the reservation provided for an entirely different class, consisting of the economically weaker sections".

(d) Permitting the State to make special provisions for admission to private unaided institutions: Reservations as a concept cannot be ruled out in private institutions where education is imparted. The view concurred with the earlier judgement in Pramati v. Society for Unaided Private Schools (2014).

7.2

Social change and contemporary tribal societies : Impact of modern democratic institutions, development programmes and welfare measures on tribals and weaker sections.

Q 1. Impact of modern democratic institutions on tribes and weaker section

Ans. The impact of modern democratic institutions upon Indian tribes was truly realised with the enactment of the 73 rd and 74th Constitutional Amendments of 1992 and the Panchayats (Extension to the Scheduled Areas) Act, 1996.

Positive Impact: The Panchayati Raj system had enabled the tribal people to better organise and represent themselves in the politicoadministrative set-up of the state. They have thus become more efficient in deriving constitutional, legal, and developmental benefits through the Panchayati Raj Institutions (PRIs).

The provisions of PESA, 1996, have enabled tribal areas to manage their resources and regulate their affairs in a democratic manner. For instance, the Gonds of Mendhu Lekha village (Maharashtra), through their Gram Sabha, have been accorded the rights to collect and dispose of bamboo by the government. The Pullangi Gram Panchayat in Andhra Pradesh, which includes households of Kondareddis, a PVTG, decided to stop the brewing and consumption of country liquor due to its adverse effects.

Another big impact of PRIs has been that tribes have become more aware and have been able to protect their local interests, even in the face of adversity. For instance, in Niyamgiri (Odisha), the Gram Sabhas of 12 tribal villages inhabited by Dongria Kondh unanimously rejected a mining project, resisting the threats and pressure tactics applied to silence them. The government had to recognise their decision and stop the project.

Even in non-tribal areas, PRIs have facilitated the participation of tribal leaders through the provision of reservations.

Negative Impact: In areas where the statutory PRIs have not been compatible with the traditional political structure, there has been a decline of traditional tribal leadership like the Mahanto and Pahan, along with tribal panchayats like the Praha of Oraon and Rai Sabha of Gonds. At best, their role has been restricted to solving family and marriage disputes.

It has also been observed that at times, statutory PRIs are dominated by non-tribal and outside leadership or by affluent tribal people. *N. Prasad (1992)* has described that this new leadership is more oriented towards their own personal needs and similar to the mainstream political culture.

29th Commission for SC and ST Reports:

1. Traditional institutions are isolated and have no role.
2. Formal institutions are ineffective and cause social discord.
3. The institutional dichotomy of roles left tribal members confused and disillusioned.

Besides the PRIs, the reservation policy and vote-bank politics in general have led to the politicisation of tribes,thereby increasing their awareness of constitutional rights. This had led to the emergence of young and educated tribal leaders fighting for change.

Dr. B.D. Sharma (former Commissioner of SCs and STs) has said that the need is to facilitate harmony and coexistence between statutory and traditional panchayats with well-defined roles and tribal participation.

The convergence of New and Old Village communities coming together as a group to deal with all outsiders, including government departments, is an optimal approach (Rai Sabhas model of Adilabad in A.P.).

Q 2. PESA Act

Ans. Broadly endorsing the recommendation of the Bhuria Committee, Parliament passed the Provision of Panchayats (Extension to Scheduled Areas) Act, 1996.

This Act exclusively empowers Gram Sabha to:

1. Safeguard and preserve (a) the traditions and customs of people and their cultural identity; (b) community resources; and (c) the customary mode of dispute resolution.
2. Carry out executive functions to (a) approve plan, programme for social and economic development (b) Identify person as beneficiary under poverty alleviation and other programme (c) Issue certificate of utilization of funds by Panchayats.

PESA also empowers Gram Sabha/Panchayat at appropriate level with:

1. Right to mandatory consultation in land acquisition, resettlement and rehabilitation of displaced persons.
2. Mandatory recommendation for license/lease of mines and concession for exploitation of minor minerals.
3. Ownership of Minor forest produce (MFP).
4. Regulate sale/consumption of intoxicants.
5. Control over money lending to ST.
6. Prevent land alienation and restore alienated land.

Its effective implementation will not only bring development but deepen democracy in 5th Schedule Areas. Ministry of Panchayati Raj adds that – Of 94 PESA district, 36 are Extremist Affected district (EAD) and of 76 EAD, 32 are PESA district.

The major impediments to PESA:

1. Responsibility of creating assonance of State legal enactment with PESA lies with State Legislature. Eg. Take Madhya Pradesh law, provision of consultation before land acquisition, recommendation before grant of license for minerals, ownership of MFP in Panchayat/Gram Sabha do not find place thereby highly deviated.
2. Incompatibility between provision of PESA and other laws have not been removed like Forest Act, 1929, Mines and Mineral Act, 1957, LAAR, 2013, etc.
3. Multiplication of parallel committees and agencies like ITDP (Integrated Tribal Development Project) which do not have coordinated relations with panchayats.
4. Lack of interface between panchayat and delivery system.
5. Lack of finances to execute work.
6. Working structure and orders of the Ministry of Panchayati Raj vs. the Ministry of Tribal Affairs.

Mungekar Committee Recommendation:

1. Gram Sabha must be given top priority by all concerned authorities, irrespective of the position they may hold in the system.
2. Adaptation of the law through the governor's notification covering all items of PESA.
3. Devolving power to the Gram Sabha under PESA should be treated as sacrosanct. Any attempt to misuse or mislead the Gram Sabha should be treated as an offence against democracy.
4. A participatory approach to programme implementation should be a mandatory pre-requisite for programme implementation.

The 2nd ARC strongly recommends all legislation be modified to bring it into conformity with this Act, and at the earliest, capacity building needs to be done.

Case Study

- Adivasi woman sarpanch belonging to Mahadev Koli tribe of Maharashtra named Usha Supeensured participation and representation of Adivasi women in the decision-making process (Mahila Gramme Sabha was created). This woman's concerns over menstruation, violence by her husband, an alcohol ban, etc. were listened to, and steps were taken to address them.
- Chhavi Rajawat, an MBA graduate, became sarpanch of Soda village, Rajasthan, and showcased how effective change can be brought in by working on electricity, health, and education facilities.

Q 3. Discuss the impact of development programmes and welfare measures on the Indian tribes

Ans. In pursuance of the constitutional provisions and the spirit of Tribal Panchsheel, a number of developmental programmes and welfare measures have been undertaken by the Indian State for the betterment of tribes.

Impact: The policy of affirmative action, along with the Tribal Sub-Plan, has led to an increase in developmental indicators for tribes. For instance, the literacy rate for STs has improved from 42.1% in 2001 to 59% in 2011. The Gross Enrolment Ratio (GER) for ST students at the Senior Secondary (Classes XI–XII) level has increased from 35.4% in 2013–14 to 43.1% in 2015–16. The infant mortality rate has declined from 62.1 (2005–06) to 44.4 (2015–16). The under-five mortality rate has declined from 95.7 (2005–06) to 57.2 (2015–16), and institutional delivery has increased from 17.7% in 2005–06 to 68% in 2015–16.

Several developmental schemes and financial aid have facilitated tribal people leaving their traditional economic livelihood and pursuing new economic activities, especially commercial agriculture and entrepreneurship. The NSSO surveys have recorded a continuous increase in the average income of ST households, along with a sharp rise in government and private services and self-employment.

The reservation policy has led to the politicization of tribes, thereby increasing their awareness of constitutional rights. This has led to emergence of young and educated tribal leadership fighting for change. H.M. Mathur says that development has succeeded in creating positive change among tribes.

However, the more affluent and vocal sections among the tribes have cornered most of the benefits. As a result, new 'tribal elites' have emerged. This has led to stratification among the tribes and inequitable development.

Moreover, to gain their rightful benefit from the welfare schemes, tribes have had to increase their contacts with the bureaucracy and mainstream society. At times, this has led to their exploitation and discrimination, especially in government schools and offices.

Finally, it is seen that, in the name of tribal development, others' will and models have been imposed on tribes. Often, development packages are not compatible with their culture and are thus not digested by the tribal folk. Chaudhary, in "Introduction to Tribal Transformation in India," pointed out salient facets of change:

1. Transformation from marginalised existence to acute awareness of civil rights
2. Progress has not met expectations due to a deficiency in programme implementation and a lack of sympathy and insight from the administration.
3. The elite class emerged through the present democratic institutions and cornered development benefits.

Dr. B.D. Sharma (former Commissioner of SCs and STs) has said that we need to redefine our model of development. For our developmental schemes and welfare measures to be successful, they must be accessible to the last tribal and blend with, not cut across, the tribal values and customs.

Case Study

- **Hunter and Gatherer:** *P. Reddy's* study of the Chenchu resettlement scheme found that little time was allowed for their reorientation into agriculture, poor management of agriculture operations by project officers, and insensitivity of officers to the social organisation of Chenchu. This actively discouraged Chenchu resettlement.
- **Artisan:** Gadgil and Guha pointed out how certain artisan activities, such as iron smithy, totally died out, and Agarias and Asurs had to resort to poor agriculture or wage earning.
- **Shifting Cultivations:** Partial success seen in Tripura resettlement of Jhum towards plantation, horticulture, and animal husbandry.
- **Agriculturalist Mohapatra's** study of Mayurbhanj points out that the creation of charge needs sustained effort. The introduction of technological charges should be synchronised with the agricultural ritual cycle and the role of tribal priests.

7.3

The concept of ethnicity; Ethnic conflicts and political developments; Unrest among tribal communities; Regionalism and demand for autonomy; Pseudo-tribalism. Social change among the tribes during colonial and post-Independent India.

Q 1. Concept of Ethnicity

Ans. According to the Oxford dictionary, the word ethnicity means the fact or state of belonging to a social group that has a common national or cultural tradition. Horowitz understands ethnicity as a sense of collective belonging, which could be based on common descent, history, language, culture, area, or religion, or a combination of these.

According to Giddens, ethnicity refers to the cultural practises and outlooks of a given community of people that set them apart from others. According to the above definitions, ethnicity includes features such as:

1. Refer to cultural practises.
2. People see themselves as culturally distinct from other groups.
3. Have different languages, histories, religions, dresses, etc.
4. It is socially mobilised and historically defined.
5. Purely a social phenomenon over time.
6. The young assimilate beliefs and norms via socialisation.
7. It is fluid and changing—where groups and regroups itself as an adaptive strategy in response to situations.

But the contemporary political usage has been restricted to a "quasi-national kind of minority group' within a state that somehow has not achieved the status of a nation.

- It is important to understand that national demand for sovereignty comes from territorially concentrated groups like Kashmiris, Sikhs, SL Tamils, Quebecs, etc.
- Ethnicity is also used as an ideology and device to gain concessions and have a say in the power structure.
- Ethnicity is manifested in Indian polities not merely due to grass-roots discontent but also due to the creation of vested political interests.

Impact of ethnicity and conflicts:

1. Regionalism, e.g., the Gorkhaland and Bodoland movements
2. Secessionism: demand for a separate nation, e.g., the Naga Movement.
3. Social tensions.
4. Dysfunctional developmental process.

Combating Ethnicity:

1. To foster loyalty to the nation, i.e., higher-order loyalty, it is necessary to satisfy lower-level loyalty, i.e., loyalty to one's region, caste, religion, etc.
2. Participation of ethnic groups in modernization and developmental processes
3. Effective implementation of the 5th and 6th Schedules and constitutional rights of linguistic and religious minorities
4. Respecting and protecting tribal culture and practises
5. Preventing the forced imposition of outside culture on ethnic minorities
6. Effective enforcement of laws protecting minority rights, e.g., tribal sub-plan Ethnicity, which is partially ascribed but largely constructed for collective action in pursuit of the interests of a group, must be in sync with the fundamentals of our Constitution, *i.e.,* sovereignty, unity, and integrity of the nation.

Q 2. Ethnic conflicts and Political Developments

Ans. Ethnicity refers to expressive aspects of ethnic identities and the process of transformation of a group into a subjectively self-conscious community having psychological unity of kind and involving complex processes.

Ethnic groups are based on three predominant attributes: biological, like descent and kinship; cultural, like language and religion; and territorial, like region and locality.

The ethnic conflicts are mainly dependent on two factors:

1. Necessary conditions like socio-economic ones: poverty, inequality, land alienation, exploitation, unemployment, underdevelopment, and an influx of migrants. Though it provides a social base for ethnic conflicts but they depend on sufficient conditions.
2. Sufficient conditions include the emergence of strong leadership, political competition and manipulation, casual and unwise government policies, and the availability of foreign support. Unless these sufficient conditions become active or powerful, these movements fail to find their language of expression.
   - Change in the demographic profile of states like Maharashtra, Assam, or Tripura due to the influx of migrants It has aggravated local competition for scarce resources and the publication of the ideology of 'sons of soil'. In the case of Tripura, tribals decreased from 64% to 29%.

Year	1874	1911	1991
Tribal in Tripura out of total pop.	64%	36%	29%

   - Scholars like Rajni Kothari have argued that the formation of ethnic identity gains momentum when the dominance of the majority over the minority becomes a fact. E.g., construction of the Hindutva agenda VHP's attempt to create division between "we Hindus' and 'they Muslims' or an attempt by VHP to build up the Ayodhya issue.
   - Political personalities like Shibu Soren, Bal Thackeray, and K. Chandrashekhar Rao used the sentiments of the masses to build movements. The demand for separate states of Andhra Pradesh, Punjab, Nagaland, and Uttarakhand were not conceded until it achieved political significance.

Case Study

1. **Punjab:** Sikhs in Punjab, with a developed sense of cultural destruction, faced discrimination in economic and political matters. Initially, agitation focused on demands like Chandigarh, water redistribution, and territorial demarcation. But the centre bottlenecked these issues for a long time. It later led to the demand of Khalistan and subsequent actions by the government, leading to Operation Bluestar, the Delhi riots, etc.
2. **Telangana Movement:** It refers to the creation of Telangana from pre-existing Andhra. New State corresponds to the Telegu-speaking portions of the erstwhile princely States of Hyderabad. After struggling for a decade, it was formed in 2014.

The imaging of individuals as national communities as well as the collection of subnational identities like regional, religious, linguistic, or tribal are not antagonistic. Even those insurgent groups that look anti-national finally compromise on political and economic gains. Ethnic movements, as in Jharkhand or Telangana, may work as organs of civil society to strengthen democracy. Hence, they must be viewed from a wider perspective.

Case Study

- **Politicisation of Ethnicity: A Study on the Bodos and the Koch-Rajbongshis of Assam by Dipika Paul**

The discourse on the politicisation of ethnicity sees ethnicity as a "political phenomenon" in modern society and argues that it shouldn't be researched independently of politics. The analysis of this interaction between politics and ethnicity was attempted in the discussion on the movement of identity assertion by the Bodos and Koch Rajbongshsis. The study demonstrates that a variety of variables, including state policies, dominant groups' chauvinistic attitudes, elites, and ethnic organisations at various times, contributed to the politicisation of ethnicity among these two ethnic groups. As a result, it is possible to view the discourse surrounding the politicisation of ethnicity as a key method for comprehending the current ethnic movements.

- **Ethnic Diversity, Autonomy, and Territoriality in Northeast India: A Case of Tribal Autonomy in Assam**

Different tribes in Northeast India continue to call for the establishment of new states and territorially delineated autonomous councils notwithstanding the creation of a number of new states. This is due to the fact that the majority of tribes in the area believe that maintaining and developing their socio-cultural identities depend on having an acceptable share of political power. Although reasonable, such cultural and developmental objectives encounter difficulties whenever they are linked to exclusive administrative borders for self-governance. Community disputes over land and territoriality so persist in making Northeast India a region of constant upheaval and crises. Additionally, the majority of the councils failed to influence the minds and hearts of the smaller tribal groups under their jurisdiction. Many times, these groups considered the councils as an instrument of suppression.

For instance, there is a distinct distinction between Bodos and non-Bodos, like the Adivasis, in the BTC region. Even the formation of the BTC had been rejected by the latter. The creation of the council was criticised by non-Bodos as evidence that the government had given in to their 'gun culture' and the militant Bodos. Their main defence was that because the Bodos made up just roughly 25% of the overall population in the BTC region, they were ineligible to rule over the remaining 75% of the population. They said that by creating the BTC, non-Bodo communities were reduced to the status of second-class citizens, giving the Bodos the chance to mistreat them.

The non-Bodos further contended that a mixed-population area could not support the idea of "territorially defined autonomy" for a certain group. Territorial autonomy, they claimed, "will encourage other ethnic groups in the state to raise the demand to carve out territories along ethnic lines." Similar divisions exist between Karbis and non-Karbis groups like the Kukis in the autonomous district of Karbi Anglong. The autonomous area is solely the home of the Karbis, who consider all other people to be'settlers'. One example of this is the 2003 Kuki-Karbi conflict. Other councils are experiencing a similar circumstance as well. These councils have therefore failed to use the local initiative and guarantee that the public is involved in the development processes.

Along with these councils' ineffectiveness, there has been an increase in militant separatist groups along tribal lines with competing claims that try to establish exclusive homelands. Violent confrontations such as the Kuki-Karbi war, the Hmar-Dimasa conflict in North Cachar Hills in 2003, and the Bodo-Santhals fight in Kokrajhar and Bongaigaon in the 1990s were caused by their disputing claims. The numerous Bodo factions are still engaged in intra-faction violence as they attempt to dominate Bodo politics. Tribals in Northeast India have primarily understood the district/territorial council requirement under the Sixth Schedule as an "ad hoc and intermediary arrangement" between tribal councils and statehood.

Additionally, they now think that these councils might result in statehood, as they did for Meghalaya and Mizoram. In light of this, the Karbis and the Dimasas have intensified their call for the establishment of independent states. Similar to how the BTC was established, other plain tribes are also calling for the establishment of territorial councils similar to the BTC for themselves. The Bodo people anticipate the creation of a separate Bodoland state soon. The majority of the tribes in Northeast India now believe that having a sufficient amount of political authority is a must for maintaining their cultural identity and, more importantly, for their overall development. These goals are not only realistic but also legitimate. But once such goals become inescapably linked with exclusive administrative limits for "self-governance," they begin to run into trouble. Such demands call for careful analysis given the nature and scope of ethnic diversity in Northeast India in general and Assam in particular, both in terms of plurality and shared physical and cultural space.

Q 3. Unrest among tribal communities

Ans. A.B. Vardhan comments that British imperialists deliberately isolated tribals from the rest of the population as they were aware of the explosive potential of tribals. However, they were open to Christian missionaries, landlords, moneylenders, etc. to exploit them.

Although instances of tribal unrest existed in pre-colonial times, the colonial period marked the onset of such cases at a widespread level. Unfortunately, this has continued in independent India as well.

Factors Responsible:

1. **Historical experience:** During the colonial phase, the British opened up the tribal areas, leading to the exploitation of the tribal resources and people. Thus, even today, tribals remain wary of outsiders. E.g., the Sentinelese of the Andamans is extremely hostile towards outsiders today due to their exploitation by the British in the late 19th century.
2. **Relationship with the Hindu society:** A lower position in the tribe-caste continuum coincides with social, economic, and political deprivation, leading to a feeling of frustration among the tribes. If doors to achieving a higher ranking are closed off, this often leads to unrest.
3. **Demographic imbalance:** Tribes such as those of the North-East have often complained of the influx of nontribals into their ancestral homes, rendering them a minority in their own region.
4. **Industrialization and urbanisation:** these modern forces have led to the exploitation of tribal resources, land alienation and displacement of tribes, and an influx of outsiders. E.g., the Jharkhand movement arose due to the exploitation of the region's mineral and forest resources in the name of development without passing on equitable benefits to the local tribes.
5. **Unfair treatment by the government:** When the tribals witness the government being more inclined towards the interests of non-tribals, they feel betrayed, leading to unrest. E.g., the Pathalgadi Rebellion boiling in the tribal villages of Jharkhand today was induced by the state government's continuous attempts to amend the tenancy laws in favour of outsiders. The Shilu A.O. Report (1969) points towards lethargy and indifference when dealing with tribes.
6. **Cultural orientation:** If the tribals have a vastly divergent cultural orientation from mainstream society, it often leads to contra-acculturation. Also, an educated section turns the unrest into an organised movement. E.g., the Naga secessionist movement is driven by English-educated elites who, due to their Western cultural orientation, have never identified themselves as part of Indian society.

Way Ahead: The Expect Group of the Planning Commission in 2006 came out with a report titled "Challenges of Development in Maoist-Affected Tribal Areas". It linked extremism to deeper faults in governance, land alienation, unemployment, and inequality in society. The situation has been compounded by the heavy use of the coercive apparatus of the state in forests, negating all democratic principles. Gross misuse of the Land Acquisition Act is one of the sore points in this situation. The Expert Group has tried to project an open approach rather than a security-centric one. It was argued that land-related factors play an important role in the growth of Maoism. It has asked the government to take legal measures to ensure landless people get land. It recommended that FRA be implemented in full earnest.

Srinivas and Sanwal say that for most tribes in the North-East, the experience of being part of a nation is recent, and the difficulty in quickly and unqualifyingly accepting this fact needs to be sympathetically reviewed. Tribal people fear losing their identity in the ocean of Hindu nationalism.

Case Study

- **Manipur Violence**

The protests were triggered by the Manipur High Court's direction to the State to pursue a 10-year-old recommendation to grant Scheduled Tribe (ST) status to the non-tribal Meitei community.

The Court's order has brought the historical tensions between the valley-dwelling Meitei community and the state's hill tribes to a boil.

Violence started: A 'tribal solidarity march' was organised by the All Tribal Students' Union of Manipur (ATSUM) against the order of the High Court. Violent clashes broke out at various places in Manipur during the course of this march.

Which are the major communities residing in Manipur?

The State is like a football stadium with the Imphal Valley representing the playfield at the centre and the surrounding hills the galleries.

The valley, which comprises about 10% of Manipur's landmass, is dominated by the non-tribal Meitei. This area yields 40 of the State's 60 MLAs.

The hills comprising 90% of the geographical area are inhabited by more than 35% recognised tribes. This area sends only 20 MLAs to the Assembly.

Why does the Meitei community want ST status?

There has been an organised push in support of this demand since 2012, led by the Scheduled Tribes Demand Committee of Manipur (STDCM). In their plea before the High Court, it was argued that the Meitei community was recognised as a tribe before the merger of the princely state of Manipur with the Union of India in 1949. It lost its identity as a tribe after the merger. The demand for ST status arose from the need to preserve the community, and save the ancestral land, tradition, culture and language of the Meiteis.

As per the arguments forwarded by the community in the court: The community has been victimised without any constitutional safeguards to date. The Meitein/Meetei have been gradually marginalised in their ancestral land. Their population which was 59% of the total population of Manipur in 1951 has now been reduced to 44% as per 2011 Census data.

Why are tribal groups against ST status for Meiteis?

The tribal groups say the Meiteis have a demographic and political advantage besides being more advanced than them academically and in other aspects. The Meiteis are a dominant group controlling the state and its apparatuses. Hence, the claim that Meiteis need ST status to protect their culture and identity is self-defeating. They feel the ST status to the Meiteis would lead to loss of job opportunities and allow them to acquire land in the hills and push the tribals out.

Is this demand the only reason for the conflict rocking the state currently?

Unrest has been brewing among the hill tribes of the state for a number of reasons. Pro-government groups in Manipur claim that some tribal groups with vested interests are trying to scuttle Chief Minister's crusade against drugs. The anti-drug drive began with destroying poppy fields and the theory that illegal settlers from Myanmar are behind clearing forests and government lands to grow opium and cannabis. These settlers are ethnically related to the Kuki-Zomi people of Manipur. The first violent protest in March was against the eviction of the residents of a Kuki village. Kuki groups have claimed that the survey and eviction is a violation of Article 371C, which confers some administrative autonomy to the tribal-dominated hill areas of Manipur. The large-scale arson and violence, on May 3 and 4, followed a tribal solidarity rally against the reported move to include the Meiteis in the ST list.

- **Komaram bheem**

Komaram Bheem's efforts are still significant in light of the decades-long Adivasi fight for patta rights; he serves as an example of a revolutionary icon for all Adivasi movements and serves as a reminder of the nation's and state's unfulfilled promises to the Adivasis. In the Gond Adivasi group, Komaram Bheem is held in the highest regard and revered as a deity (pen). Every year on Aswayuja Powrnami, the Gonds mark the anniversary of Bheem's passing. On this day, a celebration honouring his life and struggles is held at Jodeghat. After a protracted battle and 72 years after his passing, Komaram Bheem's statue was finally erected in Hyderabad's Tank Bund in 2012. Komaram Bheem will always be remembered as the champion and icon of the legendary Adivasi "Jal Jangal Jameen" uprising.

- **Forest satyagraha**

The tribal people of Tamora village in Chhattisgarh opposed the British using Gandhi's nonviolent strategy of satyagraha in the jungle. Dayabati was the movement's coordinator. Beginning in 1930, the British introduced a law known as the "forest law," which forbade people from bringing their pets into the forest to use them as fodder and required them to keep them indoors. In the course of the forest satyagraha, forest laws were broken in a number of ways, including by leaving cattle to graze in forbidden forests, by taking wood and leaves from these forests without first getting permission from the forest authorities, and by socially boycotting British employees of the revenue and forest departments.

Q 4. Regionalism and demand for autonomy

Ans. Regionalism means becoming affiliated with one particular region and claiming to belong to that region. The best way to understand tribal regionalism may be to study it within a socio-economic, geographical, and political framework. Regional movements aim to attract the attention of the centre to local problems. It has been a common phenomenon in India that whenever local needs and aspirations are ignored for longer periods, when people start feeling that the state is not fulfilling their expectations, separatist tendencies may emerge. With the emergence of separatist tendencies, identification of oneself with a region gets boosted, and this gives rise to regionalism which plays an important role in separatist movements.

But regionalism in India has also developed among certain tribals due to cultural contacts. It started in regions that were underdeveloped and exploited in every aspect. An important example of regionalism among Indian tribes is the "Jharkhand Movement," which asked for an entirely separate tribal region. The tribal cultural zone of Jharkhand is an aggregate of the cultures of different tribes such as Mundas, Oraon, Ho, Santhal, etc. The "Jharkhand Party" was formed in 1950 and claimed 15-20 districts of Bihar, West Bengal, Madhya Pradesh, and Odisha as the

Jharkhand region. In the 1970s, more efforts were made to promote a common culture, language, script, and identity. One such proof is the publication of a magazine called "Jai Jharkhandi" in Nagpuri dialect. In 1973, the "Jharkhand Mukti Morcha" was formed and demanded a separate Jharkhand State. Due to their efforts, a separate Jharkhand state was created in 2000 A.D.

When we consider the North East, the regionalist movement of Naga is worth mentioning. They formed the "Naga National Front" and demanded a separate region for themselves. But roots can be traced as far back as 191 8, when an organisation called the "Naga Club" was formed. They demanded Naga be left to themselves when the British quit India. However, demand for a separate political identity gained real momentum with the emergence of the Naga National Council in 1946. This movement for succession from India led to unity among Naga tribes into one ethnic political block. Later in 1963, a separate state, Nagaland, was created. However, state problems were not solved, as reflected in the National Socialist Council of Nagaland's demands.

Causes:

1. Rooted in the structure of society and geography
2. Based on ethnic, linguistic, and geographical diversity
3. Imbalanced economic development in Jharkhand
4. The impractical application of the CrPC to peaceful protestors led to further regionalism. E.g., HaiemendorfGond case study
5. Language loss or cultural loss Eg. Dimasa.

Dr. Ram Dayal Munda (VC, Ranchi University) found middle and lower levels of government officials to have little commitment towards tribal welfare. The government took away forests to manage them scientifically. However, they mismanaged forests, gave outsiders preferential treatment in hiring, and land alienation continues unabated.

Way Forward:

1. Policy of accommodation rather than assimilation.
2. M.N. Srinivas has suggested that for neutralising regional movements, positive socio-economic measures should be taken by the government. Implement constitutional provisions in letter and spirit and give tribal people a legitimate share in the fruits of development.

Conclusion: The positive aspect of these regional movements is that they have served to transform yesterday's ethnic rebels into tomorrow's responsible rulers. As shown in *Das Gupta's* work, regions, after gaining autonomy, have settled down to work out constructive partnerships with national leadership, national economic planning, and the national administrative system. It deserves to be tackled with care, sympathy, and appreciation for long-suppressed tribal aspirations.

Case Study

- **Nagaland: Commission on the Register of Indigenous Peoples submits recommendations**

The report of the commission was finally presented during the recently concluded Monsoon Session of the state assembly, two years after the Nagaland government's proposed Register of Indigenous Inhabitants of Nagaland (RIIN) drew criticism from various quarters, including tribal bodies and civil society, forcing the government to immediately convene a commission to examine the issues and submit recommendations. Following several talks with tribal organisations, civil society, and NGOs, the commission on RIIN, headed by the former chief secretary Banuo Z. Jamir, presented its report to the state administration.

The commission stated that, despite taking into account various points of view, it was its firm position that December 1, 1963—the day Nagaland attained statehood—should be used as the cutoff date to determine whether a person qualifies as a resident of Nagaland, regardless of whether they are indigenous, a tribal nonindigenous to Nagaland, or a non-tribal.

The commission advised that information provided for each individual should first be verified at the family level in the village, followed by confirmation from clan and khel, before the village council certifies the document, which would then be submitted to the deputy commissioner, in order to ensure that authentication of an individual's identity is carried out without influence or manipulation. The commission suggested setting up a panel to be in charge of verifying the membership of different such communities. The commission advised that the state government explore passing legislation to give legitimate individuals access to the complete RIIN process, including the issue of the indigenous inhabitant certificate (IIC) and permanent resident certificate (PRC).

Q 5. Pseudo-tribalism

Ans. Tribalism refers to the possession of a strong ethnic or cultural identity that separates oneself as a member of one group from members of another.

Pseudo-tribalism refers to the process by which a non-tribal group claims the status of a tribe in order to enjoy unintended concessions and privileges in employment, education, and other developmental activities. It also means that tribal groups may continue to claim ST status even though they are well advanced in terms of socio-economic and religious status.

Different Scenario:

1. **Different recognition in different States:** Lambadas, Banjaras, ST in Andhra, SC in Karnataka, OBC in Delhi Hence, they immigrate to different places to take advantage.
2. **Identical names:** Goudu of Agency tracts are pastoral tribes, but Gowda and Goundla are from plains.
3. **Tribalisation:** In Bastar district, initially tribes were displaced for irrigation projects, but later land got vacant and was illegally occupied by adjacent castes, who adopted hunting and rituals of the tribe. M.N. Srinivas considers tribals a model of Sanskritization to overcome untouchability and social exclusion in the Hindu social system and fight oppression.
4. **Desanskritization:** Many Brahmins and Rajputs settled in Khasa village, Dehradun. Adopted non-vegetarians, drank liquor, and married Khasa girls; thereby, they claim tribal status and enjoy benefits (D.N. Majumdar).
5. **Economic advancement:** modernization of Garo and Khasis under Christian missionaries but still corner benefits under ST status
6. **Retribalization:** Gonds converted into Raj Gonds under the influence of Sanskritization. Later came the reservation, and they wanted it. Thereby, they retribalized mainly for reservations.

Impact:

1. Pseduo-tribes take advantage of the benefits given in the Constitution to ST.
2. Genuine tribes are not getting actual benefits and remain behind in development.

Conclusion: One of the important functions of the Ministry of Tribal Affairs is the scheduling and descheduling of communities. The Constitution enjoins on the state special responsibility for the protection and development of ST.

Case Study

- **Many get false community certificates to take away the opportunities of Scheduled Caste and Scheduled Tribe candidates.**

In Nirguna v. The Chairman and ors., the Madras High Court expressed concern about people who do not belong to the Scheduled Caste or Scheduled Tribe (SC/ST) communities obtaining false SC/ST community certificates and thereby denying them opportunities in elections, educational admissions, or employment. Many people who do not belong to a Scheduled Caste or Scheduled Tribe obtain fictitious certificates declaring their community status as such in order to run in elections for local offices or constituencies reserved for SC or ST candidates, to apply for seats in educational institutions designated for SC or STs, or to obtain employment under the SC or ST category, violating the rights of deserving candidates who do belong to these groups.

There are numerous examples before this court where members of other communities get counterfeit SC/ST community certificates from officials, who also blithely provide such certificates for a variety of reasons, infringing the constitutional rights of SC/ST people. The order said that by obtaining such fraudulent certifications, undeserving individuals unfairly benefit and violate the rights of SC/ST community members. The Bench asked the state government to respond to a suggestion made by the Court to name Revenue Divisional Officers in each district who may be exclusively authorised to issue nativity certificates, income certificates, and community certificates after conducting a proper investigation in order to stop such malpractices.

Q 6. Social change among the tribes during colonial and post-Independent India

Ans. According to L.K. Mahapatra, "social movement occurs when a fairly large number of people, or an otherwise identifiable segment of the population, deliberately band together for collective action in order to act, reconstitute, reinterpret, restore, supplant, or protect some portions of their culture or social order, or to better their life chances by redistributing power of control in society".

COLONIAL:

K.S. Singh divided this into three phases:

- 1st: 1795–1860: This coincided with the establishment of the British Empire.
- 2nd: 1861–1920: Intensive Colonialism, during which merchant capital penetrated tribal economies.
- 3rd: 1921 –1947: 1921 -1947- Participation in the nationalist movement and launching of the agrarian and separatist movements.

A few movements worth mentioning are:

- Santhal Rebellion (1855–1857)—Peasant revolt due to the land-acquiring policy of British-appointed zamindars and the nexus of moneylenders and traders. It was led by Sidhu and Kanhu, but at the end, 23000 Santhal tribals were killed.
- Munda Revolt (1895–1901)—British replacement of the traditional Khuntkari system by the Zamindari system was the main reason. It was led by Birsa Munda but suppressed by the harsh actions of the British. Britishers passed the Tenancy Act of 1903, which recognised the Khuntkari system.
- Other uprisings, like Kuki, Khasi, etc., took place in the north-east.

Causes:

1. **K.S. Singh:** The land problem, i.e., how the British enforced their law, is one of the main causes of rebellion, as seen in the Birsa Munda case. Conservation of forests is Mundas' traditional right. In the 1896–97 and 1899–00 famines, Mundas suffered losses of cattle and lives.

2. **Ghanshyam Shah:** Deprivation of tribal people of their forest rights and harassment by the forest bureaucracy were the main reasons.
3. **Haimendorf:** The British encouraged outsiders to enter their wasteland and exploit them.

Post-Independence: The situation for tribals did not change much. Many revolts broke out after independence as well. K.S. Singh has classified tribal movements into four categories: agrarian, Sanskritization, cultural, and political.

1. **Agrarian and Forest:** restricted to only some regions Forest Satygraha by Gond in MP, the "tree war' in Orrisa against deforestation of Sal trees, and the Chipko Movement are a few among these.
2. **Sanskritization:** More spread in middle India due to which many tribal groups lost their culture and identity. Sant Samaj movement led by Gahira Guru among Kawar and Bhagat movements from M.P., Gujarat, and Rajasthan
3. **Cultural:** Sarna Dharma, centred around Sarna, or sacred groove, started as a religious movement among tribals in 1961; similarly, others like the Birsa cult and the Bonga cult had an impact on tribals.
4. **Political:** Movements like Jharkhand Mukti Morcha, Gond Raj, etc. for autonomy

The most striking ones:

1. **Naga Separatist Movement:** Started in 1918 with the foundation of the Naga Club. In 1946, it was renamed Nagaland National Council but asked for a separate state comprising Nagaland, A.P., Assam, Myanmar, etc. In 1980, due to failures in talks with India, NSC formed two organisations in 1988: NSCM (IM) and NSCM (K). Goal Common: "Greater Nagaland"
2. **Naxalite Movement:** In 1967, it started out in Naxalbari, West Bengal, as tribals exploited by higher caste zamindars. This movement started as retaliation with armed methods and has now spread to Chhattisgarh, Odisha, A.P., and eastern India.
3. Tribal protest against projects (Vedanta, Posco, etc.)

Causes:

1. Industrialization, urbanisation, and globalisation: the privatisation of land, along with its alienation by industries, has led to a breakdown of the self-sufficient tribal economy. There is rising individualism, consumerism, and migration among tribes. This has caused a shift to nuclear families and a decline in kinship values.
2. Development programmes and policies - The more affluent and vocal sections among the tribes have cornered the benefits of the "scheduled tribe" tag. As a result, they have emerged as the new 'tribal elites.' This has led to stratification among the tribes.
3. Modern democratic institutions—tribal panchayats like the Praha of Oraon and Rai Sabhas of Gonds—have suffered a decline in authority due to the Panchayati Raj Institutions (PRIs). However, where the PRIs have been compatible, the traditional political organisation has been retained culturally while becoming more organised and efficient.

For proper integration and inclusive development of tribals, *Dr. B.D. Sharma,* in a letter to the President of India, emphasised the following:

1. Land records are properly maintained, and tribals don't suffer in litigation.
2. Surplus land is distributed to tribals.
3. Review the Land Acquisition Act.
4. Ensure minimum wages.
5. FRA, 2006, implements it in letter and spirit.
6. The Abolition of Bonded Labour Act, 1976, was implemented sternly.
7. A credit facility is easily available to tribals.

8. Joint forest management should be ensured.
9. Customary tribal laws should be codified and respected.
10. Protect and promote tribal languages
11. Restoration of people's right to live in dignity and freedom.

Conclusion: Even today, tribal conflicts for autonomy, rights, and even identity persist in some form or another throughout the nation. The need of the hour is to understand their culture before making decisions and involving them in any policy that affects them.

Case Study

- **Identity Politics in the Hill Tribal Communities :**

As an illustration of the tribes' loss of identity, see Tripura. When the Khasi elders urge their fellow tribesmen to remain watchful about the rise of non-tribal population in the state, they use the non-tribal dominance in Tripura as an illustration. It is used as rationale for calls for tighter controls on non-tribal residents of the state's economic activity. Such limitations, set in accordance with the Constitution's Sixth Schedule, aid in lessening competition between the populations of tribes and non-tribes in the open market.

Even after the construction of distinct hill states for the tribal people, the relationship between development and underdevelopment remained the same. Previously, it involved Assamese hill tribals and plains people; currently, it involves the numerous tribes within the same state. Due to their numerical disadvantage, the less developed tribes in these states feel oppressed by the tribes who make up the majority. These tribes, feeling abandoned, have begun calling for either increased autonomy or their own states. On the other hand, the more advanced tribes have begun to view the less advanced tribes as a "burden" on the state's resources. This is possibly the rationale behind the Khasis' backing of the Garos of Meghalaya's quest for a separate "Garoland." Even the state's official websites do not provide a list of all the tribes that live there, a practise that suggests that different tribes in tribal states have different statuses.

- **Remembering Budhu Bhagat! Tribal Hero Who Stood Against Forced Labour, Economic Exploitation By Britishers**

Many of the demonstrations against the British government were conducted by tribal people while India fought for its independence. The nation observed their battle evolving into a revolution while they were utilising traditional weapons like swords and bows, which made their defence of their homeland and people all the more admirable. Among these warriors was Budhu Bhagat, a revolutionary. Budhu Bhagat, who was born on February 17, 1792, was an Oraon from the village of Silagai in what is now the state of Jharkhand. He has been practising swordsmanship and archery since he was a young boy. Bhagat always intended to get involved in an armed conflict against the British government because of his intense animosity towards them and their control over his territory, according to a local publication.

Budhu Bhagat organised the Larka insurrection in 1832 and inspired the tribal people to rise against the British and landlords' unjust authority. Bhagat and his supporters engaged in combat using ad hoc weapons, including axes, arrows, and bows. People used to think of Budhu Bhagat as a divine manifestation due to his organising skills. People in Ranchi and the adjacent districts of Chhota Nagpur were greatly influenced by the freedom warrior and were willing to give their lives in support of his cause. He gave the natives guerrilla warfare training and instructed them to fight for their rights. By utilising the impenetrable jungles and impassable hills, he repeatedly defeated the English soldiers. The hit-and-run tactics of Budhu soldiers caused heavy casualties among the British soldiers, who were unaware of the terrain of the region. The British authorities saw Bhagat as a serious threat and offered a reward of 1,000 rupees on his head, which was a significant sum at the time. On February 13, 1832, the British encircled Silagai village and started firing in an attempt to apprehend Budhu Bhagat and his friends. Bhagat and his allies fought until they died using just swords and an axe against the sophisticated firearms and weapons of the British army. Bhagat was shot during the battle and passed away while defending his country.

8

Impact of Religion on Tribal, Tribe, and Nation State

8.1

Impact of Hinduism, Buddhism, Christianity, Islam and other religions on tribal societies.

Q 1. Hinduism and Tribal

Ans. Hinduism is polytheistic, as are tribals; therefore, proximity between the two is natural. But the impact of Hinduism on tribalism is not due to coercion because Hinduism is not propagating its religion. Impact has been mainly due to cultural contact with peasants, neighbours, travellers, pilgrims, Sadhus, Sanyasis, etc.

- The study of two major Central Himalayan tribes, the Tharus of U.P. (Srivastava) and the Khasas of Uttarakhand (Majumdar), reveals that they have a tribal matrix but are intermingled with Hindu ways of life. Tharus have succeeded in getting accepted as Thakur by wearing sacred thread, establishing marriage relationships with Thakur, and modelling rites-de-passage in accordance with Hinduism. Similarly, the culture of Khasas in the Central Himalayas has been modelled on the ways of life of Rajputs and Brahmins in neighbouring plain areas.
- ButMajumdar also explained the concept in which transculturation among Hos of Jharkhand took place towards Gops (Hindu Caste), and Gops adopted tribal ways of life, and one cannot distinguish between Hos and Gops.
- In middle India, Bhumij of M.P. (Surjit Sinha) has been so greatly influenced by the Kshatriya model of Sanskritization that, in 1935, they formed the "Bhumij Kshatriya Association" to intensify Sanskritization.

Effects:

Negative:

1. According to *Ghurye,* tribes have always been in contact with Hindus, and they have assimilated to various degrees. He called tribes "backward Hindus".
2. Replacement of tribal ritual by complicated Hindu ritual.
3. Introduction of child marriage and gender disparity.
4. Decline of the youth dormitory, which created tensions.
5. Replacement of bride price by dowry.
6. Exploitation of premarital and extramarital sex among tribals.

Positives:

1. A new socio-cultural system based on reason, rationality, and modernity. E.g., Raghuvanshi of Bengal got the gotra system from Hindus and endogamy from tribals.
2. Opening up a new way of life based on Hinduism for tribals.

   However, in recent decades, fringe elements of militant Hinduism have been aggressively mooing tribals in the name of Ghar-Vapsi. Vishwa Hindu Sammelan by VHP at Jhabua in M.P. in 1999 converted 50000 tribals to Hinduism. The annual Shabari Sammelan of Gujarat points towards the aggressive campaign of these fringe elements to convert tribals to Hinduism.

Conclusion: Competition in the propagation of religion and faith in secular India has the dangerous potential of promoting the worst form of communalism. Let tribes enjoy their cultural autonomy, make their own decisions, and participate in the nation-building process as equal partners in progress, relating their self-respect and keeping their heads high.

Case Study

- **Tribal-Hindu Conflict:**

Tensions between Adivasi groups and BJP members have been brought on by a dispute over the flying of a flag on August 9 atop the statue of Rana Punja Bhil, a historical figure revered by the tribal Bhil community. Adivasi organisations and Hindu organisations were at odds over tribal heritage even during the Amagarh Fort dispute.

Q 2. Christianity and Tribal

Ans. Christianity is monotheistic while tribals are polytheistic; therefore, conversion of tribals to Christianity is quite a painful process for the first generation of converts, as tribals have to leave their worldview and total way of life, including ancestor worship. Though Christianity was introduced in India in the first century A.D., its impact on tribal communities started mainly after 1813, when Christian missionaries were allowed entry into tribal areas.

The first impact was felt by Khasis (1830), Oraon (1980), and Bhils (1880). According to estimates, tribal Christians comprise one-sixth of the total Christian population in India. The major concentration is in the northeast Himalayas. Among Garos, Nagas, and Mizos, the Christian population ranges from half to almost full. In middle India, the highest number exists among Mundas (one-fourth), Oraons (one-fourth), etc. In Oraons, Christianity has replaced the old faith in the Sarna religion (Sahey). As a result, there have been vast sociological changes in festivals, village organisation, rites-de-passage, economic life, etc.

In most cases, adoption of Christianity was a reaction of tribal groups to ruthless exploitation by Hindu landlords and moneylenders. A case in point is the Kol Rebellion and the spread of Christianity on the Chotanagpur plateau. The north-eastern region has also felt the most radical transformation as a consequence of the spread of Christianity.

Impact:

Positive:

1. Spread of formal and modern education and healthcare.
2. Monogamy and discourage divorce.
3. Increased self-image and identity.

4. Abolition of the practise of burying a newborn child with the mother if the mother dies at the time of childbirth E.g. Mizo.
5. Christian missionary started homes for motherless babies, *Animesh Roy* studied among Mizo.
6. Abstain from drinking rice beer among Naga tribes: Konyak and Ao Naga.

A case study of the impact of Christianity on the Vaiphei tribe of Manipur by *Dr. Heena Vaiphei* depicts that Christianity served as a platform for interclan or intertribal solidarity. Practise of offering sacrifices to please God in the form of food or meat given up. Education increased rapidly, healthcare improved, use of modern utensils and furniture increased, etc.

Negative:

1. Rob them of cultural autonomy.
2. Vertical division in tribal society between Christians and non-Christians, e.g., Khasi (Meghalya).
3. Migration to urban centres
4. Tribal practise and belief degenerated.
5. Youth dormitory abondon.
6. A new faith replaces tribal belief.
7. Rise of consumerism (private property).
8. Elwin is a missionary anxious for tribals to convert to Christianity.
9. K.N. Sahay's study of converts to Christianity in Chotanagpur believed that they were superior and practised world's best religion.

But now there is a trend in which revival movements are led by non-Christian Adivasis to identify them with traditional norms of society. In recent decades, conflict between Christian missionaries and fringe elements of militant Hinduism has been on the rise. The murder of Dr. Staines and his two sons, as well as the Kandhamal riots of 2007, reflect the friction between aggressive Hinduism and Christianity.

Case Study

- **Tribes in Arunachal Pradesh feel pushed to resist conversions to Christianity.**

In Arunachal Pradesh, there is a rising push to withdraw the Scheduled Tribes (ST) certificate given to anyone who has converted to a different faith. The campaign is intended for tribal members who have accepted Christianity. People who identify as Christians make up 30.26% of the population. Hindus are the second most numerous ethnic group in the state, making up 29.04% of the 13.84 lakh people that live there. To prevent conversions to Christianity, the RSS has been actively encouraging indigenous faith adherents of the state to institutionalise and record their religious practises. The execution of the anti-conversion law, the removal of converted tribal members from the Scheduled Tribes list, and renaming the existing Department of Indigenous Affairs into the Department of Indigenous Faith and Cultural Affairs are the three main objectives of the Indigenous Faith and Cultural Society of Arunachal Pradesh (IFCSAP).

Q 3. Islam and Tribal

Ans. As far as Islam is concerned, it could not penetrate tribal regions mainly because it is highly dogmatic in nature and lacks patronage from Muslim rulers. There was an absence of missionaries, and hence it was left to Sufi saints and preachers to spread it. That is why we find marginal impact in tribal regions.

Siddhis of Gujarats, Gujjars of N-W region, section of Bhils, Dhankasis, Kotis of Rajasthan, pastoral community like, Bakarwal of J&K have embraced Islam. Lakshadweep is only example where wholesome conversion to Islam taken place where communities like Keya, Malmi etc., exists.

Due to influence of Islam, changes observed:

1. Matrilineal feature of these tribes have changed towards patrilineal (K.S. Singh).
2. Islamic Personal Law prevails. (Shariat Law).
3. Cross cousin marriages prefered.
4. Celebration of festivals like birthday of Prophets.
5. Mat ruling in Islam particularly in context of Lakshadweep studied by Leela Dubey and Kutti.

Contact of Islam with tribal communities like Gujjar, Bakarwal has brought changes in their dress pattern and food habits. Some older beliefs have become obsolete today.

Wherever Islam got tribal followers, it was because Islam developed in a nomadic socio-cultural setting and its social structure had a tribal egalitarian character. However, Muslim tribal societies may show marked internal differentiation in structure and organisation.

Conclusion: Competition in the propagation of religion and faith in secular India has the dangerous potential of promoting the worst form of communalism. Let tribes enjoy their cultural autonomy, make their own decisions, and participate in the nation-building process as equal partners in progress, developing their self-respect and keeping their heads high.

Q 4. Buddhism and Tribal

Ans. Buddhism emerged as a distinct religion in the 6th century BCE, founded by Lord Buddha. Despite gaining the patronage of prominent rulers in the ancient period, Buddhism vanished from the Indian mainland starting in the medieval period.

As far as Buddhism is concerned, only some tribal groups came under its impact because adopting Buddhism demanded that they forfeit their culture completely, which is difficult because of the nature-man-spirit complex. Few tribes like the Bhotiya of the NW Himalayas, Lepchas, Chakmas, and Nagas of the NE, and some tribes of J&K, Ladakh and Arunachal came under their impact.

Tribes of Western Arunachal Pradesh inhabiting the highlands of Kameng, Subansiri, and Siang districts are followers of Mahayana Buddhism.

Khampti inhabiting the foothills of Lohit district follow the Hinayana version of Buddhism. Those who took to Buddhism maintained gompas, sacred places where images of Buddha are installed and holy books kept. One or more sacred specialists, known as lamas, are attached to the gompa. Almost every Khampti and Singhpo village has a monastery locally known as Bapuchang. Singhpo living as neighbours of Khamtis have followed them, and the majority of them accepted Hinayana Buddhism.

Buddhism also exists among Sherdukpens and Monpa, particularly Mahayana Buddhism, but they also worship their tribal deities. This shows that even the adoption of Buddhism could not cut through traditional beliefs and practises. Though Buddhism is gradually penetrating their society in the realm of ethics and social organisation, local little traditions are too deeply embedded to be given up easily.

Conclusion: Competition in the propagation of religion and faith in secular India has the dangerous potential of promoting the worst form of communalism. Let tribes enjoy their cultural autonomy, make their own decisions, and participate in the nation-building process as equal partners in progress, relating their self-respect and keeping their heads high.

Case Study

- **Tribals and Their Religion by VK Bahuguna**

In actuality, all Indians must have formerly belonged to one or more tribes; it is only the imbalanced modern evolution that currently distinguishes between tribal and non-tribal people. Unfortunately, the tribal and nontribal verbosity of our constitution is also a prison. The heated argument that tribals don't follow a particular religion is essentially proselytization-oriented, with churches in India spreading politically driven and foreignfunded propaganda. The Sanatana Dharma, or Hinduism as it is currently known, has all the components of tribal religion. In tribal communities, natural worship predominates in terms of divinity, and many Hindu traditions and holidays are influenced by them. Several politicians' claim that aboriginal people never practised organised religion does not hold water if we see the history of the country. The first organised census was conducted in 1871, and the first synchronised census was conducted in 1881. In these two censuses, 95% of the tribal population identified as Hindu. Due to interpretational prejudice during the census, just 2% of people from the North East declared a tribal religion. Only 3% of people were shown to practise a tribal religion in 1891, whereas the majority were Hindus. Christianity-related census data from 1891 was also gathered. Tribals who participated in the 1951 first census after gaining independence indicated their religion as Hinduism in 97–98% of cases. It wasn't until many years later, when Christian missionaries began winning over the tribal people in central and eastern India, that Hinduism's reverence for nature was methodically attempted to be separated from it. As shown in the rock sculptures, the Tripuri, Jamatias, and other tribes of Tripura have been worshipping Shiva. Similar to the Sarna approach to divinity, which regards all natural objects as sacred, it is centred on the adoration of nature and spiritual beings. Many tribal groups in Jharkhand and the surrounding states adhere to this religious system, which is completely reflected in their social and cultural lives. Due to the census staff's classification of such tribal beliefs as "other," the "other" category for religion in the census after independence led to this confusion. A few political elites are using well-planned propaganda to isolate the tribal community from the majority of Sanatana Dharma. Christian missionaries and the Naxalites are aiding and abetting this effort.

India is home to followers of all major religions in the world. Though the overwhelming majority of people still maintain their separate existence and their exclusive beliefs and practises, more than 90% of Indian tribes are oriented towards Hinduism and are passing through different stages of Hinduization. More than 90% of the tribal population of western, middle, central, and southern India is Hindu. The Hindu population is scattered all over the country. On a rough estimate, around 5% of tribal populations adhere to Christianity, which is largely concentrated in Assam, Meghalaya, Nagaland, Manipur, and Mizoram. Christian tribal populations are found in Kerala, A&N, M.P., Orissa, and Bihar. As far as Islam and Buddhism are concerned, followers of these faiths among tribals are around 0.21% and 0.89, respectively. Other religions beliefs hardly figure in tribal India, and their followers may be there in an insignificant and inconsiderable number. Siddhi's of Gujarat, Gujjars of N.W., Bakarwals of J&K, some parts of Bhils, Kotas, and Dhankasis are examples of Muslim tribes. Almost the entire population of Lakshadweep is Muslim, and this is the only place where they have any significant presence. The impact of Buddhism can be seen in Bhutiyas, Lepcha, Chakmas, some Nagas, and some tribes of the Arunachal and Ladakh regions.

8.2

Tribe and nation state—a comparative study of tribal communities in India and other countries.

Q 1. Tribe and Nation State–a comparative study of tribal communities in India and other countries

Ans. The nation-state is defined as an area where the cultural boundaries match up with the political boundaries. The ideal of a nation-state is that the state incorporates people of a "single ethnic" stock and cultural traditions. However, India is a multiethnic nation and a melting pot of numerous races and ethnic identities.

But at the same time, it is equally important that Indian ethnic groups, including many tribal groups, share a common history with different traditions and languages. While the socio-cultural mechanisms have kept them in contact, the contact on governance is only a post-independence phenomenon.

The first contact of the nation-state with tribal communities was not very encouraging. It led to the exploitation of tribals due to the continuation of colonial policies, and extra time was taken to change them. E.g., state reorganisation was delayed and kept for administrative convenience. It resulted in tribal movements in Chhattisgarh, Jharkhand, and some other parts of the North East. Also, conflicts and regionalism strengthened due to resource exploitation, increased problems in tribal life, etc.

But in the last 2–3 decades, significant results have been achieved by the implementation of PESA and the Forest Right Act (FRA) of 2006. Set up of a Ministry and National Commission for Schedule Tribes, thus providing control and an important say to tribals in governance and development. The 5th and 6th Schedules have provided strength to local tribal governance bodies.

Thus, the integration of tribals in the nation-state has again gained pace, and efforts are on to remove the distrust created in the tribals earlier. The issue of governance seems to have been settled in most of the tribal regions.

A Comparative Study of Tribal Communities in India and Other Countries:

India: In ancient times, various tribes were autonomous, but after colonisation, they were subjugated. After Independence, they were given constitutional protection in the form of the 5th and 6th Schedules, and they were also provided with many constitutional provisions. Many other programmes and schemes are launched for their development. But much more needs to be done for their development, as many tribes like Kuki, Naga, Bhil, Oraon, etc. revolted against the government in sites like Nagnd, Manipur, etc.

Erstwhile USSR: From the time of Lenin, various tribes like the Adyghe, Bashkirs, Chenchus, Khakas, Yakuts, etc., got reservations and better status in the country. However, later governments didn't pay special attention to their welfare, although some programmes were launched for their development. Thus, when their aspirations were not fulfilled, they revolted. For example, Khurds and Chechan revolted against the government for their various demands.

USA: Here the indigenous groups faced discrimination, large-scale killings and persecution, and racism. No right to vote was given to them until 1930. Many tribes, like the Red Indians and Zuni Indians, were kept in sanctuaries. The USA has taken "affirmative action" for indigenous groups via the

Declaration of Indian Rights, 1954. Affirmative action is defined as the practise of improving the educational and job opportunities of members of groups that have not been treated fairly in the past because of their race, sex, etc.

Almost similar action, i.e., "protective discrimination," is taken by the Indian Government for STs. Protective discrimination is the policy of granting special privileges to underprivileged sections of society and giving preferences in admission to public educational institutions and public employment to weaker sections of society.

But there are some similarities and dissimilarities between them, like:

Similarities: They provide support to the marginalised sections of society. They help to correct historical wrongs. They help to create confidence among these sections and improve their involvement in the nation.

Dissimilarities: while protective discrimination is given in the Constitution of India and institutionalised, no such provisions are given in the American Constitution. While protective discrimination is made to remove the high inequalities and caste hierarchies of the old Hindu religion, affirmative action is based on the unfair treatment expended by the white majority on other races and women.

Australia: Many tribes in Australia, like the Aruntas, Kareras, etc., also faced much discrimination in the past. Many were rejected from their lands by white settlers. They were exploited a lot, but now the government has taken many measures to improve their condition, like making multiculturalism the official policy since 1974.

South America: The rapid economic transformation of South American nation-states spells irreversible changes for the tribes. The Amazonian tribes, such as the Awa of Brazil and the Aymara of Chile, among several others, are being displaced due to major developmental projects and rapid deforestation in the Amazon basin. Meanwhile, tribes like the Mapuche in southern Chile, Huaorani in Ecuador and Maya in Central America have all been affected by decades of civil war, drug mafia, and international conflicts.

Africa and Saudi Arabia: The condition of tribes in Africa was not good during colonial rule. They faced many atrocities and remained as slaves. The hunting-gatherers, like the Bushmen of the Kalahari, the Batwa of Uganda, and the Ogiek of Kenya, are the most affected groups. They have lost their forestlands due to privatisation, mining projects, and the establishment of wildlife sanctuaries. Tribes like the Nuer and Dinka have been affected by perpetual civil war with the state and internal states.

Q 2. Indigenous people and UN Convention

Ans. There are over 476 million indigenous people living in 90 countries across the world, accounting for 6.2 percent of the global population. Of those, there are more than 5,000 distinct groups. Indigenous people speak an overwhelming majority of the world's estimated 7,000 languages. They are nearly three times as likely to be living in extreme poverty compared to their non-indigenous counterparts.

Indigenous peoples have in common a historical continuity with a given region prior to colonisation and a strong link to their lands. They maintain, at least in part, distinct social, economic, and political systems. They have distinct languages, cultures, beliefs, and knowledge systems. They are determined to maintain and develop their identity and distinct institutions, and they form a non-dominant sector of society.

The right to self-identification: The UN Declaration on the Rights of Indigenous Peoples does not include a definition of indigenous peoples. According to the Declaration, self-identification as indigenous is considered a fundamental criterion. The Declaration refers to their right to determine their own identity or membership in accordance with their customs and traditions.

Indigenous peoples face many challenges. These include:

1. Denial of their right to control their own development based on their own values, needs, and priorities
2. Lack of, or very poor, political representation
3. Lack of access to social services

Often, indigenous peoples are excluded or poorly represented in decision-making processes on matters that directly affect them and are not consulted about projects affecting their lands or the adoption of administrative or legislative measures that may affect them. Also, they are often displaced from their ancestral lands as a result of ventures such as the exploitation of natural resources.

Discrimination against Indigenous Peoples is racial discrimination.

The Committee on the Elimination of Racial Discrimination has made it clear that discrimination against indigenous peoples is racial discrimination. It has interpreted non-discrimination as the protection of aspects of indigenous cultural identity and language and the offer of economic and social development, effective participation, and rights over lands, territories, and resources.

The United Nations has highlighted the problem of discrimination against indigenous peoples since the first Decade to Combat Racism and Racial Discrimination in 1973–1982. This concern led to the establishment in 1982 of the United Nations Working Group on Indigenous Populations, which articulated their needs and aspirations in the landmark Declaration on the Rights of Indigenous Peoples adopted in September 2007 by the UN General Assembly.

Durban Declaration and Programme of Action: The Durban Declaration of 2001 acknowledges the basic human rights and fundamental freedoms of indigenous peoples. It emphasises, among other things:

1. The right of indigenous peoples to be free and equal
2. The right to self-determination and to freely determine their political status and freely pursue their economic, social, and cultural development
3. The right to practise and revitalise their cultural traditions and customs
4. The right to establish and control their educational systems
5. The right to participate fully at all levels of decision-making in matters that may affect their rights, lives, and destinies
6. The right to their lands, territories, and resources
7. The right to be secure in the enjoyment of their own means of subsistence and development

Despite the progress that has been made, achieving significant recognition of and improvements in the human rights of peoples who have endured centuries of exploitation and marginalisation remains a tremendous challenge for governments and the United Nations system.

Case Study

- **Hadzabe Tribe**

A hunter-gatherer tribe in Tanzania with a 40,000-year history acquires legal control over their ancestral territories, giving them the ability to defend their forests against farmers and herders attempting to destroy the land. Since then, deforestation in the core Hadzabe territory has decreased while significantly increasing in the surrounding area. African wild dogs, lions, leopards, and endangered elephant populations have all increased, and the Hadzabe have made over US$450,000 from trading carbon offsets. The Hadzabe UNDP Equator Prize, which honours indigenous peoples' efforts to eliminate poverty through the conservation and sustainable use of biodiversity, was given in recognition of this outstanding advancement.

Q 3. Indian Tribal Case studies

Ans. **Bhil:** The Bhil are one of the largest tribal groups, living in Chhattisgarh, Gujarat, Karnataka, Madhya Pradesh, Maharashtra, Andhra Pradesh, and Rajasthan. The name is derived from the word 'billu', which means bow. The Bhil are known to be excellent archers, coupled with deep knowledge about their local geography. Traditionally, experts in guerrilla warfare were mostly farmers and agricultural labourers. They are also skilled sculptors. Bhil has traditional medical specialists: Budwa (Shaman), Huvarki (traditional birth attendant), Vaidu (herbalist), and Had Vaidu (bone setter), with some communities having male midwives. Bhil women wear traditional saris, while men are dressed in long frocks and pyjamas. The woman put on heavy ornaments made of silver and brass, along with rosaries of beads, silver coins, and earrings.

Munda: Munda are a tribe belonging to the Chotanagpur plateau, spread across Jharkhand, Chhattisgarh, Madhya Pradesh, Odisha, Tripura, and West Bengal. A Munda is defined by his or her surname, which is based on natural elements such as trees, animals, and birds.

Mundas are fond of dance and music; their songs evoke nature in all its glory. Nupur (an anklet) is a special dance form that involves wearing a nupur on the ankles and dancing in chorus. They observe many festivals, the most important being Magha or Ba, a Thanksgiving festival celebrated in spring. Since ancient times, the Munda have been wanderers and hunters; more recently, they have become cultivators. Buried ancestors are treated as guardian spirits of the 'khunt," or genealogical family, symbolised by the sasandiri, the burial stone.

Baiga: The Baiga, meaning sorcerers, are one of the particularly vulnerable tribal groups (PVTGs) and are spread across Chhattisgarh, Jharkhand, Bihar, Odisha, West Bengal, Madhya Pradesh, and Uttar Pradesh. Traditionally, the Baiga lived a semi-nomadic life and practised slash-and-burn cultivation. Now, they are mainly dependent on minor forest products for their livelihood.

Bamboo is the primary resource that they use to build houses as well as household items such as fans and baskets. Known for collecting honey using traditional techniques, the Baiga also have an in-depth knowledge of folk medicine. They have a rich cultural heritage with unique styles of music, dance, and dance dramas. After a death in the family, the Baiga just leave the house and build another. Tattooing is an integral part of Baiga culture—every age and body part has a specific tattoo reserved for the occasion.

Kokna: The Kokna are a major tribe found in Gujarat, Maharashtra, Karnataka, Rajasthan, Dadra, and Nagar Haveli. According to anthropologists, the ancestors of the Kokna tribe were the primary inhabitants of the Konkan region, and it is from their ancient dialects that the present-day Konkani language has evolved. The Kokna are known for making masks, bamboo, wooden crafts, brass, and copper motifs. Kokna artists can craft ordinary wooden tobacco containers into beautiful works of art. The tribe celebrates Bohada, the famous festival of masks, which is a combination of dance and drama, during March and April. Various facial expressions are intricately highlighted in the masks. The Kokna have their own traditional panchayat that solves disputes and conflicts within the community.

Madia: The Madia live in Chhattisgarh, Maharashtra, Madhya Pradesh, and Odisha. There are two major groups: the Bada Madia, mostly concentrated in the dense forest around the Laheri hills, and the Chota Madia, which lives on plains. They are primarily a hunting-gathering tribe. The Madia are skilled in bamboo and take special care while cutting so as not to damage the roots. Every Madia village has a ghotul (youth dormitory), where young boys and girls learn various life skills and several aspects of their culture, including song, dance, and playing musical instruments. When a Madia man is engaged, he must carve a Mundha, a decorative wooden pillar to be kept in front of the ghotul during his marriage ceremony. The Mundha is perhaps the most superior example of skill in wood carving.

Santhal: The Santhal are the largest and one of the oldest tribes in India. They are spread across Assam, Bihar, Chhattisgarh, Jharkhand, Odisha, and West Bengal. From time immemorial, they have cleared forests, tilled the land, and produced food for subsistence. They are also well-versed in the arts of hunting and sericulture. The Santhal system of governance, known as Manjhi-Paragana, can be compared to local self-governance. Panchayats are a common feature, with clusters of 50–200 villages forming mega panchayats.

Dancing and singing as a group are integral parts of Santhal culture. One of the most studied tribal religions in the country, the Santhals worship Marang Buru or Bonga as their supreme deity. The weight of belief, however, falls on a court of spirits (Bonga), who are believed to handle different aspects of the world and who must be placated with prayers and offerings in order to ward off evil. A characteristic feature of the Santhal village is a sacred grove on the edge of the settlement, considered the home of spirits.

Warli: The Warli are spread across Thane, Nashik, and Dhule districts of Maharashtra, Valsad district of Gujarat, Karnataka, Goa, and the Union territories of Dadra and Nagar Haveli and Daman and Diu. The Warli are small-scale cultivators and cultivate rice, pulses, and vegetables. They also sell toddy, mahua, and fuel wood to their tribesmen and neighbouring communities for a living. Warli are nature worshippers. Warli art stems from their belief system, shaped by their centuries-old subsistence on forest land. The Warli did not have a written word until recent times, and their art was a way of transmitting their belief systems from one generation to the next. Their drawings revolve around community traditions, the tools they use, and their association with nature.

Birhor: The Birhor are a nomadic hunting-gathering tribe found in Jharkhand and neighbouring areas of Chhattisgarh, West Bengal, Odisha, Bihar, and Madhya Pradesh. They have been classified as a particularly vulnerable tribal group. Tribe members practise shifting cultivation. Birhor live in small settlements called *tanda* at the edge of the forest. Expert hunters use nets and snares to catch small animals and birds. Nets made of strong fibre spread from tree to tree are used to trap monkeys. They also collect honey. The practise of bartering still exists. The Birhor religion presents a mixture of animism, animatism, naturalism, worship, and belief in spirits.

Abhuj Maria: Abhuj Maria lives a life of isolation from the outside world. A subtribe of the Gond, they can be found in the secluded enclaves of Narayanpur tehsil in Bastar, Chhattisgarh. They are one of the few tribes that have managed to keep their quintessential culture alive. Members of the tribe love to adorn themselves with multiple iron rings strung around their necks. The Abhuj Maria are mainly slash-and-burn cultivators, though they also practise some form of settled cultivation. Korsa, kolha (types of millets), and rice are their main outputs. The tribe's main festival is Kaksar, which is celebrated in June. The other important festival is Kudin, which is marked to honour the clan gods before the beginning of the harvest season.

Gond: Gonds, one of the largest tribal groups in the world, are mostly found in Chhindwara district of Madhya Pradesh, Bastar district of Chhattisgarh, and parts of Maharashtra, Andhra Pradesh, Gujarat, Jharkhand, Karnataka, Telangana, Uttar Pradesh, West Bengal, and Odisha. Gonds are subdivided into four tribes: Raj Gonds, Madia Gonds, Dhurve Gonds, and Khatulwar Gonds. Their staple foods are two kinds of millet: kodo and kutki. Rice is mostly consumed during festival feasts. Gonds believe that earth, water, and air are ruled by gods.

Apatani: The Apatanis of Arunachal Pradesh donned nose plugs and tattoos on their faces. While one theory says that women wore them to make themselves less attractive to abductors, another says it helped them find a husband. The people of the Apatani group from Arunachal Pradesh collectively work on each other's farms and help each other out. The wastewater from farms is collected in a pond and used for farm fishing. Abundance reflects itself in many spheres of their lives.

Konyak: Konyaks are an isolated ethnic group of headhunters that reside in the interiors of Nagaland. Their stories are like the modern-day Mahabharata and Ramayana. Konyaks were known to rip heads off when they attacked villages of rival tribes. Those who came back with their heads intact were considered warriors. It was believed that headhunting brought prosperity and benefits to their farm yield.

Drokpas: The Drokpas of Ladakh sported goatskin capes, hand-made beaded and oxidised silver jewellery, and headgear adorned with flowers to attract men. Although not in practise anymore, the community traditionally engaged in wifeswapping. Public displays of affection were encouraged in the community. They lived a freer life as compared to many other tribes. The members of the community are believed to be descendants of Alexander the Great's army. From zero-waste practises to a strong sense of community, the sustainable way of life has been practised by them for years now. Technology, digitization, and westernisation, however, are changing many important aspects of these groups, from their dressing and food habits to traditions passed down through generations. Even in the remotest areas, people have access to mobile phones, the Internet, and televisions, he points out.

Case Study

- **Who are the Hakki Pikki ?**

More than 181 members of the Hakki Pikki tribal community from Karnataka were stuck in violence-hit Sudan. Who are the Hakki Pikki, and why did so many travel to far-away Sudan?

The Hakki Pikki is a tribe that lives in several states in west and south India, especially near forest areas. Hakki Pikkis (Hakki in Kannada means 'bird' and Pikki means 'catchers') are a semi-nomadic tribe, traditionally of bird catchers and hunters.

According to the 2011 census, the Hakki Pikki population in Karnataka is 11,892, and they live primarily in Davangere, Mysuru, Kolar, Hassan, and Shivmogga districts. In different regions, they are known by different names, such as Mel-Shikari in northern Karnataka and Maharashtra.

Mr. Gangadhar, Vice Chancellor of Chamarajanagar University and an anthropologist who has conducted a study on the tribe, said, "The Hakki Pikki move in groups from place to place in search of livelihood. They are divided into four clans, called Gujaratia, Panwar, Kaliwala, and Mewaras. These clans can be equated with castes in traditional Hindu society. In the olden days, there was a hierarchy among the clans, with the Gujaratia at the top and the Mewaras at the bottom. The forest is the main natural resource of the Hakki Pikki."

- **Where do they live?**

The Hakki Pikki people are believed to hail originally from the bordering districts of Gujarat and Rajasthan. According to Gangadhar, they came to the south in search of game. "To Karnataka, they seem to have arrived via Andhra Pradesh, as they still remember a place called Jalapally near Hyderabad as their ancestral home, where their forefathers lived for a considerable period. They are now spread across south India," he said.

Till a few years ago, women used to wear the ghagra (skirt) common in Rajasthan, although now they wear saris and other garments.

9

Tribal Administration and the Role of Anthropology in Tribal Development, Rural Development, and Various Movements

9.1

History of administration of tribal areas, tribal policies, plans, programmes of tribal development and their implementation. The concept of PTGs (Primitive Tribal Groups), their distribution, special programmes for their development. Role of N.G.O.s in tribal development.

Q 1. History of Tribal Administration

Ans. The history of tribal administration is divided into two phases: before 1947 and after 1947.

Before 1947: British administrators were the first to try to grapple with the problem of administrative tribal areas. The British did come into contact with the tribes during their efforts to consolidate the Indian Empire. The Britishers did everything to ensure that the tribes remained isolated from the rest of the Indian masses because they realised the potentiality of Indian tribes as explosive forces in any national movement. Thus, the tribals were isolated, and their places of habitation were declared prohibited areas.

The first serious attempt made by the British rulers in India to deal with the tribes was in connection with the Paharias, or Malers, of Rajmahal Hills, who had risen in revolt against the Hindu zamindars. They were at first subdued in a clash of arms, but soon after, a policy of pacification was decided upon. Bribes were paid under the name of pensions to the tribal leaders, and they were asked to report all outbreaks. At the foot of the hills, lands were granted to retired or disabled soldiers, and thus a ring-fence of military-minded people was created around the Paharias. Afterwards, in 1782, on the recommendation of *Cleveland*, this tribal tract was withdrawn from the jurisdiction of the ordinary courts, and the local courts, comprising local leaders, were set up, and these courts were given civil and penal jurisdiction over the Hill tract. These courts collectively came to be known as the Hill Assembly, and they had the power to inflict even capital punishment.

Having achieved the objective of internal justice and peace through the creation of the Hill Assembly, Cleve Land tried to solve another important problem: the problem of encroachments by non-tribals. The lands held by the Paharias were formed into government estates, held by them directly from the government and free from rent. This whole tract came to be known as "Daman-i-koh". In this way, the problematic Paharias or Malers were pacified, and all the rules were made in Law and Regulation I of 1796. With the passage of time, the prestige of the Hill

Assembly dwindled, and Regulation I of 1796 was replaced by Regulation I of 1827, which brought the Paharia and other adjacent tribes under the partial jurisdiction of ordinary courts. At this stage, some other tribal groups also rebelled. In this context, such uprisings as the Ho mutiny of Singbhum in 1831, the Kond uprising of 1846, and the Santhal rebellion of 1855 are worth mentioning. The main causes of these uprisings and disturbances were almost always the same, *i.e.,* the deep resentment and dissatisfaction created as a result of exploitation by non-tribals.

The concept of the Inner Line Permit comes from the colonial area. Under the Bengal Eastern Frontier Regulation Act, 1873, the British framed regulations restricting the entry and regulating the stay of outsiders in designated areas. The ILP system is in force in four Northeastern states — Arunachal Pradesh, Nagaland, Mizoram and now Manipur — and no Indian citizen can visit any of these states without permit unless he or she belongs to that state, nor can he or she overstay beyond the period specified in the ILP this stage, the idea that distinct and special arrangements were necessary for isolated tribal regions gained acceptance. Thus, the British government finally decided on a policy of segregating the tribes into special areas where their lives could be adequately protected. Keeping this purpose in mind, an Act was passed in 1874 to specify tribal areas into Scheduled Districts. This act provided for the appointment of special officers to administer civil and criminal justice, to superintend the settlement and collection of public revenue and matters relating to rent, and to conduct the administration within the Scheduled Districts. It also provided for the extension, by notification, in Scheduled Districts of laws enforced in any part of British India with such special restrictions and modifications as were deemed fit. These areas were reconstituted under Section 52A of the Government of India Act of 1919. Tribal areas covered under the Scheduled District Act were removed from the purview of the legislature. These areas were divided into two categories: (i) wholly excluded areas and (ii) areas of modified exclusion. But the limits of exclusion differed in extent and degree. Under the Government of India Act, 1935, these areas were declared “excluded areas” and “partially excluded areas”.

The Government of India Act, 1935, provided that no act of the Federal Legislature or the Provincial Legislature would apply to these areas except on the direction of the Governor, who was empowered to make such exceptions and modifications as he considered necessary. It also enabled the governor to make regulations for the peace and good governance of the areas. Reservation of seats for tribal areas was also made in the local legislatures of Madras, Bombay, Bihar, the Central Provinces, Assam, and Orissa. This policy remained in existence until 1947.

After 1947: After independence, the nation witnessed a considerable awakening about the welfare of the tribal people. In order to promote the integration of the tribal people with the rest of India, the Constitution provided special safeguards for the tribal communities for a period of 10 years. This has continued to be extended until now.

A Tribal Welfare Department was set up in 1951 for the protection and advancement of tribal, and with the help of various provisions of the Constitution, a new line of administration was chalked out.

Articles 244 and 244(A) under Part X of the Constitution provide for the administration of scheduled areas and tribal areas. The Scheduled Areas are governed by the provisions contained in the Fifth Schedule, and the Tribal Areas are governed by the provisions of the Sixth Schedule.

Administration of Scheduled Areas: Since Independence, the President has issued two orders, i.e., the Scheduled Areas (Part A States) Order 1950. These orders declared certain tribal areas as Scheduled Areas in the States of Andhra Pradesh, Bihar, Gujarat, Madhya Pradesh, Maharashtra, Orissa, Rajasthan, and Himachal Pradesh.

The Scheduled Areas have been constituted with the following two clear objectives:

- To assist the tribals in enjoying their existing rights without any hindrance from others.
- To develop the scheduled areas and protect and promote the interests of the scheduled tribes.

The Scheduled Areas are administered under the Fifth Schedule of the Constitution. The main features of the Fifth Schedule are: Special Legislative Powers of the Governor, the Governor's Report to the President, and the Tribal Advisory Council.

Sixth Schedule: It applies to tribal areas within the states of Assam, Meghalaya, Mizoram, and Tripura. The tribal areas have been defined under the Sixth Schedule and cover only those areas that are specified in that schedule. The Parliament may, by law, make changes in the areas included in this schedule.

Tribal areas enjoy full autonomy in respect of matters falling within their jurisdiction. These areas may be called "states within a state." It provided the tribal people with the power of self-management through autonomous districts and autonomous regions.

Role of the Traditional Tribal Council and the advent of Panchayati Raj: The institution of the Traditional Tribal Council is as old as tribal society. Decisions of councils on social, religious, and economic matters are law to tribals because they are based on their social customs and religious rites.

The introduction of the statutory panchayati system has weakened traditional tribal councils, but these statutory panchayats have adopted all the functions of traditional tribal councils with the added responsibility of implementing developmental works.

The 1961 Report of the Scheduled Area and Scheduled Tribes Commission remarks that the foundation of tribal life should not be destroyed. The traditional tribal councils should not disappear. They should be revised where they are weak and encouraged where they are strong.

Case Study

- **Adivasis, the Fifth Schedule, and Urban Development: A Study of Greater Ranchi by Aashish Khakha**

The Indian Constitution's Fifth Schedule was formed for the specific management of tribal territories to avoid land alienation through land transfer regulation, where no land or immovable property in these areas can be transferred by way of sale or lease to individuals other than the tribals or Adivasis. However, when state-led urban development projects are carried out in Jharkhand, a state that is included in the Fifth Scheduled Area, one finds a flagrant violation of not only the Fifth Schedule of the Constitution but also of historical laws like the Chhotanagpur Tenancy (CNT) Act (1908). The construction of Greater Ranchi, Jharkhand's new capital township, is one such example of progress. On former Heavy Engineering Corporation Limited (HECL) land in the Dhurwa neighbourhood, this township is being constructed on the outskirts of the city. After displacing the local Adivasi population, the state donated this land to the business.

Q 2. Fifth Schedule

Ans. Since Independence, the President has issued two orders, *i.e.,* Scheduled Areas (Part A States) Order 1950. These orders declared certain tribal areas as Scheduled Areas in the States of Andhra Pradesh, Bihar, Gujarat, Madhya Pradesh, Maharashtra, Orissa, Rajasthan, and Himachal Pradesh.

The Scheduled Areas have been constituted with the following two clear objectives:

- To assist the tribals in enjoying their existing rights without any hindrance from others.
- To develop the scheduled areas and protect and promote the interests of the scheduled tribes.

The Scheduled Areas are administered under the Fifth Schedule of the Constitution. The main features of the Fifth Schedule are the Special Legislative Powers of the Governor, the Governor's Report to the President, and the Tribes Advisory Council.

(a) Special Legislative Powers of the Governor: The Governor of a State having Scheduled Areas has been vested with special legislative powers in two ways: (i) Legislation by notification, and (ii) Legislation by regulation.

Legislation by notification: The Governor of a State having Scheduled Areas is responsible for deciding whether an Act of Parliament or of the State Legislature is suitable or unsuitable for Scheduled Areas. He may withhold or modify the application of the law that is not suitable for such areas. The notification can be issued by the governor without any reference either to the Tribal Advisory Council or to the President.

Legislation by Regulation: The Governor has been empowered to make regulations for peace and good government in Scheduled Areas. Such regulations may, in particular:

i) Prohibit or restrict the transfer of Scheduled Area land by or among members of the tribes or STs.
ii) Regulate the allotment of Scheduled Area land to members of the tribes or STs.
iii) Regulate the carrying on of the business of moneylenders by persons who lend money to the members of the tribes or STs in such Scheduled Areas.

The regulation-making power of the Governor for peace and good government in the Scheduled Area shows the concern of the framers of the Constitution to protect the interests of the tribals in land and against exploitation by moneylenders. The regulation-making power of the Governor is subject to the following two limitations:

- Such a regulation should be based on the previous consultation of the Tribal Advisory Council.
- Regulations should be submitted to the President and shall not have effect until assent is given by him.

(b) Governor's Report: The Union Government has been made responsible for providing guidance for the administration of the Scheduled Areas. The Fifth Schedule lays down mechanisms for keeping the Union Government informed of the situation in tribal areas. It provided that the Governor of each state having Scheduled Areas is required to submit to the President of India an annual report or a report at such intervals as may be required by the Union Government. The submission of the report by the Governor is intended to enable the Union Government to decide how best it can discharge its responsibility towards the tribes. On this basis, the Union Government may issue directives to the State for better administration of the Scheduled Areas.

(c) Tribal Advisory Council: Clause 4 of the Fifth Schedule of the Constitution provided for Tribal Advisory Councils (TAC) in each state having Scheduled Areas. Besides, if the President so directs, it may also be established in states that do not have scheduled areas. The councils have been established in all the eight states of Andhra Pradesh, Bihar, M.P., Maharashtra, Gujarat, H.P., Rajasthan, and Orissa, which have scheduled areas. In addition, tribal advisory councils have also been established in two states that do not have scheduled areas, namely, Tamil Nadu and West Bengal.

The Tribal Advisory Council consists of no more than 20 members. Of these, three-fourths should be the representatives of the STs in the legislative assembly of the state. In the event that the number of representatives of the STs in the assembly of the state is less than the number of seats in the Tribal Advisory Council, the remaining seats shall be filled by other members of the tribes in the state. Governors are required to make rules prescribing the mode of appointment of members to the Council and its workings, etc. In all states, these councils are headed by the chief ministers. The Fifth Schedule provides that it shall be the duty of the Tribal Advisory Council to advice on such matters pertaining to the welfare and advancement of the tribes and STs in the state as may be referred to them by the Governor. The introduction of PRIs has weakened the traditional tribal councils in some places.

However, in practise, the Xaxa Committee points out a number of contradictions with the spirit of these constitutional provisions:

1. Irregularity of Submission of Report: According to the Bhuria Committee Report (2002–2004), the States of Andhra Pradesh sent the report of 1994–2000 at the time of report writing. The Ministry of Tribal Affairs Report 2013 points out that except Gujarat, no other state has submitted its report for that year.
2. The committee observes that reports are depletive, casually and haphazardly constructed, and tend to heavily borrow from reports of the tribal welfare department.
3. Governors exercise discretionary powers under the Fifth Schedule only on the advice of the Council of Ministers, killing the responsibility given to them.
4. A detailed study of the minutes of the meetings of the tribes of the Tribal Advisory Council by the Asian Indigenous and Tribal People Network reveals that the meetings of the council are tokenistic and critical issues are rarely discussed.
5. The members of the TAC have few powers, even in terms of what can be discussed at council meetings. For instance, the Chhattisgarh TAC rules state that no issues can be discussed in the meeting unless notified.
6. Even when issues are taken up by TAC, it has been noted that there is rarely any sustained and consistent engagement.

Mungekar Committee recommendation for Schedule Area:

1. There is a need to stop the practise of routinely extending all laws to Schedule areas without consciously adapting laws to Schedule areas.
2. In-depth situational analysis of the problem of unrest in Schedule Areas, thereby covering all its facets with a response strategy.
3. The Office of the Governor in Schedule Area should have a separate, well-staffed, and well-equipped office to take care of ST matters.
4. All tribal left-out areas must be brought under the 5th Schedule within 2 years.
5. Governor Report: The government report should present an overall assessment of the tribal situation in the state with special reference to weak spots and corrective action and discontinue the present practise of being a routine exercise that too not every year.

Bhuria Committee Recommendation for Schedule Area:

6. The report of the governor should be forwarded directly to the president instead of to the Ministry of Tribal Affairs and within the specified time limit.
7. A tribal subplan was placed before the tribal advisory council.
8. Institutional buildup, like the legal cell set up in the Tribal Development Department to appraise the impact of legislation on tribal.

Q 3. Sixth Schedule

Ans. The Sixth Schedule applies to tribal areas within the states of Assam, Meghalaya, Mizoram, and Tripura. The tribal areas have been defined under the Sixth Schedule and cover only those areas that are specified in that schedule. The Parliament may, by law, make changes in the areas included in this schedule.

Tribal areas enjoy full autonomy in respect of matters falling within their jurisdiction. These areas may be called "states within a state." It provided the tribal power of self-management through autonomous districts and autonomous regions. The writ of the Parliament or the State Legislature does not run automatically unless extended to the tribal areas by notification of the Governor.

Autonomous Districts and Autonomous Regions:

Part I:

- North Cachar Hills District.
- Karbi Anglong District
- Bodoland Area District.

Part IIa:

- Tripura Tribal Areas District

Part II:

- Khasi Hill District.
- Jaintia Hill District.
- Garo Hill District.

Part III:

- Chakma District
- Maua District
- Lai District

Each autonomous district has a district council for its administration. A district council consists of no more than 30 members. Of these, not more than four members are nominated by the governor, and the rest are elected on the basis of adult suffrage. The District Council consists of territorial constituencies, and each of them is a single-member constituency. The governor may fix the total number of members of the council. He may reserve all the constituencies for the tribals and bar the non-tribals from contesting the elections in such areas.

Powers of the District Councils and Regional Councils: District Councils and Regional Councils shall have the power, with respect to all areas under their respective jurisdiction, to make laws with respect to the following subjects:

1. the allotment, occupation, or use of land other than any land that is a reserve forest;
2. the management of any forest that is not a reserve forest;
3. the regulation of the practise of shifting cultivation;
4. the establishment of village or town committees;
5. any other matter relating to village or town administration;
6. appointment or succession of chiefs or headsmen;
7. the inheritance of property;
8. marriage, divorce, and
9. social customs.

All laws so made shall be submitted to the Governor, and until assented to by him, they shall have no effect. The autonomous District Councils and Regional Councils, in respect of areas under their control, may constitute Village Courts for the trial of cases between parties belonging to Schedule Tribes within their respective areas. The councils will administer justice under the All-India Civil and Penal Codes, modified by local customs.

The District Council may establish, construct, and manage primary schools, dispensaries, markets, cattle ponds, roads, road transport, and waterways in the district.

The governor enjoys a unique position in relation to autonomous districts. Broadly speaking, his position may be equated to that of the presidents in relation to states.

Each district and regional council shall have their own fund. All money received shall be credited to that fund. The governor may make rules for the management of the fund. These councils shall have the power to assess and collect revenue with respect to lands under their control in accordance with the principles followed by the government of the state. The councils shall have power to levy and collect all or any of the following taxes within their jurisdiction:

1. taxes on professions, trades, etc.
2. taxes on animals, vehicles, and boats,
3. taxes on the entry of goods into a market for sale,
4. taxes for the maintenance of schools, dispensaries, and roads.

The District Council may make regulations for the regulation and control of money-lending or trading within the district by persons other than STs residing in the district.

The Governor may at any time appoint a commission to report on the work of these councils. He is also empowered to annul or suspend the councils whenever he is satisfied that their activities are likely to endanger the safety of India.

However, the Xaxa Committee observes contradictions in the spirit of those constitutional provisions:

1. In many cases, the state government functions through the council, particularly through the blocking of funds. The powers and responsibilities given to them have not materialised into financial autonomy.
2. The autonomy of autonomous district councils is restricted in several respects. For example, in Meghalaya, the autonomy of the ADC is curtailed in Section 12A, which states that the state government has precedence over those passed by councils.
3. Considerable powers have been handed over to the governor, like deciding whether laws made by the state legislature are applicable to the autonomous district or not. The governor also has the power to dissolve the autonomous district.
4. There is a significant degree of variation in the functions delegated to various autonomous councils. For instance, the Bodoland Traditional Council has more power than others. It resulted in other areas demanding more power.
5. There is no mandatory time limit for the reconstitution of the ADC once it is dissolved, and hence its location can be postponed indefinitely.
6. Minority groups are not adequately represented in the ADC. Even those groups that are indigenous to the region, such as smaller tribal groups, do not have any representation.

The Xaxa Committee has recommended rectifying these anomalies:

1. Autonomous councils must be covered under the State Finance Commission, which is empowered to periodically review financial positions and lays down principles of resource devolution.
2. ADC should be reconstituted within 6 months after dissolution.
3. There should be provisions for the representation of minority groups.
4. Traditional political institutions in the village hamlet should be formally recognised by the state.
5. Extend the 6th Schedule pattern to 5th Schedule areas.

B.D. Sharma, in his book "Tribal Affairs in India," illustrated the need for better implementation of the 6 th Schedule.

Q 4. Approaches for Tribal Development

Ans. For long periods, there was frictionless co-existence between tribal folks and Hindu caste society in the true sense of the word (Haimendorf). But the physical isolation of most aboriginal tribes came to an end when modern means of communication like roads and railways were introduced in the early 20th century, coupled with the sudden growth of the Indian population.

D.N. Majumdar, commenting on the lives and deaths of many primitive tribes in India, has enumerated causes like:

1. Tribal land used for shifting cultivation has been taken away.
2. Quarrying in bid-owned land is not allowed except with payment of a licence fee.
3. Capture marriage is an offence under the IPC.
4. A new market concept affected tribal financially.
5. Judicial officer not able to give satisfactory justice.
6. Modern education has caused more harm.

7. Missionary efforts demeaned their own culture.
8. Contact based diseases for which they don't have indigenous pharma.

S.C. Dube presented four main approaches to tribal development as: (i) political; (ii) religious; (iii) voluntary agencies; (iv) anthropological; while *L.P. Vidyarthi* has differentiated the political from the administrative approach.

Political Approach: The political approach to tribal welfare may be understood in the context of the pre-independence and postindependence periods. The creation of 'excluded' and 'partially excluded areas' resulted in separate political representation for tribal. The main policy was isolationism during colonial rule.

The post-independence period has given rise to several protective, relief, and development measures. These measures initiated a programme to bring tribals into the national mainstream, whereas the most desirable course would be to work for the integration of tribals in regional and national settings.

Administrative Approach: The Tribal Development Administration has been criticised because:

(i) There is a lack of common goals in government sectors, which leads to coordination problems among various development programmes.
(ii) Ignorance of administrators regarding tribal ways
(iii) Lack of understanding between social scientists and administrators

There is a need to make tribal administration better adapted to the environment of tribal culture. Integration can be developed only through building up a spirit of teamwork and a high level of morale through democratic leadership on the part of the administration.

Religious Approach: Many religious agencies (Christian missionaries, Arya Samaj, Rama Krishna Mission, etc.) are engaged in work for tribal welfare in different parts of the country.

Elwin comments that the missionaries are anxious to see primitives transformed, their inferior social customs and ideas eliminated, and their identity assimilated into the Christian Church.

K.N. Sahey corroborates that because of their feeling of cultural and religious superiority, they are responsible for disturbing tribal cultural integration and inculcating a feeling of inferiority in Adivasi. This resulted in a rift between Christian and non-Christian tribal groups.

Voluntary Agencies Approach: In post-independence, voluntary social service organisations (Bhartiya Adimjati Sewak Sangh, Bhartiya Depressed Classes League, All India Backward Classes Federation, etc.) have done considerable humanitarian work in tribal areas, but often their spirit of service was not matched by their understanding of tribal problems. They sometimes went into tribal areas with ready-made solutions. They failed to realise that well-intentioned reforms may be injurious to tribes in terms of socio-cultural life (L.P. Vidyarthi).

➢ **Anthropological Approach:** A sector of politicians and social workers has labelled anthropologists as isolationists. Elwin's concept of creating "ethnological parks" for tribals was most often misunderstood. Actually, there is not one anthropological approach, but many, and instead of offering ready-made solutions, anthropologists think of possible solutions.

According to B.K. Roy Burman, welfare and development activities should be concerned with:

➢ Satisfy minimum needs
➢ Control and management of productive resources
➢ Employment optimised

- Broad-based participation of the population in the development process
- Socio-cultural and political aspects of national integration

Conclusion: In the words of B.D. Sharma, approach, first and foremost, it requires an empathetic and willing bureaucracy. If we are to achieve true tribal development, we must redefine our model of development. Otherwise, the wheels of development will break sooner rather than later.

Q 5. Policies for Tribal Development

Ans. The Constitution of India states, "The State shall still promote with special care the educational and economic interests of weaker sections of the population, in particular SC and ST, and shall protect them from social injustice and all forms of exploitation" under Article 46.

However, different policies have been put forward for tribal development, as follows:

i. **Policy of Isolation:** The British Indian Government and Administration followed the policy of segregation, in which specific permissions are needed from the administration for entire tribal areas. The policy of isolation resulted in a lack of communication, hampering the task of development. Even in the postindependence period, the policy of segregation continued for a while. Verrier Elwin, advisor in tribal affairs to the Government of Assam, recommended the isolation of tribals in certain extreme cases. The step was taken to avoid the exploitation of tribal people, which somehow resulted in this segregation.

However, tribes have been living in complete isolation since ancient times, but they had physical proximity and cultural contact with neighbouring communities. However, there was no external pressure to get assimilated or to get isolated.

As pointed out by Elwin, isolation may be good for protecting tribal culture. However, he failed to understand that it is not the solution to tribal problems. If isolated, they can never participate in national development roles, nor can they share the fruits of development.

Thakkar Bappa criticised the idea that isolationist-policy anthropologists want tribals as specimens by keeping them isolated.

ii. **Policy of Assimilation:** Another approach to tribal development is the assimilation of the tribal population with the rest. It is a continuous process, and the main reason has been cultural contacts with the neighbour. Some have converted to Hinduism, some have adopted Christianity, and a few others have embraced Islam. This policy is promoted by the religious approach and the voluntary agency approach. Dube has given a five-fold classification:

1. Aboriginals living in seclusion
2. Tribal groups with some village folk associations
3. Tribals living in mixed villages
4. Tribals are forced to live as untouchables.
5. Tribals enjoy high status.

The above classification keeps different tribes at different levels in the scale of the tribe-caste continuum, a concept given by F.G. Bailey.

Ghurye has called them "backward Hindus. For a large tribe, some sections have been assimilated into the Hindu fold, while a major chunk remains tribal.

The policy of assimilation would result in the assimilation of tribals into the neighbouring mainstream, resulting in their losing their own cultural identity and assimilation. It will also limit confrontations with neighbouring communities.

However, to compel tribal people to get assimilated into the majority population would be a violation of human rights as well as the constitutional spirit, which guarantees every community the right to maintain their culture, language, and traditions.

(iii) Policy of Integration: J.L. Nehru, along with V. Elwin, initiated the integration approach in 1958 and gave the concept of Tribal Panchsheel, which has five fundamental principles for tribal development as follows:

1. People should develop along the lines of their own genius, and we should avoid imposing anything on them. We should try in every way to encourage and promote their traditional art and culture. E.g., the Jarawa tribe, due to tourist encroachment, is facing the spread of infections and diseases.
2. Tribal rights to land and forests should be respected. e.g., the Vedanta Project, opposed by the Dongria Kond tribe.
3. We should try to train and build up a team of their own people to do the work of administration and development. Some technical personnel from outside will no doubt be needed, especially in the beginning. But we should avoid introducing too many outsiders into tribal territories. E.g., along with using modern medicine, the help of shamans must be sought.
4. We should not overadministrate these areas or overwhelm them with a multiplicity of schemes. We should rather work through and not in rivalry with their social and cultural institutions. E.g., while introducing modern democratic institutions, traditional tribal leadership should be taken into confidence.
5. We should judge results not by statistics or the amount of money spent but by the quality of human characters that are evolving. e.g., how much literacy and nutritional status improved rather than focusing on the amount of money spent.

The policy of integration not only upholds the constitutional spirit but also includes tribal communities in the stream of development without impeding on their cultural practises. It will build tribal capacity to decide their own path of development along with their cultural and social norms.

According to L.P. Vidyarthi, the relevance of Tribal Panchsheel lies in the evergreen blueprint it provides for tribal development. We should not impose our own model of development on tribal communities. Developmental solutions should be compatible with the culture of tribes, in particular their nature-man-spirit complex. Otherwise, they will become more harmful than beneficial. Further, only tribal officers should be deployed in tribal areas. If the need arises for outside help, then non-tribal officers who have an anthropological bent of mind should be deployed.

Case Study

- **Lakshadweep Development Authority Regulation 2021 (LDAR)**

In a letter to Vice President Venkaiah Naidu and Governor Arif Mohammed Khan, three prominent individuals, including former Lakshadweep administrator Wajahat Habibullah, who also served as Chairman of the National Commission for Minorities, claimed that the Lakshadweep Development Authority Regulation 2021 (LDAR) will destroy the delicate ecosystem of the coral islands and the lives and livelihoods of the islanders. Recent policy changes were unilaterally and arbitrarily made without taking into account community livelihood practises, land use, land ownership, or the exploitation of maritime resources. The invasion of their food philosophy (beef ban, opening of booze stores, etc.), which violated their culture and traditions, was only the icing on the cake. The letter from the three individuals claimed that they would also dismantle their customary systems of democratic decentralisation- based decision-making. The islands required equitable government, access to safe and secure healthcare, education, food security, and livelihood possibilities connected to their ecosystem, which included abundant tuna fish resources in the nearby oceans. The Andaman, Nicobar, and Lakshadweep: An Environmental Impact Assessment by renowned ecologist Cecil J. Saldanha summarised the development plans for the islands created under the direction of the government's former Island Development Authority, which was presided over by Prime Ministers from Rajiv Gandhi to A.B. Vajpayee. To maintain resource access, human rights, secularism, democracy, and the ethnic diversity of the island population, all programmes being designed would need a vision that considered a collaborative approach rather than being forced from the top. The Preamble of the Indian Constitution would be upheld through prompt intervention in these matters.

Q 6. Plans for Tribal Development

Ans. Soon after independence, planned development was adopted as a national policy.

Need for Plans and Programmes:

Report of the Task Force on the Development of Tribal Areas (1975):

1. Northern areas from Ladakh to Tarai in U.P. tribals suffer due to the remoteness of their habitats and difficult climatic conditions.
2. Eastern, Central, and Western Zone tribals suffer from land alienation, indebtedness, and outsider exploitation of resources.
3. Southern zones suffer due to the primitive economy of Podu culture (shifting cultivation) and the prevalence of the Muttadari system of land tenure.
4. Andaman and Nicobar and Lakshadweep tribals suffer due to a subsistence economy based on fishing and the cultivation of coconuts.

Common problems due to:

5. Difficult terrain.
6. Overspending on social and religious ceremonies
7. Low rate of literacy.
8. Dependent on natural items and lack of motivation for making profit.

A programme of community development was launched in the first five-year plan, but tribal areas were more difficult, sparsely populated, and hilly.

Thus, a massive programme of integrated development was initiated by organising 43 special "Multipurpose Tribal Blocks" during the second five-year plan in areas with tribal concentration. Top priority was given to education, followed by communication, agriculture, animal husbandry, and medical facilities.

In the third 5-year plan, integrated development benefits were made available to all tribal areas through 489 tribal development blocks opened by the end of 1966–67 (Elwin Committee and Dhebar Commission). During this time, economic uplift was the top priority, followed by education, health, housing, and communication.

An expert committee was set up under the chairmanship of S.C. Dube to advice on the new formula during the fifth 5-year plan. On recommendation of this Committee, the concept of "tribal sub-plan" was adopted, i.e., the situation in regions of tribal concentration and areas with dispersed tribal populations is different; hence, the sub-plan concept evolved. It is not a scheme, but a new approach. The broad objectives of TSP are to narrow the gap between the level of development in tribal areas and other areas and improve the quality of life in tribal communities. The TSP areas in different states and UT are grouped as 194 Integrated Tribal Development Project (ITDP) operational areas.

During the Sixth Plan, the Modified Area Development Approach (MADA) was adopted to cover smaller areas of tribal concentration as part of the TSP strategy. The most backward groups among tribal primitive tribes are given special attention by preparing special schemes.

The 8th Plan stressed an income generation programme with special reference to PTG (primitive tribal groups). The **9th Plan** aimed at intellectual property rights protection, economic protection from external forces, empowerment of tribal groups, and a separate plan for "primitive tribes" through micro-projects.

The 10th Plan worked to provide legislative measures to tribal communities, thereby making them free from manual scavenging.

11th 5-year plan: the basic theme was inclusive growth. It was aimed at providing basic facilities for tribal development. In the 10th and 11th Plans, educational facilities like residential schools, ashram schools, and hostels for ST were largely promoted.

12th 5-year Plan: The basic theme was faster, more inclusive, and sustainable growth. In this regard, the government constituted a committee under *Prof. Xaxa* to look into the socio-economic and educational problems of tribals.

Bodies and institutions formed: A dedicated Ministry of Tribal Affairs, created in 1999, is responsible for the overall policy, planning, and coordination. Besides the Ministry, a number of bodies have been created since the 1970s to work for tribal development.

The National Scheduled Tribes Finance and Development Corporation (NSTFDC), 2001, and the State STFDCs provide financial assistance under various schemes, especially pertaining to self-help groups and skill development. The Tribal Cooperative Marketing Development Federation of India Limited (TRIFED) is involved in the marketing of tribal products.

The Integrated Tribal Development Agencies (ITDAs) administer the developmental projects and have jurisdiction over the ITDPs, Modified Area Development Approaches (MADAs), and clusters.

Tribal Research Institutes (TRIs) have been set up to provide research, training, and support services to tribal people and government officials. The Anthropological Survey of India (AnSI) also plays a significant role in conducting anthropological studies on tribes.

Impact:

1. According to the Shilu Ao Committee, the result achieved has not been commensurate with the expenditure incurred. For example, the failure of housing schemes—tiled houses constructed in the midst of forests have remained abandoned due to the wrong assumption of planners that what is good for people in the plains should be equally good and acceptable to tribes.
2. The Planning Commission observed that the multiplicity of agencies has resulted in the diffusion of responsibility, inadequate control, and difficulty in identifying officials concerned with specific programmes.
3. Ram Dayal Munda observes that land alienation continues unabated, and outsiders continue to get corruption, training, and employment. Corruption and favouritism continue to thrive in an alien political culture.
4. Delays in implementation of the recommendations of the Schedule Area and Schedule Tribe Commission There has been no conscious attempt, except by the Andhra government, to ensure that tribals receive a reasonable share of the benefits from the general development programme. These led to unsatisfactory results.

Xaxa Committee Recommendations to Address Issues:

1. Gram Sabha consent should be mandatory for the acquisition of land by the government for its own use as well.
2. Minerals should be exploited by tribal people themselves; form registered ST cooperative societies.
3. Penalty on officers who delay the application of the PESA Act.
4. Inclusion of local culture, folklore, and history in the curriculum can help children understand the relevance of education in their lives.
5. Tribal people need a specially designed health plan. 'Tribal Health Plan' should become an essential feature of NHM and TSP.
6. The participation of women in the FRA process has to be increased.
7. Committee should be set up to investigate R&R in all medium and major projects of the last 50 years.

With the replacement of the Planning Commission by Niti Ayog, the onus of tribal welfare lies on Niti Ayog. Aspirational district planning is a step in the right direction, but still, a lot needs to be done.

Q 7. Tribal Sub-plan

Ans. At the end of the 4th 5-year plan, it was realised that funds were directed to non-tribals in Tribal Development Blocks. The Tribal Sub-Plan (TSP) Strategy was evolved by the Expert Committee set up by the Ministry of Education and Social Welfare in 1972 under the Chairmanship of S.C. Dube and L.P. Vidyarthi for rapid socioeconomic development of tribal people and adopted for first time in fifth 5-year Plan, continuing since then.

Salient features:

1. **TSP** is a plan within the ambit of a state or UT plan meant for the welfare and development of tribals. Such a plan is part of the overall plan of the state, or UT, and is therefore called a sub-plan. The benefits percolating from TSP to tribals are in addition to those percolating from the overall plan of the state or UT.
2. The most significant aspect is to ensure the flow of funds for TSP areas in at least equal proportion to the ST population of each state and UT.
3. **Sub-plans:**
   1. Identify resources for TSP areas.
   2. Prepare a broad framework for development.
   3. Define an administrative strategy for implementation.

Broad objectives:

1. Substantial reduction in poverty and unemployment.
2. Creation of productive assets in favour of ST to provide them with livelihood opportunities on a sustained basis.
3. Provision of social, physical, and financial security for them against all types of exploitation and oppression.
4. Generate employment.
5. Develop agri-economy.

Strategy spells out the problem of tribes in two parts:

1. Areas with more than 50% tribal concentration and schedule areas
2. Areas with dispersed tribal populations besides having primitive tribal groups as special groups. State plans of the state or UT for category (i) are really tribal development plans, and no sub-plan is necessary. For category (ii), sub-plans are needed.

The region of tribal concentration or sub-plan in each state comprises a number of viable project areas known as Integrated Tribal Development Projects (ITDP). However, funding comes from state plans, special central assistance to TSP, sectoral programmes of central ministries, etc.

Weakness:

1. Provision of a smaller TSP budget in the annual plan in comparison to the tribal population E.g., in the 2015-16 budgets, allocation to Adivasis was only Rs. 19,980 crores, while it should have been Rs. 40,014 crores towards TSP (8.6% of plan outlay).
2. Annual plans do not have any realistic physical targets for TSP schemes.
3. On behalf of the government, there is no periodical benchmark to look at the socio-economic status of tribal people in TSP areas and no vision document for long-term goals.
4. In Odisha, TSP funds are diverted for infrastructure development.
5. The ST development department is spending less than the desired level of expenditure earmarked for various purposes.

Mungekar Committee Recommendation:

1. There should be a separate budget head for each ministry or department in TSP.
2. A minimum of 8% of the budget fund of the Ministry concerned with social sector programmes is allocated towards TSP.
3. TSP funds should be non-lapsable and non-divertible.
4. Every ministry shall prepare an ST-specific annual tribal sub-plan.
5. There shall be a committee called the Committee for Approval and Monitoring of the Annual TSP of the Central Ministry or Department.
6. At the state level, the Department of Tribal Affairs should plan and devise a TSP programme for Scheduled Areas.

Bhuria Committee Recommendation:

7. TSP should be placed before the Tribal Advisory Council for their advice.
8. Every state TSP should earmark programmes specifically for women's planning and implementation (at least 30%).

TSP is currently being monitored by MoTA based on an online monitoring system, developed on the lines of the NITI Ayog monitoring framework.

Q 8. Programmes of Tribal Development

Ans. Though primary responsibility for promotion of economic, educational and social development of ST rests with all Central Ministries, Ministry of Tribal Affairs (MoTA) complement their efforts by way of development intervention in critical sectors through "specially tailored schemes". Ministry administers various Central Sector and Centrally Sponsored Schemes besides two Special Area Programme *viz.* Special Central Assistance to TSP and Grant-in-aid under Article 275(1).

Broad arenas:

1. **Education:** Education received top priority in recent plans to facilitate educational development among ST. The scheme of post-matriculation scholarships for ST was started in 1948 with the objective of providing financial assistance to students to complete their education. For the first time in 1954–55, an overseas scholarship for ST was given with preference for studies in science and engineering. A programme was enacted in 1961 –62 to provide separate hostels for ST girls with the aim of providing residential facilities to tribal girls in pursuit of education. In 1980–90, separate hostels for ST boys also started. The scheme of Ashram School in TSP areas has been operational since 1990–91 with the objective of promoting educational facilities to ST students, including PVTG, in tune with their social and cultural milieu. A follow-up education programme has been introduced for tribal students who wish to clear AIS through competition.
2. **Economic Empowerment:** Economic development among tribals largely depends upon agriculture and allied activities. Besides, forest resources and minor forest produce contribute to the tribal economy.
   a. **Agriculture and allied activities:** a large number of tribals follow shifting cultivation. Steps taken to regulate it. In Tripura, out of about 27,000 families practising shifting cultivation, about 2/3 have changed to settled agriculture. They were allocated 2 acres of cultivable land and some costs for seeds, implements, etc. In Rajasthan, HYV of maize and paddy was introduced with success in tribal areas.
   b. **Animal Husbandry and Fisheries:** In Chotanagpur, some bulls have been distributed free of charge by Tribal Development Blocks. Special steps have been taken in tribal Bihar (now Jharkhand) by the Fishery Dept. under the programme of tank renovation and bringing them under pisciculture.

c. **Forests:** Tribal economies and lives revolve around fruits. In order to save tribals from exploitation by private traders and offer them remunerative prices, the Tribal Co-operative Marketing Development Federation of India (TRIFED) was set up by the GOI in 1987. TRIFED functions both as a service provider and a market developer for tribal products. In 2013–14, the scheme "Mechanism for Marketing MFP through MSP and Development of the Value Chain for MFP" was introduced.

d. **Scheme of Vocational Training Centres** in Tribal Areas Launched in 1992–93 to develop skills among ST youth to enable them to gain employment and self-employment opportunities. Training is provided through ITI polytechnics, computer training centres, etc.

e. **Govt. of India launched the Vanbandhu Kalyan Yojana** during 2014–15 for the holistic development of tribals across the country. It ensures a goods- and service-oriented approach while striking at critical gaps through the convergence of resources and institutional mechanisms.

3. **Health:** In the medical field, more PHC centres are opening. In M.P., an ayurvedic section was added in remote tribal areas. The Tribal Affair Ministry operates a scheme of grant-in-aid to voluntary organisations working for the welfare of STs and a scheme of grant-in-aid to NGOs for running bedded hospitals and mobile dispensaries in tribal areas.
4. **Social Justice:** Protection of Civil Rights Act, 1955, and SC and ST Prevention of Atrocities Act, 1989, are two legal instruments to prevent all types of social discrimination, like untouchability and exploitation. A scheme for the development of PVTG was launched in 1998–99 for the survival, protection, and development of PVTG in fragile living conditions and a declining population trend. Grant-in-Aid under Article 275(1) is 100% financial assistance provided to states through MoTA for the welfare of ST and upgradation of administration in tribal areas. PESA, 1996, and FRA, 2007 are other two fundamental acts to bring justice for ST.

Impact: The impact of the tribal welfare and developmental programmes has been mixed and uneven. There are both positive and negative aspects to the impact. The impact varies in degree not only between two different tribes but also within the same tribe.

The People of India project was completed in 1994. It studied 635 tribal communities and came out with some quantitative data on tribal participation in the mainstream and their response to developmental efforts:

1. According to the project, politically, there has been a rise in political leadership, with a number of tribes playing leadership roles at various levels, like village panchayat, regional, and national levels.
2. In the field of education, the literacy rate has increased and the dropout rate has decreased.
3. In the field of health, 53% of tribes have expressed a favourable attitude towards modern medicine. There is a decline in the death rate and an increase in the birth rate.
4. In the field of economic development, many tribal communities are aware of and participate in self-employment schemes initiated by the government. E.g., agriculture, animal husbandry, piggery, poultry, pisciculture, smallscale industries, etc.
5. On miscellaneous fronts, the coverage of electronic media in tribal areas has increased. The net effect is that an elite stratum of entrepreneurs, teachers, administrators, engineers, doctors, and defence personnel has been created.

A study by Gadgil and Guha on hunting and gathering tribes like the Jenukuruba and Chenchu of Andhra Pradesh points out that the Jenukurbas, with their vast traditional knowledge of the forest, now help the forest department in the rearing of elephants and collection of forest produce, earning a mere subsistence but creating huge revenue for the forest department. Some Chenchu have taken to crime, which is a failure of tribal development programmes.

Case Study

- **Technology eases the path for the weary nomads in J&K**

To facilitate their yearly journey, the nomadic groups of J&K have been given smart cards and free transportation. The Gujjars and Bakerwals, a nomadic clan in Jammu and Kashmir, have been making gruelling treks on foot as part of their periodic migration to locate better pastures for their livestock for millennia. They frequently lose livestock to mishaps and difficulties along the journey, as well as occasionally losing family members. To assist them in travelling vast distances faster and more safely, transit services and technological advances have been made available this year. The J&K Tribal Affairs Department has polled 98,000 of these families to map their travel patterns.

- **Killing two birds with a solitary out-of-box idea**

IFS Ananda Reddy in Nasik district replaces slingshots with sports equipment and books so that birds are saved and tribal children turn into sports champions.

- **Odisha publishes India's first encyclopaedia on tribal communities**

To preserve the long-standing and distinctive traditions of tribal communities, Odisha became the first state in the nation to launch an encyclopaedia on tribal cultures. 418 research papers on the tribes, including 13 particularly vulnerable groups, are included in the five edited volumes of the "Encyclopaedia of Tribes in Odisha," produced by the Scheduled Castes and Scheduled Tribes Research and Training Institute and the Odisha State Tribal Museum.

- **An IAS officer's journey towards bettering the lives of tribals**

Pravir Krishna, the managing director of TRIFED, has written a book titled "Tryst With the Tribes: Tales From Tribal Heartlands" that details his experiences dealing with tribal people. The book "Tryst With the Tribes: Tales From Tribal Heartlands" tells the tale of a young IAS officer who fell in love with the tribal heartlands of India and how these encounters altered him irrevocably. When Krishna, an IAS officer from the Madhya Pradesh cadre and a member of the 1987 batch, was appointed collector and district magistrate of Sarguja, a tribal district in Madhya Pradesh, in 1994, he first experienced the harsh realities of the exploitation of tribal people. He was so profoundly impacted by it that he set out on a mission to improve the lives of indigenous people. Since then, he has contributed to establishing a climate in which tribals trade freely and earn more. The author has provided a number of practical suggestions for transforming symbolic legislation for the tribes into a more robust strategy for tribal development that is based on enhancing self-help, using local resources, the traditional and sound skills and knowledge banks of the tribes, and the necessity of developing enterprises based on these resources. When he conceptualised and led the Imli Andolan of Bastar, which assisted 30 lakh tribal people in getting a fair value for their commerce and taking control of their futures, Krishna gained the moniker "Imli Krishna." The book is a labour of love that required a lot of sweat, effort, and perseverance. It explains how a bureaucrat took the "Imli Andolan" and turned it into what Krishna affectionately refers to as the "Tribal AMUL Transformation."

- **Jantatiya Gaurav Diwas**

Every year on November 15th, the Janjatiya Gaurav Divas will be observed to honour the tribal people's contributions to the preservation of cultural heritage and the promotion of Indian values like patriotism, bravery, and hospitality. They organised a number of tribal uprisings against British colonial control in various parts of India. These tribal groups include, among others, the Tamars, Santhals, Khasis, Bhils, Mizos, and Kols. In addition to a few social programmes in Bhopal, the PM opened the Birsa Munda Museum in Ranchi. Even the Rani Kamlapati railway station in Bhopal has been dedicated to the country by the PM. On November 15th, Birsa Munda, who is worshipped as God by tribal people all over India, also celebrates his birth anniversary.

- **Mission Connect Paderu**

Despite being referred to as a "smart city," the scenery of the Agency regions in the Visakhapatnam district is in stark contrast. The tribal areas frequently lag behind in acquiring access to even the most basic facilities, like power and public transportation, due to poor road connectivity, accessibility to healthcare, a lack of drinkable water, and other factors. In order to start addressing the problems the tribal people were having, Mallikarjuna launched "Mission Connect Paderu," which paved the ground for a long-term development plan.

The initiative intends to develop infrastructure in the Agency areas in an effort to lessen the load on those who still carry "doli" (a homemade stretcher) to help meet the emergency needs of the tribals, provide improved drinking water facilities, and facilitate motorable roads. The goal is to provide a motorable route for the tribal members to access, even if it is not a blacktop road. The plan is to improve the tribal region's currentinfrastructure over the next three years by including the industries as partners in CSR projects.

Q 9. ITDP

Ans. ITDP (Integrated Tribal Development Projects) are administrative units adopted by a number of states for the purpose of delivering programmes and services to tribal individuals, households, and habitations. To date, about 194 ITDPs have been set up in various states.

A unit of planning is an ITDP in the state; it is smaller than a district but bigger than a block. The ITDP programme takes the form of a Project Report, while the State programme takes the form of a Sub-plan. Since socio-economic conditions vary from one region to another and even within the same region, the strategy for each ITDP needs to be worked out separately with reference to its problem. A district approach has to be adopted for different sub-regions, even within the same project area. Thus, the schematic formula approach was discarded as a matter of planning for ITDP.

ITDP refers to the entire development process in an area. It is not a special project for which special staff is assigned. The entire administrative and developmental structure in the project area should form the implementing machinery for the total project programme.

Here, programmes are to be built up from below, and flexibility is central to their approach. Before adding new institutes, existing ones need to be optimised. E.g., before taking on a new drinking water programme, existing ones need to be utilised.

They are responsible for infrastructure development, income generation activity, health, and education service delivery, as well as implementing FRA within their areas.

Andhra Pradesh provides a good model of ITDA, where each unit is equipped with engineering, health, and education personnel accountable to the project manager. The government has established a single-line administration system in ITDA areas with the objective of an integrated approach to development for tribal people in sub-plan areas. Various departments were brought under the Project Office, ITDA.

Issues according to Mungekar's Report:

1. ITDP has over the years become an agency engaged in rituals of coordination but without content. They have become defunct and subservient to District Area Development Agencies (DRDA). They work just with the 2 crore or so annual funds from MoTA.
2. Tribals are bewildered in the face of numerous departments and a lack of technical staff in ITDP like the Engineering Wing with ITDP.

Recommendations according to the Mungekar Report:

1. There is a strong need to resuscitate ITDP by restrengthening and revamping it to be able to implement agencies for the new proposal deal.
2. The process of planning should begin with ITDP and move to block units. Competent microplanning units should be established at the state and ITDP levels.

Case Study

- **ITDA (Eturnagaram)**

The Integrated Tribal Development Agency (ITDA), Eturnagaram, is not in good shape. The ITDA doesn't do anything other than exist in name alone. They revealed an unpleasant truth. The ITDA appears to be understaffed. But when the ITDA was scrambling for money to carry out developmental activities like the Giri Vikas initiative, the economic support scheme, etc., In contrast, the Adivasis are fighting back against the revenue and forest officials because the government has not yet done anything to settle the land issues. The Scheduled Tribes and Other Traditional Forest Dwellers (RoFR) Act of 2006 is unconcerned by the forest department. Even the pattas that some Adivasis have are of little concern to them. Because of this, not all of the local farmers were receiving Rythu Bandhu benefits. Officials reject Rythu Bandhu in the name of allotted or forested property, according to Rao. It has been discovered that more than 4,200 farmers had their Rythu Bandhu support halted for a variety of reasons. Since the handover, the government has not yet appointed a project officer (PO) to the Eturnagaram ITDA. As of now, the Mulugu District Collector is in control of the ITDA. As the government had issued funding under the leadership of the Tribal Welfare Department, PO's absence had an effect on how work was progressing. The last meeting of the ITDA's governing body took place more than two years ago. In actuality, the regulating body needs to review the progress of the developmental programmes in its command area once every three months.

Q 10. Concept of PTGs (Primitive Tribal Groups), their distribution and programmes for development

Ans. The President of India appointed the Dhebar Commission in 1961 to inquire into the working of constitutional provisions as provided to Schedule Tribes. This commission found that a section within ST is still backward and lags any type of development. Consequently, during the 4–5th year plan, the Planning Commission appointed the Shilu Ao Committee in order to judge the level of development among STs. This committee also supported the report of the Dhebar Commission. Thus, during the fifth five-year plan, a sub-category is created and 53 tribal groups are identified, who are termed primitive tribal groups. Presently, there are 75 such groups, and Maram of Manipur is the latest entry. PTGs comprise 27 lakh people and are spread over 14 states and 1 U.T. In 2006, they were renamed PVTG (Particularly Vulnerable Tribal Groups). Some of them are: Boda, Birhors, Chenchus, Jorawas, Juangs, Kamars, Kurumbas, Totos, Rajis, Onges, Mal Paharias, Shompen, Marams, Lodhas, Paniyans, Irulas, etc.

Main criteria followed to classify PTG:

1. Pre-agricultural level of technology
2. Low or negligible literacy rate.
3. Stagnant or declining population.
4. Subsistence level of the economy.

Problem of PTG:

1. Loss of customary habitats and livelihood resources due to non-recognition of their rights.
2. It led to hunger, malnutrition, ill health, and the erosion of traditional occupations, which threatened their survival. Some are on the verge of extinction, including the Shompen, Jarawas, and Sentinalese of Andaman and Nicobar.
3. Poor functioning of PDS and ICDS and poor health services in PVTG areas
4. Lack of baseline surveys conducted
5. Extremely low level of awareness regarding rights

Case Study: *Jayanta Kumar Nayak* studied the Mankindias of Odisha. They are in an oscillation from huntergatherer to wage labourer. However, due to undernutrition and hunger, their population size is declining. However, they continue to live a gregarious life with strong bonds of sociality.

Measures to bring improvement: The Central Government has taken many measures for their development. Huge funds are allocated to the concerned state to launch various programmes for PTGs. A Central Sector Scheme was launched in 1998–99 with a view to building houses for them, constructing link roads, and providing them with health and education facilities. Certain social schemes, like the Janshree Bima Yojna, were also introduced. A Conservative and Community Development Scheme was launched in 2006 and 2007 for the overall development of PVTGs, and by this scheme, huge funds were allocated during the 11 th and 12th Five-Year Plans.

The Central Government also directed the concerned state governments to launch various pilot projects and action plans for their development. The Ministry of Tribal Welfare raised the Centre Sector Scheme with effect from April 1, 2015, with an intuition to protect, develop, and reduce vulnerability among them. 100% financial assessment provided by the Centre to the State Government for construction of houses, development of roads, introduction of health and medical facilities, installation of non-conventional sources of energy, etc., in other areas. Outcome Analysis:

Research Study (2015) on Effectiveness Measurement of Development Interventions among PVTGs in Nine PVTGOccupying States of India:

- As per the existing strategies of resource sharing between the centre and states, there has been an adverse effect on the implementation of development interventions due to improper coordination between the state and the centre. Sometimes the state utilises the funds allotted to it under Art. 275(1) and Central Assistance to the TSP area for purposes other than those for which they have been stipendiated. The incomplete houses under the Birsa Munda housing scheme for PVTGs in Jharkahand are one manifestation of such coordination and cooperation.
- Livelihood strategies and design development programmes for PVTGs are not based on people's felt needs and priorities. Often, the implementing authorities, such as SO/PA and other concerned development personnel, decide the strategies and design development programmes on behalf of PVTGs without the consent of the beneficiaries. However, states like Gujarat Tribal Development have addressed the livelihood strategies of PVTGs for economic enhancement through dairy farming and mango saplings through NGOs, which is pleasing. Similarly, the government of Andhra Pradesh made a dent in enhancing the livelihood strategy of PVTGs by implementing tribal tourism by supplying mechanised boats and ensuring 40% reservation of tourist bookings in favour of PVTGs. Besides this, Andhra Pradesh leads other state governments in implementing livelihood strategies for women SHGs by supplying tractors for community use as well as for income generation.
- Contrary to the conventional notion of developing the PVTGs and mainstreaming them through development interventions, it was observed that the culture of the PVTGs no longer remained conserved and, in many cases, had been subjected to distortions.

Recommendation of the National Advisory Council for PVTG:

1. MOTA should facilitate a specially designed census for PVTG that covers their enumeration, health, education, and housing.
2. Prepare the vulnerability index for PVTG.
3. Generate awareness about the vulnerability of PVTG and the need to respect, protect, and recognise their rights, especially to their land and customary habits.
4. Control factors that contributed to protecting the PVTG population: a special food security programme; controlling malaria, viral hepatitis, anaemia, deworming, etc. ICDS activities, IEC campaign, sanitation programme enhancement
5. Institutionalise the participatory process.

Case Study

- **Denying access of Particularly Vulnerable Tribal Groups to Contraceptive Services: A Case Study among the Baiga Community in Chhattisgarh, India**

The most vulnerable of India's indigenous populations are designated as Particularly Vulnerable Tribal Groups (PVTG), including the Baigas. The government restricted their access to permanent contraceptive methods in 1979 as a measure to stop their population decline, which was mostly caused by high mortality, and this restriction is being enforced as a prohibition. Out of proportion to district and state averages, the Baiga experience extreme poverty and poor nutritional status. 61.3% of the women surveyed have had four or more pregnancies, and 61.3% have lost a child at least once while pregnant or later. Baiga women are denied access to contraceptive services because of the forehead tattoo that serves as an identifier for them. They frequently lack access to even interim solutions. They have become even poorer as a result of this forceful policy. The right to get contraceptive services has been demanded by the Baigas. A breach of the rights to selfdetermination, bodily autonomy, and reproductive and human rights is the denial of contraceptive services.

- **Pradhan Mantri PVTG Development Mission**

In presenting the Union Budget 2023–24 to Parliament, the Union Minister for Finance and Corporate Affairs stated, "We envision a prosperous and inclusive India, in which the fruits of development reach all regions and citizens." The Finance Minister announced the commencement of the Pradhan Mantri PVTG Development Mission in order to enhance the socioeconomic circumstances of the especially vulnerable tribal groups (PVTGs). "This will flood PVTG families and habitations with basic amenities like secure housing, clean drinking water and sanitary facilities, improved access to education, health, and nutrition, road and telecom connectivity, and sustainable livelihood opportunities," she continued. The Finance Minister added that under the Development Action Plan for the Mission, Rs. 15,000 crore will be made accessible over the following three years for the Scheduled Tribes.

Q 11. Role of N.G.O.s in tribal development

Ans. Non-governmental organisations (NGOs) are not-for-profit organisations that are independent from states and international governmental organisations. As per the Dhebar Commission, an NGO like BASS has played no small part in helping the government shape its tribal welfare policy at the stage of the preparation of the Constitution.

NGO's are playing a key role in development programmes, particularly in the Third World, and the reasons are:

1. Government machinery has failed to deliver goods.
2. Government officials fail to empathise with the local population.
3. Government officials lack the real commitment and dedication that personnel of NGOs possess.
4. Red tapism and corruption in government departments are so rampant that rural or tribal people do not get work done unless they pay a certain percentage as a bribe to officials.
5. It generates employment for youth along with the development of the masses.

The first major involvement was seen in 1921 with the establishment of Bhil Seva Mandal by A.V. Thakkar. Soon after independence, Dr. Rajendra Prasad founded Bhartiya Admijati Sevak Sangh (BASS) in 1948. Hundreds of organisations are now associated with BASS. It has involved itself in welfare activities relating to every walk of tribal life. It also publishes newsletters, pamphlets, and journals dealing with tribal problems and organises seminars.

Another significant welfare organisation is Vanavasi Kalyan Ashram, which focuses on indigenous tribes in remote areas of India and has branches all over India. These branches focus on agriculture, healthcare, child education, and sports and culture in their respective regions.

Other prominent: Kruthi NGO, making a bridge school for Koyas, displaced due to the Godavari delta, for providing non-formal vocational education. Ekal Vidyalaya exists with the vision of "One Village, One Teacher, One School". Tata Institute of Social Sciences (TISS), Indian Red Cross Society, Ramakrishan Mission, Arya Samaj, All India Harijan Sevak Samaj, etc. are a few others.

B.K. Roy Burman has emphasised the role of non-governmental organisations (NGOs) in a number of seminars:

1. Advisory and consultative role as they have good rapport with tribal
2. Implement government programmes at the last mile.
3. Compliment government action as they do not have bureaucratic procedural norms.
4. Alternative to formal organisation.
5. Direct contact with people.

Government Support:

- CAPART set up.
- Financial assistance to the NGO to implement the government scheme
- Diversified work to NGO like women, water, sanitation, land issues, etc., apart from health and education

In India, CAPART has been the chief organisation for funding NGOs and voluntary organisations for developmental works relating to housing, water, health, sanitation, etc.

Issues:

1. There are more than 3 million non-governmental organisations that either do not have a sound academic base or are not honest. E.g., in 2014, 75% of respondents did not submit audited accounts.
2. CAPART's nine regional centres closed in 2013–14 because of rampant corruption.
3. These are 14,000 NGO with FCRA, and half of them have been derecognized by the centre in the last 3 years for misuse of funds or anti-government activity.
4. Some NGOs work for religious conversions.
5. Shilu Ao found a tendency for NGO operations to be restricted to more developed tribal areas.

To solve these issues and utilise the expertise of NGOs, the government should identify honest NGOs, train them to achieve their objectives, and release proper funds for them.

The 2nd ARC says that there should be an independent body like the National Accreditation Council for certification of voluntary organisations that seek funding from government agencies. According to the Dhebar Commission, personal touch given by NGOs can harness the latent touch energies of the masses into a useful channel for their development.

Case Study

- **CSR: Piramal Foundation campaigns to dispel vaccine hesitancy across tribal districts in India.**

The Aashwasan campaign was started by the Piramal Foundation in association with the Ministries of Health and Family Welfare, Tribal Affairs, and USAID under the auspices of Anamaya, Tribal Health Collaborative, in an effort to combat COVID-19 vaccine hesitancy, encourage COVID-appropriate behaviour, and proactively identify tuberculosis cases among India's tribal population. The campaign will cover all villages and blocks with more than 25% tribal residents in 177 tribal districts in stages. 49 tribal districts served around 10 lakh beneficiaries. Discuss vaccine acceptance with religious leaders, indigenous healers, Panchayati Raj organisations, community influencers, and young people.

The key objectives of Aashwasan are to: (1) generate awareness of COVID-19 and COVID Appropriate Behaviour (CAB); (2) reduce vaccine hesitancy; and (3) improve epidemic preparedness by involving community influencers, faith leaders, tribal healers, and others. (4) Build awareness of TB, identify people with presumptive TB, and link them with public services for screening, diagnosis, and treatment.

- **Conservation and Preservation of the Tribal Museum and Rare Books on Tribals at the BAJSS Building at Jhandewala, New Delhi**

The National Tribal Research Institute, New Delhi, under the mentorship of TRI Uttarakhand, signs a MoU with the Bharatiya Adim Janajati Seva Sangathan (BAJSS), New Delhi, to preserve, protect, and digitise rare books on tribals and to renovate and digitise the tribal museum.

- **Volunteers keep the learning boat afloat for tribal kids in Jharkhand.**

Globally, the COVID-19 epidemic has wrought an unprecedented revolution in education, and its ramifications are now being felt in other spheres of society. Since the lockdowns began in March 2020, the number of young girls being married off at young ages and forced to perform hard labour has increased alarmingly in the state of Jharkhand. The National Family Health Survey (NFHS-5)'s most recent findings show that in Jharkhand, 32.2% of all girls and 36.1% of rural girls are married before the age of 18. However, only 60.2% of girls under the age of six in rural areas are able to attend school.

The lives of Talamani Soren and Sona Murmu of Bhognadih village in the Barhait block of Sahibganj, a remote district of Jharkhand, have seen a glimmer of optimism despite this grim situation. For the past few months, the girls have regularly attended an informal school where they have been learning Hindi and English, as well as reading, writing, and speaking. These tribal girls are among 350 children undergoing the pandemic-induced lockdown who are receiving free education because of the Sido-Kanhu Murmu Hul Foundation's efforts.

9.2

Role of Anthropology in Tribal and Rural Development.

Q 1. Role of Anthropology in tribal development

Ans. Development means qualitative growth in body and mind. Tribals have been the most marginalised section in colonial and postcolonial days. Therefore, anthropologists have a key role in their development. Anthropology as a discipline has the following distinguished characteristics:

1. **Holistic Approach:** This involves the study of human beings in terms of the entire pattern of their lives. An anthropologist studies biological, social, economic, and linguistic aspects and integrates them to study them holistically. E.g., during rehabilitation in development projects, connection with nature should be taken into account (Nature-Man-Spirit Complex).
2. **Comparative Theme:** Anthropology focuses on comparing and contrasting the information available about different communities.
3. **Cultural Relativism:** It is reinforced by *Malinowski* and suggested that an anthropologist must evaluate culture and think in the same way as natives without any bias. E.g., while implementing a ban on the slaughter of cattle, tribal dependence on animals for food should be taken into account.
4. **Participant Observation Method:** It is a fieldwork technique in which an anthropologist stays with the community for a long period of time as a member and then obtains the data from observation. It is the most accurate fieldwork technique. E.g., D.N. Majumdar's Study of the Ho Tribe.

The holistic approach, belief in cultural relativism, and strong humanitarian tradition put anthropology on a different pedestal. By virtue of their vast experience of fieldwork for more than 150 years among simple societies, anthropologists have accumulated a vast treasure of knowledge. Among tools of data collection, participant observation gives an insidious view, which provides a different angle to look at tribal development. Therefore, the role of anthropology is much more significant in tribal development.

- Elwin advised the government on NEFA and the policy of Tribal Panchsheel.

- S.C. Roy, as a member of the Bihar Legislative Assembly, upheld the cause of tribal people.
- In India, under the chairmanship of S.C. Dube, the Tribal Sub-Play strategy is the first step towards the rapid socio-economic development of tribals under the aegis of applied anthropology.
- L.P. Vidyarthi introduced action anthropology research programmes among the Birhar, a nomadic tribe of South Bihar, and Prof. Bhowmik undertook the developmental work among the Lodhas, ex-criminal tribes of Midnapur District of West Bengal.
- L.P. Vidyarthi, in his book "Applied Anthropology in India," suggested that anthropologists are not merely "social doctors" who can diagnose the evils of society but "social engineers" who can reconstruct a healthy society. Because anthropologists study cultural relativism objectively,

There is a difference in the way an administrator and an anthropologist look at tribal development. Development means growth plus change. It involved both material and human factors. Administrators measure development in terms of material and quantified indicators such as rate of growth, national income per capita, etc., whereas to an anthropologist, such a mechanical concept of development is unacceptable. He has consistently emphasised that socio-cultural factors are integral to growth. While striving for the development of a group or area, due emphasis has to be given to traditional values and historical experience. An anthropologist tries to understand the inside view of the problems and provide concrete and pragmatic recommendations to the government.

Another point that puts an anthropologist on a different pedestal is that he is not obsessed with ends alone. For him, means are as important as ends because he understands that coercive means could prove counterproductive in any scheme for tribal development. Development has to come by integrating tribals with the mainstream along with their own genius and culture. Rather than imposing development from outside, it should be induced from inside.

Even after four decades of tribal development, no substantial results have been observed. This state of affairs is also due to the fact that administrators have failed to appreciate that anthropologists are the only ones who can guide and advice most effectively in matters concerning tribal people. It is high time that administrators as generalists and anthropologists as specialists come together to collaborate in a spirit of collaboration to make the tribal development programme a success. In this way, anthropology can be used to the best advantage of society in general and tribal people in particular.

Q 2. Role of Anthropology in rural development

Ans. The importance of knowledge of anthropology for efficient administration was first realised as early as 1807, when the Court of Directors of the East India Company made a formal decision that such knowledge would be of great use for the administration of the country. To this effect, *Dr. Francis Buchnon* was appointed by the Governor General in Council to undertake an ethnographic survey of the inhabitants of Bengal and their religion. Later, *Risley, Dalton,* etc. were deputed by the British government to prepare handbooks, monographs, etc. on tribe and caste in India.

But their stand was generally condemned at the government level. They were even ignored except in museum and survey work. In the 1960s and 1970s, after seeing the disastrous results of wrong approaches, the government realised the importance of anthropologists. This started reflecting in the composition of tribal research institutes, tribal advisory councils, the committee of the planning commission, etc.

George Foster has put three merits of anthropology:

1. Anthropology from a point of view
2. As a storehouse or treasure of factual information;
3. Distinct research methodology.

Edward Jay says that the double advantage of an anthropologist's long residence in an area and concerted effort to learn and understand qualifies them as the only outsider able to give recommendations for action.

Anthropologists have conducted village studies in India since the 1950s. Important ones include:

1. S.C. Dube's Indian Village
2. M.N. Srinivas's India's Villages
3. McKim Marriott's Village India, among others.

Key concepts emerged from such village studies as:

1. Sanskritisation
2. Dominant Caste
3. Jajmani System
4. Universalization and parochialization
5. Disintegration of joint families

These works broke the book's view of rural society and the caste system. They showed how the Indian villages were part of the wider society and civilization and not mere little republics as had been established by colonial studies.

Anthropologists have not only helped illustrate the complex social life of rural India but also traced the impact of modern forces and globalisation on Indian villages.

Limitations:

1. Most anthropologists are ignored by administrators, and their inputs are not used in policy making.
2. Anthropologists themselves stress more about academic concerns.
3. More studies focus on the cultural, social, and religious aspects of society than on economic aspects.
4. Lack of finding and inter-disciplinary nature with subjects like sociology.

B.K. Roy Burman says that anthropologists advocate alternate strategies for development by stressing on:

1. Small, localised micro-projects
2. Involvement of NGOs
3. Sustainable Development-Oriented Programmes
4. People-focused and people-led development, not government-led development

The World Bank acknowledged anthropologist contributions in its Annual Report (1997) - To gain a better understanding of the pathology of poverty, banks, in several cases, include sociological and anthropological assessments as part of project design and appraisal.

L.P. Vidyarthi, in his "Applied Anthropology in India," suggested that an anthropologist is not merely a social doctor who diagnoses the evils of society but a "social engineer' who reconstructs a healthy society.

Case Study

- **Navigating Business Through an Anthropological Lens by Tulsi Menon**

Tulsi Mehrotra Menon discusses using anthropological techniques to determine how a brand will fit into actual customers' lives as opposed to trying to make them fit the brand's ideal. She argues that applying cultural insights and taking a more human-centric approach can result in solutions that are more practicable and marketable. Tulsi Mehrotra Menon was raised and educated in Bangalore and graduated from Macalester College with a degree in anthropology. Tulsi returned to India in order to apply anthropological techniques in an Indian corporate setting. She joined The Womb, one of the earliest branding and advertising firms in India, looking for an anthropologist since she wanted to investigate the use of anthropology in a more consumerfocused industry. She acquired the skills necessary to transform cultural insights into useable, marketable solutions at The Womb. She is interested in investigating how anthropological practises might be applied in a variety of fields and companies that have not traditionally made use of anthropology.

- **Understanding digital anthropology**

The anthropological study of how people interact with technology in the digital age is known as "digital anthropology." Between Industry 1.0 and Industry 4.0, the human race has advanced. Throughout this trip, we have also changed in terms of habits and skills. Nightlife was unheard of before the development of electricity. Following each stage of human evolution, we began performing actions that were previously regarded as impossible, oftentimes without even realising it. For instance, we now accept work in cities that are far from our hometowns. Rakim thinks that after the digital change, people will continue to develop. For instance, as of right now, when a doctor, driver, or any other professional service provider retires, they take all of their expertise and experience with them. Data on the medical history of the family may now be saved, and insights can be drawn from it thanks to big data and artificial intelligence. Many of us have a tendency to take selfies and publish them right away on social media. Our subconscious mind compels us to check the likes and comments on our social media posts. So, in a sense, we are developing new habits as a result of digitalization. And the thought processes of our sub-conscious mind now include these habits. This idea is already being used by FAAAN (Facebook, Amazon, Apple, Alphabet, and Netflix) companies. 'M-Pesa' was primarily responsible for meeting financial needs in Africa. One of the most popular mobile money services in Africa is M-Pesa. The main requirement in this instance was to trade money between two people. Each person has an essential need that must be recognised and met. Once more, this calls for a shift in the way their subconscious minds think. The majority of tasks will be completed by machines in the future. However, machines lack a subconscious mind. Raktim envisions a day in the future when machines and people will work together to improve the world. The human race will then undergo the next stage of evolution.

- **Anthro-Vision: A New Way to See in Business and Life**

The award-winning journalist and Cambridge social anthropology Ph.D. presents a strong, comprehensible case for the commercial relevance of her academic field in Anthro-Vision. Tett discovers that anthropology imparts this value in three different ways: by making the unfamiliar weird, by making the familiar odd, and by enhancing awareness of social silence. Business executives, investors, legislators, economists, technologists, financiers, physicians, lawyers, and accountants can all benefit from the insights provided by anthropological instruments.

9.3

Contributions of anthropology to the understanding of regionalism, communalism and ethnic and political movements.

Q 1. Contributions of anthropology to the understanding of regionalism, communalism and ethnic and political movements

Ans. As per *David Mandelbaum* (1980), the three hallmarks of anthropology—holistic view, cultural relativism, and participant observation—facilitate an in-depth understanding of every aspect of a subject's life with desired objectivity and empathy. This makes an anthropologist the best suited to work on understanding regionalism, communalism, ethnicity, and political movements.

Regionalism: Expressing attachment to one's own region and to the people inhabiting that region is called regionalism. The crux of regionalism lies in the imbalances between regions created by economic development. In all regional movements, the protest is against equality because not all regions benefit equally from development and modernization. In the case of tribal societies, the problem of ethnicity and region has surfaced in certain areas. Numerically, big tribal groups have taken up their cause and have finally demanded a separate region for themselves; the most significant movements are the Naga movement, the Jharkhand movement, etc.

Communalism arises in society when a particular religious group tries to promote its own interests at the expense of others. The British had sown the seeds of communalism in India by dividing the people of various communities and spreading a feeling of distrust among them. Different communal organisations are found in India that has created hatred among the people of various religious communities by propagating communalism.

Ethnicity refers to expressive aspects of ethnic identities and the process of transformation of a group into a subjectively self-conscious community having psychological unity of kind and involving complex processes. The ethnic conflicts are mainly dependent on two factors: necessary conditions like socio-economic ones like poverty, inequality, land alienation, exploitation, unemployment, underdevelopment, and the influx of migrants. Though it provides a social base for ethnic conflicts, they depend on sufficient conditions. Sufficient conditions include the emergence of strong leadership, political competition and manipulation, casual and unwise government policies, and the availability of foreign support. Unless these sufficient conditions become active or powerful, these movements fail to find their language of expression. Change in the demographic profile of states like Maharashtra, Assam, or Tripura due to the influx of migrants This has aggravated local competition for scarce resources and the publication of the ideology of 'sons of soil'.

Several Indian anthropologists have written about these phenomena:

1. Ram Dayal Munda (VC, Ranchi University) found middle and lower levels of government officials to have little commitment towards tribal welfare. The government took away forests to manage them scientifically. However, they mismanaged the forests. Outsiders are given preference in employment. Land alienation continues unabated.
2. M.N. Srinivas has suggested that for neutralising regional movements, positive socio-economic measures should be taken by the government. Implement constitutional provisions in letter script. Legitimate share in the fruits of development.
3. Das Gupta says that regions, after gaining autonomy, have settled down to work out constructive partnerships with national leadership, national economic planning, and the national administrative system. It deserves to be tackled with care, sympathy, and appreciation for long-suppressed tribal aspirations.
4. Srivastava says that one of the key factors in communal politics in India is the communal politics of Britishers and the bitter experience of partition.
5. Emile Durkheim says that there is a psychological cause for communalism—the labelling theory of Muslims getting tagged as terrorists.
6. S.C. Dube's study of Sharimpet village showed Muslim and Hindu interaction with each other during festivals.
7. N.K. Bose's study, 'Gandhian Values Unite India," showed takeover and equality among all religions.
8. A Study on the Bodos and the Koch-Rajbongshis of Assam by Dipika Paul. The study shows that multiple factors, such as state policies and the chauvinistic attitudes of dominant groups, elites, and ethnic organisations at different points in time, led to the politicisation of ethnicity among these two ethnic groups. Therefore, the discourse of the politicisation of ethnicity can be considered a significant approach to understanding present-day ethnic movements.

According to *Ghurye*, "the political aspect, the administrative unity, and the political participation in it of the individual citizens are political integration, and in combination with social integration, it makes up a complex that is designated as national integration".

A detailed discussion of the issue of national integration regarding tribals was taken up in a "Seminar on Tribal Situation in India" held at the Indian Institute of Advanced Study, Shimla. The seminar recommended proper use of the mass media for the realisation of tribal integration with the national mainstream. To achieve this process, the following statements were issued by various scholars assembled in the seminar:

1. The press, radio, and other mass media have an important role to play in bridging the prevailing gulf of ignorance, misunderstanding, and prejudice between tribals and non-tribals. They could explain to the nontribals the aspirations of the tribals. Further, they could make clear to the tribals that many of the difficulties faced by them are more or less common to the other underprivileged sections of Indian society with whom they must join hands to find a common solution.
2. Special attention should also be given to the production of popular books for children and adults and textbooks designed to promote knowledge and appreciation of the different cultures inhabiting this ancient land. In devising schemes of national service for studies, care should be taken to ensure that tribal students work in non-tribal areas and non-tribals in tribal areas wherever practicable.
3. The development of communications and more satisfactory contacts between people of diverse backgrounds would naturally result in a good deal of give and take, leading to further enrichment of the content of the national culture.

Case Study

- **Identity Politics on the Hill Tribal Communities in North-Eastern India**

The fight to keep the Sixth Schedule's restrictions in place reflects identity politics. A few years ago, the Khasi Students Union in Meghalaya began a campaign to get the Khasi language added to the Indian Constitution's Eighth Schedule. The students believed that by receiving such accreditation, the Union Public Service Commission would accept their language as a valid writing medium for the several competitive exams that it holds. A few Khasi intellectuals pleaded with the union's leaders to end the agitation and drop the demand. They claimed that if their language were listed on the Eighth Schedule, it would indicate that it had advanced, and as a result, their civilization would likewise have advanced. The intellectuals forewarned the students that their society would forfeit all previous benefits received under the Sixth Schedule in such a scenario. The union renounced their request. After a while, the union brought up this demand once more, and this time it was met with sympathy from both the administration and those who had previously opposed it. Cases like the one mentioned above and others highlight the conundrum that tribal communities face when engaging in identity politics. They fear losing their "tribal identity" and all the advantages that come with it if they choose the route of economic growth. They risk extinction if they do not follow the path of development.

- **Pathalgarhi Movement (Tribal Movement/Tribal Issue PESA)**

The Union Government retracted the 2006 FRA modification that would have diminished tribal control over forests. In order to promote simpler land acquisition rules, the state government also dropped proposed revisions to the Santhal Paragnas Tenancy Act of 1876 and the Chotanagpur Tenancy Act of 1908. The PESA of 1996's provisions and proper implementation, however, were displayed on stone slabs buried on the outskirts of the settlement as a form of protest by the tribal population.

- **Pew Research (2021) provides data-backed evidence of the nature of Indian secularism**

Data-supported evidence of the nature of Indian secularism is provided by Pew Research (2021). Although they live apart, Indians simultaneously profess a commitment to religious tolerance and a constant preference for preserving their religious communities in distinct areas. While some people may desire to see their nation become a "melting pot" of many religious identities, our statistics indicate that many Indians would rather have their nation be more like a patchwork cloth, or thali, with distinct boundaries between communities.

Q 2. Anthropological Survey of India

Ans. The Anthropological Survey of India (AnSI) is the only research organisation to pursue anthropological research in a government setting. In 1945, the Anthropology Section of the Zoological Survey was carved out to become AnSI.

It is a premier research organisation under the Ministry of Culture. It is headquartered in Kolkata. It conducts bio-cultural investigations on the Indian population and collects and preserves documents of scientific interest about the people of India. It contributes to the biological, social, and cultural heritage of India.

Objectives:

1. To study tribes and other communities from both a biological and cultural point of view.
2. To study and preserve human skeletal remains from modern and anthropological sources.
3. To collect samples of the art and craft of the tribes of India.
4. To function as a training centre for advanced students in anthropology and for administration.
5. To publish the results of research.

One of the most remarkable projects was 'People of India'. It generated a brief anthropological profile of all communities in India and the impact of development on them. Around 4635 communities' fields were tasted, identified, and studied. 4,000 maps were prepared showing their distribution.

During the past 5 years, certain research projects done:

1. Study of denotified, nomadic, and seminomadic communities (2019).
2. Community health, disease, and genetic structure of the Indian population (2005)
3. Development and sustainability (2007-8)

There is a demand for more funding for R&D, more manpower, and bringing it under the Ministry of Tribal Affairs.

Case Study

- **Gandhian Insights into Applied Anthropology Journal by AnSI**

1. Ralph Nicholas, who is also well recognised for his work on the Bengali rural festival of Gajan, emphasised that the festival's emphasis on equality and human community—which shares many characteristics with Gandhi's yatra—embodied the equality of all citizens in the democratic India for which he gave his life. Participating in a variety of Durga Puja roles is similar to the healthy society Gandhi envisioned.
2. Professor Syiemlieh (former chairman of the UPSC) notes that although Gandhi was not the only national figure to visit the northeast, his direction and call were stirring and had a lasting impact, particularly on the Gandhian way of life, which is followed by many people in this region.
3. According to cultural anthropologist Kakali Chakrabarty, Gandhi believed that tribes should be contacted without resorting to violence, respecting the tenets of a democratic society as well as the inherent equality and oneness of all people.
4. Dr. Srivastava, Director of AnSI, stated that a closer examination reveals Gandhi's life and work were heavily influenced by anthropology. Gandhi seminars had already been held by AnSI in several of our regional hubs.

10

Ethnographic Profile of Tribes in Jammu and Kashmir UT and Ladakh UT

1. Gaddi

The Gaddis are shepherds who primarily live in Jammu's mountainous terrain. The majority of them are dispersed over the areas of Billawar, Ramban, Doda, Poonch, Anantnag, Basohli, Ram Nagar, and Udhampur. They have a mysterious past and origin, and there is no reliable documentation to support this. They were said to have originated in the plains of the combined Punjab and Sind provinces. The Gaddis travelled from place to place till they settled in the landlocked region of Bharmour (Himachal Pradesh). They were granted gaddi, or the right to rule, by Lord Shiva, who also decreed that only they could reside and rule in the area. They later came to be known as these individuals, and they referred to us as the Gaddis. Although the Gaddis are not vegetarians, they avoid eating beef. Maize, wheat, and rice are their main sources of nutrition. They eat grains and many kinds of pulses, and they cook using mustard oil. They snuff and chew tobacco simultaneously. A multitude of subsects, including Aralu, Beloria, Katoch, Chaak, Krokar, Jarwa, Lalhal, Shundal, Parihar, and Veerpuri, make up the Gaddis.

These compounds tend to be grouped according to the Rajput and Brahman lineages. The Gaddis practise exogamy within their gotras and endogamy within their communities. The members of the household get along well with one another. Unless they are of a criminal nature and must be handled by the state's judicial laws, disputes are typically resolved by mutual reconciliation. In all spheres of life, women are viewed as less important than men, and although they take part in all socioeconomic activities, they are not competing on an equal footing with their male counterparts. The majority of women work in farming, caring for animals, and other similar fields. For their homes, they serve as fuel gatherers and water bearers. Most of the ladies now weave wool blankets and clothing as well. Despite having the right to vote, women hardly participate in politics on an active basis. They are docile and subservient, yet they also put in a lot of effort. Land and woods are the Gaddis' main economic resources. The Gaddis, who work as shepherds, are constantly forced to transfer their flock of sheep and goats from one pasture to another and from one area to another. Their other economic pursuits include settled agriculture and the trade in animal sales. In addition to engaging in their ancestral activity, the Gaddis also practise settled agriculture, which significantly reduces their reliance on the official market. On a local level, the Gaddis have village panchayats. Village panchayats are diverse in nature, and although they lack statutory authority, their primary duty is to exercise social control. Hinduism is practised by the Gaddis. All of the significant Hindu religious holidays, including Diwali, Lohri, Janmashtami, Shivratri, and Rakshabandan, are observed by them. Seasonal holidays like Pitrolu and Shari are also observed by them. They perform with a ponoth, a traditional musical instrument. Men and women both take part in dancing. They are beginning to value formal education; however, guys are given priority over girls in pursuing it. Most boys only complete high school, and many of them enrol in colleges. Most girls only complete their basic education, while a handful makes it to high school. Social and financial issues contribute to the girls' dropping out of school. Boys are forced to discontinue their formal education primarily for financial reasons and to increase family income. Despite having a positive view of contemporary Medicare, the Gaddis mostly rely on traditional Medicare because it is available.

2. Gujjars:

The Gujjars are a well-known pastoral, semi-nomadic group. They went from Gujarat to Jammu and Kashmir, where they got their name. They are dispersed throughout the state's districts, including Jammu, Anantnag, Rajouri, Poonch, Pulwama, Ramban, Doda, Kishtwar, Shopian, Kulgam and Srinagar. The area where they reside and go to find pasture has a frigid environment with low humidity, little rainfall, few woods, and moderate to heavy winter snowfall. The Pir Panjal and Himalayan ranges encircle the steep terrain. Gujri is the name of the Gujjar language. When speaking with others, they use Punjabi, Hindi, and Kashmiri. Salwars, beards, kameez shirts, and long turbans are the community's distinctive clothing items. Women cover their heads with a particular style of cap called a topi. The majority of the adult members wear mehndi or henna-dyed beards.

The Gujjar are meat eaters who eat fish, poultry, goats, and sheep. Maize, rice, wheat, and pulses like moong (green gram) and moth (brown gram) are their main sources of sustenance. They enjoy eating bread and salty seafood. The Gujjars are socially divided according to occupation and faith. There are two groups of Gujjars in Kashmir: Jamindar and Dodhi. While the Dodhi Gujjars mostly depend on the sale of milk and milk products as well as the contract rearing of buffaloes, the Jamindar Gujjars are primarily involved in agriculture. The Muslim Gujjars are organised into a number of exogamous gotras that govern marriage relationships, including Kasana, Chechi, Padhana, Lodha, Khatana, Paswar, and Bangri. They see themselves as being in the middle of the regional social structure, and other people concur. Endogamy is always upheld and regarded as the law of marriage at the religious and communal levels. When choosing a bride for marriage, cousins are given favour. Parallel and cross-cousin marriages are both common. Negotiations are used to finalise weddings, but love marriages do occur. Although polygamy is permitted by Sharia (Islamic law), monogamy is the norm. Relationships between family members are built with appropriate respect for the elders and love for the children. The family's eldest member is regarded as the head and is given responsibility for managing family issues.

Women are treated equally and have significant roles in the social, religious, and economic areas of life among the Gujjars. They continue to work on home duties. In addition to helping their male counterparts with agricultural tasks, their responsibilities also include milking cattle, gathering firewood and fodder, and providing drinkable water. Along with keeping tabs on the family's spending, they also work hard to earn money for the household. The Gujjars observe the customs associated with birth, marriage, death, and other social events with tremendous fervour and excitement.

As mentioned earlier, in Jammu and Kashmir, there are two distinct subgroups of Gujjars: Jamindar and Dodhi. The Dodhi Gujjars are only pastoralists, but agriculture and animal husbandry are the main occupations of the Jamindar Gujjars. They continue to roam between low and high and high and low altitude hills in search of pastures for their buffaloes, which are the foundation of their entire business. Their main source of income is the sale of milk and dairy products. On occasion, they raise buffalo under contract. They also engage in agriculture as a secondary occupation, but only during the winter, when they remain in their natural environment. They give the land to sharecroppers in other seasons.

Although the majority of milk and milk products are sold in cities, they are occasionally traded with other items while on their summer pasture. More territory belongs to the Jamindar Gujjars than the Dodhi Gujjars. Although there is no system of bonded labour among them, family members' children do occasionally work in the paddy and corn fields.

They serve as grazers as well. Even if they now pursue other traditional occupations, including commerce, government and private jobs, and even the military, pastoralism is still thought of as their traditional occupation. To settle disagreements within the community, the Gujjars have their own biradari panchayat.

The Gujjars are Muslims. They go to mosques and other holy sites on certain occasions. Additionally observed are Id-ulZuha, Id-ul-Fitr, Shab-e-Qadr, Urs-e-Nabi, the Prophet's birthday, Id-ul-Milad, and Miraj-e-Alam. The Prophet's hair relic is on exhibit at the Hazratbal shrine on his birthday. They take part in the Urs, for example, the Urs-e-Shah Hamdan. Although the Gujjars do not have a unique art or craft, a handful of their people are skilled at creating specific knitted items from sheep's wool. Women sing folk songs at various social gatherings; however, there isn't a traditional musical instrument in the area. In order to find green pasture for their cattle, they go from high mountain ranges to low mountain ranges, and while they do so, they build friendly relationships with both Muslim and non-Muslim groups in the area where they set up camp. Given that the Bakarwal are regarded as a subset of the Gujjar, their relationships with them are very close. Due to their nomadic lifestyle, the Gujjar have a negative attitude towards formal education, especially in regards to the education of women. Most boys study until the first grade, while a few have advanced. The Jammu and Kashmir government established a few mobile primary schools to educate the local children, but the programme was not effective because the children were moved to new locations with harsh temperatures and challenging access, only staying a brief time in each camp. They still favour conventional indigenous treatments and pay little attention to the modern medical system.

3. Bakarwal

Sheep and goat herders are known as the Bakarwal, one of the pastoral communities in the state of Jammu and Kashmir. The term comes from the word bakariwale, which means a goat herder or a sheep and goat breeder. The Bakarwal started arriving in Kashmir in quest of greener pastures, and the SWAT region is thought to be their ancestral homeland. The community moved to the Kashmir Valley in the latter part of the nineteenth century. Although they are scattered across practically all of the districts in the state, they are primarily concentrated in the districts of Rajouri, Poonch, Udhampur, Kathua, Kupwara, Badgam, Baramulla, Pulwama, Jammu, and Doda. Although they write in Arabic and speak Kashmiri, the Gujjars' primary dialect, Gujri, is used to refer to them.

The Bakarwals eat largely vegetarian food, and their staples include maize, rice, wheat, and pulses like musur, black gram, urad, and moong (green gram). Although there is no social stratification in the neighbourhood, there is a modest difference in the size of the sheep flock, educational attainment, and economic standing. Although they believe they are in the middle of the regional social structure, others see them as being at the bottom. At the local level, endogamy is always preserved. Although polygamy is also acceptable in the culture, monogamy is the norm. According to the residential norms, patrilocal women must help with household chores such as milking animals, gathering fuel and grain, bringing potable water, buying necessities, and caring for injured cattle. Livestock is essential to the Bakarwal people's economy. Despite owning agricultural land and working in various related fields, these are regarded as secondary employment. By transporting tourists' luggage to the valleys of Sonemarg, Gulmarg, Pahalgam, and Bhaderwah, they can also make money from the tourists.

To resolve conflicts within the community, the Bakarwals have their own Biradari Panchayat. The Nambardar (headman), who leads the panchayat, is chosen by voice vote. Village statutory panchayats resolve inter-ethnic or land conflicts where they are natively found. These panchayats seek to promote the village's growth and wellbeing. They observe many Muslim holidays in various months. At various social gatherings, women sing folk music. They continue to favour their own traditional Medicare system because contemporary Medicare's amenities are not always available where they camp.

4. Bot/Bodh

The Ladakhi Bodh, Ladakhspa, or Botriksha are essentially Tibetans; it is from this region that they obtain their names of Pot, Bot, or Bhotta. Before the Aryan Dards began to immigrate to Ladakh, the North Indian people known as the Mons lived in Ladakh. Following their enslavement, the Mons received a very low standing in Ladakhi society. The hierarchy of the population is clearly defined and reflected in the seating arrangements made at public events, with subgroups such as Gyalpo (rulers), Kahlon (ministers), Mangriks (farmers), and Ringan (lower occupation groups) being among the most prominent. They reside in the regions of Zanskar (the "land of white copper"), Nubra, Ladakh, Kishtwar, Udhampur, and Reasi, which are distinguished by their high mountains, little to no precipitation, significant snowfall, and a barren, brown terrain with perpetual snow on barren hilltops. They converse in Bodhi among one another.

Women have the ability to inherit property, take part in all socioeconomic activities, manage the family's money, engage in self-employment, and work in white-collar positions. At the bridegroom's home, the ceremony is performed while the pair is shielded from evil spirits by prayers. Handicrafts, horticulture, small-scale enterprises, grinding, wood carving, transportation, etc. are examples of auxiliary economic resources.

The goba is in charge of the village elders' committee, which regulates social behaviour by resolving family conflicts, divorce-related issues, water-sharing disputes, the collection of livestock tax, and intercommunity disputes. The Gelukpa, Drokpa, and Neima subsects of Buddhism make up the Mahayana sect, which is practised by the Bodhs of Ladakh. Polyandry is deemed to be a bad practise as well. Elders, however, believe that religious observance is declining and that they are simultaneously being culturally assimilated by the nearby majority populations. Lamas are skilled in engraving, carving, painting, and drawing. The Bodhs have reached a high level of literacy and pursue higher education at the institutions in Jammu and Kashmir. They support small families and have a positive outlook on family welfare programmes.

5. Balti

The majority of Muslims (Shia) in Ladakh are Balti. They appear to be immigrants from Baltistan (Tibet Minor), a nearby region with Skardo as its capital. They are dispersed over Kupwara, Ganderbal, Kargil, Ladakh, and Baltistan. The locals converse with outsiders in Urdu, write among themselves in Arabic script, and speak to one another in Balti. Based on their social identities, the Baltis are split. Neither at the community level nor at the village level is endogamy effectively upheld as a regulation of marriage. Cross and parallel cousin marriages are also acceptable. For the purpose of marriage, the following kinds of kin are forbidden: (i) children of a mother and a sister; (ii) siblings of common parents; and (iii) offspring of a woman who has acted as a wet nurse. The common style of marriage is monogamous marriage. The nikah, which comes in two varieties: nikah-e-inqatai (breakable marriage contract) and nikah-e-daimi (permanent marriage contract). The former is referred to as muta, and both Baltis and Shia Muslims in general and Shia Muslims in particular recognise this kind of marriage.

Every household has a male head that has complete control over how the family's financial resources are allocated and distributed. In interfamilial social interactions, he represents the family, demands the respect of children, and shows them love. The Balti women engage in activities outside of the home as well as inside of it. For the harvesting of juniper plants that keep her home and hearth warm during the lengthy arctic winters, she treks 5 to 7 kilometres every day. The participation of women in ritual performance is equal to that of men. Agriculture and trade made up the Balti people's traditional economies. The majority of artisan crafts, including masonry, carpentry, milling, shoemaking, and tailoring, are specialised among the Baltis, who are not only self-sufficient but also offer their services to the Brokpa for a set cost.

6. Brokpa, Drokpa, Dard, and Shin

Brokpa, Drokpa, Dard, and Shin are a category of Scheduled Tribes under the Indian Constitution. The tribes in this category speak Dardic languages. These tribes are primarily found in the districts of Kargil, Baramulla, and Leh. They are mostly Muslims, but there are also some Buddhists and Hindus among them. The "Brokpa, Drokpa, Dard, and Shin".

Tribes' demographic data is combined for the Indian Census. This group is known collectively as the Dards. The tribes included in this category are as follows: Baramulla's Shina or Dard-Shin tribe; Ladakh's Drokpa (Shin) and Brokpa (Minaro) tribes in the Dha-Hanu region.

Gurez and Tulail in Baramullah are home to the Dard-Shin tribe, often known as the Shina people. A distinctive Shinaspeaking Dard tribe that has been shut off from its mainland Astore, Gilgit, and Chilas by the Line of Control resides in the Gurez valley. They converse in the Shina language's Astori dialect.

In the Drass valley of Kargil, there is a Muslim Dard tribe known as the Drokpa or Shin. They are also referred to as "the Shin" because of their language, "Shinna," which belongs to the Dard group of languages in the non-Sanskritic IndoEuropean family. They are also thought to have originated in Dardistan. They uphold certain traditions that they bring with them from their own country, even if they claim to be Sunnis. They converse in the Shina language's Astori dialect.

Buddhist Dards, known as Brokpa or Minaro, speak the Brokskat language. They can be found in the area of the Aryan Valley. While Ladakhis refer to them as Brokpa or Dokhpa, they go by the name "Minaro". They converse in the Eastern Dardic language family through the Brokskat or Minaro dialect. The ancient "Minaro" religion (spirit worship) is one of the two faiths practised by the Minaro. Tibetan Buddhism is the alternative.

Under the Scheduled Tribes of the former Jammu and Kashmir, these Scheduled Tribes are referred to as a "group of Dardic Tribes". Other non-tribal Dardic people, like the Kashmiri, do exist in the state, though. According to the most recent research, the term "Dardic" is neither linguistic nor ethnic; it is only a suitable geographical expression used to officially choose the Indo-Iranian language that retains the archaic characteristics that are spoken in the north-western Himalayas and in the Hindu Kush. The people who speak these languages do not share a common ethnicity. Additionally, it is impossible to link the languages to a single linguistic tree model.

7. Brokpa

The Muslim Dards, known as the Brokpa, can be traced back to the Aryans. The name "hill dwellers" is derived from the two terms broq (hills) and pa (people). They go by the name Shin. The settlements in the Kargil and Suru valleys are home to the Brokpas. They communicate with others in Balti, Bodhi, or Urdu while speaking Shina among themselves. For writing, they employ the Balti script. Well-educated Brokpas have developed solid Arabic and Persian language skills.

Men do not display any identity markers, but women can be identified by their customary Dard hats, which are decorated with household items and flowers from their own kitchen gardens. They consume yak meat and are not vegetarians. Eggs are moderately consumed, while fish is not. The staple foods are grim (baked barley) and kachi (parched grim flour), with mutton and green vegetables serving as side dishes. Rice is only infrequently eaten. Fruits that may be found nearby, including apricots and apples, are consumed in large quantities. Their major beverage is cha, or tea.

The populace is split up into many Gatti (lineages). Every Gatti is made up of different Khandan (families). The various gattis are not ranked in any particular order. Although it is typically an endogamous entity, intra-Gatti weddings frequently occur because there aren't any acceptable mates. The populace is divided into a number of hierarchically superior categories, such as the sheikh (artisan class). The denomination of the sect is another factor in their split. The Brokpa are both Shia (Ethna-e-Ashari) and Sunni people, and they are unwilling to form marriage connections. The culture of Brokpa is controlled by men. Women take an active part in farming, gathering fuel, and performing rituals. Legal village panchayats have not been successful in advancing issues or involving citizens in decision-making. Since gaining independence, many elections have been held, and the populace has a high level of political awareness. Folk songs have a deep oral legacy among the Brokpa. The state government's many development initiatives have received a generally favourable reception from the Brokpa people, who have also shown considerable enthusiasm.

8. Champa

The Champa, also known as the Changpa, live in the icy deserts and northern plains that separate Tibet from Ladakh. They communicate with one another in Bodhi, but they speak Changskhat to each other. They use the Bodhi script. They consume meat, cat yak, and kiang (wild asses) and are not vegetarians. Tsampa (powdered barley) and yak and kiang meat make up the staple diet. Although tea with salt (cha) is the daily beverage, chang is the main beverage.

The Fangpa (sedentary) and the Phalpa (nomadic) are two subgroups of the Champas. They have an elite class among them known as Nono. The stratification is solely based on economic status and level of accomplishment. There are no restrictions on intermarrying between the three portions. Girls get married at 16, while boys get married at 18. To the extent of one-third, women have the right to inherit their parents' property. They are actively involved in the family's economic endeavours. Yak and goat herds are the primary sources of income for the Champa people. The population resides on land owned by the Hemis Gompa rather than having their own landholdings.

The traditional forum for dispute resolution is Goba. The legally required Gram Panchayats have failed to enter this hostile territory. As regulated courts of justice have grown in popularity, Goba is gradually losing its power over the populace. They are members of the Buddhist Drokpa sect. In their cultural framework, religion is fundamental. They have places of pilgrimage in Hemis and Dharamshala.

9. Dokhpa/Drokpa

Drokh or Dokh, in its literal sense, refers to a meadow, and Dokhpa/Drokhpa refers to the inhabitants of the meadow. The Dokhpas are thought to be the immediate ancestors of the Dards, who are reported to have moved from Gilgit. The Dokhpas are described as valiant people by historians. Four villages, Hanu and Da in Ladakh and Darsik and Gorkone in Kargil, are home to the Dokhpa people. Because there is a lot of water, the Dokhpas' primary vocations are agriculture and horticulture, where they even currently reside. Buckwheat, millets, and naked barley are the principal crops farmed.

Their cash crops, which are the primary source of their revenue, include tomatoes, apricots, and grapes. Speaking Droskhat among themselves, the Dokhpas talk in Ladakhi or Urdu with strangers. They employ the Bodhi script. The headgear, the distinctively half-shaven heads, and the gown are the characteristics of the Dokhpa attire. Women are particularly drawn to needlework.

They also eat vegetables, grains, and meat. Poultry, eggs, and anything made from cow's milk are absolutely forbidden. There is gurgur chai (salted tea) in their diet. Fruits are consumed in huge numbers, notably the apricots and grapes that are cultivated in profusion. Everyone in the neighbourhood drinks chang, an alcoholic beverage made locally from barley. The Drokhpas are made up of a few clans called phasphuns, and intermarriage is allowed between them. Singing, dancing, and drinking are all prevalent throughout this significant festive occasion. The Dokhpa's primary line of work is agriculture. Raising sheep and cattle is another aspect of the Dokhpa's economy. Among the Dokhpas, craftspeople and artisans like barbers, tailors, etc. are noticeably lacking.

The only authority known to the Dokhpas is the headman, who goes by the name Makdom. He was chosen democratically. He is the one who makes crucial decisions affecting the community as a whole and guards its interests. They hold faith in demons, spirits, and gods. Lower-level educational facilities are offered. Both boys and girls attend school at very low rates. Even the students who attend these institutions don't appear to gain much.

10. Mon

Ladakh's Mons are a group of people who play the flute. They don't have any titles, synonyms, or subgroups. They are known as Dolba by Ladakh's Buddhists. The Mons were classified as Rungnum (lowest class) in the 1911 census report. principal concentration The Tibeto-Burman-originating city of Leh is home to the Mon people, who can be found on high terraces overlooking it. They employ the Bodhi script. Several of them converse in Urdu with others. They present themselves in traditional Ladakhi Buddhist garb. Men don a Ladakhi cap, a goncha (long cat), a shakten (shirt), sherak (trousers), and a belt made of colourful cloth around the waist. They also wear shoes made of leather or wool. The women are covered in a scarf over their heads, goncha, and perak (woollen boots). They have Mongoloid features. The Mon consumes beef and is not a vegetarian. Barley and wheat make up their stable diet. Gram, urad, moong, and peas are the pulses used. The medium for cooking is mustard oil. Sattoo is the main meal item. Potatoes, turnips, gurgur (salty tea), and chang (barley beer), all of which are consumed often throughout the day, are made from the flour of roasted wheat and barley.

Social distinctions don't exist among the Mons. However, there are exogamous gyuts (blood connections). The community's members don't all share the same last name. At the local level, endogamy is practised, although it is not strictly observed. A few marriages have taken place outside of the group. The Bhotos, or Ladakhi Buddhists, often do not gift or accept brides from the Mons because they view them as being of poor social standing. Contraception is not used. The Mons have mixed extended families. The family is led by the father. The Mon women are involved in farming, animal husbandry, fuel gathering, bringing drinkable water, child care, food preparation, housekeeping, etc. In contrast to the lads, the girls receive tender care while bringing the bride price. Women and men have the same status. Land serves as the primary economic resource for the Mons. In the past, the monastery or the Raja would give the monks some land in exchange for the services they offered. When there are celebrations or rites, their main job is to play the flute. The community's residents also work as wage labourers, run their own businesses, or provide services. A couple of them are active-duty soldiers. They do not occupy any positions of leadership in the village council because of their poor social rank. They use the community elders to mediate their own issues. They identify as Buddhists. They can go to the gompas or the monastery to worship and make offerings to the idols of Lord Buddha.

11. Gara/Garra

Mongoloid ancestry can be used to pinpoint the origin of the Gara, a group of blacksmiths in Ladakh known as Garba in the Kargil district. They are mainly found in Leh, but there are also a few scattered individuals in the Kargil district. Their homes in Leh are set on the Ladakh range at a high elevation with a view of the Indus River and its tributaries. They can speak some Urdu, and they speak Ladakhi. Bodhi is their written script. They present themselves in traditional Buddhist Ladakhi garb. Men dress in a long coat called a goncha, shirts called shaktens, a belt around the waist called a sherak, and boots made of wood and leather. The goncha, perak, firoza, which is a scarf worn on the head, and chertor woollen or leather footwear are worn by the women.

The Garas consume beef and are not vegetarians. Grim (naked barley) and wheat are their main sources of sustenance. The pulses consumed are peas, urad, moong, and grain. Chang is a common alcoholic beverage made from barley. They do not frequently smoke. Social distinctions are nonexistent. However, there are exogamous gyuts (blood relatives) and rikanum (occupational groups). The gyuts have no particular names, yet the locals are aware of each one. Endogamy is used in local communities. The Mon, Beda, and Bhotos (Ladakhi Buddhists) are the only groups from which the Garas can obtain wives. The most common type of marriage is monogamy. Respect for the elderly and love for children are the cornerstones of interpersonal relationships. Homework is primarily carried out by women. Major domestic tasks include caring for children, preparing meals, getting water, and gathering fuel. When crops are being sown and harvested, they also work in the fields. Women have the same standing as men. The Garas are an agrarian people. They assist the local population by mending iron hearths, kitchenware, and other agricultural equipment. They make iron stoves, windows, doors, sickles, spades, hammers, and knives. In addition to supplying the requirements of the locals, they also advertise their finished goods in the Leh market.

The Garas do not have any positions of leadership in the village council due to their poor socioeconomic rank. They rarely go before the village council to resolve issues; instead, they turn to the elders in their local neighbourhood. A gara is never favoured in disputes with the Bhotos or the Ladakhi Buddhists. Relations between communities are founded on reciprocal reliance. The Bhotos, the majority group of Ladakhi Buddhists in the area, view the Garas as their servants. There are not much business owners, academics, and people working in white collar jobs, doctors, or engineers in the community. Because the Bhoto students will have to wish and salute, the Bhotos do not want a Gara as a teacher. Both boys and girls desire formal education, but due to discrimination from the dominant population, the community is unable to send its children to school. Dropouts are more prevalent in this neighbourhood. The Gara people are Buddhists. Each family has a chotkang (place of worship) in the home, which is typically in the kitchen and is lit by an oil lamp. The gompa is open to community members; however, they are not permitted to become lamas.

Case Study

- **Who are the Paharis and Paddaris, proposed for ST status in J&K?**

The government has brought a Bill to include four communities in the list of Scheduled Tribes (STs) in Jammu and Kashmir: “Gadda Brahmin”, “Koli”, “Paddari Tribe”, and “Pahari Ethnic Group”.

The Constitution Jammu and Kashmir) Scheduled Tribes Order (Amendment) Bill, 2023 is one of the four Bills relating to the Union Territory that were introduced in Lok Sabha.

ST communities now

The dominant ST communities in J&K are the Gujjars and Bakerwals, who mainly live in the districts of Rajouri, Poonch, Reasi, Kishtwar, Anantnag, Bandipora, Ganderbal, and Kupwara. Most of them, especially the Bakerwals, are nomadic — they migrate with their livestock to the higher reaches in the summer, and return before the onset of winter.

With a population of almost 18 lakh, the Gujjar-Bakerwal are the third largest group after Kashmiris and Dogras in J&K. They were given ST status in 1991, along with the two smaller groups of Gaddis and Sippis. This entitled these four communities to 10% reservation in government jobs and admission to educational institutions; in 2019, they were empowered politically after the Centre announced a 10% quota for them in Lok Sabha and Assembly seats in J&K.

The proposed expansion of the ST list has triggered unrest among the Gujjar-Bakerwal, who apprehend a shrinking of their share of the quota benefits pie. The Bill says the amendment "may entail additional expenditure on account of benefits to be provided to persons belonging to the said [four] communities".

Gujjar-Bakerwal leaders are especially agitated with the proposed ST status for Paharis and Paddaris. Gadda Brahmins and Kolis are very small communities; also, according to the protesters, Gadda Brahmins are a branch of the Gaddis while Kolis are a sub-caste of Sippis—both these communities are already in the ST list.

Pahari Ethnic Group

The Paharis are Hindus, Muslims, and Sikhs, and include people of Kashmiri origin who settled in the districts of Rajouri and Poonch over a period of time. There are upper caste Hindus among the Paharis; also people who were displaced from Pakistan Occupied Kashmir.

In 1989, the J&K government led by Farooq Abdullah recommended that Paharis should be included in the list of STs along with the Gujjars, Bakerwals, Gaddis, and Sippis. However, the recommendation was rejected by the Registrar General of India on the ground that there was no caste/ tribe of that name in its records.

In response to popular demand from Paharis living in the border areas of Rajouri and Poonch districts — who argued that they lived in the same areas as the Gujjar-Bakerwals and faced similar social and educational backwardness — the Farooq government set up an Advisory Board for Development of Pahari Speaking People. The Board defined Paharis as all people living in Rajouri and Poonch except those who were STs.

As the Paharis continued to clamour for ST status, the Centre sought repeated clarifications from the J&K government. In 2012-13, the J&K government commissioned a study by Prof Amin Peerzada of Kashmir University, which its report supported the Paharis' demand. The PDP-BJP government led by Mehbooba Mufti sent the report to the Centre with its supporting recommendation; however, the case was rejected once again on the ground that Paharis were not an ethnic group.

Earlier in 2014, the Omar Abdullah government had brought a Bill proposing a 5% quota for Paharis, but Governor N N Vohra refused his assent to the Bill.

The Paharis finally got 4% reservation in jobs and educational institutions in 2019, when Satya Pal Malik was Governor. Also in 2019, the Justice (retd) G D Sharma Commission was appointed to identify groups that were socially, educationally, and economically backward. The Commission in its report recommended ST status for Gadda Brahmins, Kolis, Paddari Tribe, and Pahari Ethnic Group. The report was sent to the Tribal Affairs Ministry, and the Registrar General approved it in 2022.

Paddari Tribe

They live in the remote Paddar area of the hilly Kishtwar district. Spread over two tehsils, the Paddari homeland borders Zanskar (Ladakh) in the north and the east, Pangi in Himachal Pradesh in the south, and the rest of J&K in the west.

The 2011 census recorded the Paddari population at 21,548, comprising 83.6% Hindus, 9.5% Buddhists, and 6.8% Muslims. The people of the area, including those who have come from elsewhere to settle there, speak the Paddari language. Like in the case of the Paharis.

Bibliography

- Nadeem Hasnain . *Indian Anthropology*. 6th ed., Palaka Prakashan.
- Nadeem Hasnain . *Tribal India*. 6th ed., Palaka Prakashan.
- D.K. Bhattacharya. *An Outline of Indian Prehistory*. 8th ed., Palaka Prakashan.
- Akshat Jain IAS. *Anthropology Demystified*. 1st ed., Jice Publications.
- Dr Sudhir Kumar. *Anthropology Test Series Material*.
- Vaid's ICS. *Study Material for Anthropology*.
- Laurels institute. *Study Material for Anthropology*.
- "Bhuria Commission Report, Mungekar Committee Report, NAC Recommendations for PVTGs, Xaxa Committee Report." *https://tribal.nic.in/Statistics.aspx*.
- "India Hosted Youngest Populations of 'Acheulean' Human Ancestors: Study." *The Indian Express*, 6 Oct. 2021, indianexpress.com/article/technology/science/india-hosted-youngest-populations-of-acheulean-human-ancestors-study-7556077.
- "Palaeolithic Cave Paintings Found in Corner of NCR Could Be Among Oldest." *Hindustan Times*, www.hindustantimes.com/india-news/palaeolithic-cave-paintings-found-in-corner-of-ncr-could-be-among-oldest-in-the-country-101626201354624.html.
- "Fossil of Earth's Oldest-known Mammal, Dickinsonia, Found in Madhya Pradesh." *Deccan Herald*, 3 May 2021, www.deccanherald.com/science-and-environment/fossil-of-earths-oldest-known-mammal-dickinsonia-found-in-madhya-pradesh-981952.html.
- "Prehistoric Rock Paintings Found in Telangana, History Enthusiasts Believe They Date Back 10k-30k Years." *The Indian Express*, 13 May 2022, indianexpress.com/article/cities/hyderabad/prehistoric-rock-paintings-telangana-7915834.
- Agencies. "Two Human Skeletons From Indus Valley-era Found in Rakhigarhi - the Shillong Times." *The Shillong Times*, 9 May 2022, theshillongtimes.com/2022/05/09/two-human-skeletons-from-indus-valley-era-found-in-rakhigarhi.
- Staff, The Wire. "New Study Suggests Indus Valley People Spoke Ancestral Dravidian Language – the Wire Science." *New Study Suggests Indus Valley People Spoke Ancestral Dravidian Language – the Wire Science*, 17 Aug. 2021, science.thewire.in/the-sciences/nature-study-ancestral-dravidian-language-indus-valley-elephant-pilu.
- "India Now Has More Women Than Men: 8 Major Findings From NFHS-5 Data." *India Now Has More Women Than Men: 8 Major Findings From NFHS-5 Data*, www.dailyo.in/variety/india-population-demography-decline-nfhs-5-data-34869.
- KUSHAGRA PRASAD M.Phil Scholar (MDU,Rohtak). "THE DOMINANT CASTE IN HARYANA: MAPPING OUT THE DOMINANCE OVER THE YEARS." *International Journal of Science, Engineering and Management (IJSEM)*, vol. 6, no. 2.
- Akhyai Jyoti Mahanta. "Inter-Caste Marriage: An Untold Saga of Oppression in a Vaishnava Monastery of Assam." *Indian Sociological Society*, vol. 5.
- Pinaki Das. "Kharchi Puja, Synthesis of Tribal and Hindu Culture, Begins in Tripura." *Outlook India*, 17 July 2021.
- Malik, Col Yuvraj. "Kashi-Tamil Sangamam: Shared Knowledge, Shared Traditions." *Times of India Blog*, 26 Nov. 2022, timesofindia.indiatimes.com/blogs/voices/kashi-tamil-sangamam-shared-knowledge-shared-traditions.

- "A Unique Initiative by Tribal Affairs Ministry in Aurangabad;" *Press Information Bureau*, pib.gov.in/Pressreleaseshare.aspx?PRID=1744809.
- "India's Leopard God, Waghoba, Aids Wildlife Conservation in the Country." *WorldAtlas*, 29 Jan. 2022, www.worldatlas.com/articles/india-s-leopard-god-waghoba-aids-wildlife-conservation-in-the-country.html.
- "The Two Day Global Buddhist Summit 2023 Concludes With New Delhi Declaration." *Press Information Bureau*, pib.gov.in/Pressreleaseshare.aspx?PRID=1918640.
- *PM Addresses on Occasion of 150th Birth Anniversary of Shri Vijay Vallabh Surishwar Ji via Video Message*. pib.gov.in/Pressreleaseshare.aspx?PRID=1871041.
- GatewayHouse, and Sukh Deo Muni. "Islam in India's Soft Power - Gateway House." *Gateway House*, 28 June 2018, www.gatewayhouse.in/islam-india-soft-power.
- Jessymol M.V, and Dr. Avinuo Chupuo. "Impact of Christianity on Naga Culture." *IJCRT*, vol. 9, no. 10.
- Joshi, P. C. "Professor Vinay Kumar Srivastava: A Life Full of Academic Humility." *Journal of the Anthropological Survey of India*, vol. 70, no. 1, SAGE Publications, June 2021, pp. 157–61. *Crossref*, https://doi.org/10.1177/2277436x211016688.
- "Gaon Connection Releases 'The State of Rural India Report 2020', a Unique Compendium of Ground Reports From Rural India - Gaonconnection | Your Connection With Rural India." *Gaonconnection | Your Connection With Rural India*, 29 Dec. 2020, en.gaonconnection.com/gaon-connection-releases-the-state-of-rural-india-report-2020-a-unique-compendium-of-ground-reports-from-rural-india.
- "Supreme Court to Rule on Quota for Dalit Muslims, Christians | India News - Times of India." *The Times of India*, timesofindia.indiatimes.com/india/wont-wait-for-panel-sc-to-rule-on-quota-for-dalit-muslims-christians/articleshow/99445174.cms.
- "Karnataka Govt. Decision Scrapping 4% Quota to Muslims Will Not Be Implemented Till May 9: Supreme Court." *Karnataka Govt. Decision Scrapping 4% Quota to Muslims Will Not Be Implemented Till May 9: Supreme Court - the Hindu*, 25 Apr. 2023, www.thehindu.com/news/national/karnataka-govt-decision-scrapping-4-quota-to-muslims-will-not-be-implemented-till-may-9-supreme-court/article66776612.ece.
- Rana P.B. Singh. "Ethno-geography of the Sun Goddess Festival, 'chhatha', in Bhojpur Region, India: From Locality to Universality." *Asiatica Ambrosiana*.
- Dept. of Rural Development Govt. of Telangana . "Transforming Villages – Convergence of MGNREGS." *https://rural.nic.in/sites/default/files/TELANGANA.pdf*.
- UNESCO. "Mobile Vaani." *https://unesdoc.unesco.org/ark:/48223/pf0000258878*.
- Mallika Bhagat. "Ink of Life: This Artist Is Archiving India's Indigenous Tattoos." *https://www.outlookindia.com/outlooktraveller/explore/story/71692/ink-of-life-this-artist-is-archiving-indias-indigenous-tattoos*, 29 Jan. 2022.
- Walter Fernandes. "Land Alienation and Rural Development in Northeast India." *Indian Sociological Society*, vol. 1 (1), Apr. 2017, pp. 31–47.
- Moushumi Basu. "Frequent Floods in the Brahmaputra Are Eating Away at Assam's Tribal Lands." *https://scroll.in/article/1013881/frequent-floods-in-the-brahmaputra-are-eating-away-at-assams-tribal-lands*.
- "Child Marriage Rears Its Ugly Head in Rajasthan." *Child Marriage Rears Its Ugly Head in Rajasthan - the Hindu*, 24 Nov. 2022, www.thehindu.com/news/national/child-marriage-rears-its-ugly-head-in-rajasthan/article66180810.ece.
- "&Lsquo;Pathshalas&Rsquo;Making Change in Tribals&Rsquo; Life." *The New Indian Express*, 13 May 2023, www.newindianexpress.com/thesundaystandard/2022/jan/16/pathshalasmaking-change-in-tribals-life-2407304.html.
- "Govt Taking Measures to Upgrade All Eklavya Model Schools: Tribal Affairs Minister." *The Indian Express*, 13 July 2021, indianexpress.com/article/education/govt-taking-measures-to-upgrade-all-eklavya-model-schools-tribal-affairs-minister-arjun-munda-7402574.

- "With National Education Policy Mandate, Odisha Bats for Mother Tongue of Tribals." *With National Education Policy Mandate, Odisha Bats for Mother Tongue of Tribals - the Hindu*, 19 Nov. 2021, www.thehindu.com /news/national/other-states/with-national-education-policy-mandate-odisha-bats-for-mother-tongue-of-tribals/article37588923.ece.
- "Shaala Sangwari: Killing Two Birds With One Stone." *Shaala Sangwari: Killing Two Birds With One Stone*, 29 Nov. 2019, www.downtoearth.org.in/blog/forests/shaala-sangwari-killing-two-birds-with-one-stone-68063.
- "Fight Against Covid-19: Odisha's Bonda Tribe Shows the Way." *Bonda Tribe | Fight Against Covid: Odisha's Bonda Tribe Shows the Way - Telegraph India*, 13 June 2023, www.telegraphindia.com/india/fight-against-covid-odishas-bonda-tribe-shows-the-way/cid/1848530.
- "TRIFED, UNICEF& WHO Promote Health With Livelihood Activities Through a Focussed Vaccination Campaign in Tribal Districts." *Press Information Bureau*, pib.gov.in/PressReleseDetail.aspx?PRID=1758962.
- "Country's First Report on Tribal Health Still Awaits Implementation." *Country's First Report on Tribal Health Still Awaits Implementation - the Hitavada*, www.thehitavada.com/Encyc/2022/3/6/Country-s-first-report-on-tribal-health-still-awaits-implementation.html.
- "Giri Poshana Is the War Waged Against Hunger." *The New Indian Express*, 7 May 2023, www.newindianexpress.com /states/telangana/2022/jan/02/giri-poshana-is-the-war-waged-against-hunger-2402142.html.
- Surjit Singh. "HOW SALT APPROACH IS TRANSFORMING FARMERS' LIVES IN NE INDIA ." *https://yourstory.com/mystory/how-salt-approach-is-transforming-farmers-lives-in-z0e7r9btz3.*
- "Anthropological Survey of India Builds Tribal Hut Replicas to Promote Unique Heritage." *Anthropological Survey of India Builds Tribal Hut Replicas to Promote Unique Heritage - the Hindu*, 6 Nov. 2022, www.thehindu.com/sci-tech/science/anthropological-survey-of-india-builds-tribal-hut-replicas-to-promote-unique-heritage/article66104425.ece.
- "IIT Kanpur Bags Award for 'Tech for Tribals' Programme to Connect Tribals With Global Markets." *India Today*, 14 Aug. 2021, www.indiatoday.in/education-today/news/story/iit-kanpur-bags-award-for-tech-for-tribals-programme-to-connect-tribals-with-global-markets-1840768-2021-08-14.
- "TRIBES INDIA VAN DHAN to Expand Online Marketing in a Big Way by Tying up With Big Basket, MoU Signed Between TRIFED and Big Basket." *Press Information Bureau*, pib.gov.in/Pressreleaseshare.aspx?PRID=1756421.
- "Amazon India Launches Karigar Mela in Partnership With Tribes India." *Amazon India Launches Karigar Mela in Partnership With Tribes India - the Hindu*, 30 Aug. 2021, www.thehindu.com/business/amazon-india-launches-karigar-mela-in-partnership-with-tribes-india/article36182937.ece.
- "Under Police's Initiative, 300 Tribal Youths in Naxal-hit Gadchiroli Get Jobs in Different Fields." *The Economic Times*, economictimes.indiatimes.com/news/india/under-polices-initiative-300-tribal-youths-in-naxal-hit-gadchiroli-get-jobs-in-different-fields/articleshow/88612983.cms.
- "Attempt to Revive Covid-hit Dhokra Tribal Craft in Odisha." *India Today*, 14 Feb. 2022, www.indiatoday.in/india/story/dhokra-traditional-handicraft-artisan-odisha-handicraft-1912903-2022-02-14.
- "A Tale of 2 Villages: How Dhinkia and Nuagaon Have Fared Different Between 2 Steel Projects." *A Tale of 2 Villages: How Dhinkia & Nuagaon Have Fared Different Between 2 Steel Projects*, 18 Jan. 2022, www.downtoearth.org.in/news/governance/a-tale-of-2-villages-how-dhinkia-nuagaon-have-fared-different-between-2-steel-projects-81166.
- "Tribal Communities Suffer When Evicted in the Name of Conservation." *Tribal Communities Suffer When Evicted in the Name of Conservation*, 7 May 2019, www.downtoearth.org.in/blog/forests/tribal-communities-suffer-when-evicted-in-the-name-of-conservation-64376.
- "Loktak Lake: The Human and Environmental Costs of Hydropower." *Loktak Lake: The Human and Environmental Costs of Hydropower – the Diplomat*, 11 Dec. 2021, thediplomat.com/2021/12/loktak-lake-the-human-and-environmental-costs-of-hydropower.

- "No Means No: Kinnaur Tribals Oppose Hydropower Plant to Protect Fragile Ecology | NewsClick." *NewsClick*, www.newsclick.in/no-means-no-kinnaur-tribals-oppose-hydropower-plant-protect-fragile-ecology.
- "Forest Conservation Rules Infringe Upon Land Rights of Tribespeople: ST Panel Chief." *Forest Conservation Rules Infringe Upon Land Rights of Tribespeople: ST Panel Chief - the Hindu*, 20 Oct. 2022, www.thehindu.com/sci-tech/energy-and-environment/national-commission-for-scheduled-tribes-asks-centre-to-put-new-forest-conservation-rules-on-hold/article66035744.ece.
- "Ensure Patta and Effective Implementation of Forest Rights Act for Tribal People: Study." *Ensure Patta and Effective Implementation of Forest Rights Act for Tribal People: Study - the Hindu*, 18 Aug. 2021, www.thehindu.com/news/cities/Coimbatore/ensure-patta-and-effective-implementation-of-forest-rights-act-for-tribal-people-study/article35987689.ece.
- Mrs. Sephali Pradhan. *GLOBALISATION AND ITS EFFECT ON TRIBAL DEVELOPMENT*.
- Mrs. Sephali Pradhan. "GLOBALISATION AND ITS EFFECT ON TRIBAL DEVELOPMENT." *INTERNATIONAL JOURNAL FOR INNOVATIVE RESEARCH IN MULTIDISCIPLINARY FIELD*, vol. 1, no. 3, Oct. 2015.
- IndiaSpend.com, Abhijit Mohanty. "In Odisha, an Adivasi Community Is Using Traditional Farming to Fight Climate Change." *Scroll.in*, 26 Sept. 2021, scroll.in/article/998817/in-odisha-an-adivasi-community-is-using-traditional-farming-to-fight-climate-change.
- Jayashree Ambewadikar. "Interlinking Discrimination , Poverty and Social Exclusion of Scheduled Castes in Rural India ." *Semanticscholar*.
- "The Constitution (One Hundred and Twenty-seventh Amendment) Bill, 2021." *The Constitution (One Hundred and Twenty-seventh Amendment) Bill, 2021*, 9 Aug. 2021, prsindia.org/billtrack/the-constitution-one-hundred-and-twenty-seventh-amendment-bill-2021.
- Sharma, Padmakshi. "Breaking | Supreme Court Upholds 10% Reservation for Economically Weaker Section (EWS) in Education and Public Employment by 3:2 Majority." *Supreme Court Upholds EWS Quota by 3:2 Majority; CJI Lalit & Justice Bhat in Minority*, 7 Nov. 2022, www.livelaw.in/top-stories/supreme-court-10-reservation-for-ews-economically-weaker-section-in-education-public-employment-213437.
- Dipika Paul. "Politicisation of Ethnicity: A Study on the Bodos and the Koch-Rajbongshis of Assam." *Indian Sociological Society*, vol. 4 (1), Apr. 2020, pp. 4–28.
- ThemeGrill. "Komaram Bheem: A Forgotten Adivasi Leader Who Gave the Slogan 'Jal Jangal Jameen' – Adivasi Resurgence." *Komaram Bheem: A Forgotten Adivasi Leader Who Gave the Slogan 'Jal Jangal Jameen' – Adivasi Resurgence*, 16 Oct. 2016, adivasiresurgence.com/2016/10/16/komaram-bheem-a-forgotten-adivasi-leader-who-gave-the-slogan-jal-jangal-jameen.
- "On Gandhi Jayanti, Know the Importance of Forest Satyagraha." *Hindustan Times*, 2 Oct. 2021, www.hindustantimes.com/india-news/on-gandhi-jayanti-know-the-importance-of-forest-satyagraha-101633131489931.html.
- "Nagaland: Commission on Register of Indigenous Inhabitants Submits Recommendations." *Hindustan Times*, 12 Aug. 2021, www.hindustantimes.com/cities/others/nagaland-commission-on-register-of-indigenous-inhabitants-submits-recommendations-101628757634007.html.
- Emmanuel, Meera. "Many Get False Community Certificates to Take Away Opportunities of Scheduled Caste/ Scheduled Tribe Candidates: Madras High Court Raises Concern." *Bar And Bench - Indian Legal News*, 26 June 2021, www.barandbench.com/news/litigation/false-community-certificates-scst-candidates-madras-high-court.
- Nazir, Tashafi. "Remembering Budhu Bhagat! Tribal Hero Who Stood Against Forced Labour, Economic Exploitation by Britishers." *Remembering Budhu Bhagat! Tribal Hero Who Stood Against Forced Labour, Economic Exploitation by Britishers*, 17 Feb. 2022, thelogicalindian.com/history/remembering-tribal-hero-budhu-bhagat-33997.
- "Tribes in Arunachal Pradesh Feel Push to Resist Conversions to Christianity." *Tribes in Arunachal Pradesh Feel Push to Resist Conversions to Christianity - Frontline*, 20 Oct. 2022, frontline.thehindu.com/the-nation/tribes-in-arunachal-pradesh-feel-push-to-resist-conversions-to-christianity/article66013399.ece.
  "Hadza." *Hadza*, education.nationalgeographic.org/resource/hadza.

- Aashish Khakha. "Adivasis, the Fifth Schedule and Urban Development: A Study of Greater Ranchi." *Indian Sociological Society*, vol. 3 (2), Oct. 2019, pp. 78–89.
- "Former Lakshadweep Administrator, Two Others Demand Roll Back of LDAR 2021." *Former Lakshadweep Administrator, Two Others Demand Roll Back of LDAR 2021 - the Hindu*, 28 May 2021, www.thehindu.com/news/national/kerala/former-lakshadweep-administrator-two-others-demand-roll-back-of-ldar-2021/article34665067.ece.
- "Technology Eases Path for the Weary Nomads in J&K." *Technology Eases Path for the Weary Nomads in J&K - the Hindu*, 8 Oct. 2022, www.thehindu.com/news/national/technology-eases-the-path-for-seasonal-migration-of-nomads-in-jk/article65982543.ece.
- "Killing Two Birds With Solitary Out-of-box Idea." *The New Indian Express*, 7 May 2023, www.newindianexpress.com /thesundaystandard/2021/aug/15/killing-two-birds-with-solitary-out-of-box-idea-2344810.html.
- "Odisha Publishes India's First Encyclopedia on Tribal Communities." *Hindustan Times*, 27 Sept. 2022, www.hindustantimes.com/india-news/odisha-publishes-india-s-first-encyclopedia-on-tribal-communities-101664282139388.html.
- SNS. "An IAS Officer's Journey Towards Bettering Lives of Tribals - the Statesman." *The Statesman*, 1 Jan. 2022, www.thestatesman.com/books-education/ias-officers-journey-towards-bettering-lives-tribals-1503035380.html.
- Devalla, Rani. "Visakhapatnam: 'Mission Connect Paderu' to Enhance Quality Life of Tribals." *Visakhapatnam: "Mission Connect Paderu" to Enhance Quality Life of Tribals*, 8 Oct. 2021, www.thehansindia.com/news /cities/visakhapatnam/visakhapatnam-mission-connect-paderu-to-enhance-quality-life-of-tribals-710107.
- Adepu Mahender . "Mulugu: Tribal Welfare, a Myth ." *https://www.thehansindia.com/telangana/mulugu-tribal-welfare-a-myth-725728Mulugu: Tribal Welfare, a Myth https://www.thehansindia.com/telangana/mulugu-tribal-welfare-a-myth-725728*, 22 Jan. 2022.
- "PRADHAN MANTRI PVTG DEVELOPMENT MISSION TO BE LAUNCHED WITH AN OUTLAY OF Rs.15000 CRORE." *Press Information Bureau*, pib.gov.in/Pressreleaseshare.aspx?PRID=1895298.
- "CSR: Piramal Foundation Campaigns to Dispel Vaccine Hesitancy Across Tribal Districts in India." *Indic CSR*, 4 Mar. 2022, indiacsr.in/csr-piramal-foundation-campaigns-to-dispel-vaccine-hesitancy-across tribal-districts-in-india.
- "Volunteers Keep the Learning Boat Afloat for Tribal Kids in Jharkhand." *Tribuneindia News Service* m.tribuneindia.com/news/schools/volunteers-keep-the-learning-boat-afloat-for-tribal-kids-ir jharkhand-374455.
- Tulsi Menon. "Navigating Business Through an Anthropological Lens." *https://youtu.be/EKfHbRFZpR*
- "Digital Transformation Involves Cultural Transformation and Digital Anthropology Is the Key to D That, Says Thought Leader Raktim Singh." *Fortune India: Business News, Strategy, Finance and Corpora Insight*, www.fortuneindia.com/enterprise/digital-transformation-involves-cultural-transformatio digital-anthropology-is-the-key-to-do-that-says-thought-leader-raktim-singh/105517.
- "Anthro-Vision: A New Way to See in Business and Life." *https://www.youtube.com/watch?v=PWcC7DBSo6*
- "Explained: What Is the Pathalgadi Movement, and What Is JMM Govt's Stand on It?" *The Indian Expre* 22 Dec. 2020, indianexpress.com/article/explained/explained-what-is-pathalgadi-movement-and-wh is-the-jmm-govts-stand-on-this-7114979.
- "Explained: Religions in India, 'Living Together Separately.'" *The Indian Express*, 7 July 20 indianexpress.com/article/explained/explained-religions-in-india-living-together-separately-73940
- "AnSI Explores 'The Anthropologist' Gandhi on His 150th Birth Anniversary." *AnSI Explores 'T Anthropologist' Gandhi on His 150th Birth Anniversary - the Hindu*, 26 Jan. 2020, www.thehindu.co news/national/ansi-explores-the-anthropologist-gandhi-on-his-150th-birth-anniversa article30659718.ece.